3RD EDITION

GREAT AMERICAN VACATIONS

Fodor's Travel Publications, Inc.
New York • Toronto • London • Sydney • Auckland
http://www.fodors.com/

ISBN 0–679–03027–1

Fodor's Great American Vacations

Editor: Chelsea S. Mauldin

Editorial Contributors: Jenner Bishop, Jeremy Braddock, Marianne Camas, Deke Castleman, Jeanne Cooper, Katherine Culkin, Mark Evans, Janet Foley, Julie Getzlaff, Daniel Gibson, Tara Hamilton, Deborah Hawkins, Herb Hiller, Katherine Imbrie, Helen James, Bud Journey, Jeff Kuechle, Susan Ladd, Jonathan Landreth, Dale Leatherman, Janet Lee, Karl Luntta, Oliver McCurnin, Rathe Miller, Candy Moulton, Marty Olmstead, Jane Onstott, Mark Potok, Mary Ellen Schultz, Alison Stern, Carol and Dan Thalimer, Michael Tisserand, Kristin Visser, Bruce Walker, Loralee Wenger, Tom Wharton, Paul Williams, Dick Willis, Sharron Wood

Creative Director: Fabrizio La Rocca

Cartographers: David Lindroth, Inc.; Maryland Cartographics

Cover Photographs: Nicholas Devore, Photographers/Aspen (American flag); Larry Lee/Westlight (Statue of Liberty); Phil Schermeister, Photographers/Aspen (San Francisco); Craig Aurness/Westlight

Cover Design: Tigist Getachew

Special Sales

Fodor's Travel Publications are available at special discounts for bulk purchases for sales promotions or premiums. Special editions, including personalized covers, excerpts of existing guides, and corporate imprints, can be created in large quantities for special needs. For more information, contact your local bookseller or write to Special Markets, Fodor's Travel Publications, 201 East 50th Street, New York, NY 10022. Inquiries from Canada should be directed to your local Canadian bookseller or sent to Random House of Canada, Ltd., Marketing Department, 1265 Aerowood Drive, Mississauga, Ontario L4W 1B9. Inquiries from the United Kingdom should be sent to Fodor's Travel Publications, 20 Vauxhall Bridge Road, London SW1V 2SA.

CONTENTS

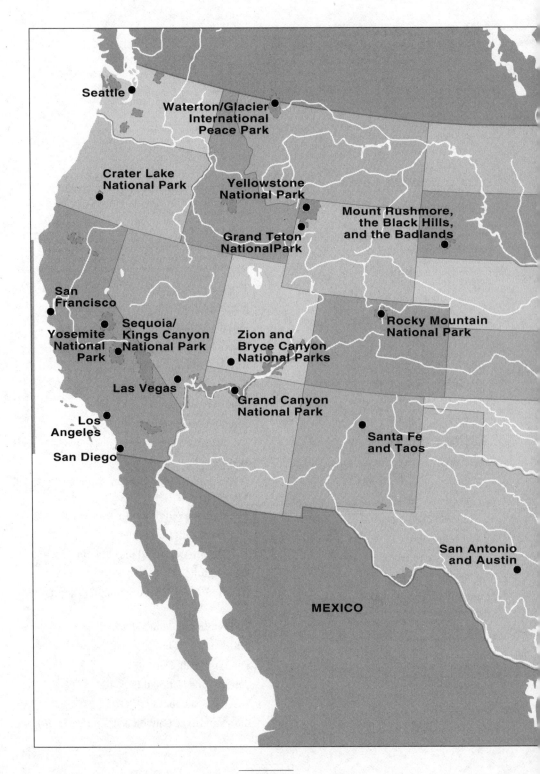

Seattle

Waterton/Glacier
International
Peace Park

Crater Lake
National Park

Yellowstone
National Park

Mount Rushmore,
the Black Hills,
and the Badlands

Grand Teton
NationalPark

San
Francisco

Sequoia/
Kings Canyon
National Park

Zion and
Bryce Canyon
National Parks

Rocky Mountain
National Park

Yosemite
National
Park

Las Vegas

Grand Canyon
National Park

Los
Angeles

Santa Fe
and Taos

San Diego

San Antonio
and Austin

MEXICO

CANADA

Mackinac Island

Minneapolis and St. Paul

Wisconsin Dells

Chicago

The Lincoln Trail

Mammoth Cave National Park

Branson

Nashville

Memphis

Hot Springs and the Ozarks

The Natchez Trace

New Orleans

The Texas Gulf Coast

Niagara Falls

Pennsylvania Dutch Country

Gettysburg

Shenandoah Valley and Charlottesville

Great Smoky Mountains National Park

Charleston

Savannah and the Golden Isles

Walt Disney World and the Orlando Area

Greater Miami

Everglades National Park

The Maine Coast

The White Mountains

Boston

Newport

Cape Cod

New York City

Philadelphia

Washington, D.C.

WIlliamsburg

The Outer Banks

THE UNITED STATES

guide to the USA like no other, *Great American Vacations* is a vacation planner for exploring 50 of the nation's most-beloved destinations. Whether you're thinking about a weekend getaway or a cross-continental vacation marathon, we've got great planning advice, sightseeing tips, listings of affordable places to eat and sleep, and the best spots for shopping, entertainment, and outdoor fun. Since so many Americans are hitting the road—often with kids, dogs, and a trailer in tow—this book pays particular attention to places that are easy to explore and fun for the whole family, but that won't empty your wallet.

Besides the 48 classic American vacation spots fully updated and revised from last edition—shimmering metropolises, awe-inspiring national parks, sites steeped in the nation's heritage, and quiet regions full of the flavor of small-town America—new to the guide are two of the country's most popular leisure destinations: Branson, Missouri, the country-music show capital, is now the second-favorite driving destination in the United States (only the Orlando area attracts more visitors). Mackinac Island, a historic and bed-and-breakfast-studded island in Lake Huron, is a romantic, four-season retreat for honeymooners and couples of all ages.

We hope this guide becomes a valuable reference tool that you use again and again. To that end, everyone who has contributed to *Great American Vacations* has worked hard to make it accurate. Since the passage of time can bring changes, however, it's always a good idea to call ahead and confirm information—particularly if you're making a detour to visit specific sights or attractions. All prices and open times are based on information supplied to us at press time; Fodor's cannot accept responsibility for any errors that may have occurred.

We would love your feedback, positive or negative, so please send us a letter or postcard—you can address it to Great American Vacations Editor, Fodor's Travel Publications, 201 East 50th Street, New York, NY 10022. We'll look forward to hearing from you. In the meantime, whether you're off to far-flung states or rediscovering your own backyard, have a wonderful trip!

Essential Information

o matter what your destination, your vacation can run more smoothly with advance planning. What follows are a few things to consider to make your trip easier.

BUS TRAVEL

Bus service in North America—though fairly economical—has not been a first-class means of travel in recent years. But **Greyhound Lines** (tel. 800/231–2221) and other bus companies are taking great pains to improve service. New amenities may include an onboard host/hostess, meals, and VCRs. A number of discount passes are also available.

CAMERAS AND CAMCORDERS

If your camera is new or if you haven't used it for a while, shoot and develop a few rolls of film before you leave. Always store film in a cool, dry place—never in the car's glove compartment or on the shelf under the rear window. Before your trip, also test your camcorder, invest in a skylight filter to protect the lens, and charge the batteries. The **Kodak Information Center** (tel. 800/242–2424) answers consumer questions about film and photography. Fodor's also publishes the *Kodak Guide to Shooting Great Travel Pictures* ($16.50; available at bookstores or from Fodor's Travel Publications, tel. 800/533–6478), which has hundreds of tips and photos on everything from how to shoot common travel subjects—markets, beaches, architectural details, and so on—to how to compensate for various light and weather conditions.

CAR TRAVEL

AUTO CLUBS Members of the **American Automobile Association** (AAA) receive emergency road services, free maps, itineraries, tour books, information about road and weather conditions, and travel-agency services. To join AAA, check your phone book for the nearest club or contact the national organization (1000 AAA Dr., Heathrow, FL 32746-5063, tel. 800/222–4357).

RENTAL CARS **Cutting Costs.** To get the best deal, book through a travel agent and shop around. Major companies have programs that discount their standard rates by 15% to 30% if you make the reservation before departure (anywhere from 24 hours to 14 days), rent for a minimum number of days (typically three or four), and prepay the rental. When pricing cars, ask where the rental lot is located. Some off-airport locations offer lower rates—even though their lots are only minutes away from the terminal via complimentary shuttle. You may also want to price local car-rental companies, whose rates may be lower still, although service and maintenance standards may not be up to those of a national firm. Also ask your travel agent about a company's customer-service record. How has it responded to late plane arrivals and vehicle mishaps? Are there often lines at the rental counter, and, if you're traveling during a holiday period, does a confirmed reservation guarantee you a car?

Insurance. When you drive a rented car, you are generally responsible for any damage or personal injury that you cause as well as damage to the vehicle. Before you rent, see what coverage you already have by means of your personal auto-insurance policy and credit cards. Rental companies sell insurance, known as a collision damage waiver (CDW), that eliminates your liability for damage to the car; it's always optional and should never be automatically added to your bill. California, New York, and Illinois have outlawed the sale of CDW altogether.

Surcharges. Before picking up the car in one city and leaving it in another, ask about drop-off charges or one-way service fees, which can be substantial. Note, too, that some rental agencies charge extra if you return the car *before* the time specified on your contract. Fill the tank when you turn in the vehicle to avoid being charged for refueling at what you'll swear is the most expensive pump in town.

Toll-Free Numbers. Here are toll-free numbers for some of the top rental agencies: **Alamo** (tel. 800/327–9633; but located at only the biggest airports), **Avis** (tel. 800/331–1212), **Budget** (tel. 800/527–0700), **Dollar** (tel. 800/800–4000), **Hertz** (tel. 800/ 654–3131), **National** (tel. 800/227–7368), and **Thrifty** (tel. 800/367–2277). When you call, ask about seasonal promotions, discounts, and possible tie-ins with hotels, airlines, and family attractions.

CREDIT CARDS AND OPEN HOURS

CREDIT CARDS The following credit-card abbreviations are used throughout this guide: AE, American Express; D, Discover; DC, Diner's Club; MC, MasterCard; V, Visa. It's always a good idea to call ahead and confirm an establishment's credit-card policy.

HOURS The open hours listed in this guide often do not include seasonal variations and holiday closures. Always call ahead.

HEALTH AND SAFETY

Before you leave home, check with your insurance company to see whether you are covered for hospital emergency room or doctors' visits while in the state you are visiting, and remember to bring insurance cards and forms for every member of the family.

If you're staying in a hotel, resort, or family camp, especially in a rural area, ask about the availability of health care there, including the location of the nearest hospital. Some resorts and camps have medical personnel on staff. Most hotels can furnish lists of local pediatricians and doctors or contact one for you.

A FIRST-AID KIT No matter where you're traveling, it's always a good idea to have basic medical supplies on hand. Some necessities include Band-aids, gauze pads, and tape; antiseptic cream; thermometer and vaseline; needle and tweezers for splinters or removing ticks, plus matches so you can sterilize the instruments; aspirin or other pain relievers, and if you have kids, children's acetaminophen; a small first-aid book.

LODGING

CAMPING Often the most reasonably priced campgrounds with the most compelling sites operate under the auspices of the **National Park Service** (Dept. of the Interior, Washington, DC 20240). For campgrounds run by other operations, your best source of nationwide info on both public and private parks is the **National Association of RV Parks and Campgrounds** (AVRC, 8605 Westwood Center Dr., Suite 201, Vienna, VA 22182, tel. 800/477–8669).

HOTELS The hotels that dominate the nation's lodging landscape offer widely different services and amenities. You may want to ask these questions when booking a room: Does the property have parking, is it in a garage or open lot, and is there a parking fee? Is there a restaurant on the premises, and is room service available around the clock? Is there an in-room phone, a TV, or cable channels? Will they hold your reservation if you arrive late? The following are toll-free numbers for the major hotel chains: **Adams Mark** (tel. 800/231–5858), **Best Western** (tel. 800/528–1234), **Clarion** (tel. 800/252–7466), **Colony** (tel. 800/777–1700), **Comfort** (tel. 800/228–5150), **Days Inn** (tel. 800/547–7878), **Doubletree** (tel. 800/528–0444), **Four Seasons** (tel. 800/332–3442), **Guest Quarters** (tel. 800/424–2900), **Hilton** (tel. 800/445–8667), **Holiday Inn** (tel. 800/465–4329), **Howard Johnson Hotels** (tel. 800/446–4656), **Hyatt** (tel. 800/233–1234), **Inter-Continental** (tel. 800/327–0200), **Marriott** (tel. 800/228–9290), **Meridien** (tel. 800/543–4300), **Quality Inn** (tel. 800/228–5151), **Radisson** (tel. 800/333–3333), **Ramada** (tel. 800/228–2828), **Red Lion** (tel. 800/547–8010), **Ritz-Carlton** (tel. 800/241–3333), **Sheraton** (tel. 800/325–3535), **Stouffer** (tel. 800/468–3571), **Westin** (tel. 800/228–3000), **Wyndham** (tel. 800/822–4200).

LODGING ALTERNATIVES Consider religious retreats, guest houses, college dormitories, and home exchange. The directory **Budget Lodging Guide** lists college dorms and university apartments that can cost as little as $15 a night. It can be ordered from B&J Publications (Box 5486, Fullerton, CA 92635, tel. 714/525–6625 or 800/525–6633). *A Guide to Monastic Guest Houses,* by Robert J. Regalbuto (published by Morehouse, Box 1321, Harrisburg, PA 17105, tel. 800/877–0012), lists mostly Roman Catholic and Episcopalian guest houses and is available at bookstores or from the publisher. For home exchange, go through an established organization. The **Vacation Exchange Club** (Box 650, Key West, FL 33041, tel. 800/638–3841) and **Loan-a-Home** (2 Park La., Apt. 6E, Mount Vernon, NY 10552, tel. 914/664–7640) specialize in home exchange.

MONEY MATTERS

ATMS You can use ATMs to withdraw money from a bank account or get cash advances on a credit-card account if your card has been programmed with a personal identification number, or PIN. Before leaving home, check on frequency limits for withdrawals and cash advances. Cirrus, Plus, and many other networks connecting automated-teller machines operate nationally. For specific **Cirrus** locations, call 800/424–7787. For **Plus** locations, call 800/843–7587 and enter the area code and first three digits of the number you're calling from (or of the calling area where you want an ATM).

On cash advances you are charged interest from the day you receive the money from ATMs as well as from tellers. Transaction fees for ATM withdrawals outside your home turf may be higher than for withdrawals at home.

TRAVELER'S CHECKS Whether or not to buy traveler's checks depends on where you are headed; take cash to rural areas and small towns, traveler's checks to cities. The most widely recognized are American Express, Citicorp, Thomas Cook, and Visa, which are sold by major commercial banks for 1% to 3% of the checks' face value—it pays to shop around. Both American Express and Thomas Cook issue checks that can be countersigned and used by you or your traveling companion. You can cash them in banks without paying a fee (which can be as much as 20%) and use them as readily as cash in many hotels, restaurants, and shops. Record the numbers of the checks, cross them off as you spend them, and keep this information separate from your checks.

PACKING

Necessities like batteries, film, and sunscreen lotion are available almost anywhere, but as a traveler you may end up buying them at shops on the tourist track, where prices can be high; stock up in advance to save money. If you plan on hiking or camping during the summer, insect repellent is a must. Bring an extra pair of eyeglasses or contact lenses in your carry-on luggage, and if you have a health problem, pack enough medication to last the trip. Don't put prescription drugs or valuables in luggage to be checked—it could go astray. Also don't forget the addresses of offices that handle refunds of lost traveler's checks. If you have kids still in diapers, buy them (along with wipes) at local supermarkets—hotel sundry shops usually don't sell them, though they do sell toothpaste, aspirin, and other adult toiletry needs.

PACKING FOR CHILDREN **Clothing:** Plan on layers so you can add and subtract as needed and remember that all-cotton clothing takes a long time to dry. Let kids help select; forget about taking items you like and they don't unless you really want to spend time on your vacation arguing. Be sure everyone in the family takes comfortable walking shoes—nothing ruins the fun of sightseeing like blistered feet.

Infants: As a minimum, bring diaper-rash cream, a pacifier (and a spare), formula or juice plus extra bottles and nipples, a square of plastic for diaper changing and mattress protection, plastic bags for laundry, bibs, and a couple of baby blankets (use folded as a pillow, spread out as a play spot, to pad a car seat, and so on).

OTHER ESSENTIALS Some other useful items are: flashlight (with extra batteries), can opener, Swiss army knife (any kind of folding knife will do), sewing kit, and almost the most important thing—all sizes of locking plastic bags, in which you can stash everything from a wet bathing suit to soap to a snack to a precious collection of acorns. If your kids are little, bring safety plugs for electrical outlets and a small plug-in night-light.

TIPS FOR FAMILIES WITH CHILDREN

Many local public libraries, museums, parks and recreation departments, and YMCA/YWCAs have special events throughout the year for children of all ages. Check local newspaper listings for such activities as plays, storytelling, sporting events, and so forth.

ACCOMMODATIONS Many kids prefer to stay in a chain hotel or motel rather than a very individual hotel. Part of that is knowing what to expect—one Howard Johnson's looks much like another, including the restaurants—and let's face it, kids are more comfortable with what's familiar. Hotels and resorts now actively court family business, offering such special deals as allowing kids to stay free in a room with their parents (although the maximum age to qualify as a child ranges from 12 to 17). Others let families rent adjoining rooms at discounts, which is a great way for parents to have some privacy. You can get the same effect, often for less money, by staying at an all-suite hotel, an increasingly popular choice for families. Some chains offer free or discounted meals (usually only to kids under 13).

Finding bed-and-breakfasts that welcome young children can be difficult. Many are filled with fragile antiques, serve communal breakfasts of fruit, bran muffins, and yogurt (not exactly child pleasers), and seldom have TV in the rooms.

PUBLICATIONS **Family Travel Guides Catalogue** (Carousel Press, Box 6061, Albany, CA 94706, tel. 510/527–5849) publishes a catalogue of general and specialized travel guides that includes books of games and short "travel papers" on specific cities and areas.

Family Travel Times (45 W. 18th St., 7th Floor Tower, New York, NY 10011, tel. 212/206–0688) is a national newsletter that offers a wealth of helpful tips and up-to-date advice on traveling with children.

Specialty Travel Index (305 San Anselmo Ave., San Anselmo, CA 94960, tel. 415/459–4900) lists a number of specialized family vacation offerings, including grandparent-grandchild tours, rafting trips, and more.

TRANSPORTATION **Traveling By Plane:** The annual February–March issue of *Family Travel Times* details children's services on dozens of airlines. Many offer special meals for babies and older children if you request them when you reserve. Playing cards, coloring books and crayons, games, and puzzles are just some of the in-flight entertainment provided. For other useful tips on air travel with children from toddlers to teens, send for the free pamphlet, "When Kids Fly" put out by Boston's Logan Airport (Massport Public Information Program, Boutwell One, Logan International Airport, East Boston, MA 02128). Be sure to include a self-addressed stamped envelope.

When you make plane reservations, be sure to state the ages of your children and ask about discounts and special packages available for families. Though it's no longer the norm, some airlines still offer children's discounts on certain flights, and infants under two generally fly free on domestic flights when they're held on a parent's lap.

If you'd like a bassinet—not available on all airlines—be sure to request one when you make a reservation. You'll need a bulkhead seat for a bassinet, but be warned—the seat trays in the bulkhead usually fold out of your chair arm and are impossible to use with a child on your lap. You can bring an FAA-approved car seat aboard, but your airline may charge you for the seat to put it in—ask when booking. If you will want formula or baby food on the flight, be sure to request it.

Traveling By Train: With room for fidgety kids to roam about, train travel can be a great alternative for vacationing families. Snack bars, rest rooms, and water fountains help kids fend off travel boredom; reclining seats, overhead luggage racks, and even sleeping compartments on long-distance routes make travel hours relatively comfortable. Children aged 2–15 ride for half fare on Amtrak when accompanied by an adult paying full fare. Children under two ride free.

TIPS FOR OLDER TRAVELERS

ASSOCIATIONS The **American Association of Retired Persons** (AARP, 601 E St. NW, Washington, DC 20049, tel. 202/434–2277) has two programs for independent travelers: The Purchase Privilege Program offers discounts on hotels, airfare, car rentals, RV rentals, and sightseeing; the AARP Motoring Plan, provided by Amoco, furnishes emergency road-service aid and trip-routing information for an annual fee of $39.95 per person or couple. AARP members must be 50 years or older; annual dues are $8 per person or couple.

Contact the **National Council of Senior Citizens** (membership $12 annually; 1331 F St. NW, Washington, DC 20004, tel. 202/347–8800) for other discounts on lodging, car rentals, and other travel products, along with magazines and newsletters.

DISCOUNTS While 65 is the age most people associate with the term senior citizen, you can be a lot younger and still obtain certain discounts offered to older travelers—if you're over 50, you're probably eligible for reduced rates on rooms, fares, packages, admission prices, and more. Many senior discounts are not advertised, so mention your senior-citizen status up front when booking hotel reservations, not when checking out, and before you're seated in restaurants, not when paying your bill. Note that discounts may be limited to certain menus, days, or hours. When renting a car, ask about promotional car-rental discounts—they can net lower costs than your senior-citizen discount.

The **Golden Age Passport** is a lifetime pass to all parks, monuments, and recreation areas run by the federal government. Permanent U.S. residents 62 or older may pick them up in person at any of the national parks that charge admission; there is a one-time $10 fee. The passport covers the entrance fee for the holder and anyone accompanying the holder in the same private vehicle. It also provides a 50% discount on camping, boat launching, and parking. Proof of age is required. The **Golden Eagle Pass** offers similar advantages to people under 62 for $25 a year. Call or write the National Park Service (Attn: Public Inquiries, Box 37127, Washington, DC 20013, tel. 202/208–4747).

PUBLICATIONS *The Senior Citizens Guide to Budget Travel in the United States and Canada,* by Paige Palmer, is from Pilot Books (103 Cooper St., Babylon, NY 11702, tel. 516/422–2225). *The 50+ Traveler's Guidebook: Where to Go, Where to Stay, What to Do,* by Anita Williams and Merrimac Dillon (St. Martin's Press, 175 5th Ave., New York, NY 10010, tel. 212/694–5151 or 800/288–2131), offers many useful tips.

TRANSPORTATION **Amtrak** offers senior citizens (65 and over) a 15% discount on all round-trip travel. This discount is available without restrictions except for during holiday periods of heavy travel. Check the price of excursion tickets first as these are often cheaper. **Greyhound** offers senior citizens (64 and older) a 10% reduction on regular fares Monday through Thursday, and a 5% reduction on weekends.

TIPS FOR TRAVELERS WITH DISABILITIES

ACCOMMODATIONS When discussing accessibility with an operator or reservationist, ask hard questions. Are there any stairs, inside or out? Are there grab bars next to the toilet and in the shower/tub? How wide is the doorway to the room? To the bathroom? For the most extensive facilities, meeting the latest legal specifications, opt for newer accommodations, which more often have been designed with access in mind.

ASSOCIATIONS Several organizations provide travel information for people with disabilities, usually for a membership fee, and some publish newsletters and bulletins. Among them are the **Information Center for Individuals with Disabilities** (Fort Point Pl., 27–43 Wormwood St., Boston, MA 02210, tel. 617/727–5540 or 800/462–5015 in MA; TTY 617/345–9743); **Mobility International USA** (Box 3551, Eugene, OR 97403, tel. and TTY 503/343–1284), with affiliates in 30 countries; **MossRehab Hospital Travel Information Service** (1200 W. Tabor Rd., Philadelphia, PA 19141, tel. 215/456–9603, TTY 215/456–9602); the **Travel**

Industry and Disabled Exchange (TIDE, 5435 Donna Ave., Tarzana, CA 91356, tel. 818/368–5648); and **Travelin' Talk** (Box 3534, Clarksville, TN 37403, tel. 615/552–6670).

DISCOUNTS All U.S. citizens and permanent residents with mobility problems or vision or hearing impairments are entitled to a $10 lifetime pass to all federally operated parks, monuments, historic sights, recreation areas, and wildlife refuges that charge entrance fees. The **Golden Access Passport,** which must be obtained in person from a federally operated park or recreation area, also provides a 50% discount on federal fees charged for facilities and services, such as camping and parking.

PUBLICATIONS Several publications for travelers with disabilities are available from the **Consumer Information Center** (Box 100, Pueblo, CO 81009, tel. 719/948–3334). Call or write for a free catalogue of current titles. **Twin Peaks Press** (Box 129, Vancouver, WA 98666, tel. 360/694–2462 or 800/637–2256) publishes the *Directory of Travel Agencies for the Disabled*; the *Directory of Accessible Van Rentals* for campers and RV travelers; and *Wheelchair Vagabond,* a collection of personal travel tips. The **Sierra Club** (730 Polk St., San Francisco, CA 94109, tel. 415/776–2211) publishes *Easy Access to National Parks.* **Fodor's** publishes *Great American Vacations for Travelers with Disabilities* (available in bookstores, or call 800/533–6478).

TRANSPORTATION **Amtrak** (TTY 800/523–6590) offers all passengers with disabilities a 25% discount on regular fares (children [ages 2–11] with disabilities get a 25% discount on already lower children's fares). All trains and all large stations have accessible toilets, though some of the region's smaller, unmanned stations do not. Reserve tickets 48 hours in advance. While **Greyhound** (TTY 800/345–3109) buses have no special facilities, an attendant can ride for free if a written request is presented. **Avis, Hertz,** and **National** can provide hand controls with advance notice.

TRAIN TRAVEL

Amtrak (800/872–7245 [USA–RAIL]) is the national passenger train line. For frequent train travelers, 15- and 30-day regional passes are a good value, allowing unlimited stopovers along the route. Peak season, when fares are highest, is from June through August. No reservations are required on Amtrak, but to avoid lines at departure time you can buy tickets in advance from a station agent or travel agent. For an Amtrak Travel Planner, *Amtrak's America,* which includes information on each train route as well as complete vacation packages, tips for traveling with children, and suggestions on what to do on board, call 800/321–8684.

Boston
Massachusetts

Updated by Jeanne Cooper

ew England's largest and most important city, the cradle of American independence, Boston, Massachusetts, dates from 1630—far older than the republic it helped to create in the days of its vigorous youth. Its most famous buildings are not merely civic landmarks but national icons; its great citizens are not the political and financial leaders of today but the Adamses, Reveres, and Hancocks who lived at the crossroads of history and myth. In modern times, only the Kennedy clan has come close to rivaling their lore.

At the same time, Boston is a contemporary center of high finance and higher technology, a place of granite-and-glass towers rising along what were once rutted village lanes, dwarfing the commercial structures that stood as the city's largest just a generation ago. In this other Boston, Samuel Adams is the name of a premium beer and the price of condominiums is as hot a topic as taxation without representation ever was. The area's enormous population of students, artists, academics, and young professionals has made it a haven for foreign movies, cafés, bookstores, racquetball, trendy nightclubs, and unconventional politics. Happily, these elements peacefully coexist alongside the more subdued bastions of Yankee sensibilities.

Best of all, Boston is meant for walking. Most of the city's historical and architectural attractions are located within compact areas, and Boston's varied and distinctive neighborhoods only begin to reveal their character and design to visitors who take the time to stroll through them.

ESSENTIAL INFORMATION

WHEN TO GO The best times to visit Boston are late spring and the months of September and October. Like other American cities of the Northeast, Boston can be uncomfortably hot and humid (75°–80°) in high summer and freezing cold (25°–30°) in the winter. Yet the city is not without its pleasures in these seasons. In summer there are Boston Pops concerts on the Esplanade, harbor cruises, and a score of sidewalk cafés. In winter there is Christmas shopping on Newbury Street, the symphony, the theater, and college drama and music seasons.

Each September, Boston and Cambridge welcome thousands of returning students, along with the perennially wide-eyed freshmen beginning their four-year (or longer) stays in the Hub, as residents call the twin cities. University life is a big part of the local atmosphere.

Autumn is a fine time to visit the suburbs. The combination of bright foliage and white church steeples may have been photographed countless times, but it will never become clichéd. The shore routes are less crowded in spring and fall, nearly all the lodging places and restaurants are open, and the Atlantic is as dramatic as ever.

BARGAINS Although most Boston museums charge admission, several offer a period when admission is free or reduced: the Museum of Fine Arts (tel. 617/267–9300), Wednesday 4–9:45; the Museum of Science (tel. 617/723–2500), November–April, Wednesday 1–5; the Gardner Museum (tel. 617/566–1401),

Wednesday 11–5; the Children's Museum (tel. 617/426–8855), Friday 5–9; and in Cambridge, the three Harvard art museums (tel. 617/495–9400), Saturday morning.

TOURIST OFFICES Greater Boston Convention & Visitors Bureau (800 Boylston St., Prudential Center, Boston 02199, tel. 617/536–4100 or 800/888–5515). **Boston Common Visitor Information Center** (147 Tremont St., tel. 617/426–3115) is at the beginning of the Freedom Trail. **National Historic Park Visitor Center** (15 State St., Boston 02109, tel. 617/242–5642) is across from the Old State House.

EMERGENCIES Police, fire, and ambulance: Dial 911. **Hospitals:** Massachusetts General Hospital (55 Fruit St., tel. 617/726–2000). **Doctors:** MGH Physician Referral Service (tel. 617/726–5800). **Dentists:** Dental emergencies (tel. 508/651–3521). **Pharmacies:** CVS (Porter Square Shopping Plaza, Voit St. at Massachusetts Ave., Cambridge, tel. 617/876–5519); Walgreens (757 Gallivan Blvd., Dorchester, tel. 617/282–5246).

ARRIVING AND DEPARTING

BY PLANE Logan International Airport (tel. 617/973–5500) is served by most major airlines.

Between the Airport and Downtown. Only 3 miles—and Boston Harbor—separate Logan International Airport from downtown, yet it can seem like 30 miles when you're caught in one of the traffic jams that clog the two tunnels for cars that go under the harbor (a third tunnel has been slated for bus and commercial use).

By Subway: The **MBTA Blue Line** (tel. 800/235–6426) from Airport Station travels to downtown 5:30 AM–1 AM daily, for 85¢; allow 15 to 25 minutes' travel time to downtown. Free shuttle buses connect the subway station with all airport terminals.

By Water Shuttle: The **Airport Water Shuttle** (tel. 800/235–6426) takes seven minutes and charges under $10 to cross Boston Harbor and arrive at Rowes Wharf downtown; from here, though, you may need to hail a cab to your final destination. The shuttle leaves every 15 minutes on weekdays and every 30 minutes on weekends. Free shuttle buses connect the ferry terminal with all airport terminals.

By Taxi: Cabs can be hailed outside any terminal; fares are $12–$15 downtown assuming moderate traffic, and travel time is 20–40 minutes. Call 617/561–1751 for cab information.

By Minibus: City Transportation (tel. 617/561–9000) leaves the airport every 30 minutes and serves major downtown hotels; the cost is approximately $7.50.

BY CAR Boston is reached via I–93 (also called the Southeast Expressway or the John F. Fitzgerald Expressway) from the south, via the Massachusetts Turnpike (I–90, a toll road) from the west, and via I–93 and U.S. 1 (from I–95) from the north. Traveling between Boston and Cambridge, Storrow Memorial Drive runs along the Charles River on the Boston side (the busier and faster route) and Memorial Drive (affording more scenic views of Boston) on the Cambridge side.

BY TRAIN Amtrak (tel. 800/872–7245) stops at South Station (at Atlantic Ave. and Summer St., tel. 617/482–3660) from points south and west of Boston. **North Station** (Causeway and Friend Sts., tel. 617/722–3200) is used by commuter trains serving points within the state north and west of the city.

BY BUS Greyhound Lines (tel. 800/231–2222) connects Boston's South Station with all major U.S. cities. **Peter Pan Bus Lines** (Atlantic Ave. opposite South Station, tel. 617/426–7838) connects Boston with points in New England and New York. **Plymouth & Brockton Buses** (tel. 508/746–0378) opposite South Station at Peter Pan terminal serves towns on Cape Cod. **Concord Trailways** (tel. 800/639–3317) at Peter Pan terminal has service to Maine.

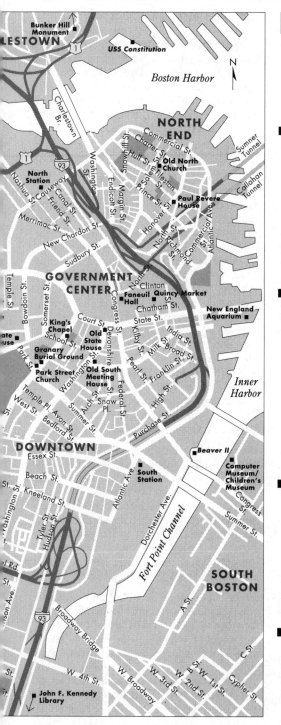

Boston is a walker's city; you're likely to move faster and see more when you stay on foot. If you get tired, the city's subway and trolley systems are efficient. And if it's late, taxis are plentiful.

BY CAR If you must bring a car into the city, stick to the major thoroughfares and park in a lot—no matter how expensive ($10–$15 for a few hours or a full day)—rather than on the streets. Meter maids in Boston are ruthless, and the maze of one-way streets drives even the locals crazy. Major public parking lots are located at Post Office Square, Government Center, Faneuil Hall, the Prudential Center, Boston Common (underground), and Copley Place.

BY SUBWAY The **MBTA** (tel. 617/722–3200 or 800/392–6100), commonly called the T, operates subways, elevated trains, and trolleys along four connecting, color-coded lines. The Park Street station is the major transfer point for the Red and Green lines; the Orange and Blue lines intersect at State Street. Trains operate from 5:30 AM to 12:30 AM. The fares are reasonable and one-, three-, and seven-day tourist passes can be purchased at the Park Street or airport stations, as well as at Bostix and the Boston Common Visitor Information Booth.

BY BUS MBTA bus routes crisscross the metro area and extend farther into the suburbs than the trolleys or subway. But for the uninitiated or those in a hurry, routes and stops on the street are difficult to pinpoint. Local fares must be paid on board with exact change, and buses operate approximately 6:30 AM–1 AM. Pick up a map at the Park Street station or call 617/722–3200 or 800/ 392–6100.

BY TAXI Cabs are easily hailed on the street and can also be found at hotel taxi stands. Companies offering 24-hour radio-dispatched taxi service include **Checker** (tel. 617/536–7000) and **Independent Taxi Operators** (tel. 617/426–8700). The rate is about $1.60 per mile.

REST STOPS Public rest rooms can be found in Quincy Market near Faneuil Hall, the National Historic Park Visitor Center at 15 State Street, downtown at South Station, and in the Copley Place mall off Copley Square.

GUIDED TOURS **Orientation:** The trolley tours (although some are actually on buses) cover all the popular sights with informative narration and plenty of stops for boarding/reboarding. You'll find information booths for the trolleys at Boston Common or Copley Square, including those for **Beantown Trolleys** (tel. 617/236–2148), **Blue Trolley** (tel. 617/876–5539), and **Old Town Trolley** (tel. 617/269–7010), which also has a tour of Cambridge. Fares average about $16 for adults, $6 for children. **Boston Duck Tours** (tel. 617/723–3825) uses restored World War II amphibious vehicles to explore the city and the Charles River; it departs from the Aquarium (no stops for reboarding) and fares are under $20.

Special Interest: Boston Park Rangers (tel. 617/635–7383) lead nature walks through the city's almost 200 parks. **Samuel Adams Lager Brewery** (Jamaica Plain, tel. 617/522–9080) offers 90-minute tours with a tasting at the end. The **New England Aquarium** (Central Wharf, off Atlantic Ave., tel. 617/973–5277) sponsors five-hour whale-watching cruises May to early October, and **Boston Harbor Cruises** (1 Long Wharf, tel. 617/227–4320) offers trips to the Harbor Islands and whale-watching cruises from mid-April through December.

Walking: The **Historic Neighborhoods Foundation** (99 Bedford St., tel. 617/426–1885), a nonprofit educational foundation, offers informal guided walking tours of Beacon Hill, the North End, and Chinatown for $5. For more information on walking tours of Boston, *see* Outdoor Activities, *below.*

EXPLORING

Boston can be seen as a series of concentric circles, with the oldest and most famous attractions clustered within easy walking distance of the State House. Many attractions are on the Freedom Trail, marked by a line of red paint or contrasting brick on streets and sidewalks (*see* Walking *in* Outdoor Activities, *below*). Boston's remarkable compactness is a boon for the pedestrian explorer; indeed, in central Boston there should be no other kind.

Back Bay, a neighborhood 11 blocks long by six blocks wide, properly begins with the Public Garden, the oldest botanical garden in the United States. Its pond has been famous since 1877 for its swan boats, which cruise during the warm months of the year. While Commonwealth Avenue resembles a Parisian boulevard, Newbury Street is a town-house version of New York's 5th Avenue. On Boylston Street, the commercial spine of Back Bay, is Copley Square, a civic space that is defined by the stately Copley Plaza Hotel, Trinity Church (Henry Hobson Richardson's masterwork of 1877), and the imposing Boston Public Library. A few blocks farther down Boylston Street is the **Prudential Center Skywalk** with an observatory offering fine views of Boston, Cambridge, and the suburbs to the west and south. *Skywalk: 800 Boylston St., tel. 617/236–3318. Open daily. Admission charged.*

Beacon Hill, a mostly residential neighborhood behind and to the west of the State House, is full of classic Federal-style brick row houses, brick sidewalks, and gas lanterns. Search out Chestnut and Mt. Vernon streets, two of the prettiest streets in America; Louisburg Square, a handsome 1840s townhouse "development"; and Acorn Street, a narrow span of cobblestones lined with tiny row houses and doors to private gardens.

Boston Common is the oldest public park in the United States and undoubtedly the largest and most famous of the town commons around which all New England settlements were once arranged. On the north side of the Common is the **State House,** arguably the most architecturally distinguished of American seats of government, where free tours are given weekdays. At the **Park Street**

Church, on the corner of Tremont and Park streets, the hymn "America" was first sung, and William Lloyd Garrison began the campaign against slavery. Next door is the **Granary Burial Ground,** where Samuel Adams, John Hancock, and Paul Revere are buried. *State House: Park and Beacon Sts., tel. 617/727–3676. Open weekdays. Admission free. Park Street Church: Open late June–late Aug., Tues.–Sat. Admission free. Granary Burial Ground: Open daily. Admission free.*

Cambridge (actually its own city, reached from Boston via the Red Line to Harvard Square or three other stops) is home to Harvard University and the Massachusetts Institute of Technology (MIT). Harvard's three exhibition halls—the Fogg Art Museum, the Sackler Museum, and the Busch-Reisinger Museum—include art from every major period and from every corner of the world. Walking-tour brochures for Revolutionary and Old Cambridge can be obtained at Cambridge Discovery (tel. 617/497–1630), an information booth near the entrance to the Harvard MBTA station. *Fogg Art and Busch-Reisinger museums: 32 Quincy St.; Sackler Museum: 485 Broadway; tel. 617/495–9400. Open daily. Admission charged.*

Charlestown, over the Charlestown Bridge, is home to the undefeated **USS *Constitution*** (nicknamed "Old Ironsides"), the oldest commissioned ship (1797) in the U.S. Navy. She is moored at the Charlestown Navy Yard, a national historic site. Take Main Street to Monument Street and walk straight uphill to reach the historic **Bunker Hill Monument.** Only the hearty need ascend the 295 steps (there is no elevator). *USS* Constitution*: tel. 617/242–5670. Open daily. Admission free. Bunker Hill Monument: Monument Sq., tel. 617/242–5641. Open daily. Admission free.*

The **Christian Science Church Center** in the Back Bay is the mother church of the Christian Science faith, established here in 1879. The 670-foot reflecting pool is a pleasant place to stroll around, and the Maparium, a 30-foot stained-glass globe, gives you the feeling of walking through the world on a glass bridge. *175 Huntington Ave., tel. 617/450–*

3790. Church open Tues.–Fri. and Sun.; Maparium open Tues.–Fri. Admission free.

Downtown Boston—the financial district—is home to several stops on the Freedom Trail. At the corner of Tremont and School streets stands **King's Chapel,** where Paul Revere's largest, and in his opinion his sweetest-sounding bell, chimes. Two blocks from King's Chapel (down School Street, with the Parker House Hotel on your right), on Washington Street at the corner of Milk, is the **Old South Meeting House.** Samuel Adams called a town meeting here to discuss dumping dutiable tea into Boston Harbor. A right turn onto Washington Street from the doorstep of the Old South will take you to the **Old State House,** the seat of the Colonial government from 1713 until the Revolution. *King's Chapel: 58 Tremont St., tel. 617/227–2155. Open Tues.–Sat. Admission free. Old South Meeting House: 310 Washington St., tel. 617/482–6439. Open daily. Admission charged. Old State House: 206 Washington St., tel. 617/720–3290. Open daily. Admission charged.*

Faneuil Hall (pronounced Fan'l), on Merchants Row in downtown Boston, was erected in 1742 to serve as both a place for town meetings and a public market. Inside Faneuil Hall are dozens of paintings of famous Americans and the headquarters and museum of the Ancient and Honorable Artillery Company of Massachusetts. **Quincy Market,** right behind Faneuil Hall, consists of three structures that originally served as a retail and wholesale meat and produce distribution center; today the area is a model of urban renewal, with specialty foods, restaurants, bars, market stalls, and shops. *Open daily. Admission free.*

Isabella Stewart Gardner Museum is a monument to one woman's taste (and despite the loss of a few masterpieces in a daring 1990 robbery, still a trove of paintings, sculpture, furniture, and textiles) housed in an Italian-style villa. The collection includes works by Titian, Matisse, Van Dyck, Rubens, and Botticelli. *280 The Fenway, tel. 617/566–1401. Open Tues.–Sun. Admission charged.*

John F. Kennedy Library, south of the city but accessible via a free shuttle from the JFK/UMass stop on the Red Line, is the official repository of this native Bostonian's presidential papers, desk, and other personal belongings. Changing exhibits and movie and video presentations illustrate historic events from his era. *Columbia Pt., South Boston, tel. 617/929–4523. Open daily. Admission charged.*

Museum of Fine Arts has holdings of American art that surpass those of all but a few other American museums, plus the most extensive collection of Asiatic art under one roof, and a European collection representing the 11th through the 20th centuries. *465 Huntington Ave., tel. 617/267–9300. Open Tues.–Sun. Admission charged.*

Museum of Science has more than 400 exhibits covering astronomy, anthropology, and earth sciences. Also housed here are the Hayden Planetarium and the Mugar Omni Theater. *Science Park, across the Charles River on Green Line, tel. 617/523–6664. Open daily. Admission charged.*

The **North End** has been Italian Boston since the early 20th century; Italian grocers, cafés, festivals honoring saints, and encroaching gentrification characterize the narrow and winding streets of the present-day neighborhood. Salem and Hanover streets are particularly active and colorful. Off Hanover Street is the oldest house in Boston, the **Paul Revere House,** built nearly 100 years before Revere's midnight ride through Middlesex County. Head right on Hanover Street and make a left onto Tileston Street. At the end of Tileston Street make a right on Salem Street to find the **Old North Church** (the oldest church in Boston), where two lanterns in its steeple signaled Paul Revere on the night of April 18, 1775. *Paul Revere House: 19 North Sq., tel. 617/523–2338. Open Apr.–Dec., daily; Jan.–Mar., Tues.–Sun. Admission charged. Old North Church: tel. 617/ 523–6676. Open daily, except Thanksgiving. Admission free.*

The **Waterfront** is home to several popular Boston attractions. Behind Quincy Market

and to the south is the **New England Aquarium,** where you'll find a hands-on tide pool and more than 2,000 species of fish, sharks, turtles, and sea lions. Walk along Atlantic Avenue to the Congress Street Bridge to board the Boston Tea Party Ship, *Beaver II,* a replica of one of the ships that was forcibly boarded and unloaded on the night Boston Harbor became a teapot. Across the bridge is the **Computer Museum,** with exhibits for young and old hackers alike. Next door, the **Boston Children's Museum** has a multitude of hands-on exhibits designed with kids in mind. *Aquarium: Central Wharf, tel. 617/973–5200. Open daily. Admission charged. Boston Tea Party Ship* (Beaver II) *and Museum: Congress Street Bridge, tel. 617/338–1773. Open Mar.–Nov., daily. Admission charged. Computer Museum: 300 Congress St., tel. 617/ 423–6758. Open May–Aug., daily; Sept.– Apr., Tues.–Sun. Admission charged. Children's Museum: 300 Congress St., tel. 617/426–6500, TTY 617/426–5466. Open Labor Day–mid June, Tues.–Sun. 10–5; mid-June–Labor Day, daily 10–5 and Fri. until 9 PM. Admission charged.*

HOTELS AND INNS

Lodging in Boston will be your biggest expense. Some expensive hotels offer reasonably priced weekend packages, but availability varies. With all the colleges, businesses, conventions, and historic attractions in the area, hotels generally maintain a very high rate of occupancy; to avoid frustration, do not arrive without a confirmed reservation. Consider using a reservations firm such as A Bed & Breakfast Agency of Boston (tel. 617/720–3540 or 800/248–9262) or Bed & Breakfast Associates Bay Colony (tel. 617/ 449–5302 or 800/347–5088) to find affordable home-style accommodations. Keep in mind that hotel prices generally do not include fees for parking, if available. Price categories for double occupancy, excluding 9.7% tax, are Very Expensive, over $145; Expensive, $105–$145; Moderate, $80–105; and Inexpensive, under $80.

BACK BAY **Beacon Guesthouses.** These furnished studio apartments in converted town houses (similar to European pensions) offer basic accommodations. All have private baths and kitchenettes. *248 Newbury St., 02116, tel. 617/266–7142, fax 617/266–7276. 20 rooms. MC, V. Inexpensive.*

Copley Square Hotel. One of Boston's oldest hotels (1891) and best values, this centrally located hotel has a European flavor and rooms of various sizes—from singles to family suites. *47 Huntington Ave., 02116, tel. 617/536–9000 or 800/225–7062, fax 617/236–0351. 143 rooms. Use of health club (for a small fee). AE, DC, MC, V. Expensive.*

57 Park Plaza/Howard Johnson. The location is part Park Square and part theater district, which makes this clean and serviceable property popular with both business travelers and tourists. *200 Stuart St., 02116, tel. 617/482–1800 or 800/468–3557, fax 617/451–2750. 370 rooms. Heated indoor pool, sauna, sundeck. AE, D, DC, MC, V. Expensive.*

Newbury Guest House. This four-story town-house bed-and-breakfast has small but attractive hotel-style rooms with phones, TVs, and reproduction Victorian furnishings. A complimentary breakfast buffet is served in the courtyard-level dining room. *261 Newbury St., 02116, tel. 617/437–7666 or 800/437–7668, fax 617/262–4243. 32 rooms. AE, D, DC, MC, V. Moderate.*

CAMBRIDGE **Cambridge House.** This antiques-filled gracious old home, listed on the National Register of Historic Places, offers rooms in several buildings (some with private baths), full breakfast, afternoon tea and sherry, and evening wine and cheese—and it's only a short walk to the MBTA Red Line. *2218 Massachusetts Ave., 02140, tel. 617/491–6300 or 800/232–9989, fax 617/868–2848. 16 rooms, 12 with private bath. Free parking. AE, D, DC, MC, V. Expensive–Very Expensive.*

Harvard Manor House. This functional and clean five-story motel in Brattle Square, minutes from Harvard Square, offers the largest rooms in the area for the price. *110 Mt. Auburn St., 02138, tel. 617/864–5200 or 800/458–5886, fax 617/864–2409. 72 rooms. AE, D, DC, MC, V. Expensive.*

Susse Chalet Cambridge. Rooms at the Susse Chalet are clean but sparse, and the location is a bit isolated from most shopping areas and sights. However, you're only a 10-minute car or subway ride from Harvard Square; it's within walking distance of the MBTA Red Line terminus, but take a cab back at night. *211 Concord Tpke., 02140, tel. 617/661–7800 or 800/258–1980, fax 617/868–8153. 78 rooms. Free parking. AE, D, DC, MC, V. Inexpensive.*

SOUTH END **Chandler Inn.** On the corner of Berkeley Street close to the Back Bay, in a still-gentrifying neighborhood with a large gay community, this simple hotel attracts clients who enjoy the urban scene. *26 Chandler St., 02116, tel. 617/482–3450 or 800/842–3450, fax 617/542–3428. 56 rooms. Lounge. AE, D, DC, MC, V. Moderate.*

THEATER DISTRICT **Tremont House.** The lobby, with its high ceilings, marble staircase, lots of gold leaf, and four-tier chandelier, denotes a grandeur that is not reflected in the rooms themselves; both the guest rooms (furnished with 18th-century Thomasville reproductions) and the bathrooms are small. Rates can soar in peak months, so be sure to ask if the more reasonable bed-and-breakfast package or other discounts are available. *275 Tremont St., 02116, tel. 617/426–1400 or 800/331–9998, fax 617/482–6730. 281 rooms. Laundry service, no-smoking floor. AE, D, DC, MC, V. Expensive.*

MOTELS

MODERATE **Comfort Inn** (Rte. 1, Saugus 01906, tel. 617/324–1900 or 800/228–5150, fax 617/321–9018). 117 rooms; free parking. **Holiday Inn** (55 Ariadne Rd., Dedham 02026, tel. 617/329–1000 or 800/465–4329, fax 617/329–0903). 200 rooms; free parking.

INEXPENSIVE **Red Roof Inn** (650 Cochituate Rd., Framingham 01701, tel. 508/872–4499 or 800/843–7663, fax 617/972–2579). 170 rooms; free parking.

DINING

The main ingredient in Boston's restaurant fare is still the bounty of the North Atlantic, the daily catch of fish and shellfish that appears on virtually every menu. Seafood or no, the choice of dining experience in Boston has expanded to include a variety of ethnic cuisines beyond French and Italian; Thai and Indian restaurants, for example, are often attractive, affordable options. Price categories per person, excluding 5% tax, service, and drinks, are Expensive, over $25; Moderate, $15–$25; and Inexpensive, under $15.

BACK BAY **Legal Sea Foods.** The atmosphere at Legal's is bustling and the cuisine simple but delectable—choose from raw, broiled, steamed, or baked seafood. There's a café version two doors down and there are two outposts at either end of the Prudential Center/Copley Place malls. *64 Arlington St., Park Sq., Boston Park Plaza Hotel, tel. 617/ 426–4444. AE, D, DC, MC, V. Moderate.*

Parish Cafe. The area's top chefs each contributed an innovative sandwich recipe to this bistro, which spills out onto Boylston Street in season and stays open late. Combinations include ham and cheese on banana bread and grilled mushrooms with walnut-onion pesto on focaccia; generous accompaniments include navy-bean or chunky red-potato salad. *361 Boylston St., tel. 617/ 247–4777. AE, DC, MC, V. Inexpensive.*

Turner Fisheries. This tastefully decorated dining room and jazz lounge offers a wide selection of seafood, but any meal should begin with the rich chowder, which has been inducted into the city's Chowderfest Hall of Fame. *10 Huntington Ave., Westin Hotel, tel. 617/424–7488. AE, D, DC, MC, V. Moderate.*

BEACON HILL **Bangkok Seafood.** Choose from an assortment of mild to spicy curries to go with your choice of meat, seafood, or vegetables at this reliable Thai restaurant

close to the Common and Public Garden. *26 Charles St., tel. 617/248–9535. AE, MC, V. Inexpensive.*

Figs. This tiny offshoot of a popular Charlestown restaurant, known for its cracker-thin, wood-grilled pizzas, also serves delectable Italian-style sandwiches and salads at lunch and savory pastas at dinner. When the line is long, get takeout, or leave your name and window-shop on Charles Street. *42 Charles St., tel. 617/742–3447. AE, DC, MC, V. Inexpensive–Moderate.*

CAMBRIDGE **Grendel's Den.** Housed in a former Harvard College fraternity building, Grendel's has an unusually warm and clubby atmosphere, a downstairs bar, and an eclectic assortment of cuisines, including Middle Eastern, Greek, Indian, and French. *89 Winthrop St., tel. 617/491–1160. AE, D, DC, MC, V. Inexpensive–Moderate.*

Iruna. This plain but popular Spanish restaurant in Harvard Square serves up paella, fresh seafood, and salads. There is outdoor dining in warm weather. They serve wine, beer, and sangria only. *56 John F. Kennedy St., tel. 617/868–5633. AE, D, MC, V. Moderate.*

CHINATOWN **Imperial Teahouse Restaurant.** Its lively second floor is a large, airy dining room with the most extensive dim sum selection in Chinatown; dim sum denotes both the meal (a Chinese brunch served daily 9–3) and the variety of dumplings and buns, tiny chicken, shrimp, and other foods that you select from passing carts and pay for by the item. *70 Beach St., tel. 617/426– 8543. AE, DC, MC, V. Inexpensive–Moderate.*

FANEUIL HALL **Union Oyster House.** The best feature of Boston's oldest restaurant, established in 1826, is the shellfish bar where the oysters and clams are fresh and well chilled—a handy place to stop for a dozen oysters or cherrystone clams on the half shell. *41 Union St., tel. 617/227–2750. AE, D, DC, MC, V. Moderate.*

NORTH END **Daily Catch.** This tiny restaurant, with long lines after 6:30 PM, has an open kitchen and its menu posted on blackboards. Dishes include calamari cooked every way imaginable and healthy servings of other fresh seafood and pasta including lobster *fra diavolo* and linguine with clam sauce. *323 Hanover St., tel. 617/523–8567. No credit cards. Inexpensive.*

Felicia's. A place for solid Italian home cooking (good enough for Luciano Pavarotti when he's in town), Felicia's serves up such specialties as chicken *verdicchio* (stewed in white wine), veal *margherita* (sautéed in white wine, garlic, and capers), and cannelloni in a dark, second-floor, traditional Italian restaurant. *145A Richmond St., tel. 617/523–9885. AE, DC, MC, V. Moderate.*

SOUTH END **Addis Red Sea.** Across from the Boston Center for the Arts and Hamersley's Bistro, this attractive Ethiopian restaurant serves mild and spicy meat and vegetable stews, eaten with pinches of a pancakelike bread called *njera. 544 Tremont St., tel. 617/426–8727. MC, V. No lunch weekdays. Inexpensive.*

Hamersley's Bistro. Rave reviews and chic black-and-white decor are the norm here, where specialties include a garlic and mushroom sandwich served as an appetizer, bouillabaisse (ingredients change with the season), and roast chicken with garlic, lemon, and parsley. *578 Tremont St., tel. 617/267–6068. MC, V. Expensive.*

THEATER DISTRICT **Brew Moon.** In a stylish, stenciled setting, this upscale brew pub offers gourmet interpretations of bar snacks, sandwiches, and more substantial fare; you can make a meal of appetizers. *115 Stuart St., tel. 617/523–6467. AE, DC, MC, V. Inexpensive–Moderate.*

WATERFRONT **Eastern Pier.** An extensive menu of traditional Mandarin and Szechuan cuisine, with an emphasis on fresh seafood, brings diners to this restaurant, tucked away across the street from Jimmy's Harborside, amid other larger waterfront seafood establishments. *237 Northern Ave., tel. 617/423–7756. AE, D, DC, MC, V. Inexpensive–Moderate.*

No-Name Restaurant. Beginning as a nameless hole-in-the-wall for Fish Pier workers, the No-Name now attracts suburbanite families, tourists, and businesspeople—but the staples still include such seafood as boiled lobster, broiled scallops, and the fish of the day. *15½ Fish Pier off Northern Ave., tel. 617/338–7539. No credit cards. Inexpensive–Moderate.*

SHOPPING

Boston has its fair share of places to spend money, and its two daily newspapers, the *Globe* and the *Herald,* are the best places to learn about sales. Most of Boston's stores and shops are located in an area bounded by Quincy Market, the Back Bay, downtown, and Copley Square. There are few outlet stores in the area, but there are plenty of bargains, particularly in the world-famous Filene's Basement. Cambridge has an attractive mall in the Lechmere area and myriad smaller shops in Harvard Square.

SHOPPING DISTRICTS **Back Bay** is home to Newbury Street, where the town-house stores run from expensive and chic near the Public Garden to cheap and hip near Massachusetts Avenue, and Boylston Street, with more than 100 stores spread out over a seven-block area. **Cambridgeside Galleria** (tel. 617/621–8666), a three-story mall between Kendall Square in Cambridge and the Museum of Science, has more than 60 shops, including the larger anchor stores of Filene's, Lechmere, and Sears. It's accessible via the Green Line.

Copley Place (tel. 617/375–4400), an indoor shopping mall connecting the Westin and Marriott hotels near Copley Square, is a blend of the elegant, the unique, the glitzy, and the overpriced. The Neiman Marcus department store anchors 87 stores, restaurants, and cinemas. Prices in the shops on the second level tend to be a bit lower; skywalks connect it to the Prudential Center complex anchored by Saks Fifth Avenue.

Downtown Crossing (on Washington St. across from Boston Common), is the city's traditional shopping area. Here are Filene's, Jordan Marsh, and the Jewelers' Building (with many fine discount jewelers) as well as a pedestrian mall with outdoor food and merchandise kiosks, street performers, and benches.

Faneuil Hall Marketplace, between Government Center and the waterfront, has hundreds of small shops, kiosks of every description, street performers, and Quincy Market, with more than a hundred international food stalls. Be prepared for crowds, especially on the weekends. On Friday and Saturday, Haymarket—a crowded jumble of outdoor fruit and vegetable vendors, meat markets, and fishmongers—is in full swing.

Harvard Square in Cambridge has more than 150 stores within a few blocks, including, in the middle of it all, Out-of-Town News (Harvard Sq., tel. 617/354–7777) with dozens of current international periodicals. In addition to the surprising range of items found in the square, Cambridge is a great place to find new and used books.

DEPARTMENT STORES **Filene's** (426 Washington St., tel. 617/357–2100), a full-service department store, is famous for its two-level bargain basement, where items are automatically reduced in price according to the number of days they've been on the rack. Competition for goods can be stiff down here, so if you see something you want, buy it—it probably won't be there the next day. **Harvard Coop Society** (1400 Massachusetts Ave., Cambridge, tel. 617/492–2000), established in 1882 as a nonprofit service for students and faculty, is now a full department store best known for its extensive collection of records and books. **Jordan Marsh Company** (450 Washington St., tel. 617/357–3000) has been New England's largest department store since the 1860s.

SPECIALTY STORES **Antiques:** Charles Street on Beacon Hill offers a full range of antiques for browsers and buyers. **Books:** The Brattle Bookstore (9 West St., tel. 617/542–0210) is Boston's best used and rare bookshop; if the book you want is out of print, the Brattle either has it or can probably find it. **Clothing:**

You'll find all the chain stores in Boston; for unique men's and women's clothing, try Jasmine (37A Brattle St., Cambridge, tel. 617/354–6043) or the many boutiques on Newbury Street. **Crafts:** The Society of Arts and Crafts (175 Newbury St., tel. 617/266–1810) offers an excellent assortment of quality handicrafts. **Food:** Savenor's (160 Charles St., tel. 617/723–6328) carries outstanding cheeses, breads, and produce for picnic fixings. **Gifts:** The Women's Educational and Industrial Union (356 Boylston St., tel. 617/536–5651) has a wide array of cards, decorative gifts, children's items, and antiques. **Jewelry:** Shreve, Crump & Low (330 Boylston St., tel. 617/267–9100), one of Boston's oldest and most respected stores, offers a complete line of the finest jewelry, china, crystal, and silver.

OUTDOOR ACTIVITIES

The mania for physical fitness is big in Boston. Lots of people bicycle to work, and runners and roller skaters are seen constantly on the Storrow Memorial Drive Embankment, which flanks the Charles River. Most public recreational facilities, including swimming pools and tennis courts, are operated by the Metropolitan District Commission (tel. 617/727–9547).

BIKING Boston's flat terrain and well-marked bike paths are well suited for bicycling. The Dr. Paul Dudley White Bikeway, approximately 18 miles long, runs along both sides of the Charles River from Watertown Square to the Museum of Science. Free bike-route maps are available from the **Bicycle Coalition of Massachusetts** (214A Broadway, Cambridge 02139, tel. 617/491–7433). Bikes may be rented at the **Community Bike Shop** (496 Tremont St., tel. 617/542–8623).

JOGGING A jog along the grassy shores of the winding Charles River, from the Hatch Shell on the Esplanade to the Harvard/JFK Street Bridge and then back again on the Cambridge side, is a popular 7- or 8-mile circular route for conditioned city joggers. For shorter trips, many hotels provide jogging maps for guests. Another excellent source of information is the **Bill Rodgers Running Center** (Quincy Market, tel. 617/723–5612).

SWIMMING Two convenient and clean public swimming pools are located downtown: **Lee Pool** (tel. 617/523–9746), off Charles Street on the banks of the Charles River, and a **city-operated pool** (tel. 617/635–5235) off Commercial Street in the North End, which overlooks Boston Harbor and the USS *Constitution*. Both pools are open in July and August only.

TENNIS **Charlesbank Park** (Charles St.) is open from April to November and has lighted courts, available on a first-come, first-served basis.

WALKING The grandmother of all historical walks is the **Freedom Trail,** a 3½-mile walk that winds past 16 of Boston's most important historic attractions, including the Old State House, the Paul Revere House, and the USS *Constitution*. Its path is delineated by a red line marked on the sidewalk, beginning on Boston Common and ending in Charlestown. The 1½-mile self-guided **Harborwalk** traces Boston's maritime history. The 1.6-mile **Black Heritage Trail** explores the history of the city's 19th-century black community. The **Women's History Trail** celebrates notable contributions by Bostonian women. Maps for each of these four trails are available at the **Boston Common Visitor Information Center** (146 Tremont, tel. 617/426–3115) and the **National Historic Park Visitor Information Center** (15 State St., tel. 617/242–5642).

ENTERTAINMENT

Boston is a paradise for patrons of all the arts, from the symphony orchestra to experimental theater and dance to Orson Welles film festivals. Thursday's *Boston Globe* "Calendar" and the weekly *Boston Phoenix* provide comprehensive listings of events for the coming week. If you want to attend a specific performance, it would be wise to buy tickets when you make your hotel reservations. **Bostix** (Faneuil Hall Marketplace and Copley Square, tel. 617/723–5181) is Boston's largest official entertainment information center. Half-price, cash-only tickets are sold here for the same day's performances.

DANCE The **Boston Ballet** (tel. 617/695–6950 or 617/931–2000 for tickets) is the city's premier company, dancing at the Wang Center for the Performing Arts October through May. **Dance Umbrella** (tel. 617/492–7578) is one of New England's largest presenters of contemporary dance; performances are scheduled throughout Boston and throughout the year.

FILM The **Loews Nickelodeon Cinema** (606 Commonwealth Ave., tel. 617/424–1500) presents first-run independent and foreign films as well as revivals. In Cambridge, try the **Brattle Theater** (40 Brattle St., tel. 617/876–6837) for classic movies.

MUSIC For its size, Boston is the most musical city in America. Of the many contributing factors, perhaps most significant is its abundance of universities and other institutions of learning, which are a rich source of performers, music series, performing spaces, and audiences. Boston's churches also offer outstanding, and often free, music programs; early music, choral groups, and chamber groups also thrive here. Check Saturday's *Boston Globe* for listings of musical events.

Classical. One of the world's most perfect acoustical settings, **Symphony Hall** (301 Massachusetts Ave., tel. 617/266–1492) is home to the Boston Symphony Orchestra September–April. On Wednesday evenings the orchestra has open rehearsals, and tickets for these evenings are less expensive and easier to obtain. From May through July, the Boston Pops take over Symphony Hall with its upbeat, lighter renditions of the classics.

Jazz. The **Plaza Bar** (Copley Plaza Hotel, Copley Sq., tel. 617/267–6495) is an ornate, high-ceilinged piano bar. In Cambridge, **Scullers** (The Guest Quarters Suite Hotel, 400 Soldiers Field Rd., tel. 617/783–0811) books national and regional acts, and at the **Regattabar** (The Charles Hotel, Bennett and

Eliot Sts., tel. 617/864–1200), top names perform in a spacious and elegant club.

Pop. In summer, **Harborlights Pavilion** (Fan Pier, Northern Ave., tel. 617/931–2000 for tickets) seats 4,800 under an attractive white tent with beautiful harbor and city views; top national acts in country, folk, pop, and rock perform. The cluster of small clubs around Kenmore Square and Cambridge's Central Square present a wide roster of local and national acts in all genres year-round.

SPECTATOR SPORTS Sports are as much a part of Boston as codfish and Democrats, and the zeal of Boston fans can be witnessed year-round. April through September, the **Boston Red Sox** (tel. 617/267–8661 or 617/267–1700 for tickets) play baseball at Fenway Park, accessible via the Kenmore stop on the Green Line. The **Boston Celtics** (tel. 617/523–3030 or 617/931–2000) shoot hoops in the new FleetCenter on Causeway Street, accessible via the North Station stop on the Orange and Green lines, from November through April. The **Boston Bruins** (tel. 617/227–3223) are on the ice there from October through April. From September through December, the **New England Patriots** (tel. 800/543–1776) play football at Foxboro Stadium (best reached by car), 45 minutes south of the city.

THEATER Although Boston is no longer the tryout town for Broadway that it once was, it still hosts national tours, with a growing number of local theaters. Commercial theaters clustered in the Theater District include the **Colonial** (106 Boylston St., tel. 617/426–9366), the **Shubert** (265 Tremont St., tel. 617/426–4520), and the **Wang Center** (270 Tremont St., tel. 617/482–9393). Highly regarded local companies include the **American Repertory Theatre** (Loeb Drama Center, Harvard University, 64 Brattle St., tel. 617/495–2668); the **Huntington Theatre Company** (264 Huntington Ave., tel. 617/266–0800), affiliated with Boston University; **Charles Playhouse** (74 Warrenton St., tel. 617/426–5225), home of *Shear Madness*; and the **Lyric Stage** (140 Clarendon St., tel. 617/437–7172).

Branson
Missouri

Updated by Alison Stern

oday Branson seems like a ready-made phenomenon, an apparition with a sort of "Build it and they will come" inevitability. By now most people have at least heard of this booming Ozark town, even if they can't place it on the map. After all, Branson has hit the charts with nearly 40 theaters boasting more than 50,000 seats! That's a greater capacity than all the Broadway theaters combined can offer. Even more impressive is Branson's place as the second most popular driving-vacation destination after Walt Disney World and the Orlando area, with more than 6 million visitors annually. And the number keeps growing. Indeed, gazing down the neon landscape of the Strip (a 5-mile-long highway lined with theaters, shops, and restaurants), it's difficult to think of Branson as a place with a past, rather than one with a continually expanding future.

Yet there was a Branson even before it was anointed in 1991 by *60 Minutes* as the "Country Music Show Capital of the Universe." The nickname has stuck, somewhat to the chagrin of locals who want to stress that there's more to Branson than country music, Andy Williams, and Shoji Tabuchi. The region includes theme parks galore, enough to keep the kids entertained for days, as well as the lush, rolling Ozark countryside, where lots of outdoor activities are possible amid a wealth of natural and man-made resources. In fact, a 10-minute drive will take you to Taneycomo, Table Rock, and Bull Shoals lakes (*see* Outdoor Activities, *below*) for some of the best boating and bass fishing in the country.

This chapter merely scratches the surface of all the activities and entertainment that await you on your Branson vacation. For more details, pick up *Fodor's Branson: The Official Travel and Souvenir Guide to America's Music Show Capital.*

ESSENTIAL INFORMATION

WHEN TO GO Memorial Day through Labor Day is the traditional peak season for Branson, when all the headliners—and tour buses—are in town. Branson Country Spring (mid-March–May) and Ozark Mountain Christmas (mid-November–December) also draw crowds for festivals, concerts, and special shows and sporting events. Don't bother visiting between New Year's and the spring extravaganza, as many theaters, hotels, and restaurants close.

FESTIVALS AND SEASONAL EVENTS Branson **Country Spring (mid-Mar.–May):** Among the celebrations, designed to promote tourism during the shoulder season, are the Americana Branson Jam, a huge film festival, the Bass Pro Spring Fishing Classic and the White Bass Round-Up, and the seasonal opening of the 20-mile Dogwood Trail. **Country Crafts Show and Sale (July–Aug.):** If you adore knickknacks, this is the time to pick up everything from soaps to saddles. **Fall Harvest Festivals (mid-Sept.–late Oct.):** Apple bobbing and scarecrow building are just two of the autumn activities at this festival celebrating the region's bounty. **Ozark Mountain Christmas (Nov.–Dec.):** Drawing more than 400,000 visitors a year are such yuletide

attractions as a 40-foot-high nativity scene glowing atop the rocky bluffs above Branson, an Adoration Parade with marching bands and beautiful floats, and the Festival of Lights—a blazing stream of lights lining the highway from Springfield to Branson.

BARGAINS Downtown hotels are cheaper and more basic than the accommodations that are along the Strip and closer to the theaters. When dining out, look for restaurants that offer buffets; breakfasts, for example, can be found for as little as a few dollars. Early-bird specials, offered at most restaurants between 4 and 6 PM, are another way to eat on the cheap. Although most theater tickets are competitively priced, combination tickets can sometimes save you a few dollars, so look around for joint-owned ventures such as Silver Dollar City and the Grand Palace or White Water.

TOURIST OFFICE Branson/Lakes Area Chamber of Commerce (Box 1897, 269 W. Rte. 248 at Rte. 65, Branson 65615, tel. 417/334–4136, fax 417/334–4139).

EMERGENCIES Dial 911 or call the following numbers. **Police:** Branson Police Department (tel. 417/739–2131). **Fire:** Branson Fire Department (tel. 417/334–2600). **Hospital:** Skaggs Community Hospital (N. Business Rte. 65 at Skaggs Rd., tel. 417/335–7000; ambulance, 417/334–1441). **Dental:** Branson Dental Center (1034 W. Main St., tel. 417/334–6120). **Pharmacies:** Family Discount Drug (650 N. Rte. 65, tel. 417/334–1390), Master's Pharmacy (811 S. Commercial St., tel. 417/334–6665), and Wal-Mart (2050 W. Rte. 76, tel. 417/334–5005).

ARRIVING AND DEPARTING

BY PLANE The closest major commercial airport is **Springfield Regional Airport** (tel. 417/869–0300), located 40 miles north of Branson. **American Eagle** (tel. 800/433–7300), **Northwest Airlink** (tel. 800/225–2525), **TWA** (tel. 800/221–2000), and **USAir** (tel. 800/428–4322) offer daily service via their respective hubs.

Regional carrier **Lone Star Airlines** (tel. 800/877–3932) offers limited service to Harrison's tiny Boone County Airport (tel. 501/741–3433), 35 miles south of Branson on U.S. 65. There is no shuttle service between Harrison and Branson.

Between Springfield Airport and Branson: The **Show-Me Shuttle Service** (tel. 417/883–7900 or 800/795–7555) schedules several round-trips daily for $40 per person, as well as service between Branson and Tulsa, Oklahoma. **Branson Shuttle** (tel. 417/335–4466) runs regularly between the airport and Branson for $60 per person one-way; group discounts are available.

Branson City Cab (tel. 417/334–5678) and **A-1 Shuttle and Taxi** (tel. 417/335–4486) can arrange airport transfers from Springfield for about $60 each way. Reservations are required.

BY BUS Greyhound Bus Systems (tel. 800/752–4841) runs daily service from most major North American gateways to Springfield (803 St. Louis St. and National St., tel. 417/862–5097) and Branson (1911 Main St., Branson Welcome Center, tel. 417/337–9323).

BY CAR Branson is known as a rubber-tire destination, because the majority of visitors here have come by car from within a 500-mile radius. Branson is 40 miles south of Springfield along U.S. 65, a scenic, well-maintained highway. During winter watch for icy conditions.

GETTING AROUND

BY CAR Highway 76 (a.k.a. "The Strip") is Branson's main drag, along which are most of the town's theaters and restaurants. Traffic is often a problem, especially during lunch (11:30–2), at dinner (5–7:45), and when shows let out (9:15–11). To help remedy the traffic problem, Branson has created "Time Saver" routes, which are marked with color-coded guitar icons and will help you steer clear of traffic. Pick up a map from the chamber of commerce for details on the red, yellow, and blue routes.

BY TAXI A-1 Shuttle & Taxi (tel. 417/335–6001) and **Branson City Cab** (tel. 417/334–5678) offer 24-hour service throughout Branson Lakes region. Destinations along the Strip cost about $8–$10; outlying areas such as Shepherd of the Hills and Silver Dollar City could cost as much as $15.

BY FOOT Although the Strip runs only about 5 miles from downtown to the last theater, Branson is not a comfortable place to explore on foot. The terrain can be hilly, and Highway 76 is an extremely busy thoroughfare. Outlying attractions must be reached by car or taxi.

EXPLORING

THE THEATERS AND THE STARS The primary attractions in Branson are the stars and their theaters. Since there are breakfast, matinee, and evening shows, your day can be filled with entertainment—but only if come when the headliners are in town. Most stars remain in Branson from May through October, and some extend their schedules into November and December for Ozark Mountain Christmas. Since the theaters' show offerings can change rapidly, we've listed only address, phone, capacity, and months open below; call for current information on who's playing and when. Reservations are recommended for all shows.

Baldknobbers Jamboree Theater. *2845 W. Rte. 76, tel. 417/334–4528. 1,700 seats. Open May–mid-Dec.*

Moe Bandy's Americana Theater. *2905 W. Rte. 76, tel. 417/335–8176. 950 seats. Open late Mar.–Nov.*

Boxcar Willie Theater. *3454 W. Rte. 76, tel. 417/334–8696. 901 seats. Open late Apr.–late Oct.*

Braschler Music Show Theater. *Gretna Rd., 2 blocks north of intersection of Hwys. 76* and 165, tel. *417/334–4363. 720 seats. Open May–Oct.; limited schedule Nov.–Dec.*

Glen Campbell's Goodtime Theater. *Rtes. 248 and 65, tel. 417/336–1220. 2,200 seats. Open May–early Dec.*

Campbell's Ozark Country Jubilee Theater. *3115 W. Rte. 76, tel. 417/334–6400 or 800/365–5833. 650 seats. Open year-round.*

Roy Clark Celebrity Theater. *3425 W. Rte. 76, tel. 417/334–0076. 1,000 seats. Open late Mar.–Nov.*

Country Tonite Theater. *4080 W. Rte. 76, tel. 417/334–2422. 2,000 seats. Open mid-Mar.–mid-Dec.*

Dixie Stampede Dinner Theater. *1527 W. Hwy. 76, tel. 800/520–5544. 1,000 seats. Open Apr.–Dec.*

Gettysburg Theater. *2211 S. Hwy. 248, tel. 417/334–8400. 922 seats. Open year-round.*

Mickey Gilley Theater. *3455 W. Rte. 76, tel. 417/334–3210. 950 seats. Open Apr.–early Dec.*

Grand Palace. *2700 W. Rte. 76, tel. 417/334–7263 or 800/572-5223. 4,000 seats. Open Apr.–Dec.*

Cristy Lane Theater. *3600 W. Rte. 76, tel. 417/335–5111. 1,300 seats. Open Feb.–Dec.*

Wayne Newton Theater. *3701 W. Hwy. 76, tel. 417/336–6220. 2,000 seats. Open Mar.–Nov.*

Tony Orlando Yellow Ribbon Music Theater. *Rte. 165 at 3220 Falls Pkwy., tel. 417/335–8669. 2,000 seats. Open mid-Mar.–Dec.*

Osmond Family Theater. *3216 W. Rte. 76, tel. 417/336–6100. 1,300 seats. Yakov Smirnoff: tel. 800/336–6542. Open Apr.–mid-Dec.*

Presley's Mountain Music Jubilee Theater. *2920 W. Rte. 76, tel. 417/334–4874. 2,000 seats. Open Apr.–Oct.; limited schedule Nov.–mid-Dec.*

Charley Pride Theater. *Wildwood St. and Gretna Ave., tel. 417/337–7433 or 800/242–7539. 1,974 seats. Open mid-Apr.–mid-Dec.*

Pump Boys and Dinettes Theater. *Rte. 165 at Green Mountain Dr., tel. 417/336–4319. 600 seats. Open year-round.*

76 Music Hall. *1919 W. Rte. 76, tel. 417/335–2484. 500 seats. Open year-round.*

Shenandoah South Theater. *Rte. 248 and Shepherd of the Hills Expressway, tel. 417/336–3986. 3,000 seats. Open year-round.*

Jim Stafford Theater. *3444 W. Rte. 76, tel. 417/335–8080. 1,100 seats. Open mid-Apr.–mid-Dec.*

Shoji Tabuchi Theater. *3260 Shepherd of the Hills Expressway, tel. 417/334–7469. 2,000 seats. Open Apr.–Dec.*

Thunderbird Theater. *2215 W. Hwy. 76, tel. 417/336–2542. 650 seats. Open Apr.–Dec.*

Mel Tillis Theater. *Rte. 248, tel. 417/335–6635. 2,672 seats. Open Apr.–Dec.*

Bobby Vinton's Blue Velvet Theater. *2701 W. Rte. 76, tel. 417/334–2500 or 800/872–6229. 2,000 seats. Open Apr.–mid-Dec.*

Lawrence Welk Champagne Theater. *1984 Rte. 165, tel. 417/337–7469 or 800/505–9355. 2,268 seats. Open Apr.–Dec.*

Andy Williams' Moon River Theater. *2500 W. Rte. 76, tel. 417/334–4500. 2,000 seats. Open May–mid-Dec.*

THEME PARKS

Most of the theme parks lie within 10 miles of Branson proper and are easily reached by car. They are all family-oriented, and most have retained at least a piece of Branson's past, with living-history demonstrations and costumed staff recalling yesteryear.

Mutton Hollow Entertainment Park and Craft Village. The idyllic retreat in the Harold Bell Wright novel, *Shepherd of the Hills* (see Shepherd of the Hills Homestead, *below*), was the inspiration for this charming re-creation pioneer village. The beautifully landscaped gardens are laced with silvery brooks, and the streets are lined with more than 30 crafts shops, three music theaters, restaurants, a museum that was formerly Harold Bell Wright's home, and a country-fair area, all carefully modeled on historic photos. *Hwy. 76 and Shepherd of the Hills Expressway (western end of Strip), tel. 417/334-4947. Open late Mar.–Oct., daily; Nov.–Dec., Thurs.–Sun., for Ozark Mountain Christmas celebration. Admission charged for rides and entertainment.*

Shepherd of the Hills Homestead and Outdoor Theater. At the turn of the century, writer Harold Bell Wright made a trip from upstate New York to the Ozarks in the hope that the mountain air would help him recover from tuberculosis (which it eventually did). While here he was befriended by a local family, the Rosses, who permitted him to camp on their homestead while he regained his health and strength. His experiences inspired the bucolic novel *Shepherd of the Hills,* which was based on his encounters with the family and other memorable hill folk.

Since the 1940s, an outdoor stage epic based on the novel has been performed at the Ross's former home, which is now a National Literary Landmark. "Shepherd of the Hills," presented in a theater that can (and often does) hold 2,500 audience members, is monumental in every way: There are 80 actors, 58 animals, three buggies, four wagons, a 1906 DeWitt automobile, and a virtual arsenal of 12-gauge shotguns and 45-caliber pistols. After "Shepherd of the Hills" shuts down for the season, a drama called "The Newborn King" takes the outdoor stage, also with great fanfare.

During the regular season there's a Jeep-drawn wagon tour of the 160-acre site that takes in "Old Matt's" cabin, a gristmill, a flag museum, a playground, a dilapidated 1901 church on Inspiration Point, and the 230-foot Inspiration Tower. The tower affords a sensational 360° view of the countryside from the observation deck, which is reached by elevator. *W. Hwy. 76 (2 mi west of Shepherd of the Hills Expressway), tel. 417/334-4191. Homestead Park open Apr.–Oct; Shepherd of the Hills Theater open May–Oct; Christmas Show open Nov.–Dec; Inspiration Tower open year-round. Admission charged; combination tickets available.*

Silver Dollar City (SDC). Marvel Cave, an underground complex of winding passageways and striking calcite and limestone formations, first opened to the public in 1894. Today the cave is one of the main attractions within Silver Dollar City, a remarkable re-creation of an 1890s town that was developed to entertain the cavern's many visitors. Beyond the usual theme-park attractions—water rides, roller coaster, Ferris wheel, petting zoo, and nine theaters presenting musical and dance revues—SDC is most notable for its 50 crafts and food shops, most built from local materials and staffed by artisans and actors who take their 19th-century Ozarks theme seriously. Weekends in high season (May–October) can be a madhouse, so visit during the week to avoid the worst crowds. *Indian Point Rd. (off W. Hwy. 76, 3 mi west of Branson), tel. 800/572-5223. Open year-round. Admission charged.*

WATER, WATER EVERYWHERE

Ride the Ducks. Take the 70-minute tour of a military museum in one of 30 amphibious vehicles that transported troops and equipment over land and water during World War II. At the end of the tour, the ducks splash down into Lake Taneycomo for a quick sightseeing cruise. (Sit in front if you want to get wet.) *W. Hwy. 76, tel. 417/334-5350. Open daily Apr.–Oct., with tours every 15 mins; daily Nov. and Feb., but tours are less frequent, so call ahead. Admission charged.*

Sammy Lane Pirate Cruises. The *Sammy Lane,* a 49-person passenger boat, will whisk you off on a 70-minute Lake Taneycomo adventure. You'll hear the history of the White River (dammed to become Taneycomo and Table Rock lakes) before you tangle with a fearsome band of pirates who are after the gold that the *Sammy Lane* picked up from the Boston Ridge Gold Mine. *280 N. Lake Dr., tel. 417/334-3015. Open Apr.–Oct., with 10 cruises daily. Admission charged.*

Waltzing Waters. Depending on your mood, you may find this water show with rows of lighted fountains coordinated with thunderous show tunes either hokey or mesmerizing—or maybe a bit of both. More than 40,000 gallons of water, in flumes up to three-stories high, form twirling lariats, three-tier wedding cakes, and even the Manhattan skyline. An engineer runs the sophisticated, 200-button control panel during the show, but audience members can make the waters dance after the performance. *W. Hwy. 76 (west end), tel. 417/334–4144. Open year-round. Reservations recommended for groups of 15 or more. Admission charged.*

White Water. You won't think Branson is landlocked when you're relaxing under palm trees by a blue grotto, playing beach volleyball, bobbing in the wave pool, or cooling off on one of the water slides or raft rides at this water park. *3505 W. Hwy. 76, tel. 417/334–7488. Open daily Memorial Day–Labor Day. Admission charged.*

MUSEUMS

Bonniebrook. In 1907 illustrator Rose O'Neill retreated to Bonniebrook (an Ozark home she bought for her parents), where as she slept one night some small, plump, impish figures appeared to her in a dream. A year later the Kewpies made their first appearance in illustrations for the *Ladies Home Journal,* and soon they were reproduced as the now-famous dolls. Today, the Bonniebrook Historical Society runs this home as a museum commemorating Rose and her creations. *481 Rose O'Neill Rd., Walnut Shade, MO (just east of Hwy. 65, 9 mi north of Branson), tel. 417/561–4797. Open Apr.–Sept., daily 7–5. Admission charged; group rates available.*

Boxcar Willie Museum. This museum is joyously crammed with seemingly everything Box picked up while on the road. He's cataloged all of his obsessions, including railroad, airplane, and recording memorabilia; Roy Rogers paraphernalia; Elvis's rocking chair; and even the cockpit of the KC97 WWII fighter plane around which his adjoining theater was constructed. *3454 W. Rte. 76, tel. 417/334–8696. Open Apr.–late Oct., Mon. and Wed.–Sat. Admission charged.*

Civil War Museum. This museum, opened in 1993, houses one of the state's largest private collections of Civil War memorabilia, with Union artifacts gathered on one side, Confederate on the other. *Shepherd of the Hills Expressway (off W. Hwy. 76), tel. 417/334–1861. Open Apr.–Oct., Mon.–Sat. 9–6, Sun. 1–6. Admission charged.*

Ralph Foster Museum at the College of the Ozarks. Among the many attractions at the College of the Ozarks are greenhouses with some 7,000 plants; a weaving studio; a fruitcake-and-jelly kitchen where more than 25,000 cakes are baked annually; and Edward Mills, a replica of an old-fashioned mill, where students grind whole-grain meal and flour. The main reason to visit the college, however, is the astounding Ralph Foster Museum (a.k.a. "The Smithsonian of the Ozarks"), named in honor of the man who founded KWTO radio station in Springfield, Missouri, and who gave many country stars their first break on his "Ozark Jubilee" show. More than 750,000 items are displayed on the museum's three crowded floors. Among the most notable exhibits are Grammy certificates, gold records, and old fiddles; collections of rare Kewpies and ethnic dolls; the original *Beverly Hillbillies* buggy; and a large gun collection. *College of the Ozarks, Point Lookout, tel. 417/334–6411, ext. 3407. Open Mon.–Sat. 9–4. Admission charged.*

Ripley's Believe It or Not Museum. As you approach this museum devoted to the macabre and the bizarre, you may wonder, "Was there an earthquake?" The edifice is uniquely designed with an ominous crack running down the center—a tribute to seismologists who predicted a "Really Big One" for Missouri (which sits on the New Madrid Fault) in 1990. (It never happened.) Displays include such oddities as the World's Largest Ball of Nylon String, weighing 7 tons; collections of antique bedpans, chimney pots, and toilet seats; and New Guinea penis sheaths, which protect the wearer against insect bites. *3326 W. Hwy. 76, tel. 800/998–4418. Open daily 9 AM–10 PM. Admission charged.*

OTHER ATTRACTIONS

Ozarks IMAX Discovery Center. Award-winning IMAX film technology allows audiences not only to see a movie but to feel like part of the action. The giant curved screen can create the sensation that you're hanging over the rim of the Grand Canyon, wandering amid penguins in Antarctica, sinking with the *Titanic,* or on stage with the Rolling Stones. The IMAX Center also features 14 shops and a full-service restaurant. *3069 Shepherd of the Hills Expressway (off W. Hwy. 76), tel. 417/335–4832. Open Jan.–Mar., daily 9:30–7:30; Apr.–Dec., daily 8:30 AM–11:30 PM. Admission charged.*

Stone Hill Winery. Although the Stone Hill vineyard is in Hermann, 220 miles away on the Missouri River, the Branson facility blends and bottles many of the wines. You can take a free tour of the winery and learn how the grapes are grown, crushed, and fermented. The tour ends with a wine tasting. *Hwy. 165 (south of W. Hwy. 76), tel. 417/334–1897. Tours and tastings free. Open Mon.–Sat. 8:30–6, Sun. noon–6.*

Talking Rocks Cavern. Discovered in 1883, this cavern is essentially a giant room with an incredible variety of calcite formations created over eons by dripping water. Among the most spectacular sights are the 100-foot-tall Cathedral (which you can actually walk through), the towering Powell's Column, and the Angel, a formation with "wings." *Hwy. 13 (1 mi south of Branson West, about 8 mi from the Strip), tel. 800/600–2283. Open Apr.–Sept., daily 9:30–5; Oct.–mid-Dec. and mid-Jan.–Mar., Fri.–Tues. 9:30–5. Admission charged.*

LODGING

The Branson Lakes region offers a range of accommodations from houseboats to bed-and-breakfast inns; the following selection includes B&Bs, basic hotels, and motels that are in Branson proper and lie mostly in the Inexpensive–Moderate range. Some expensive accommodations are also represented. Although not listed here, Branson also has a good selection of full-service resorts that are mostly situated along the lakes and tend to be very expensive. Price categories for double occupancy, excluding tax, are Expensive, $100–$150; Moderate, $50–$100; and Inexpensive, under $50.

MODERATE–EXPENSIVE **Holiday Inn Crowne Plaza.** This property is Branson's largest, and is less noisy than some others since it's on a side street, just off the Strip. Rooms are huge and are done in elegant, dark, mountain colors. *120 S. Wildwood Dr., tel. 417/335–5767, fax 417/335–7979. 500 rooms. Restaurant, bar, pool, exercise room. AE, D, DC, MC, V.*

Lodge of the Ozarks. The small but sophisticated lobby, with marble, tile, and polished wood furnishings, strikes an immediate note of class as you enter this reasonably priced but posh property. Choose from oversize standard rooms in soothing earth tones to suites with wet bar and Jacuzzi. *3431 W. Hwy. 76, tel. 417/334–7535, fax 417/334–6861. 190 rooms. Restaurant, bar, pool. AE, D, MC, V.*

Palace Inn. This well-situated hotel is another Branson bargain with high-quality rooms and relatively low rates. The hospitable lobby evokes a genteel southern sitting room, and although accommodations are on the small side, they are pleasingly decorated. *2820 W. Hwy. 76, tel. 417/334–7666, fax 417/334–7720. 164 rooms. Restaurant, bar, pool. AE, D, MC, V.*

Settle Inn. The huge green-and-white buildings recall grand hotels of a bygone era. What the hotel is most noted for, however, is its theme suites (OK Corral Room, Coca Cola Room, Big Top Room), which are at once kitschy and fun. *3050 Green Mountain Dr., tel. and fax 417/335–4700. 300 rooms. Restaurant, bar, pool. AE, D, MC, V.*

MODERATE **Branson Hotel.** Built in 1907, this B&B is the oldest accommodation in Branson. Each room is individually decorated with a mix of antiques and period reproductions but also has modern conveniences such as cable TV and full baths. *214 W. Main St., tel. 417/335–6104. 9 rooms. No credit cards.*

Inn at Fall Creek. This idyllic B&B feels like it's in the middle of the countryside yet is only a few minutes' drive from the Strip. Farmhouse antiques were patiently culled from barn sales and decorate the inn. *391 Concord Ave., tel. 417/336–3422. 4 rooms. MC, V.*

INEXPENSIVE-MODERATE **Branson Towers Inn.** The handsome exterior has a plantation-mansion look that complements the gracious lobby, with its ornate woodwork, an imposing double staircase, and marble floors. Rooms are slightly spartan but fresh, with wine-color carpets, salmon walls, and floral spreads and curtains. *236 Shepherd of the Hills Expressway, tel. 417/336–4500, fax 417/334–6838. 210 rooms. Restaurant, pool. AE, D, DC, MC, V.*

Days Inn of Branson. Tour groups often stay at this hotel because it's so big, cheap, and accommodating. Since it's located on a side street just off the Strip, the property offers convenience without the noise of hotels on the main thoroughfare. *3524 Keeter St., tel. 417/334–5544, fax 417/334–2935. 425 rooms. Restaurant, pool. AE, D, DC, MC, V.*

Dutch Kountry Inn. Children especially enjoy this property, thanks to a fairy-tale-theme miniamusement center where they can explore a windmill and clamber through a model of Mother Hubbard's shoe. Family units include sleeping lofts, and honeymoon suites have a whirlpool tub. Children under 16 stay for free. *2425 W. Hwy. 76, tel. 417/335–2100, fax 417/334–5738. 291 rooms. Restaurant, pool. D, MC, V.*

Edgewood Motel. The Edgewood and its adjacent sister property, the Shadowbrook, are set amid 25 acres of gardens and shade trees. Rooms, decorated in maroon, jade, and dark blue, are huge, if a little spare. *W. Hwy. 76, tel. 417/334–1000, fax 417/334–0476. 297 rooms. Restaurant, pool. AE, D, MC, V.*

Great Western Inn. This is one of the typical big bargains on the Strip: The billboard outside advertises rooms for $14 and up. Furnishings are clean, if a little frayed at the edges, and the inn offers all of the amenities you'd expect from higher-end properties. *3110 W. Rte. 76, tel. 417/334–8998. 41 rooms. Pool. AE, D, MC, V.*

Music Country Motor Inn South. This basic motel's advantages are its good rates and location near the Andy Williams, Bobby Vinton, and Grand Palace theaters. The rear-building rooms are much quieter than those near the street. *2834 W. Rte. 76, tel. 417/334–1194, fax 417/334–7760. 113 rooms. Pool. AE, D, MC, V.*

Queen Anne Motel. Sister properties Queen Anne I and Queen Anne II combine the amenities of a motel with the ambience of a B&B. The larger-than-average rooms are daintily decorated in coral and salmon colors, with dark, polished headboards and armoires. *3510 W. Rte. 76, tel. 417/335–8100, fax 417/335–8204. 40 rooms. Pool. AE, D, MC, V.*

Seven Gables Inn. You'll receive a gracious welcome at this cozy property just off of the Strip. Standard rooms have maroon carpets and cherry two-poster beds; several rooms have whirlpool tubs. *305 Rte. 165 S, tel. 417/334–7077 or 800/280–7077, fax 417/335–3629. 130 rooms. Pool. AE, D, MC, V.*

DINING

Branson's gastronomic options range from buffet-style breakfasts with bacon and eggs to international smorgasbords featuring Mexican, Italian, Greek, and Chinese fare. The following selection includes only properties in Branson proper. Price categories per person, excluding drinks, service, and tax, are Expensive, over $20; Moderate, $10–$20; and Inexpensive, under $10.

CONTINENTAL Buckingham's. What's most memorable about this restaurant is its African motif, with elaborate masks and faux leopard- and zebra-skin seat covers. The food, while not nearly so exotic, is quite tasty. Try Maryland crab cakes with aioli or a shrimp kabob with tangy coffee-barbecue sauce. *2820 W. Hwy. 76, tel. 417/337–7777. AE, D, MC, V. No lunch Mon.–Sat. Expensive.*

Paradise Grill. If you're in the mood for fun food you'll probably enjoy this jazzy restaurant. The slyly sophisticated menu lists items such as Squawking Nachos (smoked chicken, *caciotta* goat cheese, and two salsas) and Wild Things (wild mushrooms, leeks, and Brie on focaccia), among other standouts. *3250 Shepherd of the Hills Expressway, tel. 417/337–7444. AE, D, DC, MC, V. Inexpensive–Moderate.*

Upstairs at Jim's. This cozy aerie above the Jim Stafford Theater looks like a fairy-tale set, with murals of trees, animals on the walls, and painted cobblestone paths on the floors. The menu is concise, with a few homemade offerings each day; you can usually count on a chicken and a meat dish, as well as bountiful salads. *3440 W. Rte. 76, tel. 417/335–8080. AE, D, MC, V. Moderate.*

COUNTRY Bob Evans General Store and Restaurant. Local musicians pick and fiddle on the porch, and artists display Ozarks crafts and offer demonstrations outside of this re-creation 1900s general store. Breakfasts are excellent, with scrumptious muffins and cinnamon-raisin biscuits. *801 W. Main St., tel. 417/336–2023. No reservations. AE, MC, V. Inexpensive.*

Shack Cafe. Opened as a takeout food shack in 1904, this café has evolved into a respectable restaurant that charmingly recalls the turn of the century. Owner Arena Creekmore serves stick-to-the-ribs meals with generous sides of homemade mashed potatoes. *108 S. Commercial St., tel. 417/334–3490. No reservations. No credit cards. Inexpensive.*

FAMILY-STYLE McGuffey's. There are now four McGuffey's locations in Branson, but the original was built by Andy Williams, whose theater is next door. Traditional favorites such as broiled chicken and deep-fried shrimp head up the family-style menu. *2600 W. Hwy. 76, tel. 417/336–3600. Reservations recommended. AE, D, MC, V. Moderate.*

Sadie's Sideboard. The woodsy, rustic decor at Sadie's down-home eatery may make you forget that you're right on the Strip. The all-you-can-eat buffets feature more than 20 items, including broiled chicken, pot roast, and peel-and-eat shrimp. *2840 W. Hwy. 76, tel. 417/334–3619. No reservations. AE, MC, V. Inexpensive–Moderate.*

ITALIAN Rocky's. Locals come to this popular downtown spot for the publike ambience and hearty portions served up with lots of garlic and attitude. Numerous superb pastas are on the menu, as well as expert renditions of such classics as chicken piccata and veal marsala. *120 N. Sycamore, tel. 417/335–4765. AE, D, DC, MC, V. Closed Sun. Moderate.*

MEXICAN AND TEX-MEX Gilley's Texas Cafe. The list of entrées offered at Mickey's place goes on for pages, but some favorites are fajitas, big beef burgers, barbecue chicken, and ribs. Margaritas are the drink of the house, and if you're lucky you might get to share the cantina with Mickey after his show. *3457 W. Hwy. 76, tel. 417/335–2755. No reservations. AE, D, DC, MC, V. Moderate.*

STEAK AND BARBECUE B.T. Bones Steakhouse. The menu won't "steer" you wrong, especially if you order one of the many cuts of thick, juicy steak (all Iowa choice, cut fresh daily in house). There's usually entertainment here nightly, from music to comedy to magic. *2346 Shepherd of the Hills Expressway, tel. 417/335–2002. AE, D, DC, MC, V. Moderate–Expensive.*

Uncle Joe's Bar-B-Que. "You'll wanna lick your fingers right down to your toes," brags the menu about the messy, delicious, hickory-smoked ribs and chicken served in dinosaur-size portions at tables dressed in red-and-white checked tablecloths. *2819 W. Hwy. 76, tel. 417/334–4548. No reservations. D, DC, MC, V. Inexpensive.*

OUTDOOR ACTIVITIES

BOATING, FISHING, AND WATER SPORTS The Branson/Lakes region, comprising Lake Taneycomo, Table Rock Lake, and Bull Shoals Lake, attracted sportspeople and nature lovers long before the stars spread their glitter down Highway 76. These megalakes, formed by a series of dams on the White and James rivers, offer water sports from canoeing to jet skiing, as well as some of the finest bass and trout fishing in the country. The lakes are meticulously maintained by the U.S. Army Corps of Engineers, and the splendor of the surrounding multicolored bluffs and virgin forest has been well preserved.

Boating and Other Water Sports. Table Rock offers the most activities, including scuba diving and sailing. Wave runners, Jet Skis, and water skis are all available for rent at several marinas. Some Bull Shoals marinas also rent jets and water skis, but they're less in demand as most people prefer to enjoy the tranquil setting. Taneycomo is limited to pontoons, bass boats, and fishing boats.

Fishing. All anglers must purchase either a three-day ($8), 14-day ($15), annual nonresident ($25), or annual resident ($8) fishing permit, available at any bait shop. Trout fishermen must also buy a Missouri Trout Stamp, available at bait shops for $6.

Swimming. While there are several beaches and coves, especially on Table Rock and Bull Shoals, these should not be confused for classic Caribbean crescents. They are made of predominantly small gravel, not sand, and while buoy markers demarcate a safe swimming zone, there are no lifeguards.

CYCLING AND IN-LINE SKATING There are suitable trails in **North Beach City Park** (Lake St., Branson, tel. 417/335–3085). While short, they're relatively flat and consistently paved, with some lovely peaceful vistas of Lake Taneycomo.

GOLF There are five excellent golf courses in the Branson area, but the only championship contender is the par-70, 6,200-yard course at **Pointe Royale Golf Club** (Rte. 165, Branson, tel. 417/334–4477), where water comes into play on several holes. The other courses include **Holiday Hills Resort & Golf Club** (E. Rte. 76, Branson, tel. 417/334–4443), **Oakmont Community Golf Course** (Rte. 86, Ridgedale, tel. 417/334–1572), **Kimberling Hills Country Club** (1 Lakeshore Dr., Kimberling City, tel. 417/739–4370), and **Lake Taneycomo Golf Course** (Rte. 160, Forsyth, tel. 417/546–5454).

HIKING Don't plan to do any arduous wilderness trekking in the Ozarks: The gentle mounds and hollows are better suited to brisk walks. The **Mark Twain National Forest** (Ava Ranger District, Bus. Rte. 5S, Box 188, Ava 65608, tel. 417/683–4428) is 1.5 million acres, with more than 63,000 acres congressionally designated as wilderness. A gentle, 3-mile trail winds through **Table Rock Lake State Park** (Rte. 165, 7 mi southwest of Branson, tel. 417/334–4704), beginning at Indian Point. The comparatively rugged trails winding through the **Busick Wildlife Area** (15 mi north of Branson, entrance off Rte. 65, no phone) are popular with mountain bikers, as well as hikers. The trails in **Henning Conservation Area** (W. Hwy. 76, just east of Shepard of the Hills Homestead, tel. 417/334–3324) are rich in indigenous flora. If you don't want to venture off alone, contact **Scenic Trails Vacations** (Box 785A, Ava 65608, tel. 800/322–5048), which organizes day walks and biking/hiking trips throughout the region.

Cape Cod
Massachusetts

Updated by Karl Luntta

The craggy peninsula called Cape Cod—jutting into the open Atlantic and separated from the Massachusetts mainland by the 17.4-mile Cape Cod Canal—offers the visitor a ruggedly beautiful coast and well-preserved towns and farmscapes dating from Colonial times. Provincetown, with its bright, gay, muscular nightlife, is another story altogether.

The Cape is only about 70 miles from end to end and no more than 20 miles wide; you can make a cursory circuit of it in a day. Most visitors, however, prefer to settle into a hotel or bed-and-breakfast and wander no farther than the nearest beach or clam bar. Though overdevelopment has bred some ugly strip malls and tourist traps, much of the land is now permanently protected. Paved trails wander through nature preserves, which protect the natural beauty of the pine forests, marshes, swamps, and cranberry bogs. Thanks to the establishment of the Cape Cod National Seashore, one can walk for almost 30 miles along the dune-backed Atlantic beach, seeing few traces of human habitation.

Through the creation of many national historical districts, similar protection has been extended to some of the area's oldest and loveliest settlements. Along tree-shaded country roads you'll see traditional saltboxes and Cape Cod–style cottages, their shingles weathered to a silvery gray, with soft pink roses spilling across them or massed over low, split-rail fences. You'll also pass many working windmills and white-steepled churches, taverns, and village greens that epitomize old New England. The onetime artists' colony of Provincetown—still alive with art, and the Cape's prime people-watching town—offers a cheerful, back-to-back mix of tiny waterfront shops.

ESSENTIAL INFORMATION

WHEN TO GO Cape Cod's climate is milder than the mainland's, with average minimum and maximum temperatures of 63°–78° in July and 25°–40° from December through February. Winter sometimes brings bone-chilling dampness and winds, but very little snow as a rule. Memorial Day through Labor Day (and in some cases through Columbus Day) constitutes the high season, when the weather makes you think nothing but "beach" and everything is open; unfortunately, it is also a time of higher prices, crowds, and traffic. In fall, the moorland turns rich autumn colors and the mild weather and thinned-out crowds make exploring a pleasure. Unpredictable spring arrives late. Though winter is a time when many activities and facilities shut down, romantic country inns offer cozy rooms with canopy beds and fireplaces at as much as 50% below summer rates.

BARGAINS Factory outlets are scattered throughout the Cape, a number of them along Route 28 east of Hyannis. The visitor centers of the Cape Cod National Seashore offer free slide shows, exhibits, and free or inexpensive nature-oriented programs and tours. Most of the historical museums throughout the Cape charge only nominal fees. In the off-season especially, many restaurants offer early-bird specials and weekend buffets.

TOURIST OFFICES **Massachusetts Office of Travel & Tourism** (100 Cambridge St., 13th Floor, Boston 02202, tel. 617/727–3201 or 800/227–6277). **Cape Cod Chamber of Commerce** (junction of Rtes. 6 and 132, Hyannis 02601, tel. 508/362–3225).

EMERGENCIES **Police, fire,** and **ambulance:** Dial 911. **Hospitals:** Cape Cod Hospital (27 Park St., Hyannis, tel. 508/771–1800). Falmouth Hospital (100 Ter Heun Dr., Falmouth, tel. 508/548–5300).

ARRIVING AND DEPARTING

BY PLANE **Barnstable Municipal Airport** (Rte. 28 rotary, Hyannis, tel. 508/775–2020) is the Cape's main air gateway, with frequent flights to Martha's Vineyard and Nantucket islands. **Provincetown Municipal Airport** (Race Point Rd., tel. 508/487–0241) offers year-round scheduled flights to Boston, plus charters anywhere (regular charters from New York arrive on summer weekends). Both airports are only a few minutes from the town center. There are private airports in Falmouth, Marstons Mills, and Chatham.

BY CAR From Boston (60 miles), take Route 3, the Southeast Expressway, south to the Sagamore Bridge. From New York (220 miles), take I–95 north to Providence; change to I–195 and follow signs for the Cape to the Bourne or Sagamore bridges. At either bridge, take Route 6 to reach the central and eastern towns. At the Bourne Bridge, Route 28 leads south to Falmouth and Woods Hole.

BY TRAIN Amtrak (tel. 800/872–7245) offers limited weekend summer service to the Cape; the rest of the year, there is connecting bus service from the Boston train station.

BY BUS Bonanza Bus Lines (tel. 508/548–7588 or 800/556–3815) serves the Cape from several East Coast cities, with connections from points beyond. **Plymouth & Brockton**

Street Railway (tel. 508/775–5524 or 508/775–5514) has routes from Boston and Logan International Airport.

BY BOAT From Memorial Day into October, passenger ferries between Boston and Provincetown are operated by **Bay State Cruise Company** (Boston, tel. 617/723–7800 or Provincetown, tel. 508/487–9284; 3 hrs) and by **Capt. John Cruises** (tel. 508/747–2400 or 800/242–2469 in MA; 1½ hrs) in Plymouth.

GETTING AROUND

BY CAR AND RV For touring the Cape, a car is necessary; public transportation is very limited. Traffic in summer can be maddening, especially on Route 28 along the busy south shore and on Route 132 near Hyannis center. Route 6 is a limited-access highway running the entire length of the Cape through the sparsely populated center. During summer, Route 6 is often congested at the bridges with incoming traffic on Fridays and Saturdays and outgoing traffic on Sundays. On the north shore, take the Old King's Highway, or Route 6A, a scenic country road paralleling Route 6. When you're in no hurry, use the back roads.

BY BUS The **Cape Cod Regional Transit Authority** (tel. 800/352–7155) provides bus service between Hyannis and Woods Hole, with many stops, every day but Sunday. **Plymouth & Brockton Street Railway** (tel. 508/775–5524) has service between Sagamore and Provincetown, with stops, and **Bonanza Bus Lines** (tel. 508/548–7588 or 800/556–3815) plies the route between Bourne, Falmouth, Woods Hole, and Hyannis.

BY BOAT The **Steamship Authority** runs car ferries to Martha's Vineyard out of Woods Hole (tel. 508/548–3788; 45 min) and to Nantucket out of Hyannis (tel. 508/771–4000; 2¼ hrs) year-round. **Hy-Line** (tel. 508/778–2600) carries passengers and bicycles to both islands, May–October, out of Hyannis. Hy-Line offers inter-island travel June–September.

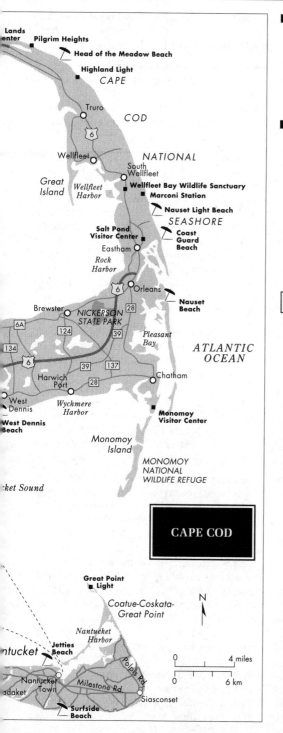

CAPE COD

REST STOPS The Herring Run visitor center, on Route 6 between the Bourne and Sagamore bridges, has rest rooms, a good view of the Cape Cod Canal, picnic tables, and access to the canal bike path. The Cape Cod National Seashore visitor centers have public rest rooms as well as picnic areas.

GUIDED TOURS **Hy-Line** (Ocean St. Dock, Pier 1, tel. 508/778–2600) offers one-hour narrated tours of Hyannis Port Harbor. **Cape Cod Scenic Railroad** (Main and Center Sts., Hyannis, tel. 508/771–3788) runs 1¾-hour excursions (seasonal) between Sagamore and Hyannis, with stops at Sandwich and the Canal. In season, Cape Cod National Seashore (*see* Exploring, *below*) offers guided walks, nature trips, self-guided trails, and more.

EXPLORING

Route 6A from Sandwich east (about 50 miles) is part of the Old King's Highway historic district. Among the charms of this tree-shaded country road are beautifully preserved saltboxes and Cape Cod–style cottages, a number of small museums, and fine crafts, book, and antiques shops. In fall, foliage along Route 6A is bright because of the many ponds and marshes, and in Sandwich you can watch the berries being harvested in flooded bogs. The Cape Cod National Seashore offers dramatic and unspoiled ocean vistas. For outdoors enthusiasts, the Cape offers walking, bicycling, and horseback-riding trails through diverse environments, as well as a number of nature preserves.

Sandwich is the oldest town on the Cape. A pleasant stroll through its center, a perfectly preserved old New England village just off Route 6A, offers the **Sandwich Glass Museum** (129 Main St., tel. 508/888–0251; open Apr.–Oct., daily; Nov., Dec., Feb., Mar., Wed.–Sun.; admission charged) and the **Thornton W. Burgess Museum** (4 Water St., tel. 508/888–4668; open daily, winter hrs vary; donations accepted), dedicated to the children's-book author and his Old Briar

Patch characters. At the center of it all is idyllic **Shawme Pond** and the waterwheel-operated **Dexter Gristmill.**

Heritage Plantation, reached from Sandwich center via Grove Street, is a complex of museums devoted to classic cars, military memorabilia, Americana, and more, all set on 76 beautifully landscaped acres. Walking paths weave through the extensive day-lily, herb, rhododendron, and other gardens. *Intersection of Grove and Pine Sts., tel. 508/ 888–3300. Open Mother's Day–Oct., daily. Admission charged.*

Sandy Neck Beach, farther east on Route 6A (take a left on Sandy Neck Rd., next to Sandy Neck Hotel), is a 6-mile stretch of sand and dunes that makes for excellent beach walks, including a glimpse of a privately owned, nonoperational lighthouse.

Yarmouth Port, east of Barnstable Village on Route 6A, boasts impressive former captains' homes, some now bed-and-breakfasts; **Hallet's Store,** a still-operating country drugstore preserved as it was in 1889; and **Parnassus Bookshop,** an old barn brimming with books. Behind the post office are the **Botanical Trails of the Historical Society of Old Yarmouth,** 50 acres of woodlands, a pond, an 1873 chapel, and marked trails with benches (small admission to trails). A left off Route 6A onto Center Street (follow signs to Gray's Beach) leads to **Bass Hole Boardwalk,** over a marshy creek.

Dennis hosts the **Cape Museum of Fine Arts,** an exhibition gallery that features works by local and international artists, as well as lectures and avant-garde films at the nearby Reel Art Cinema. *Rte. 6A, on Playhouse grounds, tel. 508/385–4477. Open daily. Admission charged for nonmembers.*

Brewster, farther east on Route 6A (past Dennis, whose backstreets have a well-preserved Colonial charm) has a number of attractions. Among them are **Sydenstricker Glass** (tel. 508/385–3272; open Apr.–Oct., daily; Jan.–Mar., Thurs.–Sun.), a gallery and glass decoration facility, and the **New England Fire & History Museum** (tel.

508/896–5711; open mid-May–Labor Day, daily; Labor Day–Columbus Day, weekdays; admission charged).

Cape Cod Museum of Natural History offers nature and marine exhibits, as well as self-guided walking trails through 80 acres of forest, marshland, and ponds. *Rte. 6A, Brewster, tel. 508/896–3867. Museum open daily. Admission charged for museum; trails free.*

Hyannis, on the south shore's Route 28, is the busy commercial hub of the Cape, with a lively downtown and the John F. Kennedy Memorial, a quiet esplanade with a fountain pool overlooking boat-filled Lewis Bay. The John F. Kennedy Museum (397 Main St., tel. 508/775–2201; open daily; donations accepted) displays photographs, memorabilia, and historical documents from the Kennedy era. Nearby, in Hyannis Port, is the Kennedy family compound (closed to the public).

Chatham, east of Hyannis on Route 28, sits at the bent elbow of the Cape, with water on three sides. A traditional town, it boasts gray-shingled houses with tidy awnings and cheerful flower gardens, an attractive Main Street with crafts and antiques shops, and scenic walking and biking loops around coves and ponds. Chatham Light, a working lighthouse, offers a view of the harbor, the offshore sandbars, and the ocean beyond.

The **Cape Cod National Seashore** is a 30-mile stretch between Eastham and Provincetown that is protected from development. It includes spectacular beaches, dunes, and other habitats, making for excellent swimming, fishing, bicycling, horseback riding, bird-watching, and nature walks. The nine self-guided walking trails include the moderately difficult 1¼-mile Atlantic White Cedar Swamp Trail in Wellfleet and two easy ones in Truro—the ¾-mile Pilgrim Spring Trail (through wild woodland leading to the spring where a Pilgrim expedition once stopped) and the ½-mile Cranberry Bog Trail. Visitor information, slide shows, and many programs are located at the **Salt Pond Visitor Center** (Rte. 6, Eastham, tel. 508/ 255–3421; open Mar.–Dec., daily; Jan.–Feb., weekends) and the **Province Lands Visitor Center** (Rte. 6, Provincetown, tel. 508/487–1256; open Apr.–Thanksgiving, daily).

Provincetown, at the farthest tip of the Cape, is reached via Route 6 East, past the fishing-and-art village of Wellfleet and Truro's Highland Light (Thoreau slept here), high atop an eroding cliff. A place of creativity and infinite diversity, Provincetown mixes Portuguese fishermen with painters, poets, writers, and tourists, many of whom come to enjoy the freedom of a town with a large, visible gay population. In summer, crowds throng the many art galleries, shops, restaurants, and nightspots that line Commercial Street, the 3-mile main street. Get a good overview of it all from atop the **Pilgrim Monument,** a 252-foot granite tower with a museum of local history at its base. *Tel. 508/ 487–1310. Open Nov.–Mar., call for hrs; Apr.–Oct., daily. Admission charged.*

Martha's Vineyard, an island off the south shore, supports six towns, varying from the tidy, polished former whaling port of Edgartown, with its fashionable shops and well-preserved architecture; to Oak Bluffs, where 300 tiny cottages trimmed in Victorian gingerbread are gathered around the open-air tabernacle of the Methodist Camp Ground; to the sparsely developed towns of Chilmark and Gay Head, where scenic roads lead to the dramatically striated Gay Head Cliffs, high above the ocean.

Nantucket, once the whaling capital of the world, is a smaller island farther south than the Vineyard, giving it a more remote feeling. It is blessed with a remarkably preserved 17th- to 19th-century town, where cobblestone streets are lined with hundreds of weathered gray-shingled antique houses. Along with more than a dozen historical museums, the island offers the seaside village of Siasconset, where tiny cottages are dressed in masses of climbing pink roses. Several paved bike paths traverse the island, a third of which is open moorland and other protected conservation land. Like the Vineyard, Nantucket boasts excellent white-sand beaches and coastal scenery.

THE NATURAL WORLD Whale-watching tours are offered from spring into fall. At the main center, Provincetown's MacMillan Wharf, **Dolphin Fleet** (tel. 508/349–1900 or 800/826–9300; Apr.–Oct.) and **Portuguese Princess** (tel. 508/487–2651 or 800/442–3188) conduct tours narrated by scientists. From Barnstable Harbor, there's **Hyannis Whale Watcher Cruises** (Mill Way, tel. 508/ 362–6088 or 800/287–0374 in MA; Apr.–Nov.).

Monomoy National Wildlife Refuge (tel. 508/945–0594), two barrier-beach islands off Chatham, provide nesting and resting grounds for 285 bird species. White-tailed deer also live on Monomoy, and harbor seals frequent the shores in winter. Tours to the islands are offered by the **Cape Cod Museum of Natural History** (tel. 508/896–3867) and the **Massachusetts Audubon Society** (tel. 508/349–2615). The Audubon Society's 750-acre **Wellfleet Bay Wildlife Sanctuary** (off Rte. 6, South Wellfleet, tel. 508/349–2615) is a more accessible spot for bird-watching and offers evening bat watches.

HOTELS AND INNS

With a tourism-based economy, the Cape abounds in lodging choices. A number of appealing bed-and-breakfasts in old sea captains' houses are located along Route 6A from Sandwich to Brewster, as well as in Falmouth. Route 28, in the very commercial section between Hyannis and Orleans, has many motels in all price ranges. Price categories for double occupancy, excluding 9%–10% tax, are Expensive, $100–$150; Moderate, $75–$100; and Inexpensive, under $75. (B&Bs listed here may not have TVs or phones in guest rooms. Fax numbers are listed where applicable.)

BREWSTER **Isaiah Clark House.** Colonial decor and homey antiques echo the flavor of this 18th-century B&B, set on 5 acres with gardens, fruit trees, and a pond in a rural stretch of Route 6A; full breakfast is served. *1187 Rte. 6A, Box 169, 02631, tel. 508/896–2223 or 800/822–4001, fax 508/896–7054. 7* *rooms. Turndown service, piano. AE, D, MC, V. No smoking. Moderate–Expensive.*

Old Sea Pines Inn. This B&B in a former girls' school features a broad front veranda, a spacious common room with fireplace, antiques-furnished guest rooms (many large, some with fireplace or enclosed sunporch, a few tiny and very cheap singles), full breakfasts, and afternoon tea in winter. *2553 Main St. (Rte. 6A), Box 1026, 02631, tel. 508/896–6114, fax 508/896–8322. 19 rooms, 2 suites. AE, D, DC, MC, V. No smoking. Inexpensive–Moderate.*

CHATHAM **Moses Nickerson House Inn.** This inn, situated in an 1839 house, is characterized throughout by superb taste in decorating, a love of fine antiques, and warm, thoughtful service (including full breakfast and afternoon wine or tea). *364 Old Harbor Rd., 02633, tel. 508/945–5859 or 800/628–6972. 7 rooms (some with fireplaces). Turndown service. AE, MC, V. No smoking. Expensive.*

FALMOUTH **Capt. Tom Lawrence House.** A prim white house with cupola, set back on a lawn shaded by old maple trees, this 1861 whaling captain's house is an intimate B&B (full breakfast) with rooms romantically decorated in antique and painted furniture, French-country wallpapers, and queen canopy or king beds. *75 Locust St., 02540, tel. 508/540–1445 or 800/266–8139, fax 508/457–1790. 6 rooms. Air-conditioning. MC, V. No smoking. Moderate.*

Coonamessett Inn. Complemented by fine, gracious dining New England style, suites are nicely decorated in bleached woods or pine with antique and reproduction furnishings and set in five Cape Cod–style buildings arranged around a landscaped lawn near a wooded pond. *Jones Rd. and Gifford St., Box 707, 02541, tel. 508/548–2300, fax 508/540–9831. 25 suites, 1 cottage. 2 restaurants, clothing shop. AE, DC, MC, V. Expensive.*

Village Green Inn. This B&B, set in a turreted Victorian facing the green, offers spacious guest rooms with antique beds, lovely wallpapers and hardwood floors, elaborate

woodwork, and some working fireplaces, as well as full breakfasts. *40 Main St., 02540, tel. 508/548–5621. 4 rooms, 1 suite. Bicycles. AE, MC, V. No smoking. Closed Jan.–Mar. Expensive.*

HYANNIS AREA **Harbor Village.** Set in pine/woods by a swimming beach is this family-oriented community of Cape Cod–style cottages, most with a water view and all homey, nicely furnished, clean, and fully equipped, including fireplaces, barbecue grills, and decks. *Marstons Ave., Box 635, Hyannis Port 02647, tel. 508/775–7581. 20 units. Maid service. No credit cards. Closed Nov.–Apr. Weekly rentals only during high season. Expensive.*

Inn on Sea Street. A charming, relaxed B&B a walk away from the beach and downtown, this 1849 Victorian home is furnished with country antiques and lacy fabrics and offers excellent breakfasts served with china, silver, and crystal. *358 Sea St., Hyannis 02601, tel. 508/775–8030. 9 rooms, 1 cottage. AE, D, MC, V. Smoking discouraged. Closed mid-Nov.–Mar. Inexpensive–Moderate.*

PROVINCETOWN **Fairbanks Inn.** Guest rooms in the 1776 main house and other buildings offer four-poster and canopy beds, antiques, and Oriental rugs on wide-board floors; some have TVs, fireplaces, or kitchens. *90 Bradford St., 02657, tel. 508/487–0386. 15 rooms, some with shared bath. Continental breakfast included, rooftop sundeck. AE, D, MC, V. Moderate.*

The Masthead. Unpretentious but cheerful seaside accommodations offer cooking facilities, cable TV, phones, air-conditioning, and decks, some overlooking the beach. *31–41 Commercial St., 02657, tel. 508/487–0523 or 800/395–5095, fax 508/487–9251. 8 rooms, 6 apartments, 3 efficiencies, 4 cottages. AE, D, DC, MC, V. Moderate–Expensive.*

SANDWICH **Dan'l Webster Inn.** This large, traditional New England inn in the center of town has an excellent restaurant as well as guest rooms redecorated with reproduction furnishings—some with canopy beds, fireplaces, or whirlpools, and one with a baby grand piano. *149 Main St., 02563, tel. 508/ 888–3622 or 800/444–3566, fax 508/888– 5156. 46 rooms and suites. Pool, access to health club and golf club, room service, turn-down service, air-conditioning, gift shop. AE, D, DC, MC, V. Moderate–Expensive.*

MOTELS

MODERATE **Captain's Quarters** (Rte. 6, Box Y, North Eastham 02651, tel. 508/255–5686 or 800/327–7769, fax 508/240–0280). 75 rooms; Continental breakfast included, pool, beach shuttle, bikes, volleyball, tennis courts. **Hampton Inn Cape Cod** (1470 Rte. 132, Hyannis 02601, tel. 508/771– 4804 or 800/999–4804, fax 508/790–2336). 104 rooms; Continental breakfast included, pool, saunas, fitness room. **Wellfleet Motel & Lodge** (Rte. 6, Box 606, South Wellfleet 02663, tel. 508/349–3535 or 800/852– 2900). 65 rooms; breakfast room, bar, pool.

INEXPENSIVE **Handkerchief Shoals Motel** (Rte. 28, Box 306, South Harwich 02661, tel. 508/432–2200). 26 rooms; pool. **Sandy Neck Motel** (669 Rte. 6A, corner of Sandy Neck Rd., East Sandwich 02537, tel. 508/ 362–3992 or 800/564–3992, fax 508/362– 5170). 11 rooms, 1 efficiency; minifridges.

CAMPGROUNDS

For a listing of the Cape's many private campgrounds, contact the Cape Cod Chamber of Commerce. No camping is permitted on the Cape Cod National Seashore itself.

Bourne Scenic Park. Sites are in a wooded area by the Bourne Bridge and the Cape Cod Canal. Amenities include a saltwater swimming pool and summer recreation programs. *Near Bourne Bridge underpass, north side of Canal (Scenic Hwy.), Bourne 02532, tel. 508/ 759–7873. 475 RV and tent sites, hookups ($22), no hookups ($20); showers, bathrooms, LP gas available, picnic tables, barbecue areas, store. No reservations. No credit cards.*

Nickerson State Park. The most popular site for those who like camping closest to nature, Nickerson is almost 2,000 wildlife-filled acres of white pine, hemlock, and spruce forest, dotted with opportunities for trout fishing, walking or biking along 8 miles of paved trail, canoeing, sailing, motorboating, and bird-watching. *Rte. 6A, Brewster 02631, tel. 508/896–3491. 418 RV and tent sites, no hookups ($6); showers, bathrooms, picnic tables, barbecue areas, store. No credit cards.*

Scusset Beach State Reservation. The reservation is set on 360 acres near the canal, with a beach on the bay. Sites are behind dunes in an open area. Its pier is a popular fishing spot; other activities include biking, hiking, swimming, and hunting. *140 Scusset Beach Rd., off Rte. 3, Sandwich (Buzzards Bay 02532), tel. 508/888–0859. 104 RV and tent sites, hookups ($9), no hookups ($6); showers, bathrooms, picnic tables, barbecue areas. No reservations. No credit cards.*

DINING

The area offers a wide variety of fresh fish and shellfish. Each restaurant has its version of New England clam chowder, a milk- (sometimes cream-) based soup including chunks of potatoes and salt pork. Other area specialties are Wellfleet oysters and buttery-sweet bay scallops. A long history of Portuguese immigration accounts for the variety of Portuguese dishes encountered, such as kale soup or *linguiça* (a spicy sausage). Though most Cape restaurants serve traditional Yankee fare in casual settings, a few offer haute cuisine. Price categories per person, excluding 5% tax, service, and drinks, are Moderate, $15–$27, and Inexpensive, under $15.

BREWSTER **Brewster Fish House.** Traditional New England cuisine with a contemporary, light touch is the specialty of this small, intimate restaurant in the center of Brewster; besides salmon and swordfish, indulge in poached sole, lobster, and a variety of fresh-made chowders. The building, which falls into the "very old" category, used to be a carnation farm and fish market. *2208 Main St., Rte. 6A, tel. 508/896–7867. No reservations. MC, V. Inexpensive–Moderate.*

DENNIS **Gina's by the Sea.** An intimate—and sometimes crowded—fireplace-warmed bistro by the bay, Gina's serves some of the tastiest northern Italian and seafood dishes in town. *134 Taunton Ave., tel. 508/385–3213. No reservations. AE, MC, V. Moderate.*

HYANNIS **Baxter's Fish N' Chips.** On busy Lewis Bay, Baxter's serves possibly the best fried clams on the Cape, as well as other fried, baked, and broiled fresh fish and offerings from a summer raw bar. *Pleasant St., tel. 508/775–4490. MC, V. Moderate.*

Fazio's Trattoria. Drop in for excellent Italian fare—from soup to salad and pasta to pizza, the food is fresh and delicious—and the warm, cozy atmosphere, enhanced by Fazio's wood-burning brick oven. *586 Main St., tel. 508/771–7445. MC, V. Inexpensive–Moderate.*

Up the Creek. This comfortable, casual spot offers a varied menu but specializes in seafood, including seafood strudel (pastry filled with lobster, shrimp, crab, cheese, and more) and excellent baked stuffed lobster. *36 Old Colony Rd., tel. 508/771–7866. AE, D, DC, MC, V. Inexpensive.*

MASHPEE **The Flume.** This clean, plain fish house, decorated only with a few Indian artifacts and crafts, offers a small menu of straightforward food, including outstanding chowder, fresh broiled fish, fried smelts and clams, and Indian pudding. *Lake Ave. (off Rte. 130), tel. 508/477–1456. MC, V. Inexpensive–Moderate.*

ORLEANS **Land Ho!** Decorated in a jumble of quarter boards and business signs, this landmark eatery with a lending rack of daily newspapers serves kale soup that has made *Gourmet* magazine, plus hearty sandwiches, grilled fish in summer, and very good chicken wings, chowder, and fish-and-chips. *Rte. 6A, tel. 508/255–5165. No reservations. MC, V. Inexpensive–Moderate.*

PROVINCETOWN **Lobster Pot.** A wide selection of seafood (including 2-pound-plus lobsters and full clambakes), award-winning chowder, and home-baked breads and desserts are the specialties at this family-operated, casual restaurant with a glass-walled dining room overlooking the water. *321 Commercial St., tel. 508/487–0842. No reservations. AE, D, DC, MC, V. Moderate.*

The Moors. This unique restaurant, constructed of flotsam and jetsam found on Cape beaches and studded with nautical decor, specializes in seafood and Portuguese cuisine, such as kale, *chourico*, and linguiça soups; marinated swordfish steaks; and chicken with Madeira. *5 Bradford St. Ext., tel. 508/487–0840. AE, D, DC, MC, V. Moderate.*

SAGAMORE **The Bridge.** The Bridge specializes in Yankee pot roast, homemade pasta, and seafood dishes in a quiet setting by the Sagamore Bridge. *Rte. 6A, tel. 508/888–8144. D, DC, MC, V. Inexpensive–Moderate.*

Sagamore Inn. Home-style Italian dishes like flawless eggplant Parmesan and rich chicken cacciatore, along with seafood specialties, are served in an old-Cape, family atmosphere. *Rte. 6A, tel. 508/888–9707. AE, MC, V. Inexpensive–Moderate.*

SANDWICH **Bee-Hive Tavern.** Solid family dining in a cozy tavern is what the Bee-Hive is all about. The eclectic menu includes baked scrod, Cajun rib eye, lobster pie, tabbouleh and hummus salads, and much more. *406 Rte. 6A, tel. 508/833–1184. No reservations. MC, V. Inexpensive.*

Sandy Neck Restaurant. Basic New England seafood fare and the old standards, burgers and sandwiches, are offered by this cozy, wood-paneled restaurant at the entrance to Sandy Neck Beach. For that seafood indulgence, try the Dory Platter, featuring clams, shrimp, scallops, mussels, and fish. *Rte. 6A, tel. 508/362–2943. D, MC, V. Inexpensive.*

YARMOUTH PORT **Jack's Outback.** This quirky place where customers get their own coffee serves good American home cooking, such as pot roast and mashed potatoes with gravy, superb soups, and simple but exceptional desserts. *161 Main St., tel. 508/ 362–6690. No reservations. No credit cards. Inexpensive.*

SHOPPING

Crafts—from exquisite blown glass to earthy pottery and homespun country creations— are a specialty of this area, along with antiques and art. Shoppers can look for antique and new examples of scrimshaw— the art of etching finely detailed designs of sailing ships and sea creatures onto whalebone or teeth (today, a synthetic substitute).

SHOPPING DISTRICTS Provincetown is an important art center, boasting a number of internationally recognized artists. Wellfleet is a vibrant center for more local art and crafts. Route 6A from Sandwich to Brewster hosts many crafts, antiques, and antiquarian bookshops; it also abounds in gift shops.

Hyannis's Main Street is the Cape's largest, including souvenir-type shops, ice-cream and candy stores, and miniature-golf places. Chatham's Main Street is more genteel, with more upscale merchandise in art and crafts galleries and antiques and clothing stores.

MALLS AND OUTLETS The **Cape Cod Mall** (between Rtes. 132 and 28, Hyannis, tel. 508/771–0200) includes Jordan Marsh, Sears, and Filene's among its 90 shops and a food court. **Falmouth Mall** (Rte. 28, Falmouth, tel. 508/540–8329) has Bradlees, Sears, T. J. Maxx, and 30 other shops. **Cape Cod Factory Outlet Mall** (Factory Outlet Rd., Exit 1 off Rte. 6, Sagamore, tel. 508/ 888–8417) features more than 20 outlets, including Corning/Revere, Carter's, Gitano, and Bass Shoe. The **Factory Shoe Mart** (Rte. 28, Dennis Port, tel. 508/398–6000; Rte. 28 at Deer Crossing, Mashpee, tel. 508/477– 0017) carries all the brand names.

FLEA MARKETS AND FARM STANDS The **Wellfleet Drive-In Theatre** (Rte. 6, Eastham– Wellfleet line, tel. 508/349–2520) is the site of a giant flea market (weekends in spring; Wed., Thurs., and weekends July–fall). **Fancy's Farm Stands** (199 Main St., Orleans, tel.

508/255–1949; Rte. 28, West Chatham, tel. 508/945–1949) sell local and exotic produce, fresh-baked breads and pastries, and more.

OUTDOOR ACTIVITIES

BEACHES Swimming is possible from about mid-June sometimes into October at more than 150 ocean and freshwater beaches. Those on the bay are generally colder than Nantucket Sound beaches, on the south shore. Dune-backed ocean beaches on the National Seashore are cold and often have serious surf, but they are also the most beautiful; all have lifeguards, showers, and rest rooms. Old Silver Beach in North Falmouth has a sandbar that keeps it shallow at one end. Sandy Neck Beach in West Barnstable is a beautiful 6-mile barrier beach between the bay and the marshland.

BIKING The premier bike path is the easy-to-moderate 20-mile Cape Cod Rail Trail; between Dennis and Eastham, it passes salt marshes, cranberry bogs, ponds, and Nickerson State Park in Brewster, with 8 miles of its own trails through forest. On either side of the Cape Cod Canal is an easy, straight 6- to 8-mile trail overlooking the bridges and canal traffic. The Shining Sea bike path is an easy 3½-mile route between Falmouth and Woods Hole that dips into woods as it skirts the coast.

The Cape Cod National Seashore maintains three bike trails: a 1⅗-miler through apple and locust groves to Coast Guard Beach in Eastham; an easy, 2-mile route amid dunes and marshes to Head of the Meadow Beach in Truro; and a 5¼-mile more strenuous loop in the Province Lands through dunes, woods, and marshes, with a picnic grove en route.

For bike rentals, contact: **Rail Trail Bike Rentals** (Brewster, tel. 508/896–2361), **Idle Times Bike Shop** (Brewster, tel. 508/896– 9242 or Eastham, tel. 508/255–8281), or **P & M Cycles** (Buzzards Bay, near Cape Cod Canal, tel. 508/759–2830).

FISHING A license is needed to fish in the hundreds of freshwater ponds and is available at town halls and tackle shops, such as the **Goose Hummock Shop** (Rte. 6A, Orleans, tel. 508/255–0455; Rte. 28, West Yarmouth, tel. 508/778–0877). There's good angling for blues, bass, and more along the canal; deep-sea fishing boats operate out of Hyannis, Falmouth, Provincetown, and elsewhere.

GOLF More than 45 courses dot the Cape and islands, including the championship layouts at **New Seabury** (Shore Dr., Mashpee, tel. 508/477–9110) and **Ocean Edge** (1 Villagers Rd., Rte. 6A, Brewster, tel. 508/896–5911).

HIKING AND WALKING The Cape Cod National Seashore has nine self-guided trails (*see* Exploring, *above*). Lifecourse (Access and Old Bass River Rds., South Dennis) is a 1½-mile jogging trail through woods with 20 exercise stations. Bike trails also make good walking trails, but watch your back!

ENTERTAINMENT

CONCERTS The **Cape Cod Melody Tent** (W. Main St., Hyannis, tel. 508/775–9100) presents top names in summer concerts (country, jazz, rock) and comedy. Traditional band concerts are held in most towns throughout the summer; Chatham's are the most famous (Fridays at 8 PM), with dancing and sing-alongs.

DINNER SHOWS AND THEATER The top summer-stock venues are the **Cape Playhouse** (off Rte. 6A, Dennis, tel. 508/385–3911 or 508/385–3838) and the **Academy of Performing Arts** (120 Main St., Orleans, tel. 508/255–1963). The **Barnstable Comedy Club** (Main St., tel. 508/362–6333), contrary to its moniker, presents a wide range of music and drama.

Charleston
South Carolina

Updated by Katherine Culkin

Late in the 20th century, Charleston, South Carolina, still resembles an 18th-century etching come to life—its low-profile skyline punctuated by the spires and steeples of nearly 200 churches. Parts of the historic district seem frozen in time: Block after block of old buildings have been restored for residential or commercial use. After three centuries of epidemics, earthquakes, fires, and floods, Charleston prevails and is today one of the nation's best-preserved historic cities.

Along the Battery (pronounced *bah*-try in Charlestonese), on the point of the narrow peninsula bounded by the Ashley and Cooper rivers, handsome mansions surrounded by gardens face the harbor. Built with high ceilings and large rooms opening onto broad piazzas to catch sea breezes, their distinctive style is reflective of the West Indies. Before settling in the Carolinas in the late 17th century, many British colonists first went to Barbados and other Caribbean islands and learned to build houses suitable for that warm and humid climate.

Each year, from mid-March to mid-April, many private homes and gardens are opened to visitors. Then in late May to early June, the city's vibrant cultural life finds its greatest expression in the renowned Spoleto Festival USA and Piccolo Spoleto, when hundreds of local and international artists, musicians, and other performers fill the city's streets and buildings with sound and spectacle.

ESSENTIAL INFORMATION

WHEN TO GO In spring, riots of azaleas, daffodils, wisteria, and Carolina jessamine light the old city with an ethereal glow. Summer days may be warm and humid, but even then, evening breezes make the temperature bearable, and brightly hued oleanders, cannas, and crape myrtle bloom in abundance. Autumn days are often clear and sparkling, and roses may last into December. Expect chilly days and some rain—rarely snow—in winter. Then, too, many lodgings and restaurants offer attractively priced package plans.

BARGAINS The Citadel Corps of Cadets Dress Parade, held at the famed military college's Summerall Field every Friday at 3:45 PM, is open to the public. Also free is admission to the Citadel's Memorial Military Museum. Free concerts—a variety of jazz, classical, and folk music—are often held Sunday afternoon between 4 and 5 PM during the academic year in Hampton Park, located on Rutledge Avenue near the Citadel.

TOURIST OFFICES **South Carolina Division of Tourism** (Box 71, Columbia 29202, tel. 803/734–0235). **Charleston Trident Convention and Visitors Bureau** (Box 975, Charleston 29402, tel. 803/853–8000). You can pick up free maps and information at the **Visitor Information Center** (375 Meeting St., Charleston 29401, tel. 803/724–7474).

EMERGENCIES Fire, police, and **rescue squad:** Dial 911. **Hospitals:** Charleston Memorial Hospital (326 Calhoun St., tel. 803/

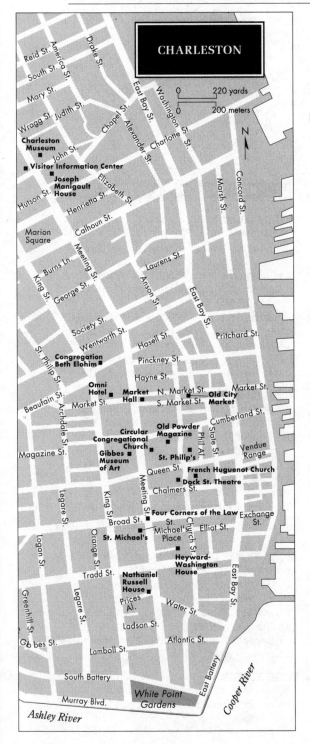

CHARLESTON

0   220 yards
0   200 meters

N

Charleston Museum

Visitor Information Center

Joseph Manigault House

Marion Square

Congregation Beth Elohim

Omni Hotel · Market Hall · N. Market St. · Old City
Market St.   S. Market St.   Market

Old Powder Magazine
Circular Congregational Church
Gibbes Museum of Art   St. Philip's
Cumberland St.
Vendue Range
Queen St.   French Huguenot Church
Chalmers St. · Dock St. Theatre

Four Corners of the Law · Exchange St.
Broad St. · St. Michael's Place · Elliot St.
St. Michael's

Heyward-Washington House

Nathaniel Russell House
Prices Al.   Water St.

Ladson St.

Atlantic St.

Lamboll St.

South Battery

White Point Gardens

Murray Blvd.

Ashley River

Cooper River

577–0600) and Roper Hospital (316 Calhoun St., tel. 803/724–2000) have emergency rooms that are open all night.

ARRIVING AND DEPARTING

BY PLANE Charleston International Airport, in North Charleston, on I–26, 12 miles west of downtown Charleston, is served by Delta, United, and USAir. Taxi fare into town costs $12–$14.

BY CAR I–26 traverses the state from northwest to southeast and terminates at Charleston. North–south coastal route U.S. 17 passes through Charleston.

BY TRAIN **Amtrak** (tel. 800/872–7245) trains between New York and Florida stop at Charleston. Taxi fare into town costs $7–$10.

BY BUS **Greyhound Lines** (3610 Dorchester Rd., tel. 800/231–2222) connects Charleston with cities throughout the country.

GETTING AROUND

BY CAR A car is the most practical means of visiting outlying attractions. Within the compact historic district, it's advisable to park and explore on foot, by bicycle, or on a carriage tour.

BY BUS There's **citywide bus service** (tel. 803/745–7928) and the **Downtown Area Shuttle** (tel. 803/724–7368), known as DASH, with trolley-style vehicles that provide fast service downtown and through the historic district on weekdays.

BY TAXI Cabs must be ordered by phone from **Yellow Cab** (tel. 803/577–6565) or **Safety Cab** (tel. 803/722–4066).

REST STOPS There are public rest rooms in the visitor center and in all museums.

GUIDED TOURS Nonstop harbor tours are offered aboard the *Charlestowne Princess* by **Gray Line Water Tours** (tel. 803/722–1112 or 800/344–4433). **Fort Sumter Tours** (tel.

803/722–1691) includes a stop at Fort Sumter in its harbor tour. Motor-coach tours are run by **Gray Line** (tel. 803/722–4444), **Adventure Sightseeing** (tel. 803/762–0088), **Carolina Lowcountry Tours** (tel. 803/797–1045 or 800/621–7996), and **Doin' The Charleston Tours, Inc.** (tel. 803/763–1233 or 800/627–4487). Carriage tours through the historic district are available from **Charleston Carriage Company** (tel. 803/577–0042), **Old South Carriage Tours** (tel. 803/723–9712), and **Palmetto Carriage Works** (tel. 803/723–8145). **Historic Charleston Walking Tours** (tel. 803/722–6460) and **Charleston Strolls** (tel. 803/766–2080) offer guided walking tours of the historic district. The **Charleston Tea Party Walking Tour** (tel. 803/577–5896) includes tea in a private garden. **Unique Tours, Inc.** (tel. 803/860–3469) offers 90-minute ghost tours of some of Charleston's most prominent haunted dwellings.

EXPLORING

If you're fascinated by history and architecture, you should plan at least three days for in-depth sightseeing of Charleston's house museums and churches, which are concentrated in the historic district. Nature lovers will want to save a day or so for exploring some of the city's outlying gardens.

For a good overview of the historic district, start at the **Visitor Information Center** (where you can park your car) to see *Forever Charleston,* a 24-minute slide and voice show of images and sounds of Charleston. *Tel. 803/724–7474. Open daily. Admission charged.*

Cross the street to visit the **Charleston Museum,** at the corner of John Street, the nation's oldest city museum, now housed in a $6 million contemporary complex. Founded in 1773, it's one of the South's major cultural repositories and is especially strong on South Carolina decorative arts. *360 Meeting St., tel. 803/722–2996. Open daily. Admission charged.*

You next come to the **Joseph Manigault House,** an outstanding example of Adam-style architecture. A National Historic Landmark, it was designed by Charleston architect Gabriel Manigault in 1803 and is noted for its carved wood mantels, elaborate plasterwork, and the curving cantilever staircase that graces the entrance hall. *350 Meeting St., tel. 803/722–2926. Open daily. Admission charged.*

You should now get your car from the visitor center and drive south along Meeting Street to explore the market area. En route, you can turn right on Hasell Street, where you'll spot **Congregation Beth Eloim,** the birthplace in 1824 of American Reform Judaism. It is the second-oldest synagogue in the United States and is considered one of the nation's finest examples of Greek Revival architecture. *90 Hasell St., tel. 803/723–1090. Open weekdays. Admission free.*

Follow King Street one block south to Market Street, where you can park in one of the area's garages. **Market Hall,** built in 1841 and modeled after the Temple of Nike in Athens, is the site of the **Confederate Museum.** Operated since 1898 by the Daughters of the Confederacy, it displays flags, uniforms, swords, and other memorabilia. *188 Meeting St., tel. 803/723–1541. Open weekends noon–5. Admission charged.*

The **Old City Market,** between Market Hall and East Bay Street, is a series of low sheds that once housed colorful produce and fish markets. There are still vegetable and fruit vendors (who may protest vigorously if you attempt to photograph them), but there are now also restaurants and shops.

Omni Hotel at Charleston Place (130 Market St.), the city's only world-class hotel, is worth a visit for tea or Sunday brunch even if you're not staying there.

Gibbes Museum of Art, 1½ blocks south on Meeting Street, has notable collections of American art, including 18th- and 19th-century portraits of Carolinians. Don't miss the intricately detailed miniature rooms. *135*

Meeting St., tel. 803/722–2706. Open daily. Admission charged.

Circular Congregational Church, across the street from the Gibbes, is most unusual in design. Legend says its corners were rounded off so the devil would have no place to hide. *150 Meeting St., tel. 803/577–6400. Call for hrs. Admission free.*

Old Powder Magazine is around the corner. Built in 1713 and used as a powder store-house during the Revolutionary War, it's now a museum with costumes, furniture, armor, and other artifacts from 18th-century Charleston. *79 Cumberland St., tel. 803/722–3767. Open weekdays. Admission charged.*

St. Philip's Episcopal Church, about half a block south on Church Street, was established in 1670 as the Mother Church of the Province. The present building was constructed from 1835 to 1838. Its churchyard includes graves of statesman John C. Calhoun, DuBose Heyward (author of *Porgy*), and other notable South Carolinians. *146 Church St., tel. 803/722–7734. Call for hrs. Admission free.*

The **Dock Street Theatre,** across Queen Street, was built on the site of one of the nation's first playhouses. It combines the reconstructed early Georgian theater and the preserved Old Planter's Hotel (circa 1809). *135 Church St., tel. 803/723–5648. Open weekdays. Admission charged.*

The **French Huguenot Church,** across the street, is one of the nation's few remaining Huguenot churches. Services are conducted in a blend of French and English. *110 Church St., tel. 803/722–4385. Open weekdays. Donations accepted.*

The **Four Corners of the Law,** at the intersection of Meeting and Broad streets, has structures representing federal, state, city, and religious jurisdiction. The County Court House, U.S. Post Office and Federal Court, and City Hall occupy three corners, and **St. Michael's Episcopal Church,** the fourth. Modeled after London's St. Martin's-in-the-Fields and completed in 1761, this is Charleston's oldest surviving church. *Broad*

and Meeting Sts., tel. 803/723–0603. Open Mon.–Sat. Admission free.

Walk east along Broad Street for one block, and turn south on Church Street. Near the end of the block, the **Heyward-Washington House,** built in 1772, was where George Washington stayed during his 1791 visit. It's notable for fine furnishings by such local craftsmen as cabinetmaker Thomas Elfe. *87 Church St., tel. 803/722–0354. Open daily. Admission charged.*

Walk south on Church Street to the end of the block, then west one block on Tradd Street and a half block south on Meeting Street. The **Nathaniel Russell House,** built in 1808 and headquarters of the Historic Charleston Foundation, is one of the nation's finest Adam-style structures. Its interior is notable for ornate detailing, lavish period furnishings, and a "flying" staircase that spirals three stories with no apparent support. *51 Meeting St., tel. 803/723–1623. Open daily. Admission charged.*

After touring the historic district, drive 2 miles east on U.S. 17, over the Cooper River Bridge, to Mount Pleasant. **Patriots Point Naval and Maritime Museum** is the world's largest facility of its kind. Berthed there are the aircraft carrier *Yorktown*, nuclear merchant ship *Savannah*, World War II submarine *Clamagore*, cutter *Ingham*, and destroyer *Laffey*. *Charleston Harbor, tel. 803/884–2727 or 800/327–5723. Open daily. Admission charged.*

Fort Sumter National Monument, on a man-made island in the harbor, was the site of the first shot fired in the Civil War. On April 12, 1861, Confederate forces at Fort Johnson opened fire on Sumter's Union troops, who surrendered after a 34-hour bombardment, leaving the fort in Confederate hands for nearly four years. National Park Service rangers conduct tours of the restored fort, which was a heap of rubble by the war's end. *Tel. 803/722–1691. Open daily. Admission free.*

West of the Ashley River via Route 171, 3 miles from town, is **Charles Towne Land-**

ing State Park at the site of the original 1670 Charleston settlement. There's a reconstructed village and fortifications, and you can walk or bicycle through extensive English gardens, rent kayaks to explore the park's waterways, or take a tram tour. *1500 Old Towne Rd., tel. 803/852–4200. Open daily. Admission charged.*

Drive west of Charleston on the Ashley River Road (Route 61) to visit several historic mansions and gardens. **Drayton Hall,** 9 miles west of Charleston, was built between 1738 and 1742 and was owned by members of the Drayton family for seven generations. A National Historic Landmark, it is considered the nation's finest example of Georgian Palladian architecture. The only Ashley River plantation house to survive the Civil War intact, it has been left unfurnished to highlight its unusual ornamental details. *Ashley River Rd., tel. 803/766–0188. Open daily. Admission charged.*

At **Magnolia Plantation and Gardens,** a mile or so farther north, the informal gardens begun in 1686 have one of the continent's largest collections of azaleas and camellias. Tours of the manor house reflect plantation life. Nature lovers may canoe through a waterfowl refuge or walk or bicycle on wildlife trails in the garden's 500 acres. *Ashley River Rd., tel. 803/571–1266. Open daily. Admission charged.*

Middleton Place, 4 miles farther north, has the oldest landscaped gardens in the United States (they date from 1741). Much of the mansion was destroyed in the Civil War, but the restored south wing houses impressive collections of silver, furniture, and paintings. In the stable yard, a living outdoor museum, authentically costumed craftspeople demonstrate spinning, blacksmithing, and other plantation-era domestic skills. *Ashley River Rd., tel. 803/556–6020 or 800/ 782–3608. Open daily. Admission charged.*

Cypress Gardens lies about 24 miles north of Charleston via U.S. 52. On boat tours or waterside trails, you can explore swamp gardens vibrant with azalea, camellia, daffodil, wisteria, and dogwood blossoms. Peak sea-

son is usually late March into April. *U.S. 52, tel. 803/553–0515. Open daily. Admission charged.*

THE NATURAL WORLD Francis Marion National Forest, about 40 miles north of Charleston via U.S. 52, comprises 250,000 acres of swamps, oak and pine trees, and little lakes thought to have been formed by meteors. It's an excellent spot for hiking, picnicking, camping, boating, and swimming. At the park's Rembert Dennis Wildlife Center (off U.S. 52 in Bonneau), deer, wild turkey, and striped bass are raised and studied.

HOTELS AND INNS

Rates tend to increase during the Spring Festival of Houses and Gardens and the Spoleto Festival USA, when reservations are essential. During Visitors' Appreciation Days, from mid-November to mid-February, discounts as high as 50% may apply. Lodgings in surrounding areas are usually cheaper than those on the peninsula. For a Courtesy Discount Card, write to the Charleston Trident Convention and Visitors Bureau (Box 975, Charleston 29402, tel. 803/853–8000). Price categories for double occupancy, excluding 5% tax, are Expensive, $90–$120; Moderate, $51–$89; and Inexpensive, $50 and under.

EXPENSIVE **Battery Carriage House.** One of Charleston's earliest inns, this renovated 1845 mansion hosts 10 carriage-house units and overlooks the Battery and West Point Gardens. Rooms are handsomely furnished with period antiques, and evening turndown service is offered with chocolate and brandy. *20 S. Battery St., 29401, tel. 803/ 727–3100 or 800/775–5575, fax 803/727– 3130. 10 rooms. Continental breakfast included. AE, D, DC, MC, V.*

Indigo Inn. Rooms here, elegantly furnished with 18th-century antiques and reproductions, face a picturesque interior courtyard, and there are eight slightly more expensive suites and rooms in nearby Jasmine House, a pre–Civil War Greek Revival building. *1 Maiden La., 29401, tel. 803/577–5900 or 800/845–7639, fax 803/577–0378. 40 rooms. Afternoon refreshments, Continental breakfast, concierge. AE, MC, V.*

Meeting Street Inn. Rooms in this handsome 1870 house are furnished with reproduction four-poster beds, and all open onto a piazza. *173 Meeting St., 29401, tel. 803/723–1882 or 800/842–8022, fax 803/577–0851. 54 rooms. Whirlpool tubs, lobby bar, suite for meetings. AE, DC, MC, V.*

Sheraton Charleston Hotel. Some of the spacious rooms and suites in this 13-story hotel outside the historic district overlook the Ashley River, and decor is highlighted by Queen Anne reproductions. *170 Lockwood Dr., 29403, tel. 803/723–3000, fax 803/720–0844. 337 rooms. Dining room, cocktail lounge with dancing and live entertainment, pool, concierge, free parking. AE, D, DC, MC, V.*

Vendue Inn. Near the waterfront, this European-style inn in a renovated 1828 warehouse offers antiques-furnished public areas and guest rooms, along with deluxe suites in adjacent Vendue West, a restored 1800 house. Continental breakfast and afternoon wine and cheese are included. *19 Vendue Range, 29401, tel. 803/577–7970 or 800/845–7900, fax 803/577–2919. 34 rooms. Dining room, bar, concierge, parking. AE, D, MC, V.*

MODERATE **Comfort Inn Riverview.** This modern seven-story motor inn has some rooms overlooking the Ashley River. Continental breakfast is included. *144 Bee St., 29401, tel. 803/577–2224, fax 803/577–0361. 128 rooms, 2 with kitchenettes and whirlpools. Pool, fitness center, free parking. AE, D, DC, MC, V.*

Quality Inn Heart of Charleston. Spacious and cheerful rooms, some with balconies, are decorated with 18th- and 19th-century reproductions. *125 Calhoun St., 29401, tel. 803/722–3391, fax 803/577–0361. 126 rooms, 4 suites. Restaurant, lounge, pool, coin laundry. AE, D, DC, MC, V.*

INEXPENSIVE-MODERATE **Days Inn Historic District.** This conveniently located economy inn is attractively furnished. *155 Meeting St., 29401, tel. 803/722–8411, fax 803/723–5361. 124 rooms. Dining room, cocktail lounge, pool, garage. AE, D, DC, MC, V.*

Howard Johnson Riverfront. Overlooking a scenic stretch of the Ashley River, this inn near downtown is adjacent to the Citadel and has rooms with private balconies. Morning coffee is included. *250 Spring St., 29403, tel. 803/722–4000, fax 803/723–2513. 152 rooms. Dining room, cocktail lounge, pool. AE, D, DC, MC. V.*

MOTELS

MODERATE **Best Western Inn** (1540 Savannah Hwy., 29407, tel. 803/571–6100, fax 803/766–6261). 87 rooms; Continental breakfast, pool, wading pool. **Hampton Inn Riverview** (11 Ashley Pointe Dr., 29407, tel. 803/556–5200, fax 803/556–5200, ext. 177). 173 rooms, 3 with refrigerators; Continental breakfast, pool, fishing, and marina. **Holiday Inn Riverview** (301 Savannah Hwy., 29407, tel. 803/556–7100, fax 803/556–6176). 181 rooms with balconies; dining room, cocktail lounge, pool, exercise room, coin laundry. **Shem Creek Inn** (1401 Shrimp Boat La., 29464, tel. 803/881–1000 or 800/523–4951, fax 803/849–6969). 50 rooms with balconies; Continental breakfast, near downtown. **Quality Suites** (5225 N. Arco La., North Charleston 29418, tel. 803/747–7300, fax 803/747–6324). 168 rooms, 13 with whirlpools; complimentary beverages, VCRs and microwaves, cocktail lounge, pool with gazebo, sauna, exercise room. **Town and Country Inn** (2008 Savannah Hwy., 29407, tel. 803/571–1000 or 800/334–6660, fax 803/766–9444). 122 rooms, 20 with kitchenettes; restaurant, piano bar, sports bar, indoor and outdoor pools, spa, sauna, fitness center with racquetball courts.

INEXPENSIVE **Airport Inn** (4620 Dorchester Rd., 29405, tel. 803/747–7500, fax 803/747–9951). 104 rooms; Continental breakfast, small pool, coin laundry, VCR rentals.

Comfort Inn Airport (5055 N. Arco La., North Charleston 29418, tel. 803/554–6485, fax 803/566–9466). 122 rooms, 20 with whirlpools; pool, whirlpool, sauna, exercise room, coin laundry. **Days Inn–Patriot's Point** (261 Hwy. No. 17 Bypass, Mount Pleasant 29464, tel. 803/881–1800, fax 803/881–3769). 131 rooms; coffee shop, pool, pets accepted. **Dorchester Motor Lodge** (I–26 and Dorchester Rd., 29405, tel. 803/747–0961, fax 803/747–3230). 459 rooms; dining room, coffee shop, cocktail lounge, live entertainment, pool, coin laundry. **Econo-Lodge** (4725 Arco La., North Charleston, 29405, tel. 803/747–3672, fax 803/744–0953). 89 rooms; Continental breakfast, pool. **Fairfield Inn** (7415 Northside Dr., North Charleston 29420, tel. 803/572–6677, fax 803/764–3790). 119 rooms; small pool. **Hampton Inn** (4701 Saul White Blvd., North Charleston 29418, tel. 803/554–7154, fax 803/566–9299). 125 rooms; Continental breakfast, pool, airport transportation. **Holiday Inn Express North** (2070 McMillan St., 29405, tel. 803/554–1600, fax 803/554–1600, ext. 303). 97 rooms, some with whirlpools; outdoor pool, coin laundry. **La Quinta Motor Inn** (2499 La Quinta La., North Charleston 29418, tel. 803/797–8181, fax 803/569–1608). 122 rooms; pool. **Masters Economy Inn** (6100 Rivers Ave., North Charleston 29418, tel. 803/744–3530, fax 803/744–3530). 150 rooms, 26 with kitchenettes; pool, coin laundry.

DINING

Fresh seafood is abundant in and around Charleston, and there's Continental and American cuisine to please the most sophisticated palate. She-crab soup originated in the low country, and it's not to be missed. Neither are benne (sesame-seed) wafers, along with such coastal specialties as sautéed shrimp and grits. During peak times (mid-March–early June), reservations should be made for dinner. Price categories per person for a three-course meal, excluding 5% tax, service, and drinks, are Moderate, $15–$30, and Inexpensive, under $15.

MODERATE **Barbadoes Room.** Step through the Barbadoes's distinctive arches for an elegant dining experience. Seafood and low-country cuisine share the bill of fare in this large, airy, plant-filled enclave reminiscent of the Caribbean. *Mills House Hotel, Queen and Meeting Sts., tel. 803/577–2400. AE, DC, MC, V.*

Carolina's. Charleston's "Big City" bistro, this chic dining room is decorated in shades of black lacquer, white, and peach. You'll enjoy creative modern Carolina cuisine, including grilled seafood and beef. *10 Exchange St., tel. 803/724–3800. AE, MC, V.*

East Bay Trading Company. Coastal seafood, lamb, Carolina quail, and international specialties are showcased on three dramatic antiques-adorned levels around an atrium in this former warehouse. *161 E. Bay St., tel. 803/722–0722. AE, MC, V.*

82 Queen. The 82 Queen—occupying unique, pink stucco buildings that date from the 18th century—was recently voted the best restaurant in Charleston by locals; don't skip town without trying such low-country favorites as the first-rate crab cakes. *82 Queen St., tel. 803/723–7591. AE, MC, V.*

Library at Vendue. Three small, interconnected dining rooms provide an intimate atmosphere in which to enjoy steak, crab, and shrimp. The rooftop bar boasts a beautiful view of Charleston Harbor that's considered one of the best in the city. *19 Vendue Range, tel. 803/723–0485. AE, D, MC, V.*

Mint Juleps. Set in a 19th-century Victorian home, this low-key establishment features Southern regional cooking, with many dishes based on the owner's family recipes. Specialties include fried green tomatoes, bronzed grouper, and, of course, mint juleps; in addition to fine food, the establishment prides itself on a mere $10 markup on each bottle on its splendid wine list. *68 Queen St., tel. 803/853–6468. AE, D, MC, V.*

INEXPENSIVE–MODERATE **Shem Creek Bar & Grill.** This pleasant dockside spot is perennially popular for its oyster bar and wide variety of seafood entrées, including a steam pot big enough for two, with lobsters, clams, and oysters with melted lemon butter or hot cocktail sauce. *508 Mill St., Mount Pleasant, tel. 803/884–8102. MC, V.*

INEXPENSIVE **Athens.** Baby squid in lemon, moussaka, spinach pie, and other delights rival those served in Greece's top tavernas, and the bouzouki music is straight from the *plaka* in Athens. *325 Folly Rd., Cross Creek Shopping Center, James Island, tel. 803/ 795–0957. AE, MC, V.*

A.W. Shucks. The atmosphere at Shucks is friendly and casual—the perfect environment for lingering over fresh seafood or a plate of beef, chicken, or pasta. *35 Market St., tel. 803/723–1151. AE, D, MC, V.*

California Dreaming. Crowds come to this high-volume eatery in a stone fort on the Ashley River for terrific views of the harbor and bountiful platters of barbecued chicken and the catch of the day. *1 Ashley Pointe Dr., tel. 803/766–1644. AE, MC, V.*

Magnolias. At this local favorite, located in Charleston's original Customs House, the egg rolls (stuffed with collard greens and chicken) and the skillet-seared yellow-grits cake manage to taste simultaneously "uptown" and "Down South." *185 E. Bay St., tel. 803/577–7771. AE, MC, V.*

Slightly North of Broad. Describing itself as a "Maverick Southern Kitchen," this downtown eatery offers such twists on tradition as grits with shrimp, quail filled with herbed chicken mousse, barbecued tuna, and scallops and sausage. *192 E. Bay St., tel. 803/ 723–3424. AE, MC, V.*

SHOPPING

Visit the **Old City Market** at East Bay and Market streets for interesting, varied shopping. Next to the colorful produce market is the open-air flea market with crafts, antiques, and memorabilia. Here (and at stands along U.S. 17, near Mount Pleasant) women weave distinctive baskets of straw, sweet grass, and palmetto fronds. A portion of the Old City Market has been converted into a complex of specialty shops and restaurants.

Other complexes are **Rainbow Market** (in two connected 150-year-old buildings), **Market Square,** and **State Street Market.** There are many antiques shops along King Street. **Historic Charleston Reproductions** (105 Broad St., tel. 803/723–8292) sells superb replicas of Charleston furniture and accessories, as does the **Thomas Elfe Workshop** (54 Queen St., tel. 803/722–2130).

OUTDOOR ACTIVITIES

BIKING The historic district is level and compact, ideal for biking, and many city parks have trails, as does Palmetto Islands County Park. You can rent bikes at the **Bicycle Shop** (tel. 803/722–8168) and **Carolina Carriage Company** (tel. 803/723–8687), which also rents tandems.

FISHING Fresh- and saltwater fishing is excellent along 90 miles of coastline. Surf fishing is permitted on many beaches, including Palmetto Islands County Park's.

GOLF Public courses include **Charleston Municipal** (tel. 803/795–6517), **Patriots Point** (tel. 803/881–0042), and **Shadowmoss** (tel. 803/556–8251). The Charleston Trident Convention and Visitors Bureau has a list of area courses, including those at private resorts where the public may play when space permits.

SWIMMING People swim from April through October. Public beaches are at Beachwater Park on Kiawah Island; Sullivan's Island; Folly Beach County Park and Folly Beach, on Folly Island.

TENNIS Courts are open to the public at **Farmfield Tennis Courts** (tel. 803/724–7402) and **Shadowmoss** (tel. 803/556–8251).

WALKING AND JOGGING Walking is the locomotion of choice all over the historic district. Jogging paths wind through Palmetto Islands County Park, and Hampton Park has a fitness trail.

Chicago
Illinois

Updated by Julie Getzlaff

Chicago has everything for city lovers: culture, commerce, historic buildings, public transportation, ethnic neighborhoods, chic boutiques, and grit and grime. Masterpieces of skyscraper architecture embrace the curving shore of Lake Michigan, creating one of the most spectacular skylines in the world. An elegant system of boulevards and parks encircles the central city.

Home to the blues and the Chicago Symphony, to storefront theaters and the Lyric Opera, to neighborhood murals and the Art Institute, Chicago has come a long way in shedding its rough-and-tumble image as "city of the big shoulders," immortalized in the writings of Theodore Dreiser, Upton Sinclair, and Carl Sandburg. The infamous stockyards have long been closed, and the steel mills to the south lie largely idle. Except for a few bullet holes in the masonry around the Biograph Theater (where John Dillinger was shot), few traces remain of the disreputable 1920s gangster period that made Chicago infamous around the world; the Biograph itself is now run by the Cineplex Odeon chain, and Chicago has become, for better or worse, a hub of finance second only to New York. But Chicagoans remain friendly in the midwestern manner: helpful and generally lacking in pretense.

Long and thin (in many spots less than 10 miles wide), Chicago proper hugs the shore of Lake Michigan. Many of the major attractions are clustered within a mile of the lakefront, either in the Loop (defined by the tracks of the elevated train) or near the Loop, in the Near North Side.

ESSENTIAL INFORMATION

WHEN TO GO Travelers whose principal concern is to have comfortable weather for touring the city may prefer spring or fall, when moderate temperatures can make it a pleasure to be out and about, and the city's cultural institutions are well into their seasons.

Summertime brings many opportunities for outdoor recreation. Yet the temperatures will climb to the 90s in hot spells, and the humidity can be uncomfortably high. In more temperate times, the presence of Lake Michigan has a moderating effect on the city's weather, keeping it several degrees cooler in summer, a bit warmer in winter.

Those winters can see very raw weather, and occasional news-making blizzards and temperatures in the teens (or even in the single or negative digits in December and January) are to be expected. There are January sales to reward those who venture out, and many indoor venues let one look out on the cold in warm comfort.

BARGAINS **Museums:** There's free admission to most major museums on one day a week: The Art Institute and the Museum of Contemporary Art are free on Tuesday; the Chicago Academy of Sciences and the Chicago Historical Society, Monday; and the Field Museum of Natural History and the Museum of Science and Industry, Thursday. The Chicago Children's Museum is free Thursday evening. The Chicago Cultural Center, the Czechoslovakian Society of American Heritage Museum and Archives, the David and Alfred Smart Museum of Art, the Mexican Fine Arts

CHICAGO

Lincoln Park Zoo
and Conservatory,
Baha'i House
of Worship

*Lake
Michigan*

Chicago
Historical
Society

Schiller   St.

Goethe   St.

Division   St.

John Hancock
Center

Water
Tower   Pumping
Station

Chicago   Huron

Terra Museum

Ontario
Museum of
Contemporary Art

Navy Pier

Grand   Ave.

Chicago River

State of
Illinois Center

Chicago
Cultural
Center

Daley Center

Chicago
Temple

First
National
Plaza

Art
Institute

Brookfield Zoo,
Oak Park
W.   Jackson

Sears
Tower   Jackson

Congress

Harold
Washington
Library
Center

*Chicago
Harbor*

*Grant
Park*

W.   Taylor

Roosevelt   St.

Shedd
Aquarium

Adler
Planetarium

Field Museum
of
Natural History

*Meigs
Field*

8th   St.

Museum of
Science and Industry,
University of Chicago

0   880 yards

0   804 meters

Carroll   St.
Fulton   St.
Lake   St.

Randolph   St.
Washington   St.

Madison   St.
Monroe   St.

Turning
Basin

North

Ave.   64

N

Center Museum, the Museum of Broadcast Communications, and the Oriental Institute are free every day.

Music and Other Performances: *The Reader* (a free weekly newspaper available at many stores and restaurants, mostly on the city's North Side) lists times and locations for the free choral programs, recitals, and other performances given at area churches and music schools. The University of Chicago Concert Office (tel. 312/702–8068), the American Conservatory of Music (tel. 312/263–4161), and Chicago Musical College of Roosevelt University (tel. 312/341–3780) also host free programs. The Chicago Cultural Center (78 E. Washington St., tel. 312/346–3278) has free concerts Wednesday at 12:15 PM and various other noontime programs throughout the week. During the summer months, Chicago is host to myriad free music festivals; all the local papers and magazines advertise such events.

Shopping: In recent years, more and more discount and outlet stores have begun to sprout up around the city, especially on or near Clybourn Avenue on the Near North side. Some of the better stores include Crate & Barrel Outlet Store (800 W. North Ave., tel. 312/787–4775), Filene's Basement (830 N. Michigan Ave., tel. 312/482–8918; 1 N. State St., tel. 312/553–1055), The Gap Factory Outlet (2778 N. Milwaukee Ave., tel. 312/252–0594), Land's End Outlet (2121 N. Clybourn Ave., tel. 312/281–0900), and Spiegel (1105 W. 35th St., tel. 312/254–0091).

TOURIST OFFICES The **Chicago Office of Tourism** (Chicago Cultural Center, 78 E. Washington St., 60602, tel. 312/744–2400 or 800/487–2446, fax 312/744–2359) maintains two walk-in centers, one at the Chicago Cultural Center, the other at the Historic Water Tower in the Park (806 N. Michigan Ave.).

EMERGENCIES **Police, fire,** and **ambulance:** Dial 911. **Hospitals:** Northwestern Memorial Hospital (250 E. Superior St. at Fairbanks Ct., Near North, tel. 312/908–2000), Rush Presbyterian St. Luke's Medical Center

(1653 W. Congress Pkwy., near the Loop, tel. 312/942–5000). **Pharmacies:** Walgreen's (757 N. Michigan Ave., tel. 312/664–8686) is open 24 hours.

ARRIVING AND DEPARTING

BY PLANE All major airlines serve **O'Hare International Airport** (tel. 312/686–2200), 20 miles northwest of downtown Chicago and the busiest in the world. Midway Airlines, Delta, Northwest, Southwest, and USAir are just some of the growing number of airlines that serve smaller, less congested **Midway Airport** (tel. 312/767–0500), 7 miles from downtown on the southwest side.

Between the Airports and Hotels: Metered taxi service is available from both airports to Near North and downtown; expect to pay $30–$40 plus 15% tip for the 20- to 30-minute ride (which can stretch to more than an hour during rush hours) from O'Hare and $15–$25 plus tip for the 20- to 30-minute ride from Midway. Don't accept any offers of "limo service"; these services are unregulated and may cost you more than a licensed cab.

Continental Airport Express (tel. 312/454–7799) operates minivans from both airports to major Near North and downtown hotels; one-way fares from O'Hare and Midway are $10–$20.

The **Chicago Transit Authority** (CTA; tel. 312/836–7000) has a rapid-transit station at O'Hare in the underground concourse in Terminal 3. The first downtown stop is at Washington and Dearborn streets; from there you can take a taxi to your hotel or change to other rapid-transit lines. In recent years, the CTA opened the much-awaited "Orange Line," which runs from Midway Airport to the Loop. The stop at Adams Street and Wabash Avenue is the closest to the hotels on South Michigan Avenue. For other hotels, the simplest strategy is to alight anywhere in the Loop and hail a cab. The fare from both airports is reasonable. The CTA is best avoided late at night.

BY CAR The main arteries through Chicago are I–90/94 (from the north and the south) and I–55 (from the southwest). Coming from the south, I–94 branches off I–80 south of the city and merges with I–90 to become the Dan Ryan Expressway. Coming from the north, I–90 merges with I–94 at Montrose Avenue, about 3 miles south of the city's northern border, to become the John F. Kennedy Expressway.

BY TRAIN Amtrak (tel. 800/872–7245) offers service to **Union Station** (Jackson and Canal Sts., tel. 312/558–1075).

BY BUS Greyhound Lines (tel. 800/231–2222) has nationwide service to its main terminal (630 W. Harrison St.). **Indian Trails** (tel. 312/928–8606) also serves this terminal from Indiana and Michigan. This station is not within easy walking distance of anywhere you're likely to be staying, so be prepared to take a cab.

GETTING AROUND

Chicago's planners followed a grid pattern in laying out the city's streets. Madison Street is the baseline for streets and avenues that run north–south; Michigan Avenue (for example) is North Michigan Avenue above Madison Street, South Michigan Avenue below it. House numbers start at 1 at the baseline and climb in each direction, generally by 100 a block. Thus the Fine Arts building at 410 South Michigan Avenue is four blocks south of Madison Street. Each increment of 800 in any direction is about a mile, so it's easy to calculate how far you have to walk between locations. Even-numbered addresses are on the west side of the street, odd numbers on the east side.

For streets that run east–west, State Street is the baseline; 18th Street (for example) is East 18th Street east of State Street and West 18th Street west of State Street. House numbers start at 1 at the baseline and rise in each direction, east and west. Even-numbered addresses are on the north side of the street, odd numbers on the south side.

BY CAR It's best to leave your car behind for most city-based excursions and use Chicago's extensive network of buses and rapid transit. Street parking is difficult or impossible downtown and only a little better in the neighborhoods; "permit parking" has taken over some of the more affluent residential areas, making it illegal for nonresidents to park on side streets. Parking lots and garages charge $7–$20 a day.

A car is convenient if you plan to visit the outlying neighborhoods or suburbs. The following Interstate highways lead to the suburbs: I–94 for the North Shore and the south suburbs, I–90 for northwest, I–290 for western, and I–55 or I–57 for the southwest.

BY BUS, SUBWAY, AND EL TRAIN Buses travel all major arteries, both north–south and east–west, stopping only at posted bus stops (usually every other corner). The standard CTA bus fare is slightly less on weekends than on weekdays; the fare for mass-transit trains (known as the El) is the higher rate all times. Dollar bills are accepted for both buses and trains. The cheapest way to travel the CTA is to buy a roll of 10 tokens good for buses and the El at currency exchanges or at Jewel and Dominick's supermarkets. Transfers cost a small amount and must be purchased when you board the first bus or train. Bus and El information and maps are available by calling the **RTA Information Center** (tel. 312/836–7000).

BY TAXI The principal taxi companies are **Yellow Cab Company** and **Checker Cab Company** (both at tel. 312/829–4222), **American United Cab Company** (tel. 312/248–7600), and **Flash Cabs** (tel. 312/561–1444). Drivers expect a 15% tip. A short hop from the Near North to the Loop costs $5–$10, including tip. Keep in mind that city cabs can drop passengers off in the suburbs but can't pick them up there.

REST STOPS North Michigan Avenue's three vertical malls have rest rooms: Water Tower Place (835 N. Michigan Ave.), Chicago Place (700 N. Michigan Ave.), and the 900 North Michigan Avenue building. Downtown you can find public rest rooms at the Harold

Washington Library Center (400 S. State St.), Marshall Field (111 N. State St.), Carson Pirie Scott (1 S. State St.), and the Chicago Cultural Center (78 E. Washington St.). In Lincoln Park there are rest rooms at the Lincoln Park Zoo (2200 N. Cannon Dr.), the Chicago Historical Society (1601 N. Clark St.), and North Avenue Beach.

GUIDED TOURS Orientation: The **Chicago Motor Coach Company** (tel. 312/922–8919) operates double-decker tour buses that give one-hour narrated tours of Chicago landmarks ($10 adults, $6 senior citizens and children). Climb on at the Sears Tower (233 S. Wacker Dr. at Jackson Blvd.), the Field Museum (E. Lake Shore Dr. at Roosevelt Rd.), the Art Institute (S. Michigan Ave. and Adams St.), or the Water Tower (Michigan Ave. at Pearson St.). **Wendella Sightseeing Boats** (400 N. Michigan Ave., tel. 312/337–1446) ply the Chicago River and Lake Michigan April–October, leaving from the north side of the Michigan Avenue Bridge. The cost of the guided tour is $10 adults, $8 senior citizens, $5.50 children. **Mercury Skyline Cruises** (tel. 312/332–1353), offering similar tours and prices, leave from the south side of the bridge.

Special Interest: The Chicago Architecture Foundation offers many worthwhile tours, including walking tours of the Loop and several other historic neighborhoods, bus tours, museum tours, and an architectural river cruise. Tour times vary and prices are $5–$17 per person depending on the tour. For information, call the **CAF Tour Center** (224 S. Michigan Ave., tel. 312/922–8687). The Tour Center also has maps and self-guided tours, as well as architecture-related books and gifts.

EXPLORING

With careful planning, you can hit Chicago's high points in three or four days—but it would take weeks to exhaust all of the city's possibilities. Architecture buffs should be sure to tour the Loop, Hyde Park, and the suburb of Oak Park. Shoppers will want to stop in at Marshall Field & Co.'s State Street flagship store—past its prime but still one of the world's great department stores—and cruise the swanky shops on North Michigan Avenue. For a great view of the city's skyline, go to Navy Pier at the east end of Grand Street (600 E. Grand St.), or to the tree-lined promenade of Olive Park, which extends north into the lake at the same place.

Adler Planetarium. Stargazers love the Planetarium, which offers exhibits about the stars and planets, an ever-changing program of Sky Shows, and a hot line that gives information on the current month's skies. *1300 S. Lake Shore Dr., tel. 312/322–0304, sky information tel. 312/322–0300. Open daily. Admission free; admission charged for sky shows.*

The **Art Institute** has one of the world's most renowned collections of French Impressionism, as well as outstanding Medieval and Renaissance works and fine holdings in Asian art and photography. If you're interested in architecture, don't miss the reconstruction of the trading room from Louis Sullivan's Chicago Stock Exchange Building, demolished in 1972. If you're bringing the kids, start your tour at the downstairs Children's Museum, where youngsters can choose from over 20 fun and educational "gallery games" that will keep them entertained throughout your visit. *Michigan Ave. at Adams St., tel. 312/443–3600. Open daily. Admission charged Wed.–Mon.; free Tues.*

Baha'i House of Worship (100 Linden Ave., Wilmette, tel. 708/853–2300), the national headquarters of the Baha'i faith, is an elegant, nine-sided building that incorporates a wealth of architectural styles and religious symbols. To get there, take Lake Shore Drive north to its end, then follow the signs for Sheridan Road. You'll cross the Chicago city limits and drive through Evanston to reach Wilmette.

Brookfield Zoo. The animals here inhabit naturalistic settings, including a rocky seascape for seals and sea lions, a marsh, and Tropic World, which simulates Asian, South American, and African rain forests. The Children's Zoo features animals that may be petted, and the Seven Seas Panorama offers daily dolphin shows that are perennial favorites. To reach the zoo, take I–290 (Dwight D. Eisenhower Expressway) west to 1st Avenue and follow the signs. *8400 W. 31st St., Brookfield, tel. 708/485–2200. Open daily. Admission charged; ½ price Tues., Thurs.*

Chicago Academy of Sciences. Despite its scholarly name, this is not an institution of learning but a museum specializing in the natural history of the Midwest. The permanent displays include detailed dioramas; the Academy also features an ever-changing number of lively interactive exhibits that are especially fun for kids. *2001 N. Clark St., tel. 312/871–2668. Open daily. Admission charged Tues.–Sun.; free Mon.*

Chicago Children's Museum offers 57,000 square feet of fascinating and educational exhibits for children, including an early-childhood exhibit with a kid-size neighborhood, a hands-on art studio, science exhibits on subjects from recycling to invention, and an activity-filled exhibit that provides kids and adults with tools for addressing prejudice and discrimination. *Navy Pier, 600 E. Grand Ave., tel. 312/527–1000. Open Tues.–Sun. Admission charged; free Thurs. evening.*

Chicago Historical Society has permanent and changing exhibits on Chicago's past, plus a long-running exhibit on the roots of the Civil War. *1601 N. Clark St. at North Ave., tel. 312/642–4600. Open daily. Admission charged Tues.–Sun.; free Mon.*

Field Museum of Natural History. This gorgeous Georgia marble museum is worth visiting for its architecture alone; however, it also happens to be one of the best natural-history museums in the country. From the two-part Life Over Time exhibit that traces the evolution of life over 3.5 billion years to the eerie Mastaba tomb complex from ancient Egypt, the size and breadth of the museum's collections are staggering. Kids will enjoy all the exhibits, but particularly Place for Wonder, which lets youngsters handle everything from gourds to a ½-ton

stuffed polar bear. *Lake Shore Dr. at E. Roosevelt Rd., tel. 312/922–9410. Open daily. Admission charged Thurs.–Tues.; free Wed.*

John Hancock Center. It may no longer be the city's tallest building, but this handsome skyscraper still offers impressive vistas, particularly from the 95th floor Signature Room Lounge, where you can gaze down upon the city and the lakefront for hours while you sip an expensive cocktail or soda. There's also an observation deck on the 96th floor, but since there's an admission charge, the Signature Room is a better bet. *875 N. Michigan Ave., tel. 312/751–3681. Open daily. Admission charged for observation deck.*

Lincoln Park Zoo and Conservatory offers the best fauna and flora to be found within the city limits. The zoo includes a "koala condo," a seal pool, a rookery, a new big-cat house, and a Farm-in-the-Zoo. The conservatory has permanent exhibits of many exotic plants as well as seasonal flower shows. Lincoln Park itself, which stretches between 1600 and 5600 North along the lakefront, has rolling lawns, beaches, statuary, tennis courts, and a golf course. *Zoo: 2200 N. Cannon Dr., tel. 312/742–7695. Conservatory: 2351 N. Stockton Dr., tel. 312/ 294–4770. Open daily. Admission free at both.*

The **Museum of Contemporary Art,** started by a group of art patrons who found the Art Institute unresponsive to modern work, concentrates on 20th-century art, principally from after 1940. *237 E. Ontario St., tel. 312/ 280–5161. Open Tues.–Sun. Admission charged Wed.–Mon.; free Tues.*

The **Museum of Science and Industry** is a massive structure dating from the 1893 World's Fair. Among the many kid-friendly exhibits are a 1,200-foot-long model of the Santa Fe Railroad, a German U-boat captured during World War II, a coal mine, and an impressive domed Omnimax theater that shows entertaining educational films on a huge five-story screen that gives viewers the feeling of being inside the movie. Visit during the week if you can—the museum tends to be crowded on weekends. *57th St. at Lake*

Shore Dr., tel. 312/684–1414. Open daily. Admission charged.

Navy Pier. Recently renovated, this 1916 commercial shipping pier now houses shopping promenades, numerous restaurants, an enclosed ice-skating rink, a 1,500-seat theater, an IMAX movie theater, the Chicago Children's Museum (*see above*), and an outdoor park featuring gardens, fountains, a beer garden, a carousel, and a giant 15-story Ferris wheel. The Pier is also home port to a number of the city's popular tour and dinner cruise vessels. *600 E. Grand Ave., tel. 312/ 595–7437.*

Oak Park, a suburb of Chicago, contains the largest collection of Wright-designed buildings in the world, including the Frank Lloyd Wright Home and Studio. Also in Oak Park is Wright's poured-concrete Unity Temple (875 Lake St., tel. 708/383–8873), built in 1905 for a Unitarian congregation on a budget. Take I–290 (Eisenhower Expressway) to Harlem Avenue. Turn right and drive north on Harlem to Chicago Avenue. Then turn right and drive three blocks to Forest Avenue. *Frank Lloyd Wright Home and Studio: 951 Chicago Ave., Oak Park, tel. 708/ 848–1500. Open daily. Admission charged.*

Outdoor sculptures by famous artists are scattered throughout the Loop. Look for the Picasso at the Daley Center (Washington and Dearborn Sts.), the Miro at the plaza of the Chicago Temple (77 W. Washington St.), Claes Oldenburg's giant baseball bat at 600 West Madison Street, a Chagall mosaic at First National Plaza (Monroe and Dearborn Sts.), a Dubuffet outside the State of Illinois Center (Randolph and Clark Sts.), and a Calder stabile (a sculpture that looks like a mobile) at 230 South Dearborn Street. There's also a Calder mobile in the lobby of the Sears Tower (233 S. Wacker Dr.).

River North, bordered on the south by the Chicago River, on the north by Chicago Avenue, on the east by Clark Street, and on the west by Sedgwick Avenue, has more than 70 small art galleries offering all manner of specialties from furniture to fantasy. Galleries can be found at 750 North Orleans Street at Chicago Avenue, 301 West Superior Street at Franklin Street, and 311 West Superior Street at Orleans Street. Many galleries are closed on Sunday or Monday. For current exhibits, pick up the *Chicago Gallery News* at a Tourist Information Center (*see* Tourist Offices, *above*). Most galleries have openings the first Friday evening of every month, and gallery hopping is customary and free. Small shops and restaurants abound here as well.

Sears Tower, the Western Hemisphere's tallest building at almost 1,500 feet, offers vertigo views of the city from its 103rd-floor Skydeck. There's an admission fee, so be sure to check the visibility rating before you board the elevator to the Skydeck. Before you leave, see the fantastic Calder mobile sculpture *Universe* in the lobby near the Wacker Drive entrance. *233 S. Wacker Dr., tel. 312/875–9696. Open daily. Admission charged for Skydeck.*

John G. Shedd Aquarium gives you a chance to see sharks, eels, turtles, and other marine life without ever getting your feet wet. Its Oceanarium is the world's largest indoor marine-mammal facility; it is also quite controversial, as several of the migratory beluga whales that have been kept here have died. *1200 S. Lake Shore Dr., tel. 312/ 939–2438. Open daily. Admission charged.*

Terra Museum contains Ambassador Daniel Terra's private collection of American art. The intimate galleries include pieces by Andrew Wyeth, Edward Hopper, John Singer Sargent, Winslow Homer, and Mary Cassatt. *666 N. Michigan Ave., tel. 312/664– 3939. Open Tues.–Sun. Admission charged.*

University of Chicago, located off the still-visible Midway of the 1893 Columbian Exposition in Hyde Park, is home to two museums: the David and Alfred Smart Museum of Art, with exhibits of Renaissance through modern art, and the Oriental Institute, which specializes in the ancient Near East. The Gothic campus is a pleasant place to stroll, and there are several excellent bookstores in the neighborhood, including Powell's (1501 E. 57th St., tel. 312/

955–7780) for used books, 57th St. Books (1301 E. 57th St., tel. 312/684–1300), and the Seminary Cooperative Bookstore (5757 S. University Ave., tel. 312/752–4381). *Smart Museum: 5550 S. Greenwood Ave., tel. 312/702–0200. Open Tues.–Sun. Admission free. Oriental Institute: 1155 E. 58th St., tel. 312/702–9521. Open Tues.–Sun. Admission free.*

HOTELS AND INNS

Most travelers to Chicago will want to stay on the Near North Side or in the Loop, near many of the major cultural institutions, shopping areas, and architectural masterpieces. Accommodations are cheaper near O'Hare Airport, where there are lots of hotels and motels, but it's drab, and the trip into town can take up to an hour at peak traffic times or in bad weather. Most city hotels have special weekend rates; be sure to inquire when making reservations. Auto club or AARP members may also qualify for discounts. Loop hotels generally cost slightly less than those in the Near North, but the neighborhood can get a little creepy late at night. The streets are livelier on the Near North Side, and there's a better assortment of restaurants and nightspots.

Chicago hosts some of the world's largest conventions; it's nearly impossible to get a hotel room at any price during one of these gargantuan gatherings, and bargain rates are suspended. The tourist board can give you information on when conventions are scheduled. Some hotels charge $5–$10 more per night from April to October. Price categories for double occupancy, excluding 12.4% tax and service charges, are Expensive, $150–$200; Moderate, $100–$150; and Inexpensive, under $100.

THE LOOP **The Blackstone.** The ornate lobby gives a clue to what this grand hotel once was; if it ever gets the renovation it sorely needs, the prices will skyrocket. For now, you get basic accommodations (there's no room service) in a great location. *636 S. Michigan Ave., 60605, tel. 312/427–4300*

or *800/622–6330, fax 312/427–4736. 305 rooms, 25 suites. Restaurant, lounge, jazz club, access to health club, theater. AE, D, DC, MC, V. Moderate.*

Essex Inn. This pleasantly decorated modern building just south of the "best" stretch of South Michigan Avenue is a good place for large groups. Although not glamorous, the hotel is nicely situated opposite Grant Park and operates a free shuttle bus to North Michigan Avenue. *800 S. Michigan Ave., 60605, tel. 312/939–2800 or 800/621–6909, fax 312/939–1605. 234 rooms, 21 suites. Restaurant, lounge, outdoor heated pool. AE, D, DC, MC, V. Inexpensive.*

Grant Park Hotel. Taken over and completely refurbished by Best Western, the Grant Park is near the museums at the south end of the park. *1100 S. Michigan Ave., 60605, tel. 312/922–2900 or 800/528–1234, fax 312/922–8812. 172 rooms. Restaurant, outdoor pool, exercise room and sauna, on-site parking (fee). AE, D, DC, MC, V. Moderate.*

Ramada-Congress Hotel. Renovations have spruced up the rooms at this large, turn-of-the-century hotel, which was apparently built in pieces, with some sections grand and distinctive and others more modern and characterless. The location, however, is excellent. *520 S. Michigan Ave., 60605, tel. 312/427–3800 or 800/635–1666, fax 312/427–3972. 818 rooms. 2 restaurants, bar, health club. AE, DC, MC, V. Moderate.*

NEAR NORTH, RIVER NORTH, LINCOLN PARK, AND LAKEVIEW **City Suites Hotel.** This small, quaint hotel offers a lot of character and comfort at an excellent price. Located in the Lakeview neighborhood on the city's north side, it's just a short cab ride from downtown and is close to some of the city's best restaurants, shopping, nightlife, and theater. It's a great choice if you're looking for something out of the ordinary. *933 W. Belmont Ave., 60657, tel. 312/404–3400 or 800/248–9108, fax 312/404–3405. 15 rooms, 30 suites. Parking, room service. AE, D, MC, V. Inexpensive.*

Claridge Hotel. Intimate rather than bustling, this '30s-vintage hotel in the Gold Coast, north of the Michigan Avenue shopping district, was tastefully renovated several years ago. Four floors are designated for non-smokers. *1244 N. Dearborn Pkwy., 60610, tel. 312/787–4980 or 800/245–1258, fax 312/266–0978. 162 rooms, 4 suites. Continental breakfast included, restaurant, bar, access to nearby health club, valet parking, concierge, limousine service. AE, D, DC, MC, V. Moderate.*

Comfort Inn of Lincoln Park. At the northern edge of Lincoln Park, this basic but comfortable establishment is removed from the Loop and the Near North Side but is convenient to the lakefront neighborhoods of Lincoln Park and Lakeview. *601 W. Diversey Pkwy., 60614, tel. 312/348–2810 or 800/221–2222, fax 312/348–1912. 74 rooms. Continental breakfast included, parking. AE, D, DC, MC, V. Inexpensive.*

Hotel Inter-Continental Chicago. In 1988 the Inter-Continental Hotel acquired the adjacent Forum Hotel and underwent a $130 million renovation. The result is a huge, chic hotel with a plush lobby, spacious guest rooms, and a host of amenities including an Italianate junior-Olympic-size swimming pool built in 1929. The location on North Michigan Avenue can't be beat, either. *505 N. Michigan Ave., 60611, tel. 312/944–4100 or 800/327–0200, fax 312/321–8877. 844 rooms, 42 suites. 2 restaurants, lounge, 24-hr room service, health club, pool, concierge, business center, valet parking. AE, D, DC, MC, V. Expensive.*

Inn of Chicago. An excellent location and simple but attractive rooms make this property a very good value—except during conventions, when the rates increase. *162 E. Ohio St., 60611, tel. 312/787–3100 or 800/528–1234, fax 312/573–3140. 357 rooms, 26 suites. Restaurant, lounge, access to nearby health club, valet laundry, valet parking. AE, D, DC, MC, V. Moderate.*

Lenox Suites. This all-suites hotel was completely renovated in 1995; the expanded lobby and guest suites are now decorated in jewel tones, and amenities include kitchenettes with coffeemakers in each suite and complimentary daily newspaper, coffee, juice, and bottled water. *616 N. Rush St., 60611, tel. 312/337–1000 or 800/445–3669, fax 312/337–7217. 325 suites. 2 restaurants, 2 bars, wet-bar kitchens, concierge. AE, D, DC, MC, V. Moderate.*

Raphael. European-style multilingual service, tastefully furnished rooms with refrigerators, and a '30s-vintage building make the Raphael a very classy hotel at a reasonable price. *201 E. Delaware Pl., 60611, tel. 312/943–5000 or 800/821–5343, fax 312/943–9483. 172 rooms. Restaurant, lounge, health-club access (fee), valet parking. AE, D, DC, MC, V. Moderate.*

River North Hotel. This pleasant, modern hotel is one of the few in the River North gallery district, and it's a bit less expensive than comparably equipped hotels along Michigan Avenue. Amenities include coffeemakers and coffee in every room, and complimentary newspaper and juice daily. *125 W. Ohio St., 60610, tel. 312/467–0800 or 800/727–0800, fax 312/467–1665. 148 rooms, 58 suites. Restaurant, lounge, indoor pool, health club, valet, concierge, free parking. AE, D, DC, MC, V. Moderate.*

DINING

Once a steak-and-potatoes town, in the last decade Chicago has blossomed into a food lover's haven. Steaks, ribs, Italian beef, and the ubiquitous Vienna Hot Dog have been augmented by many excellent French and Italian restaurants, plus a variety of more exotic cuisines from Middle Eastern to Thai and Vietnamese. Most of the establishments below are in the Near North, River North, and Loop areas, within walking distance of the major hotel districts, with a few out in the city's residential neighborhoods and ethnic enclaves.

Ethnic restaurants are everywhere in Chicago. Try Greektown (Halsted and Madison Sts.), Chinatown (Wentworth Ave. and

23rd St.), and Little Italy (Taylor St. between Racine Ave. and Ashland Ave.). Chinese and Vietnamese restaurants can be found on Argyle Street between Broadway and Sheridan Road; Indian restaurants line Devon Avenue between 2200 West and 3000 West; and Thai, Japanese, Chinese, Korean, Jamaican, and Ethiopian restaurants fill Clark Street from Belmont Avenue to Addison Street.

Price categories per person for a three-course meal, excluding 8½% tax, service, and drinks, are Expensive, over $30; Moderate, $18–$30; and Inexpensive, under $18.

THE LOOP, GREEKTOWN, AND CHINATOWN **The Berghoff.** Traditional German food, lighter lunches, and house-label light and dark beer are the hallmarks of this Loop institution, whose cavernous, wood-paneled dining room serves a large business lunch crowd with dispatch. *17 W. Adams St., tel. 312/427–3170. AE, DC, MC, V. Closed Sun. Moderate.*

Courtyards of Plaka. This sophisticated Greektown restaurant offers standard as well as less familiar Greek dishes, plus whole sea bass, shellfish, and broiled pork chops. Live music and white tablecloths make it the most upscale spot in the area. *340 S. Halsted St., tel. 312/263–0767. AE, D, DC, MC, V. Moderate.*

Emperor's Choice. This sophisticated but comfortable restaurant demonstrates that Chinese seafood can go well beyond plates of shrimp and vegetables; the house specialties—octopus, squid, tuna, and shellfish cooked in a variety of ways—are fresh and expertly prepared. *2238 S. Wentworth Ave., tel. 312/225–8800. AE, D, MC, V. Moderate.*

New Rosebud Cafe. This popular restaurant in Little Italy specializes in old-fashioned southern-Italian cooking, with one of the best red sauces in town, and exquisitely prepared pastas. Expect to wait, even with reservations. *1500 W. Taylor St., tel. 312/942–1117. AE, D, DC, MC, V. Closed Sun. No lunch Sat. Moderate.*

Three Happiness. The dim-sum brunch here is one of the best in town—those in the know arrive at 9:30 AM in order to get a table when the doors open at 10. Lunch and dinner are available, too. *2130 S. Wentworth Ave., tel. 312/791–1229. AE, D, DC, MC, V. Inexpensive.*

NEAR NORTH, RIVER NORTH, AND LINCOLN PARK **Eccentric.** Talk-show star Oprah Winfrey is a partner in this combination French café/Italian coffeehouse/English pub, and her horseradish mashed potatoes are not to be missed. Steaks and chops are excellent, too. The adjacent Big Bowl Cafe offers a less expensive but equally appealing menu in a casual, friendly setting. *159 Erie St., tel. 312/787–8390. AE, D, DC, MC, V. No lunch weekends. Moderate–Expensive.*

Ed Debevic's. Brave the crowds (or go at off-hour) to savor the high-camp decor—and surprisingly good food—of this 1950s-style diner. *640 N. Wells St., tel. 312/664–1707. AE, D, DC, MC, V. Inexpensive.*

Foodlife. Hamburgers, veggie burgers, pot stickers, quesadillas, couscous, fresh vegetable and fruit juices—you can find just about anything at this international restaurant–food court. Upon entering, you're issued a credit card, on which you may charge food from any of the dozens of food stands. It's a great place for families, people on a budget, or those who are pressed for time. *Water Tower Place, 845 N. Michigan Ave., tel. 312/335–3663. No reservations. AE, D, DC, MC, V. Inexpensive.*

Frontera Grill. Authentic Mexican food that goes far beyond chips and salsa is served up at this casual café, along with such dishes as charbroiled catfish (Yucatán-style) and skewered tenderloin with *poblano* peppers, red onion, and bacon. Expect a crowd. *445 N. Clark St., tel. 312/661–1434. AE, D, DC, MC, V. Closed Sun., Mon. Moderate–Expensive.*

Hatsuhana. The best sushi and sashimi in Chicago are supplemented by extensive and unusual daily specials, including steamed baby clams in sake and broiled king mackerel with soybean paste. *160 E. Ontario St.,* tel. 312/280–8287. Reservations advised. AE, DC, MC, V. Closed Sun. No lunch Sat. Moderate–Expensive.

Pizzeria Uno. Chicago deep-dish pizza got its start here, and Uno still offers the genuine article with a variety of toppings. For a shorter wait, try Pizzeria Due (same ownership and menu, different decor, and longer hours) one block away. Uno: 29 E. Ohio St., tel. 312/321–1000; Due: 619 N. Wabash Ave., tel. 312/943–2400. AE, D, MC, V. Inexpensive.

Reza's. Chicagoans flock here for mouthwatering Persian cuisine at excellent prices. The portions are large, and everything is delicious, especially Reza's Special Chicken, a tangy chicken kebab with grilled vegetables, served over rice laced with dill and lima beans. The food is great at both locations, but the restaurant in Andersonville (N. Clark St.) has better ambience. 432 W. Ontario, tel. 312/664–4500; 5255 N. Clark St., tel. 312/561–1898. Reservations accepted. AE, MC, V. Inexpensive.

Scoozi! A big tomato hangs outside this huge, noisy, trendy place that serves up delicious country-style Italian dishes; try the osso buco (braised veal shanks in roasted vegetables). Be prepared for crowds. 410 W. Huron St., tel. 312/943–5900. AE, DC, MC, V. Moderate.

Un Grand Cafe. This relaxed, attractive, Montmartre-style bistro uses fresh American produce to create such simple French dishes as cassoulet, onion soup, steak frites, and various fish dishes with vegetables. 2300 N. Lincoln Park W, tel. 312/348–8886. No reservations. AE, D, DC, MC, V. No lunch. Moderate.

LAKEVIEW AND NORTH **Ann Sather.** Expect a wait on weekend mornings at these cheery Swedish restaurants, where locals come for omelets, Swedish pancakes, and the renowned cinnamon rolls. Lunches and dinners feature hearty, uncomplicated home cooking. 5207 N. Clark St., tel. 312/271–6677; 929 W. Belmont Ave., tel. 312/348–2378. AE, MC, V. Inexpensive.

Mia Francesca. Delicious, authentic Italian cooking; a chic, tightly spaced dining room; and very reasonable prices make the waits at this Lakeview restaurant uncommonly long. If you can wait an hour or two for a table, you're in for a treat. 3311 N. Clark St., tel. 312/281–3310. No reservations. MC, V. Moderate.

Pasteur. Steamy and often packed on weekends, this Vietnamese restaurant has an extensive menu; try the noodle salads and the do-it-yourself barbecued-beef appetizer. 4759 N. Sheridan Rd., tel. 312/271–6673. AE, MC, V. No lunch weekends. Moderate.

P.S. Bangkok. Choose from over 100 mild or spicy entrées at this popular Lakeview Thai restaurant. The decor is soothing, with wood-paneled walls and several statues of Buddha smiling benevolently down upon the room. There's also a great Sunday brunch buffet. 3345 N. Clark St., tel. 312/871–7777. AE, D, DC, MC, V. Moderate.

SHOPPING

SHOPPING DISTRICTS, MALLS, & DEPARTMENT STORES Chicago's two main shopping areas are North Michigan Avenue (between the Chicago River and Oak Street) and the Loop. At the north end of Michigan Avenue, top designers have shops on Oak Street between Michigan Avenue and State Street.

Three "vertical malls" line Michigan Avenue, offering mid- to high-priced clothing, trinkets, and housewares. **Chicago Place** (700 N. Michigan Ave.) is anchored by Saks Fifth Avenue; the top level has a food court with a variety of quick dishes available. **Water Tower Place** (835 N. Michigan Ave.) has Lord & Taylor, a branch of Marshall Field & Co., and movie theaters. **900 N. Michigan Ave.** has Bloomingdale's, Henri Bendel, and a movie theater.

While in the Loop, visit **Carson Pirie Scott & Co.** (1 S. State St.) and look for the ornate Louis Sullivan ironwork on the main entrance at State and Madison. Chicago's second major department store is **Marshall Field & Co.** (111 N. State St.); the basement of the flagship store has a food court serving everything from soup to hot entrées to ice cream, while the Walnut Room offers more traditional fare—it's also the site of the store's celebrated giant tree at Christmas.

The **North Pier complex** (435 E. Illinois St.), on the lake just south of Navy Pier, is teeming with small, fascinating shops, including a seashell store, a hologram showroom, and the City of Chicago Store, which sells unusual souvenirs such as street signs. There's also a bicycle museum, several restaurants, a food court, and an arcade that features virtual-reality games. It's an ideal place to bring the kids.

SPECIALTY SHOPS **Books:** The **Borders** (830 N. Michigan Ave., tel. 312/573–0564) three-level megastore has 140,000 book, 60,000 music, 8,000 video, and 2,000 CD-ROM titles. There's also a wide selection of magazines and a comfy café. What more could you want?

Gifts: For souvenirs of Chicago, try the **City of Chicago Store** (435 E. Illinois St., North Pier complex, tel. 312/467–1111) or the **Chicago Architecture Foundation Shop and Tour Center** (224 S. Michigan Ave., tel. 312/922–3432). You can easily please any chocolate lover with a box of Marshall Field's Frango mints, possibly the best of Chicago's edible souvenirs; pick them up at **Water Tower Place** (835 N. Michigan Ave.) or at the main **Marshall Field** (111 N. State St.).

Housewares: Visit the palatial **Crate & Barrel** (646 N. Michigan Ave., tel. 312/787–5900).

Music: For all genres of music, check out **Rose Records** (214 S. Wabash Ave., tel. 312/987–9044). **Jazz Record Mart** (444 N. Wabash Ave., tel. 312/222–1467) has the city's largest collection of jazz music.

OUTDOOR ACTIVITIES

BEACHES Public beaches and promenades line much of the lakefront. The most popular beaches are Oak Street Beach and North Avenue Beach. South of Oak Street Beach is a concrete promenade with a swimming area, popular for lap swimming, that has lifeguards from Memorial Day through Labor Day.

JOGGING, WALKING, & BIKING A 19-mile jogging, walking, in-line skating, and bicycle path with mileage markers stretches along the lakefront through Lincoln and Grant parks. Enter at Oak Street Beach (across from the Drake Hotel), at Grand Avenue underneath Lake Shore Drive, or by heading through Grant Park on Monroe Street or Jackson Boulevard until you reach the lakefront. It's populated in the early morning and late afternoon (especially if you head north from the Loop), but beware after dark and in the more desolate section south of McCormick Place. Walkers and runners should always be on the lookout for speeding cyclists.

Bicycles can be rented at Fullerton Avenue near the exit from Lake Shore Drive, and from **Turin Bicycles** (tel. 312/923–0100) in the North Pier complex. For more information on biking in Chicago, contact the **Chicagoland Bicycle Federation** (343 S. Dearborn St., Suite 1017, Chicago 60604, tel. 312/427–3325).

SPECTATOR SPORTS The **Chicago Blackhawks** play hockey October–April at the new **United Center** (1901 W. Madison St., tel. 312/455–4500). The **Chicago Bulls** also play at the United Center, November–May. The **Chicago Bears** play football at **Soldier Field** (425 E. McFetridge Dr., tel. 708/615–2327), August–January. From April to October, the **Chicago Cubs** play at **Wrigley Field** (1060 W. Addison St., tel. 312/404–2827), mostly during the day; their starting time is usually 1:20 PM. The **Chicago White Sox** play at **Comiskey Park** (333 W. 35th St., tel. 312/924–1000) April–October; their games usually begin at 7:30 PM.

TENNIS The Chicago Park District maintains hundreds of courts, most of which can be used free of charge. Public courts can be rented at the **Daley Bicentennial Plaza**

(Grant Park, 337 E. Randolph Dr., tel. 312/ 294–4790). The 12 hard-surface, lighted courts are open April–October. Call the day before you want to play to reserve a court. They fill up fast for early morning, late afternoon, and weekends but are easier to get midday.

ENTERTAINMENT

For listings of the city's theater, music, comedy, and other nightlife events, check the Friday section of the *Chicago Tribune,* the Weekend section of the *Sun-Times,* the second section of *The Reader* (this free weekly paper is distributed on Thursday in stores and restaurants on the Near North side), or the monthly *Chicago* magazine. Visitors looking for "Rush Street," Chicago's legendary nightlife and music scene, will be disappointed to find that it has moved to Division Street and is much diminished.

COMEDY The **Improv** (504 N. Wells St., tel. 312/782–6387) is a good place to catch up-and-coming talents. **Second City** (1616 N. Wells St., tel. 312/337–3992) has launched the careers of some of the great comics of the past 30 years, including Mike Nichols, Elaine May, Dan Aykroyd, John Belushi, and Bill Murray, but its recent track record is spotty—check current reviews before you go. **Zanies** (1548 N. Wells St., tel. 312/337–4027) has nurtured the careers of well-known comedians such as Judy Tenuta.

DANCE The **Hubbard St. Dance Company** (tel. 312/663–0853) is the city's premier modern dance troupe. The **Joseph Holmes Dance Theater** (1935 S. Halsted St., tel. 312/942–0065) houses another professional dance troupe that's worth watching.

FILM The **Art Institute Film Center** (Columbus Dr. at Jackson Blvd., tel. 312/ 443–3737) has special showings and series. The **Fine Arts Theaters** (410 S. Michigan Ave., tel. 312/939–3700) show first-run foreign and art films. The **Music Box Theater** (3733 N. Southport Ave., tel. 312/871–6604), a lovingly restored '20s movie palace

with twinkling stars on the ceiling, shows classics, animation, and offbeat first-run movies.

MUSIC **Blues:** Local talent is to be found at **Blue Chicago** (937 State St., tel. 312/642–6261), located in the heart of the Loop. **B.L.U.E.S.** (2519 N. Halsted St., tel. 312/ 528–1012) is cramped and smoky—basically the perfect setting in which to hear the blues. Buddy Guy uses his connections to get some of the hottest blues musicians into his club, the aptly named **Buddy Guy's Legends** (754 S. Wabash Ave., tel. 312/427–0333).

Classical and Opera: The **Lyric Opera** (Civic Opera House, 20 N. Wacker Dr., tel. 312/ 332–2244) has name stars at name prices, and tickets are hard to come by. **Orchestra Hall** (220 S. Michigan Ave., tel. 312/435–6666) hosts concerts by both the Chicago Symphony and a host of individual performers and smaller groups.

Jazz: The **Gold Star Sardine Bar** (680 N. Lake Shore Dr., tel. 312/664–4215) packs them in, as its name implies. Once a favored hangout of Al Capone, the **Green Mill** (4802 N. Broadway, tel. 312/878–5552) has been renovated and still books great jazz performers—go early on weekends if you want a seat. The **Jazz Showcase** (Blackstone Hotel, 636 S. Michigan Ave., tel. 312/427–4846) is good for serious listening, nationally known acts, and an unusual no-smoking policy. **Pops for Champagne** (2934 N. Sheffield Ave., tel. 312/472–1000) is a large, elegant room that offers a champagne bar in addition to the music.

THEATER Theater lovers will find a wealth of large and small acting companies doing everything from splashy Broadway musicals to avant-garde performance art. Most Chicago theaters are in residential neighborhoods north of the Loop; some well-known off-Loop theater groups include Steppenwolf, Remains Theater, Wisdom Bridge, the Body Politic, and Pegasus Players. For information about half-price tickets, call **Hot Tix** (108 N. State St., tel. 312/ 977–1755).

The **Auditorium Theater** (50 E. Congress Pkwy., tel. 312/922–2110) mounts touring productions of hit Broadway musicals. **Candlelight Dinner Playhouse** (5620 S. Harlem Ave., Summit, tel. 708/496–3000) matches mediocre food with outstanding productions of Broadway musicals; the dinner-theater package is a good deal, or you can go just for the show. The **Court Theater** (5535 S. Ellis Ave., tel. 312/753–4472) in Hyde Park performs Shakespeare and modern classics, with mixed results. Behind the Art Institute, the venerable **Goodman Theater** (200 S. Columbus Dr., tel. 312/443–3800) mounts consistently popular and interesting productions of classics and new plays.

Crater Lake National Park
Oregon
Updated by Jeff Kuechle

ixty-eight hundred years ago, Mt. Mazama, then one of the highest peaks in Oregon, decapitated itself in an eruption 42 times the magnitude of the 1980 eruption of its northern neighbor, Mt. Saint Helens. Forty-two-and-a-half cubic *miles* of rock was pulverized into fragments and sent screaming into the sky; some of the building-size debris landed as far away as present-day Saskatchewan. Incandescent lava and boiling mud, moving on superheated gas, carbonized surrounding forests; Indian camps as far as 70 miles away were buried beneath a rain of hot ash, pumice, and rock. The mountain collapsed inward on itself, leaving a smoking void where its graceful summit once had been.

Rain and snowmelt eventually filled this caldera, creating a lake of such guileless purity that even today sunlight penetrates to a depth of 400 feet. This mountain, enclosing a bowl filled with water of intense blue, is now Oregon's most famous tourist attraction, Crater Lake National Park.

A remote place, Crater Lake lies 143 miles from the nearest major city, Eugene. Comprising only 183,224 acres (among the smallest national parks in the West), Crater Lake Park is sometimes criticized as having little to offer other than its breathtaking lake—at 1,932 feet, the deepest in the United States. But if Crater Lake lacks the three-ring grandeur of Yellowstone or Yosemite, it also lacks the crowds. Only 500,000 annually visit Crater Lake, compared with the millions that throng other "brand-name" national parks each year.

The lack of crowds has less to do with a dearth of activities than with the fact that Crater Lake remains an undiscovered gem among national parks. The lake and its eerie, volcano-tortured environs merit more than a passing glance; the grandeur of this place puts many in a mood as reflective as the lake itself. Here is one of the great showcases for Nature the Builder, who from cataclysm has created something to awe generations.

ESSENTIAL INFORMATION

WHEN TO GO The peak visitor months at the park are July and August, but keep in mind that when you're above 7,000 feet in the Cascades, summer is a relative thing—midsummer snowstorms on the rim of Crater Lake are not uncommon. Although surrounding lower valleys often reach 110° during the summer, the park's high elevation usually keeps temperatures at a breezy 75°–80°, even during the hottest months.

Mid-September is the ideal time to visit Crater Lake: The days are still warm and clear, but the crowds thin considerably. The only caveat is that at this elevation, on any given night the temperature can fall below freezing—even after a day with temperatures in the 70s.

The lake's main source of replenishment is snow, with the vast majority falling from November to late May. Except for Mt. Rainier, no other national park receives as much annual snowfall as Crater Lake. (A year without at least 25 feet of snow at Rim Village is considered a drought, and drifts of up to 50 feet are not uncommon.)

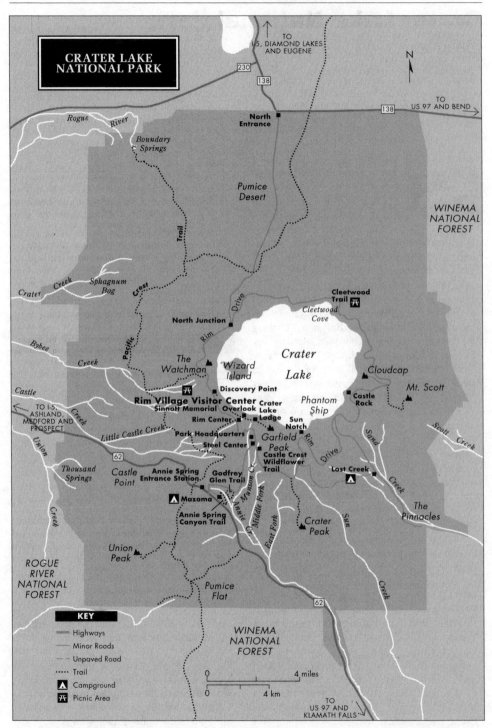

CRATER LAKE
NATIONAL PARK

TO
I-5, DIAMOND LAKES
AND EUGENE

230

138

TO
US 97 AND BEND

138

North
Entrance

Rogue River

Boundary
Springs

Pumice
Desert

WINEMA
NATIONAL
FOREST

Crater Creek

Sphagnum
Bog

Trail

Cleetwood
Trail

Cleetwood
Cove

North Junction

Pacific Crest

Rim Drive

Crater
Lake

Bybee Creek

The
Watchman

Wizard
Island

Discovery Point

Cloudcap

Mt. Scott

Castle Creek

TO I-5,
ASHLAND,
MEDFORD AND
PROSPECT

Rim Village Visitor Center
Sinnott Memorial   Overlook
Rim Center
Park Headquarters
Steel Center

Little Castle Creek

Crater
Lake
Lodge

Phantom
Ship

Castle
Rock

Sun
Notch

Garfield
Peak

Castle Crest
Wildflower
Trail

Rim Drive

Scott Creek

Last Creek

Union Creek

Thousand
Springs

62

Castle
Point

Annie Spring
Entrance Station

Godfrey
Glen Trail

Mazama

Annie Spring
Canyon Trail

Annie Creek

Middle Fork

Munson Cr.

East Fork

Crater
Peak

Sun Creek

The
Pinnacles

ROGUE
RIVER
NATIONAL
FOREST

Union
Peak

Pumice
Flat

62

WINEMA
NATIONAL
FOREST

N

KEY

Highways
Minor Roads
Unpaved Road
Trail
Campground
Picnic Area

0   4 miles
0   4 km

TO
US 97 AND
KLAMATH FALLS

FESTIVALS AND SEASONAL EVENTS 2nd Sat. in Aug.: Rim Run is a high-altitude road race along Rim Drive. As many as 500 runners compete in the 5-K, 10-K, and marathon-length events. The run is Crater Lake's only special event of note, and both lodging and restaurant space are at a premium during this week.

BARGAINS For those who can handle the steep, 2-mile round-trip hike to the dock, the two-hour boat tour of Crater Lake is spectacular and well worth the cost of approximately $11.75.

The 360° panorama of Rim Drive provides priceless photographic opportunities found nowhere else in the world.

TOURIST OFFICES Ashland Chamber of Commerce and Visitor Center (110 E. Main St., Ashland 97520, tel. 503/482–3486). **Roseburg Visitor Information Center** (410 S.E. Spruce St., Roseburg 97470, tel. 503/672–2648). **Crater Lake National Park** (Box 7, Crater Lake 97604, tel. 503/594–2511).

EMERGENCIES Police, fire, and **ambulance:** Dial 911. **Doctors:** Rogue Valley Medical Center (2825 Barnett Rd., Medford, tel. 503/773–6281) is closest to the park's year-round access point. **Dentists:** Workinger Dental Group (832 Crater Lake Ave., Medford, tel. 503/772–3411) accepts emergency patients without appointments or gives referrals if necessary.

ARRIVING AND DEPARTING

BY PLANE The closest airport of any size is **Jackson County Airport** (Medford, tel. 503/772–8068), 64 miles southwest of the park in Medford, with daily service from United and Horizon airlines. There is no public transportation to Crater Lake.

BY CAR I–5, Oregon's main north–south route, lies about 60 miles west of the park boundary. State Routes 62 and 138 connect Crater Lake with I–5 to the south and north, respectively. The drive from Medford (which skirts Rogue River for more than 40 miles) takes about two hours via Route 62. Roseburg is about 2½ hours to the west of Crater Lake on Route 138, which goes through the beautiful Umpqua National Forest. The park is about 250 miles from Portland—drive time about six hours.

BY BUS Greyhound Lines (tel. 800/231–2222) makes stops in Roseburg, Chemult, Bend, Klamath Falls, Medford, and Grants Pass. No public transportation is available to the park from any of these locations.

BY TRAIN Amtrak (tel. 800/872–7245) stops in Klamath Falls. Car rentals are available here, but there is no public transportation to the park.

GETTING AROUND

BY CAR A car, abetted by a pair of reliable hiking shoes, is the best way to get around within the park. The 33-mile Rim Drive encircles the lake, providing access to more than a dozen viewpoints that are generally less than a mile off the road.

REST STOPS Public rest rooms with flush toilets are available at Steel Information Center, at Mazama Campground near the south entrance, and at Rim Village on the south side of the lake. The designated picnic areas on Rim Drive (The Watchman, Cleetwood Cove, and Skell Head) all have chemical toilets.

EXPLORING

Crater Lake National Park encompasses more than 400 square miles of high alpine meadows, bare pumice plains, deep canyons, snowy peaks, and, of course, the geological rarity for which the park is named—a crater-bound lake. You can easily tour the park in a day, though two to three days will make for a richer, more relaxing experience. Admission to the park is about $5 if you visit by car and a little less if you walk in.

Ranger-led talks explain the origin of Crater Lake. In summer, the talks take place at the Sinnott Memorial Overlook in Rim Village, where a scale model of the lake adds to your understanding of the tectonic forces at work even today. The park rangers giving the 10- to 15-minute presentations are well prepared and welcome questions. An 18-minute video providing an overview of the park is shown every half hour at Steel Information Center. The video has some very good footage, but the scope of the lake does not fit well on the small screen. Unless you hit the park on one of its snowy or foggy days, a trip to the rim gives you a much better sense of things.

The Watchman, an 8,035-foot-high precipice complete with a lookout tower, gives one of the most impressive views of the lake. After a 0.7-mile hike (short but steep), you can look down 2,000 feet into the lagoon of Wizard Island. The trail to the Watchman leaves Rim Drive near Lightning Springs, just clockwise around the lake from Rim Village.

The 33-mile-long **Rim Drive** affords views from every possible angle. A nonstop drive, without pauses for sightseeing, will take more than an hour because of the road's meanderings. Frequent stops for viewpoints or short hikes easily make this a half-day trip. Virtually all daylight hours are good for the journey; you might want to travel clockwise so that you reach the east side of the lake as the sun is going down over the western rim. All along Rim Drive are scenic turnouts and picnic areas.

The **Boat Tour** of the lake offers the only opportunity to get a firsthand look at the surface of the lake, since private boats are not permitted to sail here. Ninety-five percent of the people who visit Crater Lake never actually touch the water of the lake itself, primarily because it lies at the bottom of a steep mile-long trail. But the opportunity to cruise this unique lake is not to be missed.

The boat tours transport you past Wizard Island, the ghostly Phantom Ship, along lichen-stained cliffs towering nearly 2,000 feet overhead and into hidden coves, where the cobalt-blue depths shade gradually to the clean, rocky bottom of the lake, visible hundreds of feet down. Bring your camera—

the tour provides ample opportunities for picture taking.

You can get off the boat at **Wizard Island** and spend the day hiking, fishing, picnicking, and, for the truly intrepid, swimming in the incredibly clear but cold(!) 45° water—and then hop the last launch back at about 6:30 PM. Run by a park concessionaire, the tours employ specially built launches that carry about 60 passengers on a two-hour circuit. Depending upon the weather and how well the boats have weathered the winter, boat tours usually commence by late June and cease in mid-September. *Tel. 503/594–2511. 1st of 9 daily tours leaves Cleetwood Cove dock on lake's north side at 10 AM; last departs at 4:30 PM. Admission charged.*

Cloudcap Lookout, across the lake, is another must-see. From this higher vantage point, the view is more expansive, including Wizard Island and breathtaking perspectives of the lake.

The Pinnacles is a spooky area of strangely beautiful volcanic spires, accessible via a 7-mile-long spur road leaving Rim Drive near Kerr Notch. The road dead-ends at the Pinnacles, so the weary sightseer must double back, seeing the same things twice. Castle Creek Canyon, on the park's southwest side, also has spires, some 100 feet high.

The **Annie Spring Canyon Trail,** which takes off from Mazama campground, is a sturdy jaunt but still easy compared to the rim hikes. The 2-mile loop threads through Annie Creek Canyon, giving views of the narrow cleft, scarred by volcanism and blooming with lichens. Watch for water ouzels—sprightly diving birds with cheerful songs—which wander along the bottom of nearby Annie Creek looking for their meals.

Castle Crest Wildflower Trail wanders for about a mile along the upper reaches of Munson Creek near Steel Information Center. The creekside walk is easy going, and in July the wildflowers are in full fragrant force.

Godfrey Glen Trail, farther down the Munson Valley, loops through a suspended valley for about 2 miles. Deer are frequently seen here, and the flowers are plentiful.

THE NATURAL WORLD The glittering lake and its stunning surroundings are, of course, the park's main natural attractions. But don't overlook the evidence of Mt. Mazama's violence: charred stumps and logs protruding from vast beds of pumice; frozen rivers of lava; and the eerie Pinnacles, a lunar landscape of hollow spires of ash and pumice, fused by escaping jets of white-hot gas.

Nature has healed herself here, as she always does. Sixty-eight hundred years after the fact, the slopes of Mt. Mazama are covered with old-growth forests and delicate alpine meadows; black bear, deer, bobcat, foxes, marmot, and elk call Crater Lake home. In its shadowed depths swim prodigious trout, some 3 feet in length.

Within the lake itself are other geologic features of note. Wizard Island, a near-perfect 700-foot-high cinder cone, is a volcano within a volcano. Near the southeast portion of the lake is the Phantom Ship, a tattered, eerie island of basalt that, in certain lights, resembles an early 20th-century battleship.

HOTELS AND INNS

Accommodations are extremely limited in or near the park; in fact, there are fewer than 220 motel units of any kind within a 25-mile radius of Crater Lake. The good news is that prices are low, especially during the winter. However, campsites are plentiful, and camping is probably the most congenial option available, so you may want to consider bringing your camping gear or RV.

If it's luxury you crave, the Medford–Ashland area (about 70 miles southwest of Crater Lake via Route 62) has the Pacific Northwest's best concentration of upscale bed-and-breakfast inns, with a sumptuous network of restaurants and shops to serve them. Contact the Ashland Chamber of Commerce and Visitor Center (110 E. Main St., Ashland 97520, tel. 503/482–3486) or the Ashland Bed and Breakfast Reservation Net-

work (tel. 503/482–2337) for information and reservations.

Price categories for double occupancy, without 9% tax, are Expensive, $70–$110; Moderate, $50–$70; and Inexpensive, under $50.

CRATER LAKE NATIONAL PARK Crater Lake Lodge. Perched on the rim of the caldera, this historic old lodge was nearly destroyed by the park's savage winters. Just renovated from the foundation up, it reopened its doors in the summer of 1995. The guest rooms, freshly decorated in a sophisticated but authentically rustic style, are a welcome oasis of comfort in the park. Nearly half the rooms have lake views. *Box 7, Crater Lake 97604, tel. 503/594–2211. 71 units with bath. Restaurant. MC, V. Expensive.*

Mazama Village. The only other lodging within the park is this 80-unit motel complex near Highway 62. Built in low-slung, four-story buildings meant to weather the winter, the accommodations are basic, with few frills. *Box 128, Crater Lake 97604, tel. 503/594–2511. 80 units. MC, V. Moderate.*

DIAMOND LAKE Diamond Lake Resort. On a mountain lake 25 miles northwest of Crater Lake, this large resort has 50 modern, plain motel rooms and 40 simple, rustic cabins. *Diamond Lake 97731-9708, tel. 503/793–3333. 90 units with bath. 3 restaurants, lounge, fishing, boat rentals. MC, V. Moderate.*

PROSPECT Prospect Historical Hotel & Motel. Built in 1889, this lovely old roadhouse hotel looks as if it were part of a set from an old John Ford movie. After a long hiatus, it reopened in 1990. Presently, there are eight smallish (but comfortable) rooms in the main hotel; out back are 14 new motel rooms that are larger and better for families. By car you're 34 miles from the entrance to Crater Lake. *391 Millcreek, Prospect 97536, tel. 503/560–3664, fax 503/560–3825. Restaurant, lounge, cable TV. MC, V. Moderate.*

Union Creek Resort. The '30s-vintage lodge and adjacent cabins here at Union Creek are listed on the National Register of Historic Places. Cabins range from very small sleeping cabins to creekside A-frames with decks;

the nine heavy-timbered lodge rooms are more colorful, but they're cramped and sometimes noisy. *Prospect 97965, tel. 503/560-3565. 13 cabins, all with private bath; 9 lodge rooms, all with shared bath. Restaurant. MC, V. Inexpensive–Moderate.*

CAMPGROUNDS

Crater Lake National Park has two camping areas—the large (198-site) Mazama Campground and the smaller, more remote (16-site) Lost Creek Campground. Reservations are not accepted, but spots are usually available on a daily basis. During the peak months of July and August, it's a good idea to arrive before noon in order to secure a spot. The maximum stay at both campgrounds is 14 days. Within an hour's drive of the park are 900 other National Forest campsites.

Lost Creek Campground. In order to keep the atmosphere more primitive, RVs are not allowed here. The road to Mazama is steep enough—a 3,000-foot gain from Union Creek to Steel Information Center—and if you drive to Lost Creek you can add another 10 miles of narrow curves. This tiny but spectacular campground on the east flank of the park has two advantages over Mazama: It's less crowded, and it's on the road to the Pinnacles, an eerily beautiful region of weird volcanic spires. *Box 7, Crater Lake 97604, tel. 503/594-2211. 16 tent sites ($6); flush chemical toilets and running water only. No reservations.*

Mazama Campground. This well-maintained campground, conveniently near the park's main (Route 62) entrance, has some popular sites overlooking Annie Creek Canyon. The road in is steep and winding, particularly for RVs, but the high Cascades views and proximity to both the lake and the Annie Creek Trail make the drive worthwhile. *Box 7, Crater Lake 97604, tel. 503/594-2211. 198 RV and tent sites, no hookups ($10); showers, bathroom, picnic tables, laundry facilities, barbecue areas, and camper store. No reservations.*

DINING

If you can't survive without morning espresso and duck à l'orange, Crater Lake may not be the national park for you. However, the reopening of the Crater Lake Lodge's fine dining room has improved the situation somewhat. In addition to the lodge fare, fast food and picnic supplies are the only sources of nourishment available within the park; it's so isolated that few other dining options exist nearby. The Medford–Ashland area, about 80 miles south of the park on Route 62, has southern Oregon's broadest array of dining options. Price categories per person, excluding tax, service, and drinks, are Expensive, $15–$25; Moderate, $8–$15; and Inexpensive, under $8.

CRATER LAKE NATIONAL PARK **Crater Lake Lodge.** Tender steaks and fresh local trout and seafood, simply prepared, form the backbone of the menu here. A variety of Oregon wines is offered as well as some great microbrews to complement the entrées. With its fantastic lake views, however, the lodge's fine dining room offers more nourishment for the soul than for the body. *Rim Village, tel. 503/594-2511. MC, V. Closed Sept.–May. Moderate–Expensive.*

Lao Rock Cafeteria. This barnlike cafeteria, where diners eat family-style at long tables, features hot dishes and simple sandwiches. *Rim Village, tel. 503/594-2511. MC, V. Inexpensive.*

The Watchman. One of the more sophisticated dining options within the park, the full-service Watchman offers an array of steak and seafood choices. *Rim Village, tel. 503/594-2511. MC, V. Closed Sept.–May. Moderate.*

Wizard Pizza. This Crater Lake institution is known for its fresh-baked pizza and fried chicken. As an added bonus, they'll deliver to the nearby campgrounds. *Rim Village, tel. 503/594-2511. MC, V. Closed Sept.–May. Inexpensive.*

DIAMOND LAKE **The Cafe.** The resort's small, informal ground-floor café is best suited for hearty breakfasts and lunches. *Diamond Lake Resort, tel. 503/793–3333. MC, V. Inexpensive–Moderate.*

South Shore Pizza Parlor. This workmanlike pizza parlor is on the south side of Diamond Lake. *Diamond Lake, tel. 503/793–3333. MC, V. Inexpensive.*

Thielsen Room. Upstairs at Diamond Lake Resort is this rustic dining room serving up such specialties as prime rib and chicken cordon bleu. *Diamond Lake Resort, tel. 503/793–3333. MC, V. Inexpensive–Moderate.*

MEDFORD–ASHLAND **Chata.** Locals rave about the food, the service, and the warm atmosphere at this eastern European restaurant. Try the *piroshki* (meat- or vegetable-filled dumplings in a delicate sour-cream sauce) or the *co za bimba* ("What a party!" in Polish)—a thick T-bone steak sautéed with fresh mushrooms, so named because that's what someone in meat-scarce Poland might say if presented with such a feast. *1212 S. Pacific Hwy., Talent (just north of Ashland on Rte. 99), tel. 503/535–2575. MC, V. Moderate.*

Chateaulin. One of southern Oregon's most romantic restaurants occupies a brick-and-ivy storefront a block from the Shakespeare Festival center. The elegant, traditional French fare and local wines lure diners from as far away as Portland. *50 E. Main St., Ashland, tel. 503/482–2264. AE, DC, MC, V. Expensive.*

Thai Pepper. This local favorite serves fiery and satisfying (if not scrupulously authentic) Thai food in a soothing creekside setting; although it's above Ashland Creek, it feels like a small café in downtown Bangkok. *84 N. Main St., Ashland, tel. 503/482–8058. MC, V. Moderate.*

PROSPECT **Beckies Cafe.** This local institution has been serving up toothsome home-cooked trout and succulent huckleberry pie to hungry locals for more than 60 years. *Rte. 62, Union Creek Resort, Prospect, tel. 503/560–3563. MC, V. Inexpensive.*

Prospect Hotel Restaurant. The dining room of this beautiful old hotel serves up hearty Mexican food (and margaritas by the liter) in surprisingly civilized surroundings. *391 Millcreek, Prospect, tel. 503/560–3664. MC, V. Inexpensive.*

SHOPPING

The only shopping within the park is at the spartan Rim Village Gift Shop (tel. 503/594–2211). Historic Jacksonville, its artsy neighbor Ashland, and Medford all have their share of intriguing galleries, gift shops, flea markets, and food and wine stores. Jacksonville is especially noted for its western antiques shops.

ANTIQUES Ashland Antique Emporium (90 N. Pioneer, Ashland, tel. 503/482–9668) sells antiques and collectibles from this century. The Main Antique Mall (30 N. Riverside, Medford, tel. 503/779–9490) is the largest antiques emporium in southern Oregon, offering pieces from a variety of periods and styles. The Jacksonville Chamber of Commerce (185 N. Oregon St., Jacksonville, tel. 503/899–8118) has maps pinpointing shops in downtown Jacksonville.

OUTDOOR ACTIVITIES

BEACHES You're welcome to swim in Wizard Island's lagoon, even though it has no beach. But remember: Composed entirely of snowmelt, the water in Crater Lake is very cold—45°–55° year-round.

BIKING The 33-mile Rim Drive is popular for bicyclists, although no designated bicycle path exists, and the road is steep and narrow in places. No bike rentals are available in the park.

FISHING A state fishing license is not required, but access to the lake is limited; if you want to fish, try the area near the boat launch or take poles on the boat tour and cast from Wizard Island. Rainbow trout and kokanee salmon lurk in Crater Lake's aquamarine depths, some growing to monster lunker size. The problem is finding them—or, rather, because no organic bait is allowed, getting them to bite.

GOLF The nearest courses are in Medford, Klamath Falls, Oakridge, and Roseburg. The free guide "Oregon Golf Courses" is available at most information centers.

HIKING The Herculean, 2,500-mile Pacific Crest Trail passes just west of Crater Lake. For easier hikes, try the trails—ranging from short nature loops to rugged mountain tracks—that crisscross the 280-square-mile park. For more information, obtain a copy of the *Crater Lake Trail Guide,* available at the park information centers at Rim Village and at Steel Information Center.

RAFTING There are no rafting venues within the park, but the nearby Rogue River is a world-famous rafting spot. For information on companies that provide rafting opportunities, contact Oregon Guides and Packers (Box 10841, Eugene 97440, tel. 503/683–9552).

SKIING Equipment rentals are available at Rim Village (tel. 503/594–2511). Crater Lake has no maintained trails; most cross-country skiers follow a portion of Rim Drive as best they can. The road is plowed to Rim Village but may be closed temporarily due to severe storms. There is downhill skiing at Willamette Pass, 50 miles north of Crater Lake, and at Mt. Ashland, 85 miles southwest.

ENTERTAINMENT

During the summer, the Park Service offers free slide shows or short films at an outdoor amphitheater near Mazama Campground. The shows are well attended by overnight visitors; check park bulletin boards for dates, times, and meeting points.

More than 100,000 theater lovers converge on Ashland for the annual Oregon Shakespeare Festival (tel. 503/482–4331), which runs from February to October.

From late June through September, the Peter Britt Festival (tel. 503/773–6077) includes open-air concerts by a veritable who's who of nationally known jazz, bluegrass, folk, and classical music performers. The concerts are held in the historic gold-rush town of Jacksonville.

Everglades National Park
Florida

Updated by Herb Hiller

Think of the Everglades as a vast, shallow "river of grass" that covers much of the lower half of the Florida peninsula, fanning out from Lake Okeechobee and creeping southward to Florida Bay and the Gulf of Mexico. Of some 4.3 million acres of subtropical, watery wilderness, more than 1.5 million belong to Everglades National Park, a mere 35 expressway miles from downtown Miami.

In 1947, what is now the park's southeastern corner was named Everglades National Park; the Ten Thousand Islands area was added in 1957. Everglades is now one of the country's largest national parks and its only subtropical one. A wetland of international importance, it is recognized by the world community as a World Heritage Site and an International Biosphere Reserve.

The Glades, as the park is often called by Floridians, is a place of wide horizons, seemingly endless plains covered with tall saw grass and dotted with islands of hardwood trees called hammocks, mangroves filled with nesting birds, salt marshes sprinkled with blooming wildflowers, and sloughs teeming with fish and other wildlife. The park features wildlife rarely seen in the United States, such as the crocodile, wood stork, bald eagle, and gentle manatee. The park is also the last refuge for 14 officially listed rare and endangered species, among them the Florida panther, American crocodile, Everglades snail kite, and paurotis palm tree. Unfortunately, the park is also the most endangered in the national park system, its fragile environment besieged by agricultural and industrial activities and encroaching urban development.

Lakes south of Orlando collect their waters in the marshy origins of the Kissimmee River, which in turn spills its waters into Lake Okeechobee. The lake drains into the Everglades' shallow river of grass, which feeds these fresh waters into the salt waters of Florida Bay. Bay waters finally slosh east through channels between the Florida Keys, bathing the coral reefs at the fringe of the Atlantic in liquid sustenance. This system connects nearly all of central and south Florida—a distance of more than 200 miles across a slope of only 20 feet. Therein lies both the system's glory and, for the past century, its instability.

Development has wreaked havoc with this watershed. Impurities from sewage and agricultural wastewater contaminate the system, and flood and irrigation engineering along rivers and lakes disrupts the natural flow of water into the Glades. For the animal and plant life evolved with the natural system, the engineered arrangement proves catastrophic.

Priorities change, however, and new policies hold promise for the endangered Everglades system. Tourism and fishing interests, conservationists, and the park management have pushed for improvement. Congressional appropriations to study restoration of the Everglades have increased, and the state is reconfiguring a crucial flood-control canal in the same area in order to allow more natural flooding. Although the future of the Ever-

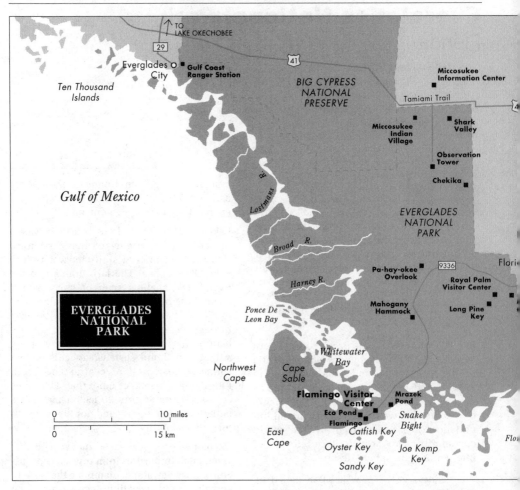

Map labels:
TO LAKE OKECHOBEE
29
Everglades City
Gulf Coast Ranger Station
Ten Thousand Islands
41
BIG CYPRESS NATIONAL PRESERVE
Miccosukee Information Center
Tamiami Trail
Miccosukee Indian Village
Shark Valley
Observation Tower
Chekika
Gulf of Mexico
Lostmans R.
EVERGLADES NATIONAL PARK
Broad R.
9336
Flori
Harney R.
Pa-hay-okee Overlook
Royal Palm Visitor Center
EVERGLADES NATIONAL PARK
Ponce De Leon Bay
Mahogany Hammock
Long Pine Key
Whitewater Bay
Northwest Cape
Cape Sable
Flamingo Visitor Center
Mrazek Pond
Eco Pond
Snake Bight
Flamingo
0   10 miles
0   15 km
East Cape
Catfish Key
Oyster Key
Joe Kemp Key
Sandy Key
Flo

glades is still uncertain, the signs are no longer unrelentingly bleak.

Today, people come to Everglades National Park from all over the world. A marked inland Wilderness Waterway trail for canoes and boats twists 99 miles through marine and estuarine areas. Shorter aquatic trails offer opportunities to explore the backcountry. A canopy-covered tram turtles its way along a 15-mile road through an ecologically rich area. Mid-December through Easter, visitors can enjoy a plethora of ranger-guided activities, including lectures and boat tours.

ESSENTIAL INFORMATION

WHEN TO GO The park has two seasons: wet (the mosquito season) and dry (the tourist season). The ebb and flow of life has been controlled for centuries by this deluge-and-drought pattern. The dry winter months (mid-November–mid-April) are the most popular time to visit, since the "skeeter meter" records bearable levels and the temperatures range from the 40s at night to the 80s during the day. Lower water levels make the trails drier and easier to navigate, and wildlife viewing is at its peak. Activities and

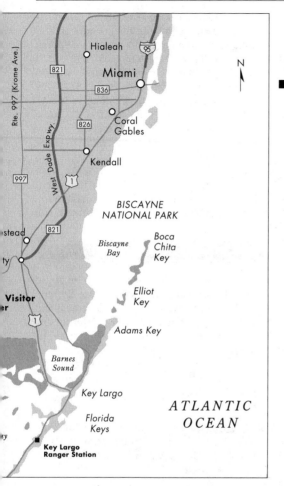

Map labels: Rte. 997 (Krome Ave.), Hialeah, 821, Miami, 836, West Dade Expwy, Coral Gables, 826, Kendall, 997, 1, 821, stead, ty, Visitor er, BISCAYNE NATIONAL PARK, Biscayne Bay, Boca Chita Key, Elliot Key, Adams Key, Barnes Sound, Key Largo, Florida Keys, ATLANTIC OCEAN, Key Largo Ranger Station, N

summer season can have its upside. Crowds thin out and the less expensive, off-season commercial lodging and service rates go into effect.

BARGAINS Everglades National Park offers free ranger-led hikes, bicycle tours, bird-watching tours, and canoe trips year-round, although the number and variety are greatest from mid-December through Easter, and some (such as the canoe trips) are not offered during the summer months. Among the more popular are a 50-minute walk around the Taylor Slough (departing from Royal Palm Visitor's Center); a 15-mile, two-hour tram tour to view wildlife at Shark Valley; and a 90-minute "Early Bird Special" focusing on bird life (from Flamingo at 7:30 AM). You can get your feet wet on "Slough Slogs" through the saw-grass marshes (from Royal Palm and Shark Valley; wear long pants and lace-up shoes). The canoe trips leave from Flamingo and the Gulf Coast. For monthly listings of ranger tours and information on reservations, contact the park (*see* Tourist Offices, *below*).

Everglades National Park's Golden Age Passport for U.S. citizens or permanent residents 62 years and older entitles the bearer and accompanying passengers to free park entry and a 50% discount off campground fees and car parking fees. Passports are issued at the park with proof of age.

TOURIST OFFICES Tropical Everglades Visitors Association (160 U.S. 1, Florida City 33034, tel. 305/245–9180 or 800/388–9669). **Everglades National Park** (40001 SR 9336, Homestead 33034, tel. 305/242–7700). **Everglades Area Chamber of Commerce** (U.S. 41 and Rte. 29, Box 130, Everglades City 33929, tel. 813/695–3941).

EMERGENCIES Police, fire, and ambulance: Dial 911. In Everglades National Park (tel. 305/242–7700, or the Gulf Coast Ranger Station, tel. 813/695–3311), the rangers perform police, fire, and emergency medical functions; look for rangers at park visitor centers and information stations or phone

special programs are in full flush during the winter—but so are the prices and the crowds (although there are no fees at any time of year for National Park Service programs).

The short "hump" seasons of spring and fall can be good times to visit. The summer season (June–October) brings sudden daily torrents of rain—as much as 12 inches in one day, high humidity, intense sun, and temperatures in the 80s and 90s. The mosquito population burgeons. (The pamphlet entitled "The Mosquito and You" is worth picking up.) But if you arm yourself with insect repellent, sun protection, and rain gear, the

the park switchboard. **Hospitals:** SMH Homestead Hospital (160 N.W. 13th St., Homestead, tel. 305/248–3232) has 24-hour emergency room services. For the Gulf Coast Everglades area, Naples Community Hospital (350 7th St. N, Naples, tel. 813/262–3131) provides 24-hour emergency service. **Doctors:** Physician Referral Service (tel. 305/633–2255 or 813/436–5430).

ARRIVING AND DEPARTING

BY PLANE **Miami International Airport** (MIA; tel. 305/876–7000) is the closest commercial airport to Everglades National Park, 34 miles from Homestead and 83 miles from the Flamingo Resort in the park.

Between the Airport and Hotels. Eleven-passenger air-conditioned vans operate 24 hours a day on demand between MIA and Homestead. The shuttle leaves from the Super Shuttle booth (tel. 305/871–2000) outside most luggage areas on the lower level. The cost is $35–$40 for the first person, and $5–$10 for each additional person traveling together, depending on the destination.

Metrobus (tel. 305/638–6700 for schedule) runs on Route 1A from MIA to Homestead during peak weekday hours (6:30–9 AM and 4–6:30 PM). Greyhound Lines (tel. 800/231–2222) makes three trips daily from its depot (4111 N.W. 27th St., Miami, tel. 305/871–1810), stopping at the Homestead Bus Station (5 N.E. 3rd Rd., tel. 305/247–2040). To connect with one of Greyhound's buses, you can take an ARTS (Airport Region Taxi Service) cab from MIA to the depot for about $5.

Taxis are available at the airport. To return to MIA from the Homestead–Florida City area, reserve a cab through South Dade Taxi (tel. 305/256–4444).

BY CAR From the north, the main highways to Homestead/Florida City are U.S. 1, the Homestead Extension of the Florida turnpike, and Krome Avenue (Route 997/Old U.S. 27).

From Homestead to Everglades National Park's Main Visitor Center (11 mi) or Flamingo (49 mi), take U.S. 1 or Krome Avenue south to Florida City and turn right (west) onto Route 9336. To reach the park's western gateway at Everglades City, take U.S. 41 (the Tamiami Trail) west from Miami (77 mi), turn left on Route 29 for 3 miles. En route from Miami, 34 miles west, you will find the Shark Valley entrance to the park. To reach the south end of Everglades National Park in the Florida Keys, take U.S. 1 south from Homestead. It's 27 miles to the Key Largo Ranger Station, located between mile markers 98 and 99 on the Overseas Highway.

GETTING AROUND

You can walk, drive, or cycle the length of the park's main road, Route 9336, but you might want to drive this 38-mile stretch and save your walking legs for exploring the numerous marked trails leading off from the highway. At Flamingo you can hike or bike on several trails or view the backcountry by boat (the only way to explore the mangrove islands and estuaries of the Gulf Coast is by boat).

REST STOPS All of the park's visitor centers—Main Visitor Center, Royal Palm, Flamingo, Shark Valley, and Gulf Coast—have rest rooms.

GUIDED TOURS Concession-operated boat tours are available at Flamingo and Everglades City; concession-operated tram tours are offered at Flamingo and Shark Valley. **TW Recreational Services** offers several boat tours and a two-hour tram tour (November–April only) at Flamingo (tel. 305/253–2241 from Miami or 813/695–3101 from the Gulf Coast; reservations advised).

TRF Concessions operates the popular two-hour tram tour at Shark Valley (tel. 305/221–8455); reservations are recommended December–March.

Everglades National Park Boat Tours (tel. 813/695–2591 or 800/445–7724 in FL) offers several cruises from the Gulf Coast

Visitor Center in Everglades City. Particularly popular is the Ten Thousand Islands Tour, where you might see manatee and nesting osprey.

Majestic Tours (Box 241, 33929, tel. 813/695–2777) are led by exceptionally well-informed guides, Frank and Georgia Garrett. Their 3½- to four-hour trips, on a 24-foot pontoon boat, depart from Glades Haven, just shy of a mile south of the circle in Everglades City. Tours are limited to six passengers and include brunch or afternoon snacks.

EXPLORING

Everglades National Park is open daily; admission is $5 per car (good for seven days) or free to Golden Access Passport holders. Begin your tour of the park at the **Main Visitor Center** (park headquarters) where you can obtain much free visitor information as well as buy a variety of books and souvenirs. *11 mi west of Homestead on Rte. 9336, tel. 305/242–7700. Open daily. Admission free.*

Everglades National Park's main road, Route 9336, begins at the Main Visitor Center and winds for 38 miles, ending in Flamingo. Leading off from the main road are more than a dozen marked walking trails. A slew of free ranger-conducted walking tours—such as "Slough Slogs," where you can get your feet wet and experience the real Everglades—and canoe trips are offered from mid-December through Easter.

As you head deeper into the Glades, notice the prairies of 10-foot-high saw grass (an ancient sedge) bordering the road to the **Royal Palm Visitor Center.** Here you will find the ½-mile Anhinga Trail, one of the best wildlife-viewing trails in the United States. The trail is a combination of pavement and boardwalk that cuts through the Taylor Slough—a marshy river that's home to alligators, turtles, marsh rabbits, anhingas, herons, fish, and purple gallinules. Another ½-mile trail, the Gumbo Limbo, also originates here.

This one winds through a junglelike grove of tropical trees, orchids, and ferns. Each trail takes about 30 minutes to complete. The Visitor Center has a small bookshop, vending machines, and a museum exhibiting the park's ecosystems. *Tel. 305/242–7700. Open daily. Admission free.*

Back on Route 9336, you come to **Long Pine Key,** a 7-mile network of trails running through a pine forest, which was largely destroyed by Hurricane Andrew. Continue until you get to the **Pahayokee Overlook.** Midway along this ¼-mile boardwalk trail is an observation tower overlooking a sea of grasses punctuated by tree islands called hammocks—a panorama that gave the Glades its name. Vultures, blackbirds, hawks, snakes, and the occasional alligator can be seen along this trail.

From here, the road turns south to **Mahogany Hammock,** a damp, dark jungle of massive mahogany trees and rare paurotis palms. A ½-mile, elevated boardwalk trail with railways and benches along the way circles through the hammock.

Bird-watchers will want to stop at **Mrazek Pond,** just off the main road before coming to Flamingo, and **Eco Pond,** between the Flamingo Visitor Center and the Flamingo campgrounds. Wood storks, ibis, egrets, and herons are just some of the birds that spend the winter here.

The road ends at **Flamingo,** where, at sunset, you can watch hundreds of wading birds head out to roost on the protected mangrove islands of Florida Bay. With campgrounds, a motel, restaurant, marina and store, boat tours, and several canoe and hiking trails, Flamingo is an excellent base for exploring the southwestern Glades, along with the winding, mangrove-lined rivers, channels, and keys of Florida Bay. At the visitor center look for the Flamingo restaurant and lounge, a gift shop, and the Buttonwood Patio Bar. *Tel. 305/242–7700 (Park Service), tel. 305/253–2241 (Flamingo Lodge). Visitor center open daily. Admission free.*

From the Tamiami Trail (U.S. 41), a separate park entrance leads you to **Shark Valley,** where you can stroll the ½-mile Bobcat Trail (a boardwalk) through the saw-grass prairie or travel a 15-mile road that loops through a shallow waterway called the Shark River Slough. You can hike, bicycle, or take a two-hour tram tour around this loop road, likely spotting alligators, and sometimes otters, snakes, turtles, snail kites, and numerous birds along the way. An observation tower midway along the loop provides a spectacular view of the "river of grass." The visitor center has displays and books available, and there are vending machines. *Park Information, tel. 305/221–8776; tram reservations, tel. 305/221–8455. Open daily. Admission charged.*

Just west of Shark Valley, the **Miccosukee Indian Village** welcomes visitors. Facilities include a restaurant, museum, and store. For a fee you can watch Native American families cook and make clothes, dolls, beadwork, and baskets. You can also see alligator-wrestling demonstrations or, for a separate fee, go on an airboat ride to a typical Glades hammock-style Miccosukee campsite. Information on the tribe's history and on special events is available at the Information Center (¼ mile east of the village, next to the restaurant). *Tamiami Trail, 25 mi west of Miami, tel. 305/223–8380. Open daily. Admission charged.*

Midway between Shark Valley and Route 29 you will pass the Oasis Visitor Center for the **Big Cypress National Preserve.** Here you can find interpretive materials about the Big Cypress, a preserve of wet prairies, marshes, and stands of Spanish moss–draped cypress trees. Watch for alligators sunning themselves on the banks of the canal that parallels the road.

To reach the western entrance to Everglades National Park, turn left (south) from Tamiami Trail onto Route 29, drive 3 miles through Everglades City to the **Gulf Coast Ranger Station.** The visitor center offers exhibits, information, gifts, snacks, and the required free permits for backcountry camp-

ing. This is also the place to arrange with the park concessionaire for boat tours to the Ten Thousand Islands region of the park or to rent canoes for exploring the backcountry waterways (*see* Guided Tours, *above;* Canoeing, *below). Gulf Coast Ranger Station, Rte. 29, Everglades City 33929, tel. 813/695–3311. Open daily. Admission free.*

HOTELS AND INNS

If you plan to spend a lot of time in the Everglades, stay either in Everglades National Park itself or 11 miles away in the Homestead–Florida City area, where there are a number of reasonably priced motels. If you plan to spend only a day in the Everglades, you may prefer to stay in the Greater Miami or Greater Fort Lauderdale areas. Hotel and motel accommodations are also available on the Gulf Coast in Everglades City and Naples. All the accommodations listed below are convenient to Everglades National Park. Price categories for double occupancy, excluding 6% tax, are Moderate, $85–$95, and Inexpensive, $50–$85.

EVERGLADES CITY **Ivey House.** Exemplary innkeepers Catlin McLeod and Lee Lambert run this plain, trailerlike but historic, clean, homey, and bargain-friendly house for the folks who operate North American Canoe Tours (*see* Canoeing *in* Outdoor Activities, *below*). Men's and women's baths with multiple showers and toilets are down the hall, but the rooms are private and impeccable, with twin beds, nightstand, luggage rack, and towel bar. *107 Camellia St., Everglades City 33929, tel. 813/695–3299, fax 813/695–4155. 10 no-smoking rooms share baths. Cold breakfast included in rate, breakfast room, small library, coin laundry. MC, V. Open Nov.–Apr. Inexpensive.*

Rod & Gun Club. A Florida landmark, the Rod & Gun avowedly avoids anything computerized. Public rooms, with their dark wood walls and animal heads, and the wraparound screen porch overlooking the river take you back to the '20s and '30s, when U.S. presidents and the Barrymore clan hung out at this landmark inn on the banks of the Barron River for hunting, fishing, and boating. Rooms, which are set in duplex cottages, are spacious, with hardwood floors, green-and-pink paisley spreads and curtains, and bird prints. The plumbing is old, so be prepared for drips. *200 Riverside Dr., Everglades City 33929, tel. 813/695–2101. 25 cottage rooms. Restaurant, lounge, pool, tennis courts, boat dock. No credit cards. Inexpensive.*

FLAMINGO **Flamingo Lodge Marina & Outpost Resort.** This is the only lodging inside the park. Its rooms are basic and well kept. Though rooms face Florida Bay, they don't necessarily provide good views. A compound of cottages provides kitchens and a more set-apart feeling. If you plan to stay in winter, reserve well in advance. Some services are available only seasonally. *Box 428, Flamingo 33090, tel. 305/253–2241 or 813/695–3101 from Gulf Coast. 102 motel rooms, 24 kitchenette cottages, 1 8-person suite. Restaurant, lounge, screened outdoor pool, 50-slip marina, marina store with snack bar, coin laundry. AE, DC, MC, V. Inexpensive–Moderate.*

HOMESTEAD–FLORIDA CITY AREA **A-1 Motel.** This one-story, U-shape motel stands directly across from the Pioneer Museum, not yet reopened after Hurricane Andrew. The rooms are clean, if basic, and done in brown and tan. Some have fridges, for which there's no extra charge. The place is utterly commercial, with much paved parking space inside the U, and a pool, too. It's your best bet for cheap doubles (as low as $36) in summer. *815 N. Krome Ave., Florida City 33034, tel. and fax 305/248–2741. 45 rooms. Pool, no-smoking rooms, coin laundry. AE, D, MC, V. Inexpensive.*

Best Western Gateway to the Keys. This two-story motel sits well back from the highway and contains such amenities as full closets, a heat lamp in the bathroom, and complimentary Continental breakfast. More expensive rooms come with wet bar, fridge, microwave, and coffeemaker. Otherwise it's a standard modern motel with floral prints and twin reading lamps. *1 Strano Blvd., 33034, tel. 305/246–5100, fax 305/242–0056. 114 units. Pool, spa, laundry. AE, D, DC, MC, V. Inexpensive–Moderate.*

Days Inn. This two-story motel just at the end of the Florida Turnpike offers clean, well-maintained rooms with floral bed covers and armoires for the TV and for hanging clothes. *51 S. Homestead Blvd. (U.S. 1), Homestead 33030, tel. 305/245–1260, fax 305/247–0939. 110 rooms. Outdoor pool, restaurant, bar, no-smoking rooms, coin laundry. AE, D, DC, MC, V. Inexpensive–Moderate.*

Hampton Inn. This two-story motel just off the highway has good clean rooms and public-friendly policies, including free Continental breakfast daily, free local calls, and a movie channel available at no extra charge. All rooms have at least two upholstered chairs, twin reading lamps, and a desk and chair. Units are color-coordinated and carpeted. Baths have tub-showers. *124 E. Palm Dr., 33034, tel. 305/247–8833 or 800/426–7866, fax 305/247–8833. 122 units. Outdoor pool. AE, D, DC, MC, V. Inexpensive–Moderate.*

Super 8 Motel. Standard rooms in a pair of one-story buildings would hardly rate notice anywhere else, but in Florida City the choices are either a half category up in price or set around vast paved parking area. Avoid rooms 148–151 and 101–104, which are nearest the road. *1202 N. Krome Ave., Florida City 33034, tel. 305/245–0311, fax 305/247–9136. 52 rooms. Coin laundry. AE, D, DC, MC, V. Inexpensive.*

TAMIAMI TRAIL **Port of the Islands Resort & Marina.** A Spanish Mission–style hotel is the focal point of this resort 12 miles from the park's Gulf Coast Ranger Station, on Tamiami Trail near Everglades City. Accommodations are luxurious but reasonably priced, and amenities include boat rentals, cruises, and even a 3,500-foot private airstrip. *25000 Tamiami Trail E, Naples 33961, tel. 813/394–3101 or 800/237–4173, fax 813/394–4335. 185 rooms, 23 with kitchenettes, 5 suites. Restaurant, lounge, 2 heated* pools, fitness room, 6 tennis courts (4 lighted), boat and bike rentals, 99-slip marina, marina store, playground. AE, DC, MC, V. Moderate.

CAMPGROUNDS

Everglades National Park offers three developed campgrounds—Chekika, Flamingo, and Long Pine Key—for tents and RVs, plus 48 primitive backcountry campsites. The developed campsites have no hookups for water, electricity, or sewage; but modern rest rooms and showers, picnic tables, grills, tent and trailer pads, drinking water, and sanitary dump stations are all available. Camping is on a first-come, first-served basis, so come early, especially in the winter season when the camps fill up quickly. Both Chekika and Long Pine Key were heavily damaged by Hurricane Andrew; check with park headquarters (tel. 305/242–7700) for availability. The stay at all three campgrounds is limited to 14 days from December through March and to a total of 30 days per year.

Everglades National Park Backcountry Sites. Deep within the park there are 48 designated campsites—two accessible by land, the rest by water only. Most are beach or forest sites, but 14 are chickee sites (raised wooden platforms with thatched roofs). All have chemical toilets. Obtain free camping permits from the rangers at Flamingo or the Gulf Coast station. Permits are issued for a specific site; capacity and length of stay are limited. Call ahead for information and daily updates. *Flamingo Ranger Station, Backcountry Reservations Office, Box 279, Homestead 33034, tel. 305/253–2241, ext. 182, or 813/695–3101, ext. 182. Gulf Coast Ranger Station, Rte. 29, Everglades City 33929, tel. 813/695–3311. Sites available on first-come, first-served basis.*

Chekika. This area, with a fishing lake, was added to the park in 1991, and the campsite here offers central rest rooms, hot and cold showers, and picnic tables. Sites cost $8 in winter (they're free in summer), and there's

a $3 vehicle entrance fee. *Chekika Campground, Everglades National Park, S.W. 237th Ave. and 160th St., tel. 305/251–0371. No hookups. Register at campground.*

Flamingo. This camping area offers cold-water showers, drinking water, rest rooms, and a sewage dump station. Limited groceries and camping supplies can be purchased at the Flamingo Marina Store. *Everglades National Park, Box 279, Homestead 33030 (38 mi from Main Visitor Center), tel. 305/242–7700. 235 drive-in sites, 60 walk-in sites; no hookups ($8 per night for drive-in sites in winter, free in summer; $4 per night for walk-ins in winter and summer). Register at campground.*

Long Pine Key. Long Pine Key has no camp store, so all supplies must be obtained in Homestead. *Everglades National Park, Box 279, Homestead 33030 (6 mi from Main Visitor Center), tel. 305/242–7700. No hookups ($8 in winter; free in summer). Register at campground.*

Southern Comfort RV Resort. Ten miles from Everglades National Park, this RV-only campground, completely renovated since Hurricane Andrew, offers full hookups, a beautiful pool, a barbecue area with Tiki bar, and a recreation pavilion. *345 E. Palm Dr., Florida City 33034, tel. 305/248–6909, fax 305/242–1345. 350 RV sites (70 pull-throughs), hookups ($25 daily; $150 weekly); comfort stations with showers, laundry, store. MC, V.*

DINING

Florida is filled with restaurants, and there are good places to eat within a short drive of all the park entrances. While you can find variety in cuisine, local specialties include dolphin (known as mahimahi), grouper, yellowtail snapper, stone-crab claws, swordfish, conch soup and fritters, and fried alligator.

The list below is a selection of independent restaurants on the Tamiami Trail, in the Homestead–Florida City area, at Flamingo, and in the Everglades City area. Many of these establishments will pack picnic fare for you to take to the park, and several will prepare your catch with all the trimmings if you fillet it. You can also find fast-food establishments with carry-out service in Homestead–Florida City. Price categories per person, excluding 6% tax, service, and drinks, are Moderate, $15–$25, and Inexpensive, under $15.

EVERGLADES CITY **Oyster House.** A local favorite, this rustic, nautically decorated seafood restaurant serves up heaping plates of Blue Crab fingers, fresh Chokoloskee Bay oysters, and the ever-substantial Everglades Platter (fried gator, frogs' legs, catfish, deviled crab). A variety of Florida wines is offered, and your catch will be prepared to order. *Rte. 29 (across from Gulf Coast Ranger Station), tel. 813/695–2073 or 813/695–3423. MC, V. Inexpensive.*

FLAMINGO **Flamingo Restaurant.** The only restaurant in Everglades National Park, Flamingo offers breathtaking views of Florida Bay from the picture windows of its three-tier dining room. Alas, all the seafood is frozen. Picnic boxes are available. Between April and mid-October there is buffet service only. *Flamingo Visitor Center, Everglades National Park, tel. 305/253–2241 or 813/695–3101 from the Gulf Coast. Reservations advised. AE, DC, MC, V. Moderate.*

FLORIDA CITY **Mutineer Restaurant.** Specializing in Florida seafood, this stylish roadside restaurant, complete with an indoor/outdoor fish pond, offers bilevel dining, a nautical ambience, and the lively Wharf Lounge. Among the Mutineer's fresh seafood dishes, a standout is snapper Oscar, topped with crab and asparagus. *11 S.E. 1st Ave., tel. 305/245–3377. AE, D, DC, MC, V. Moderate.*

Richard Accursio's Capri Restaurant. A popular Italian restaurant since 1958, the Capri is known for its family atmosphere, good food, and varied menu, serving pizzas, pastas, and everything Italian. *935 Krome Ave., tel. 305/247–1544. AE, D, MC, V. Closed Sun. (except Mother's Day). Inexpensive.*

HOMESTEAD **Chez Jean Claude (JC's Place).** The garish pink-and-purple facade of this refurbished 1931 "hurricane-proof" house (it lost only two roof shingles to Hurricane Andrew) does not prepare you for the intimate, understated dining rooms, with their white linen tablecloths and fresh flowers. Homemade stews are among the French-country specialties. *1235 N. Krome Ave., tel. 305/248–4671. AE, MC, V. Closed Mon. No lunch. Moderate.*

Potlikker's. This Southern country-style restaurant takes its name from the broth left over from the boiling of greens. Live plants hang from open rafters in the lofty pine-lined dining room. Among the specialties are lemon-pepper chicken breast with lemon sauce, fresh-carved roast turkey with homemade dressing, and at least 11 vegetables served with lunch and dinner entrées. Try the 4-inch-tall frozen Key lime pie; it tastes great if you dawdle while it thaws. *591 Washington Ave., Homestead, tel. 305/248–0835. No reservations. AE, MC, V. Inexpensive.*

TAMIAMI TRAIL **Miccosukee Restaurant.** Eye-catching murals and waitresses in vibrant woven skirts prepare the way for some traditional Miccosukee Indian recipes, among them pumpkin bread, fried catfish, and Indian fry bread (slabs of dough deep-fried in peanut oil). *On Tamiami Trail near Shark Valley entrance to Everglades National Park, tel. 305/223–8380, ext. 332. No credit cards. Inexpensive.*

OUTDOOR ACTIVITIES

BIKING Bicycle rentals are available at **Flamingo Lodge Marina & Outpost Resort** (TW Recreational Services, tel. 305/253–2241 or 813/695–3101). Ask the rangers for "Foot and Canoe Trails of the Flamingo Area," a leaflet that also lists bike trails. Inquire about water levels and insect conditions before you set out. The concession at **Shark Valley** (tel. 305/221–8455) rents bikes. You may ride along the Loop Road, a 15-mile round-trip. Yield right-of-way to trams.

CANOEING The subtropical wilderness of southern Florida is a mecca for flat-water paddlers. There are six well-marked canoe trails in the Flamingo area, including the southern end of the 99-mile Wilderness Waterway from Flamingo to Everglades City. Bring your own canoe cushions, and be sure to get the required free permit from the rangers at Flamingo or the Gulf Coast station if you plan to camp overnight.

You can rent canoes at **Everglades National Park Boat Tours** (Gulf Coast Ranger Station, Everglades City, tel. 813/695–2591 or 800/445–7724 in FL), **North America Canoe Tours at Glades Haven** (800 S.E. Copeland Ave., Everglades City, tel. 813/695–4666), and **Flamingo Lodge Marina & Outpost**

Resort (Everglades National Park, Flamingo, tel. 305/253–2241).

FISHING The inland and coastal waters of the Everglades are popular for both saltwater and freshwater fishing. There are largemouth bass in freshwater ponds, while snapper, redfish, and trout can be caught in Florida Bay. The mangrove shallows of the Ten Thousand Islands yield tarpon and snook. Freshwater and saltwater fishing require separate Florida fishing licenses. Check at a park visitor center for specific fishing regulations and closed areas.

Boats can be rented at **Flamingo Lodge Marina & Outpost Resort** (Everglades National Park, Flamingo, tel. 305/253–2241). Everglades City has boat rentals, chartered fishing trips, and fishing guides in abundance. For U.S. Coast Guard licensed fishing guides try **Fishing on the Edge** (tel. 813/695–2322) or Capt. Clint Butler (tel. 813/695–4103).

Gettysburg
Pennsylvania

Updated by Rathe Miller

 annons and monuments lining the roadside signal to visitors that they have arrived in historic Gettysburg, Pennsylvania, site of perhaps the most famous battle of the Civil War (or War Between the States, depending on the side of the Mason-Dixon line from which you come). Here, for three days in July of 1863, Union and Confederate forces faced off in a bloody conflict that left some 51,000 casualties. The resulting Confederate defeat is regarded by many historians as the turning point of the war. Consecrating a national military cemetery on the site the following November, President Lincoln delivered a two-minute speech—the Gettysburg Address—that has gone down in history.

Covering over 5,000 acres, the Gettysburg National Military Park contains more than 40 miles of scenic avenues winding around the landmarks of the battle. The National Cemetery in particular is a well-shaded spot for a lovely summer stroll. The tourist district at the southern end of town offers several museums and shops, and the historic downtown area contains more than 100 buildings restored to their original Civil War charm. In all, more than 1,000 markers and monuments commemorate the battle. Those who want to skip from the Civil War era to the mid–20th century can visit the home of former president Dwight D. Eisenhower, which is right next to the park. The orchards of Adams County, just north of town, are especially beautiful to drive through in May.

A visit to Gettysburg is easily combined with a trip to the Pennsylvania Dutch country (*see* the Pennsylvania Dutch Country chapter).

ESSENTIAL INFORMATION

WHEN TO GO Summer months and weekends can be quite crowded at this popular destination. Crowds begin thinning out after Labor Day, but weekends are still busy through November, and the action picks up again beginning on Easter Sunday. The best hotel rates are November through March, but if you visit then, be aware that some museums close during the winter months.

In August, the maximum temperature averages about 90°, with punishing humidity. January and February are cold, with an average high of 30°. Spring and fall months bring changeable weather, with many warm days but brisk, cool nights.

FESTIVALS AND SPECIAL EVENTS **Late June–early July:** Gettysburg Civil War Heritage Days commemorates the Battle of Gettysburg with living history encampments, band concerts, and battle reenactments. **Early Oct.:** National Apple Harvest Festival is an old-time festival featuring apple products, live country music, arts and crafts, antique autos, steam engines, orchard tours, pony rides, and homemade foods. **Mid-Nov.:** Remembrance Day, the anniversary of Lincoln's Gettysburg Address, includes a parade and wreath-laying ceremony.

BARGAINS The Gettysburg area's chief attraction—the battlefield park itself—charges no admission fee, and the park service offers a wide variety of free walks and lectures that are not widely advertised, so be sure to ask at the visitor center for topics and schedules.

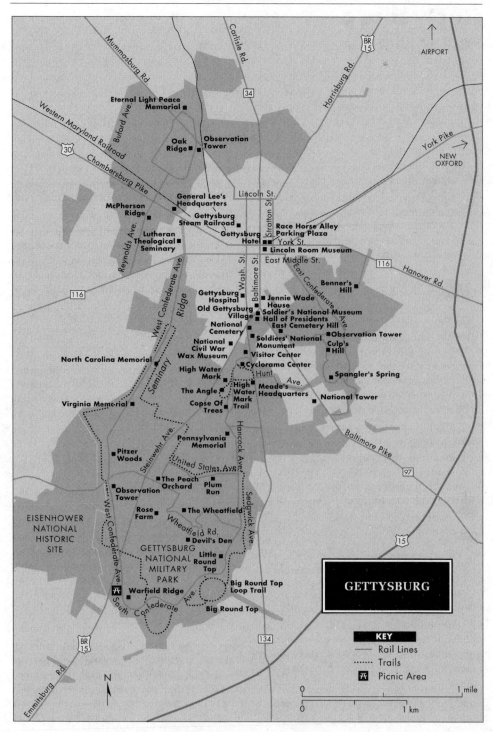

Mummasburg Rd.
Carlisle Rd.
BR 15
AIRPORT
Western Maryland Railroad
34
Eternal Light Peace Memorial
Buford Ave.
Oak Ridge
Observation Tower
Harrisburg Rd.
York Pike
NEW OXFORD
30
Chambersburg Pike
Lincoln St.
Stratton St.
General Lee's Headquarters
McPherson Ridge
Gettysburg Steam Railroad
Gettysburg Hotel
Reynolds Ave.
Lutheran Theological Seminary
Race Horse Alley Parking Plaza
York St.
Lincoln Room Museum
East Middle St.
116
Hanover Rd.
116
West Confederate Ave.
Seminary Ridge
Gettysburg Hospital
Old Gettysburg Village
National Cemetery
National Civil War Wax Museum
High Water Mark
Wash. St.
Baltimore St.
Jennie Wade House
Soldier's National Museum
Hall of Presidents
East Cemetery Hill
Soldiers' National Monument
Visitor Center
Cyclorama Center
East Confederate Ave.
Benner's Hill
Observation Tower
Culp's Hill
Spangler's Spring
North Carolina Memorial
The Angle
High Water Mark Trail
Hunt Ave.
Meade's Headquarters
Copse Of Trees
High Water Mark
National Tower
Virginia Memorial
Pennsylvania Memorial
Hancock Ave.
Baltimore Pike
Pitzer Woods
Steinwehr Ave.
United States Ave.
97
The Peach Orchard
Plum Run
Observation Tower
Rose Farm
The Wheatfield
Wheatfield Rd.
Sedgwick Ave.
15
EISENHOWER NATIONAL HISTORIC SITE
Devil's Den
GETTYSBURG NATIONAL MILITARY PARK
Little Round Top
Warfield Ridge
South Confederate Ave.
Big Round Top Loop Trail
Big Round Top
BR 15
Emmitsburg Rd.
N
134

GETTYSBURG

KEY
—— Rail Lines
.... Trails
Ⓐ Picnic Area

0 —————— 1 mile
0 —————— 1 km

TOURIST OFFICES Gettysburg Travel Council (35 Carlisle St., Gettysburg 17325, tel. 717/334–6274, fax 717/334–1166), **Gettysburg-Adams County Area Chamber of Commerce** (30 York St., Gettysburg 17325, tel. 717/334–8151), **Gettysburg Tour Center** (778 Baltimore St., Gettysburg 17325, tel. 717/334–6296).

EMERGENCIES Dial 717/334–8101 for **police, fire,** and **ambulance.** You can also call the **state police** (tel. 717/334–8111). **Hospitals:** Gettysburg Hospital (147 Gettys St., tel. 717/334–2121 or for 24-hr emergency services 717/337–4357). **Doctors:** Physician referral service (tel. 717/334–4646). **Pharmacy:** Rite Aid (236 West St., tel. 717/334–6447) is open until 9 PM Monday–Saturday.

ARRIVING AND DEPARTING

BY PLANE The closest major airport is the **Harrisburg International Airport** (tel. 717/948–3900), served by American, Continental, Delta, Northwest, United, and USAir airlines. Pick up the Pennsylvania Turnpike (I–76) from the airport and head west to Route 15, which leads about 40 miles south to Gettysburg.

BY CAR Gettysburg's major east–west corridor is Route 30, and from the north or south, Route 15.

GETTING AROUND

BY CAR A car is the most practical means of touring the Gettysburg area, although the best way to explore the downtown area is on foot. Parking in the downtown area can sometimes be a problem; the Race Horse Alley Parking Plaza off Stratton Street, behind the Gettysburg Hotel, offers covered, lighted parking.

BY TROLLEY Gettysburg's downtown area is served by a trolley. The fare is 50¢, paid to the trolley driver.

REST STOPS There are rest rooms conveniently located at the visitor center and throughout the battlefield. Rest rooms in the downtown area can be found at the Adams County Library and Adams County Courthouse, both on Baltimore Street.

GUIDED TOURS Auto tour maps can be picked up at the visitor center; auto tour tapes, which can be bought or rented at the numerous tour centers, re-create the historic three-day battle with sound effects as you drive through the battlefield at your own pace.

Gettysburg Battlefield Bus Tours (tel. 717/334–6296) offers narrated 23-mile bus tours of the battlegrounds. **Eisenhower Farm Tour** (tel. 717/334–1124) visits the president's homestead. **Gettysburg Railroad Steam Train** (tel. 717/334–6932) is a 16- or 50-mile narrated steam-train ride through the countryside. The **Association of Battlefield Guides** (tel. 717/334–1124) arranges for licensed guides to drive you through the battlefield in your car.

EXPLORING

The Gettysburg National Military Park surrounds the town of Gettysburg, and at times the two are indistinguishable. Entering town from the south, you'll discover stone walls, rolling farmlands, and stately homes that were used as hospitals during the famous battle. Many of the oak trees along the roadway have stood for more than 150 years.

GETTYSBURG NATIONAL MILITARY PARK
There are several trails for walking around the park (*see* Hiking and Walking, *below*), or you can stop at the Visitor Center (97 Taneytown Rd., tel. 717/334–1124) to pick up an auto tour map, which outlines an 18-mile driving tour to 16 marked historic sites, tracing the three-day battle in chronological order. The center also offers the **Electric Map** presentation (admission charged, sit on the south side for the best view of the action), and across the parking lot is the **Cyclorama Center,** with its 360° canvas depicting the battle (tel. 717/334–1124; admission charged).

Highlights of the auto tour include the **Eternal Peace Light Memorial**; the view from the ridge at **Little Round Top**; the **Wheatfield,** site of a particularly bloody skirmish; the **Pennsylvania Memorial,** marking the site where Union artillery held the line on Cemetery Ridge; **Culp's Hill** (an optional 5-mile loop), with its observation tower and short walking trail; **High Water Mark,** site of the battle's climax, when some 7,000 Union soldiers repulsed the 12,000 Confederate soldiers of Pickett's Charge; and the **National Cemetery,** where President Lincoln delivered the Gettysburg Address on November 19, 1863.

AROUND THE BATTLEFIELD **Eisenhower National Historic Site.** Adjacent to the park to the west is the Georgian-style farmhouse used as a retirement home by President Dwight D. Eisenhower. Shuttle buses take tours to the site from an information center on the lower level of the visitor center of the park (*see above*). *Tel. 717/334–1124. Closed early Jan.–early Feb. Admission charged.*

National Civil War Wax Museum. Just west of the National Cemetery, this audiovisual presentation brings to life some 200 Civil War figures in 30 scenes, as well as a reenactment of the Battle of Gettysburg and an animated figure of Lincoln giving the Gettysburg Address. *Bus. Rte. 15, tel. 717/334–6245. Open Mar.–weekend after Thanksgiving, daily; Dec.–Feb., weekends only. Admission charged.*

Lincoln Train Museum. A 12-minute simulated train ride brings to life Lincoln's journey from Washington to Gettysburg in 1863. *Bus. Rte. 15, tel. 717/334–5678. Admission charged.*

Hall of Presidents and First Ladies. To the north of the cemetery is a gallery displaying wax reproductions of the presidents "narrating" the story of America. *789 Baltimore St., tel. 717/334–5717. Open Mar.–Nov. Admission charged.*

Jennie Wade House. Directly north of the Hall of Presidents, you can walk through the carefully restored brick home of Jennie Wade, the only civilian to be killed in the battle of Gettysburg. *528 Baltimore St., tel. 717/334–4100. Open Mar.–Nov. Admission charged.*

Other worthwhile attractions surrounding the battlefield include **Soldier's National Museum** (777 Baltimore St., tel. 717/334–4890; open Mar.–Nov.; admission charged) with its miniature dioramas of the Civil War's 10 major battles, and the **National Tower** (999 Baltimore Pike, tel. 717/334–6754; open Mar.–Oct., daily; Nov., Fri., weekends; admission charged) for 360° views from a perch 307 feet above the battlefield.

DOWNTOWN GETTYSBURG **Lincoln Square.** The heart of Gettysburg's historic downtown area is Lincoln Square, which you can reach by following Baltimore Street north of the park to York Street. On the south side of the square, the **Lincoln Room Museum** (tel. 717/334–8188; open Mar.–Dec.; admission charged) houses the bedroom where the president finalized his famous address. On the north side of the square, the restored **Gettysburg Hotel** (tel. 717/337–2000 or 800/528–1234) was known as the vacation White House during the Eisenhower administration and hosted a number of other historic figures. Look for the Civil War–era cannonball still embedded in the redbrick building across the street.

Go west on York Street, which turns into Chambersburg Pike and takes you to **General Lee's Headquarters.** Used by Gen. Lee and his staff on the eve of July 1, 1863, this building houses one of the finest collections of Civil War relics. *Rte. 30W, tel. 717/334–3141. Open Mar.–Nov. Admission charged.*

HOTELS AND INNS

Bed-and-breakfasts with unique Civil War charm have joined the family-oriented motels throughout the Gettysburg area. Price categories for double occupancy, excluding sales tax, are Expensive, $85–$100; Moderate, $65–$85; and Inexpensive, under $65.

EXPENSIVE **Best Western Gettysburg Hotel 1797.** Built before the Civil War, this venerable stucco hotel with green-striped awnings was reconstructed from a burned-out shell and reopened in 1991. It's a cut above the motels and B&Bs that predominate in the area. *1 Lincoln Sq., 17325, tel. 717/337–2000 or 800/528–1234. 83 rooms. Suites have whirlpool tubs and fireplaces; covered parking. AE, D, DC, MC, V.*

MODERATE **Brierfield Bed and Breakfast.** Conveniently located near the major attractions, this restored 1878 house offers homey comfort, including well-furnished guest rooms and shady porches. *240 Baltimore St., 17325, tel. 717/334–8725. 3 rooms. Full breakfast included. No credit cards.*

Farnsworth House Inn. This Civil War–period B&B is an elegant Victorian house complete with actual bullet holes from the battle. Its restaurant (*see* Dining, *below*) serves authentic Civil War–era specialties. *401 Baltimore St., 17325, tel. 717/334–8838, fax 717/334–5862. 5 rooms. Full breakfast in garden included, restaurant. AE, D, MC, V.*

Hickory Bridge Farm. Set on a working 100-acre farm in the rolling orchard country of western Adams County, guests stay either in the pre-Revolutionary farmhouse or in one of two cottages. Found on the grounds are a small covered bridge, a trout stream, and a herd of Black Angus cattle. *96 Hickory Bridge Rd. (between Rte. 116 and U.S. 30, 8 mi west of Gettysburg), Oritanna 17353, tel. 717/642–5261. 7 rooms. Full breakfast included, restaurant, gift shop. MC, V.*

Little House Guest House. Originally a two-story Victorian carriage house, this small home-away-from-home with exposed brick walls and wooden beams includes a living room, an upstairs bedroom, and a kitchen. It can comfortably accommodate up to four people. *Rear 20 N. Washington St., 17325, tel. 717/334–3940. No credit cards.*

Tannery Bed & Breakfast. Located in a residential area near major attractions, this Gothic-style Victorian home, built by a Civil War veteran in 1868, has shady porches and several common rooms where guests can relax. *449 Baltimore St., 17325, tel. 717/334–*

2454. 5 rooms with bath. Continental breakfast included, off-street parking. MC, V.

INEXPENSIVE **Blue Sky Motel.** This family-owned motel 5 miles north of Lincoln Square is on a main road, but the landscaping creates a quiet country atmosphere. Guest rooms are paneled in knotty pine. Rates include complimentary morning coffee. *2585 Biglerville Rd., 17325, tel. 717/677–7736 or 800/745–8194. 16 rooms, 1 efficiency. Pool, picnic area. AE, D, MC, V.*

Homestead Motor Lodge. This small, family-owned and operated motel is clean and quiet and caters to older folks. *1650 York Rd., 17325, tel. 717/334–3866. 10 rooms. AE, D, MC, V.*

MOTELS

EXPENSIVE **Holiday Inn** (516 Baltimore St., 17325, tel. 717/334–6211 or 800/465–4329, fax 717/334–7183). 102 rooms; restaurant, lounge, pool. **Ramada Inn** (2634 Emmitsburg Rd., 17325, tel. 717/334–8121 or 800/776–8349). 203 rooms; restaurant, lounge, pool with Jacuzzi, saunas, fitness center, tennis, racquetball, chip-and-putt golf, exercise course, fishing lake.

MODERATE **Comfort Inn** (871 York Rd., 17325, tel. 717/337–2400 or 800/221–2222). 81 rooms; Continental breakfast included, indoor pool, whirlpool. **Days Inn** (865 York Rd., 17325, tel. 717/334–0030 or 800/329–7466). 113 rooms; pool, fitness center. **Holiday Inn Express** (869 York Rd., 17325, tel. 717/337–1400 or 800/465–4329). 51 rooms; indoor pool, whirlpool. **Quality Inn Gettysburg Motor Lodge** (380 Steinwehr Ave., 17325, tel. 717/334–1103 or 800/228-5151). 104 rooms; pool, fitness center, whirlpool, sauna, putting green, lounge.

INEXPENSIVE **Howard Johnson's Lodge** (301 Steinwehr Ave., 17325, tel. 717/334–1188). 77 rooms; pool, lounge, parking. **Perfect Rest Motel** (2450 Emmitsburg Rd., tel. 717/334–1345). 25 rooms, pool, picnic area. **Quality Inn—Larsons** (Rte. 30W, 17325, tel. 717/334–3141). 41 rooms; restaurant, pool, putting green.

DINING

The predominant Pennsylvania Dutch ancestry in the area is reflected on dinner menus in such dishes as chicken and dumplings or *Snitz un Knepp* (a pie made with dried apples). Restaurants serve fresh locally grown fruits and vegetables, and menus feature items "cooked from scratch." Price categories per person, excluding 6% tax, service, and drinks, are Moderate, $15–$25, and Inexpensive, under $15.

MODERATE **Blue Parrot Bistro.** This cozy bar/restaurant near Lincoln Square offers an informal, intimate atmosphere, with a dinner menu including heart-healthy pastas. You can grab a quick lunch of soup or a deli combo from the counter bar. *35 Chambersburg St., tel. 717/337–3739. MC, V.*

Dobbin House Tavern. Built in 1776, this beautifully restored building in the tourist district features light, low-calorie, and charbroiled fare, and dinners by candlelight. *89 Steinwehr Ave., tel. 717/334–2100. AE, MC, V.*

Farnsworth House Inn. The menu at this restored inn (*see* Hotels and Inns, *above*) harks back to such Civil War–era dishes as game pie, peanut soup, and spoon bread. The partially covered outdoor garden, surrounded by ivy and sculptures and serenaded by the sounds of a waterfall, is a peaceful spot in which to relax after a day of touring the battlefield. *401 Baltimore St., tel. 717/334–8838. AE, D, MC, V.*

Gettysburg Hotel 1797. The dining room in this Lincoln Square hotel is among the most elegant spots in town. The house honors former president Eisenhower and his first lady with a prime rib special in their name—the Ike or Mamie cut (the Eisenhowers were frequent dinner guests here). *1 Lincoln Sq., tel. 717/337–2000. AE, MC, V.*

Pub and Restaurant. Located on Lincoln Square, this lively publike restaurant offers a variety of pasta and seafood dishes, plus a full range of salads. *21 Lincoln Sq., tel. 717/334–7100. AE, MC, V.*

INEXPENSIVE **Food for Thought Cafe.** A favorite of the crowd from nearby Gettysburg College, this health-conscious eatery offers a coffee-shop atmosphere where you can linger as long as you like and order from a menu that includes Create-Your-Own Pita Sandwiches and organic side dishes. *48 Baltimore St., tel. 717/337–2221. No credit cards.*

Hoss's Steak and Sea House. The decor is rustic and the atmosphere family-oriented at this restaurant. Upon entering, diners order beef, chicken, ham, or seafood by number from a picture board and are then escorted to a table. Dinners include all-you-can-eat salad and dessert bar with homemade soups and warm breads. *1140 York Rd. (U.S. 30), tel. 717/337–2961. AE, D, MC, V.*

Lincoln Diner. You'll find the locals at this old-fashioned diner one block from Lincoln Square. Open 24 hours, it features fast service and Italian and Greek cooking. *32 Carlisle St., tel. 717/334–3900. No credit cards.*

Shoney's. Earth tones, rows of booths, and a glass atrium create a light, airy feeling in this '90s-style diner. The salad bar features homemade soups; the menu offers selections for children and specials for senior citizens. *Bus. Rte. 15 (adjacent to National Civil War Wax Museum), tel. 717/334–7618. AE, D, MC, V.*

Sunny Ray Family Restaurant. This restaurant, located on Route 30W, prepares food the old-fashioned way, including homemade soup and real mashed potatoes. There's a large salad bar and lighter menu selections as well. *90 Buford Ave., tel. 717/334–4816. No credit cards.*

SHOPPING

Gettysburg has numerous shops that feature handmade crafts and furniture, antiques, gifts, Civil War memorabilia, and books. Tourist shops sell T-shirts, postcards, and other less expensive keepsakes; homemade quilts and furniture, handcrafted by the local Amish community, can be found south of town. Stop at one of the many roadside markets north of Gettysburg, such as Sandoes Market, An Apple A Day, or Hollabaugh Brothers, for fresh fruits and vegetables at bargain prices.

SHOPPING DISTRICTS Downtown, along the streets radiating from Lincoln Square, you'll discover unique stores offering clothing, crafts, books, art, and hard-to-find items. In the tourist district, virtually every other shop along Steinwehr Avenue sells bullets and relics excavated from the battlefield. At **Old Gettysburg Village** (777 Baltimore St.), you'll find quaint shops, including a fudge kitchen, doll shop, general store, and military art store.

SPECIALTY STORES **Antiques:** Mel's Antiques and Collectibles (rear of 103 Carlisle St., tel. 717/334–9387; open Fri.–Sun.) has many bargains. Arrow Horse International Market and Antiques (51 Chambersburg St., tel. 717/337–2899) sells gifts, antiques, and baskets as well as vegetarian foods, international groceries, and coffee beans. You may also want to drive to New Oxford Borough, 10 miles east of Gettysburg on Route 30, which has numerous antiques shops.

Gifts: Codori's Bavarian Gift and Christmas Shop (19 Barlow St., tel. 717/334–5019; 2 York St., tel. 717/334–6371) offers German, Russian, and Scandinavian gifts, music boxes, nutcrackers, nativities, and Hummel figures. Irish Brigade Gift Shop (504 Baltimore St., tel. 717/337–2519) has a complete line of Irish jewelry, crystal, sweaters, linens, and china as well as Civil War–related items. The Country Curiosity Store (89 Steinwehr Ave. at the Dobbin House Tavern, tel. 717/334–2100) is a charming shop selling quilts, candles, bric-a-brac, and rebel flags. Gettysburg's largest gift shop may be found in the National Civil War Wax Museum (Bus. Rte. 15, tel. 717/334–6245).

War Memorabilia: The Horse Soldier (777 Baltimore St., tel. 717/334–0347) sells original military Americana, including guns, swords, documents, and photographs. For a vast selection of Civil War memorabilia, visit Farnsworth Military Impressions (401 Baltimore St., tel. 717/334–8838).

OUTDOOR ACTIVITIES

BIKING Marked bicycle routes offer a great way to discover the battlefield at your own pace. Bike rentals can be found at **Artillery Ridge Campground** (610 Taneytown Rd., tel. 717/334–1288).

HIKING AND WALKING A number of trails can be found on the Gettysburg Battlefield, including: the High Water Mark Trail (1 mile, begins at the Cyclorama Center); the Big Round Top Loop Trail (1 mile); and paths winding through the enormous rocks, caves, and crevices that hid Confederate sharpshooters in Devil's Den. For a longer hike, inquire about the 9-mile Billy Yank Trail or the 3½-mile Johnny Reb Trail. For a more contemplative experience, plan an early morning or evening walk through the National Cemetery, near the spot where Abraham Lincoln delivered the Gettysburg Address. Few others will be present at this time of day, leaving you alone with the ghosts of the past.

HORSEBACK RIDING For trail riding across the battlefield, contact **Hickory Hollow Farm** (219 Crooked Creek Rd., tel. 717/334–0349) or **National Riding Stables** (610 Taneytown Rd., tel. 717/334–1288).

SKIING Skiing during the winter months can be found at **Ski Liberty** (8 mi from Gettysburg on Rte. 116, Carroll Valley, tel. 717/642–8282) with night skiing, a 40-room hotel, and a children's center.

Grand Canyon National Park
Arizona

Updated by Jane Onstott

Neither words nor photographs can adequately describe the Grand Canyon; it must be seen up close and in person. More than 80 million years ago, a great wrenching of the earth pushed the land in the region up into a domed tableland. Ever since, the mighty Colorado River has chewed at this Colorado plateau, carving it away to create a geologic profile of the Earth's history and revealing, at the bottom of the canyon, the oldest exposed rock on the planet. This vast and beautiful scar on the surface of our planet is 277 miles long, 17 miles across at the widest spot, and nearly 6,000 feet from rim to floor at its deepest point. Above the twisting line of river rise wildly carved stone buttes, whose colors change with the time of day.

Grand Canyon National Park encompasses not just the great gorge itself, but also vast areas of scenic countryside along the North and South rims. The South Rim, at about 7,000 feet, is forested primarily by ponderosa pine, piñon pine, and Utah juniper. Shrubs include cliff rose, mountain mahogany, and fern-bush. The Kaibab Plateau on the North Rim is thickly forested with ponderosa pine, spruce, fir, and quaking aspen. Two animal species are unique to the area: the Kaibab squirrel, with its white tail and tufted ears, is found only on the North Rim, and the pink rattlesnake is found at lower elevations down in the canyon. Mule deer are frequently seen in the park as they cross the roads (so drive carefully). Coyotes are seldom seen but often heard as they howl and yip at night, and you might see hawks and ravens riding the updrafts over the canyon.

The South Rim, 91 miles from Flagstaff on U.S. 180, is more accessible, has more services and amenities, and is more crowded. The North Rim, 210 miles from Flagstaff through lonely but scenic country, is set in lush forest where you can seem to escape civilization when you're only a few yards from motels and campgrounds.

ESSENTIAL INFORMATION

WHEN TO GO You can visit the South Rim anytime of year. Because it's at 7,000 feet, the summer offers warm days, with short but sometimes frequent afternoon thundershowers, and crisp evenings. Temperatures in spring and fall generally stay above 32° and often climb into the 70s, and in winter range from around 20° to near 50°. Snow further enhances the beauty of the canyon, and the roads are kept open. The North Rim, parts of which are above 8,000 feet, is officially open from May 16 to October 21, but unexpected snow can change those dates. For information on weather, call 520/638–7888.

Nearly 5 million people visit the canyon each year; almost 90% of them head for the South Rim, and summer crowds there are enormous. You must make summer reservations months in advance. If you visit in spring, fall, or winter, the crowds will have thinned out and prices, in some cases, will be lower. For our purposes, the "summer season" covers the months of June, July, and August. "Colder months" refers to the rest of the year.

BARGAINS The Grand Canyon is quite affordable—even the dining and lodging are reasonably priced. Per-person and per-car entrance fees are low ($5–$15), and when the gatekeepers are off duty (roughly 6 PM–7 AM), you may enter the park for free. Among the free activities are lectures on the canyon's history, geology, plants and wildlife, and ancient inhabitants; visitors may also browse through the public areas and exhibits at the historic El Tovar Hotel and Bright Angel Lodge. Each day's program offerings are listed in a free newspaper, *The Guide* (available at visitor centers and at lodgings and stores), which also has an area map showing shuttle-bus routes and rest rooms. In summer at the South Rim, free brown-and-tan shuttle buses take visitors along the West Rim and to other stops in and near Grand Canyon Village.

TOURIST OFFICES **Grand Canyon National Park** (Box 129, Grand Canyon, AZ 86023, tel. 520/638–7888). For information on lodging and all other tour and recreational information inside the park, contact **Grand Canyon Park Lodges–South Rim** (Box 699, Grand Canyon, AZ 86023, tel. 520/638–2631) or **Grand Canyon Lodge–North Rim** (Box 400, Cedar City, UT 84720, tel. 801/586–7686).

EMERGENCIES Police, fire, or **ambulance:** Dial 911 (from any motel or hotel room in Grand Canyon National Park, dial 9–911). **Clinics:** Grand Canyon Clinic, Grand Canyon Village (South Rim), has medical (tel. 520/638–2551) and dental (tel. 520/638–2395) services. The North Rim Clinic at Grand Canyon Lodge has a nurse practitioner (tel. 520/638–2611). **Road Services:** the Fred Harvey Garage at Grand Canyon Village (tel. 520/638–2225) and the Chevron Station on the North Rim access road (tel. 520/638–2611, ext. 290) have road service.

ARRIVING AND DEPARTING

BY PLANE Phoenix's **Sky Harbor International Airport** (tel. 602/273–3300) is served by all major airlines and has the best connections to the **Grand Canyon Airport** (tel. 520/638–2446) on the South Rim. **McCarran International Airport** (tel. 702/261–5743), in Las Vegas, Nevada, also serves Grand Canyon. There is charter service from Flagstaff's **Pulliam Airport** (tel. 520/774–7858).

The free **Tusayan/Grand Canyon Shuttle** (tel. 520/638–2475) runs from the airport to the village of Tusayan, 6 miles south of the Grand Canyon Village on the South Rim. For a small fee, the shuttle will take you on to Grand Canyon Village. A 24-hour taxi service (tel. 520/638–2822) is also available.

BY CAR Your best access to the Grand Canyon (South Rim) is from Flagstaff (on I–40), via U.S. 180 (91 miles) or U.S. 89 north, then west on Route 64 (107 miles). The longer route is more scenic. If you are driving on I–40 from the west, the most direct route is via Route 64 from Williams (58 miles). To reach the North Rim, drive north from Flagstaff on U.S. 89 to Bitter Springs, then take U.S. 89A to Route 67 and turn south to the North Rim (210 miles).

BY TRAIN OR BUS Amtrak (tel. 800/872–7245) has daily service to Flagstaff and, April through October, from there to Williams by bus. Amtrak also arranges three-hour trips from Williams to the South Rim on a turn-of-the-century steam train; the train leaves from the historic Grand Canyon Railway station (518 E. Bill Williams Ave., Williams, 86046, tel. 520/635–4000 or 800/843–8724). **Greyhound Lines** (tel. 800/231–2222) serves Flagstaff and Williams. From Flagstaff, bus connections can be made to Grand Canyon Village and Tusayan through **Nava-Hopi Tours** (tel. 520/774–5003 or 800/892–8687).

GETTING AROUND

ON FOOT Once you reach the Grand Canyon, you don't need a car. At Grand Canyon Village, the many scenic viewing points, museums, hotels, and restaurants are within easy walking distance, and visitors can also catch a free shuttle bus (in summer) or a taxi, or sign up for bus tours. At the North Rim,

GRAND CANYON
NATIONAL PARK

TO JACOB
LAKE

N

67

KAIBAB PLATEAU

Kaibab
Lodge

De Motte
Campground

Kanab Canyon

Colorado River

North Rim
Entrance Station

Great Thumb
Point

Granite Gorge

GRAND CANYO

Supai

Point
Sublime

Havasupai
Point

Powell
Memorial

Maricopa
Point

Pima
Point

Hopi
Poin

SE

Trailview
Overlook

Lookout
Studio

Hopi
House

Visitor
Center

Mather
Point

Hermits Rest

West Rim
Drive

Bright
Angel
Trailhead

Bright
Angel
Lodge

El Tovar
Hotel

Camper
Services

South Rim
Entrance Station

Trailer
Village

GRAND
CANYON
VILLAGE

Mather
Campground

Grand Canyon
Airport

64

KEY

— Unpaved Road

⋯⋯ Trail

Ranger Station

Campground

Picnic Area

Restaurant

Lodge

0   1200 yards
0   1200 meters

180

0   10 miles
0   15 km

PAINTED
DESERT

NATIONAL PARK

Point
Imperial

Colorado River

Canyon
Lodge

Bright Angel
Point

Kaibab Trail

Angel Creek

Phantom Ranch

Cape
Royal

Yaki
Point

Granite Gorge

Grand
anyon
illage

Desert
View

Lipan
Point

East Rim
Drive

Tusayan Ruins
and Museum

64

Grandview
Point

Moran
Point

East
Entrance

TO CAMERON,
FLAGSTAFF

VILLIAMS,
GSTAFF

viewing points and other attractions are within walking distance of Grand Canyon Lodge.

BY CAR AND RV Because of the scenic drives in and around the National Park, having your own car or RV is a convenience. You can rent a car at the Grand Canyon Airport from **Budget** (tel. 800/527–0700 or 520/ 638–9360) or **Dollar Rent-A-Car** (tel. 800/ 331–6698 or 520/638–2625). At the South Rim in summer, when lodging space is tight, an RV would be an advantage. The free parking lots are large.

BY BUS AND TAXI Scenic bus tours and shuttles (some free in summer) and local taxi services (tel. 520/638–2822) provide adequate local transportation in Grand Canyon Village, nearby Tusayan, and at the North Rim (*see* Guided Tours, *below*).

The **Trans Canyon shuttle van** (tel. 520/ 638–2820) makes the 235-mile trip to the North Rim from Grand Canyon Village daily ($60 one-way, $100 round-trip). The route to the remote North Rim is never congested.

REST STOPS There are bathrooms throughout the National Park at the Visitor Center, lodgings, museums, and many viewing points. Nava-Hopi Tours buses have rest rooms.

GUIDED TOURS Tours of the Grand Canyon are available by raft, air, bus, and mule. The raft trips are relatively expensive and must be booked well in advance (*see* Outdoor Activities, *below*).

By Air: Air Grand Canyon (tel. 800/247– 4726 or 520/638–2618) operates 30- to 90-minute plane rides over the canyon from the South Rim. **Kenai Helicopters** (tel. 800/ 541–4537 or 520/638–2412) offers 30- to 50-minute helicopter tours. Additional companies operate out of the Grand Canyon Airport. All flights cost $50–$200 per person, depending on length and type of vehicle.

By Bus: The **Fred Harvey Transportation Company** (tel. 520/638–2631) in Grand Canyon Village offers motor-coach trips along the South Rim and to as far away as Monument Valley. At the North Rim, minibus tours to Cape Royal and Point Imperial can be booked at **Grand Canyon Lodge** (tel. 520/635–4000). **Nava-Hopi Tours** (tel. 800/892–8687 or 520/774–5003), in Flagstaff, runs a daily guided tour to the South Rim and East Rim that takes in the Old Cameron Trading Post, Yavapai and Mather points, and the IMAX film at Tusayan.

By Mule: Mule rides are available from both the North and South Rim. From the North Rim, one-hour, half-day, and full-day trips are offered through **Grand Canyon Trail Rides** (Box 128, Tropic, UT 84776, tel. 801/679–8665). On the South Rim, options include day treks (with lunch) and one- or two-night treks to Phantom Ranch at the bottom of the canyon; contact the **Reservations Dept.** (Box 699, Grand Canyon 86023, tel. 520/638–2401). Prices for North Rim excursions are $15–$100; the South Rim treks run a pricier $100–$350 (including lodging and meals). For either option you must be taller than 4'7", weigh less than 200 pounds, speak English, and not be pregnant. Make reservations well in advance; on short notice, North Rim trips may be a better bet.

EXPLORING

We suggest two tours to cover the main points of interest on both the South Rim and North Rim (the South Rim tour is in two parts; the first is taken on foot, the second—to the so-called West Rim—by car or bus). Unless otherwise noted, points on the tours are open daily and admission is free.

SOUTH RIM TOUR **Mather Point** offers your first look into the awesome gulf—you have an extraordinary view of the inner gorge and numerous buttes that rise out of the chasm.

The **visitor center** (tel. 520/638–7888) provides a comprehensive orientation to the Grand Canyon, information, natural-history exhibits, short movies and slide programs, and a bookstore. Park rangers are on duty to answer questions and help plan excursions.

The **Yavapai Observation Station** (tel. 520/638–7888), just over a mile northeast of the visitor center, has exhibits tracing the long geologic history of the canyon; the polarized picture windows provide excellent views into the depths of the gorge and signboards identify the features of the panorama. Buy booklets (25¢ each) here for a self-guided tour west along the rim.

The **Village Nature Trail** is a paved, level, and easy route along the canyon edge, with marvelous views. Highlights along the 2½-mile walk include **Hopi House** (tel. 520/638–2631), a multistory building that duplicates a Hopi Indian pueblo and is one of the best-stocked gift shops in the area, and **El Tovar Hotel** (tel. 520/638–2401), an imposing log-and-stone structure built in 1905 and considered one of the finest hotels in the national park system; you can browse through the rustic lobby and people-watch.

Eventually you'll reach Bright Angel Trailhead, the start of a well-maintained track that leads to the floor of the canyon. From the trailhead, you can walk directly back east past the mule barn to **Bright Angel Lodge,** another of the canyon's historic hotels. It has a dining room (full meals, light lunches) and a soda fountain and is a good spot for resting after your walk.

You can tour the **West Rim** during most of the year by car, and in summer take the free shuttle bus from the vicinity of Bright Angel Lodge. **Trailview Overlook** offers a good view of Bright Angel Trail as it loops its way down to the inner gorge. **Maricopa Point** offers a clear view of the Colorado River. The large granite **Powell Memorial** is dedicated to the early canyon explorer John Wesley Powell. **Hopi Point** looks out over the Colorado River where it is 350 feet wide, and **Mojave Point** reveals three sets of white-water rapids. At **The Abyss,** a sheer canyon wall drops 3,000 feet to the Tonto Plateau. At **Pima Point,** you'll see a clear view of the Tonto Trail, which winds more than 70 miles through the canyon. **Hermits Rest,** named for Louis Boucher, a 19th-century prospector who lived in the canyon, sells refreshments and has one of only two sets of rest rooms on the West Rim (the others are at Hopi Point).

NORTH RIM TOUR You approach the North Rim of the Grand Canyon through the Arizona Strip, the land between the canyon and the Utah border, ending with a magnificent 45-mile drive south on Route 67, along the 9,000-foot-high Kaibab Plateau. Most visitors immediately go to the historic **Grand Canyon Lodge** (tel. 801/586–7686 or 520/638–2611, fax 801/586–3157), which has a huge lounge area with hardwood floors, high, beamed ceilings, and wide windows that give a superb view of the canyon. There is also a spacious viewing deck outside.

The short trail to **Bright Angel Point** starts on the grounds of the hotel and proceeds along a crest of rock that juts out into the canyon. The ½-mile round-trip is exciting because of the sheer drop on each side of the trail. Afterward, you can lunch in the rustic stone-and-log dining room of the lodge, then browse through the nearby curio shop or take a leisurely walk down **Transept Trail,** which starts near the lodge's east patio.

To reach Point Imperial and Cape Royal, two of the North Rim's most popular viewing points, drive north from Grand Canyon Lodge, bear right at the signposted fork, and continue for 11 miles. **Point Imperial,** at 8,803 feet, the highest point on either rim, reveals not only the canyon but thousands of square miles of surrounding countryside.

Return west to a signed junction and turn left to **Cape Royal,** which is 15 miles south on the paved road. From here you can see **Angel's Window,** a giant eroded hole through the projecting ridge of Cape Royal. Near the parking area there's a wonderfully scenic spot for a picnic, with rest rooms. The nearby **Cliff Springs Trail** is an easy 1-mile walk through a heavily forested ravine to another impressive view of the canyon.

HOTELS AND INNS

Try to make summer reservations as early as possible, particularly within the park. If you can't get rooms near the canyon, you might find vacancies in Flagstaff or Williams, on the Navajo Reservation at the Cameron Trading Post (U.S. 89, tel. 520/679–2231), or in Tuba City at the Tuba Motel (U.S. 160, tel. 520/283–4545). Price categories for double occupancy, excluding 6½% tax, are Expensive, $100–$200; Moderate, $50–$100; and Inexpensive, under $50.

SOUTH RIM **Best Western Grand Canyon Squire.** The rooms at this hotel, 1 mile south of the park's entrance station, have attractive Western-style decor, and the property boasts a wide assortment of amenities. *Tusayan 86023, tel. 520/638–2681 or 800/528–1234, fax 520/638–2782. 250 units. Dining room, coffee shop, gift shop, heated pool, hot tub, sauna, air-conditioning, tennis courts, bowling alley, billiards, beauty salon. AE, D, MC, V. Expensive.*

Bright Angel Lodge. This rustic hostelry, built in 1935, sits within a few yards of the canyon rim, with rooms in the main lodge or in quaint cabins. *Box 699, Grand Canyon 86023, tel. 520/638–2401, fax 520/638–9247. 90 units. Dining room, steak house, lounge, gift shop. AE, D, DC, MC, V. Moderate–Expensive.*

El Tovar Hotel. Built in 1905 of native stone and pine logs in the style of a European hunting lodge, this is regarded as one of the finest hotels located in a national park; reservations are a must. *Box 699, Grand Canyon 86023, tel. 520/638–2401, fax 520/638–9247. 78 rooms and suites. Dining room, lounge, gift shop. AE, D, DC, MC, V. Expensive.*

Phantom Ranch. At the bottom of the Grand Canyon, accessible only to hikers or mule riders, the ranch has four 10-bed dormitories and 12 stone-and-timber cabins. Be sure to reserve ahead. *Box 699, Grand Canyon 86023, tel. 520/638–2401, fax 520/638–9247. Meals available, lounge. AE, D, DC, MC, V. Inexpensive–Moderate.*

Quality Inn. This clean, comfortable motel— with typically bland motel architecture and decor—is 1 mile south of the park's south entrance. *Tusayan 86023, tel. 800/424–6423 or 520/638–2673, fax 520/638–9537. 176 units. Restaurant, gift shop, heated pool, air-conditioning. AE, DC, MC, V. Expensive.*

NORTH RIM **Grand Canyon Lodge.** This rugged, spacious lodge, a few yards from the rim at Bright Angel Point, opened in 1937. The main building has massive limestone walls and timbered ceilings. The accommodations are in rustic cabins (four with views) and motel units scattered among the pines. *TW Services, Box 400, Cedar City, UT 84721, tel. 801/586–7686, fax 801/586–3157. 161 cabins and 40 motel units. Dining room, cafeteria, lounge, gift shop. AE, DC, MC, V. Moderate.*

Kaibab Lodge. These simple cabins 18 miles north of the canyon rim are rented in summer as hotel rooms; in winter (mid-Dec.–March) they are booked exclusively as part of two- to four-night cross-country ski packages. These packages (including meals, lodging, round-trip transportation from Jacob's Lake, ski tours, and lessons) cost $350–$560. The eight-person yurt can be pre-booked in winter only. *HC 64, Box 30, Fredonia 86022, tel. 520/638–2389 (summer), 520/526–0924 (winter), or 800/525–0924, fax 520/527–9398. 24 units and 1 yurt. Dining room, country store (summer only), gift shop, gas station, TV in lodge, no phones. D, MC, V. Moderate.*

MOTELS

These clean, no-frills lodgings on U.S. 89A, some 45 to 80 miles from the North Rim, range from Indian-style rock-and-mortar buildings to frame cabins.

INEXPENSIVE-MODERATE **Cliff Dwellers Lodge** (Marble Canyon 86036, tel. 800/433–2543 or 520/355–2228, fax 520/355–2229). 20 rooms; restaurant, general store. **Jacob Lake Inn** (Jacob Lake 86022, tel. 520/643–7232). 35 rooms; restaurant, lunch counter, general store, gift shop. **Lees Ferry Lodge** (mailing address: HC67 Box 1, Marble Canyon 86036; Lees Ferry, tel. 520/355–2231). 8 rooms,

double cabin; restaurant, gift shop, tackle shop. **Marble Canyon Lodge** (Marble Canyon 86036, tel. 520/355–2225, fax 520/355–2227). 51 rooms; restaurant, general store, coin laundry.

CAMPGROUNDS

All campgrounds here are attractively located, most of them in heavy pine forests, and they're very popular, particularly at the South Rim. If you can't get reservations, try the Kaibab National Forest, which is open to "at-large" camping.

Inside the park, camping is permitted only in designated areas, and a permit is required for camping within the canyon. Write to **Backcountry Office** (Box 129, Grand Canyon 86023, tel. 520/638–7888) as soon as possible, but not more than four months before desired reservation date.

Remember that *everything* that goes into the canyon must be packed out, even cigarette butts and used toilet paper. Gasoline and groceries are available at Grand Canyon Village, Desert View, and on the North Rim.

SOUTH RIM **Desert View Campground.** This National Park Service (NPS) campground is 25 miles from South Rim in an area generally referred to as East Rim. Still, it has a magnificent view of the canyon from the Watchtower Lookout, plus a grocery store, service station, and trading post. *Tel. 520/638–7888. 50 RV and tent sites; flush toilets. No reservations. Open May–Oct. No credit cards.*

Grand Canyon Camper Village. This privately owned campground 1 mile south of the National Park entrance on U.S. 180 is generally rated among the best in the South Rim area. *Box 490, Grand Canyon 86023, tel. 520/638–2887. 200 RV sites, 60 tent sites; flush toilets, coin-op showers, picnic tables. D, MC, V.*

Mather Campground. This popular NPS South Rim location is heavily booked in summer, so make reservations as early as possible. *Tel. 520/638–7888. 319 RV and tent sites; water, flush toilets, coin-op showers, laundry, dump station, grills, picnic tables. Reservations through Mistix, tel. 800/365–2267. MC, V.*

Trailer Village. This Fred Harvey park, near the visitor center on the South Rim, is convenient for RVs, but make reservations well in advance. *Tel. 520/638–2401, fax 520/638–9247. 80 RV sites; flush toilets, showers, laundry and grocery store nearby. MC, V.*

NORTH RIM DeMotte Campground. This attractive National Forest Service site is in an area of tall pines, 20 miles north of the North Rim. *Tel. 520/643–7395. 22 RV and tent sites; some flush toilets, barbecue grills, picnic tables. No reservations. Open May–Oct. No credit cards.*

Jacob Lake Campground. This is another Forest Service campground in the secluded pine country of the Kaibab Plateau about 45 miles north of the North Rim. *Tel. 520/643–7395. 53 RV and tent sites; some flush toilets, grills, picnic tables. Group reservations only. Open May–Oct. No credit cards.*

North Rim Campground. In a heavy grove of pines near a general store 1 mile north of Grand Canyon Lodge, this is the only designated campground inside the park at the North Rim. *82 RV and tent sites; water, flush toilets, showers and laundry, nearby dump station, grills, picnic tables. Reservations through Mistix, tel. 800/365–2267. Open May–Oct. MC, V.*

DINING

Throughout Grand Canyon country, restaurants and cafeterias cater to tourists on the move, and most places serve standard American fare, prepared quickly and offered at reasonable prices. The most serious dining is in the El Tovar Hotel, where reservations are definitely in order. Price categories per person, excluding 5% tax, service, and drinks, are Moderate, $15–$25, and Inexpensive, under $15.

SOUTH RIM Bright Angel Restaurant. This is an informal but respectable place for breakfast, lunch, or dinner in the memorable Bright Angel Lodge. Try such southwestern treats as fajitas or Indian fry-bread tacos. *At the rim in Grand Canyon Village, tel. 520/638–2401. AE, D, DC, MC, V. Moderate.*

Fred Harvey Cafeterias. These three decent, perhaps predictable, cafeterias with wide selections can be found at Maswik Lodge and Yavapai Lodge (tel. 602/638–2401) in Grand Canyon Village and at Desert View Trading Post (Rte. 64, tel. 602/638–2360). *AE, D, DC, MC, V. Inexpensive.*

Steak House. This is the place for a warm western atmosphere, right down to the checkered tablecloths. Respectable ribs, steaks, and chicken are prepared over an open juniperwood fire. *Tusayan, tel. 520/638–2780. AE, MC, V. Inexpensive.*

NORTH RIM Grand Canyon Lodge Cafeteria. Dining choices are limited on the North Rim; this is the place for burgers, pizza, and other no-frills American classics. *Grand Canyon Lodge, tel. 801/586–7686 or 520/638–2611. AE, D, DC, MC, V. Inexpensive.*

Grand Canyon Lodge Dining Room. The huge, high-ceilinged dining room serves such well-prepared entrées as grilled rainbow trout and shrimp tempura; vegetarian fare is also available. *Grand Canyon Lodge, tel. 801/586–7686 or 520/638–2611. AE, D, DC, MC, V. Moderate.*

Vermilion Cliffs Restaurant. If you make the long drive up U.S. 89 to the North Rim, you'll need at least one food stop, and this is the best along the route. It has rock walls, a rustic interior, surprisingly good American fare, and over 100 beers from around the world. *At Lees Ferry Lodge off U.S. 89A near Marble Canyon Bridge, tel. 520/355–2231. MC, V. Moderate.*

SHOPPING

At the South Rim, nearly every lodging and retail store carries Indian artifacts, Grand

Canyon souvenirs, and some casual clothing. Most of the Indian jewelry, rugs, baskets, and pottery are authentic, but several outlets deserve special mention: **Desert View Trading Post** (tel. 520/638–2360) on Route 64; **Hopi House** (tel. 520/638–2631), next door to El Tovar Hotel; and **Cameron Trading Post** (tel. 520/679–2231), 1 mile north of the junction of Route 64 and U.S. 89. **Babbitt's General Store** (tel. 520/638–2262), a good stop for all types of necessities, has branches in Grand Canyon Village, Tusayan, and Desert View.

OUTDOOR ACTIVITIES

BIKING The park has miles of scenic paved roads and dirt roads, but bicycles are not permitted on any of the walking trails. You must bring your own bike; there are no rentals available.

HIKING From leisurely walks on well-defined paths to arduous treks into the canyon and from one rim to the other, rangers can provide you with maps and information. Corridor trails, which are maintained and have toilets and emergency phones, are recommended for first-time hikers into the Grand Canyon. From the South Rim, the South Kaibab trail is the more scenic of the two.

HORSEBACK AND MULE RIDING On the South Rim, gentle horses can be rented April through November from **Apache Stables** (tel. 520/638–2891) at the Moqui Lodge in Tusayan for a variety of guided rides. There are guided mule rides from the North or South Rim (*see* Guided Tours, *above*).

RAFTING White-water raft trips through Grand Canyon can be the adventure of a lifetime. Summer reservations must be made as much as a year in advance. More than 25 companies offer multiday raft trips, among them **Canyoneers, Inc.** (tel. 800/525–0924 outside AZ or 520/526–0924), **Diamond River Adventures** (tel. 800/343–3121 or 520/645–8866), and **Expeditions, Inc.** (tel. 520/774–8176).

Smooth-water, one-day float trips—from $50–$75 per person—are run by **Fred Harvey Transportation Company** (tel. 520/638–2401), **Navi-Hopi Tours** (tel. 800/892–8687 or 520/774–5003), and **Del Webb Wilderness River Adventures** (tel. 520/645–3279).

ENTERTAINMENT

Be sure to see *Grand Canyon, Hidden Secrets* at the IMAX theater in Tusayan—it's a truly dazzling introduction to the Grand Canyon (tel. 520/638–2203). There are cocktail lounges at El Tovar (piano), Bright Angel Lodge (live entertainment), Maswik Lodge (sports bar), Moqui Lodge (live entertainment), and Grand Canyon Lodge on the North Rim.

Grand Teton National Park
Wyoming

Updated by Candy Moulton

ew Rocky Mountain vistas are more impressive than the jagged Teton Range in northwestern Wyoming. Guarding the Jackson Hole Highway (U.S. 89) like brawny, behemoth sentinels, these mountains have served as a backdrop to mountain men, cattle barons, conservationists, Hollywood cowboys, and political summit meetings. The Indians call them Teewinot—"many pinnacles." Nineteenth-century French trappers called them Les Trois Tetons—"the three breasts." The most prominent Tetons rise north of Moose Junction: 11,901-foot Nez Perce, 12,804-foot Middle Teton, 13,770-foot Grand Teton, 12,928-foot Mt. Owen, and 12,325-foot Teewinot Mountain, south to north. Beneath the Tetons stretches the 8- to 15-mile-wide by 40-mile-long valley, called Jackson Hole since the early 1800s. Through Jackson Hole, the Snake River winds in braided channels for 27 miles. Between the Snake and the Tetons lie a string of sparkling lakes: Phelps, Taggart, Jenny, Leigh, and Jackson.

Lacking the geysers, roadside wildlife, and summer traffic jams of its northern neighbor, Yellowstone National Park, Grand Teton draws a hardier sort of wilderness enthusiast: This is prime hiking, climbing, and rafting country. Still, civility abounds. You can forgo the rough outdoor life for a gentle walk around Jenny Lake, or an evening drink facing the Tetons on the Jackson Lake Lodge veranda, or a night of whooping it up in a saloon in the nearby town of Jackson.

ESSENTIAL INFORMATION

WHEN TO GO The park's July average daily maximum temperature is 81°, with an average minimum of 41°. Locals say there are three seasons: July, August, and winter. Though that's an exaggeration, snow is possible year-round. A spring of mild days and cold nights extends into June, when average highs and lows are 71° and 37°. Snow begins regularly in October, when average highs and lows are 57° and 24°. January average maximum and minimum temperatures are 25° and 2°. The park averages 49 inches of snow in January, while July and August are generally dry.

Grand Teton's crowds are smaller than Yellowstone's year-round, and they are genuinely sparse in winter, when park lodgings close. While most of Teton Park Road closes to wheeled vehicles, U.S. 89 along the park's eastern edge stays open, providing good access to cross-country ski trails and frozen Jackson Lake, which is open to snowmobiles. In April, most of Teton Park Road opens to bicyclists and foot travelers only.

BARGAINS Free ranger-led activities usually originate at Moose and Colter Bay visitor centers. They include guided walks, naturalist tours, photography workshops, and campfire programs. Some otherwise expensive lodgings offer shoulder-season (Apr.–May and mid-Oct.–late Nov.) specials.

TOURIST OFFICES Superintendent, Grand Teton National Park (Drawer 170, Moose

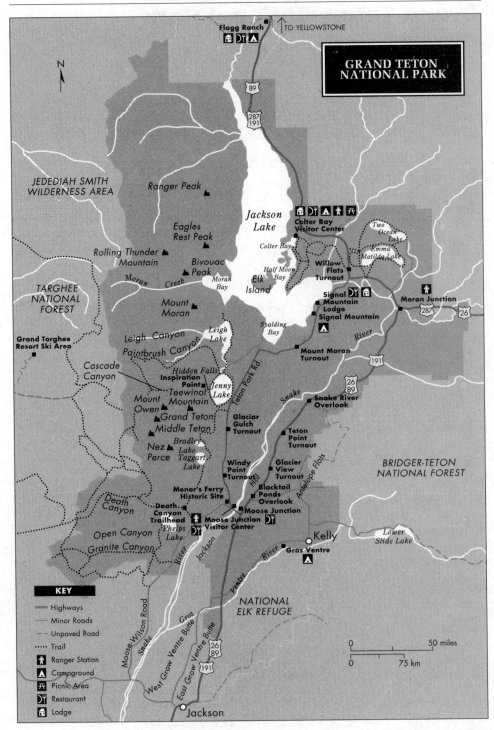

GRAND TETON
NATIONAL PARK

Flagg Ranch
↑ TO YELLOWSTONE

N

89

287
191

JEDEDIAH SMITH
WILDERNESS AREA

Ranger Peak

Jackson
Lake

Eagles
Rest Peak

Colter Bay
Visitor Center

Colter Bay

Two
Ocean
Lake

Rolling Thunder
Mountain

Bivouac
Peak

Moran
Bay

Half Moon
Bay

Emma
Matilda Lake

TARGHEE
NATIONAL
FOREST

Moran
Creek

Elk
Island

Willow
Flats
Turnout

Signal
Mountain
Lodge
Signal Mountain

Moran Junction

Mount
Moran

Spalding
Bay

287
26

Grand Targhee
Resort Ski Area

Leigh Canyon

Leigh
Lake

River

191

Paintbrush Canyon

Mount Moran
Turnout

Cascade
Canyon

Hidden Falls
Inspiration
Point
Teewinot
Mountain

Jenny
Lake

Teton Park Rd.

Snake

26
89

Snake River
Overlook

Mount
Owen

Glaciar
Gulch
Turnout

Teton
Point
Turnout

Grand Teton
Middle Teton

Nez
Perce

Bradley
Lake
Taggart
Lake

Windy
Point
Turnout

Glacier
View
Turnout

Hw

Antelope Flats

BRIDGER-TETON
NATIONAL FOREST

Death
Canyon

Menor's Ferry
Historic Site

Blacktail
Ponds
Overlook

Death
Canyon
Trailhead

Phelps
Lake

Moose Junction
Visitor Center

Moose Junction

Kelly

Lower
Slide Lake

Open Canyon

Gros Ventre

Granite Canyon

River

Jackson

River

Ventre

KEY

Highways
Minor Roads
Unpaved Road
Trail
Ranger Station
Campground
Picnic Area
Restaurant
Lodge

Moose-Wilson Road

Snake

Gros

West Grow Ventre Butte

East Grow Ventre Butte

NATIONAL
ELK REFUGE

26
89

191

0   50 miles

0   75 km

Jackson

83012, tel. 307/739–3300). **Moose Visitor Center** (same address and tel. as above). **Colter Bay Visitor Center** (same address as above, tel. 307/543–2467). Park lodging, dining, and tours: **Grand Teton Lodge Company** (Box 240, Moran 83013, tel. 307/543–2811). **Jackson Hole Chamber of Commerce** (Box E, Jackson 83001, tel. 307/733–3316). **Jackson Hole Visitors Council** (Box 982, Dept. 8, Jackson Hole 83001, tel. 800/782–0011). **Wyoming Division of Tourism** (I–25 at College Dr., Cheyenne 82002, tel. 307/777–7777 or 800/225–5996).

EMERGENCIES **Police:** Dial Park Dispatch (tel. 307/733–2880 or 307/543–2851) or Teton County Sheriff's Office (tel. 307/733–2331). **Doctors:** Grand Teton Medical Clinic (near Chevron Station, Jackson Lake Lodge, tel. 307/543–2514; June–mid-Sept.). Walk-in clinic: Emerge+A+Care (Powderhorn Mall, W. Broadway, Jackson, tel. 307/733–8002).

ARRIVING AND DEPARTING

BY PLANE **Jackson Hole Airport** (tel. 307/733–7682), 8 miles north of town off U.S. 89, receives daily flights connecting through Denver and Salt Lake City. Some lodgings provide free airport shuttle service. One-way taxi fare from the airport to Jackson is $10–$15. Taxi companies include **Buckboard Cab** (tel. 307/733–1112) and **Dollar** (tel. 307/733–0935).

BY CAR The Jackson Hole Highway (U.S. 26–89–191) is open all year from Jackson to Moran Junction, east over Togwotee Pass (U.S. 26–287) and north to Flagg Ranch, 2 miles south of Yellowstone Park's south entrance (closed in winter).

BY BUS **Greyhound Lines** (tel. 800/231–2222) has daily service to West Yellowstone and Rock Springs from Salt Lake City. There is no direct bus service to Jackson Hole.

GETTING AROUND

BY BUS **Grand Teton Lodge Company** (tel. 307/543–2811) runs buses from Jackson

Hole Airport to Jackson Lake Lodge daily. There are also shuttle buses between Jackson Lake Lodge and Colter Bay (June–mid-Sept.). Jackson's START bus line runs regularly from the Town Square to Teton Village (late May–mid-Sept., early Dec.–early Apr.).

BY CAR Starting at Moose Junction, Teton Park Road skirts the foot of the Tetons for 20 miles to Jackson Lake Junction (closed from early December through early May between Cottonwood Creek and Signal Mountain Lodge). There is a short cut from Teton Village into the park, the Moose-Wilson Road, which turns to gravel for a few miles before joining Teton Park Road at Moose Visitor Center (road closed early December through early May due to snow, and always closed to trucks, trailers, and RVs). The Jackson Hole Highway (U.S. 26–89–191) is longer than Teton Park Road but faster. Its scenic parking areas are Blacktail Ponds, Glacier View, Teton Point, and Snake River Overlook. Another series of scenic parking areas extends past Jackson Lake Junction, overlooking Jackson Lake. Scenic parking areas on Teton Park Road are Windy Point, Glacier Gulch, and Mount Moran turnouts; Moose and Colter Bay visitor centers; and Jackson Lake, Jenny Lake, and Signal Mountain lodges.

REST STOPS Both visitor centers and all three park lodges have public rest rooms. Dornan's Corner at Moose Junction and Flagg Ranch just north of the park also have rest rooms.

GUIDED TOURS **Bus and Jeep: Grayline Tours** departs Dirty Jack's Theatre (140 N. Cache St., Jackson, tel. 307/733–4325) for a daily trip to the park. The **Teton Village Tram** (tel. 307/733–2292) provides a scenic overview of Jackson Hole. **Wild West Jeep Tours** (Jackson, tel. 307/733–9036) will take you through Grand Teton backcountry June through early September. **Access Tours** (Box 2985, Jackson, WY 83001, tel. 307/733–6664 or 800/929–4811) caters to visitors with disabilities, offering multiday park tours.

Walking: Jackson Hole Museum (tel. 307/733–2414) tours historic Jackson on foot

(June–early Sept.). In the park, rangers at Moose and Colter Bay visitor centers lead guided walks both easy and strenuous—be sure to inquire.

EXPLORING

Admission to Grand Teton Park ($10 per vehicle or $4 per person on foot or bike) also buys entry into Yellowstone Park for up to one week. National Park Service Golden Age and Golden Access Passports give free entry to people over 62 and to people with disabilities. The following covers major highlights from Jackson, northward.

National Elk Refuge is home to the nation's largest elk herd. The best time to view the majestic animals is winter, when U.S. Fish and Wildlife Service sleigh rides (fee charged) take visitors close to nearly 9,000 elk. The refuge road leaving from Jackson's north end is paved for a few miles and open to visitors in summer. *USFWS, Box C, Jackson 83001, tel. 307/733–9212. Refuge Headquarters, Broadway St., 1 mi east of Jackson Town Sq. Open weekdays.*

Moose Junction Visitor Center has ranger naturalists and carries publications. Just north of the visitor center, the ½-mile Menor's Ferry Historical Trail goes past turn-of-the-century Snake River cabins and displays on Jackson Hole pioneer life. *Tel. 307/739–3300. Open daily. Admission free.*

Snake and Gros Ventre Rivers, in the park's southeast, are traverse rolling plains and river flats that attract bison, antelope, and moose. From Jackson Hole Highway, take the Antelope Flats Road at Gros Ventre toward Kelly to the paved Teton National Forest access road, which winds along the Gros Ventre River. Return to Antelope Flats Road along the Gros Ventre to rejoin Jackson Hole Highway. Halfway between Moose and Moran junctions, the Snake River Overlook surveys a sweeping bend of the Snake, with a wayside exhibit identifying Teton peaks in the background. Two miles beyond, the Cun-

ningham Cabin Trail is an easy walk to an 1890 homestead.

Jenny Lake. Take the one-way road heading south from North Jenny Lake Junction, 12 miles north of Moose. Just before you rejoin the Park Road at South Jenny Lake Junction, you'll see Jenny Lake, a favorite hiking area. The 6.6-mile Jenny Lake trail skirts the shoreline, with Teton Range views from the east shore. Cascade Canyon, the park's most popular trail, follows Jenny Lake's south shore and climbs for a gentle ½-mile to Hidden Falls. A strenuous ½ mile farther leads you to Inspiration Point and views of Jenny and Jackson lakes. The now-difficult trail continues into Cascade Canyon itself for some of the park's best Teton Range close-ups. A shuttle boat crosses Jenny Lake regularly from the marina on the east shore, eliminating 2 miles of the hike each way. *Ranger station, horseback rides (fee charged). Teton Boating Co. offers scenic cruises and lake shuttle (fees charged), tel. 307/733–2703. Open June–late Sept., daily.*

Jackson Lake. South of Jackson Lake Junction along Teton Park Road, Mt. Moran Turnout affords your first view of the northern Tetons. Just past the junction, Willow Flats Turnout completes that view: From south to north, you'll see 12,605-foot Mt. Moran, 10,825-foot Bivouac Peak, 10,908-foot Rolling Thunder Mountain, 11,258-foot Eagles Rest Peak, and 11,355-foot Ranger Peak. Also south of Jackson Lake Junction, Signal Mountain Road climbs 800 feet in 5 miles for a sweeping view of the entire 40-mile Teton Range and Jackson Hole. Visit Jackson Lake Lodge's 1920s rustic lobby, with comfortable old leather chairs and floor-to-ceiling windows overlooking the northern Tetons. From the lodge, take the Lunchtree Hill Trail, an easy ½ mile to the top of a rise overlooking Willow Flats and the northern Tetons. *Signal Mountain Lodge (tel. 307/543–2831) has a store, gas station, and marina. Open late May–mid-Sept. Jackson Lake Lodge (tel. 307/543–2811) has stores, gas station, horseback rides. Open June–mid-Sept.*

Colter Bay is the hub of park activities on Jackson Lake. One-and-a-half-hour cruises depart its marina all day: You'll see close-ups of glaciers, waterfalls, and the wild western shore of Jackson Lake (fee charged). Take the easy 3-mile circular trail from Colter Bay Visitor Center through pine forest and open meadows past Heron Pond and Swan Lake, a favorite habitat of great blue herons, moose, and beavers. Even gentler is the 1.8-mile self-guiding Colter Bay Nature Trail along the forest edge. *Visitor Center: tel. 307/739–3591. Service station, marina, tackle shop, store, boat and horseback rides. Open early May–late Sept., daily.*

THE NATURAL WORLD Over 50 types of wildflowers bloom in the park's glacial canyons in July and August—a list of these, as well as a list of the park's nearly 300 bird species, is available at Moose and Colter Bay visitor centers. Great blue herons and ospreys nest at Oxbow Bend—stop at the turnout with binoculars. White pelicans and bald eagles also fish in this prime bird habitat's shallow water. Look for hawks and falcons along Antelope Flats Road. Oxbow Bend and Willow Flats turnouts are good places for observing moose, beavers, and otters. In summer, elks and big-ear mule deer haunt forest edges along Teton Park Road at sunrise and sunset.

HOTELS AND INNS

Grand Teton National Park doesn't have Yellowstone Park's variety of inexpensive lodgings. A larger choice of lower-priced properties can be found in nearby Jackson and Teton Village ski resort (open in summer), 12 miles north of Jackson on the Moose-Wilson road (*see also* Yellowstone Park chapter). Rates at Teton Village—but not in Jackson—are often $10–$40 higher during the winter ski season. You can reserve some rooms through Jackson Hole Central Reservations (Box 510, Teton Village 83025, tel. 307/733–4005 or 800/443–6931). Price categories for double occupancy, excluding 4%

tax, are Moderate, $50–$85, and Inexpensive, under $50.

MODERATE **Best Western Inn at Jackson Hole.** Lodgepole pine beds and oak furniture lift this Teton Village inn far above the general run of chain motels. *Box 328, Teton Village 83025, tel. 307/733–2311 or 800/842–7666, fax 307/733–0844. 83 units. 2 restaurants, pool, 3 hot tubs, coin laundry, valet service, kitchens, fireplaces, room service. AE, D, DC, MC, V.*

Colter Bay Village Cabins. The log accommodations, some of them remodeled settlers' cabins, are situated on a terraced drive overlooking Jackson Lake. *Colter Bay Village, Grand Teton Lodge Co., Box 240, Moran 83013, tel. 307/543–2855, 307/543–2811 for same-day reservations, fax 307/543–2869. 209 cabins. Restaurant, coin laundry, airport shuttle. AE, DC, MC, V.*

Cowboy Village Resort. These log cabins on a quiet side street just south of downtown Jackson have porches, barbecue grills, and picnic tables. *Flat Creek Rd. off W. Broadway, Box 1747, Jackson 83001, tel. 307/733–3121 or 800/962–4988, fax 307/739–1955. 82 cabins. Kitchens. AE, D, MC, V.*

Cowboy Village Resort at Togwotee. Seventeen miles from the eastern park entrance on U.S. 26/287, this big, family-oriented resort has a log lodge and log cabins and offers horseback rides, snowmobile rentals, and other outdoor services. *Box 91, Moran 83013, tel. 307/543–2847 or 800/543–2847. 34 rooms. Restaurant, sauna, laundry room, room service, airport shuttle. AE, D, MC, V.*

Flagg Ranch Village. This sprawling year-round resort lies on the Snake River, 4 miles north of Grand Teton and 2 miles south of Yellowstone. The cabins are well equipped and ideal for families. *John D. Rockefeller Memorial Pkwy., Box 187, Moran 83013, tel. 307/543–2861 or 800/443–2311, fax 307/543–2356. 54 rooms, 6 cabins. Restaurant, grocery store, coin laundry, fireplaces. MC, V.*

Grand Targhee Resort. On the back (west) side of the Tetons, this popular ski center is also a summer resort featuring hiking trails, horseback rides, and other outdoor activities. The spacious rooms lack character, but some have fine mountain views. *12 mi east of Driggs, ID off U.S. 33. Box SKI, Alta 83422, tel. 307/353–2300 or 800/443–8146, fax 307/827–4433. 63 units. Restaurant, pool, coin laundry. AE, MC, V.*

Signal Mt. Lodge. The log cabins here have pine beds, wicker chairs, and old-fashioned lamps. Four-unit chalets have modern furnishing with kitchens. All are situated on Jackson Lake, with views of Mt. Moran from the Aspen restaurant and a back deck. *Grand Teton National Park, Box 50, Moran 83013, tel. 307/543–2831 or 307/733–5470, fax 307/543–2569. 79 cabins and rooms (some in moderate range). Restaurant, kitchens, fireplaces. AE, D, MC, V.*

Sojourner Inn. This is Teton Village's major hotel, though rooms aren't as inviting as those at the Best Western (all have mountain views, however). *Box 348, Teton Village 83025, tel. 307/733–3657 or 800/445–4655, fax 307/733–9543. 100 rooms. Restaurant, pool, sauna, valet and room service. AE, D, DC, MC, V.*

Teton Tree House. Nestled on a mountainside surrounded by huge, old pine trees, this B&B is for the health conscious, from the homemade granola, fruit juice, and whole-grain foods served at breakfast to the 95 steps you have to climb to reach the house itself. The owners provide information about hiking, maps, and the best places to see wildlife. Rooms in this modern three-story home have views of Jackson. *Box 550, 6175 Heck of a Hill Rd., Wilson, WY 82014, tel. 307/733–3233. 5 no-smoking rooms with baths. Hot tub. Reservations required. No credit cards.*

Teton View Bed & Breakfast. Between Jackson and Teton Village, this B&B has rooms with mountain views, queen-size beds, and flannel sheets; homemade pastries and breads are served. *2136 Coyote Loop, Box 652, Wilson 83014, tel. 307/733–7954. 3 rooms. Laundry room. MC, V.*

INEXPENSIVE **Camp Creek Inn.** This lodging consists of A-frames with knotty-pine interiors, 16 miles south of Jackson in Hoback Canyon. *U.S. 89, Star Rte. Box 45-B, Jackson 83001, tel. 307/733–3099 or 800/228–8460, fax 307/733–3195. 9 cabins. Restaurant, bar. MC, V.*

Colter Bay Tent Cabins. Rooms have canvas walls and sheet-metal ceilings on wood frames with bare-minimum furnishings and shared bathrooms, but the price and location are unbeatable. *Colter Bay Village, Grand Teton Lodge Co., Box 240, Moran 83013, tel. 307/543–2855, 307/543–2811 for same-day reservations, fax 307/543–2869. 72 cabins. Restaurant, airport shuttle. AE, DC, MC, V.*

The Hostel. A favorite of families and skiers, this modest, cozy Teton Village lodging, open year-round, features four twin beds (two in a bunk) per room and a lounge with a huge stone fireplace. *Box 546, Teton Village 83025, tel. 307/733–3415, fax 307/739–1142. 60 rooms. Laundry and game rooms, no room phones or TVs. MC, V.*

MOTELS

Note: all addresses are Jackson 83001.

MODERATE **Best Western Executive Inn** (325 W. Pearl St., Box 1101, tel. 307/733–4340 or 800/528–1234). 137 rooms; pool, valet and room service. **Days Inn** (1280 W. Broadway, tel. 307/739–9010 or 800/325–2525, fax 307/733–0044). 78 rooms. **Forty-Niner Motel** (330 W. Pearl St., Box 1948, tel. 307/733–7550 or 800/451–2980). 114 rooms; restaurant, valet and room service. **Parkway Inn Best Western** (Box 494, tel. 307/733–3143). 51 rooms; pool, fitness center, valet service. **Pony Express Motel** (Box 972, tel. 307/733–2658 or 800/526–2658). 41 rooms; pool. **Virginian Lodge** (750 W. Broadway, Box 1052, tel. 307/733–2792 or 800/262–4999, fax 307/733–9513). 150 rooms; restaurant, pool, kitchenettes, valet service.

INEXPENSIVE **Hoback River Resort** (U.S. 89 south of Jackson, Star Rte., Box 23, tel. 307/733–5129). 18 rooms. **Motel 6** (1370 W.

Broadway, tel. 307/733–1620). 155 rooms; pool. **Snow King Lodge Motel** (400 E. Snow King Ave., Box 1053, tel. 307/733–3480). 18 rooms; kitchenettes. **Teton Gables Motel** (Junction of Rtes. 191–189–22, Box 1038, tel. 307/733–3723). 35 rooms.

CAMPGROUNDS

The National Park Service operates five park campgrounds, each charging $10 per night on a first-come, first-served basis. No reservations are accepted; campsites fill up in July and August. Park Service campsites don't provide hookups, unlike the concessioner-operated Colter Bay RV Trailer Village and Flagg Ranch Village.

Colter Bay is busy, noisy, and fills by noon, but it's close to many activities and services. *1½ mi off U.S. 89–287, near cabins. Grand Teton National Park, Box 170, Moose 83012, tel. 307/739–3300. 310 combination sites, no hookups; showers, bathrooms, LP gas available, picnic tables, barbecue areas. No reservations or credit cards.*

Colter Bay Trailer Village, near Colter Bay Marina, is a large, often crowded RV-only park close to boat rentals, scenic cruises, horseback rides, a store, and a visitor center. *Grand Teton Lodge Co., Box 240, Moran 83013, tel. 307/733–2811. 112 RV sites, hookups; showers, bathrooms, LP gas available. Reservations advised. MC, V.*

Flagg Ranch Campground lies within a bustling tourist complex 4 miles north of Teton Park on U.S. 89–287. *Box 187, Moran 83013, tel. 307/733–8761 or 800/443–2311. 100 RV sites, 75 tent sites, hookups; showers, bathrooms, laundry, picnic tables, barbecue areas. MC, V.*

Gros Ventre is as pristine as Colter Bay is cluttered, in an isolated area frequented by moose along the Gros Ventre River; it usually doesn't fill until nightfall. *2 mi southwest of Kelly on Gros Ventre Rd., Grand Teton National Park, Box 170, Moose 83012, tel. 307/733–2880. 360 sites, no hookups;*

bathrooms, picnic tables, barbecue areas. No reservations or credit cards.

Jenny Lake is a quiet, small, lakeside campground for tents only, close to the Jenny Lake trailhead; this area is extremely popular and fills by 8 AM in July and August. *On Teton Park Rd., 8 mi north of Moose. Grand Teton National Park, Box 170, Moose 83012, tel. 307/733–2880. 49 tent sites, no hookups; bathrooms, picnic tables, barbecue areas. No reservations or credit cards.*

DINING

Several innovative area restaurants combine native game, birds, and fish (especially quail and trout) with Old World ingredients and New Age health consciousness. An alpine spaetzle-and-sausages tradition remains, but it has been enhanced over the past decade by many new poultry and pasta dishes. Wholegrain breakfasts and soups are crowding out eggs and burgers, too. Price categories per person, excluding 5% tax, service, and drinks, are Moderate, $15–$25, and Inexpensive, under $15.

MODERATE **Cadillac Grille.** As slick as it gets in Jackson, this art deco–style restaurant does nouvelle-cuisine presentations of buffalo, venison, and other native game and fish. *Cache St. on Town Sq., Jackson, tel. 307/733–3279. AE, DC, MC, V.*

Gouloff's. Across the street from the Jackson Hole Racquet Club outside town, this small, locally popular restaurant offers entrées of venison and game birds, among other specialties. *Teton Village Rd., Jackson, tel. 307/ 733–1886. AE, MC, V.*

Jackson Lake Lodge Mural Room. Wildlife and landscape paintings in this cavernous restaurant compete with striking Teton views from its grand picture windows. Large summertime crowds flock to the Mural Room for fresh beef and game, and a small selection of heart-wise entrées. *Jackson Lake Lodge, tel. 307/543–2811. AE, DC, MC, V.*

Off Broadway. Just off the main tourist prowl with a sunny deck in back, this smoke-free and health-conscious eatery has an extensive pasta and seafood selection. *30 King St., Jackson, tel. 307/733–9777. MC, V.*

Sweetwater Restaurant. This crowded local favorite serves great Greek appetizers, seafood, and vegetable dishes. Additions to this downtown, log-cabin eatery include two log-walled dining rooms and a pleasant outdoor deck. *Corner of King and Pearl Sts., Jackson, tel. 307/733–3553. AE, MC, V.*

INEXPENSIVE **Bar J Chuckwagon Suppers.** Besides an all-you-can eat meal of barbecued beef, potatoes, beans, biscuits, cake, and a drink, the Bar J offers a first-class western show most nights featuring the Bar J Wranglers. *Teton Village Rd., 1 mi from Wilson, tel. 307/733–3370. Reservations advised. AE, MC, V.*

Bubba's Bar-B-Que. Not your average beef 'n' beans joint, this local landmark features wooden booths, antique signs, and tributes to western gunmen, plus huge turkey and chicken barbecue platters. *515 W. Broadway, Jackson, tel. 307/733–2288. D, MC, V.*

The Bunnery. Whole-grain breads, pancakes, waffles, and muffins are served in a bustling nook called the Hole-in-the-Wall Mall. *130 N. Cache St., Jackson, tel. 307/ 733–5474. D, V.*

Harvest Cafe, Bakery, Natural Foods and Products. This small restaurant serves homemade Belgian waffles, cereal, and organic coffee for breakfast and has an organic salad bar, homemade breads, vegetarian soups, and chilies for lunch with most items low-fat and many dairy free as well. *130 W. Broadway, Jackson, tel. 307/733–5418. MC, V.*

Jackson Lake Lodge Pioneer Room. Nothing fancy here, just hearty soups and sandwiches served at long counters by friendly waiters and waitresses. *Jackson Lake Lodge, tel. 307/543–2811, ext. 1911. AE, DC, MC, V.*

Jedediah's House of Sourdough. Mountain-man memorabilia surround diners, who enjoy sourdough and whole-grain pancakes, waffles, and biscuits—not to mention buffalo burgers—at this laid-back, log-cabin breakfast and lunch spot. *1 block east of Town Sq., E. Broadway, Jackson, tel. 307/ 733–5671. AE, MC, V.*

SHOPPING

JACKSON Cache Creek Square, located on the corner of Cache Street and Broadway across from Town Square, includes **Teton Traditions** (western gifts, tel. 307/733–4100), the **Hole Works** (Indian and cowboy crafts, tel. 307/733–7000), and **Jack Dennis Outdoor Shop** (outdoor clothing and cowboy boots, tel. 307/733–6838). Chet's Way next door includes **Warbonnet Indian Arts** (Navajo weaving, tel. 307/733–6158). Across the Town Square's northwest corner is Gaslight Alley (corner Cache and Deloney Sts.), home to **Buckskin Mercantile** (western wear, tel. 307/733–3699), the **Shirt Smuggler** (souvenir clothing, tel. 307/733–9037), and **Valley Bookstore** (western subjects, guidebooks, tel. 307/733–4533). **Wyoming Outfitters** (corner of Center St. and Broadway, tel. 307/733–3877) is another major western-wear retailer. Jackson also has an outstanding selection of photograph and art galleries.

GRAND TETON NATIONAL PARK Jackson Lake Lodge Apparel and Gift Shops (in the lodge, tel. 307/543–2811) sells fine western wear and Indian crafts. **Signal Mountain Lodge Gift Shop and Moosle Beach Club Store** (in the lodge, tel. 307/543–2831) sell Indian crafts and outdoor clothing.

OUTDOOR ACTIVITIES

BIKING The RKO Road 4 miles north of Moose provides an easy four-hour mountain ride along the Snake River. A bike lane allows northbound bike traffic along the one-way Jenny Lake Loop Road for a one-hour ride. A four-hour, moderate ride on paved road goes from Gros Ventre Junction to Slide Lake. For bike rentals and repairs try **Teton Cyclery** (175 N. Glenwood St., Jackson, tel. 307/733–4386) or **Mountain Bike Outfitters** (at Dornan's Corners, Moose Junction, tel. 307/733–3314).

FISHING Native cutthroat, rainbow, brook, and lake trout are all caught in Teton Park waters. Unlike Yellowstone, the park requires a Wyoming fishing license (fee charged). Jenny and Leigh lakes are open all year, Jackson Lake is open January–September and November–December, and Snake River is open April–October. Only the park's northern half allows live bait.

HIKING (Note: all distances/times are round-trip, except where noted.) The park has 200 miles of hiking trails (*see* Exploring, *above,* for popular short hikes). A spur off Jenny Lake Road leads to String Lake, where the 7.4-mile, four-hour Bearpaw Lake Trail borders Leigh Lake and provides close-ups of Mt. Moran. The 11-mile, seven-hour moderate Granite Canyon Trail starts with a ride up the Teton Village Tram (fee charged) and then down through alpine meadows and sagebrush. A popular 8.8-mile, four-hour easy hike leaves Colter Bay Trailhead to follow the shore of Hermitage Point on Jackson Lake.

RAFTING The Snake River between Moran Junction and Moose is extremely popular with beginners' tour groups, drawn by its scenery and lack of white water. Float companies charge $20–$30 for 5- or 10-mile scenic trips. Try **Osprey Float Trips** (Triangle X Ranch, Moose, tel. 307/773–5500) and **Solitude Float Trips** (Moose, tel. 307/733–2871).

SKIING In Grand Teton Park, ski the gentle 6-mile Flagg Canyon Trail at Flagg Ranch Village, heading north toward Yellowstone along a cliff above the Snake River. The 3-mile Swan Lake–Heron Pond Loop near Colter Bay Visitor Center is gentler still. The 9-mile Jenny Lake Trail is mostly level. The 4-mile Taggart Lake–Beaver Creek Loop south of Jenny Lake offers easy to moderately difficult trails. **Rossignol Nordic Ski Center** (Box 290, Teton Village 83025, tel. 307/739–2629) at Teton Village rents skis and also offers 25 kilometers of trails.

Great Smoky Mountains National Park

Tennessee and North Carolina

Updated by Katherine Culkin

At the Great Smoky Mountains National Park, shared almost equally by North Carolina and Tennessee, the Southern Appalachians reach their ultimate grandeur as 16 peaks soar more than 6,000 feet. A grayish blue, smokelike haze often hovers about these magnificent peaks, given their name by the Cherokee Indians, the region's first human inhabitants. Established in 1934, the 520,000-acre park is about 60 miles long and 20 miles wide.

Mysterious and haunting, these mountains are teeming with wildlife. Because hunting is not permitted, many species have made their home in the park. You may spot deer in Cades Cove, and wild turkeys, ruffed grouse, quail, and black bears. More than 200 species of birds reside in the park at one season or another; they're especially visible during the spring and fall migrations and the summer nesting season.

Plant life in the Great Smoky Mountains National Park is among the United States' most varied. There are at least 130 native species of trees, and although much of the woodland is second growth, 110,000 acres of virgin forest remain, preserving a magnificent tract of red spruce, whose lives are measured in centuries. Wildflowers and shrubs bloom, rivers and streams are often bordered by thick stands of rhododendron, and on some "balds"—mountaintops covered only with grass or low-growing plants—there are dazzling displays of flame azalea in the spring. It is scarcely to be wondered, then, that the Great Smoky Mountains National Park is the most-visited national park.

ESSENTIAL INFORMATION

WHEN TO GO Dogwoods and hosts of wildflowers bloom from late April to mid-May. June and July bring mountain laurel, flame azalea, and rose, purple, and white rhododendrons. The primrose, sweet shrub, Indian paintbrush, Queen Anne's lace, Turk's Cap lilies, and minuscule bluets last all summer and into September. Toward late September at higher elevations, the sumac turns deep scarlet, heralding the approach of autumn. Foliage generally peaks about mid-October in the higher altitudes and lasts into early November along the intermediate and lower slopes. Numerous varieties of hardwood trees produce brilliant colors—gold, red, russet, deep scarlet, and dazzling yellow.

There is no bad or wrong time of year to visit the park. However, during July, August, and October, you may want to avoid driving the Newfound Gap Road on weekends; traffic during these peak seasons can slow to a snail's pace. Even during the summer, the weather can be crisp and cool at higher elevations. Winter temperatures can vary from moderate to bitterly cold, but the Newfound Gap Road remains open unless there's ice and snow, and the park has a certain solitary beauty—and it's uncrowded.

BARGAINS The best bargain is the park itself; admission to the Great Smoky Mountains National Park is free. Seasonal nature programs are also free and are conducted by park rangers at visitor centers and campgrounds. These programs sometimes involve

GREAT SMOKY MOUNTAINS
NATIONAL PARK

KEY

Highways

Minor Roads

Unpaved Road

Trail

Ranger Station

Campground

short walks (including sunset and twilight treks), while others are illustrated talks.

TOURIST OFFICES Superintendent, Great Smoky Mountains National Park (Gatlinburg, TN 37738, tel. 615/436–1200). **North Carolina Travel & Tourism Division** (430 N. Salisbury St., Raleigh, NC 27611, tel. 919/733–4171 or 800/847–4862 outside Raleigh). **Tennessee Department of Tourist Development** (Room T, Box 23170, Nashville, TN 37202, tel. 615/741–7994).

EMERGENCIES Police, fire, and ambulance: Dial 911 or call park headquarters at 615/436–1230.

ARRIVING AND DEPARTING

BY PLANE Tennessee's **Knoxville Airport** is approximately a one-hour drive from Gatlinburg, and the Asheville Airport in North Carolina is approximately a one-hour drive from Cherokee. Rental cars are available at both airports.

Between the Airports and the Park by Car: From Knoxville, follow U.S. 411/441 40 miles south to Gatlinburg, at the park's northern entrance. U.S. 441 (the Newfound Gap Road) runs through the park to exit outside Cherokee. From Asheville, North Carolina, take U.S. 19 west for 48 miles to the park's southern gateway town, Cherokee. From Cherokee, North Carolina, follow U.S. 441 4 miles north into the park's southern entrance. The Blue Ridge Parkway also leads westward from Asheville to its terminus just outside Cherokee.

BY BUS Greyhound Lines (tel. 800/231–2222) has service to Knoxville (100 Magnolia Ave., tel. 615/522–5144) and Asheville (2 Tunnel Rd., tel. 704/253–5353).

GETTING AROUND

BY CAR You'll need a car to tour the park. Pick up free maps and literature on the park at visitor centers near the Gatlinburg and Cherokee entrances.

REST STOPS Public rest rooms can be found at park visitor centers, campgrounds, and picnic areas.

GUIDED TOURS Bus tours—sights include Cades Cove, Newfound Gap, Clingmans Dome, and Roaring Fork—depart daily in summer from Cherokee and Gatlinburg and cost $15–$20. Contact **Acorn Vacations Step-On Guide Service** (Gatlinburg, tel. 615/436–8898 or 800/736–8898), **Mountain Tours** (Pigeon Forge, tel. 615/453–0864), and **Smoky Mountain Tours** (Gatlinburg, tel. 615/436–3471).

Backpack trips can be booked through **Back of Beyond Expeditions** (Gatlinburg, tel. 615/436–0481). Naturalist **George Ellison** (Bryson City, tel. 704/488–8782) offers guided wildflower hikes, while the **Great Smoky Mountains Institute at Tremont** (Townsend, tel. 615/448–6709) offers two- to six-day courses in backpacking, crafts, and wildlife photography.

EXPLORING

The major highway traversing the park is U.S. 441, known within the park as Newfound Gap Road. This 35-mile stretch of road connects the major gateway cities of Gatlinburg, Tennessee, and Cherokee, North Carolina, and winds past overlooks, hiking and nature trails, and several historic attractions. To get a real feel for this mountain wilderness, plan to explore Newfound Gap Road, some spur roads, and some of the park's 900 miles of hiking or horseback trails.

Our tour runs southeast, from Gatlinburg to Cherokee. As an alternate route, however, you can enter the park from Townsend, Tennessee, driving east on Route 73, which connects with Little River Road. If you choose this route, it would make sense to visit Cades Cove first, and then drive east along Little River Road to Sugarlands Visitor Center.

Sugarlands Visitor Center and **the Great Smoky Mountains National Park Headquarters** are at the park entrance, 2 miles south of Gatlinburg, Tennessee, on U.S. 441. Here you can get an introduction to the park through an audiovisual presentation and displays highlighting the wildlife, plants, and geological formations of the Smokies. From mid-April to October, rangers give campfire programs and other illustrated talks. *Tel. 615/436–1200. Open daily. Admission free.*

Cades Cove, west of the Sugarlands Visitor Center along Little River Road, is a carefully preserved historic area reflecting the heritage of pioneer settlers. For many years, families who lived here were virtually isolated from the rest of the world. You can follow an 11-mile loop road through the area, stopping at the visitor center where displays depict life here as it once was. Also along the way are hewn-log houses, small churches with their historic burial grounds, and a working gristmill. The loop road is open daily, weather permitting. *Tel. 615/448–2472. Visitor center and gristmill open mid-Apr.–Oct., daily. Admission free.*

You can also choose from about 70 miles of hiking trails at Cades Cove. Its elevation is slightly less than 2,000 feet, and if you want to head for 4,600-foot **Rich Gap,** you'll enjoy a fairly steep climb. It's especially scenic during spring wildflower season or in autumn, when the woods are aglow with color. For a more level hike, head west to **Abrams Falls,** quite dramatic if there have been recent heavy rainfalls.

The **Elkmont area,** east of Cades Cove off Little River Road, has more than 80 miles of trails. Among them are easy, relaxed walks along the Cucumber Gap and Husky Gap trails near Elkmont Campground.

Continue southeast along Newfound Gap Road, to find scenic overlooks where you can park your car and absorb the essence of these soaring forests of Canadian hemlock, red spruce, Fraser fir, yellow buckeye, and various oaks.

Along the route, too, you can explore a wealth of hiking trails, including **Alum Cave Bluffs Trail,** a 5-mile, round-trip trek (especially splendid about mid-June, when rose and purple rhododendrons usually reach peak bloom) beginning at the Alum Cave parking area and **Cove Hardwoods Self-Guided Nature Trail,** which will take you first through open areas where pioneers once farmed the land and then through virgin hardwood forest.

Newfound Gap, about midway along the Newfound Gap Road at a 5,048-foot elevation, marks the boundary dividing North Carolina and Tennessee. On a clear day, views from this majestic site on the crest of the Great Smokies are extraordinary.

The **Appalachian Trail** crosses the highway at Newfound Gap, and even if you're not a serious hiker, you'll enjoy a short walk along this famous pathway. Unfortunately, heavy usage and soil erosion have worn down the trail to solid rock in places. Serious hikers wishing to walk its entire stretch in the park can enter at Davenport Gap at the eastern end of the park or Fontana Dam at the southwestern end. It will take six to eight days to complete the trail, and there are shelters along the trail about a day's walk apart.

Clingmans Dome, the highest peak in Tennessee at 6,643 feet, can be reached by a 7-mile spur road from Newfound Gap, but keep in mind that this road is generally closed in winter. A rather steep pathway that is not too arduous leads to a mountain-top observation tower from which, good weather permitting, you'll see the mountains sweeping in every direction.

Oconaluftee Visitor Center, just inside the park's southern entrance, marks the end of your drive through the Great Smoky Mountains National Park. The adjacent Mountain Farm Museum consists of a collection of vintage structures—main house, barn, storage bins, smokehouse—suggesting the rugged, self-sufficient lifestyle of mountain people during the late 19th century. During the peak visitor season, craftsfolk demonstrate pioneer skills. Half a mile north, off Newfound Gap Road, cornmeal is produced the old-fashioned way by water-powered wheels and may be purchased at Mingus Mill. *Visitor center: tel. 704/497–9146. Open daily. Admission free. Mingus Mill: no phone. Open mid-Mar.–mid-Nov., daily. Admission free.*

HOTELS AND INNS

Accommodations range from basic, limited facilities in the Great Smoky Mountains National Park to a wide range of motor inns, lodges, and hotels in every price category in the gateway resort towns of Gatlinburg, Tennessee, and Cherokee, North Carolina.

Price categories for double occupancy, excluding tax (11¾% in Tennessee, 7½% in North Carolina), are Expensive, $76–$96; Moderate, $50–$75; and Inexpensive, under $50.

CHEROKEE **Best Western Great Smokies Inn.** This well-maintained affiliate of the international hotel group has colorful, spacious rooms and is set on gardenlike grounds landscaped with native plantings. *1 block off U.S. 441N, Box 1809, 28719, tel. 704/497–2020, fax 704/497–3903. 152 rooms. Dining room. AE, D, DC, MC, V. Moderate.*

GATLINBURG **Best Western Fabulous Chalet.** In a quiet country setting overlooking Gatlinburg, this luxurious small inn has one- and two-bedroom town houses and suites, some with fireplaces and balconies. *516 Sunset Dr., Box 11, 37738-0427, tel. 615/436–5151. 38 rooms. Continental breakfast included (in summer), heated pool. AE, D, DC, MC, V. Moderate–Expensive.*

Mid-Town Lodge. Chalet-style town houses are a favorite here: Each sports large fireplaces, loft bedrooms with king-size beds, and full bathrooms tucked under cathedral ceilings. Downstairs you'll find a well-equipped kitchen and queen-size sofa bed. Other options in this heart-of-downtown hotel include poolside rooms, luxury suites, and efficiencies. *805 Parkway, Gatlinburg 37738, tel. 615/436–5691 or 800/633–2446, fax 615/430–3602. 133 rooms, 3 with hot tubs; 8 town houses. Swimming pool. AE, MC, V. Moderate.*

Park Vista Hotel. This lavish, circular tower hotel lacks the charm you'll find in some of the region's family-run Colonial inns, but there are striking mountain views from the rooms' private balconies. *¾ mi east off U.S. 441 via Airport Rd., Box 30, 37738, tel. 615/436–9211 or 800/421–7275; in TN, 800/526–1235; fax 615/436–5141. 312 rooms. Dining room, lounge, heated indoor pool, wading pool, whirlpool. AE, D, DC, MC, V. Expensive.*

NEAR THE PARK **Fontana Village Resort.** Originally built in the 1940s to house construction workers from nearby Fontana Dam, this clustered community of cabins, cottages, and hotel rooms is far in the wild, untrammeled western reaches of the park. Rooms in the Fontana Inn are typical motel offerings; opt instead for one of the two-bedroom cottages, equipped with fireplaces and kitchens. *Fontana Dam, NC 28733, tel. 704/498–2211 or 800/849–2258, fax 704/498–2209. 80 rooms, 100 cottages. Restaurant, tennis courts, horses, boating, fishing. AE, D, MC, V. Inexpensive–Moderate.*

Wonderland Hotel. Those who loved the old Wonderland Hotel, which until 1992 was located inside the park at Elkmont, will not be disappointed by its replacement: This sprawling lodge with its rough-sawn, knotty-pine exterior adroitly re-creates the rustic appeal of the time-worn original. Rooms are furnished with reproduction antiques that seem out of place in these sylvan surroundings, but the Wonderland's location and remote setting are hard to beat. *3889 Wonderland Way, Sevierville 37862, tel. 615/436–5490 or 615/428–0779, fax 615/429–4752. 29 rooms. Restaurant, horses. No TV or phone in rooms. MC, V. Closed Jan.–mid-Mar. Moderate.*

MOTELS

MODERATE **Comfort Inn** (Box 132, Cherokee, NC 28719, tel. 704/497–2411, fax 704/497–6555). 80 rooms; pool, Continental breakfast. **Comfort Inn South** (309 Oakley Dr., Gatlinburg, TN 37738, tel. 615/436–7813, fax 615/430–3744). 93 rooms; heated pool, whirlpool. **Days Inn** (Box 1865, Cherokee, NC 28719, tel. 704/497–9171, fax 704/497–3424). 58 rooms; 2 pools, wading pool, playground, fishing. **Gazebo Inn** (417 Airport Rd., Box 435, Gatlinburg, TN 37738, tel. 615/436–2222). 60 rooms; heated pool, whirlpool. **Gillette Motel** (235 Airport Rd., Box 231, Gatlinburg, TN 37738, tel. 615/436–5601 or 800/437–0815). 80 rooms; heated pool. **Holiday Inn** (Box 1929, Cherokee, NC 28719, tel. 704/497–9181, fax 704/497–5973). 154 rooms; dining room, indoor and outdoor pools, whirlpool, sauna, game room, playground. **Homestead House** (Box 367, Gatlinburg, TN 37738, tel. 615/436–6166 or 800/233–4663). 86 rooms; Continental breakfast in lobby included, conference room, tennis, heated pool. **Howard Johnson's Motor Lodge** (559 Parkway, Box 408, Gatlinburg, TN 37738, tel. 615/436–5621, fax 615/430–4471). 252 rooms; heated pool, wading pool, coin laundry. **Lloyd's on the River** (Box 429, Bryson City, NC 28713, tel. 704/488–3767). 21 rooms; pool. **River Terrace Creekside** (125 Le Conte Creek Dr., Gatlinburg, TN 37738, tel. 615/436–4865 or 800/473–8319, fax 615/436–0214). 67 rooms; heated pool, fishing. **Rocky Waters Motor Inn** (333 Parkway, Box 230, Gatlinburg, TN 37738, tel. 615/436–

7861 or 800/824–1111, ext. C, fax 615/430–4471). 105 rooms; 2 heated pools, 2 wading pools, whirlpool, coin laundry, fishing.

INEXPENSIVE Craig's Motel (Box 1047, Cherokee, NC 28719, tel. 704/497–3821). 30 rooms; pool, wading pool, playground, fishing. **Creekstone Motel** (104 Oglewood La., Gatlinburg, TN 37738, tel. 615/436–4628). 25 rooms; heated pool, wading pool, pets accepted. **Pageant Hills Motel** (Box 172, Cherokee, NC 28719, tel. 704/497–5371). 42 rooms. **Rainbow Motel** (Box 1397, Gatlinburg, TN 37738, tel. 615/936–5887). 41 rooms; outdoor pools. **Spruce Flats Motel** (Box 94, Gatlinburg, TN 37738, tel. 615/436–4387). 31 rooms; heated pool, wading pool.

CAMPGROUNDS

The three largest and most popular developed campgrounds in Great Smoky Mountains National Park are Cades Cove and Elkmont on the Tennessee side, and Smokemont in North Carolina. From mid-May through the end of October, reservations for these sites can be made up to eight weeks in advance by calling 800/365–2267; dial the park's code, which is GREA. The seven other campsites in the park are filled on a first-come, first-served basis.

Cades Cove Campground. Cades Cove provides an excellent base for varied day hikes. Its ranger station can issue permits for backcountry camping; there are 17 backcountry campsites in the area. *10 mi southwest of Townsend, TN, via TN 73 and Laurel Creek Rd. (Gatlinburg, TN 37738, tel. 615/436–5615). 160 RV and tent sites, no hookups ($11); dump station, picnic tables, grocery store, fishing, seasonal nature programs, rental horses and bicycles, fireplaces, flush toilets, cold running water. Stay limited to 7 days May–Oct.*

Elkmont. The park's largest campground, Elkmont is nestled in a scenic wooded swatch along the Little River. Backcountry camping permits are available, and there are 13 backcountry campsites. *8 mi west of Gatlinburg, TN, via Newfound Gap Rd., Little River Rd., Elkmont Rd. (Gatlinburg, TN 37738, tel. 615/436–5615). 220 RV and tent sites, no hookups ($11); dump station, picnic tables, fishing, seasonal nature programs, fireplaces, flush toilets, cold running water. Stay limited to 7 days May–Oct.*

Smokemont. Just inside the park's North Carolina entrance, this heavily used campground along the Oconaluftee River is convenient to eastern segments of the park, which have numerous hiking and horseback trails. *6 mi north of Cherokee, NC, via Newfound Gap Rd. (Gatlinburg, TN 37738, tel. 615/436–5615). 152 RV and tent sites, no hookups ($11); dump station, picnic tables, fishing, seasonal nature program, rental horses, fireplaces, flush toilets, cold running water. Stay limited to 7 days May–Oct.*

DINING

Except for the dining room of the Wonderland Hotel, there are no restaurants or food stands in Great Smoky Mountains National Park. Gatlinburg, Tennessee, however, has a wide variety of dining establishments in every price category, and Cherokee, North Carolina, has a selection as well. Freshly caught mountain trout and country ham with red-eye gravy and grits are featured on many mountain menus, and in Tennessee, sourwood honey is often served with breakfast, and you can buy jars to take home. Price categories per person, excluding tax (7¾% in Tennessee, 4½% in North Carolina), service, and drinks, are Moderate, $10–$20, and Inexpensive, under $10.

CHEROKEE Chestnut Tree. A favorite with family vacationers, this large and airy dining room features steak, prime rib, and freshly caught mountain trout. *Holiday Inn, U.S. 19, tel. 704/497–9181. AE, D, DC, MC, V. Inexpensive–Moderate.*

GATLINBURG Apple Tree Restaurant. The East Tennessee fare here includes fried chicken, spoon bread, and a cornmeal soufflé, all served in individual portions or family style. *420 Parkway, tel. 615/453–4961. AE, MC, V. Closed Dec.–Feb. Inexpensive– Moderate.*

Burning Bush Restaurant. Antique-style furnishings evoke a Colonial atmosphere, and the menu features such dishes as broiled Tennessee quail. *1151 Parkway, tel. 615/ 436–4669. AE, DC, MC, V. Moderate.*

Ogle's Buffet Restaurant. Buffet tables groan with five choices of country-style meats such as country ham, along with farm-fresh vegetables and 70 varieties of salad fixings. You can dine in the soft green-and-beige dining room or on the patio above a turbulent mountain stream. *539 Parkway, tel. 615/ 436–4157. MC, V. Inexpensive.*

Open Hearth. There's candlelight dining at the foot of the Smokies in this perennially popular restaurant, where specialties include aged charcoal beef and rainbow trout. *1138 Parkway, tel. 615/436–5648. AE, DC, MC, V. Moderate.*

Pancake Pantry. Century-old brick, polished oak paneling, and copper accessories create a rustic ambience for enjoying such house delicacies as Austrian apple walnut pancakes. *628 Parkway, tel. 615/436–4724. No credit cards. Inexpensive.*

Smoky Mountain Trout House. This cozy restaurant serves trout prepared 12 different ways. *410 Parkway, tel. 615/436–5416. AE, DC, MC, V. Inexpensive–Moderate.*

OUTDOOR ACTIVITIES

BIKING The flat floor of Cades Cove is excellent for bicycling, and you can rent bikes at the Cades Cove general store (across from Cades Cove Ranger Station). From early May to mid-September, the 11-mile Cades Cove Auto Loop is closed to automobile traffic until 10 AM on Saturdays. Mountain bike rentals and route maps are available at **NOC Bryson City Store** (Everett St., Bryson City, tel. 704/488–2446).

FISHING You can fish year-round in the park's 600 miles of open waters. Smallmouth and rock bass and brown and rainbow trout are frequent catches, but possession of brook trout is prohibited. Anglers must purchase North Carolina or Tennessee licenses and no live bait is allowed.

HIKING The park has about 800 miles of hiking, nature, and horseback trails, including 70 miles of the Appalachian Trail. You can choose from full-day hikes, rugged backcountry treks, or easy nature trails. Pick up trail guides at the park's visitor centers, where you can also obtain backcountry camping permits.

HORSEBACK RIDING During the peak spring through autumn vacation season, you can rent horses in the park from **Cades Cove Riding Stables** (Walland, tel. 615/448–6286), **McCarter's Stables** (Gatlinburg, tel. 615/436–5345), **Smoky Mountain Stables** (Gatlinburg, tel. 615/436–5634), **Smokemont Stables** (Cherokee, tel. 704/497–2373), and **Wonderland Stables** (Sevierville, tel. 615/436–5490).

SKIING **Ober Gatlinburg Ski Resort,** outside the park but reachable from downtown Gatlinburg by car or aerial tramway, offers winter visitors the opportunity to ski eight slopes and trails, ranging from novice to expert. *1001 Parkway, Gatlinburg, TN 37738, tel. 615/436–5423 or 800/251–9202; in TN, 800/843–6237.*

Hot Springs and the Ozarks

Arkansas

Updated by Helen James

idway between the Appalachians and the Great Plains lie the velvety hills of Arkansas, a land of simple pleasures where crooked highways wind their way through peaceful mountain towns. One such settlement is Hot Springs, which grew up almost a century ago around a series of geothermal springs whose waters were said to be medicinal. Casino gambling flourished during the town's heyday in the 1910s and '20s, drawing the likes of Al Capone, Andrew Carnegie, Jack Dempsey, and Babe Ruth. Although there is no more gambling (except at the Oaklawn Park Thoroughbred racecourse), bathers still come by the thousands each year to the spas around Hot Springs National Park, at 4,900 acres the country's smallest national park.

Besides the thermal waters, other nearby attractions include Lake Hamilton, 15 minutes from downtown Hot Springs, and the Ouachita National Forest, the largest in the South. The unique lifestyle of the Ozark Mountains is well preserved today at the Ozark Folk Center near Mountain View. Musicians saw their fiddles, cloggers dance, and craftsmen show their skills and sell their wares.

In the Victorian and hilly burg of Eureka Springs, the bed-and-breakfast capital of the region, you'll find scores of gingerbread houses tucked away on shady back streets and an unrivaled concentration of artists, whose galleries and shops line serpentine Spring Street.

ESSENTIAL INFORMATION

WHEN TO GO Temperatures average in the 40s in winter and around 80° at the height of summer. The fall foliage attracts droves of visitors, which drives up rates, especially in Eureka Springs. The busiest time in Hot Springs is racing season (late Jan.–Apr.), when hotel rates jump noticeably.

TOURIST OFFICES **Arkansas Department of Tourism** (1 Capitol Mall, Little Rock 72201, tel. 800/628–8725). **Hot Springs Visitors Center** (369 Central Ave., Hot Springs National Park 71901, tel. 501/623–1433), or write to **Hot Springs Convention & Visitors Bureau** (134 Convention Blvd., Hot Springs National Park 71901, tel. 800/772–2489). The **Eureka Springs Chamber of Commerce** (visitor information center, near junction of U.S. 62 and Main St., Box 551, Eureka Springs 72632, tel. 800/638–7352).

EMERGENCIES **Police, fire brigade,** or an **ambulance:** Dial 911. **Hospitals:** St. Joseph's Regional Health Center (300 Werner Dr., Hot Springs, tel. 501/622–1000); Eureka Springs Hospital (24 Norris St., Eureka, tel. 501/253–7400).

ARRIVING AND DEPARTING

BY PLANE Most air traffic in and out of Arkansas is through **Little Rock Regional Airport-Adams Field,** served by American (tel. 800/433–7300), Delta (tel. 800/221–1212), Northwest (tel. 800/225–2525), South-

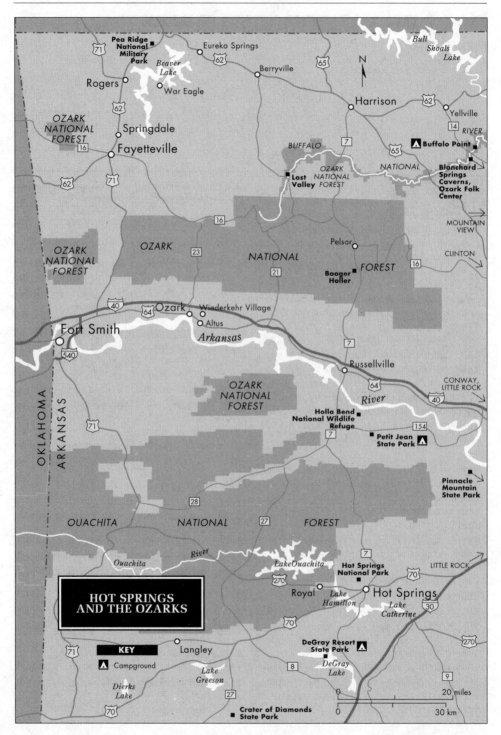

HOT SPRINGS
AND THE OZARKS

KEY

△ Campground

west (tel. 800/531–5601), TWA (tel. 800/892–2746), and USAir (tel. 800/428–4322). **Airport Shuttle** (tel. 800/643–1505) provides daily shuttle service between the airport and Hot Springs for around $20 per person.

BY CAR Two major interstate highways cross Arkansas. I–40 runs east and west; I–30 runs diagonally northeast to southwest. From the north, U.S. 65 is the fastest way into the state and is a scenic drive; U.S. 71 and U.S. 65 load in from Louisiana.

BY TRAIN AND BUS Amtrak (tel. 800/872–7245) has frequent service to Little Rock via Dallas and St. Louis. **Greyhound Lines** (tel. 800/231–2222), which serves North Little Rock from major U.S. cities, has two buses daily between Little Rock and Hot Springs.

GETTING AROUND

BY CAR A car is essential for visiting Hot Springs and the Ozarks, although Bathhouse Row in Hot Springs and Eureka Springs's central district can be explored on foot.

BY BUS AND TROLLEY Motorized trolleys travel the streets of Hot Springs. A good way to travel around Eureka Springs, especially on crowded weekends, is via the open-air buses that stop at every motel.

REST STOPS Tourist information centers with rest rooms are conveniently situated on most highways entering the state. Public rest stops are uncommon, but proprietors of roadside shops and cafés usually don't mind if travelers ask to use their facilities.

GUIDED TOURS One of the best ways to see Hot Springs is with the **White & Yellow Ducks Land & Lakes Tours** (tel. 501/623–1111), in World War II amphibious vehicles that ply local waterways and streets on 1½-hour trips. National Park rangers conduct guided thermal tours daily, starting at the Fordyce Bathhouse Visitors Center on Bathhouse Row.

EXPLORING

Outdoors people and those who like to drive could spend weeks exploring the Ozark and Ouachita Mountains around Hot Springs. Camping, hiking, and fishing opportunities abound, and the mountain vistas are one step beyond impressive. For walkers, diners, and music lovers, Hot Springs makes a good base; arts lovers will be smitten by Eureka Springs; and the Ozark Folk Center at Mountain View offers everyone an easy overview of mountain culture. Our suggested itinerary starts in Hot Springs, then travels north on scenic Route 7 (with a few side trips) to Eureka Springs, 196 miles north, and finally east along the Buffalo River to Mountain View.

Hot Springs. The central Hot Springs attraction is Bathhouse Row, within the National Park, so named for the old spas lined up along Central Avenue, two of which are open to the public. The 70-year-old **Fordyce Bathhouse Visitor Center** (tel. 501/623–1433) provides an interesting look back at local history along the row. For a quick steam, soak, or massage, make a beeline for the **Buckstaff Bathhouse** (tel. 501/623–308) which is open weekdays and a half day on Saturday.

Above the bathhouses and the historic district is the Grand Promenade, a ¼-mile walk along a shady hillside. Several trails branch off from there to climb Hot Springs Mountain, for example, the Peak Trail, which takes an hour or more coming and going. An alternative is motoring up to an overlook, but for an even better view, take the elevator 216 feet up **Hot Springs Mountain Tower** (admission charged) at the summit.

Crater of Diamonds State Park, about an hour southwest of Hot Springs, is the only diamond mine in the world open to the public. Visitors roam 40 acres that are frequently plowed to turn up fresh stones; old buildings from mining days are still on the grounds. *Off Rte. 301, Murfreesboro, tel. 501/285–3113. Open daily. Admission charged.*

Scenic Highway 7, famous for its vistas, leads north from Hot Springs toward Eureka Springs, crossing the Arkansas River at Russellville and climbing into the Ozarks. A few miles south of Russellville, turn east on Route 154 to visit **Petit Jean Mountain.** Begin at the park's visitor center or at Mather Lodge, built of stone and logs in the 1930s (*see* Hotels and Inns, *below*). A free brochure directs you on a driving tour to 16 highlights. A 3½-mile hike on Seven Hollows Trail takes you through wooded glades and an eerie place called Turtle Rocks. A good Boy Scout trail approaches 90-foot Cedar Falls along the bluffs, and Cedar Falls Trail starts at Mather Lodge and wanders all the way up the canyon (2.2 miles, 2 hours). In Rock House Cave, an ancient bluffside shelter, Indian pictographs can be discerned. *Off Rte. 154 south of Russellville, tel. 501/727–5441. Admission free.*

Booger Holler, on Route 7, 20 miles north of Russellville, is a big store where you can get crafts and Arkansas-smoked hams. Another repository of local culture is **Hankins General Store** in the tiny burg of Pelsor, where hound dogs sleep on porches and old geezers in overalls doze in rocking chairs. For a hiking diversion, take Route 16 east 6 miles to **Pedestal Rocks.** The hike, which takes about an hour, goes down a gradually sloping path through a thick forest, emerging at the edge of tablelike formations that hang above the valley below. The view and the solitude make it a classic picnic spot.

Eureka Springs. Back on Route 7, continue north to Harrison, then take U.S. 65 west to U.S. 62 to Eureka Springs. Once an enclave of 1960s counterculture, today the town draws visitors for its notable Victorian charms and its vibrant arts community. A free map and guide, distributed at all Eureka Springs galleries, highlights Spring Street, a crooked lane with a striking Old World look and feel, and its neighborhood, with scores of shops selling everything from books to regional pottery and quilts. There are plenty of restaurants in the area and four convenient historic hotels. You can spend a day walking around

the Spring Street historic district and then by car follow the signs of the "Historic Route" to see some pretty Victorian neighborhoods and an interesting church.

Pea Ridge National Military Park is one of the most quietly beautiful and stirring places in the Ozarks. The site of the Civil War battle that saved Missouri for the Union in 1862, it's worth a half-day side trip from Eureka Springs. Steeped in violent history, today it is a windswept expanse of prairies and woodland. A well-crafted car tour leads visitors from site to site, through waving green seas of tall grass, past old cannons and split-rail fences. There's a visitor center, picnic tables, a beautiful overlook, the Elkhorn Tavern, and several trails. *Off Rte. 62, tel. 501/451–8122. Open daily. Admission charged.*

The **Buffalo National River,** best known for canoeing, flows through a bluff-lined valley in a National Reservation extending west from Route 7 about 70 miles east toward Mountain View; you can rent canoes in Jasper. The area south of Yellville is one place to spend half a day, and Buffalo Point, a campground and picnic spot off Route 14, is a good place to start. There are trails for hikes of varying difficulty, cabins, and a ranger station. Take Route 14 farther south to **Rush,** an old ghost town (the turnoff is marked). The surrounding Buffalo Mining District, 1,300 acres on the National Register of Historic Places, has a network of trails that meander past old homesteads and mine shafts (the ranger station has maps).

Mountain View, nearly 60 miles east of Route 7, in the heart of the Ozarks, has managed to retain much of the musical charm of the hills; local musicians gather to play daily at about noon on the town square. At the Ozark Folk Center State Park at the edge of town, where craftsmen toil at such traditional tasks as blacksmithing, mandolin construction, and candle making, you can catch an evening concert and even stay overnight (*see* Hotels and Inns, *below*). *Tel. 501/269–3871. Open late Mar.–early Nov. Admission charged.*

In nearby **Blanchard Springs Caverns,** take an elevator 476 feet deep into the limestone heart of a mountain, where two magnificent subterranean trails wind their way through a series of dank chambers. Both trails follow a paved sidewalk most of the way and are not especially difficult; the shorter trail, Dripstone, is handicapped accessible. Farther into the park is one of the prettiest camping and picnicking sites in the state, a pair of frigid but popular swimming holes. *Blanchard Spring Caverns: 9 mi north of Mountain View via Rtes. 9 and 14, tel. 501/757–2211. Open daily Apr.–Oct.; closed Mon., Tues., and holidays Nov.–Mar. Admission charged.*

THE NATURAL WORLD Arkansas's nickname—the Natural State—is an apt one. Holla Bend National Wildlife Refuge on the Arkansas River near Russellville is a stop for migratory waterfowl and the winter home of bald eagles (binoculars are helpful). At Petit Jean State Park, birders can watch for 130 species. At Pinnacle Mountain State Park on Route 10 near Maumelle, rangers lead spring wildflower forays and autumn-foliage walks. Dogwood decorates the mountainsides from late March into mid-April; a little-known but beautiful dogwood drive is Route 16 between Pelsor and tiny Witts Spring.

HOTELS AND INNS

Arkansas has reasonably priced lodging for every taste. Rooms are most in demand in October; rates drop dramatically November–March. Price categories for double occupancy, excluding 9% tax, are Expensive, over $85; Moderate, $50–$85; and Inexpensive, under $50.

EUREKA SPRINGS **Grand Central Hotel.** The Grand Central was built in 1883, making it the oldest hotel in Eureka Springs. This Victorian masterpiece was completely renovated, and now every suite is decorated with Victoriana and antiques. *37 N. Main St., tel. 501/253–6756, fax 501/253–6050. 14 suites. AE, D, MC, V. Expensive.*

Heart of the Hills Inn. A night in this 1883 house in the historic district is a night among antiques; one room also has a hot

tub. You can take the trolley from downtown and be dropped off within spittin' distance. *5 Summit St., Eureka Springs 72632, tel. 501/253–7468. 4 rooms. Full breakfast included, off-street parking. AE, D, MC, V. Moderate.*

Palace Hotel and Bath House. A former brothel and spa within a short walk of the shopping district, this hotel has rooms that border on the luxurious and a basement spa with whirlpools and massage. *135 Spring St., Eureka Springs 72632, tel. 501/253–7474. 8 suites. Off-street parking. AE, D, MC, V. Moderate.*

HOT SPRINGS **De Gray Lakeview Cottages.** These rustic but adequate cabins are close to Hot Springs and next to a public golf course and lake. *Rte. 3, Box 450, Bismark 71929, tel. 501/865–3389. 6 cottages. No credit cards. Inexpensive.*

Spillway Resort and Marina. About 15 minutes from town, these secluded cabins with wide porches are in a tranquil lakeside compound. *Rte. 227, Box 321, Mountain Pine 71956, tel. 800/525–2516. 7 cabins. D, MC, V. Moderate.*

Vintage Comfort Bed & Breakfast Inn. The restored Queen Anne house is within walking distance of Bathhouse Row and downtown. *303 Quapaw Ave., Hot Springs National Park 71901, tel. and fax 501/623–3258. 4 rooms. Full breakfast. MC, V. Moderate.*

Wildwood 1884. This grand Victorian mansion—built in 1884 and listed on the National Register of Historic Places—is home to one of Hot Springs's nicest bed-and-breakfast inns. Antiques and period decor mesh nicely with modern, squeaky-clean facilities. *808 Park Ave., tel. 501/624–4267. 8 rooms. Full breakfast included. AE, D, MC, V. Moderate.*

Williams House Bed and Breakfast Inn. This 100-year-old Victorian brick and brownstone near Bathhouse Row shopping is well furnished and is run by a friendly hostess. *420 Quapaw Ave., Hot Springs National Park 71901, tel. 501/624–4275. 5 rooms. MC, V. Inexpensive–Moderate.*

MOUNTAIN VIEW **Commercial Hotel.** This old, comfortable inn with a bakery right on the town's musical square attracts fiddlers and banjo players to its porch daily. *Corner of Peabody and Washington Sts., Box 72, Mountain View 72560, tel. 501/269–4383. 8 rooms. AE, D, MC, V. Inexpensive.*

Ozark Folk Center. This center of culture and entertainment, roughly 2 miles outside Mountain View, has a large, quaint lodge with a rough-hewn quality about it. *Box 500, Mountain View 72560, tel. 800/264–3655. 60 rooms with bath. Restaurant. AE, D, MC, V. Inexpensive.*

PETIT JEAN **Mather Lodge.** This simple but cozy lodge atop Petit Jean Mountain, for years an attractive retreat, has wonderful views and 31 modern cabins. *Rte. 3, Box 340, Morrilton 72110, tel. 501/727–5431. 24 rooms. Restaurant. AE, MC, V. Inexpensive.*

MOTELS

MODERATE **Avanelle Motor Lodge** (1204 Central Ave., Hot Springs 71901, tel. and fax 501/321–1332). 88 rooms; restaurant, pool. **Best Western Eureka Inn** (1 Van Buren St., Eureka Springs 72632, tel. 501/253–9551). 85 rooms; restaurant, pool, racquetball, game room. **Inn of the Ozarks** (Hwy. 62W, Eureka Springs 72632, tel. and fax 501/253–9768). 122 rooms; pool, tennis court. **Ramada Inn** (218 Park Ave., Hot Springs 71901, tel. 501/623–3311, fax 501/623–8871). 191 rooms; restaurant, live entertainment, pool, exercise room.

INEXPENSIVE **Downtowner Motor Inn & Spa** (135 Central Ave., Hot Springs 71901, tel. 501/624–5521, fax 501/624–4635). 150 rooms; restaurant, bathhouse, pool. **Ozarka Lodge** (Hwy. 23S and Hwy. 62E, Eureka Springs 72632, tel. 800/321–8992, fax 501/253–8883). 45 rooms; pool. **Swiss Village Inn** (Rte. 1 at Hwy. 62E, Eureka Springs 72632, tel. 800/447–6525, fax 501/253–9541). 55 rooms; pool. **Traveler's Inn** (Rte. 1, Hwy. 62E, Eureka Springs 72632, tel. 800/643–5566). 60 rooms; pool.

CAMPGROUNDS

The U.S. Forest Service campground in the park next to **Blanchard Springs Caverns** is one of the best. Hot showers are within a short walk of most campsites, and deer in the narrow valley are a common sight around twilight. *Tel. 501/757–2213 or 800/283–2267. 32 tent sites, no RV hookups; showers, bathrooms, dump station, picnic tables, barbecue areas. Phone reservations only, 10 days in advance.*

Fourteen first-come, first-served campgrounds surround the **Buffalo National River,** all free and relatively primitive except sites at Tyler Bend and those with electrical hookups at Buffalo Point. *Box 1173, Harrison 72601, tel. 501/741–5443.*

At **Petit Jean State Park** at Morrilton, the campsites are divided into four areas, each with its own bathhouse. The park has "rent-a-camp" kits for the unequipped (available April–October). *Tel. 501/727–5441. 127 campsites, water and electric hookups; showers, bathrooms, dump station, picnic tables, barbecue areas. Reservations by phone.*

DeGray Resort State Park, 20 miles south of Hot Springs on Route 7 on a 14,000-acre lake, has a 96-room lodge, a marina with boat rentals, a public golf course, swimming, waterskiing, and hiking. *Rte. 3, Box 490, Bismarck 71929, tel. 501/865–2851. 113 tent and RV sites, hookups; showers, bathrooms, dump station, picnic tables, barbecue areas. Phone reservations.*

Hot Springs National Park's single campground, in scenic Gulpha Gorge, is 2 miles from downtown. *Off Rte. 70B, tel. 501/624–3383. 45 tent and RV campsites, no hookups; water, toilets, dump station, picnic tables, barbecue areas. No reservations.*

DINING

Although traditional pork barbecue is widespread, most barbecue restaurants now serve chicken as well. Cajun and Creole food can be found, and country cooking—chicken or beef served with vegetables, gravy and corn bread, often with fruit cobbler for dessert—is common. Price categories per person, excluding 5% tax, service, and drinks, are Moderate, $15–$25, and Inexpensive, under $15.

EUREKA SPRINGS **Bubba's.** Smoky barbecue is the specialty at this hole-in-the-wall, though zesty pork and lean chicken sandwiches are also served. *60 Kings Hwy., tel. 501/253–7706. No credit cards. Closed Sun. Inexpensive.*

Cafe Armagost. At this roadside restaurant-in-a-house, the tables are close together but the service is fast and the menu is full of good soups and salads, wonderful chicken dishes, and tasty seafood. *52 Kings Hwy., tel. 501/253–8075. AE, D, MC, V. No lunch. Moderate.*

Devito's Restaurant. Fresh fish and homemade pastas compliment a modest selection of imported wines at this excellent Italian café near shops and galleries. *5 Center St., tel. 501/253–6807. AE, D, MC, V. Closed Wed. Moderate.*

Victorian Sampler. Duck out of the historic district's shopping traffic, and grab a quiet table at this charming Victorian home; the homespun house specialties run the gamut from chicken and veggies to pork ribs and corn bread. *33 Prospect Dr., tel. 501/253–8374. D, MC, V. Moderate.*

HOT SPRINGS **Arlington Hotel.** The Continental menu is good, but the restaurant is best known for its hearty and healthy Sunday brunch. *Corner of Central and Fountain Sts., tel. 501/623–7771. AE, DC, MC, V. Inexpensive–Moderate.*

Cafe New Orleans. This restaurant across from the old Arlington Hotel is run by a group of friends from New Orleans who truly know their Creole and Cajun cooking. *210 Central Ave., tel. 501/624–3200. AE, D, MC, V. Inexpensive.*

La Hacienda. A Mexican-American family serves authentic Mexican food (with the spices toned down for an American clien-

tele) that's an especially good bargain at lunchtime. *4716 Central Ave., tel. 501/525–8203. AE, D, MC, V. Inexpensive.*

Magee's Café. This former auction house across from Bathhouse Row is a good place to unwind with a pastry and a cup of coffee. It's the sort of place where poets and folk musicians like to mingle. *362 Central Ave., tel. 501/623–4091. AE, MC, V. Inexpensive.*

McLard's. There are many barbecue joints in Hot Springs, but local aficionados claim McLard's is the best. Long lines and somewhat surly service seem to be inevitable parts of the McLard experience. *505 Albert Pike, tel. 501/624–9586. No credit cards. Closed Sun., Mon. Inexpensive.*

Mrs. Miller's. A Hot Springs institution, Mrs. Miller serves up some of the state's finest home-cooked cuisine, everything from fried quail to chicken potpie. This is the perfect stop if you're headed to Lake Hamilton. *4723 Central Ave., tel. 501/525–8861. D, MC, V. Closed Mon. No lunch. Inexpensive–Moderate.*

SHOPPING

Factory Outlet Hot Springs Stores, on Route 7, 3 miles south of the Hot Springs racetrack, is a popular discount store. On Spring Street in Eureka Springs, good deals and good quality can be found on pottery, quilts, soaps, candles, and scrimshaw. **Mountain Valley Spring Company** (150 Central Ave., Hot Springs, tel. 800/643–1501) bottles and sells the fabled water from the national park. Bring your own container and collect the thermal water for free at the two Thermal Water Jug Fountains at the end of Bathhouse Row. To buy Ouachita Mountain quartz crystals, try **Ron Coleman's Rocks-R-Gems** (tel. 501/624–7280), on Highway 70 just before Hot Springs.

OUTDOOR ACTIVITIES

CANOEING The Buffalo National River is at its best in early summer. Canoes can be rented from **Buffalo Camping and Canoeing**

(Gilbert, tel. 501/439–2888) and at half a dozen shops in Mt. Ida on Highway 27. The state tourism department distributes a floater's guide to Arkansas.

FISHING Area lakes harbor largemouth and smallmouth bass, bream, and catfish. There are trout streams in the Ozark National Forest not far from Eureka Springs. For a fishing guide, contact the **Arkansas Game and Fish Commission** (2 Natural Resources Dr., Little Rock 72205, tel. 501/223–6300).

GOLF Several courses are noted in the guide put out by the state's tourism department (tel. 800/628–8725). DeGray Resort State Park near Hot Springs has an 18-hole public course.

HIKING Arkansas has backcountry trails galore, a good many of them concentrated around the Buffalo National River, and in the Ouachita and Ozark national forests.

HORSEBACK RIDING Mountain-trail rides, hayrides, and lunch and dinner rides can be arranged at **Castleberry Stables** (tel. 501/623–6609 or 501/623–9939) outside Hot Springs.

WATER SPORTS Swimming is good at Buffalo Point on the Buffalo River, south of Yellville on Route 14. Boats can be rented for waterskiing on Lake Hamilton, Lake Ouachita, and DeGray Lake.

ENTERTAINMENT

CONCERTS The **Ozark Folk Center** (tel. 501/269–3851) at Mountain View has nightly mountain music April–October, with special monthly Sunday-night gospel concerts. In Hot Springs, the **Music Mountain Jamboree** (tel. 501/767–3841) features country and bluegrass.

HORSE RACING **Oaklawn Park** (tel. 501/623–4411) at Hot Springs has pari-mutuel betting on horse races from late January or early February (schedule varies) through most of April.

MUSEUMS At the **Mid-America Museum** (tel. 501/767–3461; admission charged) in Hot Springs, science comes to life in big exhibits such as the tornado chamber, lifelike dinosaurs, and a laser show.

Las Vegas
Nevada

Updated by Deke Castleman

Until recently Las Vegas existed for only one reason: gambling. Yes, there were cultural attractions and local events, but tens of millions of visitors came to this fantasyland for adults primarily to try their luck. With gambling becoming legalized around the country, however, the city is investing billions of dollars to turn itself into a Disney-like family destination, with a vacation's worth of fun things for kids to see and do.

Nongambling activities are proliferating as fast as casinos. Every major hotel built in the 1990s has an amusement park, high-tech entertainment, free spectacles, or a theme so fully realized as to be educational; each of the many hotels slated to open before the year 2000 has similar plans. Of course, Las Vegas is still the nation's premier gambling destination, and thanks to the subsidizing effect of casino profits, visitors can play blackjack, ride a roller coaster, stuff themselves at an all-you-can-eat buffet, or partake of dozens of other amenities at prices that are cheaper than anywhere else in the world.

A drive through town will show you an extraordinary collection of neon signs and flashing lights, especially on Fremont Street downtown. Drive only a few minutes from the flamboyant Strip and you'll discover a Southwestern landscape of red rock, Joshua trees, and yucca. To the east, 40 minutes away, are Hoover Dam, one of the greatest man-made wonders, and Lake Mead, one of the largest "artificial" lakes in the world. Zion, Bryce, Death Valley, and other natural wonders are only a few hours away.

ESSENTIAL INFORMATION

WHEN TO GO Las Vegas, the largest city in Nevada, is 2,162 feet above sea level, but the desert still defines the climate: bone-dry and hot in the summer, sunny and pleasant in spring and fall, cool and sometimes downright cold in winter. The weather is best April–May and October–November, with highs in the 70s and 80s and a low of 45°. In summer, the fierce desert sun pushes the mercury to above 110° (the heat is relatively free of humidity and more tolerable than, say, Disney World in the summer). When the sun is at its fiercest, Las Vegas lives indoors, in the hotel rooms, showrooms, and the casinos, where everything is air-conditioned.

There is neither a peak nor an off-peak season in Las Vegas. The only true slow period is right before Christmas, when quiet descends on the Strip and hotel rooms are abundant. Spring and fall tend to be busy times, as do holiday weekends year-round; New Year's Eve and Valentine's Day (when thousands of people fill the wedding chapels) and the Super Bowl (when the hordes crowd the sports books) are the busiest days of the year. Conventions frequently pack the town, so check your travel dates with the Las Vegas Convention & Visitors Authority (*see* Tourist Offices, *below*). Hotel room rates routinely fluctuate with a vengeance. Sunday through Thursday are the bargain nights (except during large conventions), while Friday and Saturday get top dollar.

FESTIVALS AND SEASONAL EVENTS In early May, the Senior Classic Golf Tournament

takes place at the Desert Inn (3145 Las Vegas Blvd. S, 89109, tel. 702/382–6616). Helldorado Days, held at the end of May, recall the Wild West with a rodeo, contests, and parades. National Finals Rodeo brings finalists to compete at the Thomas and Mack Center (tel. 702/731–2115) during the second week of December. The biggest New Year's Eve Party in the West is celebrated downtown on Fremont Street.

BARGAINS Hotel rooms, food, drink, and entertainment cost a fraction of what they would in other cities, simply because the highly profitable casinos bankroll all the other vacation necessities. Las Vegas is renowned for its cheap and ample buffets (breakfast $3–$4, dinner $6–$8; you can eat breakfast for as little as 99¢, a steak dinner for $3, and drink alcoholic beverages for free in all the casinos as long as you're playing the tables. Lounges provide free live music all over town (few have a drink minimum). Circus acts, exploding volcanoes, pirate shows, and people-watching are other good entertainment bargains. To tour the Strip inexpensively, take the local bus or trolley, both of which creep through the brightly lit district for a small fare.

TOURIST OFFICES **Las Vegas Chamber of Commerce** (711 E. Desert Inn Rd., 89109, tel. 702/735–1616). **Las Vegas Convention & Visitors Authority** (3150 Paradise Rd., 89109, tel. 702/892–0711).

EMERGENCIES **Police, fire** and **ambulance:** Dial 911. **Hospitals:** Sunrise Hospital (3186 S. Maryland Pkwy., tel. 702/731–8000) and University Medical Center (1800 W. Charleston Blvd., tel. 702/383–2000). **Doctors:** Physicians Medical Center (3121 S. Maryland Pkwy., tel. 702/732–0600). **Dentists:** Paradise Dental Center (2221 Paradise Rd. at Sahara Ave., tel. 702/735–8189). **Pharmacies:** White Cross Drugs (1700 Las Vegas Blvd. S, tel. 702/382–1733) is open 24 hours.

ARRIVING AND DEPARTING

BY PLANE Thanks to renovation, **McCarran International Airport** (tel. 702/261–5743),

slightly southeast of the city, is one of the most attractive and efficient in the nation. The least expensive mode of transportation from the airport to town is shuttle van. **Bell Trans** (tel. 702/739–7990) operates a shuttle service that costs less than $5 per person to the Strip hotels, a dollar or so more to the downtown ones. You will also find taxis lined up, mostly **Yellow, Checker, and Star** (tel. 702/873–2000). The cab ride to the Strip will cost $10–$15, and $15–$20 to downtown.

BY CAR The major highways leading to Vegas are I–15, running east from Los Angeles and west from Salt Lake City, U.S. 93 from Arizona, and U.S. 95 from Reno. If you take U.S. 93, you will drive across the top of the mighty Hoover Dam en route.

BY TRAIN **Amtrak** (tel. 800/872–7245) passes through Las Vegas. The depot is in back of the Plaza Hotel (1 N. Main St., tel. 702/386–6896)—you disembark right into a casino.

GETTING AROUND

BY CAR Las Vegas is an easy city to drive in because it is so compact. Las Vegas Boulevard runs north and south, a 3½-mile section of it known as the Strip. Here the major hotel-casinos are found, one right after the other. Every hotel has free self-parking, or have a valet do it for a customary $1–$2 tip.

BY BUS **Citizen Area Transit** (CAT, tel. 702/228–7433) runs Strip buses from the Hacienda Hotel at the southern end of the Strip to the downtown area. The buses stop at the major hotels.

BY TAXI **Desert Cab** (tel. 702/386–2687) and **Yellow, Checker, and Star Cabs** (tel. 702/873–2000) are the major cab companies in Las Vegas. It should not be necessary to call for one from major hotels, as they wait outside. This is not the case in less trafficked neighborhoods.

REST STOPS There are no public rest stops in Las Vegas. Hotels, restaurants, and gas stations provide convenient alternatives.

GUIDED TOURS Gray Line (1550 S. Industrial Rd., tel. 702/384–1234 or 800/634–6579) offers sightseeing tours of the city and its environs. Large luxury coaches do city tours (Ethel M's chocolate factory, Nevada State Museum, and such celebrity homes as Siegfried and Roy and Wayne Newton), as well as trips outside the city to Red Rock Canyon and Old Nevada, and Hoover Dam and Lake Mead.

EXPLORING

There are two separate tourist districts in Las Vegas: the older downtown section of the city, and the fabled Strip, where the glitzy new hotels are clustered.

DOWNTOWN This is where it all began for Las Vegas, back in 1905, when the San Pedro, Los Angeles, and Salt Lake Railroad founded it as a division point. After years of losing ground to the Strip megaresorts, downtown has refurbished itself with a four-block-long, 100-foot-high canopy, complete with 1.5 million lightbulbs—with the famous Glitter Gulch neon still sparkling below. Of the dozen or so hotels lining Fremont Street, the **Golden Nugget** (129 Fremont St., tel. 702/385–7111) stands out from the neon crowd, done as it is in white marble and gold.

THE STRIP This legendary area, home to 30 or so hotels, starts 2 miles south of downtown at the Sahara and keeps running south for another 3½ miles. The famous names—the Mirage, Caesars Palace, Bally's, Stardust, Sands, Flamingo—evoke images of beautiful people, mobster types, and high rollers, all throwing $100 chips around a crap table. Though no longer exclusively a playground for the rich, the Strip is still a fantasyland. Hotels worth a special visit are **Caesars Palace** (3750 Las Vegas Blvd. S, tel. 702/731–7110), with its theatrical re-creation of ancient Rome, and the **Mirage** (3400 Las Vegas Blvd. S, tel. 702/791–7111), which features an erupting volcano, a dolphin pool out back, and a glassed-in grotto for white tigers. If you are traveling with children, stop by **MGM Grand** (3805 Las Vegas Blvd.

S, tel. 702/891–1111), where you'll find the largest arcades, pool, and selection of restaurants, plus a 33-acre amusement park filled with rides for big kids and small. Everyone should visit **Luxor** (3900 Las Vegas Blvd. S, tel. 702/262–4000) for its stunning architecture, expansive atrium, and high-tech entertainment, and **Treasure Island** (3300 Las Vegas Blvd. S, tel. 702/894-7111) for its pyro-technic pirate show out front.

MUSEUMS, ATTRACTIONS, & THEME PARKS

Ethel M. Chocolate Factory is Willy Wonka come to life. Stop here to watch the candy being made on your way to the Hoover Dam. *2 Cactus Dr., Henderson, tel. 702/458–8864. Open daily.*

Grand Slam Canyon, the 5-acre indoor amusement park (under the big pink dome) behind Circus Circus, houses the world's largest indoor roller coaster, along with a flume, laser tag, kiddie rides, and a midway. *2880 Las Vegas Blvd. S, tel. 702/794–3939. Open daily. Admission charged.*

At the **Guinness World of Records Museum,** exhibits and film footage re-create record-setting events in sports, science, and entertainment. *2780 Las Vegas Blvd. S, tel. 702/792–3766. Open daily. Admission charged.*

The **Imperial Palace Auto Collection** houses 200 antique cars, including the world's largest collection of Duesenbergs. *Imperial Palace Hotel, 3535 Las Vegas Blvd. S, tel. 702/731–3311. Open daily. Admission charged (coupons for free entry distributed outside hotel).*

The **Liberace Museum** displays the master showman's pianos, flashy costumes, and extravagant automobiles. *1775 E. Tropicana Ave., tel. 702/798–5595. Open daily. Admission charged.*

At the **Nevada State Museum,** regional history is the theme indoors, while lakeside exhibits feature native plants and animals. *In Lorenzi Park, 700 Twin Lakes Dr., tel. 702/486–5205. Open daily. Admission charged.*

Omnimax Theater's 70mm films with wraparound sound focus on such stomach-hurtling subjects as rocket launches and white-water rafting. *In Caesars Palace, 3570 Las Vegas Blvd. S, tel. 702/731–7900. Open daily with shows on the hr. Admission charged.*

Scandia Family Fun Center, an outdoor game center, has batting cages and three miniature golf courses. *2900 Sirius Ave., tel. 702/364–0070. Open Mon.–Sat. Admission free (fee to play the games).*

Wet 'n Wild, a 26-acre water park, has pools, slides, and every conceivable water ride. *2600 Las Vegas Blvd. S, tel. 702/737–3819. Open mid-Apr.–Sept., daily. Admission charged.*

AROUND TOWN **Hoover Dam** is considered one of the seven man-made wonders of the world. The dam rises 727 feet high (the equivalent of a 70-story building) and is 660 feet thick at its base (greater than the length of two football fields). It was completed in 1935 for two purposes: flood control and the generation of electricity. Construction of the dam required 4.4 million cubic yards of concrete—enough to build a two-lane highway from San Francisco to New York. *On U.S. 93, 25 mi southeast of Las Vegas just outside Boulder City, tel. 702/293–8367. Open daily. Admission charged for dam tour.*

Lake Mead was created by the construction of Hoover Dam and is the largest man-made body of water in the Western Hemisphere. Its surface covers 229 square miles, and the irregular shoreline extends 550 miles; it's a popular spot for boating, swimming, or fishing. *On U.S. 93, beginning at Hoover Dam and extending northeast, tel. 702/293–8906 (Lake Mead Visitor Center). Open daily. Admission free.*

Nature enthusiasts will want to take excursions from Las Vegas into the Southwest desert. The nearest site of interest is **Red Rock Canyon,** 15 miles due west of the city. Here the rocks glow reddest and are strikingly lovely at sunrise or sunset. Farther out, 60 miles northeast of Las Vegas on I–15, is **Valley of Fire State Park,** so named for its flame-colored rock. Here, the red stone formations have been eroded into strange and wondrous shapes. Many have petroglyphs, a sort of graffiti-meets-stone-carvings, from Anasazi Indians who lived in the valley 1,000 years ago.

HOTELS AND INNS

As a rule, downtown Las Vegas hotels tend to be less costly than those on the Strip, although some lack swimming pools and most don't have tennis courts. Except for holiday weekends and peak convention periods, you should have no trouble finding a room. For hotel availability and recommendations, contact the **Las Vegas Convention & Visitors Authority Hotel and Room Reservations** (tel. 702/892–0777).

In Las Vegas, almost every hotel houses a casino. Gambling, after all, is the hotels' reason for being. Therefore the facility is not listed separately. Price categories for double occupancy, excluding 8% (Strip) and 9% (downtown) room tax, are Moderate, $50–$100, and Inexpensive, under $50.

DOWNTOWN **El Cortez.** The southwest corner of this hotel is the oldest original casino wing in the country, and the rooms in the newer tower are all minisuites. *600 E. Fremont St., tel. 702/385–5200 or 800/634–6703. 315 rooms. 2 restaurants. AE, D, DC, MC, V. Inexpensive.*

Fitzgeralds. Once the tallest building in Nevada, this luck-of-the-Irish-themed casino is still the greenest. It's a friendly place, with a free souvenir in the funbook and available rooms even during the most crowded times of year, such as New Year's Eve and the Comdex convention. *301 E. Fremont St., 89102, tel. 702/388–2400 or 800/274–5825, fax 702/388–2181. 650 rooms. 2 restaurants, lounge. AE, DC, MC, V. Inexpensive.*

Four Queens. The casino here claims the world's largest slot machine; the guest towers have 24-hour security, and the rooms are large and comfortable. *202 Fremont St., 89109, tel. 702/385–4011 or 800/634–6045.*

720 rooms. 2 restaurants. AE, D, DC, MC, V. Moderate.

Jackie Gaughan's Plaza. You're an elevator's ride away from Amtrak at this hotel, built on the site of the old Union Pacific depot. The Plaza is also the scene of the fireworks on New Year's Eve. *1 S. Main St., 89109, tel. 702/386–2110 or 800/634–6575, fax 702/382–8281. 1,034 rooms. Restaurant. AE, D, DC, MC, V. Moderate.*

THE STRIP **Circus Circus.** The first hotel in town to cater to families, this carnival-style place is ideal for the kids but a bit of a madhouse for grown-ups. *2880 Las Vegas Blvd. S, 89109, tel. 702/734–0410 or 800/634–3450. 2,793 rooms. 4 restaurants, 3 pools, RV park, midway with circus acts. AE, DC, MC, V. Inexpensive.*

Excalibur. Named for King Arthur's sword, Vegas's newest hotel, also the world's largest, is modeled after a medieval castle. *3850 Las Vegas Blvd. S, 89109, tel. 702/597–7777 or 800/937–7777. 4,032 rooms. 7 restaurants, pool. AE, D, DC, MC, V. Moderate.*

Hacienda. The southernmost hotel on the Strip, the Hacienda is refreshingly low-key (at least for Las Vegas), with a lushly landscaped pool area and one of the oldest wedding chapels in town. *3950 Las Vegas Blvd. S, 89109, tel. 702/739–8911 or 800/634–6713. 840 rooms. 3 restaurants, showroom, pool, tennis courts, RV park. AE, D, DC, MC, V. Moderate.*

Riviera. This sprawling forty-something hotel-casino has four showrooms and a 125,000-square-foot casino, second largest in the world. *2901 Las Vegas Blvd. S, 89109, tel. 702/734–5110 or 800/634–6753, fax 702/731–3265. 2,200 rooms. 5 restaurants, pool, tennis courts. AE, D, DC, MC, V. Moderate.*

Sam's Town. For 15 years, Sam's Town had 200 rooms, a western store and theme, and little else. But the hotel added a nine-story atrium surrounded by a 450-room cityscape, with trees, stone paths, rock waterfalls, and wooden bridges over creeks. The rooms facing the courtyard overlook a free laser-and-dancing-waters show twice nightly. *5111 W. Boulder Hwy., 89122, tel. 702/456–7777 or 800/634–6371, fax 702/454–8014. 650 rooms. 6 restaurants, pool, RV park. AE, D, DC, MC, V. Inexpensive.*

Stardust. A 1,000-room tower, a spectacular neon facade and sign, and 40 years on the Strip make this one of the landmark Las Vegas hotel properties. *3000 Las Vegas Blvd. S, 89109, tel. 702/732–6111 or 800/634–6757. 2,500 rooms. 5 restaurants, pool, tennis courts. AE, D, DC, MC, V. Moderate.*

Tropicana. Near the airport, the beautifully appointed grounds feature waterfalls and the lushest swimming area in town, where you can even play swim-up blackjack. *3801 Las Vegas Blvd. S, 89109, tel. 702/739–2222 or 800/468–9494, fax 702/739–2323. 1,900 rooms. 5 restaurants, showroom, 2 pools, AE, D, DC, MC, V. Moderate.*

MOTELS

MODERATE **Blair House Suites** (344 E. Desert Inn Rd., 89109, tel. 702/792–2222). 224 rooms, pool, spa. **Rodeway Inn** (3786 Las Vegas Blvd. S, 89109, tel. 702/736–1434). 97 rooms; pool.

INEXPENSIVE **Center Strip** (3688 Las Vegas Blvd. S, 89109, tel. 702/739–6066). 147 rooms with refrigerators and VCRs, pool, spa. **La Quinta** (3782 Las Vegas Blvd. S, 89109, tel. 702/739–7457). 114 rooms; pool.

DINING

You can eat very well for very little money in Las Vegas. The hotels keep food prices down to attract—and to keep—patrons inside near the slots and tables. The buffets are incredibly inexpensive and bountiful, and the coffee shops often advertise rock-bottom prices for steaks, prime rib, and lobster. Snack bars have food priced so cheaply, you wonder why they don't just give it away. Many good restaurants are found beyond the hotel area, away from the sound of slot machines, where the locals know to go.

For the restaurants listed below, price categories per person, excluding 7% tax, services, or drinks, are Moderate, $15–$25, and Inexpensive, under $15.

MODERATE **Bootlegger.** Locals flock to this popular Italian restaurant for the excellent seafood dishes, notably the lobster *diavolo*. *5025 S. Eastern Ave., tel. 702/736–4939. AE, D, DC, MC, V.*

Cafe Michelle. Crepes and salads are the primary lure at this café, where there are red-and-white checked tablecloths inside and alfresco dining under Cinzano umbrellas. *1350 E. Flamingo St., tel. 702/735–8686. AE, MC, V.*

Cathay House. Here you can enjoy a lovely view of the city while dining on spicy Szechuan cuisine. *5300 Spring Mountain, tel. 702/876–3838. AE, DC, MC, V.*

Steak House. Fine aged steaks are cooked over an open-hearth grill in this quiet, wood-paneled restaurant. *Circus Circus Hotel, 2880 Las Vegas Blvd. S, tel. 702/734–0410. AE, D, DC, MC, V.*

The Tillerman. Seafood is the favorite at this garden-setting spot, located 3 miles east of the Strip. Here the catch of the day is flown in fresh and served under an open skylight on hot desert nights. *2245 E. Flamingo St., tel. 702/731–4036. AE, D, DC, MC, V.*

INEXPENSIVE **Chicago Joe's.** The pastas at this unpretentious restaurant have a fan club of their own. *820 S. 4th St., tel. 702/382–5637. MC, V.*

Dona Maria's. The enchilada-style tamales (best with the green sauce) and other Mexican dishes are the best in town. *910 Las Vegas Blvd. S, tel. 702/382–6538. AE, MC, V.*

Old Heidelberg. Despite its German name, this small, family-run nook near the Sahara Hotel features Continental fare such as veal calvados. *604 E. Sahara Ave., tel. 702/731–5310. MC, V.*

Silver Dragon. At this replica of a Peking palace, you'll find traditional Chinese food, sweet-and-sour dishes, and lemon fish.

1510 E. Flamingo St., tel. 702/737–1234. AE, MC, V.

BUFFETS Las Vegas is famous for its lavish buffets. Nearly every hotel offers breakfast, lunch, and dinner buffets. **Circus Circus** (2880 Las Vegas Blvd. S, tel. 702/734–0411) is cheapest; at around $5 for dinner, it's always mobbed, but the food is unremarkable. The **Rio** (3700 W. Flamingo, tel. 702/252–7777) and **Palace Station** (2411 W. Sahara Blvd., tel. 702/367–2411) buffets are the best. On weekends, the better hotels serve more sumptuous buffets. The most elegant of these is the Sterling Champagne Brunch at **Bally's** (3645 Las Vegas Blvd. S, tel. 702/739–4111); it's expensive, but worth it.

SHOPPING

There are two shopping malls on the Strip: the exclusive **Forum Shops at Caesars** (3500 Las Vegas Blvd. S, tel. 702/893–4800) and the **Fashion Show Mall** (3200 Las Vegas Blvd. S, tel. 702/369–8382). In the larger hotels, such as Bally's and the Mirage, you'll also find upscale retail shops. These stores are expensive, feature designer labels, and are hardly for impulsive purchases. At the other extreme are the undeniably tacky souvenir shops, which sell T-shirts and the quintessential Las Vegas dice clock.

OUTDOOR ACTIVITIES

FISHING Fishing is a year-round activity on Lake Mead. Visitors may obtain a three-day permit from any of the marinas. The nearest one to Las Vegas is **Lake Mead Marina** (tel. 702/293–3484).

GOLF Golf is the favorite recreation of this sun-blessed city, and there are more than a dozen courses in Las Vegas Valley. The closest is found at the **Desert Inn** (3145 Las Vegas Blvd. S, tel. 702/733–4290), but it is open only to hotel guests. The **Las Vegas Golf Club** (4349 Vegas Dr., tel. 702/645–5696) and **Angel Park** (100 S. Rampart, tel. 702/254–4653) are open to the public.

SWIMMING Most hotels have swimming pools, but if you prefer the beach, try Boulder Beach on Lake Mead, next to Lake Mead Marina. The water never gets warm in the lake (heating up to about 65°), but near the shallow beach it's tolerable.

TENNIS Many of the larger hotels have courts, open to both guests and visitors (*see* Hotels and Inns, *above*).

ENTERTAINMENT

Las Vegas, of course, means showbiz, and the nightlife here is varied. You will find household-name superstars like David Copperfield and Tom Jones, and big production shows—spectacularly staged musicals, performed by scantily clad showgirls—interspersed with specialty acts. There are also smaller-scale revues and several magic acts.

With the exception of dinner shows (*see below*), performances include two cocktails with the price of admission, and that price varies. The big stars command $40–$100 a seat; big productions average $30. The small revues run about $20.

Some shows have advance ticket purchasing, while the rest are first-come, first-served. For the latter, call the hotel the day of or the day before the show to make a reservation. Count on waiting in line at the showroom for about 30 minutes before you are seated, and to get a good seat in a crowded room, you must tip the maître d'

$5–$20—depending on the performer and the number of people waiting. While tipping maître d's is a questionable practice, it's the way things are done in Las Vegas.

DINNER SHOWS The dinner show, once a Vegas institution, is vanishing from the scene. Only three hotels still have them: the **Tropicana** (3801 Las Vegas Blvd. S, showroom reservations tel. 702/739–2411), the **Flamingo Hilton** (3555 Las Vegas Blvd. S, tel. 702/733–3333), and the **Rio** (3700 W. Flamingo Ave., tel. 702/252–7777).

BIG PRODUCTION SHOWS "Jubilee" at Bally's (3645 Las Vegas Blvd. S, tel. 702/739–4567), **"Folies Bergere"** at Tropicana (3801 Las Vegas Blvd. S, tel. 702/739–2411), and **"Siegfried and Roy"** at the Mirage (3400 Las Vegas Blvd. S, tel. 702/791–7444) are some of the long-running hits.

SMALLER REVUES **"La Cage"** and **"Crazy Girls"** at the Riviera (2901 Las Vegas Blvd. S, tel. 702/734–5110), though less extravagant and less expensive than the major productions, are no less enjoyable and entertaining.

SUPERSTARS Some of the hotels featuring big-name performers are **Bally's** (3645 Las Vegas Blvd. S, tel. 702/739–4567), **Caesars Palace** (3750 Las Vegas Blvd. S, tel. 702/731–7333), and **MGM Grand** (3805 Las Vegas Blvd. S, tel. 702/891–1111). Free tourist magazines in the hotel gift shops list which stars are in town and their performance schedules.

The Lincoln Trail
Illinois, Indiana, Kentucky

Updated by Jane Onstott

Stretching from the rolling green hills of northern Kentucky to Indiana's Ohio Valley and to the wide-open prairies of southern and central Illinois, the Lincoln Trail conjures up images of log cabins, tiny farms surrounded by split-rail fences, and prairie air scented with wood smoke. Exaggerations? Not really, for you don't have to walk too far from your car to find all of these on the historic Lincoln Trail.

Abraham Lincoln's presence is still felt along the strip of middle America now known as the Lincoln Trail; dozens of spots along the trail, countless historical markers, and three national historic sites pay homage to Lincoln's memory. The Abraham Lincoln Birthplace National Historic Site, near Hodgenville, Kentucky, enshrines in a large granite memorial the tiny log cabin where Lincoln was born. Remote southern Indiana's Lincoln Boyhood National Memorial marks the farm where Lincoln labored for 14 difficult years. And in Springfield, Illinois, where Lincoln practiced law for 24 years, the Lincoln Home National Historic Site preserves the only home he ever owned, and the place where he received word of his election to the presidency in 1860.

Much of the region cut by the Lincoln Trail is rural, dotted with small towns and neat, orderly farms. Even Springfield, the Illinois prairie capital known as Mr. Lincoln's Hometown, is surrounded by seemingly endless cornfields. You won't find much glitter along the Lincoln Trail: Except for Springfield, which bustles when the legislature is in session, the pace is slow and life is fairly sedate.

ESSENTIAL INFORMATION

WHEN TO GO July and August are the trail's hottest months, when maximum temperatures often reach the upper 80s or higher, with high humidity. Winters see modest snowfall and average temperatures in the upper 20s, although freezing rain often occurs. Although the summer (June–August) is peak season, the region is perhaps loveliest in autumn, when the crowds thin out, the heat and humidity are lower, and the land is ablaze with color.

FESTIVALS AND SEASONAL EVENTS Mid-Feb.: Lincoln's Birthday is celebrated with musical programs, speakers, and other events at Hodgenville, Kentucky; Lincoln City, Indiana; and Springfield, Illinois; **2nd weekend in Oct.:** Lincoln Days, in Hodgenville, Kentucky, features rail-splitting contests, Lincoln look-alikes, and a parade.

TOURIST OFFICES Kentucky Department of Travel Development (Capital Plaza Tower, 500 Mero St., Suite 2200, Frankfort, KY 40601, tel. 502/564–4930 or 800/255–8747). **Indiana Tourism Development Division** (1 N. Capitol, Suite 700, Indianapolis, IN 46204-2288, tel. 317/232–8860). **Central Illinois Tourism Council** (629 E. Washington St., Springfield, IL 62701, tel. 217/525–7980 or 800/262–2482). **Louisville Convention & Visitors Bureau** (400 S. 1st St., Louisville, KY 40202, tel. 606/584–2121 or 800/626–5646). **Abraham Lincoln Tourism Bureau** (303 S.

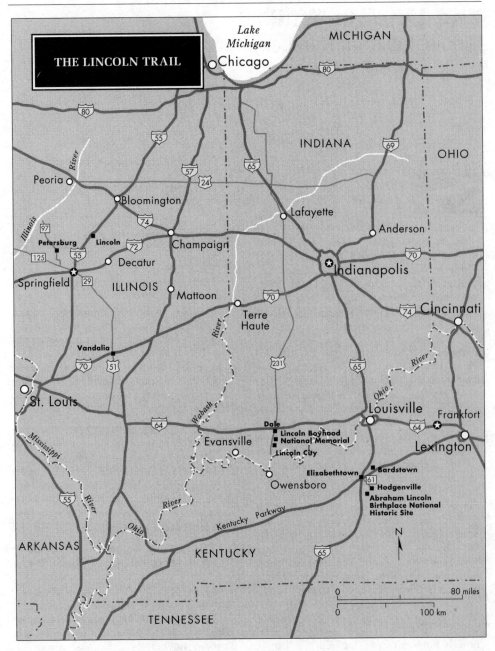

THE LINCOLN TRAIL

Kickapoo St., Lincoln, IL 62656, tel. 217/ 732–8687). **Springfield Convention & Visitors Bureau** (109 N. 7th St., Springfield, IL 62701, tel. 217/789–2360 or 800/545–7300).

EMERGENCIES **Police, fire,** and **ambulance:** Dial 911. **Doctors:** Hardin Memorial Hospital (913 N. Dixie Ave., Elizabethtown, KY, tel. 502/765–1640). St. Joseph's Hospital (1900

Medical Arts Dr., Leland Heights, Huntingburg, IN, tel. 812/683–2121). Memorial Medical Center (800 N. Rutledge St., Springfield, IL, tel. 217/788–3000).

Lincoln Home National Historic Site Visitor Center (426 S. 7th St.) and the Capitol Complex Visitor Center (425 S. College St.) have rest rooms.

ARRIVING AND DEPARTING

BY PLANE Standiford Field Airport (tel. 502/368–6524), 5 miles south of downtown Louisville, Kentucky, has scheduled daily flights by major U.S. carriers. **Capital Airport** (tel. 217/788–1060), 5 miles north of downtown Springfield, Illinois, is served by regional carriers.

BY CAR A car is the most practical means of touring the Lincoln Trail. I–65 intersects Kentucky from north to south and passes near Hodgenville's Lincoln attractions. For travelers heading to Indiana's Lincoln Boyhood National Memorial, I–64 crosses southern Indiana from east to west. In Illinois, I–55 passes through Springfield, and I–74 and I–70 lead to other Lincoln sites.

BY BUS Greyhound Lines (tel. 800/231–2222) serves the region's major hubs, but service to the historic sites and smaller towns on the Lincoln Trail is sporadic.

BY TRAIN Amtrak (tel. 800/872–7245) makes regular stops in Springfield and Lincoln, Illinois.

REST STOPS There are rest stops with rest rooms on I–65, just south of Elizabethtown, Kentucky. The park's visitor center at the Abraham Lincoln Birthplace National Historic Site, near Hodgenville, Kentucky, has rest rooms. In Indiana, rest stops on I–64, just west of Exit 57, near Dale, have rest rooms and tourist information about the entire state, and both the Lincoln Boyhood National Memorial and the adjacent Lincoln State Park offer rest rooms. In Illinois, a rest stop on I–64 at the Indiana border has rest rooms. The Vandalia Tourist Information Center, at the junction of U.S. 51 and I–74, has rest rooms. In Springfield, the Abraham

EXPLORING

You can cover the Lincoln Trail in a week to 10 days. From the beginning of the trail in Hodgenville, Kentucky, to Lincoln City, Indiana, is approximately 135 miles via I–65 and I–64. It's about another 250 miles from Lincoln City to Springfield, Illinois, via I–64 west to U.S. 51, then north to Route 29. Most of Springfield's Lincoln-oriented sites are clustered in the city's center, within easy walking distance of one another.

KENTUCKY Abraham Lincoln Birthplace National Historic Site contains Lincoln's traditional birth cabin, enshrined in a large neoclassical memorial designed by John Russell Pope. The National Park Service Visitor Center offers a short film about Lincoln's Kentucky years and displays period artifacts, including the Lincoln family Bible. *2995 Lincoln Farm Rd., Hodgenville, tel. 502/358–3874. Open daily. Admission free.*

The **Lincoln Museum,** in downtown Hodgenville, has artifacts, paintings, and artwork pertaining to Lincoln's Kentucky years and 12 life-size dioramas of scenes from the life of America's 16th president. *66 Public Sq., Hodgenville, tel. 502/358–3163. Open daily. Admission charged.*

Lincoln's Boyhood Home, 7 miles northeast of Hodgenville on Knob Creek, is a reconstructed cabin on the site where Lincoln lived from 1811 to 1816. A small museum adjacent to the cabin displays period antiques and artifacts. *7120 Bardstown Rd., tel. 502/549–3741. Open Apr.–Nov., daily. Admission charged.*

INDIANA Lincoln Boyhood National Memorial marks the site of the Lincoln family farmstead from 1816 to 1830. Operated by the National Park Service, the visitor-center museum has original Lincoln artifacts, photographs, paintings, sculpture, and a film about Lincoln's Indiana years. A walking trail leads to Lincoln's mother's grave, and the Trail of 12 Stones contains stones from significant spots in Lincoln's life. *5 mi south of I-64 Exit 57, then 2 mi east on Rte. 162, across the street from Lincoln State Park, Lincoln City, tel. 812/937-4541. Open daily. Living History Farm open mid-Apr.–Oct., daily. Admission charged.*

Lincoln State Park has a church built by Lincoln's father and a small cemetery where his sister, Sarah, is buried. The park has hiking trails and offers boating, fishing, and camping. The drama *Young Abe Lincoln* (*see* Entertainment, *below*) is presented here in the summer. *Rte. 162, Lincoln City, tel. 812/937-4710. Open daily. Admission charged.*

ILLINOIS **Vandalia Statehouse State Historic Site** was Illinois's capitol from 1834 until 1839. The Federal-style building where Lincoln served in the legislature has been restored and now holds state offices, legislator's chambers, and courtrooms with Lincoln-era furnishings. *315 W. Gallatin St., Vandalia, tel. 618/283-1161. Open Mar.–Nov., daily. Admission free.*

Lincoln Home National Historic Site preserves the home where Lincoln and his wife lived from 1844 to 1861 and is the showpiece of the restored historic area. Restored and refurbished by the National Park Service, the home contains some original furnishings. Tickets, required for guided tours, are available at the visitor center. *426 S. 7th St., Springfield, tel. 217/789-2357. Open daily. Admission free.*

Lincoln Depot Museum, two blocks east, is where Lincoln left Springfield in 1861 to assume the presidency. His impromptu farewell address ranks among his most eloquent speeches. The depot has restored waiting rooms and shows a film depicting his farewell to Springfield and the events that took place on his journey to Washington.

10th and Monroe Sts., Springfield, tel. 217/544-8695 or 217/788-1356. Open Apr.–Aug., daily. Admission free.

Lincoln-Herndon Law Offices State Historic Site, three blocks west and one block north of the depot, contains offices that Lincoln shared with his law partner, William Herndon. From 1843 to 1852, the building held the only Federal Court in Illinois. *1 S. Old Capitol Plaza, Springfield, tel. 217/785-7289. Open daily. Admission charged.*

Old State Capitol State Historic Site, across the street, is where Lincoln made his famous "House Divided" speech and argued more than 300 cases before the state supreme court. President Lincoln's body lay in state here in 1865. The magnificently restored building, with former state offices and legislative chambers, displays an actual draft of the Gettysburg Address written by Lincoln. *6th and Adams Sts., Springfield, tel. 217/785-7960. Open daily. Donations accepted.*

Lincoln's Tomb State Historic Site, 2 miles north of the Old Capitol, holds the remains of Lincoln, his wife, and three of their four children. Designed by Larkin Mead, this soaring edifice dominates a 12-acre plot and houses an impressive collection of Civil War and Lincoln statuary. At 7 PM each Tuesday from June through August, the 114th Infantry Regiment performs impressive drills in authentic Civil War uniforms. *Oak Ridge Cemetery, Springfield, tel. 217/782-2717. Open daily. Admission free.*

Lincoln's New Salem State Historic Site, 20 miles northwest of Springfield, is the restored prairie village of New Salem, where Lincoln lived from 1831 to 1837. The village museum displays New Salem artifacts, and costumed interpreters give demonstrations of weaving, candle making, and other 1830s skills. *2 mi south of Petersburg on Rte. 97, tel. 217/632-4000. Open daily. Admission free.*

Lincoln, 31 miles northeast of Springfield via I-55, is the only town named for Abraham Lincoln during his lifetime. Lincoln christened his namesake with watermelon juice on August 27, 1853; a historical marker at the Amtrak station marks the spot.

Postville Courthouse State Historic Site is a replica of the courthouse where the circuit-riding Lincoln practiced law during sessions from 1840 to 1847. The building has a small courtroom with period furnishings and photographs. *914 5th St., Lincoln, tel. 217/732–8930. Open Fri.–Sat. Admission free.*

Lincoln College Museum, in McKinstry Memorial Library, houses some 2,000 Lincoln artifacts, including items from Lincoln's Springfield home and the White House to Lincoln's assassination. In the library's presidential museum are documents bearing the signatures of all the U.S. presidents. *300 Keokuk St., Lincoln, tel. 217/732–3155. Open Feb.–mid-Dec., daily. Admission free.*

HOTELS AND INNS

Family-oriented motels remain the mainstay along the Lincoln Trail, although bed-and-breakfast accommodations are growing in popularity. Contact **Kentucky Homes Bed & Breakfast** (1219 S. 4th Ave., Louisville 40203, tel. 502/635–7341) for a brochure listing more than 100 B&Bs throughout Kentucky and southern Indiana, and for a free copy of *A Guide to Illinois Bed & Breakfasts & Country Inns*, contact the **Illinois Bed & Breakfast Association** (Box 96, Elash, IL 62028). Rates for lodging places tend to be lower before Memorial Day and after Labor Day. Price categories for double occupancy, excluding sales tax (6% in Kentucky, 8% in Indiana, and 7¼% in Illinois), are Expensive, over $85; Moderate, $50–$85; and Inexpensive, under $50.

KENTUCKY **Best Western Cardinal Inn.** This modern motel with large rooms is a 20-minute drive from Hodgenville's Lincoln attractions. *642 E. Dixie Hwy., Elizabethtown 42701, tel. 502/765–6139 or 800/528–1234. 67 rooms. Pool, coin laundry, playground. AE, D, MC, V. Inexpensive.*

Lincoln Memorial Motel. Set on part of the original Lincoln farm, adjacent to the Lin-

coln Birthplace National Historic Site, this motel is convenient to Hodgenville's Lincoln attractions. *U.S. Hwy. 31E and Kentucky Rte. 61, Hodgenville 42748, tel. 502/358–3197. 10 rooms. Pool, wading pool. AE, MC, V. Inexpensive.*

INDIANA **Stone's Budget Host Motel.** This no-frills motel in a small-town atmosphere is only 3 miles from the Lincoln Boyhood National Memorial. *410 S. Washington St., Dale 47523, tel. 812/937–4448. 23 rooms. Restaurant. AE, D, DC, MC, V. Inexpensive.*

ILLINOIS **Mansion View Inn and Suites.** This charming inn emulates the architectural style and decor of the Governor's Mansion, which is right across the street. The Mansion View has character, so it's a nice alternative to the chain hotels. *529 S. 4th St., Springfield 62701, tel. 217/544–7411 or 800/252–1083. 78 rooms, 30 suites. Restaurant next door, exercise room. AE, D, DC, MC, V. Moderate.*

Springfield Renaissance Hotel. Elegant public areas; large, comfortable rooms; attentive service; and a convenient downtown location make this hotel a good choice if you want to splurge. *701 E. Adams St., Springfield 62701, tel. 217/544–8800 or 800/228–9898. 316 rooms. 2 restaurants, cocktail lounge, entertainment, indoor pool, saunas, whirlpool, fitness center, valet service. AE, D, MC, V. Expensive.*

MOTELS

All of the following are in the Inexpensive or Moderate categories.

KENTUCKY **Days Inn** (2010 N. Mulberry Rd., Elizabethtown 42701, tel. 502/769–5522 or 800/325–2525). 122 rooms; restaurant adjacent, pool, playground. **Howard Johnson** (708 Dixie Hwy., Elizabethtown 42701, tel. 502/765–2185). 80 rooms; restaurant, pool, coin laundry.

INDIANA **Best Western Dutchman Inn** (406 E. 22nd St., Huntingburg 47542, tel. 812/683–2334 or 800/528–1234). 95 rooms;

restaurant, lounge, pool. **Holiday Inn** (951 Werrsing Rd., Jasper 47546, tel. 812/482–5555 or 800/465–4329). 200 rooms; restaurant, indoor pool, sauna, whirlpool.

ILLINOIS **Best Inns of America** (500 N. 1st St., Springfield 62702, tel. 217/522–1100). 91 rooms; Continental breakfast included, outdoor pool. **Crossroads Motel** (1305 W. Woodlawn Rd., Lincoln 62656, tel. 217/735–5571). 30 rooms; outdoor pool, playground. **Drury Inn** (3180 S. Dirksen Pkwy., Exit 94 off I–55, Springfield 62703, tel. 217/529–3900). 118 rooms; indoor pool, whirlpool, mini-suites. **Vandalia Travelodge** (1500 N. 6th St., Vandalia 62471, tel. 618/283–2363). 48 rooms; outdoor pool, playground.

DINING

The Lincoln Trail offers a selection of foods ranging from biscuits and gravy to Continental cuisine. Price categories per person, excluding tax (6% in Kentucky, 6% in Indiana, and 7¼% in Illinois), service, and drinks, are Expensive, over $20; Moderate, $10–$20; and Inexpensive, under $10.

KENTUCKY **Stone Hearth Restaurant.** This is an informal, family-oriented eatery that yet attains a certain elegance with its white-cloth dinner tables spread around the restaurant's namesake—a cozy stone hearth. The menu is long and typically all-inclusive: Pick from many grilled chicken and beef dishes or a heaping plate of pasta. *1001 N. Mulberry St., Elizabethtown, tel. 502/765–4898. AE, DC, MC, V. Moderate.*

INDIANA **Stone's Budget Host Motel.** Don't be misled simply because this family-style restaurant is located inside a motel; the dining room is packed many nights, and the food, southern Indiana home cooking, is first-rate. *410 S. Washington St., Dale, tel. 812/937–4448. AE, D, DC, MC, V. Inexpensive.*

ILLINOIS **Bauers.** In a converted historic building near the state capitol, Bauers serves broiled steaks, Continental cuisine, and a variety of fresh seafood in several cozy dining rooms. *620 S. 1st St., Springfield, tel. 217/789–4311. AE, D, DC, MC, V. Moderate–Expensive.*

Chesapeake Seafood House. A long list of seafood and beef dishes satisfy hungry Springfielders at the popular Chesapeake, located in a prim, finely restored 1850s residence. *3045 Clear Lake Ave., Springfield, tel. 217/522–5220. AE, D, DC, MC, V. Inexpensive–Moderate.*

Feed Store. Amid Springfield's Lincoln attractions, the Feed Store serves up soups, salads, and light sandwiches in a family-style setting that's often packed. *516 E. Adams St., Springfield, tel. 217/528–3355. No credit cards. Inexpensive.*

Guzzardo's Italian Villa. Hearty helpings of American and Italian dishes—from steaks and salads to seafood and pasta—have made Guzzardo's a hot spot in Lincoln. *509 Pulaski St., Lincoln, tel. 217/732–6370. No credit cards. Inexpensive–Moderate.*

Jim's Steakhouse. Broiled steaks, fresh seafood, and succulent cuts of thick prime rib are featured at this popular supper club just south of downtown. *2242 S. 6th St., Springfield, tel. 217/522–2111. AE, MC, V. Moderate–Expensive.*

Norb Andy's. This pleasantly dark downtown café offers fish, poultry, and the much-imitated horseshoe sandwich—a hot open-face blend of meat and Cheddar cheese topped with shoestring potatoes. Wednesday to Saturday you can sip coffee while groovin' to a live jazz band. *518 E. Capitol St., Springfield, tel. 217/523–7777. AE, DC, MC, V. Inexpensive.*

OUTDOOR ACTIVITIES

HIKING In Indiana, Lincoln State Park (Rte. 162, Lincoln City, IN, tel. 812/937–4710) and the Harrison-Crawford Wyandotte Complex (7240 Old Forest Rd., Corydon, IN, tel. 812/738–8232) offer several miles of hiking trails. In Springfield, Illinois, Lincoln

Memorial Garden (2301 E. Lake Shore Dr., tel. 217/529–1111), Lincoln Park (1601 N. 5th St., tel. 217/522–5431), Adams Wildlife Sanctuary (2315 E. Clear Lake, tel. 217/544–5781), and Riverside Park (4105 Sand Hill Rd., tel. 217/789–2353) have easy hiking trails; contact the Springfield Convention & Visitors Bureau (109 N. 7th St., Springfield 62701, tel. 217/789–2360 or 800/545–7300) for additional information. Also in Illinois, New Salem State Park (2 mi south of Petersburg on Rte. 97, tel. 217/632–7952) and Sangchris Lake State Park have several miles of hiking trails.

ENTERTAINMENT

CONCERTS **Lincoln Jamboree** (2579 Lincoln Farm Rd., Hodgenville, KY, tel. 502/358–3545) presents country-music concerts on Saturday nights.

SPECTATOR SPORTS The **Springfield Cardinals,** a St. Louis Cardinals class-A baseball team, play at Lanphier Ball Park (1415 N. Grand Ave. E, Springfield, IL, tel. 217/789–2352) from April through August.

THEATER The musical drama *Big River* or *Young Abe Lincoln* is presented in an outdoor amphitheater at **Lincoln State Park** (Box 7-21, Lincoln City, IN, tel. 812/937–4493 or 800/264–4223), nightly except Monday, from mid-June to late August. The **Great American People Show** (Box 401, Petersburg, IL, tel. 217/632–7755) presents *Your Obedient Servant, A. Lincoln* in an outdoor amphitheater at Lincoln's New Salem Historic Site from mid-June to mid-August.

Los Angeles
California

Updated by Jenner Bishop

hose from purportedly more sophisticated cities note what Los Angeles, California, lacks. Others from more provincial towns raise an eyebrow at what it has. Regardless of the varying opinions about Los Angeles, the city attracts people from all over—and lots of them (in 1994 alone the city hosted more than 22 million overnight visitors).

We cannot predict what *your* Los Angeles will be like. You can laze on a beach, soak up some of the world's greatest art collections, or tour the movie studios and stars' homes. You can window-shop along the luxurious Rodeo Drive in Beverly Hills or browse for hipper novelties on boutique-lined Melrose Avenue. The possibilities are endless. Indeed, you cannot do Los Angeles in a day or a week or even two. This second-largest city in America holds too many choices between its canyons and its coast to be exhausted in one trip; you will be exhausted first.

So, relax. *Everybody's* a tourist in Los Angeles. Los Angeles is a city of ephemerals, of transience, and above all, of illusion. Whether you love it or hate it, Los Angeles is an overwhelming spectacle in the best sense. There's a feeling that anything can happen—and it often does.

ESSENTIAL INFORMATION

WHEN TO GO Almost any time of year is the right time to go to Los Angeles; the climate is mild and pleasant year-round, rarely dipping lower than 60° during the day. There's no official tourist season in L.A.—it's busy all year—but crowds swell around such big events as the Rose Bowl and the Academy Awards and during school holidays. Hotel bargains occasionally become available during the summer, when Los Angeles smog can be at its worst. The rainy season usually runs from November through March, with the heaviest downpours usually coming in January. Summers are virtually rainless.

BARGAINS **Museums & Sights:** Admission to the following Los Angeles museums is free: **California Museum of Science and Industry** (tel. 213/744–7400) and **California Afro-American Museum** (tel. 213/744–7432), both in Exposition Park; **J. Paul Getty Museum** in Malibu (tel. 310/458–2003); **Los Angeles Maritime Museum** (tel. 310/548–7618); **Cabrillo Marine Museum** (tel. 310/548–7562); and the **Travel Town Museum** (tel. 213/662–5874) in Griffith Park. The **Los Angeles Municipal Art Gallery** (tel. 213/485–4581) at Barnsdale Park in Hollywood charges $1.50 for admission, but their Junior Art Center is free. Mann's Chinese Theater and the Hollywood Walk of Fame cost nothing to explore, but be sure to visit during daylight, since this section of Hollywood becomes downright seedy after dark.

People-watching: Los Angeles's street action is free and a great way to gain insight into what makes this metropolis tick. Explore West Hollywood's Melrose Avenue, a thoroughfare of flashing neon and up-to-the-second trends, and Venice Boardwalk, the bohemian corner of Los Angeles, packed with jugglers, acrobatic roller skaters, sweaty muscle builders, leftover hippies, and a parade of bikinis. Melrose activity starts about noon every day, and Venice is especially hopping on weekends, particularly after lunch.

TV Tapings: Free tickets are available for many television show tapings. **Audiences Unlimited** (100 Universal City Plaza, Bldg. 153, Universal City, CA 91608, tel. 818/506–0067) will provide you with a monthly schedule if you send them a stamped, self-addressed envelope. You can also pick up tickets in person at the Audiences Unlimited information center (Fox Plaza, 5746 Sunset Blvd., Hollywood).

Each network studio also has a ticket booth that distributes tickets on a first-come basis. Plan to pick up tickets first thing in the morning or phone ahead to check availability. **ABC** (4151 Prospect Ave., Los Angeles, tel. 310/557–7777), **CBS** (7800 Beverly Blvd., Los Angeles, tel. 213/852–2624), **NBC** (3000 W. Alameda Ave., Burbank, tel. 818/840–3537), **Fox** (5746 Sunset Blvd., Hollywood, tel. 213/856–1000).

Tickets are also given out in front of Mann's Chinese Theater, during the Universal Studios Tour, and by the Greater Los Angeles Visitors Bureau. Many shows require audience members to be at least 16 years of age.

TOURIST OFFICES **Los Angeles Convention and Visitors Bureau** (633 W. 5th St., Los Angeles, CA 90071, tel. 213/624–7300).

EMERGENCIES **Police, fire,** and **ambulance:** Dial 911. **Hospitals:** Hollywood Presbyterian (Vermont Ave. at Fountain Ave., tel. 213/913–4896) and Cedars-Sinai (Beverly Blvd. at San Vicente Blvd., tel. 310/855–6517) have 24-hour emergency rooms. **Doctors:** Physician Referral Service (tel. 213/483–6122). **Dentists:** L.A. Dental Society (tel. 213/380–7669). **Pharmacies:** Horton and Converse (6625 Van Nuys Blvd., tel. 213/873–1556) in Van Nuys and Horton and Converse (11600 Wilshire Blvd., tel. 310/478–0801) in West L.A. are open until 2 AM. Osco/Savon Drug Stores (tel. 800/627–2866) will direct you to one of their many 24-hour pharmacies.

ARRIVING AND DEPARTING

BY PLANE **Los Angeles International Airport, LAX** (tel. 310/646–5252), lies about 22 miles from downtown L.A., slightly less from Beverly Hills, and a bit more from Hollywood.

Between the Airport and Downtown: Buses operated by **RTD**, the Rapid Transit District (tel. 213/626–4455 or 800/266–6883), run every few minutes. It takes an hour to get from LAX to downtown hotels.

L.A. Taxi (tel. 213/627–7000) and **Independent** (tel. 213/385–8294) cabs, available curbside, take about 25 minutes to downtown hotels. The fare is about $30, including an airport charge.

Super Shuttle (tel. 310/417–8988) is available by calling on the courtesy phone at the baggage claim. It takes 30–40 minutes to get from LAX to downtown hotels, and the fare is around $15. Rates to other areas vary. Other shuttle services include **Best Shuttle** (tel. 310/670–7080), **Prime Time Shuttle** (tel. 310/558–1606), and **Shuttle One** (tel. 310/670–6666).

If you're coming from LAX by car, take Century Boulevard to I–405: south to Long Beach, Newport Beach, and San Diego; north to I–10E to downtown, Century City, and Hollywood. For Hollywood, take I–10 downtown, to I–110 north to U.S. 101 north to Hollywood. If it's rush hour and the freeways are jammed, an alternate route is Sepulveda Boulevard, running parallel to I–405. Follow Sepulveda north from LAX for about 2 miles. Turn right at Wilshire Boulevard, thus skirting Century City, and cut through Beverly Hills on your way downtown, or travel ½ mile farther on Sepulveda to Sunset Boulevard and turn right, which will take you through Bel Air and Beverly Hills to Hollywood.

BY CAR Los Angeles can be reached via I–5 from the north and south, or from the north coast via U.S. 101. From the east, take I–10.

DOWNTOWN

Boylston St.

Beaudry Ave.

110 Fwy.

Alpine St.

Chinatown

Ord St.

Daly St.

N. Broadway

New High St.

Spring St.

N. Main St.

Sunset Blvd.

Hollywood Fwy.

Temple St.

Union Station

Music Center

1 St.

El Pueblo State Historic Park

Olvera St.

Flower St.

Hope St.

Grand Ave.

Olive St.

Hill St.

Broadway

Spring St.

Main St.

4th St.

2nd St.

Aliso St.

Arcadia St.

101

Commercial St.

Alameda St.

Banning St.

Museum of Contemporary Art

City Hall

Little Tokyo

MONICA

MOUNTAINS

Coldwater Canyon Ave.

Ventura Fwy.

101

Los Ang

Ventura Blvd.

Laurel

Sunse

SANTA

San Diego Frwy.

0   4 miles
0   5 meters

Beverly Hills Hotel

Rodeo Dr.

Blvd.

Dr.

Oakhurst

Blvd.

BEVERLY HILLS

LOS ANGELES

University of California at Los Angeles

Monica

Ave. of the Stars

Century City

Will Rogers State Historic Park

Sunset Blvd.

Blvd.

San Vicente

18th St.

26th St.

Bundy Dr.

Veteran Ave.

WESTWOOD

Santa

Blvd.

Pico

Blvd.

Airdrome

Robertson

J. Paul Getty Museum

1

Montana

SANTA MONICA

Olympic

Sepulveda

Santa   Monica   Fwy.

Blvd.

Washington

Blvd.

CULVER CITY

Wilshire

10

Pico

Ocean

Park

Blvd.

Blvd.

Blvd.

PACIFIC OCEAN

Santa Monica Pier

1

Lincoln Blvd.

VENICE

Venice

TO LOS ANGELES INT'L AIRPORT

Venice Boardwalk

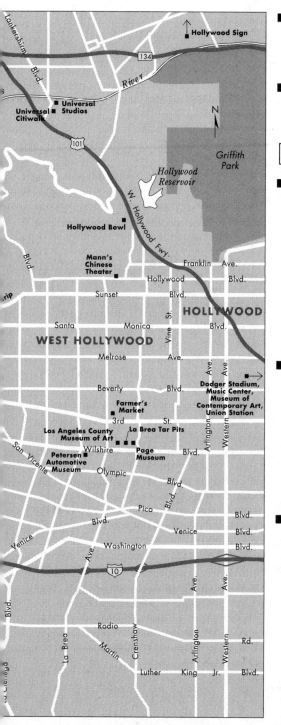

BY TRAIN **Amtrak** (tel. 800/872–7245) serves Los Angeles's famed Union Station, one of the nation's last grand railroad stations.

BY BUS **Greyhound Lines** (tel. 800/231–2222) has many drop-off stations throughout the greater Los Angeles area.

GETTING AROUND

BY CAR You'll save money if you plan your car rental (a must in this town) well in advance of your trip. Because Los Angeles is so spread out, it's impossible to negotiate without a car. The fastest way to traverse the sprawl is usually the freeway system, but at peak hours surface streets often offer the quickest route. Either way, the *Thomas Guide to Los Angeles,* an indispensable spiral-bound book of road maps that's available in bookstores and supermarkets, is the wisest $16 a visiting driver may spend.

BY BUS The city's southern California **RTD** (tel. 213/626–4455) is inexpensive, but getting from one place to another can often take a long time because buses stop frequently while traveling surface streets. If you're staying on the west side of the city, Santa Monica's **Big Blue Bus Line** (tel. 310/451–5444), featured in the 1994 movie *Speed,* offers clean, convenient, and cheap rides; worry only if you see Keanu Reeves on board.

BY LIGHT-RAIL AND TRAIN Train service in Los Angeles has improved, but it is still limited. The **Metro Blue Line** (tel. 213/972–6000) is a light-rail train that runs between downtown's Union Station and Long Beach. Its sister line, the Metro Red Line, is a subterranean train system that's still under construction; one line is operational between downtown and MacArthur Park.

Metrolink (tel. 800/621–7828) connects downtown with four outlying areas: Moorpark, San Bernardino, Santa Clarita, and Riverside. The round-trip fares range from $10 to $15, depending on your destination.

BY TAXI Avoid taxis if you can—cab rides are prohibitively expensive and not very reliable. If you must take a cab, don't expect to hail one on the street. Radio-dispatched cab companies include **L.A. Taxi** (tel. 213/627–7000) and **L.A. Checker Cab** (tel. 213/481–1234). Expect to pay a minimum of $12 for even the shortest distance.

REST STOPS Public rest rooms can be found in Griffith Park in Hollywood, MacArthur Park (6th and Alvarado St.), Roxbury Park (471 S. Roxbury Dr., Beverly Hills), and along the coast at state beaches. Also, look for public rest rooms in such large shopping centers as the Beverly Center (8500 Beverly Blvd., West Hollywood), Arco Plaza (505 S. Flower St., downtown), and Century City Shopping Center (10250 Santa Monica Blvd., Century City).

GUIDED TOURS **Orientation:** Excursions to the city's top attractions are offered by **Advantage Tours and Charter** (Box 480302, Los Angeles 90048, tel. 310/823–0321). **Oskar J's Sightseeing Tours** (4334 Woodman Ave., Sherman Oaks 91423, tel. 818/501–2217 or 800/458–2388) will pick up passengers from local hotels to tour Disneyland, Universal Studios, and other area attractions.

Special Interest: Anyone with a slightly dark sense of humor will enjoy the fascinating outings offered by **Grave Line Tours** (Box 931694, Hollywood 90093, tel. 213/469–4149), which digs up the dirt on notorious suicides and cruises the scenes of various Hollywood murders, scandals, and other crimes in a luxuriously renovated hearse that accommodates six.

EXPLORING

In a city whose residents think nothing of a 50-mile commute to work, visitors have their work cut out for them. Be prepared to put miles on your rental car.

DOWNTOWN AND ENVIRONS L.A.'s **Chinatown** runs a pale second to San Francisco's Chinatown, but it still offers visitors an authentic slice of life, beyond the tourist hokum. The neighborhood, near downtown, is bordered by Yale, Bernard, Alameda, and Ord streets, and the main street is North Broadway, where, every February, giant dragons snake down the center of the pavement during Chinese New Year celebrations.

Little Tokyo, bound by 1st, San Pedro, 3rd, and Los Angeles streets just east of downtown, is the original ethnic neighborhood for North America's largest Japanese American community. Nisei Week (*Nisei* is the name for second-generation Japanese) is celebrated here every August with traditional drums, obon dancing, a carnival, and a parade.

The **Museum of Contemporary Art** houses an impressive permanent collection of international post–World War II modern art. MOCA displays works by Mark Rothko, Franz Kline, and Susan Rothenberg in its red sandstone building, designed by one of Japan's renowned architects, Arata Isozaki. *250 S. Grand Ave., tel. 213/626–6222. Open Tues.– Sun. Admission charged, except Thurs. after 5 PM.*

The **Music Center** has been Los Angeles's cultural center since it opened in 1969. The largest theater on site, the Dorothy Chandler Pavilion, was home to the Academy Awards through 1990. The round building in the center is the Mark Taper Forum, a cozy, 750-seat theater offering experimental theater, often the prelude to a Broadway run. At the north end, the Ahmanson is the venue for many musical comedies. *135 N. Grand Ave., tel. 213/972–7211. Call for tour times. Admission free.*

Union Station, directly east of Olvera Street across Alameda, is one of those quintessentially Californian buildings that has defined Los Angeles to moviegoers around the country in the 1940s. Built in 1939, its Spanish Mission style is a subtle combination of Streamline Moderne and Moorish. The majestic scale of the waiting room is definitely worth a walk over. *800 N. Alameda St., tel. 800/872–7245.*

The **Hollywood Bowl** has hosted summer evening concerts since 1922. The shell accommodates 17,000 spectators, in boxes—where members of high society and "The Industry" often enjoy preconcert alfresco meals—or cement bleachers in the rear. Some prefer the back rows for their romantic appeal and fantastic views of the Hollywood sign. The official season begins in early July and runs through mid-September. *2301 N. Highland Ave., tel. 213/850–2000. Admission charged.*

Hollywood and Vine was once considered the heart of Hollywood. The mere mention of the intersection inspired thoughts of starlets and movie moguls passing by. These days, though, it's far from the action, with the only stars being those on the sidewalk. This corner, once the home of the famous Brown Derby restaurant, is now little more than a place for visitors to get their bearings.

The **Hollywood Sign,** with its 50-foot-high letters, is visible for miles, even on the smoggiest days. To find it, look to the Hollywood Hills that line the northern border of town. It is high on Mount Lee, north of Beachwood Canyon, which is approximately 1 mile east of Hollywood and Vine. The sign was erected in 1923 as a promotional scheme for a real-estate development called Hollywoodland. (The sign originally read "Hollywoodland"; "land" was taken down in 1949.)

Mann's Chinese Theater has finally stuck as the new name for "Grauman's Chinese." The theater opened in 1927 with the premiere of Cecil B. de Mille's *King of Kings,* and continues to show first-run movies. The hand and foot imprints of over 160 screen legends—as well as a noseprint from Jimmy Durante—are immortalized in the famous concrete slabs outside the theater; this courtyard is open free to all visitors wishing to stand in the footsteps of their favorite movie star. You'll have to buy a movie ticket to appreciate the theater's ornate interior, but it's well worth the price: As Mann's Chinese is still commonly used for Hollywood premieres, the theater boasts a state-of-the-art sound system. *6925 Hollywood Blvd., tel. 213/464–8111.*

Sunset Strip was famous in the '50s, as in *77 Sunset Strip,* but it was popular even in the 1930s, when such nightclubs as Ciro's and Mocambo were in their heyday. Drive this windy, hilly stretch of L.A. at least once to be dazzled by the hustle and bustle, the vanity boards (immense billboards touting new movies, new records, new stars), and the glitzy shops and restaurants. At Horn Street, Tower Records (a behemoth of a record store) is open until midnight every day of the week. Wolfgang Puck's world-famous Spago restaurant is also nearby, tucked half a block up the hill on Horn Street.

Universal Studios Tour offers the chance to see what happens behind the movie camera at the world's largest motion picture and TV studio. The tour includes an entertaining tram ride through the studio back lot that lets you catch a glimpses of King Kong and Jaws, as well as experience special-effects technology from the films *Earthquake* and *Backdraft.* Other attractions include "Back to the Future–The Ride," a tribute to comedienne Lucille Ball, and the "Flintstones Show." *100 Universal Plaza, Universal City, tel. 818/508–9600. Open daily. Admission charged.*

Universal CityWalk. Connecting the 18-screen Universal City Cinemas complex to the entrance of the Universal Studios Hollywood tour, this two-block-long pedestrian "Main Street" houses upscale shops and specialty restaurants among a visual feast of outrageously designed storefronts. An upside-down pink 1957 Cadillac crashing through a freeway sign, for example, makes the signage of the Hollywood Freezeway ice-cream parlor tough to miss. Gladstone's seafood restaurant has gone so far as to create a real sandy beach on the CityWalk, replete with palm trees. Taking a load off in the Center Court plaza can provide potential hours of people-watching entertainment, especially when congregations of wet kids play in the jetting waters of an underground sidewalk fountain. At night the CityWalk becomes even more dazzling, the sunlight replaced by the vivid hues from dozens of oversized neon signs, many from the Museum of Neon Art, also located on the CityWalk. *1000 Universal Center Dr., tel. 818/622–4455. Open daily after 11 AM. Admission free.*

MELROSE AVENUE AND THE WILSHIRE DISTRICT

George C. Page Museum of La Brea Discoveries is situated half underground at the tar pits, with a bas-relief on all four sides that depicts life in the Pleistocene era. The museum has a collection of over 1 million Ice Age fossils, as well as reconstructed skeletons of saber-toothed cats, mammoths, and condors. An interactive tar contraption demonstrates just how hard it would be to free oneself from the sticky mess. *5801 Wilshire Blvd., tel. 213/936–2230. Open Tues.–Sun. Admission charged; free 1st Tues. of month.*

The **Los Angeles County Museum of Art** has put the city on the map, artwise. The atrium in the Ahmanson building rises 85 feet to expose four separate levels of galleries; the museum's permanent collection of 20th-century art, in the Robert O. Anderson building, features works by Picasso, Kandinsky, and Jackson Pollock. Allow time for a stroll through the sculpture garden, home to 14 bronze works by 19th-century French master Auguste Rodin. During summer months, LACMA (pronounced LOCK-MA) sponsors its free Friday Night Jazz series, which finds hundreds of Angelinos converging on the museum patio to kick off the weekend with live jazz and refreshments. *5905 Wilshire Blvd., tel. 213/857–6111. Open Tues.–Sun. Admission charged; free 2nd Wed. of month.*

Visit **Melrose Avenue** if you're hunting for the latest fashion trends and quirky gifts. The busiest stretch, with dozens of eclectic shops and bustling restaurants, is between Fairfax and La Brea avenues, recognizable by the many wildly painted storefronts. Grab a front-row seat at one of the many outdoor cafés and soak in the colorful parade of jet-setters, trendsetters, and the occasional green-spiked Mohawk.

Petersen Automotive Museum. Pristinely restored vintage cars sit amidst an architecturally impressive re-creation of the L.A. streetscape of earlier years. Besides displaying vehicles that played a part in Hollywood history, the museum features many of Detroit's most innovative and speedy contraptions, making this collection one of the best of its type in the world. *6060 Wilshire Blvd., tel. 213/930–2277. Open Tues.–Sun. Admission charged.*

BEVERLY HILLS AND WESTWOOD The **Museum of Tolerance,** part of the Simon Wiesenthal Center, first opened its doors in 1993. Through interactive displays, hands-on computer stations, and film and video monitors, the museum aims to teach visitors about the history of racism and bigotry in America, as well as the horrors and lessons of the Shoah, or Nazi Holocaust. The museum's "Outdoor Café" exhibit reenacts a street in 1930s prewar Berlin where idle café chat turns hauntingly to concerns over the impending Nazi takeover of Germany. "Understanding the Los Angeles Riots" is an engaging interactive exhibit that poses thought-provoking questions about social justice and responsible citizenship. Original letters from Anne Frank are on display here, as well as artifacts pulled from Auschwitz and highlights of Simon Wiesenthal's life and work. *9786 W. Pico Blvd., tel. 310/553–8403. Open Sun.–Fri. morning. Admission charged.*

Many shops along **Rodeo Drive,** in Beverly Hills between Santa Monica and Wilshire boulevards, may be familiar to you because they carry the name of their famous designer/owners, such as Ralph Lauren, Armani, Ferragamo, and Gucci. These are very expensive boutiques, but fortunately, browsing is free (and fun). Several nearby restaurants have outside patios where you can sit and sip a drink while watching the fashionable shoppers stroll by.

SANTA MONICA, VENICE, AND THE COAST The **J. Paul Getty Museum,** a re-creation of a 1st-century Roman villa, contains one of the country's finest collections of Greek and

Roman antiquities. The main level houses sculpture, mosaics, and vases. Of particular interest are the 4th-century Attic stelae (funerary monuments) and the Greek and Roman portraits. On the upper level, richly brocaded walls set off paintings and furniture. All major schools of Western art from the late 13th to the late 19th century are also represented in the collection, with an emphasis on Renaissance and Baroque art. Parking reservations are required at the Getty, and there is no way to visit without using the parking lot, unless you are dropped off or take a tour bus. Construction is underway for the second Getty Museum site, an elaborate 24-acre complex high atop the Santa Monica mountains, scheduled to open in 1997. *17985 Pacific Coast Hwy., Malibu, tel. 310/458–2003. Open Tues.– Sun. Admission free.*

Santa Monica Pier is located at the foot of Colorado Avenue and is easily accessible to beachgoers as well as drive-around visitors. Cafés, gift shops, a psychic adviser, bumper cars, and arcades line the truncated pier. During summer months, Thursday evenings are particularly hopping, with bands pouring live music out into the salty sea air. The pier's 46-horse carousel, built in 1922, has seen action in many movie and television shows, most notably the Paul Newman/ Robert Redford film *The Sting. Tel. 310/ 458–8900. Closed Mon. Fee charged for riding carousel.*

Venice Boardwalk, beginning at Washington Street and running north, is the liveliest waterfront walkway in Los Angeles. The mood is something like Hippie Beach Culture meets the Turkish Bazaar. Bodybuilders are busy maintaining their impressive pecs on the adjacent beach, while locals parade their unusual breeds of dogs along the walkway. Beachfront merchants, bikini-clad in-line skaters, and street performers attract all sorts of passersby. While the boardwalk is particularly lively on weekends, it's a haven for muggers after dark; particularly avoid visiting on Sunday night, when the area transforms into turf for local gang wars.

A few hours at **Will Rogers State Historic Park** will help you understand why all of America fell in love with this cowboy/ humorist in the 1920s and 1930s. The two-story ranch house on Rogers's 187-acre estate is a folksy blend of Navajo rugs and Mission-style furniture. Rogers was a polo fan, and in the 1930s his front-yard polo field attracted such friends as Douglas Fairbanks for weekend games. The tradition continues with polo games year-round on Saturday afternoons and Sunday mornings, weather and field conditions permitting. There is a $5 entrance fee to the park, but once you're inside, everything is free. *1501 Will Rogers State Park Rd., Pacific Palisades, tel. 310/ 454–8212. Admission charged.*

HOTELS AND INNS

You can find almost any kind of accommodation in Los Angeles, everything from a simple motel that allows you to park right in front of your room to posh hotels where an attendant will whisk you off to your own private bungalow. Because L.A. is so spread out—it's actually a series of suburbs connected by freeways—it's a good idea to select a hotel not only for its ambience, amenities, and price but also for a location that is convenient to where you plan to spend most of your time. Price categories for double occupancy, excluding 14% tax, are Expensive, over $100; Moderate, $60–$100; and Inexpensive, under $60.

AIRPORT AREA **Airport Park View Hotel.** This contemporary three-story hotel located across from Hollywood Park, near the Forum, and close by the 405 freeway, offers convenient no-frills lodging. *3900 Century Blvd., Inglewood 90303, tel. 310/677–8899 or 800/793–7275, fax 310/677-6900. 178 rooms. Coffee shop, pool, free parking, free cable movies, meeting and banquet facilities. AE, DC, MC, V. Inexpensive.*

Barnaby's Hotel. This charming hotel, with spacious European-style guest rooms, is only 2½ miles south of LAX and only minutes from the beach. The hotel provides free shuttle service to the airport and to nearby shops and restaurants. *3501 Sepulveda Blvd., Manhattan Beach 90266, tel. 310/ 545–8466 or 800/552–5285, fax 310/545– 8621. 128 rooms. Restaurant, pub, lounge, pool, Jacuzzi, botanical gardens, parking, airport service. AE, DC, MC, V. Expensive.*

Crown Sterling Suites Hotel. This Spanish Mission–style all-suites hotel boasts a lovely five-story glass atrium and Japanese koi ponds. Pets are allowed. *1440 E. Imperial Ave., El Segundo 90245, tel. 310/640–3600 or 800/433–4600, fax 310/322–0954. 350 units. Complimentary full breakfast included, restaurant, indoor pool, refrigerators, microwaves, free parking, free airport transportation. AE, DC, MC, V. Moderate– Expensive.*

Red Lion Inn. Just 3 miles north of LAX near Marina del Rey, every room has its own coffeemaker and ironing board. The Culver's Club lounge offers lively entertainment and dancing. *6161 Centinela Ave., Culver City 90203, tel. 310/649–1776, fax 310/649– 6566. 368 rooms. Restaurant, lounge, pool, sauna, health club, free parking. AE, DC, MC, V. Moderate–Expensive.*

BEVERLY HILLS **Beverly House Hotel.** This is a small, elegantly furnished, European-style bed-and-breakfast hotel. Even though it's near busy areas of L.A. (Century City and Beverly Hills shopping), this hotel is quiet and actually quaint. *140 S. Lasky Dr., Beverly Hills 90212, tel. 310/271–2145 or 800/ 432–5444, fax 310/276–8431. 50 rooms. Continental breakfast included, free parking. AE, DC, MC, V. Moderate.*

DOWNTOWN AND ENVIRONS **Best Western Mayfair Hotel.** Centrally located between downtown and Hollywood near the Wilshire commercial district, this hotel has modern-style rooms with color TVs. *1256 W. 7th St., 90017, tel. 213/484–9789 or 800/821– 8682, fax 213/484–2769. 294 rooms. Restaurant, lounge, free parking. AE, DC, MC, V. Moderate.*

Figueroa Hotel. This hotel has managed to keep its charming Spanish style intact as it enters its second half century. *939 S. Figueroa St., 90015, tel. 213/627–8971 or 800/421– 9092, fax 213/689–0305. 285 rooms. Restaurant, coffee shop, lounge, pool, Jacuzzi, airport service, free parking. AE, DC, MC, V. Moderate.*

Holiday Inn L.A. Downtown. This Holiday Inn is near the Convention Center, Museum of Contemporary Art, and Dodger Stadium. A coffeemaker and hair dryer is provided in each room. Pets are allowed. *750 Garland Ave., 90017, tel. 213/628–5242 or 800/628– 5240, fax 213/628–1201. 205 rooms. Restaurant, lounge, pool, free parking. AE, DC, MC, V. Expensive.*

Inn Towne. This three-story hotel is near the convention center and a block from the famous 24-hour Pantry restaurant. *913 S. Figueroa St., 90015, tel. 213/628–2222, fax 213/687–0566. 170 rooms. Restaurant, lounge, pool, free parking. AE, DC, MC, V. Moderate.*

HOLLYWOOD AND NORTH **Hollywood Holiday Inn.** You can't miss this hotel, one of Hollywood's tallest and centrally located to all of the area's major attractions. *1755 N. Highland Ave., 90028, tel. 213/462–7181, fax 213/466– 9072. 470 rooms. Restaurant, coffee shop, pool, coin laundry, parking. AE, DC, MC, V. Expensive.*

Ramada Limited Hollywood. Renovated in 1995, this hotel boasts generous size rooms in the heart of Hollywood, as well as a free deluxe Continental breakfast. *1160 N. Vermont Ave., 90029, tel. 213/660–1788, fax 213/660–8069. 130 rooms. Heated pool, fitness center, sauna, free parking. AE, DC, MC, V. Moderate.*

Safari Inn. Often used for location filming, this hotel offers high standard services and is close to Universal Studios and NBC. Jane's Cucina Italia, off the main lobby, features a variety of pizzas and seafood as well as a full bar. *1911 W. Olive Ave., Burbank 91506, tel. 818/845–8586 or 800/782–4373, fax 818/*

845–0054. 104 rooms. Restaurant, cocktail lounge, pool, Jacuzzi, free parking. AE, DC, MC, V. Moderate.

Sunset Dunes Motel. Across the street from two TV stations, this hotel's lounge teems with local news-media folk and the occasional nervous talk-show guest. *5625 Sunset Blvd., 90028, tel. 213/467–5171, fax 213/ 469–1962. 54 rooms. Restaurant, lounge, free parking. AE, DC, MC, V. Moderate.*

SANTA MONICA AND VENICE **Carmel Hotel.** This charming 1920s hotel, one block from the beach and across the street from the Third Street Promenade (*see* Shopping, *below*), features electric ceiling fans for a tropical feel. *201 Broadway, Santa Monica 90401, tel. 310/451–2469 or 800/445–8695, fax 310/ 393–4180. 110 rooms. Restaurant, room service, parking. AE, DC, MC, V. Moderate.*

Holiday Inn Santa Monica Pier. Convenient to beaches, shopping, restaurants, and of course the Santa Monica Pier, this inn features standard Holiday Inn rooms and amenities. Pets are allowed. *120 Colorado Ave., Santa Monica 90401, tel. 310/451– 0676 or 800/947–9175, fax 310/393–7145. 132 rooms. Restaurant, lounge, pool, coin laundry, gift shop, bike rentals, valet parking. AE, DC, MC, V. Expensive.*

Marina Pacific Hotel & Suites. Facing the Pacific and one of the world's most vibrant boardwalks, this Spanish-style property, with rooms decorated in pink, is nestled among art galleries, shops, and elegant, offbeat restaurants. *1697 Pacific Ave., Venice 90291, tel. 310/452–1111 or 800/421–8151, fax 310/452–5479. 92 rooms. Restaurant, free parking, coin laundry. AE, DC, MC, V. Moderate–Expensive.*

Palm Motel. This quiet, unceremonious hotel has old-fashioned rooms. Guests are offered coffee, tea, and cookies at breakfast. *2020 14th St., Santa Monica 90405, tel. 310/452–3822. 26 rooms. Coin laundry, free parking. MC, V. Inexpensive.*

WEST LOS ANGELES **Century City Inn.** This comfortable, small hotel has rooms with VCRs, refrigerators, microwaves, coffeemak- ers, and complimentary gourmet coffees and teas. Baths boast whirlpool jets and phones. *10330 W. Olympic Blvd., 90064, tel. 310/ 553–1000 or 800/553–1005, fax 310/277– 1633. 45 rooms. Continental breakfast included, parking, laundry service, free video library. AE, DC, MC, V. Moderate–Expensive.*

Century Wilshire Hotel. Rooms in this European-style hotel near the UCLA campus feature tiled baths and homey, English-style decor. Rooms with full kitchens are available, and Continental breakfast is included. *10776 Wilshire Blvd., 90024, tel. 310/474– 4506 or 800/421–7223, fax 310/474–2535. 99 rooms. Pool, free parking. AE, DC, MC, V. Moderate.*

DINING

Once this city was known only for its chopped Cobb salad, Green Goddess dressing, drive-in hamburger stands, and outdoor barbecues; but today Los Angeles is home to some of the best French and Italian restaurants in the United States, as well as a plethora of places featuring international cuisines. Many new, good dining establishments open every week, creating stiff competition among restaurants—thus making L.A. one of the world's least-expensive big cities in which to eat. To save on meals, try the pricier restaurants at lunchtime. Locals tend to dine early, between 7:30 and 9 PM. Make reservations whenever possible.

Price categories per person, excluding 8¼% tax, service, and drinks, are Moderate, $15– $25, and Inexpensive, under $15.

BEVERLY HILLS **California Pizza Kitchen.** Unusual gourmet pizza is dished up in a contemporary setting with fast counter service and a few sidewalk tables. *207 S. Beverly Dr., tel. 310/275–1101. AE, MC, V. Inexpensive–Moderate.*

Ed Debevic's. A fun-loving '50s-style diner, replete with soda jerks and waiters who spontaneously burst into song. *134 N. La- Cienega Blvd., tel. 310/659–1952. AE, MC, V. Inexpensive.*

Grill on the Alley. This wood-paneled and brass-trimmed New York–style steak house offers basic American fare. *9560 Dayton Way, tel. 310/276–0615. AE, MC, V. Moderate.*

DOWNTOWN AND ENVIRONS **Engine Co. #28.** The ground floor of this National Historic Site building was refurbished and refitted to become a very polished, "uptown" downtown bar and grill, and it's been crowded from day one. The reason? All-American food carefully prepared and served with obvious pride. Don't miss the corn chowder and "Firehouse" chili. *644 S. Figueroa St., tel. 213/624–6996. Reservations recommended. AE, MC, V. No lunch weekends. Moderate.*

May Flower Restaurant. This luncheon spot in Chinatown features Cantonese cuisine, including a knockout rice porridge. *800 Yale St., downtown, tel. 213/626–7113. No credit cards. Inexpensive.*

Original Pantry. A tradition since 1924, especially for breakfast, this 24-hour dining spot serves up such down-home fare as ribs and chicken in a modest setting reminiscent of an old-fashioned diner. *877 S. Figueroa St., downtown, tel. 213/972–9279. No credit cards. Moderate.*

Song Hay Inn. This casual Chinese restaurant tucked inside an unobtrusive shopping center offers the best wonton soup in the city. *2720 Griffith Park Blvd., tel. 213/662–0978. MC, V. Inexpensive.*

HOLLYWOOD AND WEST HOLLYWOOD **Angeli.** This Italian cucina serving up fresh gourmet pizzas gets very busy—so make reservations. *7274 Melrose Ave., Hollywood, tel. 213/936–9086. AE, MC, V. Inexpensive.*

Authentic Cafe. Great salads are the mainstay of the multinational menu at this very active but tiny "in" spot. *7605 Beverly Blvd., Los Angeles, tel. 213/939–4626. MC, V. Inexpensive.*

Barney's Beanery. A landmark in town, this lively and very hip hangout serves up heaping portions of all-American favorites. An adjoining bar is packed on weekends, when there are long waits for a game of pool on Bar-

ney's dining-room pool tables. *8447 Santa Monica Blvd., West Hollywood, tel. 213/654–2287. AE, MC, V. Inexpensive.*

Canter's. This is the most authentic Jewish deli in the city, with great blintzes and chicken soup, and no-nonsense waitresses. *419 N. Fairfax Ave., mid-Wilshire, tel. 213/651–2030. MC, V. Inexpensive.*

Chan Dara. This restaurant serves up Thai food at its best, including such dishes as satay and barbecued chicken, in a pleasant and friendly environment. *310 N. Larchmont Blvd., tel. 213/467–1052. AE, MC, V. Inexpensive.*

Hard Rock Cafe. This rock-and-roll memorabilia restaurant sits under two large digital signs ticking away the acres of destroyed rain forest per minute and current world population estimates—only in California. The fare here is mostly burgers and heaping salads. *8600 Beverly Blvd., Beverly Center, West Hollywood, tel. 310/276–7605. AE, MC, V. Inexpensive.*

Johnny Rocket's. This new breed of the '50s diner stirs up action on the lively Melrose strip. Come here for the atmosphere and the Harley-Davidson motorcycles parked outside. *7507 Melrose Ave., West Hollywood, tel. 213/651–3361. D, MC, V. Inexpensive.*

VENICE **Rose Cafe.** Big with the beach breakfast crowd, this bright and casual café also serves up such dinner specialties as a wild-mushroom polenta and mixed-seafood grill. *220 Rose Ave., Venice, tel. 310/399–0711. AE, MC, V. No dinner Sun. and Mon. Inexpensive.*

Sidewalk Cafe. With a great view of Venice Boardwalk at its most active, this is a restaurant where the scenery never gets boring even if the service is lousy. *1401 Ocean Front Walk, Venice, tel. 310/399–5547. AE, MC, V. Inexpensive.*

WEST LOS ANGELES **Beaurivage.** If you're looking for a romantic, seaside restaurant that won't cost you an arm and a leg, come here for such Provençal favorites as mussel soup and roast duckling Mirabelle. *26025*

Pacific Coast Hwy., tel. 310/456–5733. AE, DC, MC, V. No lunch. Moderate.

Orleans. Jambalaya and gumbo, as well as terrific blackened fish and prime rib, are served up in this spacious Westside restaurant, the menu conceived by Cajun master chef, Paul Prudhomme. *11705 National Blvd., West Los Angeles, tel. 310/479–4187. AE, DC, MC, V. Moderate.*

SHOPPING

BEVERLY HILLS **Rodeo Drive** is often compared with such renowned streets as 5th Avenue in New York and the Via Condotti in Rome. Along the several blocks between Wilshire and Santa Monica boulevards, you'll find an abundance of big-name retailers. **Cartier** (370 N. Rodeo Dr., tel. 310/275–4272) offers all manner of gifts and jewelry bearing the double-C logo. **Hammacher-Schlemmer** (309 N. Rodeo Dr., tel. 310/859–7255) is a fabulous place for unearthing those hard-to-find presents for adults that never grew up. Don't explore Beverly Hills without looking around the streets that surround illustrious Rodeo Drive—there are plenty of treasures to be found on those other thoroughfares as well.

CENTURY CITY **Century City Shopping Center & Marketplace** (10250 Santa Monica Blvd., 90067, tel. 310/277–3898) sits among gleaming steel office buildings. Here, in the center of a thriving business atmosphere, is a city kind of mall—open-air. Besides the Broadway and Bullocks, both department stores, you'll find trendy boutiques filled with clothes, jewelry, and gifts. Descend down into Gelson's, L.A.'s foremost gourmet supermarket, to pick up a bite to eat, or have a submarine sandwich at Dive!, Steven Speilberg's restaurant.

DOWNTOWN Although downtown Los Angeles has many enclaves to explore, the bargain hunter should head straight for the bright orange awning of the **Cooper Building** (860 S. Los Angeles St., tel. 213/622–1139). Six floors of small shops, mostly selling women's fashions, offer 50%–70% discounts off retail prices. Grab a free map in the lobby and hit as many of the 50 shops as you can handle. Nearby are myriad discount outlets selling everything from shoes to suits to linens. The stores are open Monday–Saturday 9:30–5:30, Sunday 11–5.

SANTA MONICA In this seaside section of town you'll come across **Montana Avenue,** a stretch of a dozen blocks that has become L.A.'s version of New York City's Columbus Avenue. **A.B.S. Clothing** (1533 Montana Ave., tel. 310/393–8770) sells contemporary sportswear designed in Los Angeles. **Brenda Himmel** (1126 Montana Ave., tel. 310/395–2437) offers fine stationery and gifts. The stretch of Main Street leading from Santa Monica to Venice (Pico Blvd. to Rose Ave.) makes for a pleasant walk, with a collection of quite good restaurants, unusual shops and galleries, and an ever-present ocean breeze.

Santa Monica's newest shopping area is the renovated **Third Street Promenade,** which is closed off to vehicles between Broadway and Wilshire. The Promenade is a great place to take a stroll, browse through some uniquely California shops, and be entertained by professional street performers and inspired bums alike. Casual restaurants and specialty food stands abound, including a nifty fry joint that serves the obvious—fries—with groovy sauces far more exotic than the traditional ketchup. **Z Gallerie** (1426 3rd St. Promenade, tel. 310/394–4685) offers uniquely hip home furnishings and a gallery of mass-produced low-art posters. Also visit the three-story, 44,000 square foot Barnes & Noble (1201 3rd St. Promenade, tel. 310/260–9110), this bookstore chain's largest branch.

WEST HOLLYWOOD West Hollywood, especially **Melrose Avenue,** is great for vintage styles in clothing and furnishings. The 1½ miles of intriguing storefronts and bistros stretch from La Brea to a few blocks west of Crescent Heights; this is definitely one of Los Angeles's hottest shopping areas. **Betsey Johnson** (7311 Melrose Ave., tel. 213/931–4490) offers the designer's vivid women's fashions. **Wound and Wound** (7374 Melrose Ave., tel. 213/653–6703) displays an impressive collection of windup toys that make great inexpensive gifts. **Wacko** (7402 Melrose Ave., tel. 213/651–3811) is a wild space crammed with all manner of inflatable toys, cards, and other semi-useless items that make unforgettable Los Angeles keepsakes.

Mall Culture is alive and well and living in . . . the **Beverly Center** (8500 Beverly Blvd., Los Angeles 90048, tel. 310/854–0071). Bound by Beverly Boulevard, La Cienega Boulevard, San Vicente Boulevard, and 3rd Street, this 7-acre upscale übermall is architecturally inspired by the Pompidou Center in Paris. There are more than 200 shops, including the **Eddie Bauer Home Collection** (tel. 310/289–9809) for home furnishings and furniture. **Following Sea** (tel. 310/659–0592) has trendy eco-friendly gifts. Two stores called **Traffic** offer contemporary clothing for men (tel. 310/659–4313) and women (tel. 310/659–3438). Think again, however, should you be tempted to take in a flick while shopping here—the 13 movie-plex screens are scarcely larger than postage stamps. People-watching should provide ample entertainment, but can also be supplemented with a steaming cappuccino purchased from one of the mall's mobile espresso carts.

Venturing outside the confines of the Beverly Center will unearth some other interesting shops. **Freehand** (8413 W. 3rd St., tel. 213/655–2607) is a gallery-like venue featuring crafts, clothing, and jewelry, created predominantly by California artists; the helpful sales staff will work with any budget to come up with just the right gift.

WESTWOOD **Westwood Village,** near the UCLA campus, is a young and lively area for shopping. The atmosphere in Westwood is invigorating, especially during summer evenings, when there's a movie line around every corner, all kinds of people strolling the streets, and cars cruising along to take in the scene. **Morgan and Company** (1131 Glendon Ave., tel. 310/208–3377) is recommended for

fine jewelry. The **Wilger Company** (10924 Weyburn Ave., tel. 310/208–4321) offers fine men's clothing.

OUTDOOR ACTIVITIES

BIKING Wide bike lanes exist for a 5-mile stretch along San Vicente Boulevard in Santa Monica/Brentwood, and there are paths along the beach from Temescal Canyon to Redondo Beach. In Griffith Park, you can circle the perimeter from Riverside Drive and Los Feliz Boulevard, along the golf course, and north to Burbank in the San Fernando Valley. For rentals, try **Woody's** (3157 Los Feliz Blvd., tel. 213/661–6665) near Griffith Park, and **Spokes and Stuff** (4175 Admiralty Way, Venice, tel. 310/306–3332).

FISHING The nearest freshwater fishing is in the San Bernardino Mountains at Lake Arrowhead and Big Bear Lake, about a two-hour drive from downtown. For fishing information in the area, call 310/590–5132. Saltwater fishing is available off piers in Malibu, Santa Monica, and Redondo Beach. For deep-sea fishing, rent space on a boat from **Redondo Sport Fishing Company** (233 N. Harbor Dr., tel. 310/372–2111). Prices are $20–$30 for half- to ¾-day rentals. Pole rental is about $10, and a one-day fishing license is a little less.

GOLF City courses are economical places to tee off. Try **Rancho Park Golf Course** (10460 W. Pico Blvd., West Los Angeles, tel. 310/839–4900), or Griffith Park's **Harding Golf Course** and **Wilson Golf Course** (tel. 213/663–2555), or the nine-hole **Roosevelt Course** (tel. 213/665–2011).

HIKING For a nice 2-mile hike, check out the picturesque Hollywood Reservoir in the Hollywood Hills, reached by Beechwood Canyon. Griffith Park boasts some 53 miles of hiking trails. Call the **Sierra Club** (3345 Wilshire Blvd., Suite 508, Los Angeles 90010, tel. 213/387–4287) and participate in their guided hikes through the massive park.

HORSEBACK RIDING **Bar "S" Stables** (1850 Riverside Dr., Glendale, tel. 818/242–8443) rents horses for about $15 per hour. Horseback rides through Griffith Park are available at the park's **equestrian center** (480 Riverside Dr., Burbank, tel. 818/840–8401), including a two-hour sunset ride through the park at dusk ending at a Mexican restaurant in Burbank.

SWIMMING **Griffith Park** (3401 Riverside Dr., tel. 213/665–5188) has an Olympic-size public pool open during the summer that is usually overrun with playful children. **West Hollywood Park** (647 N. San Vicente Blvd., tel. 213/848–6534) also has a public pool. The beach communities offer ocean swimming, but expect very cold water nearly year-round and avoid winter swims—there are no lifeguards on duty at that time.

TENNIS **Griffith Park** has courts at Vermont Canyon (2715 N. Vermont, Los Angeles, tel. 213/664–3521), nestled in the Los Feliz Hills near Roosevelt Golf Course, and evening-lit courts at Riverside Drive and Los Feliz Boulevard (3401 Riverside Dr., Los Angeles, tel. 213/661–5318). There's a small court fee in the evenings and on weekends; they're free other times. Farther west, **Plummer Park** (7377 Santa Monica Blvd., West Hollywood, tel. 213/848–6530) has free tennis courts available seven days a week on a first-come, first-served basis.

ENTERTAINMENT

For the most complete listing of weekly events, pick up the current issue of *Los Angeles* magazine or a free copy of the local independent paper, *L.A. Weekly*. The "Calendar" section of the *Los Angeles Times* also offers a wide survey of Los Angeles arts events.

Most tickets can be purchased by phone (with a credit card) from **Ticketmaster** (tel. 213/480–3232), **Good Time Tickets** (tel. 213/464–7383), and **Murray's Tickets** (tel. 213/234–0123).

BALLET AND DANCE The **American Ballet Theater** performs at the **Shrine Auditorium** (665 W. Jefferson Blvd., tel. 213/749–5123) in March, and visiting companies dance at **UCLA Center for the Arts** (405 N. Hilgard Ave., tel. 310/825–2101).

CONCERTS The **Los Angeles Philharmonic** plays the **Music Center** (135 N. Grand Ave., tel. 213/972–7211) October–April; during the summer they perform at the **Hollywood Bowl** (2301 N. Highland Ave., tel. 213/850–2000). For country-and-western music, try the **Palomino Club** (6907 Lankershim Blvd., North Hollywood, tel. 818/764–4010). Admission starts at $3 and goes up depending on who's playing.

FILM The **Vista Theater** (4473 Sunset Dr., tel. 213/660–6639) shows good double bills. The **Royal Theatre** (11523 Santa Monica Blvd., West Los Angeles, tel. 310/477–5581) and the **Rialto** (1023 S. Fair Oaks Ave., South Pasadena, tel. 818/799–9567) show contemporary art films. If you just want to catch Hollywood's latest blockbuster, call 213/777–3456 to find the theater nearest you.

SPECTATOR SPORTS Although the Raiders and the Rams have left town, there are still plenty of pro teams to go around. During baseball season (April–September), the **L.A. Dodgers** play at Dodger Stadium (1000 Elysian Park Ave., tel. 213/224–1500) and the **California Angels** play at Anaheim Stadium (2000 S. Gene Autry Way, tel. 714/254–3000). The **L.A. Lakers** shoot hoops at Great Western Forum (3900 Manchester Ave., Inglewood, tel. 310/419–3182) November–April, while the **L.A. Clippers** take to the court at L.A. Sports Arena (3939 S. Figueroa St., tel. 213/745–0400). From September to April, the **L.A. Kings** (tel. 310/419–3160) hit the ice at the Great Western Forum while the **Mighty Ducks of Anaheim** face off at the Anaheim Arena (2695 E. Katella Ave., tel. 714/704–2500).

THEATER The **John Anson Ford Amphitheater** (2580 Cahuenga Blvd., tel. 213/466–1767), in the Hollywood Hills, is best known for its Summer Nights series, which features music, dance, theater, and opera under the stars. The **James A. Doolittle** (1615 N. Vine St., tel. 213/972–7211) mounts new plays, dramas, comedies, and musicals and offers a few preview nights for each show at dis-counted prices. Another less expensive alternative are equity-waiver theaters, where big-name stars are known to exercise their craft for the love of it. Check area newspapers for these listings.

Mackinac Island
Michigan

Updated by Deborah Hawkins

In 1780, fearful of an American attack during the Revolutionary War, the British moved an entire town from what is now known as Mackinaw City over icy waters to a remote island. The townspeople could never have envisioned that today nearly 1 million visitors flock to Mackinac Island (pronounced "*Mac*-i-naw, like the city) each year to absorb its rich history and natural beauty.

Mackinac Island is between three of the Great Lakes (Huron, Michigan, and Superior) in the Straits of Mackinac, where Huron and Michigan join. The region played a vital role in the northern frontier beginning in the 1600s, when the local Chippewa began trading with the French. (They also supplied the island's name, which is derived from the word "michilimacinac," meaning "great turtle"—Mackinac Island, with its rising bluffs, looks like the back of a turtle.)

In 1815, after more than 30 years of military struggles, Mackinac Island became a permanent part of U.S. territory, and in 1875 Congress created the nation's second national park on the island. The land, which now comprises more than 80% of the island's 2,200 acres, was later transferred to Michigan and became its first state park.

The island's military history and late-1800s culture come to life inside the walls of Fort Mackinac. This historic fort has been painstakingly restored (14 of its buildings are more than 200 years old), and a tour is one of the best ways to learn about the island. Be forewarned, however: The fort's cannons are fired numerous times throughout the day as part of dramatic reenactments, and although islanders have learned to take this in stride, more than a few visitors have been shaken by the blasts.

Aside from these noises, Mackinac Island has a romantic and timeless tranquility about it. Visiting is akin to traveling back about 100 years since no motorized vehicles, other than emergency ones, are allowed on the island. The only signs of the 20th century are the five-seater airplanes that fly over from St. Ignace or the catamaran that ferries you to the island. (There are no bridges leading from the mainland; the beautiful Mackinac Bridge spans the Straits of Mackinac but connects only Michigan's upper and lower peninsulas.)

Main Street winds along the harbor, and although "downtown" is not exactly peaceful, the sounds of clomping horses and bicycle bells add some charm to the noise of the crowds during peak season (July and August). A wealth of tourist attractions, such as fudge shops (an island specialty and source of the name "fudgie," humorously bestowed upon tourists), souvenir and gift shops, galleries, restaurants, bike rentals, and carriage companies, makes this the busiest spot on the island.

The island is only 8.1 miles in circumference, and a paved road circles the perimeter. A bicycle ride or carriage tour around the island is a popular way to enjoy the natural beauty of Mackinac Island State Park, which provides unique limestone formations and breathtaking views of the Great Lakes.

Lake Huron

MACKINAC ISLAND

KEY
- - - Trails
≡ Stairs

North Blodgett Tr.
gar Loaf Rd.
Bicycle Trail
Arch Rock
Rifle Range Rd.
Lime Kiln Tr.
> Tr.
Rifle Range Tr.
Quarry Tr.
Rock Trail
Manitou Trail
Winnebago
South Bicycle Trail Rd.
Arch Rock Rd.
Pottawatomie Rd.
Huron Road
Huron St.
e Rd.
Fort Mackinac
Fort St.
ll Rd.
Market Street
Main Street
Ferry Docks
valk

ESSENTIAL INFORMATION

WHEN TO GO Mackinac Island has an active year-round community of about 600 residents. The tourist season runs from mid-May to mid-October, and most accommodations are booked far in advance for July and August, when temperatures average a delightful 70°. September offers a calmer pace, since crowds have diminished and the weather is still warm (averaging 63°) during the day but cooler at night, wonderful for sound sleeping. Most of the attractions are only open during the warmer tourist season, but snow enthusiasts can still enjoy a quieter visit during cross-country skiing season, mid-December through March. Ferry service stops in January, but a 10-minute airplane flight from St. Ignace is available year-round.

FESTIVALS AND SEASONAL EVENTS **June:** The Annual Lilac Festival showcases the lilac blossoms with a celebration that includes parades and a week of family-oriented activities. **July:** The Stone Skipping Contest, as well as both the Chicago-to-Mackinac Island and Port Huron-to-Mackinac Island yacht races, feature a variety of musical entertainment and great people-watching opportunities. **Labor Day Weekend:** The Annual Mackinac Island Bridge Walk attracts thousands of people including Michigan's governor. Three days of musical entertainment keep the island hopping during the Grand Hotel's Annual Labor Day Jazz Festival (tel. 800/334–7263).

TOURIST OFFICES **Mackinac Island Chamber of Commerce** (Mackinac Island 49757, tel. 800/454–5227 or 906/847–6418, fax 906/847–3571). **Mackinac State Historic Parks Visitors Center** (Main St., Box 370 G, Mackinac Island 49757, tel. 906/847–3328). **Michigan Travel Bureau** (333 S. Capitol, Lansing 48933, tel. 800/543–2937).

EMERGENCIES **Police** and **fire:** Call 906/847–3344. **Ambulance** and **Medical Center:** Call 906/847–3542 for ambulance service and medical referrals; emergency air transportation to a hospital in St. Ignace is available.

ARRIVING AND DEPARTING

BY BOAT Since there is no bridge leading to Mackinac Island and motorized vehicles are banned, three boat companies provide the main access to the island. They operate from the towns located on either side of the bridge linking Michigan's upper and lower peninsulas (Mackinaw City on the lower peninsula and St. Ignace on the upper). The ferry lines are comparable in schedule and price, running daily from mid-April through October and averaging $12 per adult round-trip ticket for the 15-minute ride to the island. An extra charge of $3–$5 is charged to carry a bicycle on board. Parking is free for day visits and just a few dollars for overnight stays.

For those visiting the island in their own boat, complete marina services and overnight docking are available.

BY BUS Greyhound Lines (tel. 800/231–2222) stops on a daily basis in St. Ignace.

BY CAR U.S. 2 traverses the upper peninsula from the Wisconsin border into St. Ignace. Running north through the lower peninsula, I–75 leads directly to Mackinaw City.

BY PLANE Pellston Airport (tel. 616/539–8441) is the closest major airport and is serviced by United and Northwest Airlines. Wolverine Stages (tel. 616/539–8635) provides limousine service from the airport to Mackinaw City (a 20-minute drive), where you can catch a ferry to the island. Great Lakes Air (tel. 906/643–7165) also operates air-taxi service from Pellston and St. Ignace. **Mackinac Island Airport** (tel. 906/847–3231) has a 3,500-foot paved runway capable of handling charter and private aircraft.

GETTING AROUND

Visitors can walk to almost anywhere on the island, but step lightly—the main mode of transportation is horse-drawn carriage, and more than 600 horses inhabit the island during the summer months. A number of carriages are available along Main Street through private tours (hourly fare $50–$90) or "drive yourself" companies (hourly fare $30–$45). Bicycle valets will deliver your luggage from the ferry docks, leaving you to peruse the island at your leisure. Bike rentals are also available at the docks: Average rates are $3.50 an hour for singles and $5 for tandems; day rates vary, as do rental prices for three-speed and all-terrain bikes, strollers, and in-line skates.

GUIDED TOURS The **Chamber's Hotel and Visitor Information Center,** directly across from the ferry docks, has free detailed maps that highlight all the points of interest, hotels, and restaurants, perfect for a self-guided tour. **Carriage Tours, Inc.** (tel. 906/847–3325) also gives two-hour guided tours of the island.

REST STOPS Public rest rooms can be found along all ferry docks as well as at the Information Center, Fort Mackinac, and the State Park Visitors Center.

EXPLORING

Besides the many attractions on Mackinaw Island proper, there are two sites of historical interest on the mainland in Mackinaw City, one of two gateway towns to the island (St. Ignace is the other).

IN MACKINAW CITY **Colonial Michilimackinac.** This National Historical Landmark is a reconstruction of the original mainland fort and surrounding frontier fur-trading village, which was founded in 1715. Guided tours include musket and cannon demonstrations, authentic reenactments of 18th century life, an underground archaeological tunnel, a special children's tour, and more. *Exit 339 to Mackinaw City and follow signs to entrance, tel. 906/847–3328. Open mid-May–mid-Oct., daily. Admission charged.*

Mill Creek. One of the first industrial sites on the Great Lakes, this authentically reconstructed, operating, water-powered sawmill was founded in 1790 and supplied lumber for many of the buildings on Mackinac Island. Hands-on activities and artisans at work are found throughout, and park naturalists are happy to answer questions. The 625-acre park offers groomed nature trails and picnic areas. *3½ mi southeast of Mackinaw City on U.S. 23, tel. 906/847–3328. Open mid-May–mid-Oct., daily. Admission charged.*

ON THE ISLAND **British Landing Nature Center.** On the northwest side of the island, the center has exhibits that provide information about the night of July 16, 1812, when 36 British soldiers and hundreds of their Native American allies landed and captured Fort Mackinac without firing a single shot. *British Landing Rd., tel. 906/847–3328. Open Memorial Day–Labor Day, daily. Admission free.*

Butterfly House. A live butterfly display featuring several hundred butterflies encompassing over 80 different species from throughout the world. *1308 McGulpin St. behind Ste. Anne's Church, tel. 906/847–3972. Open Memorial Day–mid-Oct., daily. Admission charged.*

Fort Mackinac. Costumed interpreters demonstrate 19th-century blacksmithing and stage dramatic reenactments. Also of interest are the exhibits, artifacts, and a Discovery Room for children, where they can try on period clothing and "fire" muskets. Fourteen of the restored buildings are more than 200 years old. *E. Bluff Rd., tel. 906/847–3328. Open mid-May–mid-Oct., daily. Admission charged (includes admission to Beaumont Memorial and Indian Dormitory).*

Grand Hotel. This resort opened in 1887 and is considered one of the world's finest resorts. Visitors may stroll on its 700-foot veranda, visible from the mainland; partake of afternoon tea; meander through its gardens; peruse the historical photo collection; or even swim in the pool, built especially for the 1946 Esther Williams film *This Time for Keeps.* A special guest pass must be purchased by any visitor who is not a hotel guest. *Cadotte Ave., tel. 906/847–3331.*

Indian Dormitory. Native American culture displays and period settings are enhanced by live interpretations of life in the 1800s. *Main St., tel. 906/847–3328. Open Memorial Day–Labor Day. Admission included in Fort Mackinac fee.*

Mackinac Island State Park. A tour of the park, from the spectacular Arch Rock (a natural limestone arch that stands almost 150 feet above the water and 50 feet across) to Wildflower Trail (a small grove of wildflowers that shows a beautiful array of colors) is a must, especially since it encompasses nearly 80% of the island, covering about 1,773 acres. *Open year-round. Admission free.*

Ste. Anne's Church. Still an active parish, the church is an architectural beauty built in 1874. *Main St., tel. 906/847–3507. Open daily. Admission free.*

Stuart House Museum. Housed in millionaire John Jacob Astor's American Fur Company warehouse, built in 1810, the museum depicts the history of the bygone fur-trading era. Robert Stuart was Astor's business manager in the early 1800s and became a social leader on the island. *Market St., tel. 906/847–3783. Open Memorial Day–Labor Day. Admission charged.*

HOTELS AND INNS

Most of the bed-and-breakfasts, inns, and hotels listed below are open only in the summer. Price categories for a double room, usually including Continental breakfast, are Expensive, over $115; Moderate, $75–$115; and Inexpensive, under $75.

EXPENSIVE **Bay View at Mackinac.** When Doug Yoder restored this 1890s house, in his family for over 100 years, he kept the sitting room's tin ceiling and fireplace, the wood moldings, and the wraparound porch with panoramic views of the water. Three luxurious guest suites are new. *Summer: Main St. (Box 448), 49757, tel. 906/847–3295. Winter: 920 Cantrel Ave., Nashville, TN 37215, tel. 615/298–2759. 17 rooms, 3 suites. Ceiling fans, gallery, marine supply store, dock. MC, V. Closed Oct. 15–Apr.*

Grand Hotel. This resort opened in 1887 and has hosted celebrities, dignitaries, and politicians in elegance for decades. A dress code is enforced for guests after 6 PM, and the rates include a daily breakfast and five-course dinner. *Cadotte Ave., tel. 906/847–3331, fax 906/847–3259. 320 rooms, fans, TV available at extra charge. MC, V.*

Metivier Inn. Beautiful landscaping and a white picket fence identify this 1877 home on a quiet section of Market Street, one block from the hustle and bustle of Main Street. Soft colors and antique-style furniture lend the interior a simple, clean, and tasteful look. *Market St. (Box 285), 49757, tel. 906/847–6234. 20 rooms, 1 suite. Woodstove, cable TV. D, MC, V. Closed Nov.–Apr.*

MODERATE-EXPENSIVE Chippewa Hotel. Top-to-bottom renovations have turned this historic hotel into a downtown Victorian charmer with modern amenities and rooms elegantly couched in colorful fabrics and window treatments. Lakeside rooms are much quieter, and 26 luxury suites are available. *Box 250, 49757, tel. 800/241–3341, fax 906/847–6416. 67 rooms. Air-conditioning in lakeside suites, ceiling fans in other rooms, cable TV. AE, D, MC, V. Closed Nov.–Apr., except for 2 wks at Christmas.*

Inn on Mackinac. In the style of the Victorian "painted ladies" of San Francisco, 13 bright colors were used on this inn's exterior. While it lacks the intimacy of some other B&Bs, the attractive rooms, patio, and gardens—and proximity to the center of town—more than make up for its size. *Summer: Main St., 49757, tel. 906/847–6348 or 800/462–2546, fax 906/847–6110. Winter: Box 7706, Ann Arbor, MI 48107, tel. 313/665–5750. 44 rooms. Air-conditioning, TV. MC, V. Closed Oct. 15–Apr.*

Murray Hotel. With multiple on-site dining facilities, a professional staff, and nearly 70 rooms, the Murray has the atmosphere of a quaint 19th-century hotel. Rooms are simply decorated with floral wallpaper borders and wicker furniture. Right in the heart of downtown, the inn gets noise, but it's a great spot for people-watching. *Summer: Main St. (Box*

476), 49757, tel. 906/847–3361 or 800/462–2546, fax 906/847–6110. Winter: Box 7706, Ann Arbor, MI 48107, tel. 313/665–5750. 69 rooms. Air-conditioning, TV. MC, V. Closed Oct. 15–Apr.*

1900 Market Street Inn. Facing Marquette Park, this turn-of-the-century house has beautifully restored woodwork up the wide staircase; everything in each room, from the chintz to the wallpaper, carefully adheres to coordinated color schemes. The inn itself is relatively small, however, with only a sparse lobby and tiny front porch to gather in. *Market St. (Box 315), 49757, tel. 906/847–3811. 7 rooms. Ceiling fans, cable TV. MC, V. Closed Nov.–Apr.*

MODERATE Cloghaun Bed & Breakfast. Baskets of bright red begonias adorn both balconies here; inside, the beamed ceilings, arched windows and doors, and rosebud china set out for breakfast create a relaxed and charming atmosphere. All the rooms interconnect and can be turned into suites if desired. *Summer: Market St. (Box 203), 49757, tel. 906/847–3885. Winter: 15355 Windmill Point Dr., Grosse Pointe Park, MI 48230, tel. 313/331–7110. 10 rooms, 2 share bath. No credit cards. No smoking. Closed Oct. 15–May 15.*

Haan's 1830 Inn. This inn, built around the foundations of a log cabin dragged over the ice from the mainland during the Revolutionary War, was the first B&B on Mackinac Island. The second-story porch is a great place to relax; for more excitement, downtown is a mere three blocks away. *Summer: Huron St. (Box 123), 49757, tel. 906/847–6244. Winter: 1134 Geneva St., Lake Geneva, WI 53147, tel. 414/248–9244. 6 rooms, 2 with bath; 1 suite. Ceiling fans. No credit cards. No smoking indoors. Closed Oct. 15–mid-May.*

INEXPENSIVE Bogan Lane Inn. As the only year-round B&B on Mackinac Island, this inn is perfect for a cross-country-ski weekend or midwinter getaway, and owner Trish Martin's home-baked pastries warm up even the coldest morning. The location just off Huron Street, three blocks from downtown, is close enough for visitors to enjoy the island and far enough for them to hear only the foghorns at night. *Bogan La. (Box 482), 49757, tel. 906/847–3439. 4 rooms share 2 baths. Ceiling fans. No credit cards.*

DINING

Dining on Mackinac Island covers the gamut of every culinary desire, from elegant tableside cooking to pizza parlors and ice-cream shops. Price categories per person, excluding 6% tax, service, and drinks, are Expensive, over $25; Moderate, $15–$25; and Inexpensive, under $15.

EXPENSIVE **Grand Hotel.** The elegant, 100-foot-long lunch buffet served daily includes a large selection of entrées and great desserts; dinner is also served and a dress code is enforced. A discount to offset the cost of a guest pass is applied to any restaurant bill. *Cadotte Ave., tel. 906/847–3331. MC, V.*

MODERATE **Carriage House.** Famous for its fresh Great Lakes whitefish and located in the Iroquois Hotel, this restaurant offers gourmet dining in a relaxed setting overlooking the water. *Main St., tel. 906/847–3321. D, MC, V.*

Pink Pony. Located in the Chippewa Hotel, this is a lively nightspot as well as restaurant with entertainment starting after the dinner hour. The menu covers the gamut for lunch and dinner, but their crab legs and pasta are popular choices. *Main St., tel. 906/847–3341. AE, D, MC, V.*

INEXPENSIVE **Horn's Gaslight Bar.** You can enjoy burgers, steaks, and, at dinner, Mexican food, accompanied by a piano player and dancing. *Main St., tel. 906/847–6154. AE, D, MC, V.*

Pub Oyster Bar. Serves up seafood chowder, homemade pizza, and, of course, oysters. *Main St., tel. 906/847–3454. AE, MC, V.*

SHOPPING

A throng of over 50 souvenir shops, fudge shops, clothing stores, art galleries and T-shirt emporiums crowd a three-block area of Main Street selling everything from plastic back-scratchers and moccasins to hand-crafted pottery and original paintings. The **Loon-Feather** (tel. 906/847–3591) offers a nice balance between popular tourist items and unique treasures. The **Grand Hotel Gift Shops** (Grand Hotel, tel. 906/847–3331) offer elegant shopping and art galleries. **Harry's Old Time Photos** (Main St., tel. 906/847–3522) offers period clothing for a fun "historical" souvenir.

OUTDOOR ACTIVITIES

GOLF The **Grand Hotel** (tel. 906/847–3331) offers a challenging 18-hole course. Call ahead to arrange tee times.

HORSEBACK RIDING **Cindy's Riding Stable** (Market St., tel. 906/847–3572) offers western-style riding on marked trails only. Beginners are welcome, but the age limit is eight.

ENTERTAINMENT

Entertainment and nightlife is mild on the island compared to a city, but the people-watching and sunsets make up for it. Some of the local pubs may provide music at night and the **Mission Point Theatre** (Main St., tel. 906/847–3312) features weekly new movie releases during the summer months.

The Maine Coast
Maine

Updated by Jeanne Cooper

he coast of Maine conjures up images of stern gray rocks, crashing surf, austere spruce-fringed bays, and horizons broken by distant blue islands. While you don't have to hunt very hard to find these, you'll find that Maine's coast presents other, very different images as well.

South of the rapidly gentrifying town of Portland, you'll find long stretches of hard-packed white-sand beach bordered by nearly unbroken ranks of beach cottages, motels, and oceanfront restaurants. Kennebunkport, now world famous because of summer resident George Bush, is a classic old New England port town of stately white clapboard houses, velvety green lawns, and rambling Victorian summer "cottages."

Just north of Portland you'll come upon still another Maine coast scene: the shopping mecca of Freeport, where some 3.5 million shoppers a year descend on L.L. Bean and the more than 100 upscale outlets that have grown up in its shadow.

The quick changes continue as you move "downeast": You'll pass picturesque Wiscasset and Boothbay Harbor, one of the yachting capitals of New England and the perfect place to jump on a cruise boat; Camden, the premier town on Penobscot Bay and the headquarters of the East Coast's largest windjammer fleet; and finally Mount Desert Island, where you'll find the highest mountain on the East Coast, the nation's second most popular national park, and some of the most glorious scenery anywhere in the world.

And so it goes. If you search long enough, you can find just about anything on Maine's immense coastline—except warm water. The icy water temperature takes some getting used to, but true devotees wouldn't want it any other way.

ESSENTIAL INFORMATION

WHEN TO GO In July, the hottest month of the year, maximum temperature averages 76°. Mainers will tell you that fog is their air-conditioning: It does keep things cool in the summer, but it can also obstruct views and make sailing impossible. The ocean moderates winter's chill (January's average high temperature is 31°), but the damp can make you *feel* the cold bitterly.

Although July and August are peak season, Maine is at its best after Labor Day: Rates drop, crowds thin out, foggy days are less common, and mosquitoes vanish. Leaves begin turning in late September, and temperatures usually remain mild into October. Spring in Maine tends to be rather damp and chilly; many seasonal attractions and businesses don't open until Memorial Day or even mid-June, so be sure to call ahead.

FESTIVALS AND SEASONAL EVENTS Early Aug.: **Maine Lobster Festival,** Rockland, is a public feast held on the first weekend of the month (tel. 207/596–0376). The **Maine Festival,** the state's premier arts fair, brings together musicians, artists, and craftspeople for four days in Brunswick (tel. 207/772–9012).

BARGAINS Lobsters, as one might expect, are far cheaper in Maine than just about anywhere else in the country. Also, roadside stands offer blueberries and other fresh produce, often using an honor system for payment, at very low prices.

Factory outlets, concentrated in Kittery, Wells, Freeport, and Ellsworth, and sprinkled along Coastal Route 1, are your best bet for bargain sportswear, shoes, and housewares. Weekend yard sales (a popular summer pastime), church bazaars, and town fairs are a treasure trove for low-priced antiques and handmade crafts; check the local paper or small-town stores for information.

TOURIST OFFICES Maine Publicity Bureau (Box 2300, Hallowell 04347, tel. 207/623–0363 or 800/533–9595). Acadia National Park (Box 177, Bar Harbor 04609, tel. 207/288–3338). Bar Harbor Chamber of Commerce (Box BC, Cottage St., Bar Harbor 04609, tel. 207/288–3393 or 800/288–5103). Boothbay Harbor Region Chamber of Commerce (Box 356, Boothbay Harbor 04538, tel. 207/633–2353). Freeport Merchants Association (Box 452, Freeport 04032, tel. 207/865–1212). Kennebunkport Chamber of Commerce (Box 740, Kennebunk 04043, tel. 207/967–0857). Greater Portland Chamber of Commerce (145 Middle St., Portland 04101, tel. 207/772–2811).

EMERGENCIES Maine State Police (Augusta, tel. 800/452–4664; Gray, tel. 800/482–0730; Houlton, tel. 800/924–2261; Orono, tel. 800/432–7381). Police, fire, and ambulance: Dial 911 in most urban areas; 911 statewide service is expected by 1997. Doctors: Kennebunk Walk-In Clinic (Rte. 1N, tel. 207/985–6027). Penobscot Bay Medical Center (Rte. 1, Rockland, tel. 207/596–8000).

ARRIVING AND DEPARTING

BY PLANE Maine's major airports are Portland International Jetport (tel. 207/774–7301) and Bangor International Airport (tel. 207/947–0384); each has scheduled daily flights by major U.S. carriers. Bar Harbor Airport, 8 miles northwest of Bar Harbor, is served by Colgan Air (tel. 207/667–7171).

BY CAR AND BUS I–95 is the fastest route to and through Maine from coastal New Hampshire and points south, but it turns inland at Brunswick. The often scenic Route 1 parallels the coast from Kittery to Machias.

GETTING AROUND

BY CAR AND BUS The most practical means of touring the coast is by car. *Maine Map and Guide,* available free from the Maine Publicity Bureau, is useful. Greyhound Lines (tel. 800/231–2222) and Vermont Transit (tel. 207/772–6587) connect towns in Maine with cities in New England. Concord Trailways (tel. 800/639–3317) operates express buses from Boston to Portland and Bangor, as well as along some coastal routes.

REST STOPS Both the Kittery Information Center (off northbound I–95) and the Yarmouth Information Center (off I–95 at exit 17) have rest rooms as well as extensive tourist information about the entire state. You can exit from here onto coastal Route 1. On Route 1, midway between Wiscasset and Newcastle, is one of the state's prettiest rest stops overlooking Sherman Lake, with rest rooms. On the approach to Acadia National Park, just south of Trenton, there is an information area with rest rooms on Thompson Island on Route 3.

GUIDED TOURS Golden Age Festival (5501 New Jersey Ave., Wildwood Crest, NJ 08260, tel. 609/522–6316 or 800/257–8920) offers a four-night bus tour geared to senior citizens, with outlet shopping, a Boothbay Harbor boat cruise, and stops at Pemaquid Point, Mount Battie, and Acadia National Park.

EXPLORING

Those interested in history and architecture should stop at York, Kennebunkport, Portland, and Castine—a comfortable three- or four-day trip. Nature enthusiasts will want to bypass the crowded southern coast and visit one of the outer islands before hitting the trails of Acadia National Park.

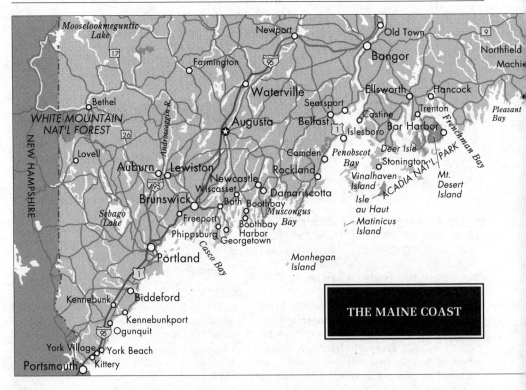

THE MAINE COAST

The Yorks, a cluster of villages along coastal Route 1A (just east of Route 1), contain the **York Village Historic District,** where a number of 18th- and 19th-century buildings have been restored and maintained by the Old York Historical Society. Stop at the Jefferds Tavern to buy admission tickets for all buildings. *Rte. 1A, tel. 207/363–4974. Open mid-June–Sept., Tues.–Sun. Admission charged.*

Ogunquit, due north of York on Route 1, is a resort town with a good stretch of sand beach. Perkins Cove, a neck of land connected to the mainland by a pedestrian drawbridge, is a picturesque jumble of seabeaten fish houses restored as shops and restaurants. You can walk from here to the Marginal Way, a mile-long footpath that hugs the shore.

Kennebunkport, reached by making a right turn off Route 1 onto Route 9 at Cozy Corners, is a town to stroll through. Don't miss

Dock Square, the busy town center, with its shops and galleries, and the grand ship captains' homes along Maine, Pearl, and Green streets. Drive up Ocean Avenue past Victorian seaside mansions to Cape Arundel (you'll glimpse the entrance to former president Bush's house on the ocean side). Nearby Kennebunk is a little calmer in season, and closer to the sandy stretch of Kennebunk Beach.

Portland, Maine's largest city, can be reached by taking Exit 6A off I–95 onto Route 295 and then taking Exit 5 onto Congress Street, which runs the length of the city. Part of a growing arts district, the distinguished **Portland Museum of Art** has a strong collection of seascapes by such masters as Winslow Homer (on view summer only), John Marin, and Andrew Wyeth, plus works by Renoir, Monet, and Picasso. *7 Congress Sq., tel. 207/ 775–6148. Open Tues.–Sun. (and Mon. July– Columbus Day). Admission charged; free Thurs. night.*

Campobello
Island

Grand Manan
Island

Cutler

onesport

N

NOVA
SCOTIA

CANADA

ATLANTIC OCEAN

0   40 miles

0   60 km

Zwicker. There's also an apprentice shop on the extensive grounds where you can watch boatbuilders at work. Boat trips on the Kennebec River are also available. *243 Washington St., Bath, tel. 207/443–1316. Admission charged.*

Wiscasset, north of Bath, is a pretty village where you can take the scenic **Maine Coast Railroad** on a 1½-hour round-trip to Newcastle, followed by a 1½-hour sail down the Sheepscott River on a 51-foot wooden boat. *Water St., Wiscasset, tel. 207/882–8000 or 800/795–5404. Open Memorial Day–Labor Day, daily; weekends in fall. Admission charged.*

Due south on Route 27 is **Boothbay,** home of the **Boothbay Railway Village,** where you can ride 1½ miles on a narrow-gauge steam train through a re-creation of a turn-of-the-century New England village to an antique auto display. *Rte. 27, Boothbay, tel. 207/633–4727. Open mid-June–mid-Oct., daily. Admission charged.*

Boothbay Harbor, a couple miles south on Route 27, is a busy town that's worth wandering through. Park at the waterfront, stroll along Commercial and Wharf streets, and leave time for a harbor cruise. Return to Route 1 and continue northeast through Newcastle and Rockland.

Camden, 8 miles north of Rockland on Route 1, is the famous resort town "where the mountains meet the sea"—the mountains being the Camden Hills (a 6,000-acre state park), the sea being Penobscot Bay. The hike up to the summit of Mount Battie in Camden Hills State Park is mildly strenuous.

From Camden, continue north and east on Route 1 through tiny Lincolnville, where you can catch the ferry to Isleboro, bustling Belfast, and onto **Searsport,** the antiques capital of Maine and home of the **Penobscot Marine Museum,** which includes a captain's house, real and model ships, and art exhibits. *Church St. at Rte. 1, Searsport, tel. 207/548–2529. Open Memorial Day–Oct. 15, daily. Admission charged.*

Portland's **Old Port Exchange** is a bustling waterside district of late-19th-century brick warehouses renovated with shops, galleries, and restaurants. Wander down Exchange, Union, and Fore streets, and end up at Custom House Wharf off Commercial Street. Casco Bay Lines (tel. 207/774–7871) offers a variety of cruises and mail-boat ferry service to Portland's many islands from its terminal at Commercial and Franklin streets.

Freeport, on Route 1, 15 miles northeast of Portland, is the home of 24-hour-a-day retailer **L. L. Bean** (Rte. 1, tel. 800/341–4341) along with dozens of outlets selling designer clothes, shoes, housewares, and toys at marked-down prices.

Bath, 19 miles north on Route 1, has been known for shipbuilding since 1607. The town's **Maine Maritime Museum** offers nautical exhibits, including ship models, journals, photographs, artifacts, and the 142-foot Grand Banks fishing schooner *Sherman*

Castine is a picturesque village 15 miles southwest of Route 1 near Bucksport. Battled over by the English, French, and Dutch in the 17th century, this town is filled with historic markers, including ruins of a British fort. It's also home to the Maine Maritime Academy, which often brings special ships to the harbor.

East of Penobscot Bay, Acadia is the informal name for the area that includes Mount Desert Island and its surroundings: Blue Hill Bay; Frenchman Bay; and Ellsworth, Hancock, and other mainland towns. **Bar Harbor,** 15 miles south of Ellsworth on Route 3, is the most popular spot on Mount Desert Island for dining and shopping. Hotels, restaurants, and shops are clustered along Main, Mount Desert, and Cottage streets. Nearby, **Acadia National Park** attracts more than 4 million visitors a year and offers 34,000 acres of woods and mountains, lakes and shore, footpaths for hiking, and carriage paths for biking or cross-country skiing. Stop at the visitor center at Hulls Cove and then pick up the Park Loop Road. Good day hikes include the Great Head Loop, a 1½-mile trail from Sand Beach around a rocky promontory above the sea; the 3-mile loop trail around mountain-ringed Jordan Pond in the center of the park; and the 2½-mile hike up Penobscot and Sargent mountains from Jordan Pond.

THE NATURAL WORLD Wildlife on the coast includes harbor seals, guillemots, common eiders, loons, and the occasional peregrine falcon and bald eagle, as well as ubiquitous herring gulls, cormorants, and black-backed gulls. Puffins nest on Matinicus Rock, off the outer island of Matinicus (the ferry leaves from Thomaston), which is itself a marvelous place for bird-watching, as is Monhegan Island (the ferry leaves from Port Clyde). Reid State Park, south of Bath on Route 127, is an ideal place to take in the variety of Maine's coastal habitats, from salt marsh to sand dune.

HOTELS AND INNS

Bed-and-breakfasts and Victorian inns have joined the family-oriented motels of Ogun-quit, Boothbay Harbor, Bar Harbor, and the Camden region. Kennebunkport has the greatest variety of accommodations on the south coast, although prices tend to run high. You'll find better value in towns a bit off the track, such as Bath and Belfast. Rates often drop sharply during the off-season. Price categories for double occupancy, excluding 7% tax, are Expensive, $80–$100; Moderate, $60–$80; and Inexpensive, under $60.

BAR HARBOR **Wonder View Motor Lodge.** While the rooms are standard motel accommodations, this place is distinguished by its extensive grounds, views of Frenchman Bay, and the location opposite the Bluenose ferry terminal. Pets are accepted. *Rte. 3, Box 25, 04609, tel. 207/288–3358 or 800/341–1553. 82 rooms with bath. Dining room, pool. AE, MC, V. Moderate–Expensive.*

BATH AREA **Fairhaven Inn.** This cedar-shingled house, circa 1790, has airy guest rooms furnished with handmade quilts and four-poster beds. A lavish breakfast is included. *RR 2, Box 85, North Bath 04530, tel. 207/443–4391. 7 rooms, 5 with private bath. Hiking and cross-country ski trails. MC, V. Inexpensive–Moderate.*

BELFAST **Londonderry Inn.** This restored 1803 farmhouse, just a mile from Belfast, offers spotless, cheery, country-style rooms with views of fields and full country breakfasts. *Star Rte. 80, Box 3, 04915, tel. 207/338–3988. 5 rooms, with shared bath. AE, D, MC, V. Inexpensive.*

BOOTHBAY HARBOR **Brown's Wharf.** All the rooms have private balconies facing the water in this centrally located motel where fishermen can tumble right out of bed and onto a charter boat. *Atlantic Ave., 04538, tel. 207/633–5440. 70 rooms. Restaurant, lounge, docking facilities. AE, MC, V. Expensive.*

The Pines. This motel, just a mile from the center of town, offers more seclusion, more space, and far better value than the cluster of motels on and around the harbor. *Sunset Rd., Box 693, 04538, tel. 207/633–4555. 29 rooms with bath. Pool, playground, tennis court. AE, D, MC, V. Inexpensive–Moderate.*

CAMDEN **Maine Stay.** This intimate bed-and-breakfast backs right up to a state park and is also within walking distance of Camden's harbor and shops. The enthusiastic innkeepers will help plan your excursions along the coast. *22 High St. (U.S. Rte. 1), Camden 04843, tel. 207/236–9636. 8 rooms, 6 with private bath. MC, V. Moderate–Expensive.*

Windward House. A choice bed-and-breakfast at the edge of town, this Greek Revival house of 1854 features rooms with romantic furnishings. The hospitality is attentive and gourmet breakfasts may include quiche, apple puff pancakes, or peaches-and-cream French toast. *6 High St., 04843, tel. 207/ 236–9656. 7 rooms with bath, 1 suite. AE, MC, V. Expensive.*

CASTINE **Castine Inn.** This pretty, pale-yellow Victorian inn with extensive gardens is steps from Castine's small harbor. The dining room, decorated with whimsical murals of the historic town, is known for savory breakfasts (free to guests) and for gourmet but moderately priced dinners. *Box 41, Main St., Castine 04421, tel. 207/326–4365, fax 207/326–4570. 20 rooms, 3 suites, with bath. Restaurant, lounge. MC, V. Moderate–Expensive.*

KENNEBUNKPORT **Green Heron.** Right on Ocean Avenue, a mile from busy Dock Square, this unpretentious inn near the beach on a river cove, provides its loyal clientele with rustic hospitality and hearty breakfasts. *Box 2578, 04046, tel. 207/967– 3315. 10 rooms and small cottage, all with bath. No credit cards. Moderate–Expensive.*

Waldo Emerson Inn. A handsome 18th-century shipbuilder's mansion, this inn is in Kennebunk, near the famous Wedding Cake house. It radiates warmth with cozy antique furnishings (a quilt store is on the premises) and working fireplaces. A fresh-baked breakfast is included. *108 Summer St., Kennebunk 04043, tel. 207/985–4250. 4 rooms with bath. AE, MC, V. Moderate–Expensive.*

PORTLAND **Hotel Everett.** In Portland's arts district, this homey, European-style hotel has simple accommodations and low rates. It's within walking distance of several major attractions. *51A Oak St., 04101, tel. 207/ 773–7882. 49 rooms, 5 with private bath. MC, V. Inexpensive.*

Inn at St. John. At the grittier, lower end of downtown on Congress Street, a short drive or walk to most tourist sites, this renovated inn offers clean, European pensionlike lodging for travelers on a budget. A breakfast of coffee, juice, and pastry is included. *939 Congress St., 04102, tel. 207/773–6481, fax 207/773–8412. 30 rooms, 15 with private bath. Laundry, bike storage, free parking. AE, D, DC, MC, V. Inexpensive.*

SEARSPORT **Captain Albert Vinals Nickels Inn.** Set back from busy Route 1 with 6½ acres of quiet Penobscot Bay waterfront, this impressive Victorian bed-and-breakfast includes a restored ballroom, a kitchen that can serve 100, and spacious public rooms. One large suite has a library and sweeping bay view. *Rte. 1, Box 38, Searsport 04974, tel. 207/548–6691 or 800/343–5001. 9 rooms, 4 with private bath. AE, MC, V. Inexpensive–Expensive.*

SOUTHWEST HARBOR **Seawall Motel.** This plain but clean two-story inn, on the quiet side of Mount Desert Island, sits a few feet from the seawall and about 1½ miles from Southwest Harbor. It's also close to the park trails. The dining room overlooks the ocean and the second-floor rooms also have great views. *Rte. 102A, Manset 04656, tel. 207/ 244–9250. 24 rooms with bath. Restaurant. AE, D, MC, V. Inexpensive–Moderate.*

YORK **Dockside Guest Quarters.** On an 8-acre private island in the middle of York Harbor, the lodgings include rooms in the main house, with country decor, and multiunit modern cottages, with harbor and ocean views. Continental breakfast is included; the airy waterfront restaurant specializes in seafood. *Box 205, York 03909, tel. 207/363– 2868, fax 207/363–1977. 13 rooms (8 suites), 11 with private bath. Restaurant, cruises. MC, V. Moderate–Expensive.*

MOTELS

MODERATE **Beachwood Resort** (272 Mills Rd.; Rte. 9, Kennebunkport 04046, tel. 207/967–2483). 112 rooms; pool; tennis court. **Day's Inn Kittery/Portsmouth** (2 Gorges Rd.; Rte. 1 Bypass, Kittery 03904, tel. and fax 207/439–5555). 108 rooms; restaurant, lounge, pool. **Highbrook Motel** (94 Eden St., Bar Harbor 04609, tel. 207/288–3591 or 800/338–9688, fax 207/288–3678). 26 rooms. **Navigator Motor Inn** (520 Main St., Rockland 04841, tel. 207/594–2131, fax 207/594–7763). 82 rooms; restaurant, lounge, across from ferry to Vinalhaven and North Haven. **Snow Hill Lodge** (Rte. 1, Box 550, Lincolnville Beach 04849, tel. 207/236–3452). 30 rooms.

INEXPENSIVE **Admiral's Ocean Inn** (Rte. 1, Box 99A, Belfast 04915, tel. 207/338–4260, fax 207/338–2707). 18 rooms and 2 suites; Continental breakfast included, pool, pets permitted. **Coastline Inn** (80 John Roberts Rd., South Portland 04106, tel. 207/772–3838 or 800/470–9494, fax 207/772–4238). 54 rooms, Continental breakfast included. **Gull Motel** (Box 811, Belfast 04915, tel. 207/338–4030). 14 rooms. **Moorings Inn** (Box 744, Southwest Harbor 04679, tel. 207/244–5523 or 207/244–3210). 19 rooms and 3 cottages; bicycles, canoes, outdoor gas grill. **Water Crest** (Box 37, Rte. 1, Wells 04090, tel. 207/646–2202, fax 207/646–7067 or 207/646–4826). 19 rooms and 43 cottages; playground, shuffleboard, picnic tables.

CAMPGROUNDS

The three campgrounds within Acadia National Park—Blackwoods and Seawall on Mount Desert Island and the Duck Harbor camping area on Isle au Haut—are extremely popular during the summer months. You can reserve ahead at Blackwoods for June 15–September 15 by contacting Mistix (Box 85705, San Diego, CA 92138, tel. 800/365–2267). Seawall accepts no reservations. You can reserve a lean-to site at Isle au Haut by mail only; write Acadia National Park (Box 177, Bar Harbor 04609) after April 1 for the application.

Blackwoods. Set in a dense grove of spruce and fir on the east side of the island, Blackwoods is the largest of the in-park campgrounds and the closest to the busy Park Loop Road. *Acadia National Park, Box 177, Bar Harbor 04609, tel. 207/288–3338. 299 RV and tent sites, no hookups; flush toilets, picnic tables, barbecue areas. Maximum stay 14 nights.*

Duck Harbor. Accessible only by mail boat, the rugged and remote Isle au Haut offers camping at five Adirondack-style lean-tos in a spruce forest a few yards from the steep, rocky shore of Duck Harbor. *Acadia National Park, Box 177, Bar Harbor 04609, tel. 207/288–3338. 5 lean-tos, no tent or RV sites, no hookups; outhouses only, picnic tables, barbecue areas. Maximum stay 3 nights.*

Seawall. On the quieter west side of Mount Desert Island, Seawall is removed from the worst of summertime congestion. The dramatic Seawall rocky beach and picnic area are a short walk away, and you can drive easily to the town of Southwest Harbor. *Acadia National Park, Box 177, Bar Harbor 04609, tel. 207/288–3338. 212 RV and tent sites, no hookups; flush toilets, picnic tables, barbecue areas. Maximum stay 14 nights.*

DINING

Dining in Maine means lobster; virtually every harbor town has a stand selling lobster rolls (a toasted sandwich) and a lobster pound where you can crack open the boiled creature by yourself. Shrimp and crab are also caught in the cold waters off Maine, and they are often served in imaginative combinations with lobster, haddock, salmon, and swordfish. Price categories per person, excluding 6% tax, service, and drinks, are Moderate, $15–$25, and Inexpensive, under $15.

BAR HARBOR **Jordan Pond House.** Oversize popovers and tea are a tradition at this rustic restaurant in Acadia National Park. The dinner menu features lobster stew and fisherman's stew. *Park Look Rd., tel. 207/276–3316. AE, D, MC, V. Moderate.*

Lompoc Cafe. Middle Eastern and vegetarian options offer a respite from seafood at this pleasantly low-key brew pub. Beer enthusiasts will want to try the Coal Porter. *36 Rodick St., tel. 207/288–9392. D, MC, V. Inexpensive.*

BATH **Kristina's Restaurant and Bakery.** This old frame house is home to some of the finest baked goods on the coast as well as to New American cuisine dinners of fresh seafood and grilled meats. *160 Centre St., tel. 207/442–8577. D, MC, V. Inexpensive–Moderate.*

BOOTHBAY HARBOR **Andrew's Harborside.** The harbor view and outdoor deck overshadow the standard offerings of fried and broiled seafood at this family-oriented eatery. *8 Bridge St., tel. 207/633–4074. AE, DC, MC, V. Moderate.*

CAMDEN **Cappy's Chowder House.** Touristy, sometimes raucous, but always cheerful, Cappy's serves burgers, chowders, and seafood in a nautical setting jam-packed with couples, families, visitors, and locals. *1 Main St., tel. 207/236–2254. No reservations. MC, V. Open for 3 meals year-round. Moderate.*

CASTINE **Bah's Bake House.** The porch overlooks the harbor at this bakery and coffee shop, which offers hearty sandwiches and soups, and a variety of other items including a delicious Thai noodle salad. Don't forget to try one of their fresh pastries. *Water St., tel. 207/326–9510. MC, V. No dinner. Inexpensive.*

Castine Inn. Decorated with a town mural and overlooking a garden porch, this inn's restaurant is open to the public for breakfast and dinner. The menu features traditional New England fare—the plump crab cakes are superlative, but you can't go wrong on any order. *Main St., tel. 207/326–4365. MC, V. No lunch. Moderate.*

FREEPORT **Harraseeket Lunch.** Escape Freeport's shopping frenzy at this no-frills lobster pound offering seafood baskets and lobster dinners, served indoors or out. *Main St., South Freeport, tel. 207/865–4888. No credit cards. Inexpensive.*

KENNEBUNKPORT **Alisson's.** A bright family restaurant in the heart of town, Alisson's has soups, salads, and chicken dishes plus the usual seafood and a generous lobster roll. *5 Dock Sq., tel. 207/967–4841. AE, D, MC, V. Inexpensive.*

OGUNQUIT **Hurricane.** It may be tough to get a table without reservations at this gourmet restaurant with an ambitious chef, but it's well worth a try. Lobster gazpacho or roasted corn and tomato soup paired with one of the "small plates," such as chicken satay or salmon napoleon, makes a great light meal. Don't miss the spectacular ocean view. *Perkins Cove, tel. 207/646–6348. Reservations advised. AE, D, DC, MC, V. Moderate.*

Ogunquit Lobster Pond. Select your lobster live, then dine under the trees or in the rustic dining room of the log cabin. Steamed clams, chicken, and children's fare are also available. *Rte. 1, tel. 207/646–2516. AE, MC, V. Moderate.*

PORTLAND **Cafe Uffa!** Open for dinner and Sunday brunch, this funky favorite in the city's arts district offers seafood and innovative vegetarian dishes—both often mesquite grilled and seasoned with chiles. Brunch includes breakfast items accompanied by thick, chewy bread. *190 State St. (at Congress St.'s Longfellow Sq.), tel. 207/775–3380. MC, V. No lunch. Inexpensive.*

Hu-Shang Exchange. When the urge for Chinese food strikes, come to this softly lit, soothing restaurant for both mild and spicy specialties such as lamb with ginger and scallions or moo shu shrimp. *29–33 Exchange St., tel. 207/772–1000. AE, D, MC, V. Moderate.*

Madd Apple Cafe. Inside the Portland Performing Arts Center you'll find this cozy bistro. Here, Southern flair is given to New England seafood—shrimp cakes with Louisiana remoulade and vegetable *boudin. 23 Forest Ave., tel. 207/774–9698. AE, MC, V. Closed last 2 wks in June. No lunch. Moderate.*

WALDOBORO **Moody's Diner.** This big, bustling, roadside diner serves fresh-baked pies and home-cooked standards in a setting of neon, chrome, and linoleum. *Rte. 1, tel. 207/832–5362. No credit cards. Inexpensive.*

SHOPPING

FACTORY OUTLETS The success of **L.L. Bean** (95 Main St., Rte. 1, tel. 800/341–4341) has fostered the growth of a great retail marketplace in the Freeport area, with scores of factory outlets. Notable outlets in the area include **Calvin Klein** (11 Bow St., tel. 207/865–1051), the **Patagonia Outlet** (9 Bow St., tel. 207/865–0506), and **Mikasa Store** (31 Main St., tel. 207/865–9441). Kittery, Wells, and Ellsworth also have a concentration of outlets.

FLEA MARKETS AND ANTIQUES Searsport hosts a number of large flea markets throughout the summer months—and you'll also find some along the busy stretches of Route 1. Kennebunkport, Wells, and Searsport are the best places to go for antiques; west of Ellsworth off Route 1 is the immense **Chicken Barn** (tel. 207/667–7308), which has thousands of antiques, collectibles, and used books.

OUTDOOR ACTIVITIES

BEACHES Maine's ocean temperatures are slightly warmer south of Portland, but most people still find the water too cold for prolonged swimming. York, Ogunquit, Wells, Kennebunk Beach, and Old Orchard Beach have long sandy beaches open to the public.

BIKING The back roads around Kennebunkport, Camden, and Deer Isle are well suited to biking, as are the carriage paths of Acadia National Park. The **Maine Publicity Bureau** (tel. 207/623–0363 or 800/533–9595) includes a statewide list of bike rentals in its tourist package.

BOATING AND SAILING Motorboats and sailboats may be rented at most towns on the coast, including Kennebunkport, Boothbay Harbor, Rockland, Camden, and Bar Harbor. You can rent canoes or kayaks for trips in the Acadia region at Bar Harbor and Ellsworth. Organized boating excursions depart from Portland and Boothbay harbors.

FISHING **Maine Department of Inland Fisheries and Wildlife** (State House Station 41, Augusta 04333, tel. 207/287–2871) has the latest information on lake and river fishing regulations and seasons; **Marine Resources** (State House Station 21, Augusta 04333, tel. 207/624–6550) has the same on the coastal areas. Deep-sea fishing cruises operate out of Portland and Boothbay harbors.

HIKING Acadia National Park and Camden Hills State Park offer the most extensive trail systems (*see* Exploring, *above*). Also try the Beehive Trail off Acadia's Park Loop Road, the easy Ocean Trail that follows the dramatic coastline from Sand Beach to Otter Point, and the moderately steep Gorham Mountain Trail that skirts the Cadillac Cliffs.

Mammoth Cave National Park
Kentucky

Updated by Katherine Culkin

ammoth Cave National Park, in south-central Kentucky, has something you can't lay eyes on anywhere else on the planet: a hole in the ground with 330 miles of winding subterranean passages. It's a first-class natural wonder, as reliably awe-inspiring as that other famous hole in the ground, the Grand Canyon. (The second-longest cave on earth, Optimisticeskaya, in Ukraine, is barely a *quarter* as long as Mammoth.)

The cave's marvels range from 192-foot-high Mammoth Dome to 105-foot-deep Bottomless Pit; from a rugged climb called Mt. McKinley to a drifting voyage on the River Styx, 360 feet down, where eyeless fish swim; from a saltpeter mine abandoned after the War of 1812 to a tuberculosis hospital abandoned after an ill-advised experiment in 1843; from an unforgiving passage called Fat Man's Misery to a vaulting chamber known as—what else?—the Grand Canyon.

The cave itself is millions of years old—mummified remains of early Native Americans have been found in its depths. Its official history, however, only began in the 1790s, when, according to legend, a buckskin-clad hunter named Houchins stumbled across its entrance while tracking a wounded bear. But it was not until later in the 19th century that the cave became a popular tourist attraction. Stagecoaches and a railway brought the first visitors. Edmund Booth, a well-known actor, gave readings in the cave. And Jenny Lind, the Swedish nightingale, sang in one of its chambers.

As the cave gained fame, it inevitably became a bone of contention for real-estate entrepreneurs. Once it was discovered the public would pay to see the natural wonder, would-be owners offered competing tours of "the greatest cave that ever was," and for a time, a circus-hawker mentality prevailed. All that came to an end, however, in the 1940s, when Mammoth Cave was declared a national park. For the 50 years since, the park has been a refuge from the hectic and a place for discovery.

ESSENTIAL INFORMATION

WHEN TO GO Mid-March to mid-April is the best time to visit the park. Redbud and dogwood trees are in bloom, and springtime temperatures average 65°. Be aware, though, that temperatures can climb well into the 80s and dip down into the 30s. Five inches of rainfall are normal for this time of year, with occasional severe thunderstorms. Because the park is only moderately crowded in early spring, cave tours are not fully booked—though reservations are always advisable—and the hotels offer their off-season rates, at least until April 15.

Fall is also a glorious time in the park. The weather cools, the crowds thin out, and the trees are ablaze with color. If you're just interested in viewing the caves, winter is the time to do so (the tours are underbooked, and you have the guides to yourself), but organized park activities are sharply curtailed, and the area seems to sink into hibernation.

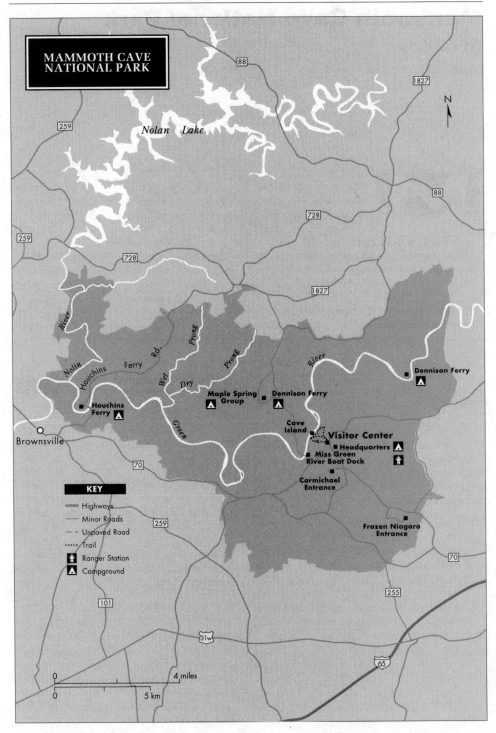

**MAMMOTH CAVE
NATIONAL PARK**

88

1827

259

N

Nolan   Lake

259

88

728

728

1827

259

728

River

Nolin

Houchins

Ferry   Rd.

Wet   Prong

Prong

Dry

River

Dennison Ferry

**Maple Spring
Group**

Dennison Ferry

**Houchins
Ferry**

Green

**Cave
Island**

Visitor Center

Headquarters

**Miss Green
River Boat Dock**

Brownsville

70

**Carmichael
Entrance**

KEY

Highways

Minor Roads

Unpaved Road

Trail

Ranger Station

Campground

259

**Frozen Niagara
Entrance**

70

255

101

31W

65

0   4 miles

0   5 km

FESTIVALS AND SEASONAL EVENTS **Apr.:** Wild-flower Month at Mammoth Cave National Park; daily nature walks, bus tours and special programs. **Weekend after Memorial Day:** Glasgow Highland Games at Barren River Lake State Resort Park (35 mi south on U.S. 31E); a gathering of Scottish clans with such sporting events as battle-ax throwing and tossing the Kyber. **Early Aug.:** Cave City Arts & Crafts Fair (9 mi east of the park on Hwy. 70); artisans from across the nation display and sell their wares. **Early Sept.:** Watermelon Festival, Tompkinsville (40 mi southeast on Hwy. 63); crafts, live entertainment, and ripe thumpers. **Last weekend in Oct.:** Hart County Tobacco Festival, Munfordville (15 mi northeast on I–65). **Mid-Dec.:** Christmas Sing in the Cave, with subterranean holiday music performed by a local choir.

BARGAINS At Campfire Circles at night, the rangers speak gratis about the region's plants and animals and the cave's distinctive history. For a leisurely stroll of an hour and a half, join the Wildflower Walks, offered free to acquaint visitors with the park's seasonal blossoms.

Take a ferry ride across Green River at the Green River or Houchins dock. Ferries operate daily, except under high-water conditions, at no charge. The park's extensive nature trails, of course, are there for the asking.

TOURIST OFFICES **Mammoth Cave National Park** (Park Office, Mammoth Cave 42259, tel. 502/758–2251). **Edmonsen County Recreational Tourist & Convention Commission** (Box 353, Brownsville 42210, tel. 502/597–2819). **Cave City Tourist & Convention Commission** (Cave City 42127, tel. 502/773–3131).

EMERGENCIES **Police:** Kentucky State Police (Bowling Green, tel. 502/782–2010). **Hospitals:** T. J. Samson Community Hospital (North Race St., Glasgow, tel. 502/651–4444); HCA Greenview Hospital (1801 Ashley Circle, Bowling Green, tel. 502/781–4330); Cavernar Memorial Hospital (Highway 31W, Horse Cave, tel. 502/786–2191). **Doctors:** The Medical Center at Bowling Green (Bowling Green, tel. 502/781–2150). **First aid within the park:** weekdays, the Chief Ranger's Office (tel. 502/758–2251); weekends, the Chief Guide's Office (tel. 502/758–2321).

ARRIVING AND DEPARTING

BY PLANE Two major airports serve the area: Louisville's **Standiford Field** (tel. 502/367–4636) and **Nashville International Airport** (tel. 615/275–1675) in Tennessee. Each is about 90 miles from the park. You'll need to rent a car; both airports have Alamo, Avis, Budget, Dollar, Hertz, National, and Thrifty branches. From Standiford Field, drive west on I–264 to I–65 (5 miles from downtown Louisville), take I–65 south to Exit 53 at Cave City, then follow KY 70 west about 9 miles to the park. From Nashville, take I–65 north to Exit 48 at Park City, then follow KY 255 west about 8 miles to the park.

BY CAR Coming from either north or south, 1–65 provides the best access. From the north, take Exit 53 at Cave City to Route 70 west and drive 9 miles to the park's visitor center. From the south, take Exit 48 at Park City to Route 255 west and drive 8 miles to the visitor center. Cumberland Parkway runs through hardwood ridge country, a more scenic, less direct route.

BY BUS **Greyhound Lines** (tel. 800/231–2222) offers bus service to Cave City, 10 miles from Mammoth Cave National Park.

GETTING AROUND

BY CAR A car is the only viable method of transportation within the park.

REST STOPS Three rest areas on I–65 provide rest rooms and tourist information: one, north of Exit 53; a second, south of Exit 43; a third, north of Exit 28. The visitor center at the park also has rest rooms and a full array of maps and brochures.

GUIDED TOURS Guided tours of the cave depart daily from the visitor center. The

Historic Tour (2 hours, 2 miles) takes you through the more famous passages, past mining operations from the War of 1812 and prehistoric artifacts. The Frozen Niagara (2 hours, ¾ mile) displays spectacular rock formations that resemble a giant, multicolored waterfall. The Half-Day Tour (4½ hours, 4 miles) invites the more ambitious to explore canyons and tubelike passages. During the summer, the Lantern Tour (3 hours, 3 miles) recreates the eeriness of the cave in days before electricity. Most tours are moderately strenuous and demand some climbing and stooping. Prices are under $10 for adults, under $5 for children. Reservations are advised at all times and are a must in summer.

EXPLORING

It is possible to see the cave in half a day and be on your way (*see* Guided Tours, *above,* for more information). It is preferable, however, to linger in the park and explore the riches of "the surface world." As this cluttered planet goes, Mammoth Park is still a fairly pristine place. If you get off the beaten path, it's possible to recapture a bit of the Kentucky that old Houchins, the cave's supposed discoverer, knew.

FLORA & FAUNA Along the backcountry trails, you can spot red foxes, opossums, raccoon, and rabbits. A variety of birds will trill in startled protest when strangers invade their territory. Joppa Motor Trail, southwest of the visitor center, is an excellent place to catch a glimpse of wild turkeys and the region's white-tailed deer.

Wildflowers bloom throughout the park from April through September, 200 species in all. Spring brings trillium and the humble daisy; midsummer, the rarer orchid. In August, honeysuckle fills the air with its extravagant sweetness. And in September, the primrose dots the woods with color.

The 7 miles of forest trails, leading from the visitor center, contain some very old, unusually large sycamores, beeches, and tulip poplars. Along the far ridge, stands of oaks and hickories abound. The Big Woods, off Little Jordan Road, is considered virgin forest. Its trees loom up, darkly austere, impenetrable.

HIKING TRAILS Nature trails beckon the hiker; the most popular are listed here.

Cave Island Nature Trail. This mile-long path begins at the cave mouth and winds through the woods past the River Styx Springs, named for its black-colored waters. En route, see limestone deposits shaped like jagged ice crystals.

Heritage Trail. This ¾-mile path, not far from the visitor center, makes for a pleasant afternoon stroll. Along the way, see wildflowers, trees, and the Old Guides Cemetery, where the first cave explorers are buried. Stop at Sunset Point, a spectacular lookout, in time to watch the sun go down.

OTHER PARK ATTRACTIONS **Ganter Cave.** Within park boundaries, this less-traveled cave is open to exploring for qualified cavers. Requirements are stiff for safety reasons. Groups are limited to four to nine adults, with one experienced caver for every two novices. Approval is needed from the Chief Ranger's Office (tel. 502/758–2251).

Green River. Twenty-five miles of this river flow through the park, its waters a shaping force in the cave. You can cross the Green River by ferry for free (*see* Bargains, *above*) or take a paddle wheeler down it. From April through October, the *Miss Green River* makes several cruises daily. On the twilight cruise, you may spot deer on the shoreline under the gentle cover dusk provides. Tickets for the paddleboat may be purchased at the visitor center.

BLUE GRASS COUNTRY This picturesque part of Kentucky is a half day's ride from Mammoth Cave. Take the scenic route: South on 1–65 to Cumberland Parkway, east on the Cumberland to I–75, then north on I–75 to Lexington. The route connects with several points of interest. South of I–75, near Middlesboro, is the Cumberland Gap, the historic gateway to the West, where early pioneers thrust their way through the mountains into Tennessee. If there happens to be a full moon, go to Cumberland Falls nearby. It's one of two places in the world where you can see a moonbow. That's a rainbow, formed by moonlight, striking a waterfall. Return to I–75 and take Exit 95 for Ft. Boonesborough State Park, where you'll find a replica of the fort where Daniel Boone fought in the glory days. Take a look inside the cabins, too, where artisans are at work on 18th-century crafts, using period tools. Just north of Lexington on I–75, detour for the Kentucky Horse Park, which features an equestrian museum and many of the riding arts.

HOTELS AND INNS

The park boasts a single hotel, which rather resembles an inn. There are three other lodging options associated with the hotel. Spaced rectangularly around a parking lot, they have no eating facilities but are all within a five-block walk of the main hotel restaurant. Cabins, campsites, or motels in nearby towns are also available. Outside the park, Cave City has more motels than either Horse Cave or Park City. Price categories for double occupancy, excluding 9% tax, are Expensive, $50–$90; Moderate, $30–$50; and Inexpensive, under $30.

IN THE PARK **Mammoth Cave Hotel.** This clean but simple two-story inn, within steps of the visitor center, offers the best lodging in the park. The rooms are pleasant and the restaurant serves generous, country-style breakfasts. *Mammoth Cave 42259, tel. 502/ 758–2225. 38 rooms. Free parking. AE, DC, MC, V. Expensive.*

Mammoth Cave Hotel Cottages. These one-room cottages furnished in the Early American style are a ¼-mile from the main hotel. They have air-conditioning and electric heat. *Mammoth Cave 42259, tel. 502/758–2225. 10 rooms. AE, DC, MC, V. Open Mar.–Nov. Moderate.*

Sunset Point Motor Lodge. Built like an old-fashioned motor lodge around an open court, Sunset Point offers generous-size rooms and is recommended for families and larger groups. *Reservations can be made through Mammoth Cave Hotel Cottages, Mammoth Cave 42259, tel. 502/758–2225. 20 rooms. Free parking. AE, DC, MC, V. Expensive.*

Woodland Cottages. Also a ¼-mile from the main hotel, these one-to-a-room New England–style cabins are for those who favor rustic lodgings: They're not in great shape, but they're cheap. *Mammoth Cave 42259, tel. 502/758–2225. 23 rooms. Free parking. AE, DC, MC, V. Open May–Oct. Inexpensive.*

MOTELS

MODERATE **Best Western Kentucky Inn** (Box 356, Cave City 42127, tel. 502/773–2321, fax 502/773–5494). 51 rooms; pool, coin laundry. **Best Western–Mammoth Resort** (Park City 42160, tel. 502/749–4101). 93 rooms; restaurant, pool, tennis court. **Days Inn–Cave City** (Box 2009, Cave City 42127, tel. 502/773–2151, fax 502/773–4091). 110 rooms; pool, coin laundry. **Heritage Inn** (Box 2048, Cave City 42127, tel. 502/773–3121 or 800/264–1514, fax 502/773-4455). 116 rooms; pool. **Interstate Inn** (Box 397, Cave City 42127, tel. 502/773–3101, fax 502/773–6082). 140 rooms; pool. **Quality Inn** (Box 547, Cave City 42127, tel. and fax 502/773–2181 or tel. 800/228–5151). 100 rooms; adjoining restaurant, pool.

INEXPENSIVE **Budget Host Inn** (Box 332, Horse Cave 42749, tel. 502/786–2165 or 800/888–2283, fax 502/786–2168). 80 rooms; coin laundry. **Cave Land Motel** (Box 242, Cave City 42127, tel. 502/773–2321). 14 rooms; pool. **Holiday Motel** (Hwy. 31W, Cave City 42127, tel. 502/773–2301). 25 rooms; pool. **Jolly's Motel** (Box 327, Cave City 42127, tel. 502/773–3118, fax 502/773–7151). 24 rooms; pool.

CAMPGROUNDS

There are four campgrounds within Mammoth Cave National Park that allow you to camp near your car. Twelve more backcountry sites are available to hikers on foot. All are in beautiful, natural settings. Like the park itself, the campgrounds are less crowded before Memorial Day and after Labor Day. Even in summer, however, they are run on a first-come, first-served basis; some sites are free, though prices range up to $15. The exception, Maple Springs Campgrounds, which accommodates horses, requires reservations, which can be made through the Chief Ranger's Office (tel. 502/758–2251). Backcountry sites require a permit, obtainable for free at Headquarters Campground (tel. 502/758–2212), near the visitor center.

Dennison Ferry Campground. This secluded, quite primitive campground is on the east side of the park, 7 miles from the visitor center, and borders Green River. *Mammoth Cave National Park, Mammoth Cave 42259, tel. 502/758–2212. 4 tent sites; 1 chemical toilet, picnic tables, barbecue areas. No reservations. Admission free.*

Headquarters Campground. Located a ¼ mile from the visitor center, Headquarters is larger and less rugged than the rest. *Mammoth Cave National Park, Mammoth Cave 42259, tel. 502/758–2212. 111 tent sites; RV parking, showers, bathrooms, LP gas available, picnic tables, barbecue areas. No reservations. Admission charged. No credit cards.*

Houchins Ferry Campground. Your car is the only reminder of civilization at this small campsite, 14 miles from headquarters, on the west side of the park. *Mammoth Cave National Park, Mammoth Cave 42259, tel. 502/758–2212. 12 tent sites; 2 chemical toilets, picnic tables, barbecue areas. No reservations. Admission charged. No credit cards.*

Maple Springs Campground. Because of the hitching posts, which lend an Old West flavor, these campgrounds, north of Green River, are the park's most popular. *Mammoth Cave National Park, Mammoth Cave 42259, tel. 502/758–2212. 6 tent sites; chemical toilets, picnic tables, barbecue areas,* parking *for horse trailers. Reservations required. Admission charged. No credit cards.*

DINING

Friendly southern restaurants dominate the area. Those on low-cholesterol or special diets may have a problem finding restaurants to accommodate their needs. Fast-food outlets are scattered throughout nearby towns; the restaurants listed below, however, feature regional specialties. All the restaurants here fall into the Inexpensive category: Price per person, excluding 6% tax, service, and drinks, is under $15.

INSIDE THE PARK **Mammoth Cave Hotel Restaurant.** This pleasant, busy restaurant at the inn features southern fare, such as country ham, and generous, country-style breakfasts. *Mammoth Cave, tel. 502/758–2225. AE, DC, MC, V.*

NEAR THE PARK **Bolton's Landing.** Distinctive Kentucky fare, such as catfish fried in corn meal, and the Hot Brown sandwich—turkey and chicken topped with cheese, tomatoes, and bacon, baked to perfection and served open-faced. *U.S. 31-E, Glasgow, tel. 502/651–8008. AE, DC, MC, V. Closed Sun.*

Hickory Villa Restaurant. Tourists and locals come here for the barbecued beef and chicken, slathered with a sauce said to be made from a 100-year-old recipe. *Rtes. 70 and 90, Cave City, tel. 502/773–3033. AE, DC, MC, V.*

Watermill Restaurant. Casual country food in casual country surroundings. Southern fried chicken is the house specialty. There's also an all-you-can-eat buffet. *Hwy. 70 west of Cave City, tel. 502/773–3186. No credit cards.*

OUTDOOR ACTIVITIES

BIKING A gentle-grade, mile-long bike trail runs from Headquarters Campground to Carmichael Entrance Road, skirting the edge of a bluff and passing through shaded woodlands. No bicycles are for rent in the park, however, so visitors must bring their own.

BOATING Almost 30 miles of the Green and Nolin rivers are open to boaters and canoers in the park. Unfortunately, there are no boats for rent, so visitors must provide their own crafts. The most popular boat trip launches at Dennison Ferry Campground and floats down the Green River to Houchins Ferry. The trip, which takes about six hours, carries guests past scenic woodlands and dramatic bluffs. No launch fees or permits are required for boating. However, you do need a Coast Guard–approved life preserver for each person on board.

FISHING Fishing is available year-round on both the Green and Nolin rivers. Within the park, you don't need a fishing license, but all other Kentucky state regulations apply. Check at the visitor center for specifics. If you drop a line in the water, you are likely to catch musky, bass, white perch, or catfish.

HIKING Ten hiking trails, covering about 70 miles, are open within the park's boundaries. Trails range in length from under 1 to 10 miles and are graded easy to strenuous, according to hills and inclines. Ask for trail maps at the visitor center.

HORSEBACK RIDING **Jesse James Riding Stables** (Rte. 70W, Cave City 42127, tel. 502/773–2560) rents horses by the half hour for trail rides on the 300 acres of property adjoining the stables.

ENTERTAINMENT

MUSIC **Mammoth Jamboree** (Rte. 70, Cave City, tel. 502/773–3314) has live country bands and singers year-round on Friday and Saturday nights and on major holidays.

THEATER **Horse Cave Theater** (Main St., Horse Cave, tel. 502/786–2177) produces seven plays from June through December, performed by professional players.

Memphis
Tennessee

Updated by Katherine Culkin

he Great River—the Missis-sippi—shaped and defined Memphis's early character and still gives the city and its hinterland a distinctive way of life. Before Memphis was founded in 1819 by Andrew Jackson and named by him for that other Memphis on the Nile, an Indian river culture flourished here from the 11th to the 15th century. Although a Deep South city, there are no antebellum mansions or definitive reminders of the Old South here. The city found real prosperity only in the late 19th century, when cotton and lumber barons built their imposing Victorian mansions.

Memphis, the youngest major city along the lower Mississippi, took time out to listen and invent the blues and was slow to get caught up in the Sun Belt's boom. But today, still making music, it stands tall on its high bluffs, facing the river with a burgeoning skyline. Memphis capitalizes on its location with a unique entertainment park on an island in midriver. And downtown, for years down-at-heel, has come alive with new civic improvements, including the Main Street Trolley, the Pyramid arena, and the National Civil Rights Museum.

In a trend somewhat unusual for southern cities, a flurry of adaptive-use projects has brought a rush of residents back to the heart of the city. Two former hotels, both on the National Register of Historic Places, have been converted into luxury apartments, and rehabilitated cotton warehouses overlooking the Mississippi are now condominiums.

Elsewhere downtown, Beale Street bustles with clubs and restaurants as it did in its heyday, when W. C. Handy first trumpeted his blue notes in PeeWee's Saloon. One young man, influenced by the city's blues sound, went on to become the king of rock and roll, and today crowds flock to Elvis Presley's Graceland, one of Tennessee's major showplaces.

ESSENTIAL INFORMATION

WHEN TO GO Spring and autumn are the ideal times for visiting Memphis. Many people come during the monthlong **Memphis in May International Festival,** when the summer's heat and humidity have not yet set in. Winters are generally mild, although snow and ice storms do sometimes occur.

FESTIVALS AND SEASONAL EVENTS **Jan. 8:** Elvis Presley's Birthday Tribute. **Apr.:** Dr. Martin Luther King, Jr. Memorial March. **May:** Memphis in May International Festival: food and musical, cultural, and sports events. **June:** Carnival Memphis (formerly Cotton Carnival): exhibits, music, and family activities. **July:** Mid-South Music and Heritage Festival: food, music, children's activities and cultural exhibits and demonstrations. **Aug.:** Elvis International Tribute Week: music, Graceland tours and graveside, candlelight vigil. **Sept.:** Mid-South Fair: agricultural exhibits, rides, food, games, contests, concerts, a midway, and a rodeo. **Oct.:** National Blues Music Awards "The Handys."

BARGAINS There's no admission charge at the **Beale Street Substation Police Museum**

(159 Beale St., tel. 901/528–2370); the **Crystal Shrine Grotto** (Memorial Park Cemetery, 5668 Poplar Ave., tel. 901/767–8930), a dramatic natural cavern with rock-crystal carvings; **Coors Brewery** (5151 E. Raines Rd., tel. 901/375–2100); or the **Agricenter International,** an aquaculture and farm complex (7777 Walnut Grove Rd., tel. 901/757–7777). The **Memphis Botanic Garden** (750 Cherry Rd., tel. 901/685–1566) is free on Tuesday after 12:30 PM. The **Memphis Pink Palace Museum and Planetarium** (3050 Central Ave., tel. 901/320–6320) offers free admission to museum exhibits Thursday 5–8 PM, and the zoo is free on Monday 3:30–5 PM.

TOURIST OFFICES **Tennessee Department of Tourist Development** (Room T, Box 23170, Nashville 37202, tel. 615/741–7994). **Memphis Convention and Visitors Bureau** (47 Union Ave., Memphis 38103, tel. 901/543–5300). The **Visitor Information Center** (340 Beale St., Memphis 38103, tel. 901/543–5333).

EMERGENCIES **Police, fire,** or **ambulance:** Dial 911. **Hospitals** with 24-hour emergency service include Baptist Memorial Hospital (889 Madison Ave., tel. 901/227–2727) and Methodist Hospital Central (1265 Union Ave., tel. 901/726–7000).

ARRIVING AND DEPARTING

BY PLANE **Memphis International Airport,** 9½ miles south of downtown, is served by American, Delta, Northwest, TWA, United, and USAir. **City Wide Cab** (tel. 901/324–4202) operates taxi service to downtown hotels (fares average $15–$20).

BY CAR From Memphis, I–55 leads north to St. Louis and south to Jackson, Mississippi; I–40 runs east to Nashville and Knoxville; I–240 loops around the city.

BY TRAIN AND BUS Amtrak (tel. 800/872–7245) serves Memphis with the City of New Orleans between New Orleans and Chicago. **Greyhound Lines** (203 Union Ave., tel. 901/523–7676) connects Memphis with cities and towns throughout the country.

GETTING AROUND

BY CAR Memphis attractions are spread out, so you'll need a car, though in some downtown areas you can park and walk from one to another.

BY BUS **Memphis Area Transit Authority** (tel. 901/274–6282) buses cover the city and immediate suburbs. There's short-hop service on designated buses between Front, 3rd, and Exchange streets daily from 9 to 3. The Trolley II shuttles between downtown and the Medical Center. MATA Showboat buses resembling riverboats connect attractions, restaurants, hotels, and stores daily except holidays.

BY TAXI Companies include **Yellow Cab** (tel. 901/577–7777) and **City Wide Cab** (tel. 901/324–4202).

REST STOPS Cossitt Library (Front and Monroe Sts.) and A. Schwab's Dry Goods Store (163 Beale St.) have public rest rooms.

GUIDED TOURS Graceland, Mud Island, and Beale Street tours; riverboat rides; and dinner and show tours are available from **Blues City Tours** (tel. 901/522–9229). For a horse-drawn carriage ride through downtown, contact **Carriage Tours of Memphis** (tel. 901/527–7542). **Cottonland Tours** (tel. 901/774–5248) conducts three-hour tours to downtown highlights and Graceland. **Gray Line** (tel. 901/948–8687) offers downtown, nightlife, Elvis Memorial, and Mud Island tours. **Heritage Tours** (tel. 901/527–3427) explores the city's black-culture sites. From March to December, the **Memphis Queen Line** (tel. 901/527–5694) runs 1½-hour sightseeing cruises; it also offers dinner and moonlight cruises with entertainment by the area's top bands.

EXPLORING

You should plan to explore Memphis in segments, beginning with the central city and branching outward (not all attractions listed below are located on the map). The city is laid out in a grid system. Madison Avenue divides north from south; Main Street separates east from west (Main is called Main Street Mall on the North side; its South side dead-ends in E. H. Crump Boulevard).

The **Visitor Information Center** on Beale Street is a good place to start a walking tour. Here you can pick up free maps and brochures and park free. On leaving the center, turn left and walk a few steps to the **W. C. Handy Memphis Home and Museum,** which displays photographs, sheet music, and other memorabilia of the Father of the Blues. *352 Beale St., tel. 901/522–1556. Open Tues.–Sun. Admission charged.*

From the home, turn right and walk west past Handy Park, between 3rd and Hernando streets, to admire a statue of W. C. Handy clutching his famed trumpet. Continue west through the **Beale Street Historic District.**

A. Schwab's Dry Goods Store (163 Beale St., tel. 901/523–9782) is an old-fashioned, 118-year-old dry-goods store where Elvis purchased some of his glitzy threads. You'll find everything from top hats and tambourines to women's dresses up to size 60 and men's trousers up to size 74. It's also a great place to pick up cheap souvenirs.

Walk two blocks west, board the trolley at Main and Beale, and travel south to Calhoun. Walk two blocks east.

The **National Civil Rights Museum** opened in 1991 at the historic Lorraine Motel, where Dr. Martin Luther King, Jr., was assassinated. The museum features exhibits and interactive displays tracing the history of the American Civil Rights movement. *450 Mulberry St., tel. 901/521–9699. Closed Tues. Admission charged.*

From the museum take the trolley to the north end of Main Street and walk one block west to **The Pyramid,** a $65 million entertainment and sports arena honoring Memphis's Egyptian heritage, opened in 1991. A massive stone statue of Ramses guards the 32-story structure, which seats 22,000. Seasonal tours are offered. *1 Auction Ave., tel. 901/521–9675. Tours available.*

Take the footbridge or monorail from 125 Front Street to **Mud Island,** a 52-acre river park situated a few blocks south of The Pyramid. In the park there's a five-block-long scale model of the river that replicates its every twist, turn, and sandbar from Cairo, Illinois, to New Orleans. There are shops, restaurants, a swimming pool and beach, an amphitheater for big-name entertainment, and the World War II B-17 bomber *Memphis Belle. Tel. 901/576–7241. Open daily. Admission charged.*

From Mud Island you'll want to retrieve your car and drive east from downtown for 1 mile, along Union Avenue. **Sun Studio,** at Union and Marshall, is the birthplace of rock and roll. Sam Phillips opened it in 1950 and recorded such acts as Elvis Presley, Jerry Lee Lewis, B. B. King, Howlin' Wolf, Muddy Waters, Carl Perkins, and Roy Orbison. The studio is open daily for continuous, 30-minute tours, and it still operates as a studio by night. *706 Union Ave., tel. 901/735–3670. Admission charged.*

Drive north to Poplar Avenue and head east toward Overton Park, where you can visit the **Memphis Zoological Gardens and Aquarium,** one of the South's most notable zoos. It houses more than 400 species on 70 wooded acres. As part of a $22 million expansion, a new Cat Country exhibition opened in 1993, followed by the opening of the Primate World and Children's Village in 1994. There's also a 10,000-gallon aquarium, a large reptile house, and an African veld setting for larger creatures. *2000 Galloway Dr., Overton Park, tel. 901/726–4787. Open daily. Admission charged; free Mon. 3:30–5 PM.*

Memphis Brooks Museum of Art has collections spanning eight centuries, including Italian Renaissance works; English portraits; Impressionist and American modernist paintings; and a large display of Doughty Bird figurines. *Overton Park, tel. 901/722–3500. Closed Mon. Donations accepted.*

Southeast of the park is the **Memphis Pink Palace Museum and Planetarium,** next to the 1920s pink marble mansion built by Clarence Saunders, founder of the Piggly Wiggly supermarket chain. A 165-seat planetarium and changing exhibits on natural and cultural history include a hand-carved miniature three-ring circus, full-scale replica of America's first self-service grocery store, and a life-size triceratops dinosaur that roars and stomps. *3050 Central Ave., tel. 901/320–6320. Open daily. Admission charged.*

The **Children's Museum of Memphis** is a short drive west of the Pink Palace. An interactive museum for children and their families, the museum offers a child-size version of a working city, including a real fire engine and police motorcycle. *2525 Central Ave., tel. 901/458–2678. Closed Mon. Admission charged.*

Graceland, 12 miles southeast of town via the I–55 south, is Memphis's most-visited attraction. A guided tour of the colonial-style mansion once owned by Elvis Presley reveals the spoils of stardom—from his gold records to his glittering show costumes—and a circuit of the grounds leads to his tomb. *3675 Elvis Presley Blvd., tel. 901/332–3322 or 800/238–2000 outside TN. Open daily. Admission charged.*

Chucalissa Indian Village, 10 miles southwest of downtown, preserves traces of the simple river culture that existed from AD 1000 to 1500. Ongoing archaeological excavations of the reconstructed site are conducted by Memphis State University. In the C. H. Nash Museum at the village, you'll see prehistoric tools, pottery, and weapons, plus a free slide presentation. Near the museum, Choctaw Indians skillfully fashion jewelry, weapons, and pottery, all of which are for sale. *1987 Indian Village Dr., tel. 901/785–3160. Closed Mon. Admission charged.*

HOTELS AND INNS

Memphis hotels and motor inns are especially busy in May and June and in mid-August, on the anniversary of Elvis's death. Bed-and-Breakfast in Memphis (Box 41621, 38174–1621, tel. 901/726–5920) arranges accommodations in a wide range of private lodgings. Price categories for double occupancy, excluding 13¼% tax, are Expensive, $70–$125; Moderate, $50–$70; and Inexpensive, under $50.

EXPENSIVE **French Quarter Suite Hotel.** All the one-bedroom suites in this charming New Orleans–style inn have living rooms and whirlpool tubs, and some have balconies. *2144 Madison Ave., 38104, tel. 901/ 728–4000, fax 901/278–1262. 104 suites. Dining room, lounge with entertainment, pool, health club. AE, D, DC, MC, V.*

Holiday Inn Crowne Plaza. This sleek 18-story hotel, adjacent to the Convention Center, offers a concierge floor and ample reading areas and lighting in its spacious rooms. *250 N. Main St., 38103, tel. 901/527– 7300, fax 901/526–1561. 406 rooms. Restaurant, lobby piano lounge, indoor pool, health club, sauna. AE, D, DC, MC, V.*

Memphis Airport Hotel and Conference Center. Guest rooms rise around a five-story, plant-filled atrium, and some suites have kitchenettes. *2240 Democrat Rd., 38132, tel. 901/332–1130, fax 901/398–5206. 380 rooms. Restaurant, nightclub, indoor and outdoor pools, 2 fitness centers, 2 tennis courts, jogging track. AE, D, DC, MC, V.*

MODERATE **Guest House Inn.** All rooms in this standard two-story chain inn have private patios. *3280 Elvis Presley Blvd., 38116, tel. 901/345–1425, fax 901/345–1425. 122 rooms. Restaurant, pool, wading pool, playground. AE, D, DC, MC, V.*

Hampton Inn Airport. Spacious, well-lighted rooms in this contemporary inn have Scandinavian-style teak furnishings, though a convenient location close to the airport is the real draw. *2979 Millbranch Rd., 38116, tel. 901/396–2200, fax 901/396–7034. 128 rooms. Pool. AE, D, DC, MC, V.*

Lowenstein-Long House. If you're into Victoriana, you may want to opt for this landmark mansion on an acre of lawn; rooms are spacious, with high ceilings and large baths. *217 N. Waldran St., 38105, tel. 901/527–7174. 8 rooms. Kitchen, laundry. No credit cards.*

INEXPENSIVE **Days Inn Memphis Airport.** This motor inn near Graceland has light, well-maintained, spacious rooms. *1533 E. Brooks Rd., 38116, tel. 901/345–2470, fax 901/398–2899. 242 rooms. Dining room, lounge with entertainment, heated pool. AE, DC, MC, V.*

La Quinta Motor Inn–Medical Center. This two-story inn near the medical center and midtown attractions has spacious, well-maintained but visually plain rooms. *42 S. Camilla St., 38104, tel. 901/526–1050, fax 901/525–3219. 130 rooms. Pool. AE, D, DC, MC, V.*

MOTELS

MODERATE **Best Western Riverbluff Inn** (340 W. Illinois Ave., 38106, tel. 901/948– 9005, fax 901/946–5716). 99 rooms; restaurant, lounge, pool, coin laundry. **Comfort Hotel Airport** (2411 Winchester Rd., 38116, tel. 901/332–2370, fax 901/398–4085). 211 rooms; dining room, lounge, pool, exercise room, lighted tennis courts.

Days Inn Downtown (164 Union Ave., 38103, tel. 901/527–4100, fax 901/525–1747). 106 rooms; restaurant, coffee shop, lounge. **Holiday Inn–Overton Square** (1837 Union Ave., 38104, tel. 901/278–4100, fax 901/272– 3810). 175 rooms; dining room, lounge, pool, parking garage.

INEXPENSIVE **Hampton Inn–Medical Center** (1180 Union Ave., 38104, tel. 901/ 276–1175, fax 901/276–4261). 126 rooms; Continental breakfast. **Quality Hotel** (3222 Airways Blvd., 38116, tel. 901/332–3800, fax 901/345–2448). 123 rooms; dining room, lounge, pool, sauna, coin laundry. **Wilson World Hotel** (3677 Elvis Presley Blvd., 38115, tel. 901/332–1000, fax. 901/366– 6361) 134 rooms; microwaves in some rooms.

DINING

Memphis, the "pork barbecue capital of the universe," also offers Cajun and Creole,

French, Italian, Greek, Mexican, and Asian food. But many restaurants now serve heart-healthy and vegetarian dishes, and you can order grilled or poached seafood or other entrées without sauce. Price categories per person, excluding 8¼% tax, service, and drinks, are Moderate, $15–$25, and Inexpensive, under $15.

MODERATE **Landry's Seafood House.** This rustic riverfront warehouse, one of Memphis's busiest eateries, offers simple, consistently well-prepared entrées like shrimp in brown butter and flounder stuffed with shrimp and crabmeat. *263 Wagner Pl., tel. 901/526–1966. AE, MC, V.*

Marenas. A different Mediterranean cuisine is featured each month at this unique midtown restaurant; one month it may be French, another Egyptian or North African. *1545 Overton Park, tel. 901/278–9774. AE, DC, MC, V.*

Paulette's. This cordial country-inn dining room specializes in filet mignon, grilled seafood and poultry, and homemade soups. If you enjoy decadent dessert crepes, Paulette's is a must. *Overton Sq., 2110 Madison Ave., tel. 901/726–5128. AE, DC, MC, V.*

Salsa. Fresh tortilla chips and tangy salsa, plus enchiladas and other Mexican specialties are popular choices at this lively Southwestern-style cantina. *6150 Poplar, tel. 901/683–6325. AE, DC, MC, V.*

INEXPENSIVE **Automatic Slim's Tonga Club.** Southwestern cuisine with a Caribbean twist is the hallmark of this trendy downtown eatery. Jamaican jerk chicken or tomato-basil soup and vegetarian black beans are dinner favorites; for dessert try the taco-shaped cookie stuffed with creamy custard and berries. *83 2nd St., tel. 901/525–7948. AE, MC, V.*

Cafe Roux. Don't fret if Louisiana isn't on your itinerary: Spicy Cajun and Creole dishes are what put chef Michael Cahhal's Cafe Roux on the culinary map. Outstanding entrées include the rich Acadian catfish, thick jambalaya, fried-oyster po'boys, and beignets. *7209 Winchester Ave., tel. 901/ 755–7689; 94 S. Front St., tel. 901/525–7689. AE, DC, MC, V.*

Charlie Vergos' Rendezvous. In a back-alley basement crammed with memorabilia and bric-a-brac, this popular establishment serves what many experts swear are the choicest barbecued ribs and pork-loin plates in the world. *General Washburn Alley at 52 S. 2nd St., tel. 901/523–2746. AE, MC, V.*

Corky's. Arguably Memphis's most popular barbecue restaurant, Corky's draws huge crowds who routinely endure hour-long waits for smoke-flavored, slow-cooked pork ribs (wet or dry). Less filling are the juicy pork sandwiches topped with coleslaw. *5259 Poplar Ave., tel. 901/685–9744. AE, D, DC, MC, V.*

Huey's. This friendly neighborhood bar and restaurant is a Memphis institution. Patrons have voted "Huey Burgers" the best in town for years running. *1927 Madison Ave., tel. 901/726–9767; 2858 Hickory Hill, tel. 901/ 374–4373. AE, MC, V.*

Little Tea Shop. Since 1918, this homey restaurant has attracted luncheon crowds for its first-rate southern cooking. Traditional favorites include turnip greens, corn streaks, and chicken salad. *69 Monroe Ave., tel. 901/ 525–6000. No credit cards.*

Spaghetti Warehouse. Pasta, salads, and a hearty minestrone draw crowds to this whimsically renovated downtown warehouse. Kids should enjoy eating in a restored trolley car in the center of the dining room. *40 W. Huling Ave., tel. 901/521–0907. DC, MC, V.*

SHOPPING

With four suburban branches, **Goldsmith's** (tel. 901/766–2200) is Memphis's major department store, but you'll find a wider selection in the Beale Street Historic District, which is crammed cheek-to-jowl with galleries and souvenir stores. **Hickory Ridge Mall** (tel. 901/795–8844) in suburban, southeast Shelby County, is one of the city's nicest malls, with dozens of department stores, boutiques, a cineplex, food court, and indoor children's carousel. Six shops at **Graceland** sell every possible kind of Elvis memorabilia. Twenty miles east of downtown Memphis, the **Belz Factory Outlet Mall** (3536 Canada Road, Exit 20 off I–40 in Lakeland, tel. 901/386–3180) is a direct factory outlet with bargains galore in its 50 stores.

OUTDOOR ACTIVITIES

HIKING There are trails at **Shelby Farms Plough Recreation Area** (tel. 901/382–2249), **Lichterman Nature Center** (5992 Quince Rd., tel. 901/767–7322), and at **T. O. Fuller State Park** next to Chucalissa Indian Village (tel. 901/543–7581).

TENNIS The **Memphis Park Commission** (tel. 901/325–5759) operates several facilities that offer tennis lessons and golf.

ENTERTAINMENT

The **Memphis International Cultural Series** stages world-class art and historical exhibitions each summer at the Memphis Cook Convention Center (One Convention Plaza, tel. 901/576–1231 or 800/755–8777; admission charged).

For live blues and dancing, try **Rum Boogie Cafe** (182 Beale St., tel. 901/528–0150); the **Omni New Daisy Theatre** (330 Beale St., tel. 901/525–8981) stages blues, jazz, and rock concerts. For the best in live blues, check out **B.B. King's Blues Club** (143 Beale St., tel. 901/527–5464).

Miami

Florida

Updated by Herb Hiller

Olé Miami!—city of choice for meetings of chiefs of state from around the Americas, the hemisphere's most active free-trade zone, and hub of Latin American air travel. Only two generations ago, Miami still slumbered during the summer, seasonally reviving with runaway hordes from miserable northern winters. Yet today you can believe the hype when this metropolis of more than 2 million residents calls itself the capital of Latin America.

As a resort destination, Miami has never ranked better. Blue sea beckons beyond broad beaches. The Art Deco District's steadily improving hotels, brilliant restaurants, and celebrity café society make South Beach the lure of paparazzi from around the world. The city boasts franchises in all four major-league sports, as well as annual world-class golf and tennis events.

On the cultured side, acclaimed opera, ballet, and symphonic troupes call Miami home. So does a stable of celebrated writers (many affiliated with the *Miami Herald,* one of the best dailies in America), and a pop music scene that ranges from MTV Latino to some of the brightest upcoming rock-and-roll, blues, jazz, and world-beat musicians, all of whom appear up and down South Beach, and across the bay downtown and in Coconut Grove.

With all its gifts, Miami remains one of the bargain vacation cities of the world.

ESSENTIAL INFORMATION

WHEN TO GO The best months for weather—when evenings are cool and the humidity relents—are mid-November through mid-April. Most affordable time of year is between Easter and Memorial Day, and again between Labor Day and mid-December. Between mid-December and mid-March, cold fronts can blow in and lower overnight temperatures to near freezing, leaving daytime temperatures barely into the 70s. Most nights are in the 50s, days reaching to the low 80s. Early spring and late fall are pleasant but between mid-April and mid-October temperatures can reach into the 90s. Humidity is oppressive June through October. But since everything is air-conditioned and the beach and ocean are otherwise the place to be, vacationers find Miami bearable any time of year. Early fall's low rates come coupled with the tail end of hurricane season (which begins in June). Hurricane reporting typically provides alerts days in advance. Rain otherwise tends to fall in afternoon showers.

FESTIVALS AND SEASONAL EVENTS Miami has festival fever. Every week of the year shows a calendar of several events, climaxing over New Year with the nationally televised **Orange Bowl festivities** (tel. 305/371–3351). In mid-January, Art Deco Weekend spotlights Miami Beach's historic district with an **Art Deco street fair** (tel. 305/672–2014) featuring crafts, food, and live entertainment. Mid-February brings the **Coconut Grove Art Festival** (tel. 305/447–0401), the

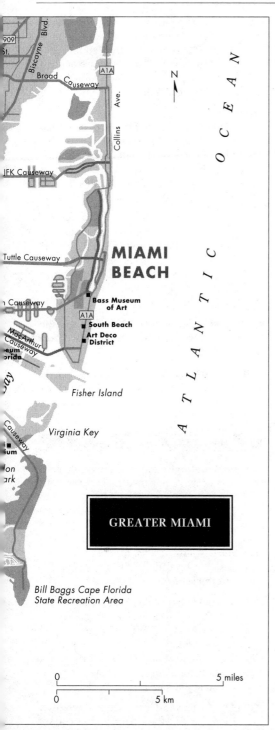

MIAMI
BEACH

Bass Museum of Art

South Beach Art Deco District

Fisher Island

Virginia Key

GREATER MIAMI

Bill Baggs Cape Florida State Recreation Area

OCEAN

ATLANTIC

0   5 miles
0   5 km

state's largest. **Carnival Miami** (tel. 305/ 644–8888), in early March, is a celebration staged by the Little Havana Kiwanis Club. On the first weekend in June, the **Miami-Bahamas Goombay Festival** (tel. 305/443–7928) in Miami's Coconut Grove celebrates the city's Bahamian heritage. For a complete list of Miami festivals, contact the **Dade County Cultural Affairs Council** (111 N.W. 1st St., Suite 625, Miami 33128, tel. 305/ 375–4634).

BARGAINS Beaches are free from the foot of Miami Beach all the way up through Sunny Isles. Free music performance takes place daily at Bayside Marketplace (*see* Shopping, *below*). The New World Symphony (*see* Entertainment, *below*) typically introduces its fall season with a series of free concerts at its Lincoln Theatre site; a monthly Musicians' Forum is performed by symphony members. For children's activities, free publications worth looking into include "A Kid's Guide to Greater Miami," which lists festivals and special events; and the "Arts in Education Directory" (tel. 305/375–4634 for both). The monthly "South Florida Parenting" (4200 Aurora St., Coral Gables, tel. 305/448–6003), provides a calendar of events, restaurant reviews by kids, and recommendations of places to visit, among other information. It's available at more than 2,200 locations, including libraries and children's retail stores. For a listing of national, state, and county parks (typically with only nominal admission), contact the Greater Miami Convention and Visitors Bureau (*see* Tourist Offices, *below*).

TOURIST OFFICES **Greater Miami Convention and Visitors Bureau** (701 Brickell Ave., Suite 2700, Miami 33131, tel. 305/539–3000 or 800/283–2707) has a satellite tourist center at Miami International Airport. **Greater Miami Chamber of Commerce** (1601 Biscayne Blvd., Miami 33132, tel. 305/350–7700). Well informed about the south side of the metropolis and the Upper Keys is the **South Dade Visitor Information Center** (160 U.S. 1, Florida City 33034, tel. 305/245–9180 or 800/388–9669, fax 305/247–4335).

EMERGENCIES **Police, fire, and ambulance:** Dial 911.

The following **hospitals** have 24-hour emergency rooms. In Miami Beach: Mt. Sinai Medical Center (off Julia Tuttle Causeway, I–195 at 4300 Alton Rd., Miami Beach; emergency, tel. 305/674–2200; physician referral, tel. 305/674–2273). In the north: Golden Glades Regional Medical Center (17300 N.W. 7th Ave., North Miami, tel. 305/652–4200). In central Miami: Jackson Memorial Medical Center (1611 N.W. 12th Ave., near Dolphin Expressway, Miami; emergency, tel. 305/585–6901; physician referral, tel. 305/547–5757). In the south: Baptist Hospital of Miami (8900 N. Kendall Dr., Miami; emergency, tel. 305/596–6556; physician referral, tel. 305/596–6557).

24-Hour Pharmacies: Eckerd Drug (1825 Miami Gardens Dr. NE, at 185th St., North Miami Beach, tel. 305/932–5740; 9031 S.W. 107th Ave., Miami, tel. 305/274–6776). Terminal Rexall Pharmacy (Concourse F, Miami International Airport, Miami, tel. 305/876–0556). Walgreen (500-B W. 49th St., Palm Springs Mall, Hialeah, tel. 305/557–5468; 12295 Biscayne Blvd., North Miami, tel. 305/893–6860; 5731 Bird Rd., Miami, tel. 305/666–0757; 1845 Alton Rd., Miami Beach, tel. 305/531–8868; 791 N.E. 167th St., North Miami Beach, tel. 305/652–7332).

ARRIVING AND DEPARTING

BY PLANE **Miami International Airport** (MIA) (tel. 305/876–7000) is 8 miles west of downtown Miami.

Between the Airport and Center City. For taxi service from the airport to hotels in the airport area, ask a uniformed county taxi dispatcher to call an Airport Region Taxi Service (ARTS) cab for you. These special blue cabs offer a short-haul flat fare in two zones: An inner-city ride is about $6; an outer-city fare is around $10. Maps are posted in cab windows. Approximate fares from MIA in normal cabs are: $10 to Coral Gables, $15–$20 to downtown Miami, and $25–$30 to Key Biscayne. Flat fares to the beaches range from $38 to northernmost beaches to $22 from 63rd Street south to the foot of Miami Beach. These fares are per trip, not per passenger, and include tolls and $1 airport surcharge. A taxi from MIA to the Port of Miami costs $16.

SuperShuttle vans operate 24 hours a day and shuttle between MIA and all destinations in Dade, as far north as Palm Beach County, as far south as the Lower Keys. It's best to make reservations 24 hours in advance. *Tel. 305/871–2000 or 800/874–8885. Lower rate for 2nd passenger in same party.*

BY CAR The main highways into Greater Miami from the north are Florida's Turnpike (toll) and I–95. From the northwest and west, take I–75 or U.S. 27 into Miami. From the south, use U.S. 1 and the Homestead Extension of Florida's Turnpike.

BY TRAIN **Amtrak** (tel. 800/872–7245) runs twice daily between Miami and New York City.

BY BUS **Greyhound Lines** (tel. 800/231–2222) buses stop at five bus terminals in Greater Miami.

GETTING AROUND

Miami is laid out on a grid with four quadrants—northeast, northwest, southeast, and southwest—which meet at Miami Avenue and Flagler Street. Miami Avenue separates east from west, while Flagler Street separates north from south. *Avenues* and *courts* run north–south; *streets, terraces,* and *ways* run east–west. And *roads* run diagonally from northwest to southeast.

Many named streets also bear numbers. For example, Le Jeune Road is also Northwest and Southwest 42nd Avenue. Also, Hialeah has its own grid, with Palm Avenue separating east from west and Hialeah Drive separating north from south. Your best bet is to use a good street map.

BY TRAIN Metrorail runs from downtown Miami north to Hialeah and south along

U.S. 1 to Dadeland. Trains run every five minutes during peak hours, 15 minutes other times. Trains are only crowded during rush hours. Operating hours are 5:30 AM–midnight. At the TRI-RAIL station you can transfer to the commuter train and ride to the Palm Beach International Airport. This system will also take you to several stations where you can board an Amtrak train. Information for this system is available by calling 800/874–7245.

You can switch to the Metromover, a coordinated inner-city mass-transit system, at Government Center Station. This system circles the heart of the city with extensions to the nearby north and south on twin elevated loops, linking major hotels, office buildings, and shopping areas. Its hours of operation are 6:30 AM–midnight.

BY BUS Metrobus stops are marked by blue-and-green signs with a bus logo and route information. The frequency of service varies widely. Obtain specific schedule information in advance for the routes you want to ride by calling 305/638–6700.

BY TAXI There are some 2,000 taxicabs in Dade County. While service from most Miami cab companies is wretched, one company stands out. It's actually a consortium of drivers who have banded together to provide good service; to plug into this consortium—they don't have a name, simply a number—call the dispatch service (tel. 305/888–4444). If you have to use another company, try to be familiar with your route and destination. There's no additional charge for extra passengers, luggage, or road and bridge tolls.

BY CAR You'll need a car to visit many Miami attractions and points of interest listed in this chapter, but some are accessible via public transportation. Parking downtown is inconvenient and expensive if you park in a private lot, so if you're staying outside the downtown area, leave your car at your hotel or at an outlying Metrorail station and take the train downtown.

EXPLORING

Flying into Miami International Airport, you can see that Miami is two cities divided by a bay. Downtown bustles with business and bargain-hunting shoppers from around the Americas. To the east, on the barrier islands across Biscayne Bay, beaches extend north through Fort Lauderdale beyond Palm Beach and south to Key West. Beaches claim most visitors' interest, but only splashing in the sea and forgoing the mainland would mean missing much of what makes Miami the most dynamic city in the Americas. Sample as much as you can of what's described below.

The **Art Deco District** is the only district listed in the National Register of Historic Places with all its structures—more than 800—dating from the 20th century. *Art Deco* refers to the styles of architecture that came together here in the late '20s and '30s. Its forms are eclectic, abstracted from nature (especially birds, butterflies, and flowers); from ancient Aztec, Mayan, Babylonian, Chaldean, Egyptian, and Hebrew designs; and from the streamlined, aerodynamic, and geometric shapes that flourished in the post-Depression building boom of the late '30s and early '40s. Sherbet-colored buildings with neon signs, rounded corners, vertical columns, fluted eaves, and Mediterranean arches can be found all along this mile-square, inner ear–shaped district that lies on the east side of South Beach, bordered by the ocean, Lenox Court, and 6th and 23rd streets.

Bass Museum of Art houses a diverse collection of European art, including *The Holy Family,* a painting by Peter Paul Rubens; *The Tournament,* a 16th-century Flemish tapestry; and works by Albrecht Dürer and Henri de Toulouse-Lautrec. Park behind the museum and walk around to the entrance past massive tropical baobab trees. *2121 Park Ave., Miami Beach, tel. 305/673–7530. Open Tues.–Sun. Admission charged.*

Coconut Grove is metro Miami's oldest settlement, inhabited as early as 1834 and established by 1873, two decades before Miami proper. Its early settlers included Bahamian blacks, "Conchs" from Key West, and New England intellectuals. They built a community that attracted wintering artists, writers, and scientists. By the end of World War I, more people listed in *Who's Who* gave addresses in Coconut Grove than anyplace else. The historic center of the Grove "went hippie" in the '60s. The '70s brought a laid-back funkiness, and the '80s, a teenybopper invasion. Today the tone is upscale and urban, with a mix of galleries, boutiques, restaurants, bars, and sidewalk cafés. On side streets the Grove still reflects its eclectic origins. Posh estates and rustic cottages, modest frame homes, and starkly modern dwellings all show up on neighboring blocks. Residents battle to retain native vegetation, lavishing affection on the jungle look.

Coral Castle is said to have taken Edward Leedskalnin 20 years to carve from 1,000 tons of coral as a tribute to his fiancée, who jilted him just hours before their wedding. The castle is an engineering marvel, with solar-heated bathtubs and even a coral "telescope" aimed at the North Star. Alas, the 9-ton gate on ball bearings that even a child could swing open has been conventionally remounted for safety reasons. *28655 S. Dixie Hwy., Homestead area, tel. 305/248–6344. Open daily. Admission charged.*

Coral Gables, one of the first fully planned communities in the United States, has emerged over the last 20 years as a prime headquarters for transnational companies operating in Latin America. Upscale boutiques, art galleries, several top hotels, and the best restaurants in the city can also be found. George Merrick, who carved his parents' tomato patch into lots for sale in 1921, named the streets of Coral Gables for Spanish explorers, cities, and provinces (hard-to-see names sit at ground level beside each intersection on whitewashed concrete cornerstones). Tough zoning and code enforcement have kept the Spanish Mediterranean look largely intact; there are broad boulevards, Spanish plazas and fountains, impos-

ing entrance gates, huge banyan trees, and miles of waterways weaving through the residential areas. Merrick's home, **Coral Gables House and Gardens** (907 Coral Way, tel. 305/460–5361; admission charged) faces residential Coral Way, one of the most beautiful boulevards in one of Miami's most beautiful suburbs. The house dates from 1907 and is open to the public as a house museum, but only briefly Wednesday and Sunday afternoons. Other notable structures include **Coral Gables City Hall** (405 Biltmore Way, tel. 305/446–6800) and **Venetian Pool** (2701 DeSoto Blvd., tel. 305/460–5356; admission charged), a one-of-a-kind coral rock swimming hole where nightly the city empties and refills the water, and where swimmers enjoy a beach, a cave, arched bridges, and a snack bar.

Downtown, staid-suited lawyers and bankers share the sidewalks with immigrant fruit vendors hawking their wares from pushcarts; T-shirted, uniformed tour groups from around Latin America; and European youths with backpacks. Pushing your way across narrow downtown streets you hear Spanish, Chinese, Creole, Portuguese, and even a little English now and then—a veritable babble of tongues that contributes to Miami's international flavor. The city sprang up almost overnight after Henry Flagler's railroad arrived in 1896. Through boom and bust, downtown has expanded into the bay, where its most popular visitor attractions now include Biscayne Boulevard (where late Brazilian landscape architect Roberto Burle Marx's brilliant redesign of the street is at last underway), Bayside Marketplace, and just across a new, humpbacked causeway, the Port of Miami. The best way to grasp the beautiful waterfront setting of this city is by riding the **Metromover,** an elevated, cushioned-wheel, driverless train that for 25¢ weaves you through the busiest neighborhoods without a traffic light to worry about.

Fairchild Tropical Garden consists of 83 acres—the largest tropical botanical garden in the continental United States. There's also a rare plant house, a rain forest, and a sunken garden. Ask about the new concert schedule. Tram tours leave on the hour from 10 AM until 4 PM. *10901 Old Cutler Rd., Coral Gables, tel. 305/667–1651. Open daily. Admission charged.*

Historical Museum of Southern Florida, in the Metro-Dade Cultural Center, houses hands-on displays and exhibits that interpret the South Florida experience through the ages. Displays are based on early Tequesta and Seminole Indian tribes, pirates, boom and bust years, and sunken ships. The Museum Tour concentrates on the exhibits, which cover 10,000 years of Miami's history and include a 15-minute slide show. The Curator's Cabinet Tour combines the Museum Tour with a look behind the scenes at departments visitors seldom see, including a research center with 500,000 photographs and the museum's cataloging and conservation departments. *101 W. Flagler St., Downtown Miami, tel. 305/375–1492. Open daily. Admission charged.*

Little Haiti is a 200-block area on Miami's northeast side that has become home to 60,000 of the estimated 200,000 Haitians who have settled in Greater Miami. Center your exploring around the two-block area along 54th Street from Miami Avenue to Northeast 2nd Avenue, where even the faded paint of lately colorful storefronts can't dampen the exuberant flair of the district. Storefront restaurants serve up such Creole specialties as fried goat, while local clubs pulse to the music of *compas* (a cross between salsa and merengue).

Little Havana formed 35 years ago, when the tidal wave of Cubans fleeing the Castro regime flooded an older neighborhood just west of downtown Miami. Today, with more than a half-million Cubans widely dispersed throughout Greater Miami, Little Havana remains a magnet for Cubans, other Spanish speakers, and Anglos alike, all of whom come to experience traditional Cuban culture—from the Spanish Mediterranean-style architecture to the strong Cuban coffee. A stroll down Calle Ocho (also known as Southwest 8th Street) will take you through the heart of the neighborhood. If your time is limited, explore the colorful three-block stretch from Southwest 14th Avenue to Southwest 11th Avenue. Old men in *guayaberas,* or pleated jackets, play dominoes at Domino Park on 14th Avenue while vendors hawk exotic fruits along the streets. At the northwestern edge of Little Havana, at Flagler Street and 17th Avenue, is Plaza de la Cubanidad, where redbrick sidewalks surround a water sculpture and a monument to Cuban patriots.

Lowe Art Museum has a permanent collection of 8,000 works, including Renaissance and Baroque art, American paintings, Latin American art, and Navajo and Pueblo Indian textiles and baskets. The museum also hosts traveling exhibitions. *1301 Stanford Dr., Coral Gables, tel. 305/284–3535 for recorded information or 305/284–3536 for museum office. Open Tues.–Sun. Admission charged.*

Matheson Hammock Park, Dade County's oldest and most scenic park, offers both walking and bike trails as well as lake fishing. The park's most popular feature, however, is a bathing beach, where the tide flushes a saltwater "atoll" pool through four gates. Pool lifeguards are on duty in winter 8:30–6, and in summer 7:30–7. *9610 Old Cutler Rd., Coral Gables, tel. 305/666–6979. Open daily. Small fee for parking.*

Metrozoo was devastated by Hurricane Andrew, but its 290 acres are once again the place to find koala bears, rare white Bengal tigers, Pygmy hippos, and other creatures, most of which roam free on islands surrounded by moats. The end of 1996 may see the reopening of "Wings of Asia," a 1½-acre aviary, where hundreds of exotic birds from Southeast Asia fly through a rain forest beneath a protective net enclosure. "Paws," a petting zoo for children, holds three shows daily. The zoo has 3 miles of walkways and an open-air amphitheater for concerts. *12400 S.W. 152nd St., South Dade, tel. 305/251–0400. Open daily. Admission charged.*

Miami Beach has gone from an avocado and coconut grove on a sandspit to become, in a bare 75 years and during three separate decades, one of the world's premier resorts. During its first heyday in the '20s, Miami Beach rivaled Palm Beach for attracting the rich at play. In the '50s, the Beach became the fun-in-the-sun place to celebrate post-war prosperity. In the '90s, the Beach has become one of the most talked-about and uninhibited strands in the world. Miami Beach is its own municipality, formed of 17 islands in Biscayne Bay. Its resorts and condominiums concentrate from north of Lincoln Road to 87th Street, most famous among these the Fontainebleau-Hilton. The sizzling appeal of the Beach today, however, centers around the Deco District of South Beach (see below), which now influences revival of the North Beach area newly underway.

Miami Museum of Science and Space Transit Planetarium. This is a participatory museum, chock-full of sound, gravity, and electricity displays for children and adults alike to manipulate and marvel at. A wildlife center houses native Florida snakes, turtles, tortoises, birds of prey, and large wading birds—175 live animals in all. Outstanding traveling exhibits appear throughout the year. Multimedia astronomy and laser shows are featured in the planetarium. *3280 S. Miami Ave., Miami, tel. 305/854–4247 or 305/854–2222 for planetarium show times and prices. Open daily. Admission charged.*

Miami Seaquarium presents six daily shows featuring sea lions, dolphins, and Lolita, a killer whale who cavorts in a huge tank. You can also touch the tide-pool inhabitants, feed sea lions and stingrays, watch the divers hand-feed the reef fish and moray eels, and admire sharks, manatees, and the tropical-reef fish in the 235,000-gallon aquarium. *4400 Rickenbacker Causeway, Key Biscayne area, tel. 305/361–5705. Open daily. Admission charged.*

Monkey Jungle is home to more than 400 monkeys representing 35 species—including orangutans from Borneo and Sumatra, golden lion tamarins from Brazil, and brown lemurs from Madagascar. Its rain-forest trail, damaged in the hurricane, is expected to

reopen fully in 1996. Performing-monkey shows begin at 10 and run continuously at 30-minute intervals. The walkways of this 30-acre attraction are caged; the monkeys roam free. *14805 S.W. 216th St., South Dade, tel. 305/235–1611. Open daily. Admission charged.*

Parrot Jungle & Gardens opened in 1936 and is one of Greater Miami's oldest and most popular commercial tourist attractions. It houses more than 1,100 exotic birds, including many parrots, macaws, and cockatoos which fly free. These birds will come to you for seeds, which you can purchase from old-fashioned gum-ball machines. Attend a trained-bird show, watch baby birds in training, and pose for photos with colorful macaws perched on your arms. The "jungle" is a natural hammock surrounding a sinkhole. Stroll among orchids and other flowering plants nestled among ferns, bald cypress, and massive live oaks. Other highlights include a primate show, small-wildlife shows, a children's playground, and a petting zoo. Also see the cactus garden and Flamingo Lake, with a breeding population of 75 Caribbean flamingos. *11000 S.W. 57th Ave., Miami, tel. 305/666–7834. Open daily. Admission charged.*

South Beach only yesterday was a rundown geriatric center. Today it's the deco darling of the world. A multimillion-dollar "sand-lift" has restored the beach, while a scenic boardwalk entices strollers, joggers, and people-watchers. Lincoln Road, once the 5th Avenue of the South and only recently an embarrassing derelict row, has been stunningly brought back to life. On weekends the Road rivals the pedestrian malls of Barcelona, Dublin, or Lyon for crowds and out-rivals all for free-form acting-out. The heart of South Beach (or SoBe, as it's sometimes called) is Ocean Drive, with its pastel-color Art Deco hotels and trendy outdoor cafés. Collins Avenue, one block west, features more affordable hotels, while Washington Avenue, one more block west, centers the best restaurants of SoBe. Some of the most imaginative boutiques line up along narrow, Mediterranean-styled Espanola Way.

South Miami, formerly a pioneer farming community, is now a suburb centered at the crossroads of Red Road (Southwest 57th Avenue) and Sunset Drive. Many boutiques and a few good restaurants line the streets of the town.

Virginia Key and Key Biscayne were a barely visited pair of islands until a causeway connected the two with the mainland in 1947. Parks occupy much of both keys, as well as a few expensive hotels and more affordably priced restaurants. Most appealing for visitors is the 3½-mile beach at Crandon Park with the clearest swimming waters in Miami; the Marjory Stoneman Douglas Nature Center; the Tennis Center at Crandon Park (site of the annual Lipton Championships); the Links at Key Biscayne (one of the top–rated public golf courses in America), and the Bill Baggs Cape Florida State Recreation Area, newly replanted in blight-resistant palms following obliteration of park foliage by Hurricane Andrew.

Vizcaya Museum and Gardens, an Italian palazzo perched on the shore of Biscayne Bay, was the winter home of Chicago industrialist James Deering. He designed his estate in Italian Renaissance style, with acres of elaborate, formal gardens and fountains that are unrivaled outside of Europe. The house contains 34 rooms of 15th- through 19th-century antique furniture, paintings, and sculptures in Renaissance, Baroque, Rococo, and Neoclassic styles. Guided tours are available. *3251 S. Miami Ave., Miami, tel. 305/579–2813 or 305/579–2808. Open daily. Admission charged.*

HOTELS AND INNS

Over the years, everything from small inns to splashy resorts and glassy condominiums have sprung up to meet the needs of Miami's diverse visitors. High-season rates prevail from mid-December through Easter. Most affordable seasons are between Easter and Memorial Day, and between Labor Day and mid-December. Rates go up for holiday weekends, though any time of year Miami offers bargain vacationing. The categories below are based on the high-season price—off-peak rates range 25%–50% lower. Price categories for double occupancy, excluding 8%–12% tax, are Moderate, $90–$120, and Inexpensive, $50–$90.

COCONUT GROVE Doubletree Hotel at Coconut Grove. On Bayshore Drive and close enough for walking to Grove attractions, this casually elegant high-rise with bay views matches large, airy rooms—most with balconies—with modern furnishings and good guest facilities. *2649 S. Bayshore Dr., 33133, tel. 305/858–2500 or 800/222–8733. 190 rooms, including 32 no-smoking rooms. Restaurant, piano bar, pool, 2 tennis courts, sundeck. AE, DC, MC, V. Moderate.*

CORAL GABLES Hotel Place St. Michel. Intimate, low rise, and historic, this jewel in the heart of the Gables is the city's most European hotel. Locals and visitors alike adore its romantic chic. Rooms are all different, shaped with odd angles, and filled with antiques. The lobby-level restaurant, with a sidewalk café, is one of the city's best. *162 Alcazar Ave., 33134, tel. 305/444–1666, fax 305/529–0074. 27 rooms. Continental breakfast included, restaurant, lounge, snack shop. AE, DC, MC, V. Moderate.*

DOWNTOWN MIAMI Hyatt Regency Hotel. With its complete makeover in 1995, the Hyatt is the choice of business travelers. The 24-story property adjoins the James L. Knight International Center and is within walking distance of everything in downtown. Enjoy dining and strolling alongside the Miami River, where a new gateway bridge that celebrates Miami history with sculptured detail opens before the end of 1996. *400 S.E. 2nd Ave., 33131, tel. 305/358–1234 or 800/233–1234, fax 305/358–0529. 640 rooms, including 43 no-smoking rooms. 2 restaurants, bar, pool, meeting rooms. AE, D, DC, MC, V. Moderate.*

Miami River Inn. This historic compound, the oldest continuously operating inn south of St. Augustine, has gaily painted, early-20th-century clapboard lodgings set around a pool in beautiful gardens. It's a 10-minute walk across the 1st Street Bridge to the heart of downtown. Second- and third-story rooms have stunning views of the city, but avoid the tiny rooms in building D. *118 S.W. South River Dr., 33130, tel. 305/325–0045, fax 305/325–9227. 40 rooms. Continental breakfast included, pool, Jacuzzi. AE, D, DC, MC, V. Inexpensive.*

MIAMI BEACH/NORTH BEACH **Bay Harbor Inn.** This favorite little inn of smart travelers divides its two-story lodgings between antiques-filled rooms town-side and more casual, resortlike rooms creek-side. An exceptional staff makes this the most guest-friendly lodging in the city. Rates are surprisingly affordable for the posh section of town. It's a 10-minute walk to the beach. *9660 E. Bay Harbor Dr., Bay Harbor Islands 33154, tel. and fax 305/868–4141. 38 rooms. Continental breakfast included. 2 restaurants, lounge, pool. AE, DC, MC, V. Moderate.*

Days Inn North Beach. This is the catbird's seat in the North Beach district, a seven-story hotel with modified deco styling (it dates from 1941) and a spot on the block-long shore road across from a beautiful section of beach backed by grassy dunes. Rooms are undistinguished—dark in aspect and furnished with the usuals, though including a fridge. Out front guests enjoy a lovely terrace with restaurant and bar service. *7450 Ocean Terr., Miami Beach 33141, tel. 305/866–1631 or 800/325–2525, fax 305/868–4617. 100 rooms. Restaurant, bar, dining terrace, minifridges. AE, MC, V. Moderate.*

Suez Oceanfront Resort. The carousel-striped Suez stands out along Motel Row because of its lovely public spaces, garden-like rattan-and-palm lounge, landscaped palm courtyard, and beachfront amenities, which include bar and restaurant, two pools, tennis court, and playground. Rooms, however, tend to be small (which helps keep rates affordable); the least expensive are in the north wing, with views only of the parking lot. Modified American Plan dining, fridges in all rooms and kitchens in some, and free laundry machines make staying here very price-attractive. *18215 Collins Ave., 33160, tel. 305/932–0661 or 800/327–5278; in FL, 800/432–3661; fax 305/937–0058. 150 rooms in main unit, 46 in lower-cost annex (including 54 rooms with kitchens). Restaurant, bar, freshwater and saltwater pools, children's pool, beach, lighted tennis court, shuffleboard and volleyball courts, playground. AE, D, DC, MC, V. Inexpensive–Moderate.*

MIAMI BEACH/SOUTH BEACH **Brigham Gardens.** A mother (architect) and daughter (horticulturist) team has gotten this place exactly right for South Beach. They refurbished but kept the deco and Mediterranean looks of their two buildings, added attractive tropical gardens, and converted what were apartments to 15 comfortable but unpretentious units. All feel like home. Floors are variously Cuban tile, mosaic tile, or wood, with a few carpeted; art ranges from Haitian to store-bought. Units may have interior arches, arresting alcoves, French doors, and the eight in the rear building all have private porches. All units have private baths; 12 have full kitchens, the others either fridge and microwave or fridge with microwave and hot plate. *1411 Collins Ave., Miami Beach 33139, tel. 305/531–1331. 15 units with bath. Garden, coin laundry, barbecue. AE, MC, V. Inexpensive–Moderate.*

Dorchester Hotel. Set back from the avenue for quiet rather than for grand effect, this '40s hotel is a rare Deco District lodging that offers a pool set in tropical gardens. It's five minutes by foot to Ocean Drive. Guest rooms are spacious, carpeted, outfitted with a fridge, and furnished with rattan and floral bed covers. Best buys are the rooms with a kitchenette. *1850 Collins Ave., 33139, tel. 305/534–6971, 305/531–5745, or 800/327–4739, fax 305/673–1006. 100 rooms. Breakfast room, pool, billiards, table tennis, free off-street parking, barbecues. AE, DC, MC, V. Inexpensive–Moderate.*

Kenmore Hotel. A notch better value than the Park Washington (*see below*), this three-story, 60-unit, mid-'30s hotel has an elevator, pool, large terrazzo lobby, and includes a free Continental breakfast. Rooms have pastel quilted bed covers, quiet ACs, and original Art Deco furniture. *1050 Washington Ave., Miami Beach 33139, tel. 305/674–1930, fax 305/534–6591. 60 units. Refrigerators. AE, D, DC, MC, V. Inexpensive–Moderate.*

Mermaid Guest House. Shazam! Lightning in the form of a long-haired former investment banker has transformed a Collins Avenue fleabag into this delightful guest house. Everything is framed in color: a back-of-the-house patio set in a jungle waiting to burst loose and retake Miami Beach; dresser drawers, each painted a different, vivid color; and louvered shutters outlined in bold graphics that bring the outdoor garden in. Beds are shrouded in mosquito netting, though rooms have air-conditioning (but not phones or TV), while small deco baths have tub-showers. There's a shared kitchen outside and a pay phone in the garden. A Continental breakfast is included, and frequent BYOB guest cookouts add to the family-style climate. *909 Collins Ave., 33139, tel. 305/538–5324. 10 units. Kitchen. MC, V. Inexpensive.*

Park Washington Hotel. Located two short blocks from the beach in the heart of the South Beach restaurant row, these are choice digs for dollar-mindful vacationers. An outdoor pool and friendly staff add to the appeal. Guest rooms are small, clean, with original pine deco furniture; the quietest are on the north side. In the same complex, the owners also run the Bel-Aire, where weekly rates can work out to an even better value. *1020 Washington Ave., Miami Beach 33139, tel. 305/532–1930, fax 305/672–6706 (for both hotels). 30 rooms. Refrigerators, complimentary Continental breakfast. AE, MC, V. Inexpensive–Moderate.*

Villa Paradiso. The under-furnished rooms of this guest house a block from the beach are ideal for couples traveling with their bikes, musical instruments, or anything else that needs space. These are informal spaces, converted from apartment use, and done more for cash flow than for taste. All units have full kitchen and bath. The building dates from 1935, so there are high ceilings and attractive details (wood floors, bathroom tiles, fluted fireplace hearths). Suites feature French doors and separate dining and kitchen areas. *1415 Collins Ave., Miami Beach 33139, tel. 305/532–0616, fax 305/667–0074. 17 units with bath. Coin laundry, kitchens, garden. AE, MC, V. Inexpensive–Moderate.*

MOTELS

INEXPENSIVE **Budgetel Inn.** Close to the airport, this four-story motel is part of a national chain but rates recommending because it's the best value you can find in the vicinity. Double-glazed windows minimize the roar of the air traffic overhead. All rooms have a microwave oven and small fridge. Breakfast is included in the room rate. *3501 LeJeune Rd., Miami 33142, tel. 305/871–1777 or 800/428–3438, fax 305/871–8080. 152 rooms, 25 suites. Pool, guest laundry, microwaves, refrigerators. AE, D, DC, MC, V.*

Paraclete Motel. The best budget buy in Miami, this small two-story property on Biscayne Boulevard sits a cut above its neighbors. You're also on the fringes of a red-light district, but nearby, just across Biscayne Boulevard to the east, is one of Miami's best old neighborhoods. The lobby is modest, and the rooms are plain. *7350 Biscayne Blvd., Miami 33138, tel. 305/751–1622, fax 305/759–1701. 20 rooms. Outdoor freshwater pool, guest laundry, off-street parking. MC, V.*

DINING

You can eat your way around the world in Greater Miami, enjoying just about every cuisine imaginable in upscale bistros or at sidewalk cafés. The waters off South Florida's coastline are rich in mahimahi, snapper, pompano, grouper, yellowfin tuna, and swordfish. Stone crabs are another local delicacy, but conch comes from abroad. Tropical fruits grow well here, and you'll find sauces made from papayas, mangoes, avocados, guavas, and coconuts.

A bargain feature at many Miami restaurants is the "early-bird dinner," where, for a fixed price—usually under $15—you get a full meal, which includes soup or salad, a choice of entrées with vegetables and potato, dessert, and often a soft drink. To get these meals you have to be seated by a certain time, usually before 6:30 PM. Call ahead to ask whether early-bird meals are offered, and until what time. If reservations are accepted, make one, because early birds are popular.

Casual neat clothing is acceptable at the restaurants listed below. Price categories per person, excluding 6% tax, service, and drinks, are Moderate, $15–$25, and Inexpensive, under $15.

COCONUT GROVE **Cafe Tu Tu Tango.** Artists set their easels up in the rococo-modern arcades of this eclectic café-lounge on the second story of the highly popular Coco-Walk. Outside offers some of the best people-watching in the South. Inside, beneath ceiling fans in the oak-floored dining room, guests graze on chips, dips, breads, and spreads—everything here is served in appetizer portions. House specials include frittatas, crab cakes, *picadillo* empanadas (spicy ground beef served with cilantro sour cream), and chicken and shrimp orzo paella, all to be enjoyed with some of the best sangria in the city. *3015 Grand Ave. (Cocowalk), tel. 305/529–2222. No reservations. AE, MC, V. Moderate.*

CORAL GABLES **Bugatti, the Art of Pasta.** Short on looks, long on value, this storefront restaurant in the heart of Coral Gables serves its specialties with sauces that range from classic pestos and marinaras to brandied leek and tomato sauce or smoked salmon cream. The pizzas are imaginatively topped. Try sautéed onions, Gorgonzola cheese, arugula, and walnuts. Gnocchi (potato dumplings) are also wonderful. Desserts include a *zabaione freddo* (chilled wine and Italian dipping cookies). *2504 Ponce de León Blvd., tel. 305/441–2545. No reservations. AE, DC, MC, V. No lunch Sun. Inexpensive–Moderate.*

DOWNTOWN MIAMI **East Coast Fisheries.** This family-run restaurant features fresh seafood caught by its own 38-boat fleet in the Keys. From tables along the second-floor balcony, watch the cooks grill your dinner in the open kitchen below. *360 W. Flagler St., tel. 305/373–5515. AE, DC, MC, V. Moderate.*

Granny Feelgood's. "Granny" is a shrewd gentleman named Irving Field, who caters to health-conscious lawyers, office workers, and backpackers with such specials as spinach fettuccine, grilled tofu, and grilled chicken salads. *190 S.E. 1st Ave., tel. 305/358–6233. No smoking. AE, MC, V. Closed Sun. Inexpensive.*

Las Tapas. Ordering different tapas—"little dishes" in Spanish—allows you to create your own smorgasbord of tastes in a single meal. Tapas to try include *la tostada* (smoked salmon and capers on melba toast) and *pincho de pollo a la plancha* (grilled chicken marinated in brandy); you can also order standard-size Spanish entrées. *Bayside Marketplace, 401 Biscayne Blvd., tel. 305/372–2737. AE, D, DC, MC, V. Moderate.*

LITTLE HAVANA **Casa Panza.** From the tile counter at the tapas bar to the flamenco dolls on the "men's" and "women's"—to the Spanish posters, the hanging hams, chorizos, and chilies—this little cavelike hideaway brings a trace of Spain to Calle Ocho in Little Havana. All dishes are made from scratch. Try tapas and soups to start, then big portions of shellfish, fish, the favored rice stews with clams or shrimp, or the paella for two. Traditional desserts (lemon or vanilla cremes, puddings of the region) finish meals off happily. Tuesday and Thursday evenings the tiny corner stage showcases a Spanish folkloric show. *1620 S.W. 8th St., tel. 305/643–5343. Reservations required. MC, V. Closed Sun. Moderate.*

Hy-Vong Vietnamese Cuisine. Magic continues to pour forth from the tiny kitchen of this plain little restaurant. Come before 7 to avoid a wait. Favorite dishes include spring rolls (a Vietnamese version of an egg roll, with ground pork, cellophane noodles, and black mushrooms wrapped in homemade rice paper), whole fish panfried with *nuoc man* (a garlic-lime fish sauce), and thinly sliced pork, barbecued with sesame seeds and fish sauce, served with bean sprouts, rice noodles, and slivers of carrots, almonds, and peanuts. *3458 S.W. 8th St., tel. 305/446–3674. No smoking. No credit cards. Closed Mon. and 2 wks in Aug. No lunch. Inexpensive–Moderate.*

Islas Canarias. For affordable Mediterranean dishes, choose this very casual restaurant favored by Cuban poets, pop-music stars, and media personalities for its dishes from the Canary Islands and Cuba. Choices include ham hocks with boiled potatoes and palomilla steak with fried plantains. *285 N.W. Unity Blvd. (N.W. 27th Ave.), tel. 305/649–0440. No credit cards. Inexpensive.*

MIAMI BEACH **Da Leo.** Volume keeps the mood festive and the standards high at this first-rate little Italian restaurant. Pastas, plus a few fish, veal, and chicken choices, make up most of the entrées. Prices here are only half of what you pay for the same fine Italian fare at trendy places. *819 Lincoln Road Mall, tel. 305/674–0350. No reservations. AE, DC, MC, V. No lunch weekends. Inexpensive–Moderate.*

News Cafe. Beach views plus a clientele that likes to schmooze have made the News Cafe the hippest joint on Ocean Drive. Stop in for a drink or a light meal—anything from bagels to chocolate fondue. *800 Ocean Dr., tel. 305/538–6397. AE, DC, MC, V. Inexpensive.*

Norma's on the Beach. Put this wonderfully reggae-style hole-in-the-wall near the top of your list. Color bursts from seat cushions to cut-tin Haitian tap taps on walls, and instead of bud vases on the tables, they've got entire palm trees in pots (on the floor). The cuisine combines French finesse with Caribbean seasonings. Dishes might include baby-back ribs with Appleton Rum glaze; Rasta chicken breast with *callaloo* (West Indian spinach), cream cheese, roasted sweet peppers, in a white wine sauce; or pan-sautéed pompano with a rum-banana sauce. *646 Lincoln Road Mall, tel. 305/532–2809. AE, D, DC, MC, V. Closed Mon. Moderate.*

SHOPPING

Greater Miami has more than a dozen major shopping malls, an international free zone, and hundreds of miles of commercial streets lined with shopping centers and storefronts. Major department stores abound, with many malls boasting three.

SHOPPING DISTRICTS Many garment manufacturers sell their products in the more than 30 factory outlets and discount fashion stores in the Miami Fashion District, located east of I–95, along 5th Avenue from 25th to 29th streets.

Bayside Marketplace (401 Biscayne Blvd., tel. 305/577–3344) is for people-watching as well as shopping. Buskers perform and a free stage schedules daily bands. Excursion boats that include a tall ship and a 36-foot-long Venetian gondola tie up at the marina.

In the old section known as Allapattah, the **Wholesale District** (20th St., between N.W. 17th and 27th Aves.) comprises hundreds of merchants lining either side of the street. Merchandise includes apparel, shoes and handbags, luggage and accessories, jewelry, perfumes, and electronic and pharmaceutical products, and many small, affordable restaurants are tucked in as well. The district is about 10 minutes east of Miami International Airport off the East–West Expressway.

FARMERS MARKETS The oldest is the **Coconut Grove Farmers Market** (Grand Ave., 1 block west of MacDonald Ave. [S.W. 32nd Ave.], Coconut Grove), begun in 1977. It takes place Saturdays 8 to 2 year-round. At the **Farmers Market at Merrick Park** (LeJeune Rd. [S.W. 42nd Ave.] and Biltmore Way, Coral Gables), some 25 produce and plant vendors set up in a little downtown park on Saturdays from 8 to 1, mid-January through March. Gardening workshops, cooking demonstrations, and children's activities are standard features. On Sundays November through March, the **Lincoln Road Farmers Market** sets up on Lincoln Road between Meridian and Euclid Avenues, including children's activities. A combined farmers/flea market, typically with some 500 vendors, takes place every weekend at the **Flagler Dog Track** (401 N.W. 38th Ct., Miami) from 9 to 4.

OUTDOOR ACTIVITIES

BEACHES Miami Beach is famous for its broad sandy expanse, which extends 10 miles from Haulover Cut to Government Cut. A wide boardwalk, which is popular with strollers and joggers, can be found between 21st and 46th streets. All the city beaches are free, and during the winter and summer lifeguards are on duty every day (except at Bal Harbour and Surfside beaches). Beaches are also tops on Key Biscayne.

BIKING Dade County has about 100 miles of off-road bicycling trails. Bike rentals can be found at **Dade Cycle** (3216 Grand Ave., Coconut Grove, tel. 305/444–5997), and at numerous shops in South Beach.

BOATING AND SAILING **Bayside Marketplace** (tel. 305/888–3002) offers catamaran cruises on Biscayne Bay. **Easy Sailing** (Dinner Key Marina, Coconut Grove, tel. 305/858–4001) rents 19- to 127-foot boats by the hour or for the whole day. It also offers motorboat and sailing lessons, scuba certification courses, and deep-sea fishing.

FISHING Florida's waters abound with mahimahi, pompano, snapper, grouper, yellowfin tuna, and swordfish. Half- and full-day fishing charters are available with *Abracadabra* (4000 Crandon Blvd., Key Biscayne, tel. 305/361–5625), **Blue Waters Sportfishing Charters** (16375 Collins Ave., Sunny Isles, tel. 305/944–4531), *Therapy IV* (Haulover Marine Center, 10800 Collins

Ave., Miami Beach, tel. 305/945–1578), and *Reward II* (Miami Beach Marina, 300 Alton Rd., MacArthur Causeway, Miami Beach, tel. 305/372–9470).

GOLF Florida is famous for its excellent and popular golf courses; following are some that are affordable and open to the public: **Biltmore Golf Course** (1210 Anastasia Ave., Coral Gables, tel. 305/460–5364), **Don Shula's Golf Club** (N.W. 154th St. at the Palmetto Expressway, Miami Lakes, tel. 305/821–1150), **Doral Golf Resort & Spa** (4400 N.W. 87th Ave., Doral, tel. 305/592–2000 or 800/713–6725), **Links at Key Biscayne** (6700 Crandon Blvd., Key Biscayne, tel. 305/361–9129), **Normandy Shores Golf Course** (2401 Biarritz Dr., Miami Beach, tel. 305/868–6502), **Presidential Country Club** (19650 N.E. 18th Ave., North Miami Beach, tel. 305/933–5266).

SNORKELING AND SCUBA DIVING Summer diving conditions in Greater Miami have been compared to those in the Caribbean. Winter diving can be adversely affected when cold fronts come through. Dive-boat schedules vary with the season and with local weather conditions.

Bubbles Dive Center is affiliated with PADI. Its boat, *Divers Dream,* is kept on Watson Island on MacArthur Causeway. *2671 S.W. 27th Ave., Miami, tel. 305/856–0565.*

Divers Paradise of Key Biscayne has a complete dive shop and diving-charter service, including equipment rental and scuba instruction (PADI). *4000 Crandon Blvd., Key Biscayne, tel. 305/361–3483.*

The **Diving Locker** is a PADI-affiliated dive shop that offers three-day and three-week certification courses, wreck and reef dives aboard *The Native Diver,* and full sales, service, and repairs. *223 Sunny Isles Blvd., North Miami Beach, tel. 305/947–6025.*

Team Divers, a PADI five-star facility in the Miami Beach marina, is the only dive shop in the South Beach area. Daily dives are arranged. *300 Alton Rd., tel. 305/673–0101 or 800/543–7887.*

TENNIS Greater Miami has more than a dozen public tennis centers. All charge non-residents an hourly fee. Courts can be affordably rented in Coral Gables at the **Biltmore Tennis Center** (1150 Anastasia Ave., Coral Gables, tel. 305/460–5360); in Miami Beach at the **Flamingo Park Tennis Center** (1100 12th St., Miami Beach, tel. 305/673–7761) and **North Shore Tennis Center** (350 73rd St., Miami Beach, tel. 305/993–2022); and on Key Biscayne at the **International Tennis Center** (7300 Crandon Blvd., Key Biscayne, tel. 305/365–2300).

WALKING The **Historical Museum of Southern Florida** (101 W. Flagler St., Miami, tel. 305/375–1492) conducts a series of tours throughout the Greater Miami area. The **Miami Design Preservation League** (1001 Ocean Dr., Miami Beach, tel. 305/672–2014) offers a 90-minute tour of the Art Deco District on Saturday morning at 10:30 AM (call for point of departure). Also available is the League's *Art Deco District Guide,* with six detailed walking and driving tours of the Art Deco District. **Paul George,** a history professor at Miami-Dade Community College and a former president of the Florida Historical Society, leads tours of many historic places in Miami and Fort Lauderdale. For reservations, call 305/858–6021.

ENTERTAINMENT

During the busy winter season, Miami's calendar is jammed with cultural events, gallery exhibits, concerts, lectures, and dance and theater performances. The *Miami Herald* publishes information on the performing arts every Friday in the "Weekend" section. Other good sources are *Miami Today,* a free weekly newspaper available each Thursday; *New Times,* another free weekly paper; and the *Greater Miami Calendar of Events* (for a free copy, call 305/375–4634).

CONCERTS Greater Miami moves to many beats. The **New World Symphony** (541 Lincoln Rd., tel. 305/673–3330; box office tel. 305/673–3331) is an advanced training orchestra for gifted young musicians. From October through May, the **Philharmonic Orchestra of Florida** (1680 Meridian Ave., Miami Beach, tel. 305/538–5112) performs classical music and pop concerts

DANCE Edward Villella's **Miami City Ballet** (905 Lincoln Rd., Miami Beach, tel. 305/532–7713) performs modern jazz and ballet from September through March. The earthy qualities of the flamenco can be seen in the refreshing choreography of the Spanish dance company, **Ballet Flamenco La Rosa** (1008 Lincoln Rd., Miami Beach, tel. 305/672–0552).

SPECTATOR SPORTS Daily listings of local sports events can be found in the sports section of the *Miami Herald.* Miami's NBA team, the **Miami Heat** (tel. 305/577–4328), and the **Florida Panthers** (tel. 305/768–1900, in Fort Lauderdale) of the National Hockey League play home games at the Miami Arena (701 Arena Blvd., tel. 305/530–4444). Football fans can watch the **Miami Dolphins** of the NFL and the **Florida Marlins** of the National League play at Joe Robbie Stadium (2269 N.W. 199th St., tel. 305/623–6100). The **University of Miami Hurricanes** play their championship brand of college football at the Orange Bowl (1400 N.W. 4th St., but for tickets, tel. 305/284–2655). Tickets for all teams' games can be purchased from Ticketmaster (tel. 305/358–5585).

Minneapolis and St. Paul
Minnesota

Updated by Oliver McCurnin

Minneapolis and St. Paul are known as the Twin Cities, but they are hardly identical. St. Paul has been described as the last of the Eastern cities, with its Victorian and Art Deco architecture, the domes of the State Capitol and St. Paul Cathedral, and the tooting steamboats on its 29 miles of Mississippi riverfront. Minneapolis is brasher and busier, with several new downtown skyscrapers, a contemporary sculpture garden, and a revitalized Warehouse District with appealing shops, galleries, and restaurants.

In both cities, residents have access to climate-controlled skyway systems, allowing them to drive downtown, park, and go about their daily business without once setting foot outdoors—a blessing during the long winters. Sports fans also fare well here, thanks to the local professional basketball, baseball, and football teams. The jewel of the Twin Cities is a lake system that enhances the residential areas and provides the foundation for parks filled with jogging and biking trails, beaches, and public docks. Minneapolis alone has 22 lakes.

Sibling rivalry has rewarded the 2.2 million people of the area with an envious metropolitan lifestyle. Both communities enjoy world-class orchestras, art museums, and a vibrant theater community that offers everything from Kabuki to Neil Simon. Although commonly associated with the rich heritage of its Irish, German, and Scandinavian pioneers, the area offers a cultural diversity these days that extends from its first Native American citizens to its most recent Southeast Asian settlers.

ESSENTIAL INFORMATION

WHEN TO GO Spring and fall are usually the gentlest seasons, with warm days and mild nights. Average maximum temperatures in April and May range between 56° and 68°, while average minimum temperatures fall between 36° and 48°. With its beautiful foliage, fall has become an especially popular time for tourists. Fall average maximum temperatures range from 59° to 72° and average minimum temperatures fall between 41° and 52°.

July and August can be humid, with temperatures usually at least in the mid-80s and several days that near 100°. Summer mosquitoes can also be a nuisance. Winter visitors will find daily temperatures that average in the teens, but these can dip below 0° with windchill factored in. With an average snowfall of 42 inches, January, February, and March are the best times for cross-country skiing.

FESTIVALS AND SEASONAL EVENTS **Late Jan.– early Feb.:** St. Paul Winter Carnival features ice sculptures and entertainment. **Early June:** Taste of Minnesota is four days of feasting, plus a big Fourth of July fireworks display on the State Capitol lawn. **Mid-July–Aug.:** Summerfest features Viennese waltzes, food fairs, and music at Minneapolis's Peavey outdoor plaza. **Late Aug.:** The always interesting and fun Renaissance

Festival runs until the end of September and features music, food, crafts, and activities for all ages. The Minnesota State Fair is held in St. Paul. Contact local tourist offices for information on events (*see* Tourist Offices, *below*).

BARGAINS In the summer, check out the free outdoor concerts at the Lake Harriet Band Shelter. Every six weeks, the Minneapolis Warehouse District hosts a free "gallery crawl," with show openings and refreshments; contact New North Artscape (tel. 612/337–5198). Many of the theater events offer senior-citizen discounts and lower prices for tickets sold shortly before curtain time. The Mississippi Mile public parkway on the downtown Minneapolis riverbanks has walking and biking trails, picnic spots, and a hot line for free events (tel. 612/342–1231).

TOURIST OFFICES The **St. Paul Convention and Visitors Bureau** (102 Norwest Center, 55 E. 5th St., St. Paul 55101, tel. 612/297–6985 or 800/627–6101) has current information on all upcoming events. The **Minneapolis Convention and Visitors Association** (400 Multifood Tower, 33 S. 6th St., Minneapolis 55403, tel. 612/348–4313 or 800/445–7412) and the **Minnesota Office of Tourism** (100 Metro Sq., 121 E. 7th Place, St. Paul 55101, tel. 612/296–5029 or 800/657–3700) are also helpful.

EMERGENCIES **Police, fire,** and **ambulance:** Dial 911. **Hospitals:** Hennepin County Medical Center (701 Park Ave. S, downtown Minneapolis, tel. 612/347–3131). **Doctors:** Referral Service (tel. 612/347–4262). **Road conditions:** Minnesota Department of Transportation hot line (tel. 612/296–3076).

ARRIVING AND DEPARTING

BY PLANE The **Minneapolis–St. Paul International Airport** (tel. 612/726–5555) lies south of the cities on Route 5, 8 miles from downtown St. Paul and 10 miles from downtown Minneapolis. The **Metropolitan Transit**

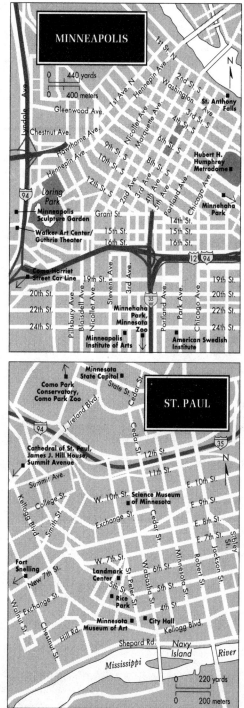

Commission (tel. 612/349–7000) provides buses between the airport and both cities. Fares are less than $2. Taxis to and from the airport take about 20 minutes from both downtown St. Paul (about $15) and downtown Minneapolis (up to $20).

To drive from the airport, take West 7th Street or Shepard Road to downtown St. Paul; for downtown Minneapolis, take Route 5 east to Route 55 north, or Route 5 west to I–35W north. Major car-rental companies are located near the baggage-claim area.

BY TRAIN The Twin Cities **Amtrak depot** (730 Transfer Rd., tel. 800/872–7245) in St. Paul serves both cities.

BY BUS **Greyhound Lines** (tel. 800/231–2222) serves both cities at St. Paul Greyhound terminal (7th St. at St. Peter St., tel. 612/222–0509) and Minneapolis Greyhound terminal (29 N. 9th St., tel. 612/371–3323).

BY CAR I–94 runs east–west through downtown Minneapolis and St. Paul and converges with I–35 (I–35E into St. Paul and I–35W into Minneapolis), a north–south artery.

GETTING AROUND

Minneapolis is spread out. You can explore downtown on foot, but for the city's far-flung sights you'll need to drive or take a bus or a cab. Downtown St. Paul and its major sights are easily explored on foot; only a few sights require a car or bus.

BY CAR In Minneapolis, Hennepin Avenue crosses the Mississippi to divide the north and south ends of town and becomes a main downtown thoroughfare. Another major artery is Lyndale Avenue, running south from the river. In St. Paul, Summit and Grand avenues run parallel with I–94; both end at the river.

BY BUS The **Metropolitan Transit Commission** (MTC, tel. 612/349–7000) runs buses in both cities. Exact fare or tokens are required,

and dollars bills are accepted. The MTC runs two transit stores (719 Marquette St., in downtown Minneapolis; 101 E. 5th St., on the skyway level, in downtown St. Paul), where you can pick up schedules and buy tokens.

BY TAXI Taxis must be ordered by phone or hired at cabstands. In Minneapolis, try **Blue and White** (tel. 612/333–3331) and **Yellow** (tel. 612/824–4444). In St. Paul, contact **Yellow** (tel. 612/222–4433) and **City Wide** (tel. 612/489–1111). **Town Taxi** (tel. 612/331–8294) serves both cities and all suburbs.

REST STOPS Public rest rooms are available at community centers in parks in both cities. Saint Paul Center and Town Square Park (Minnesota St.) in downtown St. Paul also have public rest rooms.

GUIDED TOURS Most tours are active between Memorial Day and Labor Day. **Gray Line** (tel. 612/469–5020), **Airport Express** (tel. 612/827–7777), and **Metro Connections** (tel. 612/333–8687) have tours of both cities. Mississippi River tours are provided by the **Padelford Packet Boat Co.** (tel. 612/227–1100) aboard the *Anson Northrup* and *Josiah Snelling,* modern stern-wheelers modeled after 19th-century Mississippi riverboats. Cruises on Minneapolis's Lake Harriet are offered aboard the stern-wheeler **Queen of the Lakes** (tel. 612/348–4825 or 612/348–2248).

EXPLORING

DOWNTOWN MINNEAPOLIS Downtown Minneapolis is easily walkable in any season. If the weather turns truly bitter, the skyway system connects hundreds of shops and restaurants. Following are the main attractions in or just south of downtown.

Minneapolis Institute of Arts. More than 80,000 works from every age and culture are on display here, with exhibits of photography, sculpture, paintings, drawings, and prints; free tours daily. *2400 3rd Ave. S, tel. 612/870–3131. Open Tues.–Sun. Admission free.*

St. Anthony Falls, on the edge of downtown, are harnessed by dams and bypassed by the Upper St. Anthony Lock, which allows river traffic to reach the city. An observation deck and a small visitor center have good views of lock operations and exhibits on the Mississippi. *Foot of Portland Ave., tel. 612/333–5336. Observation deck open Apr.–Oct., daily. Admission free.*

Walker Art Center. This outstanding contemporary art museum features a strong permanent collection of paintings, sculpture, prints, and photography. The center offers cultural programs regularly and adjoins the country's largest regional theater, The Guthrie (*see* Entertainment, *below*). Across from the center is the Minneapolis Sculpture Garden, the largest urban sculpture garden in the nation, with 40 fanciful creations in tree-lined plazas. The garden is linked to Loring Park and downtown Minneapolis by a footbridge. *Center: Hennepin Ave. and Vineland Pl., tel. 612/375–7600. Open Tues.–Sun. Admission charged; senior citizens free. Garden: Open daily. Admission free.*

AROUND MINNEAPOLIS **Minnehaha Park,** on the Mississippi near the airport, is home to the charming Minnehaha Falls. The Minnehaha Parkway, which follows Minnehaha Creek, offers 15 miles of jogging, biking, and roller-skating trails to Lake Harriet. *From downtown, drive on I–35W south to Rte. 62 east and then get on Rte. 55; or take Bus 7A, 7B, or 7C. Open daily. Admission free.*

Minnesota Zoo. This delightful zoo contains more than 1,700 animals and more than 2,000 plant varieties; it features six trail systems, a beaver exhibit, a koala lodge, a bird show, and camel rides. *13000 Zoo Blvd., Apple Valley, tel. 612/431–9200 or 612/432–9000. From downtown drive on I–35W south to Hwy. 62 east and follow zoo signs, or take Bus 57. Open daily. Admission charged.*

Valleyfair. This ever-expanding amusement park features everything from the basic merry-go-round to loop-the-loop roller coasters. A variety of concerts, stunt shows, and other attractions are held on a rotating basis. *Hwy. 101, Shakopee, tel. 612/445–6500. From downtown drive on I–35W south to Hwy. 101 and follow signs. Open daily. Admission charged.*

DOWNTOWN ST. PAUL Visitors can easily explore downtown on foot, either on the streets or in the skyway system (bounded by Kellogg Boulevard at the river, and 8th, Wacouta, and St. Peter streets). Buses can take you from downtown up the hill to the State Capitol, St. Paul Cathedral, and the shops on Grand Avenue.

City Hall. This 1931, 20-story building is known for its Art Deco interior, its 85-foot-long Memorial Hall, and the onyx *Indian God of Peace,* standing 36 feet high and weighing 60 tons. *4th St. between St. Peter and Wabasha Sts., tel. 612/266–8023. Open weekdays. Admission free.*

Landmark Center. This towering old federal-courts building of Romanesque Revival design faces Rice Park. It features a six-story indoor courtyard with stained-glass skylights and marble tiles. *75 W. 5th St., tel. 612/292–3225. Free guided tours, tel. 612/292–3230. Open daily. Admission free.*

Minnesota State Capitol. This noble 1905 structure contains more than 25 varieties of marble, sandstone, limestone, and granite, and its 223-foot-high dome is the world's largest unsupported marble dome. *75 Constitution Ave., tel. 612/297–3521. Open daily. Free guided tours daily.*

Rice Park. West of the museum is St. Paul's oldest urban park, only one block square. The park is a favorite with locals, who eat lunch here in warm weather. Each winter, the city's Winter Carnival ice-carving contest is held here.

Science Museum of Minnesota. This science-technology center and natural-history museum has exhibits emphasizing hands-on participation—making it very popular with children. The fantastic Omni Theater features films on topics ranging from Antarctica to space exploration. *30 E. 10th St., tel. 612/221–9488. Open daily. Admission charged.*

WEST OF DOWNTOWN ST. PAUL **Como Park.** This urban playground is home to a lake, the Como Park Conservatory (tel. 612/489–1740), the Como Park Zoo (tel. 612/488–5571), picnic areas, walking trails, and tennis and swimming facilities. *By car, take I–94 to Lexington Ave. and follow signs Open daily. Admission free.*

St. Paul Cathedral. Styled after St. Peter's in Rome, this Classical Renaissance granite domed church, completed in 1915, seats 3,000 and has stunning stained-glass windows. *239 Selby Ave., at Summit Ave., tel. 612/228–1766. Open daily. Admission free.*

Summit Avenue. This 5-mile stretch of stately homes and mansions, from the cathedral to the Mississippi, is the nation's longest expanse of intact residential Victorian architecture. F. Scott Fitzgerald lived at 599 Summit Avenue in 1918 when he wrote *This Side of Paradise*; the Governor's Mansion is at 1006 Summit Avenue. You can visit the **James J. Hill House,** an elaborate 1891 mansion that belonged to the former railroad magnate. *240 Summit Ave., tel. 612/297–2555. Open Wed.–Sat. Admission charged.*

HOTELS AND INNS

Where you want to stay may well depend on whether or not you have a car. Accommodations are cheaper outside the metropolitan area, but downtown locations offer closer proximity to the main sights. When you go also affects your decision—some hotels are attached to downtown shopping and entertainment centers by skyways to avoid the icy winters. Bargains can sometimes be found by staying at bed-and-breakfasts in the cities. For information on B&Bs, contact the Minnesota Office of Tourism (tel. 612/296–5029 or 800/657–3700). Price categories for double occupancy, excluding 7% tax, are Moderate, $50–$100, and Inexpensive, under $50.

MINNEAPOLIS **Best Western Normandy Inn.** This homey little hotel tucked between skyscrapers is no more than a 10-minute walk from the Metrodome, Convention Cen-

ter, and Orchestra Hall. *405 S. 8th St., 55404, tel. 612/370–1400 or 800/372–3131, fax 612/370–0351. 159 rooms. 2 restaurants, piano bar. AE, D, DC, MC, V. Moderate.*

Best Western Regency Plaza Hotel. The most attractive feature here is the busy downtown address—next door to the Target Center and a block away from shopping and entertainment. *41 N. 10th St., 55403, tel. 800/423–4100, fax 612/339–4765. 186 rooms, 7 suites. Restaurant, pool, free downtown shuttle bus. AE, D, DC, MC, V. Moderate.*

Holiday Inn Metrodome. A 10-minute bus ride from downtown, this showy hotel is located in the heart of a theater and entertainment district and near both the Metrodome and the University of Minnesota. *1500 Washington Ave. S, 55454, tel. 612/333–4646 or 800/465–4329, fax 612/333–7910. 265 rooms, 22 suites. Free transportation by appointment. AE, D, DC, MC, V. Moderate.*

ST. PAUL **Days Inn Civic Center.** This clean, no-nonsense downtown lodging is usually filled with folks who are attending activities across the street at the St. Paul Civic Center. *175 W. 7th St., 55102, tel. 612/292–8929 or 800/635–4766, fax 612/292–1749. 200 rooms, 5 suites. Restaurant. AE, D, DC, MC, V. Moderate.*

Excell Inn of St. Paul. This three-story hotel is near the Sun Ray Shopping Center on the eastern side of St. Paul, off I–94 and White Bear Avenue. A senior-citizen discount is offered to those 55 and older. *1739 Old Hudson Rd., 55106, tel. 612/771–5566 or 800/356–8013, fax 612/771–1262. 101 rooms, some no-smoking. AE, DC, MC, V. Moderate.*

MOTELS

All of the following are in the Inexpensive price category:

MINNEAPOLIS **Burnsville Super 8** (1101 Burnsville Pkwy., Burnsville 55337, tel. 612/894–3400 or 800/800–8000, fax 612/894–2771). 67 rooms; Continental breakfast included. **Days Inn University** (2407 University Ave. SE, 55414, tel. 612/623–3999 or 800/325–2525, fax 612/331–2152). 130 rooms; Continental breakfast included. **Prime Rate Motel** (12850 W. Frontage Rd., Burnsville 55337, tel. 612/894–8554 or 800/358–8554, fax 612/894–5828). 98 rooms; Continental breakfast included, pool.

ST. PAUL **Comfort Inn Roseville** (2715 Long Lake Rd., Roseville 55113, tel. and fax 612/636–5800 or 800/221–2222). 118 rooms; Continental breakfast included, no-smoking rooms. **Days Inn Roseville** (2550 Cleveland Ave. N, Roseville 55113, tel. 612/636–6730 or 800/325–2525, fax 612/636–5966). 115 rooms; Continental breakfast included, no-smoking rooms. **Motel 6** (2300 Cleveland Ave. N, Roseville 55113, tel. 612/639–3988, fax 612/633–5748). 113 rooms.

DINING

The Twin Cities have a growing number of northern Italian and Southeast Asian eateries. You'll also find many comfortable neighborhood spots, known either for ethnic specialties or the pleasant home cooking that seems to qualify as American cuisine these days: salads, pasta, burgers, and homemade pies. On many local menus, vegetarian entrées and fresh salads are offered. Price categories per person, excluding 6% tax, service, and drinks, are Moderate, $8–$12, and Inexpensive, under $8.

MINNEAPOLIS **Black Forest Inn.** Families, students, and artists all love the hearty German cuisine—try the schnitzel with potato pancakes and applesauce—and the varied selection of beers on tap and in bottles. In summer, be sure to request a table in the grape arbor. *1 E. 26th St., tel. 612/872–0812. AE, D, DC, MC, V. Moderate.*

Chez Bananas. This offbeat storefront café in the chic Warehouse District balances savory Caribbean food with some oddball decorations: vinyl bats, inflatable palm trees, and windup toys. *129 N. 4th St., tel. 612/340–0032. AE, DC, MC, V. Moderate.*

Giorgio's. This hip Italian café with two Uptown locations makes an authentic evening dinner with a variety of focaccias, pastas, nightly entrée specials, and Italian wines. *2451 Hennepin Ave. S, tel. 612/374–5131; 1601 W. Lake St., tel. 612/822–7071. No credit cards. Moderate.*

It's Greek to Me. Small and unpretentious, this bustling café serves some of the best Greek food in town. *626 W. Lake St., tel. 612/825–9922. MC, V. Inexpensive.*

Loring Café. The Loring offers a terrific view of handsome Loring Park, vaguely bohemian decor in the casual dining area and new formal dining room, international music nightly, one of the more experimental theaters in the Twin Cities, and an original array of dishes. *1624 Harmon Pl., tel. 612/332–1617. AE, D, MC, V. Moderate.*

The Lotus. Choose from over 150 Vietnamese dishes at this popular restaurant right in the heart of Uptown—the curried chicken and mock-duck salad are especially good. *3037 Hennepin Ave. S, tel. 612/825–2263. No credit cards. Inexpensive.*

Pasqual's. A black-bean burrito will be more than you can handle at this deli-service southwestern café. *2528 Hennepin Ave. S, tel. 612/374–1415. AE, D, DC, MC, V. Inexpensive.*

ST. PAUL **Cafe Latte.** Furiously popular with the post-theater crowd, this eclectic cafeteria is almost always jammed with devotees hungering for homemade soups, first-rate salads, stews, scones, chocolate desserts, and espresso drinks. *850 Grand Ave., tel. 612/224–5687. AE, MC, V. Inexpensive.*

Dixie's Bar & Smokehouse. This casual spot in the heart of the Grand Avenue retail district serves up an eclectic mix of southern cuisines, mixing Cajun, Creole, and Tex-Mex styles. *695 Grand Ave., tel. 612/222–7345. AE, D, MC, V. Moderate.*

Gladstone Café. Enjoy homemade muffins and soups at this popular cafeteria on the main floor of the historic Landmark Center. *75 W. 5th St., 612/227–4704. No credit cards. Inexpensive.*

Khyber Pass Café. An enthusiastic Afghani family serves their sometimes spicy native cuisine—including lamb and chicken dishes simmered with garlic or coriander chutney—in a sleepy St. Paul neighborhood. *1399 St. Clair Ave., tel. 612/698–5403. MC, V. Moderate.*

La Cucaracha. This family-run Mexican eatery has some of the best Mexican food in the Twin Cities, including a list of specialty entrées like Nina's Cactus Pepper Stew and Chilaquiles. *36 S. Dale St., tel. 612/221–9682. AE, D, MC, V. Moderate.*

Mickey's Diner. Listed on the National Register of Historic Places, this streamlined 1930s downtown diner dishes up great breakfasts and burgers. *36 W. 7th St., tel. 612/222–5633. D, MC, V. Inexpensive.*

Old City Café. The only kosher restaurant in the Twin Cities, this tiny café is also one of the area's few vegetarian restaurants, featuring Middle Eastern dishes and potato knishes. *1571 Grand Ave., tel. 612/699–5347. No credit cards. Inexpensive.*

Russian Tea House. The Tea House is a simple café that offers home-cooked Russian specialties, including a great piroshki—mild ground beef and rice baked inside a chewy, leavened roll. *1758 University Ave. W, tel. 612/646–4144. No credit cards. Inexpensive.*

SHOPPING

Museum shops often offer the best Minnesota-made wares. Try the shops at Walker Art Center in Minneapolis and Landmark Center, and the Science Museum in downtown St. Paul (*see* Exploring, *above*). **Byerly's** (3777 Park Center Blvd., St. Louis Park, tel. 612/929–2100), one of the most popular stores in the area, is a grandiose grocery with chandeliers, carpeted aisles, and gold-plated bird cages.

MINNEAPOLIS The very definition of a shopper's paradise, the **Mall of America** has over 400 stores, 14 movie theaters, 16 restaurants, and Camp Snoopy, an indoor amusement park with roller coasters and water rides. Besides the major department chains, there are such specialty shops as Legoland, a Barbie-doll store, a Native American art boutique, and a store that sells nothing but refrigerator magnets. *From downtown take I–35W south to I–494 east and follow signs, tel. 612/883–8800.*

Nicollet Mall, a mile-long pedestrian mall in the center of downtown, has skywalks connecting many of the shops and restaurants and an outdoor farmer's market on summer and fall Thursdays. It's also where you'll find Dayton's flagship department store, where downtown shoppers can pick up everything from groceries to Oriental rugs. The store offers several restaurants and snack bars.

Uptown, beginning just south of the Walker Art Center on Hennepin Avenue and culminating at the Lake Street intersection, has a variety of clothing and bookstores, coffee shops, and specialty stores. Only four blocks from popular Lake Calhoun, it's the definitive people-watching zone in Minneapolis.

ST. PAUL **Saint Paul Center** (Minnesota World Trade Center, bounded by Minnesota, Wabasha, 6th, and 8th Sts.) has major department stores and specialty shops.

Victoria Crossing (Grand Ave. and Victoria St.) is a collection of small shops, specialty bookstores, and restaurants. It provides an anchor for the dozens of shops that span Grand Avenue about 1 mile south of I–94.

OUTDOOR ACTIVITIES

For information on outdoor activities in the area, contact the **Minneapolis Parks and Recreation Board** (tel. 612/348–2226) or the **St. Paul Parks and Recreation Board** (tel. 612/266–6400).

BEACHES In Minneapolis, sun worshipers have a choice of beaches at 22 lakes; the beaches at Lake Calhoun and Lake Harriet are popular with locals. In suburban St.

Paul, Square Lake and Lake Phalen beaches are often visited; Lake Phalen has a changing house and snack bar.

BIKING/JOGGING Minneapolis offers 36 miles of bike paths, including the parkways of Minnehaha Creek, Lake Calhoun, and Lake of the Isles. Joggers and bicyclists have separate marked paths, so be sure to stay on the correct side. St. Paul offers 37 miles of biking and jogging trails; favorite paths include Summit Avenue and Mississippi Boulevard.

CROSS-COUNTRY SKIING In Minneapolis you can cross-country ski in Minnehaha Park and on several golf courses. In St. Paul, Como Park and Phalen Park are favorites for this sport.

GOLF **Minneapolis:** Hiawatha Golf Course (4553 Longfellow Ave. S, tel. 612/724–7715); Theodore Worth Golf Course (Glenwood Pkwy. and Plymouth Ave., tel. 612/522–4584). **St. Paul:** Phalen Park (1615 Phalen Dr., tel. 612/778–0424); Highland Park (1403 Montreal Ave., tel. 612/699–3650); and Como Park (1431 N. Lexington Pkwy., tel. 612/488–9673).

TENNIS Public courts can be found in Kenwood and Loring parks in Minneapolis and in Como and Phalen parks in St. Paul.

ENTERTAINMENT

For arts-events calendars, check the monthly *Mpls.-St. Paul*; the weekly *Twin Cities Reader* and *City Pages*; and the daily newspapers, the *St. Paul Pioneer Press* and the Minneapolis-based *Star Tribune*.

DANCE The **Northrop Dance Series** (tel. 612/624–2345) is a major showcase for dance in the region. The **Hennepin Center for the Arts** (tel. 612/332–4478) is home to several dance companies.

MUSIC The Minnesota Orchestra performs in **Orchestra Hall** (tel. 612/371–5656). The **Orpheum Theater** (tel. 612/339–7007) is a Hennepin Avenue mainstay that offers popular concerts. The **St. Paul Chamber Orchestra** (tel. 612/224–4222) features more than 85 concerts each year at the **Ordway Music Theater** (tel. 612/282–3000), which also hosts jazz, pop, dance theater, and mime performances.

SPECTATOR SPORTS The **Minnesota Twins** (tel. 612/375–1116) play baseball April through September, and the **Minnesota Vikings** (tel. 612/333–8828) play football August through December at Hubert H. Humphrey Metrodome (900 S. 5th St., Minneapolis). The **Minnesota Timberwolves** (tel. 612/337–3865) play basketball November through April at Target Center (600 1st Ave. N at 6th St.).

THEATER The West Bank Theater District near the University of Minnesota has the highest concentration of theaters in Minneapolis. The **Chanhassen Dinner Theatres** (tel. 612/934–1525) has four theaters under one roof. The **Guthrie Theater** (tel. 612/377–2224 or 800/848–4912) is the area's major theater, featuring avant-garde and classic plays. The **Jungle Theater** (tel. 612/822–7063) is one of the best of many independent companies.

Mount Rushmore, the Black Hills, and the Badlands

South Dakota

Updated by Dick Willis

Nature provides a fitting backdrop for the widely recognized Mount Rushmore National Memorial in western South Dakota, where the faces of former presidents Washington, Roosevelt, Jefferson, and Lincoln are carved into granite cliffs, surrounded by the Black Hills' pine-covered mountains, icy trout streams, and secluded valleys. Work on this huge memorial to democracy began in 1927 under the supervision of artist Gutzon Borglum, who employed jackhammers and dynamite to coax the presidents' images from the stone. As the crown jewel of the Black Hills' tourism industry, Mount Rushmore National Memorial hosts 2 million visitors each year. While the memorial and the facilities immediately surrounding it can become quite crowded during the busy summer season, visitors who are seeking serenity can easily retreat to the wilder seclusion of the Black Hills' backcountry or visit during the off-season.

Just a two-hour drive east, 244,000-acre Badlands National Park offers a sharp contrast in environment. The lush, pine-tree-blanketed high country of the Black Hills is a far cry from this stark, almost lunar landscape marked by sheer cliffs and buttes. Formed over the aeons by sedimentary rock deposits from the Black Hills and by ash from the volcanoes at Yellowstone Park, the eerie Badlands are home to fossils from an extinct menagerie of saber-toothed cats, giant pigs, and other unusual creatures. Once the stomping grounds of Indians and grizzled mountain men, the Badlands now offer easy driving, scenic overlooks, well-marked hiking trails, and a chance to safely experience the most desolate terrain of the Great Plains.

ESSENTIAL INFORMATION

WHEN TO GO The peak tourist season falls between Memorial Day and Labor Day, when daytime temperatures around Mount Rushmore hover in the 80s and are even higher in the Badlands. The biggest crowds arrive in early August for the Sturgis Motorcycle Classic, when thousands of bikers roar through the Black Hills on Harley-Davidsons. The sunny, warm days often linger long into the fall, though temperatures begin to dip considerably at night. Winters are very cold (with temperatures dropping into the teens), but at least during the off-season (October through May) hotel rates are often reduced by more than half.

FESTIVALS AND SEASONAL EVENTS **Easter:** A nondenominational Easter sunrise service takes place on the main view terrace at the visitor center. **June–Aug.:** Throughout summer, bands and choruses from across the country perform free concerts at the Mount Rushmore amphitheater. Contact the visitor center (tel. 605/574–2523) for a schedule of related events. **July 4:** Independence Day is always a big event at Mount Rushmore. For a schedule of events, contact the visitor center (tel. 605/574–2523).

BARGAINS All the activities and programs at Mount Rushmore National Memorial are

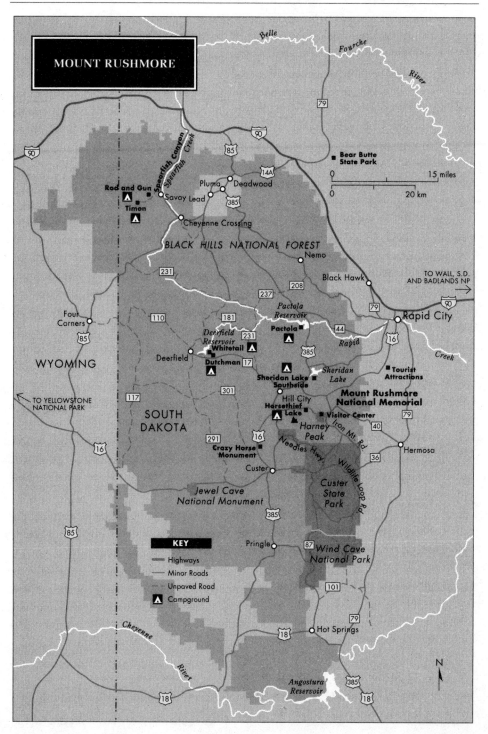

MOUNT RUSHMORE

Belle
Fourche
River

MOUNT RUSHMORE

90

79

Bear Butte
State Park

0   15 miles
0   20 km

Spearfish Canyon

Spearfish Creek

85

14A

Rod and Gun
Timon
Savoy Lead
Pluma
Deadwood
385

Cheyenne Crossing

BLACK HILLS NATIONAL FOREST

Nemo

231

237

208

Black Hawk

TO WALL, S.D.
AND BADLANDS NP

110

181

Pactola
Reservoir

79

90

Rapid City

Four
Corners
85

WYOMING

231

Pactola

44

Rapid

16

Creek

Deerfield
Reservoir
Whitetail
Deerfield
Dutchman
17

Sheridan Lake
Southside

385

Sheridan
Lake

Tourist
Attractions

Mount Rushmore
National Memorial

117

SOUTH
DAKOTA

301

Hill City
Horsethief
Lake

Visitor Center

79

40

TO YELLOWSTONE
NATIONAL PARK

291

16

Crazy Horse
Monument

Harney
Peak

Iron Mt Rd

36

Hermosa

16

Needles Hwy.

Wildlife Loop Rd.

Custer

Jewel Cave
National Monument

Custer
State
Park

385

85

KEY
Highways
Minor Roads
Unpaved Road
Campground

Pringle

87

Wind Cave
National Park

101

79

18

Hot Springs

Cheyenne
River

N

Angostura
Reservoir

385

18

18

free. In Rapid City, follow Main Street to Jackson Boulevard and turn left to reach Canyon Lake (tel. 605/394–4175). The city park there has canals and hundreds of acres of manicured grass and trees. Farther west down Jackson Boulevard is the Cleghorn Springs Fish Hatchery (tel. 605/394–2397). Several varieties of trout are spawned here by the thousands, and visitors can inspect the facilities free of charge. For a close look at some of the fossils unearthed in the Badlands, take a walk through the Museum of Geology at South Dakota School of Mines and Technology. *501 E. St. Joseph St., tel. 605/394–2467. Open daily. Admission free.*

TOURIST OFFICES South Dakota Department of Tourism (Capital Lake Plaza, Pierre 57501, tel. 605/773–3301 or 800/732–5682). **Rapid City Convention and Visitors Bureau** (Box 747, 444 Mt. Rushmore Rd. N, Rapid City 57709, tel. 605/343–1744). **Mount Rushmore National Memorial** (Box 268, Keystone 57751, tel. 605/574–2523). **Badlands National Park** (Box 6, Interior 57750, tel. 605/433–5361). **Black Hills National Forest Supervisor's Office** (RR 2, Box 200, Custer 57730, tel. 605/673–2251).

EMERGENCIES **Police:** Dial 911 or 605/394–2151. **Hospitals:** Rapid City Regional Hospital (353 Fairmont Blvd., tel. 605/341–1000). If an emergency should occur while you are in one of the parks, contact one of the patrolling park rangers or head for the nearest visitor center, where a medical-emergency team is located.

ARRIVING AND DEPARTING

BY PLANE **Rapid City Regional Airport** (tel. 605/394–4195), with several major carriers and daily flights, is the only commercial airport in the area.

BY CAR I–90 is the most direct route to the Badlands and the Black Hills. To reach Badlands National Park from I–90, take Exit 110 at Wall, or Exit 131 at Cactus Flat. To get to Mount Rushmore from I–90, take Exit 57 in Rapid City.

GETTING AROUND

BY CAR A car is the easiest way to get to Mount Rushmore, the Black Hills, and the Badlands. A free road map can be obtained from the South Dakota Department of Tourism, and more detailed maps are available at each park's visitors bureau (*see* Tourist Offices, *above*).

BY BUS The Jackrabbit Lines bus station (333 6th St., tel. 605/348–3300) in downtown Rapid City serves two regional bus lines, Jackrabbit and Powder River, both of which make connections with Greyhound Lines elsewhere.

REST STOPS Comfort stations with rest rooms are located along I–90 at Wasta between Rapid City and Badlands National Park. There are also rest rooms in the park headquarters at Mount Rushmore National Memorial and Badlands National Park. Every national forest campground has pit toilets.

GUIDED TOURS Orientation: **Gray Line of the Black Hills** (1600 E. St. Patrick St., Rapid City 57701, tel. 605/342–4461 or 800/456–4461) offers a variety of bus tours to Mount Rushmore, Black Hills National Forest, Custer State Park, and Crazy Horse Monument, all ranging in price from $9 to $28. **Stagecoach West** (Box 264, Rapid City 57709, tel. 605/343–3113) and **Golden Circle Tours** (40 5th St. N, Custer 57730, tel. 605/673–4349) offer similar tours in the same price range. Golden Circle Tours also offers a tour for under $30 to more remote spots in the Black Hills, including visits to abandoned gold mines, a picnic lunch, and a stop at Spring Creek, where guests can pan for gold and garnets.

Special Interest: Gray Line of the Black Hills runs a tour to the Black Hills Passion Play in Spearfish every Tuesday and Sunday from June through August. The bus trip and a ticket to this reenactment of the last days of Christ costs $25–$30. Gray Line also has a "Deadwood for the Day" tour to Deadwood, where gambling is the big draw. **Golden Cir-**

cle can tailor their mountain-bike tour to the ability of the participants. Bikes, helmets, and a picnic lunch are included, and a shuttle van joins the group at various points to pick up tired bikers.

EXPLORING

Mount Rushmore National Memorial, to the southwest of Rapid City, and Badlands National Park, to the southeast, are only a two-hour drive from each other. Travelers with a time restriction can see both in one day, but in order to really appreciate the natural beauty of the area, visitors should set aside at least three or four days to make a few side trips into the wilderness. All the activities in the park are free of charge.

MOUNT RUSHMORE NATIONAL MEMORIAL
Because of ongoing construction near the memorial, which is located 25 miles southwest of Rapid City on Route 16, visitors find it more convenient to leave their campers and RVs parked in campgrounds or elsewhere. It will be easier to find parking at Mount Rushmore with a smaller vehicle. Otherwise, the Mount Rushmore National Memorial can be explored on foot in just an hour or so (try to visit during the morning, when the lighting is most dramatic, or at sunset in order to see the nightly lighting ceremony). Visitors to the memorial can also stroll down the Avenue of Flags to the visitor center, where there's a video outlining Mount Rushmore's complete history. The view of the memorial from the visitor-center terrace is terrific.

Below the huge carvings is the amphitheater, where a variety of concerts are held during the summer. The nightly lighting ceremony—usually at 9 PM during the summer (the time of the ceremony varies with the sunset)—is preceded by a patriotic presentation given by one of the park rangers and a short film about the memorial. In winter the monument is lighted without much pomp shortly after dark, usually about 6 PM. *Box 268, Keystone 57751, tel. 605/574–2523. Admission free.*

Iron Mountain Road (Route 16A), a scenic drive that connects Mount Rushmore with Custer State Park in the south, was specially designed for sightseeing. As you follow the winding road through mountain passes and over old wooden bridges, notice how tunnels along the route provide glimpses of Mount Rushmore in the distance.

Custer State Park in the southern hills is home to an abundance of coyotes, eagles, antelope, mule deer, and over 1,400 buffalo. The park's Wildlife Loop Road takes about an hour to drive, and you'll spot plenty of buffalo grazing on the side of the road as you pass—these impressive beasts are dangerous, so don't get too close if you stop to take pictures.

Spearfish Canyon, found at the extreme northern end of the Black Hills Forest, is most spectacular in early October, when the aspen and birch trees lining its limestone cliffs erupt into brilliant yellows and oranges.

Commercial tourist attractions along Mount Rushmore Road to Mount Rushmore National Memorial include **Bear Country U.S.A.** (Rte. 16, Rapid City, tel. 605/343–2290), **Reptile Gardens** (Hwy. 16, Rapid City, tel. 605/342–5873), and **Marine Life Aquarium** (Rte. 16, Rapid City, tel. 605/343–7400). All of them charge admission fees of about $3.50 to $4.50 for children and $7.50 to $9 for adults; only the aquarium remains open in the winter.

The **Crazy Horse Monument,** which when completed will show a 563-foot-high stone sculpture of an American Indian sitting on a horse, is between Custer and Hill City. Continuously worked on since 1947, this monument to Native Americans is not part of the national park system, but rather, is a private family endeavor funded by admission fees. *Rte. 89, tel. 605/673–4681. Open daily. Admission charged.*

Jewel Cave National Monument and **Wind Cave National Park,** about 20 miles from one another in the southern hills, are, respectively, the second- and third-longest caves in the country. If you plan on taking a tour through one or both of the caves, be sure to bring a jacket to guard against the chilly underground temperatures. *Hot Springs 57747, tel. 605/673–2288 (Jewel Cave) or 605/745–4600 (Wind Cave). Parks open daily; caves open for tours May– Sept. Admission to parks free; cave tours $2.50–$8.*

THE BADLANDS By following U.S. 240 through Badlands National Park and stopping at the 13 scenic overlooks along this highway, you can get a good idea of what the park is like. But for a better understanding of the Badlands, leave the car behind to take a few short hikes around Cedar Pass and in the 64,000-acre Sage Creek Wilderness Area. Entrance into the park costs about $3 per car.

Cedar Pass Visitor Center on the eastern side of the Badlands National Park has exhibits on Badlands geology, wildlife, and early inhabitants. Brochures and maps detailing the area are available, and park rangers are on hand to answer questions. *U.S. 240, Box 6, Interior 57750, tel. 605/433–5361. Open daily.*

Hiking trails around the Cedar Pass Visitor Center give visitors a good opportunity to stretch their legs and get a close look at the Badlands. The trails range in length from ¼ to 5½ miles, and all are well marked. Notch Trail is a somewhat difficult hike, while Castle Trail is fairly easy but lengthy; the short Fossil Exhibit Trail features fossils displayed under glass. Information about each trail is available in the Cedar Pass Visitor Center.

Sage Creek Rim Road begins just south of the western Pinnacles entrance in Badlands National Park. The road skirts the north side of the Sage Creek Wilderness Area and runs southeast toward Cedar Pass through the Roberts Prairie Dog Town. Thirteen scenic overlooks along the way provide fine views of the Badlands' unique rock formations.

HOTELS AND INNS

Hotel rates are highest during summer but are often reduced by half or more after the peak season. The best values are found far from I–90, the main tourist route into the Black Hills. Good deals for motels in mountain surroundings can also be found in the smaller towns of Hill City, Custer, and Hot Springs, and in the outlying areas. Be sure to make your reservations well in advance since motels are often booked solid during the summer. No campgrounds or hotels are available at Mount Rushmore National Memorial, so most visitors to the memorial stay in Rapid City, Hill City, or in motels and campgrounds along the route. Visitors to the Badlands National Park can find lodging in the Cedar Pass Lodge located inside the park, or in the nearby towns of Wall and Kadoka. Price categories for double occupancy during high season, excluding taxes, are Expensive, over $70; Moderate, $50– $70; and Inexpensive, under $50.

NEAR MOUNT RUSHMORE NATIONAL MEMORIAL

Bel Air Inn. On the busiest strip in Rapid City, the Bel Air Inn is convenient to all the sights but is often noisy and lacking the charm of more secluded Black Hills lodgings. *2101 Mt. Rushmore Rd., Rapid City 57701, tel. 605/343–5126 or 800/283–4678. 30 rooms. Pool, cable TV. AE, D, DC, MC, V. Moderate.*

Castle Inn. Found on a centrally located but rather noisy street, this well-kept motel is typical of the moderately priced accommodations available in Rapid City. *15 E. North St., Rapid City 57701, tel. 605/348–4120 or 800/658–5464. 20 rooms. Heated pool, cable TV. AE, D, DC MC, V. Moderate.*

Edelweiss Mountain Lodging. The homey guest houses and cabins here—many of them former private homes—are comfortably settled among ponderosa pines on a gravel road 3 miles off Highway 385. Each cabin is unique; large groups might like the Waite cabin, which has four bedrooms and a pool table. *2780 Black Forest Rd., Rapid City 57702, tel. 605/574–2430. 18 guest houses. MC, V. Moderate–Expensive.*

Hotel Alex Johnson. This luxurious landmark hotel, with 11 stories of alpine woodwork and Indian artistry, is the most famous hotel in Rapid City: No wonder it's hosted five U.S. presidents. *523 6th St., Rapid City 57701, tel. 605/342–1210 or 800/888–2539, fax 605/342–1210. 142 rooms. Room service. AE, D, DC, MC, V. Expensive.*

Lewis Park Cabins and Motel. On a backstreet in Hill City, these 1930s cabins offer small-town living tucked away among mountain ridges and aspen trees. Each unit is furnished and has a fully equipped kitchen. The handful of motel-style rooms lack the charm of the cabins. *110 Park Ave., Box 382, Hill City 57745, tel. 605/574–2565 or 800/ 317–2565. 4 cabins, 5 rooms. D, MC, V. Inexpensive.*

Spring Creek Inn. Found in the pine-covered mountains near Hill City on Highway 16-385, the knotty-pine guest rooms here are one of the best lodging deals in the Black Hills. In summer, croquet games are set up on the grassy lawn, and fishermen angle for trout in nearby Spring Creek. *HCR 87, Box 55, Hill City 57745, tel. 605/574–2591. 12 rooms, 5 cabins, and numerous vacation homes. D, MC, V. Inexpensive.*

NEAR BADLANDS NATIONAL PARK **Cedar Pass Lodge.** Guests can gaze out at the buttes of Badlands National Park from these ideally located cabins near the park's visitor center. Built in the 1930s, the clean, carpeted cabins were remodeled in 1987, but the knotty-pine walls remain. *Box 5, Interior 57750, tel. 605/ 433–5460. 24 cabins. Restaurant nearby. AE, D, DC, MC, V. Inexpensive.*

Plains Hotel. This modern family motel near I–90 and downtown Wall is convenient for visitors to Badlands National Park. *912 Glen St., Box 393, Wall 57790, tel. 605/279–2145 or 800/528–1234, fax 605/279–2977. 74 rooms. Pool, cable TV. AE, D, DC, MC, V. Moderate.*

CAMPGROUNDS

Camping facilities abound both in and around the Black Hills and the Badlands, and while most provide water, showers, electricity, and sewage disposal, some have even more elaborate facilities. For a listing of all campgrounds, complete with maps and full descriptions, request a copy of the *South Dakota Campground Guide* from the South Dakota Department of Tourism (*see* Tourist Offices, *above*). The two national park campgrounds in the Badlands accept campers on a first-come, first-served basis, while reservations for the various Black Hills National Forest campgrounds (tel. 800/283–2267) can be made by calling well in advance of your arrival date. All the national forest campgrounds are scheduled to open on May 15. However, many will have only limited service (no rest rooms or water) until Memorial Day weekend. Many campgrounds close on September 30.

THE BLACK HILLS **Dutchman Campground.** At an elevation of 6,100 feet, this is one of the coolest spots in the Black Hills, where campers can escape from the summer heat even in July. Water is available at its 45 campsites. *Cost: Under $9. 45 sites, tent or RV; pit toilets, picnic tables.*

Horsethief Lake Campground. This is the closest public campground to Mount Rushmore National Memorial, and, as a result, it is always the most crowded. Just 1 mile west of Mount Rushmore off Highway 244, the campground offers easy access to the Norbeck Wildlife Preserve and Centennial Trail. There are 36 campsites and drinking water. *Cost: $13–$15. 36 sites, tent or RV; chemical toilet, picnic tables.*

Pactola Campground. This large campground has 80 campsites near Pactola Lake. The beautiful lakefront offers boating, fishing, and a beach. *Cost: Under $13. 80 sites, tent or RV; chemical and pit toilets, hot showers, concession store, laundry.*

Rod and Gun Campground and Timon Campground. Both of these small campgrounds offer secluded camping along Little Spearfish Creek not far from Roughlock Falls. Each has seven campsites and water. *Cost: Under $6. 7 sites, tent or RV; pit toilet.*

Sheridan Lake Southside Campground. Twelve of the campsites at this large facility are near a beach, boat ramp, and the Centennial Trail. The best spots are closest to Sheridan Lake. Drinking water is available. *Cost: Under $14. 129 sites, tent or RV, shower at beach area; pit toilet, picnic tables.*

Whitetail Campground. This campground above Deerfield Lake offers solitude and good fishing. Water is available at 17 campsites. *Cost: Under $9. 17 sites, tent or RV; pit toilet.*

THE BADLANDS **Cedar Pass Campground.** Close to the Cedar Pass Visitor's Center, this campground has very little in the way of facilities, though water is provided (except in the winter). *Cost: Under $8. 110 sites; flush toilets, picnic tables, electricity in wash house, no reservations.*

Sage Creek Primitive Campground. The key word here is *primitive.* Just south of the Sage Creek Rim Road in the Badlands Sage Creek Wilderness Area, this campground is for those who really like to rough it. This facility has no water. *Pit toilets, picnic tables.*

DINING

Most restaurants in the Badlands and Mount Rushmore are found in the towns outside the parks, and visitors should be aware that many establishments close for the winter. Those who are adventurous will want to try the local specialty—buffalo—found on the menus of several regional restaurants (raised on a number of western South Dakota ranches, buffalo meat tastes similar to beef but contains less fat and cholesterol). Price categories per person, excluding tax, service, and drinks, are Moderate, $6–$11, and Inexpensive, under $6.

INSIDE THE PARKS **Cedar Pass Lodge Restaurant.** Native American crafts decorate this small family restaurant—the park's only full-service eatery—in Badlands National Park, next to the Ben Rifel/Cedar Pass Visitor Center. The menu features tacos and quarter-pound buffalo burgers. *Cedar Pass, tel. 605/433–5460. AE, D, DC, MC, V. Inexpensive.*

NEAR THE PARKS **Alpine Inn.** Opera music and stained-glass windows enhance the ele-

gant, European atmosphere at this popular spot in the quiet logging town of Hill City. Lunch includes sandwiches and light entrees, the only dinner entrée in stock succulent 6- or 9-ounce cuts that are so reasonably priced people come from miles around and don't seem to mind a short wait. *Harney Peak Hotel, Main St., Hill City, tel. 605/574–2749. No credit cards. Inexpensive–Moderate.*

Casa Del Rey. The Americanized Mexican food served here is mild enough for almost any gringo's taste. Tortilla chips and salsa pave the way for chili *relleños*, chimichangas, and burritos. *1902 Mt. Rushmore Rd., tel. 605/348–5679. AE, MC, V. Moderate.*

Great Wall Chinese Restaurant. For years this has remained one of the most popular restaurants in Rapid City, and you may encounter a short wait before sitting down to one of their low-fat Chinese meals. Takeout is available. *315 E. North St., Rapid City, tel. 605/348–1060. MC, V. Moderate.*

Hunan Chinese Restaurant. Another popular Rapid City spot where low-fat Chinese dishes lure large crowds of locals. *1720 Mt. Rushmore Rd., Rapid City, tel. 605/341–3888. AE, MC, V. Moderate.*

Saigon Restaurant. Spicy, authentic Vietnamese and Chinese food is served in this family-run hole-in-the-wall. Here, it's the food that really counts: spicy shrimp with red sauce and onions, chicken with broccoli, and numerous ginger-inspired dishes. *221 E. North St., Rapid City, tel. 605/348–8523. No credit cards. Moderate.*

SHOPPING

GIFTS AND CRAFTS For Sioux Indian pottery, go to **Sioux Pottery Crafts** (2209 Hwy. 79S, Rapid City, tel. 605/341–3657). The largest selection of Indian art, crafts, books, tapes, and other items is available at **Prairie Edge** (606 Main St., tel. 605/341–4525).

OUTDOOR ACTIVITIES

BEACHES There are two small beaches along Sheridan Lake in the Black Hills, and Angostura Reservoir near Hot Springs is rimmed with miles of white sand. Both lakes have rest rooms, picnic tables, and barbecues, and Angostura also has a snack bar. Neither lake has lifeguards on duty. Admission charged.

BIKING The best biking in the Black Hills area is on the 5-mile-long, concrete bike path that runs along Rapid Creek in Rapid City. Bikes can be rented in Rapid City from **Mountain Mania Bicycles** (4242 Canyon Lake Dr., tel. 605/343–6596), **Two Wheeler Dealer Cycle & Fitness** (100 E. Blvd. N, tel. 605/343–0524), and the **Gold Strike** (40 N. 5th St., tel. 605/673–4349) in Custer.

FISHING Spearfish Creek and Rapid Creek are both popular spots to angle for wild brown trout. Deerfield, Sheridan, Pactola, and Stockade lakes are also good for fishing, as is small, scenic Horsethief Lake near Mount Rushmore.

GOLF Black Hills golf courses that can be used for a daily fee include **Belle Fourche Country Club** (S. Hwy. 85, Belle Fourche, tel. 605/892–3472), **Edgemont Golf and Racquet Club** (south of Edgemont, tel. 605/662–5100), **Executive Golf Course** (along Rapid Creek in Rapid City, tel. 605/394–4124), **Hart Ranch Resort** (between Rapid City and Mount Rushmore, tel. 605/341–5703), **Meadowbrook Golf Course** (3625 Jackson Blvd., Rapid City, tel. 605/394–4191), **Rocky Knolls Golf Course** (Hwy. 16 west of Custer, tel. 605/673–4481), and

Tomahawk Country Club (Hwy. 385 south of Deadwood, tel. 605/578–9979).

HIKING Dozens of trails, ranging from 100 yards to more than 100 miles, snake through the thick ponderosa pines and Black Hills spruce of the Norbeck Wildlife Preserve and the Black Elk Wilderness southwest of Mount Rushmore. A Sierra Club hiking map of the Norbeck Wildlife Preserve can be purchased from the **Sierra Club** (Box 1624, Rapid City 57709, tel. 605/348–1351) for under $5.

HORSEBACK RIDING The western-horse pack trips offered in Badlands National Park and the Black Hills by **Gunsel Horse Adventures** (Box 1575, Rapid City 57709, tel. 605/343–7608) include six- and 10-day pack trips on scenic trails through the pine forests and mountain meadows around Custer State Park and Mount Rushmore.

SKIING Two resorts in the northern hills that have downhill skiing are **Terry Peak Ski Area** (tel. 605/584–2165) and **Deer Mountain Ski Area** (tel. 605/584–3230). Two of the most popular cross-country ski trails in the Black Hills are Eagle Cliff near O'Neil Pass and Big Hill near Spearfish. Equipment rental costs $10 per day and is available at **Ski Cross Country** (701 3rd St., Spearfish, tel. 605/642–3851) and **Deer Mountain Ski Area** (near Lead, SD, tel. 605/584–2165).

SNOWMOBILING More than 300 miles of groomed snowmobile trails link the Black Hills in South Dakota and Wyoming. The most extensive trails with the best snow run through the northern Hills. Free snowmobile maps are available from the South Dakota Department of Tourism (*see* Tourist Offices, *above*).

Nashville
Tennessee

Updated by Katherine Culkin

he sprawling city of Nashville extends over eight counties in the middle Tennessee heartland, a pocket of rolling Cumberland Mountain foothills and bluegrass meadows that's one of the state's richest farming areas. Its impressive skyline, dotted with high-rise office towers, is a vivid reminder that it has been a long time indeed since Christmas Day 1779, when James Robertson and a small, shivering party of pioneers began to build a fortress and palisades on the Cumberland River's west bank.

Designated the state capital in 1843, the city began a steady growth that has accelerated mightily in the past decade. A banking and insurance hub, it is also a leading printing center for religious material. Heralded as the world's Country Music Capital and birthplace of the "Nashville Sound," it also proudly calls itself the Athens of the South. As every fan knows, it was Nashville's Grand Ole Opry that launched the amazing country-music boom when it began as radio station WSM's "Barn Dance" in 1925. The Opry performs in a sleek $15 million Opry House now, still as gleeful and down-home informal as in the early days.

Far from developing a case of civic schizophrenia at such contrasting commercial and cultural roles, Nashville has made both labels fit, becoming one of the middle South's liveliest and most vibrant cities in the process. Its role as a cultural leader is enhanced by its impressive performing-arts center and the many colleges, universities, and technical schools located here, most notably Vanderbilt University.

ESSENTIAL INFORMATION

WHEN TO GO Nashville has a temperate climate year-round. Spring and autumn are the most pleasant times of year. The summer months, especially July and August, can be very hot and humid. Winters are not usually severe, but January and early February can produce bone-rattling cold and enough snow to shut down the city. The primary tourist season runs from April through October.

BARGAINS Tapings of several TNN (The Nashville Network) television shows are open to visitors. Admission is free to "Crook & Chase," taped at 7 PM Tuesday–Friday at Jim Owens Productions (1525 McGavock St., tel. 615/889–6611; reservations required). Admission is also free to the Tennessee State Museum, Tennessee State Capitol, and Fort Nashborough. Many of the city's college art galleries can be visited without charge, and Vanderbilt often presents free concerts and plays. The parks department puts on free summer concerts and outdoor arts shows, notably the band-shell events and festivals in Centennial Park. For more information, call 615/862–8400.

TOURIST OFFICES **Tennessee Department of Tourist Development** (Room T, Box 23170, Nashville 37202, tel. 615/741–2158). **Nashville Area Chamber of Commerce** (161 4th Ave. N, Nashville 37202, tel. 615/259–4700). **Tourist Information Center** (103 Main St., at Interstate Dr., Nashville 37202, tel. 615/259–4747).

EMERGENCIES **Police, fire,** and **ambulance:** Dial 911. **Hospitals:** Centrally located Bap-

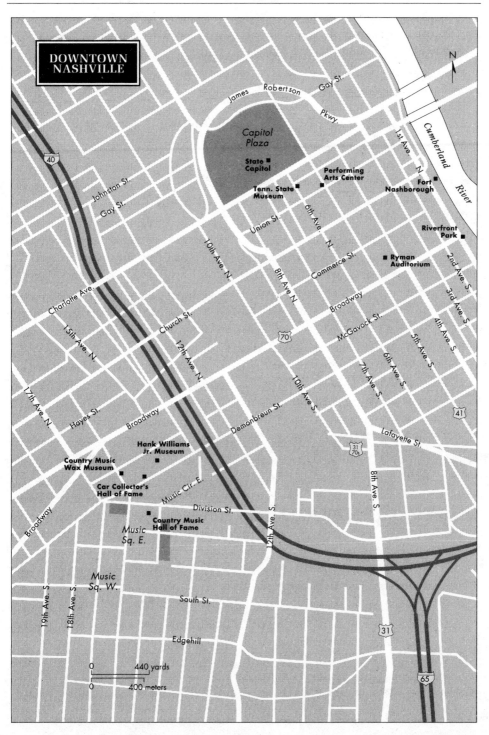

DOWNTOWN
NASHVILLE

N

James Robertson Pkwy.

Gay St.

Capitol
Plaza

State
Capitol ■

Performing
Arts Center ■

Tenn. State
Museum ■

Fort
Nashborough ■

1st Ave.

Cumberland River

Johnston St.

Gay St.

Union St.

6th Ave. N.

8th Ave. N.

Riverfront
Park ■

Commerce St.

■ Ryman
Auditorium

2nd Ave. S.

3rd Ave. S.

10th Ave. N.

Charlotte Ave.

Broadway

McGavock St.

4th Ave. S.

5th Ave. S.

6th Ave. S.

7th Ave. S.

Church St.

12th Ave. N.

15th Ave. N.

17th Ave. N.

Hayes St.

Broadway

Demonbreun St.

10th Ave. S.

Lafayette St.

Hank Williams
Jr. Museum ■

Country Music
Wax Museum ■

Car Collector's
Hall of Fame ■

Music Cir. E.

Division St.

12th Ave. S.

8th Ave. S.

Broadway

Country Music
Hall of Fame ■

Music
Sq. E.

Music
Sq. W.

19th Ave. S.

18th Ave. S.

South St.

Edgehill

0   440 yards
0   400 meters

40

70

70

41

31
70s

31

65

tist Hospital (2000 Church St., tel. 615/ 329–5555) and Vanderbilt University Medical Center (1211 22nd Ave. S, tel. 615/322–7311) have emergency rooms that are open all night. **Pharmacies:** Walgreens has four Nashville-area stores that are open 24 hours (518 Donelson Pike, tel. 615/883–5108; 5412 Charlotte Ave., tel. 615/298–5594; 2622 Gallatin Rd., tel. 615/226–7591; 15580 Old Hickory Blvd., tel. 615/333–2722).

ARRIVING AND DEPARTING

BY PLANE **Nashville International Airport,** approximately 8 miles from downtown, is served by American, Delta, Eastern, United, and USAir. Taxis are available at the terminal's ground level; the fare to downtown Nashville averages $15–$20.

BY CAR From Nashville, I–65 leads north into Kentucky and south into Alabama, and I–24 leads northwest into Kentucky and Illinois and southeast into Georgia. I–40 traverses the state east–west, connecting Nashville with Memphis and Knoxville.

BY TRAIN Amtrak does not serve the Nashville area.

BY BUS **Greyhound** (8th Ave. S and McGavock St., tel. 800/231–2222) connects Nashville with cities and towns throughout the United States.

GETTING AROUND

BY CAR Attractions are scattered, so you'll need a car. In some instances, you can park and walk from one attraction to another. Pick up a Tennessee map from a state welcome center or the Tourist Information Center; it's helpful for exploring Nashville's hinterland.

BY BUS **Metropolitan Transit Authority** (MTA; tel. 615/242–4433) buses serve the entire county. For visitors with disabilities, a wheelchair-lift van is available for downtown transport (tel. 615/351–7433). The **Nashville Trolley Company** (tel. 615/242–

4433) also offers rides in the downtown area every 10 minutes.

BY TAXI Companies include **Checker Cab** (tel. 615/256–7000), **Nashville Cab** (tel. 615/242–7070), and **Yellow Cab** (tel. 615/256–0101).

REST STOPS There are free public rest rooms at the State Capitol and the Tennessee State Museum.

GUIDED TOURS Tours that may include drives past stars' homes and visits to the Grand Ole Opry, Music Row, and historic structures are offered by **American Sightseeing** (tel. 615/256–1200 or 800/826–6456), **Gray Line** (tel. 615/883–5555 or 800/251–1864), and **Grand Ole Opry Tours** (tel. 615/889–9490). **Country & Western Round-Up Tours** (tel. 615/883–5555) offers a daily Twitty City/Johnny Cash Special motor-coach tour. **Johnny Walker Tours** (tel. 615/834–8585 or 800/722–1524) has an evening Music Village Nightlife Tour, which includes a barbecue buffet dinner and top-name country entertainment. **Belle Carol Riverboat Company** (tel. 615/244–3430 or 800/342–2355) runs Cumberland River sightseeing, luncheon, and dinner cruises that leave from the Riverfront Park dock. **Opryland USA** (tel. 615/889–6611) has daytime and dinner cruises aboard the *General Jackson*.

EXPLORING

You should plan to explore Nashville in segments. It helps to remember that the river bisects the central city; numbered avenues are west of and parallel to the river, numbered streets east of and parallel to it.

A WALKING TOUR OF DOWNTOWN Start in **Riverfront Park** and walk one block northwest on 1st Avenue.

Fort Nashborough, high on limestone bluffs overlooking the river, is the site of the Nashville founders' first 1779 log fort. In a carefully re-created fort and blockhouses, costumed interpreters depict late-18th-century frontier life. *170 1st Ave. N, tel.*

615/255–8192. Open Tues.–Sat. Admission charged.

Walk three short blocks north on 1st Avenue and three blocks west on Charlotte Avenue to the **Tennessee State Museum** in the lower level of the **James K. Polk Cultural Center.** Among the displays are a log cabin, an exhibit on Indian life, and a demonstration of early printing techniques; you'll also see Davy Crockett's powder horn and rifle, Andrew Jackson's inaugural top hat, and Sam Houston's guitar. 505 Deaderick St., tel. 615/741–2692. Open daily. Admission free.

Walk west along Charlotte Avenue to Capitol Plaza. The **Tennessee State Capitol** (1859) so impressed its architect, William Strickland, that he asked to be buried within its walls. On the grounds, among statues of Tennessee heroes, President James K. Polk and his wife are buried. Capitol Plaza and Charlotte Ave., tel. 615/741–0830. Open daily. Admission free.

Walk two blocks east on Charlotte Avenue and four blocks south on 5th Avenue. The **Ryman Auditorium and Museum,** "Mother Church" of country music, is now on the National Register of Historic Places. The home for the WSM Grand Ole Opry from 1943 to 1974 underwent a 8.5 million dollar renovation in 1994 and now seats 2,000 for jazz, classical, pop, gospel, and county-music concerts. 116 Opry Pl. (5th Ave. N), tel. 615/254–1445. Open daily. Admission charged.

THE COUNTRY MUSIC CAPITAL Continue your tour by car; take the Demonbreun Exit off I–40 to Music Row. The **Country Music Hall of Fame and Museum** displays such icons as Elvis Presley's "solid gold Cadillac" and gold-covered piano along with priceless costumes, instruments, films, and photos. Other exhibits cover Johnny Cash and the Grand Ole Opry, and a tour of the legendary RCA Studio B is included. 4 Music Sq. E, tel. 615/256–1639. Open daily. Admission charged.

The **Hank Williams Jr. Museum,** ½ block east along Demonbreun Street, displays family memorabilia of Hank Sr. and Jr. Exhibits include many of their stage costumes and guitars, along with Hank Sr.'s '52 and Hank Jr.'s '57 Cadillac. 1524 Demonbreun St., tel. 615/242–8313. Open daily. Admission charged.

Car Collectors Hall of Fame, a few doors away, displays another of Elvis's Cadillacs, the Batmobile from the Batman television series, and 50 other flashy vehicles, many with country connections. 1534 Demonbreun St., tel. 615/255–6804. Open daily. Admission charged.

At the **Country Music Wax Museum and Mall,** on the same block, more than 60 figures, dressed in original stage costumes, display the entertainers' own musical instruments. 118 16th Ave. S, tel. 615/256–2490. Open daily. Admission charged.

Opryland USA, an attraction-filled show park 15 minutes from downtown, is a must-see. "The Grand Ole Opry" now performs here each weekend in the world's largest broadcast studio (it seats 4,424). There are nearly two dozen rides, more than a dozen live shows, crafts demonstrations, restaurants, and special events. Here, too, the **Roy Acuff Musical Collection and Museum** (admission free) contains memorabilia of the "king of country music," and **Minnie Pearl's Museum** (admission free) provides a nostalgic tour of her life. 2802 Opryland Dr., tel. 615/889–6700. Open late Mar.–Oct., daily. Admission charged.

Music Valley Wax Museum of the Stars, just north of Opryland USA, contains more life-size figures of country stars. Outside, in the **Sidewalk of the Stars,** are their footprints, handprints, and signatures. 2515 McGavock Pike, tel. 615/883–3612. Open daily. Admission charged.

HISTORIC NASHVILLE To get a feeling for Nashville's history and culture, begin in Centennial Park. The renovated **Parthenon** is a replica of the Athenian original, right down to the Elgin Marbles. It contains a huge new statue of Athena and also houses an art gallery with changing exhibits. West End Ave., Centennial Park, tel. 615/862–8431. Open Tues.–Sat. Admission charged.

From Centennial Park, head west on West End Avenue and follow the signs for **Belle Meade Mansion,** a stunning Greek Revival house, the centerpiece of a 5,300-acre estate that was one of the nation's top Thoroughbred breeding farms. A Victorian carriage museum continues the equine theme. *110 Leake Ave., tel. 615/356–0501. Open daily. Admission charged.*

Take Harding Road east, turn right on Belle Meade Boulevard, and look for signs to Tennessee Botanical Gardens. **Cheekwood,** formerly the Cheek family mansion, is now a fine-arts center exhibiting 19th- and 20th-century American art and sculpture. The surrounding 55 acres of the **Tennessee Botanical Gardens** display herbs, roses, irises, daffodils, and wildflowers, and, with greenhouse, streams, and pools, is a delightful spot for a picnic. *1200 Forrest Park Dr., adjacent to Percy Warner Park and Golf Course, tel. 615/356–8000. Open daily. Admission charged.*

From here, drive east on Harding Place/Battery Lane, taking I–65 south to the first of two Harding Place exits. **Travellers' Rest** is the restored clapboard home of John Overton, law partner and mentor of Andrew Jackson. The house, decorated with period furnishings, grew from a 1799 four-room cottage to a 12-room mansion with Federal and Greek Revival additions. *636 Farrell Pkwy., tel. 615/832–2962. Open daily. Admission charged.*

Northeast of Travellers' Rest (via Harding Place and Donelson Pike) is a most impressive landmark. **The Hermitage,** which Andrew Jackson built for his beloved wife, Rachel, on 600 acres of gently rolling farmland, reflects Old Hickory's life and times in such detail it seems he has just stepped out for a moment. It is furnished with many original family pieces, and the Jacksons are buried on the grounds. The **Andrew Jackson Center** contains many Jackson artifacts, Rachel's Garden Cafe, and a museum store. A 16-minute film, *Old Hickory,* is shown in its auditorium. *4580 Rachel's La., Hermitage, tel. 615/889–2941. Open daily. Admission charged.*

THE NATURAL WORLD In the surrounding "Heartland," a bucolic enclave where meandering streams wind amid fields, orchards, and green pastures framed by white fences, many state parks (tel. 615/532–0001 or 800/421–6683) and other natural areas offer opportunities to hike or bicycle in dense hardwood forests, and to fish, swim, or go boating. Cedars of Lebanon State Park preserves the Southeast's largest remaining red cedar forest.

HOTELS AND INNS

Catering to budget-conscious tourists as well as corporate travelers, Nashville has a wide selection of accommodations. Some establishments increase rates slightly during the peak summer travel season. Price categories for double occupancy, excluding 11¾% tax, are Expensive, $80–$100; Moderate, $50–$80; and Inexpensive, under $50.

EXPENSIVE **Courtyard by Marriott–Airport.** This handsome, low-rise motor inn with a gardenlike courtyard offers some amenities you'd expect in higher-priced hotels: spacious rooms, king-size beds, and hot-water dispensers for coffee. *2508 Elm Hill Pike, 37214, tel. 615/883–9500, fax 615/883–0172. 145 rooms. Restaurant, lounge, indoor pool, sauna, whirlpool, exercise room. AE, DC, MC, V.*

Holiday Inn–Select. There's one of the popular Holidome Indoor Recreation Centers right inside the inn, so you can enjoy sports activities in any season. *2200 Elm Hill Pike at Briley Pkwy., 37210, tel. 615/883–9770, fax 615/391–4521. 385 rooms. Restaurant, lounge with live entertainment, sauna, whirlpool, coin laundry, game room, table tennis, pool tables. AE, DC, MC, V.*

Holiday Inn–Vanderbilt. Adjacent to the Vanderbilt University campus, this attractive high-rise is centrally located, with some of the city's finest restaurants nearby. *2613 West End Ave., 37203, tel. 615/326–8034, fax 615/327–8034. 300 rooms. Dining room, lounge with live entertainment, heated pool, exercise room, coin laundry. AE, DC, MC, V.*

Opryland Hotel. This sprawling complex is one of the 25 largest hotels in the world and houses several charming shops and restaurants, a 2-acre conservatory, and a radio station. Located across the street from Opryland USA, it's worth a visit even if you are staying elsewhere. *2800 Opryland Dr., 37214, tel. 615/889–1000, fax 615/871–5728. 12,800 rooms. 14 restaurants, 22 shops, pool, golf, tennis. AE, MC, V.*

Ramada Inn Across from Opryland. This well-maintained, low-rise, contemporary motor inn has well-lighted, spacious rooms and is a short drive from Opryland. *2401 Music Valley Dr., 37214, tel. 615/889–0800, fax 615/883–1230. 308 rooms. Dining room, lounge with live entertainment, heated indoor pool, sauna, whirlpool. AE, DC, MC, V.*

MODERATE **Comfort Inn–Hermitage.** Near the Hermitage, this low-rise inn offers first-rate accommodations, some with water beds or whirlpool baths. *5768 Old Hickory Blvd., 37076, tel. 615/889–5060, fax 615/871–4137. 106 rooms. Indoor and outdoor pools, sauna. AE, DC, MC, V.*

Hampton Inn–Vanderbilt. Near the Vanderbilt University campus, this contemporary inn has colorful, spacious rooms, with some no-smoking units. *1919 West End Ave., 37203, tel. 615/329–1144, fax 615/320–7112. 171 rooms. Free Continental breakfast, pool. AE, DC, MC, V.*

La Quinta Motor Inn–MetroCenter. The rooms here are especially spacious and bright, and some have full-length mirrors and recliners. *2001 Metro Center Blvd., 37228, tel. 615/259–2130, fax 615/242–2650. 121 rooms. Pool. AE, D, DC, MC, V.*

Wilson Inn. Three miles from Opryland, this five-story hotel is new, clean, and convenient. Many rooms have kitchens, and coffee and doughnuts are served in the spacious lobby. *600 Ermac Dr., 37210, tel. 615/889–4466, fax 615/889–0484. 110 rooms. AE, D, DC, MC, V.*

MOTELS

MODERATE **Best Western–Music City Inn** (13010 Old Hickory Blvd., 37013, tel. 615/641–7721, fax 615/641–6263). 144 rooms; restaurant, pool. **Days Inn–Downtown Convention Center** (711 Union St., 37219, tel. 615/242–4311, fax 615/242–1654). 100 rooms; deli, convenience market, free parking. **Drury Inn Airport** (837 Briley Pkwy., 37217, tel. 615/361–6999, fax 615/361–6999). 148 rooms; breakfast included, pool. **Family Inns of America–Nashville** (3430 Percy Priest Dr., 37214, tel. 615/889–5090, fax 615/889–5090). 57 rooms, 6 efficiencies; heated pool. **Nashville La Quinta Motor Inn** (2001 Metrocenter Blvd., Nashville 37227, tel. 615/259–2130 or 800/531–5900, fax 615/242–2650). 120 rooms; pool, cable TV. **Quality Inn Hall of Fame Hotel** (1407 Division St., 37203, tel. 615/242–1631, fax 615/244–9519). 102 rooms; restaurant, lounge with entertainment, pool. **Ramada Inn** (840 James Robertson Pkwy., 37203, tel. 615/244–6130, fax 615/742–0932). **Ramada Inn–Downtown** (303 Interstate Dr., 37213, tel. 615/244–6690, fax 615/742–0932). 120 rooms; heated indoor pool, whirlpool. 180 rooms; restaurant, lounge, pool, coin laundry, garage. **Shoney's Inn of Nashville** (1521 Demonbreun St., 37203, tel. 615/255–9977, fax 615/242–6127). 147 rooms; pool.

INEXPENSIVE–MODERATE **Best Western–Metro Inn** (99 Spring St., 37207, tel. 615/259–9160, fax 615/244–5871). 148 rooms; restaurant, pool, coin laundry. **Holiday Inn–North** (230 =W. Trinity La., 37207, tel. 615/226–0111, fax 615/228–6412). 389 rooms; restaurant, cocktail lounge, 2 pools, exercise room, coin laundry, playground.

INEXPENSIVE **Budgetel Inn** (531 Donelson Pike, 37214, tel. 615/885–3100, fax 615/871–4238). 150 rooms; pool, coin laundry. **Budgetel Inn–Nashville West** (5612 Lenox Ave., 37209, tel. 615/353–0700, fax 615/352–0361). 110 rooms; pool. **Comfort Inn–Southeast** (97 Wallace Rd., 37211, tel. 615/833–6860, fax 615/833–6860). 127 rooms; pool. **Days Inn–Nashville Central** (211 N. 1st St., 37213, tel. 615/254–1551, fax 615/256–0758). 180 rooms; restaurant, lounge, heated indoor pool, whirlpool, exercise room. **Days Inn–Trinity Lane** (1360 Brick

Church Pike, 37207, tel. 615/226–4500, fax 615/227–3604). 150 rooms; restaurant, pool, playground. **Econo Lodge** (300 Interstate Dr., 37213, tel. 615/242–9621 or 800/444–4401, fax 615/255–4544). 84 rooms; pool. **Nashville Comfort Inn Hermitage** (5768 Old Hickory Blvd., 37076, tel. 615/889–5060 or 800/221–2222, fax 615/871–4137). 100 rooms, 7 suites; pool. **Red Roof Inn** (510 Claridge Dr., 37124, tel. 615/872–0735, fax 615/871–4647.) 120 rooms.

DINING

Nashville is full of unpretentious cafés where fried chicken, catfish and hush puppies, barbecue, and buttermilk biscuits reign supreme. But more and more Music City restaurants are offering lighter cuisine and vegetarian fare. You'll find increasingly imaginative dishes in American, Continental, Chinese, Thai, Japanese, and Middle Eastern restaurants. Price categories per person, excluding 8¼% tax, service, and drinks, are Moderate, $15–$25, and Inexpensive, under $15.

MODERATE **Kobe Steaks.** Traditional Japanese decor, with shoji screens and lacquer furniture, enhances the atmosphere of this popular restaurant, where you can sit around group tables to dine on seafood or steak, prepared right there on teppan grills. *210 25th Ave. N, tel. 615/327–9081. AE, D, DC, MC, V.*

Mario's Ristorante Italiano. Country-music stars and visiting celebrities come here to see and be seen and to dine on seafood, pasta, and such northern Italian dishes as veal *saltimbocca* in this elegant Nashville institution. *2005 Broadway, tel. 615/327–3232. AE, DC, MC, V.*

Midtown Cafe. A quiet, elegant but relaxed ambience greets diners at this centrally located café just a couple of quick blocks from famous Music Row and featuring excellent seafood entrées. Many feel the Midtown offers the city's finest Caesar salad, and don't miss out on a taste of the lemon artichoke soup. *102 19th Ave. S, tel. 615/320–7176. AE, DC, MC, V.*

Morton's. The venerable Chicago steak house opened one of its eateries downtown in the shadow of the State Capitol. Huge steaks, salads, and one-pound baked spuds are the specialties. *625 Church St., tel. 615/259–4558. AE, DC, MC, V.*

106 Club. A white baby grand and a shiny, black-enamel-and-glass-brick bar set the tone in this intimate art deco dining room, where the cuisine is a mix of international favorites and such California nouvelle offerings as veal medallions with litchis. *106 Harding Pl., tel. 615/356–1300. AE, DC, MC, V.*

Peking Garden. Paper lanterns, paintings, and other traditional Chinese decor create the ideal setting for sampling a mind-boggling selection of regional Middle Kingdom food. *1923 Division St., tel. 615/327–2020. AE, MC, V.*

Sunset Grill. Pasta, veal, lamb, and seafood dishes top the menu at this midtown hot spot, where you're liable to see city business and political leaders rubbing shoulders with Nashville's biggest stars. *2001-A Belcourt Ave., tel. 615/386–3663. AE, D, DC, MC, V.*

INEXPENSIVE **Cakewalk Restaurant.** A popular spot with the Vanderbilt University crowd, this café's eclectic menu embraces healthy California and Southwest cuisine and regional favorites. *3001 West End Ave., tel. 615/320–7778. AE, D, DC, MC, V.*

Elliston Place Soda Shop. Generations of Vanderbilt students have eaten the sandwiches, plate lunches, and breakfasts at the 1950s-style booths and old-fashioned soda fountain of this landmark. *2111 Elliston Pl., tel. 615/327–1090. No credit cards.*

Faison's. Veal, poultry, seafood, and pasta attract a younger, stylish crowd to this attractively renovated bungalow bistro. *2000 Belcourt Ave., tel. 615/298–2112. AE, DC, MC, V.*

Houston's. Great burgers, salads, and delectable prime rib keep this West End Avenue restaurant hopping at noon and at night. Well worth the wait for a table, you can't go wrong with their baked-potato soup and house salad. *3000 West End Ave., tel. 615/269–3481. AE, MC, V.*

Jimmy Kelly's. This Nashville favorite has served great steaks and seafood for more than 50 years; nowadays it serves from a restored Victorian mansion. *217 Louise Ave., tel. 615/329–4349. AE, D, DC, V. Closed Sun. No lunch.*

Loveless Cafe. An institution as renowned as the Opry and the Parthenon, this laid-back establishment 20 miles southwest of downtown attracts hordes of city folks for down-home cooking. *Rte. 5, Hwy. 100, tel. 615/646–9700. No credit cards.*

Old Spaghetti Factory. Diners enjoy heaping portions of pasta, spaghetti, and veal in a converted 1890s warehouse decked with Victorian artifacts. *160 2nd Ave. N, tel. 615/254–9010. D, MC, V.*

Satsuma Tea Room. Dining at this welcoming little downtown retreat is a reminder of meals at Grandma's house, and the fresh vegetables, soups, meats, home-baked breads, and desserts are all first-rate. It's a Nashville lunch-hour institution. *417 Union St., tel. 615/256–0760. No credit cards.*

SHOPPING

ANTIQUES AND FLEA MARKETS The **Nashville Flea Market** (tel. 615/383–7636) at the fairgrounds is on the fourth Saturday of every month. And try the **Smorgasbord Antique Mall** (4144-B Lebanon Rd., tel. 615/883–5789). Murfreesboro, about 15 miles outside town, calls itself the Antique Center of the South. Pick up a free shopping guide at **Cannonsburgh Pioneer Village** (tel. 615/875–7644), a living museum of 19th-century life in the South.

COUNTRY-AND-WESTERN WEAR Stores geared to the latest look in country clothing include **Boot Country** (2412 Music Valley Dr., tel. 615/883–2661), **Loretta Lynn's Western Stores** (435 Donelson Pike, tel. 615/889–5582), and **Nashville Cowboy** (118 16th Ave. S, tel. 615/242–9497; 1516 Demonbreun St., tel. 615/256–2429).

MALLS Some of Nashville's best shopping is located in its suburban malls, most notably the **Mall at Green Hills** (2126 Abbott Martin Rd., tel. 615/298–5478), **Hickory Hollow Mall** (5252 Hickory Hollow Pkwy, tel. 615/731–6255), the **Bellvue Center** (7620 Hwy. 70 S, tel. 615/646–8690), and **CoolSprings Galleria** (1800 Galleria Blvd., tel. 615/771–2128). **Church Street Centre** (625 Church St., tel. 615/254–4260) is the major downtown shopping area.

RECORDS AND TAPES Fans can find good selections at **Tower Records** (2400 West End Ave., tel. 615/327–3722); **Ernest Tubb Record Shops** (2412 Music Valley Dr., tel. 615/889–2474; 417 Broadway, tel. 615/255–7503); and for used records, tapes, and CDs, try the **Great Escape** (1925 Broadway, tel. 615/327–0646; 111 Gallatin Rd. N, Madison, tel. 615/865–8052).

OUTDOOR ACTIVITIES

BOATING AND FISHING Boats can be rented at J. Percy Priest Lake, 11 miles east of Nashville off I–40, and Old Hickory Reservoir, 15 miles northeast of Nashville via U.S. 31 E.

GOLF Among courses open to the public year-round are **Harpeth Hills** (tel. 615/862–8493), **Hermitage Golf Course** (tel. 615/847–4001), and **Rhodes Golf Course** (tel. 615/862–8463). Hermitage is the site each April of the LPGA Sara Lee Classic.

HIKING There are extensive trails (and a nature preserve) in heavily wooded Percy Warner Park.

HORSEBACK RIDING You can go riding at **Riverwood Recreation Plantation and Riding Academy** (tel. 615/262–1794) and **Ramblin' Breeze Ranch** (tel. 615/876–1029).

ICE-SKATING September through April, there's indoor skating at **Sportsplex** (tel. 615/862–8480) in Centennial Park.

JOGGING Favorite sites include Centennial Park, the Vanderbilt University track, J. Percy Priest Lake, and Percy Warner Park.

TENNIS There are several municipal tennis facilities, and **Centennial Sportsplex Tennis Center** (tel. 615/862–8490) has grass and clay courts plus indoor courts.

ENTERTAINMENT

CONCERTS Performances by the Nashville Symphony Orchestra and out-of-town artists are staged at Andrew Jackson Hall, part of the **Tennessee Performing Arts Center** (TPAC, tel. 615/741–7975; call Ticketmaster (tel. 615/741–2787 or 800/333–4849) for information on all TPAC theaters. Chamber concerts take place at TPAC's James K. Polk Theater. Vanderbilt University stages music, dance, and drama productions (many free) at its **Blair School of Music** (tel. 615/322–7651).

NIGHTLIFE Not surprisingly, the "world's country music capital" offers down-home live entertainment at every turn. If you can attend only one event, try to make it the **Grand Ole Opry** (2804 Opryland Dr., 37214, tel. 615/889–3060); write or call for tickets in advance of your visit. You may see tomorrow's stars performing at the **Nashville Palace** (2400 Music Valley Dr., tel. 615/885–1540), the **Stock Yard Bull Pen Lounge** (901 2nd Ave. N, tel. 615/255–6464), and the **Wildhorse Saloon** (120 2nd Ave., tel. 615/256–9453). Bluegrass fans head for the **Station Inn** (402 12th Ave., tel. 615/255–3307). The songwriter's mecca is the **Bluebird Cafe** (4104 Hillsboro Rd., tel. 615/383–1461).

SPECTATOR SPORTS You can root for the AAA **Nashville Sounds,** an affiliate of the Chicago White Sox baseball team, from April through August at Herschel Greer Stadium (tel. 615/242–4371).

THEATER TPAC's Andrew Jackson Hall (*see* Concerts, *above*) hosts touring Broadway shows and ballet; the James K. Polk Theater stages local performances; and there are numerous small theater companies. The **Nashville Academy Theatre** (tel. 615/254–9103) stages children's performances.

The Natchez Trace
Mississippi, Alabama, Tennessee

Updated by Helen James

he Natchez Trace Parkway is what highways were meant to be—an uncrowded, unpretentious swath of two-lane roadway, lined by countryside that's peaceful, lush, and lovely. As the Trace, as it's called, cuts its way through rural Mississippi and Alabama on its way to Tennessee, it follows age-old trails worn by Choctaw and Chickasaw Indians. Meandering through pine forests and cypress swamps, past magnificent antebellum mansions surrounded by softly swaying oak trees, the parkway traverses a landscape redolent of the history and mystery often associated with the American South.

Flower-filled in spring, verdant in summer, and crisply colorful in fall, the Trace has changed little over the years, thanks in large part to restrictions on billboards and commercial traffic and impeccable maintenance by the National Park Service. Intended to connect Natchez and Nashville, the Natchez Trace spans 415 of its projected 445-mile course; until the remainder is completed, the temporary northern terminus is Leipers Fork, Tennessee. (For information on Nashville, *see* the Nashville chapter.) The majority of miles (313 to be exact) run diagonally from the southeast to the northwest corner of Mississippi.

ESSENTIAL INFORMATION

WHEN TO GO Traffic is rarely a problem, but summer on the Trace is always hot and humid; temperatures on the southern leg average 82° and peak in the 90s, while summer in Nashville sees temperatures hover in the low 80s. Winter on the Trace means chilly mornings and 50° afternoons. Spring and autumn are the most moderate seasons, and the most colorful, with temperatures for both in the mid-60s. Springtime also brings wildflowers, which bloom in profusion along the highway: dogwood, redbud, wisteria, and honeysuckle are unforgettable in May. Autumn colors are equally vibrant, with reds, golds, and browns intermingling with the evergreens of pine and juniper.

BARGAINS The **Tupelo Visitor Center** (tel. 601/680–4025) offers a free film on the development of Natchez Trace, plus an excellent selection of books by southern writers. The **Ridgeland Crafts Center** (milepost 102.4, tel. 601/856–7546) outside Jackson is a dogtrot cabin filled with the reasonably priced work of members of the Craftsman's Guild of Mississippi. **Grand Village of the Natchez Indians** (400 Jefferson Davis Blvd., Natchez, tel. 601/446–6502) is a fun, free roadside attraction, with an archaeological park and a museum.

TOURIST OFFICES Get the definitive free map of the route from the **Natchez Trace Parkway Visitor Center** (RR1, NT-143 [milepost 266], Tupelo, MS 38801, tel. 601/680–4025) or any of the other parkway rest stops. **Alabama Mountain Lakes Tourist Association** (Box 1075, Mooresville, AL 35649, tel. 205/350–3500 or 800/648–5381). **Metro Jackson Convention & Visitors Bureau** (Box 1450 [1150 Lakeland Dr.], Jackson, MS 39215, tel. 601/960–1891 or 800/354–7695). **Natchez Convention & Visitors Bureau** (Box 1485, Natchez, MS 39121, tel. 601/446–6345 or 800/647–6724).

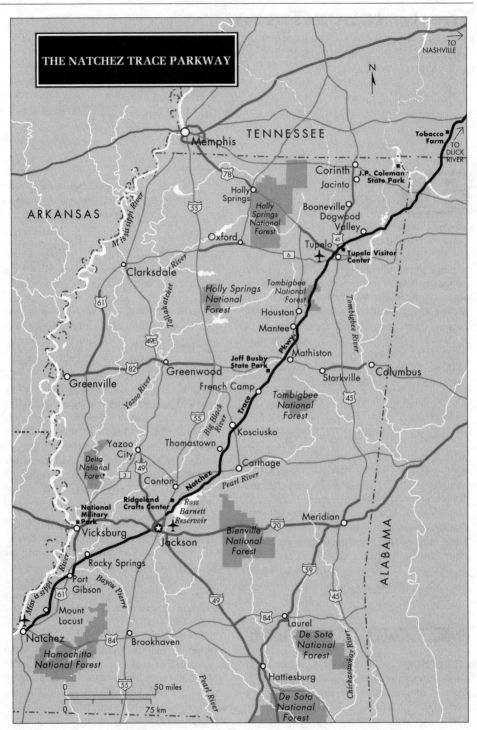

THE NATCHEZ TRACE PARKWAY

TO NASHVILLE

TENNESSEE

Memphis

ARKANSAS

78

Holly Springs

Holly Springs National Forest

Oxford

Corinth

Jacinto

J.P. Coleman State Park

Booneville

Dogwood Valley

Tupelo

Tupelo Visitor Center

Tobacco Farm

TO DUCK RIVER

55

Clarksdale

6

45

Holly Springs National Forest

Tombigbee National Forest

Houston

Mantee

Mathiston

Columbus

Starkville

61

49E

82

Greenwood

Jeff Busby State Park

Greenville

French Camp

Tombigbee National Forest

45

Yazoo City

Thomastown

55

Kosciusko

Delta National Forest

49

Canton

Carthage

Natchez

Pearl River

3

Ridgeland Crafts Center

Ross Barnett Reservoir

Meridian

National Military Park

Vicksburg

Jackson

Bienville National Forest

20

Rocky Springs

Port Gibson

61

Mount Locust

Natchez

84

Brookhaven

49

59

84

45

Laurel

De Soto National Forest

Homochitto National Forest

Hattiesburg

De Soto National Forest

0   50 miles
55

0   75 km

EMERGENCIES Police, fire, and ambulance: Dial 911 in Tupelo, Jackson, Natchez, and Alabama. For help on the Natchez Trace, dial 0 and ask for the nearest Park Ranger. **Hospitals:** North Mississippi Regional Medical Center (830 S. Gloster St., Tupelo, tel. 601/841–3000), Mississippi Baptist Medical Center (1225 N. State St., Jackson, tel. 601/968–1776), Jefferson Davis Hospital (Sgt. Prentiss Dr., Natchez, tel. 601/442–2871).

ARRIVING AND DEPARTING

BY PLANE Delta, American, Continental Express, and Northwest airlines have nonstop daily flights to Jackson's **Allen C. Thompson Field** from Dallas, Atlanta, and New Orleans, and direct service from other major cities. The airport is east of town off I–20. **Tupelo Municipal Airport** is served by Northwest Airlines and American Eagle.

BY CAR Natchez, Mississippi, the southern anchor of the Natchez Trace, is served by U.S. 61. The Natchez Trace is incomplete at Jackson, connected through the city by I–55 and I–20. From the north, U.S. 78 and U.S. 45 lead to Tupelo. Nashville, Tennessee, about 35 miles north of the Trace, is served by I–65 and I–24 from the north and south, and by I–40 from the east and west.

BY TRAIN Amtrak (tel. 800/872–7245) has frequent trains through Jackson from New Orleans and Chicago.

BY BUS Greyhound Lines (tel. 800/231–2222) offers daily service to Tupelo, Corinth, Natchez, and Jackson.

GETTING AROUND

BY CAR A car is essential along the Natchez Trace Parkway, which is designed for independent travelers.

REST STOPS The National Park Service maintains almost 20 rest stops with rest room facilities along the parkway, all clearly marked on the Park Service map.

GUIDED TOURS Jackson Tour & Travel (tel. 601/981–8415 or 800/873–8572) organizes tours along the Trace, as well as to nearby New Orleans. In Natchez, **Pilgrimage Tours, Inc.** (tel. 601/446–6631 or 800/647–6742) takes groups through 13 antebellum mansions (up to 30 during the spring and fall pilgrimage seasons), and sells separate admissions to individuals.

EXPLORING

The entire Natchez Trace Parkway could be driven in a very long day, but that's not the way to see it. Travelers who get the most out of the route take it little by little (minding the 50-mph speed limit), with frequent stops at the dozens of trails and historic sites. Four of the best stretches and the principal cities (from south to north) are noted below. Beyond the official parkway, Natchez and Jackson have enough historic diversions to make them destinations in themselves; Vicksburg and its Civil War history make it worth a half day at least. Nashville, with its glitzy music scene, is just off the northern terminus (see the Nashville chapter).

Natchez. This is a city out of time, its beautiful antebellum mansions spared the fiery fate of those in other southern towns, thanks to Natchez's sympathies for the Union. Tours can be arranged through Pilgrimage Tour Headquarters. Historic Natchez-under-the-Hill—a former red-light district overlooking the Mississippi River—is a popular area for nightlife, which includes dockside gambling.

Mount Locust to Rocky Springs (MP 15.5–54.8). At Mount Locust is a restored "stand," or inn, as it was in 1810, now a museum with interpretive programs. Coles Creek (MP 17.5) is a quiet picnic grounds, and at Bullen Creek (MP 18.4), a 15-minute trail wanders through a hardwood-pine forest. Owens Creek Waterfall (MP 52.4) has adjacent picnic tables, and the old town site of Rocky Springs (MP 54.8) can be reached by a short trail. En route, swing through the quiet town of Port Gibson, where grand historic mansions line the tree-canopied streets.

Jackson. The soul of Mississippi's capital is preserved in its old downtown architecture and several museums. The Agriculture and Forestry Museum (1150 Lakeland Dr., tel. 601/354–6113; open daily; admission charged) is a working farm. The state's Old Capitol Building is perched atop Capitol Green, with a view of the State Historical Museum (100 N. State St., tel. 601/359–1000; open daily; admission charged). The Mississippi Arts Center (201 E. Pascagoula St., tel. 601/960–1515; open Sept.–July, Tues.–Sun.; admission charged) has changing exhibits and an Impressions Gallery with interactive exhibits of electronic art. The Eudora Welty Library (300 N. State St., tel. 601/968–5811; open daily) is the biggest in Mississippi.

Vicksburg National Military Park. Adjacent to the historic river town of Vicksburg, roughly 50 miles west of Jackson, this enormous park has a visitor center and a 16-mile drive past hundreds of memorials honoring the dead of both sides in the great siege of Vicksburg in 1863. One stop on the drive is at the USS *Cairo,* the first ironclad ever sunk by an electronic mine. *Clay St. (U.S. 80), 1 mi from I–20, Exit 4B, tel. 601/636–0583. Open daily. Admission charged.*

Ridgeland Crafts Center to French Camp (MP 102.4–180.7). The crafts center has exhibits, demonstrations, and goods for sale. Reservoir Overlook (MP 105.6) gives a bird's-eye view of the lake that parallels the route for 8 miles. Cypress Swamp (MP 122) has a 20-minute wetlands trail. The Upper Choctaw Boundary (MP 128.5) is an old border marked by a line of trees with a nearby 10-minute nature trail. At Cole Creek (MP 175.6) there are wetlands walks. In autumn, sorghum is made at French Camp (MP 180.7), a settlement founded in 1812.

Jeff Busby to Tupelo (MP 193.1–266). The Jeff Busby stop and its scenic overlook is a good place to rest and refuel. North from here, the original Trace leads into the forest (MP 221.4), and a marker (MP 243.3) points out where Hernando DeSoto camped during the winter of 1540–1541. At Bynum Mounds (MP 232.4), exhibits describe the local prehistoric people. Chickasaw Council House (MP 251.1) is a pretty place for a picnic, and you can examine plants the Indians used in a short walk on the outskirts of Chickasaw Village (MP 261.8). At Tupelo, a national battlefield (MP 259.7) commemorates the battle of 1864.

Tupelo. Elvis Presley was born in this city, and locals have seen fit to restore his boyhood home (off Old Hwy. 78, at 306 Elvis Presley Dr., tel. 601/841–1245; open daily; admission charged). The Tupelo Museum (off Rte. 6W, tel. 601/841–6438; open Tues.–Sun.; admission charged) has further Presley memorabilia, as well as an old-time country store, a train depot, and an old Western Union office.

Dogwood Valley to Tobacco Farm (MP 275.2–401.4). Occasional flooding along a 20-minute trail to Donavan Slough (MP 283.3) creates a botanically interesting plant variety. At Dogwood Valley, a 15-minute nature trail wanders through a stand of trees that flower in April. At Pharr Mounds (MP 286.7), a 90-acre burial ground, you can see eight 2,000-year-old mounds and exhibits on their construction and use; Tishomingo State Park (MP 302.8) is a good overnight spot for campers. At Freedom Hills Overlook (MP 317), as the Trace begins its 33-mile run across the northwest corner of Alabama, a quarter-mile trail leads to an 800-foot vantage point. A creek-side trail at Rock Spring, Alabama (MP 330.2), wanders through a hilly forest, and wildflowers are brilliant in season along Sweetwater Branch trail (MP 363), a 20-minute walk along a fast-flowing stream. At Old Trace Drive (MP 375.8), now in Tennessee, a road follows the original Trace for 2½ miles. Tobacco Farm (MP 401.4) has a curing barn and exhibits on the agriculture of the weed; a 2-mile unpaved side road follows the original route of the Trace to several scenic overlooks.

Nashville. Best known for its music, this Tennessee city is also a repository of southern culture (*see* the Nashville chapter).

HOTELS AND INNS

The Old South comes alive in historic lodging up and down the Natchez Trace, though some places—like the ones in Vicksburg—are a few miles off the parkway. Natchez is well endowed with accommodations, and Nashville (see the Nashville chapter) has a large concentration of lodgings. Price categories for double occupancy, excluding room tax (7% in Tennessee, 6% in Mississippi), are Expensive, $85–$100; Moderate, $50–$85; and Inexpensive, under $50.

NATCHEZ **Eola Hotel.** Nicely restored to its Roaring Twenties glory, this grand old hotel—it's listed on the National Register of Historic Places—has a tiny formal lobby and somewhat cramped rooms with antique reproduction furniture; the guest house across the street has bigger rooms with balconies. *110 N. Pearl St., 39120, tel. 601/445–6000 or 800/888–9140, fax 601/446–5310. 122 rooms. Restaurant. AE, DC, MC, V. Moderate.*

Monmouth. This massive and immaculate bed-and-breakfast inn, built in 1818, sits regally on 26 verdant acres. Rooms and suites in the Main and Carriage Houses, and in the garden cottages, feature period antiques and decor. *36 Melrose Ave., 39120, tel. 601/442–5852 or 800/828–4531. 25 rooms. Full breakfast included. AE, D, MC, V. Expensive.*

VICKSBURG **Anchuca.** Visitors have rooms in the slave quarters or in the turn-of-the-century guest cottage of this oak-shaded antebellum mansion. *1010 1st East St., 39180, tel. 601/631–6800 or 800/469–2597. 6 rooms. Pool, hot tub. Breakfast and house tour included. AE, D, MC, V. Moderate–Expensive.*

Duff Green Mansion. This 1856 house, which was used as a Civil War hospital, is generously decorated with antiques, including half-tester beds. *1114 1st East St., 39180, tel. 601/638–6662, fax 601/634–1061. 7 rooms, 2 suites. Pool, courtyard, gazebo. Breakfast and house tour included. AE, MC, V. Moderate–Expensive.*

JACKSON **Edison Walthall Hotel.** Distinguished by its decor, which seems like a restoration, this hotel is outfitted with marble floors, shiny brass, and a comfortable, old-fashioned bar. *225 E. Capitol St., 39201, tel. 601/948–6161 or 800/932–6161, fax 601/948–0088. 208 rooms. Heated pool, whirlpool, airport transportation, fitness center. AE, D, DC, MC, V. Moderate–Expensive.*

DUCK RIVER **McEwen Farm Log Cabin Bed and Breakfast.** This farm near the northern end of the parkway has two comfortable cabins and a restored train station that has been turned into a two-bedroom lodge. *Box 1910, Bratton La., TN 38454, tel. 615/583–2378. 4 rooms. MC, V. Expensive.*

MOTELS

MODERATE **Executive Inn Tupelo** (1011 N. Gloster, Tupelo 38801, tel. 601/841–2222, fax 601/844–7836). 115 rooms; indoor pool, whirlpool, sauna, cable TV. **Holiday Inn–Downtown Jackson** (200 E. Amite St., Jackson 39201, tel. 601/969–5100 or 800/922–9222, fax 601/353–4333). 358 rooms; restaurant, lounge, pool. **Ramada Hilltop Natchez** (130 John R. Junkin Dr., Natchez 39120, tel. 601/446–6311 or 800/272–6232, fax 601/446–6321). 162 rooms; restaurant, lounge. **Ramada Renaissance Hotel–Jackson** (1001 Count Line Rd., Jackson 39211, tel. 601/957–2800 or 800/272–6232, fax 601/957–3191). 300 rooms; airport transportation, restaurant, live entertainment, lobby bar, gift shop, barbershop.

INEXPENSIVE **Quality Inn–Vicksburg** (I–20 Frontage Rd. S, 39180, tel. 601/634–8607 or 800/228–5150, fax 601/634–5150). 70 rooms; exercise room, whirlpool, sauna.

CAMPGROUNDS

All of the National Park Service campgrounds are open on a first-come, first-served basis and are rarely crowded. There are no hookups, no showers, and no fees. Each campground has central rest rooms with basins and flush toilets; each campsite has a picnic table and grill. For information, contact the superintendent, **Natchez Trace Park Service** (RR 1, NT143, Tupelo 38801, tel. 601/842–1572).

J. P. Coleman State Park on Pickwick Lake in northernmost Mississippi has wooded campsites and rough-hewn cabins, many on the lake. Facilities include rowboat rentals, a pool, miniature golf, and waterskiing. It is 45 minutes off the parkway, but worth the drive. *Rte. 5, Box 504, Iuka 38852 (13 mi north of Iuka off U.S. 25), tel. 601/423–6515. 47 RV sites with full and partial hookups, 16 tent sites, 10 cabins; showers, flush toilets, picnic tables, grills. Reservations required for cabins. MC, V.*

Tishomingo State Park is off the parkway in the Appalachian foothills—rare terrain in Mississippi. It has a primitive camping area, RV sites, six rustic cabins, a 13-mile nature trail through a scenic canyon, and canoe float trips. *Box 880, Tishomingo 38838 (3 mi north of Dennis off U.S. 25), tel. 601/438–6914. 62 RV sites with partial hookups, tent sites, 6 cabins; showers, bathrooms, picnic tables, barbecue areas. Reservations required for cabins. MC, V.*

DINING

Though most places along the Trace still reflect a bias for southern and Creole food, grilled entrées are replacing deep-fried offerings. Price categories per person, excluding tax (8% in Mississippi, 7¾% in Tennessee), service, and drinks, are Moderate, $15–$25, and Inexpensive, under $15.

NATCHEZ **Natchez Landing.** Tables on the porch have a view of the Mississippi and the riverboat landing below the street, a bustling 19th-century hangout for gamblers and prostitutes. Grilled catfish is a specialty, the salads are good, and the barbecue is respectable. *11 Silver St., Natchez-Under-the-Hill, tel. 601/442–6639. AE, MC, V. Inexpensive–Moderate.*

Scrooge's. This old storefront has a saloon atmosphere downstairs and quieter dining upstairs. It serves beans and rice, mesquite-grilled chicken, and a number of seafood dishes. *315 Main St., tel. 601/446–9922. AE, D, DC, MC, V. Closed Sun. Inexpensive.*

VICKSBURG **Tuminello's.** Vicksburg locals have enjoyed fresh seafood, steaks, and veal at Tuminello's since 1899, when this family-run business first opened. Almost a century later, dinner at Tuminello's remains a popular tradition. *500 Speed St., tel. 601/634–0507. AE, DC, MC, V. Inexpensive–Moderate.*

JACKSON **Gridley's.** The city's barbecue spot of choice, with well-seasoned chicken as well as ribs, this café specializes in fast service. *1428 Old Square Rd., tel. 601/362–8600. AE, D, MC, V. Inexpensive.*

Hal and Mal's Restaurant and Oyster Bar. This old warehouse, renovated with neon, 1930s memorabilia, and an eclectic mix of antiques, is the place for grilled fresh fish and grilled chicken. *200 Commerce St., tel. 601/948–0888. AE, D, MC, V. Closed Sun. Inexpensive.*

The Mayflower. A 1930s-style diner with black-and-white tiled floors, straight-back booths, and Formica-topped counters, this restaurant is known for its Greek salads and fresh fish sautéed in lemon butter. *123 W. Capitol St., tel. 601/355–4122. MC, V. Closed Sun. Inexpensive.*

Ralph & Kacoo's. This is authentic Cajun, no doubt about it. Ralph and Kacoo started in south Louisiana, and they've since introduced Jackson to crawfish étouffée and blackened catfish the way it was meant to be—down-home Louisiana style. *100 Dyess Rd. at I-55, tel. 601/957–0702. AE, D, DC, MC, V. Moderate.*

SHOPPING

Good deals on regional souvenirs can be had at the **Old Country Store** (U.S. 61, tel. 601/437–3661), a repository of local culture since 1890. For antiques and crafts, Jackson has **C.**

W. Fewel III & Co. (840 N. State St., tel. 601/355–5375) and **Bobbie King's** (Woodland Hills Shopping Center, tel. 601/362–9803).

OUTDOOR ACTIVITIES

BOATING, FISHING, WATER SPORTS Elvis Presley Lake and Campground (tel. 601/841–1304) lie on the outskirts of Tupelo, at Tishomingo State Park and J. P. Coleman State Park.

GOLF In Jackson, tee off at **Lefleur's Bluff State Park** (tel. 601/987–3998).

TENNIS In Jackson, play at **Tennis Center South** (2827 Oak Forest Dr., off McDowell Rd., tel. 601/960–1712) and **Parham Bridges Park** (5055 Old Canton Rd., tel. 601/956–1105). In Natchez, there's **Duncan Park** (Duncan St. at Auburn Ave.).

ENTERTAINMENT

There's always something doing in Natchez, and even more so now that dockside gambling has arrived. The replica paddle wheeler *Lady Luck* (tel. 601/445–0605) is permanently docked at Natchez-under-the-Hill, on the Mississippi River, and offers Las Vegas–style gambling 24 hours a day, plus food and spirits. There is no admission charge.

In Jackson, **The Dock** (Main Harbor Marina at Ross Barnett Reservoir, tel. 601/856–7765) is especially popular on Sundays. Poet's (1855 Lakeland Dr., tel. 601/982–9711) has a nightly jazz trio.

New Orleans
Louisiana
Updated by Michael Tisserand

For most visitors, New Orleans means Mardi Gras, the French Quarter, electrifying jazz, and great food. New Orleans is both an old-fashioned town with 10 historic districts and a major world city with a thriving port and an insouciant, fun-loving soul that bedevils progressives bent on jerking it into the 20th century. Its party-town reputation is well founded—local folks eagerly celebrate anything at the drop of a hat. Mardi Gras is the biggest bash in all North America, and 6 million annual visitors is the city's version of having a few friends in. Carnival season officially starts on Twelfth Night, January 6, and builds up to its frenzied culmination on "Fat Tuesday," the day before the beginning of Lent.

To experience this fun-filled city, you must go beyond the usual tourist attractions to linger in a corner grocery store, sip a cold drink in a local joint, or chat with a stoop-sitter. Orleanians love their city. They treasure tradition, bask in the sultry semitropical climate, and look at life with a laid-back attitude that makes New Orleans seem a close cousin to her Caribbean neighbors.

ESSENTIAL INFORMATION

WHEN TO GO In June, July, and August, when it can stay above 95° for weeks, merely mustering the energy to lift a mint julep may cause malaise. Happily, virtually everything is air-conditioned. June through November is hurricane season, when torrential rains and high winds can hit. During the mild winters (around 47° to 60°) high humidity puts a chill in the air. The best time to visit is early spring, when days are pleasant, nights are coolish, and the city blossoms with flowers and festivals.

If you want to peacefully savor the city's considerable charms, avoid arriving the last weekend in April—the beginning of the 10-day Jazz Fest, when hundreds of thousands of musicians and aficionados flock into town to enjoy the best of jazz, blues, Cajun, zydeco, gospel, and many other varieties of Louisiana music. And during Mardi Gras (February or March), about a million people jam the French Quarter and the Central Business District (CBD) to see the "greatest free show on earth." In summer, many hotels offer discount rates, and during the month-long Creole Christmas, which can be snow white or white hot, you can find attractive "Papa Noel" packages with low rates.

BARGAINS The ancient art of street theater is practiced in exuberant New Orleans style in Jackson Square and Woldenberg Riverfront Park. In the early 1990s, long-suffering neighbors around Jackson Square managed to get the loudest of the jazz bands banished to Woldenberg Riverfront Park, but Jackson Square abounds with tap dancers, bongo players, unicyclists, clowns, and fire-eaters, all of whom vie for attention (and loose change). New Orleans street musicians, incidentally the best in the busker business, are out in full force in all but the worst weather in the Square, the Riverfront Park, and on Royal Street; performers range from a solo vocalist doing soulful spirituals to a 10-piece Dixieland band tearing up the patch. Free concerts are performed regularly in

NEW ORLEANS

Lake Pontchartrain

New Orleans
Lakefront
Airport

METAIRIE

Lake Pontchartrain Causeway

W. Esplanade Ave.

Pontchartrain Blvd.

West End Blvd.

Robert E. Lee Blvd.

Lake Shore Dr.

Lake Shore Dr.

L.C. Simon Dr.

Hayne Blvd.

Morrison Rd.

City
Park

Oaklawn Dr.

Bonnabel Blvd.

Harrison Ave.

Canal Blvd.

Orleans Ave.

Bayou St. John

Bernard St.

Mirabeau Ave.

Paris Ave.

London Ave.

Elysian Fields Ave.

Franklin Ave.

Press Ave.

Congress Dr.

Downman Rd.

610

Causeway Blvd.

Ridgewood Dr.

TO
AIRPORT

Airline Hwy.

10

DeSaix Blvd.

New Orleans
Museum of Art

Fairgrounds
and
Race Track

Gentilly Blvd.

St. Bernard Ave.

10

Almonaster Ave.

Louisa St.

LaBarre Rd.

Metairie Rd.

Amelia Earhart St.

90

Monticello

Expwy.

Jeff Davis Pkwy.

Orleans St.

Tulane Ave.

Broad St.

Claiborne Ave.

Esplanade Ave.

Franklin Ave.

Claiborne Ave.

St. Claude Ave.

Carrollton Ave.

Claiborne

Louisiana Ave.

Napoleon Ave.

Canal St.

Louisiana
Superdome

CBD

Spanish Plaza

FRENCH
QUARTER

Royal St.

Aquarium of
the Americas

FERRY

ALGIERS

Mississippi River

River Rd.

City Ave.

Calhoun St.

St. Charles Ave.

LaSalle St.

Jackson Ave.

Greater
New Orleans
Bridge

90

Newton St.

Gen. Meyer Ave.

Blaine Kern's
Mardi Gras World

Franklin St.

Gen. de Gaulle Dr.

Audubon
Park

Zoological
Gardens

Magazine St.

Tchoupitoulas St.

GARDEN
DISTRICT

FERRY

GRETNA

Holmes Blvd.

Louisiana St.

Mississippi River

River Rd.

4th St.

90

West Bank Expwy.

23

Carol Sue Ave.

WESTWEGO

4th St.

Ames Blvd.

Barataria Blvd.

Destrehan Ave.

Peters Rd.

Manhattan Blvd.

Belle Chasse Hwy.

Lapalco Blvd.

0   1 mile
0   2 km

N

Dutch Alley at the French Market; schedules are available at the Dutch Alley kiosk. And for the price of a drink, you can hang out and hear great jazz in one of the open-air cafés of the French Market. Doors of Bourbon Street music clubs are flung wide, and you have but to lean against a lamppost and soak it in. Old-time jazz legends play nightly in funky Preservation Hall, where a mere $3 buys four hours of the best traditional jazz in the world.

For a leisurely 12-minute scenic ride, take the commuter ferry from the foot of Canal Street across the Mississippi to Algiers and back. Passage is free each way for pedestrians; motorists pay $1 per vehicle for the trip from Algiers to Canal Street.

Mardi Gras parades begin marching regularly a full two weeks before the final day, so if you book well in advance (say, a year) for the weekend before the big Mardi Gras weekend, you can get a room at a reasonable rate and still see what all the shouting's about. The Germaine Wells Mardi Gras Museum on the second floor of Arnaud's Restaurant (813 Bienville St., tel. 504/523–5433), with its dazzling display of Carnival gowns and memorabilia, is free to the public.

Park rangers of the Jean Lafitte National Park Service (916 N. Peters St., tel. 504/589–2636) conduct daily free history tours of the French Quarter and the Garden District.

TOURIST OFFICES **Greater New Orleans Tourist and Convention Commission** (1520 Sugar Bowl Dr., New Orleans 70112, tel. 504/566–5011). **Louisiana Visitor Information Center** (529 St. Ann St., Jackson Sq., New Orleans 70116, tel. 504/568–5661).

EMERGENCIES **Police, fire,** and **ambulance:** Dial 911. **Hospitals:** There are 24-hour emergency rooms at Charity Hospital (1532 Tulane Ave., tel. 504/568–2311), the Tulane University Medical Center (220 LaSalle St., tel. 504/588–5711), and Touro Infirmary (1401 Foucher St., tel. 504/897–8250). **Doctors:** Orleans Parish Medical Society (tel. 504/523–2474). **Dentists:** New Orleans Dental Association (tel. 504/834–6449). **Phar-**

macies: Walgreens (900 Canal St., tel. 504/523–7201) remains open until 9 PM, Eckerd (3400 Canal St., tel. 504/488–6661) closes at midnight, and K&B (3100 Gentilly Blvd., tel. 504/947–6611) is open 24 hours.

ARRIVING AND DEPARTING

BY PLANE **New Orleans International Airport** (tel. 504/464–0831), 15 miles west of the city in Kenner, is served by all major airlines. Ground transportation to downtown hotels takes 20–40 minutes on the **Airport Shuttle** (tel. 504/522–3500 or 800/543–6332, fax 504/592–0549; $10) and in taxis (around $20 for one or two passengers, plus $10 for each additional passenger); the **Airport Express Bus** (tel. 504/737–9611; $1.50) takes 45–60 minutes to reach Elk Place in the CBD.

BY CAR I–10 runs from Florida to California and passes directly through the city. Exit at Poydras Street for the business district; for the French Quarter, take the Vieux Carre exit.

BY TRAIN AND BUS **Union Passenger Terminal** (1001 Loyola Ave., CBD, tel. 504/528–1610) is the terminal for Amtrak (tel. 800/872–7245) trains and Greyhound Lines (tel. 800/231–2222).

GETTING AROUND

ON FOOT The best way to see the French Quarter and the Central Business District is on a leisurely stroll. The Garden District is also walkable, but you'll need transportation to get there and to other parts of town.

BY CAR The narrow streets of the French Quarter were laid out for horse-drawn rigs, not horseless carriages. Traffic is maddening during special events, parking signs are indecipherable, and illegally parked cars are towed away fast. It's best to leave your car in a secured garage.

BY STREETCAR The St. Charles Streetcar, the city's movable historic landmark, makes the picturesque 5-mile trek from the CBD to

Carrollton Avenue around the clock (but less frequently at night) through the Garden District and Uptown, past Audubon Park and Audubon Zoo. The Riverfront Streetcar connects Esplanade Avenue to the New Orleans Convention Center. The Regional Transit Authority staffs a 24-hour **route-information line** (tel. 504/569–2700).

BY BUS The Vieux Carre Shuttle, which looks like a miniature trolley, scoots around the Quarter and to the foot of Canal Street. A free map available at the Louisiana Visitor Information Center shows bus and streetcar routes most used by tourists.

BY TAXI Cabs can be hailed in the CBD and the French Quarter, but in other areas it's usually necessary to call one from **Yellow-Checker Cabs** (tel. 504/525–3311), **Liberty Bell Cabs** (tel. 504/822–5974), or **United Cabs** (tel. 504/522–9771 or 800/323–3303), many of which take credit cards ($5 minimum).

REST STOPS There are clean public rest rooms in the Jackson Brewery and Millhouse in the French Quarter, on the third level of Canal Place, the fourth level of the World Trade Center, and each level of Riverwalk in the CBD, and in department stores and hotels. During Mardi Gras and the Jazz Fest, virtually all restaurants, bars, and guest houses post REST ROOMS FOR PATRONS ONLY signs. During those special events the city sets up portable toilets in the Quarter and the CBD, but there aren't nearly enough to accommodate the huge crowds of people.

GUIDED TOURS Boat: For dinner-plus-jazz riverboat cruises, contact the *Creole Queen* (tel. 504/524–0814 or 800/445–4109). The *Natchez* (tel. 504/586–8777 or 800/365–2628) is an authentic steamboat, with the steam for the boat generated by a paddle.

Orientation: Two-hour city tours by bus are conducted by **Gray Line** (tel. 504/587–0861) and **New Orleans Tours** (tel. 504/592–1991 or 800/543–6332). **Tours by Isabelle** (tel. 504/391–3544) offers three-hour city tours in 14-passenger vans. Gray Line and New Orleans Tours also have combination city tours and riverboat rides.

Special Interest: The three above companies offer full-day bus tours of plantations, with a lunch stop. Tours of the swamps and Cajun Country are run by **Gator Tours** (tel. 504/484–6100), Gray Line, Tours by Isabelle, and **Honey Island Swamp Tours** (tel. 504/641–1769). New Orleans Tours does nighttime tours to popular jazz clubs. To visit New Orleans's famed "Cities of the Dead," contact **Save Our Cemeteries** (tel. 504/588–9357).

Walking: Daily walking tours of the Quarter that take in two museums (about 2½ hours) are led by the **Friends of the Cabildo** (tel. 504/523–3939). **Heritage Tours** (tel. 504/949–9805) offers a general literary tour and walks focusing on William Faulkner or Tennessee Williams. **Classic Tours** (tel. 504/899–1862) covers art, antiques, architecture, and history; the **Preservation Resource Center** (tel. 504/581–7032) occasionally does guided architecture tours. Voodoo tours are a specialty of the unique **Magic Walking Tours** (tel. 504/593–9693).

EXPLORING

The serpentine Father of Waters dictates directions here. The city radiates out from an 8-mile stretch between a loop of the Mississippi River and Lake Pontchartrain. Downtown, which includes the French Quarter and the CBD, is "downriver," the Garden District and Uptown are "upriver," and north and south are "lakeside" and "riverside." Free maps for self-guided walking and driving tours are available at the Louisiana Visitor Information Center (*see* Tourist Offices, *above*). Seeing and doing everything in the Quarter can take days; allow time for an afternoon or evening riverboat cruise, a day trip to the bayous or plantation country, and at least a half day each to see the Garden District, the parks, and the zoo. Some of the attractions below close on Mardi Gras Day; call ahead for hours.

AQUARIUM OF THE AMERICAS The spectacular design of the riverfront aquarium offers viewers close-up encounters with more than 7,000 aquatic creatures from the Amazon

River Basin, the Caribbean Reef, the Mississippi River, and the Gulf Coast. *Foot of Canal St., CBD, tel. 504/861–2537. Open daily. Admission charged.*

AUDUBON PARK AND ZOO Splendidly landscaped by Frederick Law Olmsted, the 340-acre park includes an 18-hole golf course, riding stables, tennis courts, picnic and play areas, hiking and biking trails, and a 2-mile jogging path with 18 exercise stations. The world-class Audubon Zoo occupies 58 acres between the park and the river. Wooden walkways lead to the Louisiana Swamp Exhibit, the tropical bird house, the flamingo pond, the sea lions, and the white tiger. The Mombasa miniature tram circles through the African Savannah. A free shuttle van runs from the Audubon Park entrance on St. Charles Avenue to the zoo, but a 25-minute walk will take you there through Oak Alley, one of the most enchanting settings in New Orleans. *6500 Magazine St., tel. 504/861–2537. Open daily. Admission charged for zoo.*

BLAINE KERN'S MARDI GRAS WORLD The largest float-builder in the world is in Algiers, an old residential district across the river from downtown. A tour here takes you through the warehouses, or dens, where the spectacular floats are constructed. Mardi Gras World provides a free shuttle that meets each incoming ferry in Algiers and transports visitors to the Blaine Kern attraction. *233 Newton St., tel. 504/361–7821. Open daily. Admission charged.*

CENTRAL BUSINESS DISTRICT **Central Business District.** One of the city's most exciting areas, where Canal Street meets the river (the "foot of Canal Street"), the CBD is within walking distance of the French Quarter and most downtown hotels. The riverfront has been dramatically developed in recent years, and here you'll find the Aquarium of the Americas, Spanish Plaza, riverboat landings, and Riverwalk (*see* Shopping, *below*). New Orleans has also entered the casino age, with several gambling riverboats located on the river and Lake Pontchartrain. Harrah's land-based casino is located in

Armstrong Park, near the French Quarter, until 1996, when operations are scheduled to begin at the permanent site at the foot of Canal Street. The Greater New Orleans Tourist and Convention Commission and the Louisiana Visitors Information Center have information on all area casinos.

CITY PARK Among the attractions in the park's 1,500 acres of greenery and scenery are lagoons for fishing or canoeing beneath moss-draped live oaks; golf courses; tennis courts; baseball diamonds; paths for jogging, hiking, and biking; a children's amusement park with a turn-of-the-century carousel; botanical gardens; a festival of holiday lights in December; and the New Orleans Museum of Art.

FRENCH QUARTER The heart and soul of the city is the original French Creole colony, which covers an easily walkable square mile. Start in Jackson Square to watch the street entertainers and to explore its historic buildings: St. Louis Cathedral, and the Cabildo and Presbytère, part of the **Louisiana State Museum complex** (tel. 504/568–6968; open Tues.–Sun.; admission charged). Royal Street has fine antiques stores and art galleries, while funky Bourbon Street is famed for its bars and music clubs. An only-in-New Orleans attraction is the **Voodoo Museum** (724 Dumaine St., tel. 504/523–7685; open daily; admission charged). At the **Musée Conti Wax Museum** (917 Conti St., tel. 504/525–2605; open daily; admission charged), lifelike figures in colorful tableaux depict the city's history. The Victorian **Gallier House** (1132 Royal St., tel. 504/523–6722; open daily; admission charged) features ornate circa-1860s furnishings, and the **Hermann-Grima House** (820 St. Louis St., tel. 504/525–5661; open daily; admission charged) offers a taste of elegant French Quarter living in the 1830s.

GARDEN DISTRICT Take the St. Charles Streetcar to 1st Street to see some of America's most palatial private houses. Walk one block toward the river to Prytania Street, 1st, 3rd, and 4th streets (which cross Prytania Street), and along St. Charles Avenue.

LAKE PONTCHARTRAIN A favorite playground for Orleanians, the 40-mile-long lake is a fit place for fishing and boating (but not swimming). The world's longest causeway crosses it to the piney woods on the north shore. Along Lakeshore Drive there are picnic grounds and marinas.

NEW ORLEANS MUSEUM OF ART A nationally recognized museum, NOMA has a large permanent collection of pre-Columbian, African, and local art, works by some European and American masters, and Fabergé eggs. In 1993, the museum completed a $23.5 million expansion and now includes 130,000 square feet of space in which to display its $200 million collection. *City Park, tel. 504/488–2631. Open Tues.–Sun. Admission charged.*

SPANISH PLAZA Several sightseeing riverboats tie up at this broad, open plaza at the foot of Canal Street. The plaza is laid with colorful mosaic tiles, and its centerpiece is a splashy fountain that's lighted at night. It is the site of the city's annual Lundi Gras bash— a free and freewheeling *bal masqué* that ushers in the final 24 hours of Mardi Gras.

HOTELS AND INNS

New Orleans has a wide variety of accomodations, including high-rise hotels, antiques-filled antebellum houses, Creole cottages, old slave quarters, and familiar hotel chains. Price categories for double occupancy, excluding 11% tax, are Expensive, $100–$125; Moderate, $75–$100; and Inexpensive, under $75.

MODERATE-EXPENSIVE Cornstalk Hotel. Individually decorated rooms with four-poster and canopy beds, armoires, fireplaces, balconies, and galleries are among the attractions of this 1816 Victorian-style house in the Lower Quarter. *915 Royal St., French Quarter, 70116, tel. 504/523–1515. 14 rooms. Free Continental breakfast. AE, MC, V.*

Crowne Plaza. A glass-and-concrete high-rise smack in the midst of the CBD, the Crowne Plaza is an upmarket Holiday Inn hotel. Public areas are spacious, with plenty of fresh flowers and greenery, and guest rooms are large and color-coordinated with good-quality spreads, drapery, and upholstery. *333 Poydras St., 70130, tel. 504/525–9444 or 800/522–6963, fax 504/568–9312. 441 rooms, 2 Jacuzzi suites. Restaurant, lounge, health club, outdoor pool, valet parking. AE, D, DC, MC, V.*

Le Pavillon. In the heart of the CBD, this European-style hotel with smart awnings, magnificent chandeliers, and rooms with high ceilings and hand-carved furnishings attracts savvy Europeans who know a bargain when they find one. *833 Poydras St., CBD, 70140, tel. 504/581–3111 or 800/535–9095, fax 504/522–5543. 219 rooms, 7 suites. Restaurant, pool, sundeck, 5 no-smoking floors, valet laundry, parking. AE, DC, MC, V.*

Radisson Hotel. Easily accessible off I–10 and about a 10-minute walk from the French Quarter, this large, full-service high-rise with modern decor is run by the Radisson chain. Rates are good for the CBD. *1500 Canal St., CBD, 70112, tel. 504/522–4500 or 800/824–3359, fax 504/525–2644. 759 rooms, 23 suites with wet bars. Restaurant, deli, pool, hot tub, exercise room, laundry, free shuttle to French Quarter, valet parking. AE, DC, MC, V.*

MODERATE Chateau Motor Hotel. Near Jackson Square, a carriageway sweeps into the small courtyard of this balconied Creole house, which has a mix of 19th-century Louisiana antiques and contemporary or traditional furnishings. *1001 Chartres St., French Quarter, 70116, tel. 504/524–9636, fax 504/525–2989. 39 rooms, 6 suites. Restaurant, pool, valet parking, free Continental breakfast. AE, DC, MC, V.*

Le Richelieu. One of the city's best bargains, the five renovated row houses that comprise this hotel near the French Market contain rooms with walk-in closets, brass and ceiling fans; many have balconies, mirrored walls, and refrigerators. *1234 Chartres St., French Quarter, 70116, tel. 504/529–2492 or 800/535–9653, fax 504/524–8179. 69 rooms, 17 suites. Coffee shop, cocktail lounge, pool, valet service, free parking. AE, DC, MC, V.*

Park View Guest House. Adjacent to Audubon Park, this 1884 Victorian mansion has brass beds, ceiling fans, splendid views in rooms facing the park, and a casual atmosphere. *7004 St. Charles Ave., Uptown, 70118, tel. 504/861–7564. 23 rooms, 8 with shared bath. Free Continental breakfast. AE, MC, V.*

Prytania Park Hotel. A half block from the St. Charles Streetcar line, this hotel complex with several balconied units comprises an 1834 town house, with exposed brick walls and period reproductions, and newer contemporary sections with lofts, refrigerators, and microwaves. *1525 Prytania St., Garden District, 70130, tel. 504/524–0427 or 800/862–1984, fax 504/522–2977. 62 rooms, 6 suites. Free Continental breakfast, free parking. AE, DC, MC, V.*

St. Charles Inn. This small, modern Uptown hotel offers good-size rooms (those on the front can be noisy) with dressing areas, a friendly staff, and the convenience of the adjacent Que Sera Restaurant. *3636 St. Charles Ave., Garden District, 70115, tel. 504/899–8888. 40 rooms. Free newspaper and Continental breakfast. AE, DC, MC, V.*

Terrell Guest House. In a somewhat neglected neighborhood that's being renovated, this 1858 mansion, with handsome double parlors and 19th-century antiques, has a room and a suite in the main house and other rooms in the carriage house and slave quarters facing a patio with a fountain. *1441 Magazine St., Lower Garden District, 70130, tel. 504/524–9859 or 800/878–9859. 7 rooms, 3 suites. Free breakfast. AE, MC, V.*

INEXPENSIVE-MODERATE **Bon Maison Guest House.** On the quiet end of Bourbon Street, this 1840 town house has simply furnished rooms in renovated slave quarters off a courtyard and in large suites in the main house atop very steep, winding stairs. *835 Bourbon St., French Quarter, 70116, tel. 504/561–8498. 3 rooms, 2 suites. Kitchenettes. MC, V.*

Hotel Villa Convento. Near the Old Ursuline Convent in the Lower Quarter, this family-run hotel occupying a three-story, 1848 Creole town house festooned with ironwork has antique reproductions in individually decorated rooms and a patio area. *616 Ursulines St., French Quarter, 70116, tel. 504/522–1793, fax 504/524–1902. 25 rooms. Free Continental breakfast. AE, DC, MC, V.*

Rue Royal Inn. A pot of hot coffee, a tin of cookies, and three Persian cats greet you in the lobby. Many rooms are pleasantly oversized in this circa-1830 home; four have balconies overlooking Royal Street. *1006 Royal St., French Quarter, 70116, tel. 504/524–3900 or 800/776–3901, fax 504/947–7454. 17 rooms. Kitchenettes, off-street parking. AE, DC, MC, V.*

INEXPENSIVE **Maison St. Charles.** You wouldn't know by the lobby's gilded tables and Frederic Remington sculptures that this is a Quality Inn—one of the chain's top-of-the-line hotels, built around five spacious, flower-filled courtyards. *1319 St. Charles Ave., 70130, tel. 504/522–0187 or 800/831–1783, fax 504/525–2218. 122 rooms, 8 suites. Restaurant, outdoor pool, heated whirlpool, no-smoking rooms, valet parking. AE, MC, V.*

St. Charles Guest House. The affable owners of this simple European-style pension, one block off St. Charles Avenue, offer rooms in three buildings (some are small, inexpensive "backpacker" rooms, with shared baths and no air-conditioning), a guide to self-conducted tours, and occasionally a home-cooked crawfish boil or red-beans-and-rice meal. *1748 Prytania St., Garden District, 70130, tel. 504/523–6556. 30 rooms, 4 with shared bath, 7 "backpacker" rooms. Common room, outdoor pool, sundeck. AE, MC, V.*

MOTELS

MODERATE **Days Inn Downtown** (1630 Canal St., 70112, tel. 504/586–0110 or 800/329–7466, fax 504/581–2253). 216 rooms, 5 suites; restaurant, pool, laundry, free parking. **Holiday Inn Downtown–Superdome** (330 Loyola Ave., 70112, tel. 504/581–1600 or 800/535–7830, fax 504/586–0833). 297 rooms, 4 suites; restaurant, pool, parking. **Holiday Inn & Holidome–New Orleans Airport** (2929 Williams Blvd., Kenner 70062, tel. 504/467–5611 or 800/465–4329, fax 504/469–4915). 303 rooms, 1 suite; restaurant, lounge, indoor pool, Jacuzzi, exercise room, laundry facilities, free parking.

DINING

New Orleans restaurants reflect 270 years of ethnic culinary overlap by the French, African, Spanish, American Indian, Caribbean, Italian, German, and Yugoslavian schools, joined in the 1980s by Asian chefs. The lines between south Louisiana's two mother cuisines—Creole and Cajun—have blurred, but simply put, Creole cuisine carries an urban gloss, epitomized by rich, creamy sauces, while Cajun food is more rough-hewn and rural. Call in advance for reservations and to find out what meals are served. Price categories per person, excluding 9% tax, service, and drinks, are Moderate, $15–$25, and Inexpensive, under $15.

MODERATE Alex Patout's. The fixed-price menus are good values in this stylish restaurant, which spotlights deep-flavored gumbo, sautéed lemon fish with a roasted-pepper sauce, eggplant stuffed with crab and shrimp, and duck with oyster dressing. *221 Royal St., French Quarter, tel. 504/525–7788. Jacket advised for dinner. AE, DC, MC, V.*

Bayona. Although chef Susan Spicer's dinner menu tops the Moderate price range, you can get a taste of her popular cuisine at lunch when prices drop to well within budget. For starters, ask for grilled shrimp with black-bean cake and coriander sauce. The grilled-quail salad comes with mixed greens and tasty surprises of raspberries, strawberries, and hazelnuts. *430 Dauphine St., French Quarter, tel. 504/525–4455. Reservations advised. Jacket advised for dinner. AE, DC, MC, V.*

Bayou Ridge Café. This popular café on the fringes of the Quarter offers a slew of salads,

including eggplant served with sun-dried tomatoes and feta, and grilled scallops with grapefruit butter. Pasta primavera is made with light olive oil, and buttery couscous is topped with spicy Moroccan vegetables. *437 Esplanade Ave., Faubourg Marigny, tel. 504/ 949–9912. AE, DC, MC, V. Closed Mon., Tues.*

Delmonico's. About as near as you can get to dining in a Garden District mansion, Delmonico's has wallpapered rooms, botanical prints, and period furnishings. Vegetable soup and okra gumbo are excellent starters; beef fillet in burgundy sauce, broiled red snapper, and broiled, stuffed shrimp make fine entrées. *1300 St. Charles Ave., Lower Garden District, tel. 504/525–4937. Reservations advised. AE, DC, MC, V.*

G&E Courtyard Grill. This chic dining room and courtyard uses fresh, organically grown herbs on dishes like grilled trout stuffed with garlic and tarragon, grilled duck with a Thai barbecue sauce and marinated Japanese cucumbers, and roasted free-range chicken with sweet peppers, capers, rosemary, and lemon. *1113 Decatur St., French Quarter, tel. 504/528–9376. AE, DC, MC, V.*

Gabrielle. This friendly Cajun-Creole restaurant is popular with locals, so make reservations. The warmed-spinach salad is recommended, as is the flavorful jerked pork rib chop, which is served with apples stewed in root beer. The extensive dessert menu includes a textbook bread pudding and a rich, chocolate-infused "Peppermint Patty." Arrive early for the *price fixe* specials. *3201 Esplanade Ave., Mid-City, tel. 504/948–6233. Reservations advised. AE, DC, MC, V.*

Galatoire's. This 90-year-old French Creole bistro, with mirrored walls, glistening brass chandeliers, and white-cloth tables, serves lumps of crabmeat atop buttery broiled pompano, spring lamb chops in béarnaise sauce, and seafood-stuffed eggplant. *209 Bourbon St., French Quarter, tel. 504/525–2021. No reservations. AE, MC, V. Closed Mon.*

Ralph & Kacoo's. Freshness and consistency are the trademarks of this seafood restaurant, where you'll find huge crowds, a long wait, and a heart-healthy menu approved by a dietitian. *519 Toulouse St., French Quarter, tel. 504/522–5226; 601 Veterans Blvd., Metairie, tel. 504/831–3177. AE, DC, MC, V.*

INEXPENSIVE **Alberto's.** A small, bohemian upstairs Italian eatery noted for unusually low prices for such standouts as cannelloni flavored with an herbed tomato-and-cream sauce and freshly made fettuccine. *609 Frenchmen St., Faubourg Marigny, tel. 504/949–5952. MC, V. Closed Sun.*

Bozo's. Bare-top tables and plain wood paneling set the tone for this no-nonsense seafood house (a favorite with locals), which serves such basics as fresh catfish and shellfish, simply but deliciously cooked. *3117 21st St., Metairie, tel. 504/831–8666. MC, V. Closed Sun.*

Casamento's. The small and immaculate family-run eatery, on the scene since 1918, serves dishes like oysters poached in seasoned milk, and impeccably fresh and greaseless fried shrimp, trout, and oysters. *4330 Magazine St., Uptown, tel. 504/895–9761. No credit cards. Closed Mon. and early June–late Aug.*

Kung's Dynasty. Crispy duck, fine double-cooked pork, tender and spicy eggplant in garlic sauce, and stir-fried oysters are among the offerings in a Garden District cottage. *1912 St. Charles Ave., Lower Garden District, tel. 504/525–6669. AE, DC, MC, V.*

Praline Connection. This neat-as-a-pin and laid-back family restaurant has stewed chicken, collard greens, sweet potato pie, corn bread, and some of the lowest prices in town. Don't leave without sampling a homemade praline from the candy store. The CBD location offers a gospel brunch on Sunday. *542 Frenchmen St., Faubourg Marigny, tel. 504/943–3934; 907 S. Peters St., CBD, tel. 504/523–3973. AE, DC, MC, V.*

Saddlery. A cheerful corner restaurant, the Saddlery serves the likes of chicken-fried steak and mashed potatoes, marvelous barbecued ribs, and mouthwatering home-baked pastries. If you're a vegetarian, ask the

chef to whip up a platter of pasta mixed with fresh vegetables. Just make sure to save room for the pies. *240 Decatur St. (at Bienville St.), French Quarter, tel. 504/522–5172. AE, DC, MC, V.*

Shoney's. An all-you-can eat breakfast buffet and a salad bar attract locals and tourists alike to the familiar chain, with its casual ambience and straightforward American food. *619 Decatur St., French Quarter, tel. 504/525–2039. AE, MC, V.*

SHOPPING

SHOPPING DISTRICTS The main shopping areas are the French Quarter and the Central Business District. Magazine Street has secondhand stores, antiques shops, and galleries, and Royal Street has more of the same, but more upscale. **Riverwalk** (1 Poydras St., tel. 504/522–1555) features more than 200 nationally known and local shops, restaurants, and cafés. In the Quarter, the Jackson Brewery, Millhouse, and Marketplace are restored historic buildings filled with specialty shops and eateries. The **Community Flea Market** (French Market at Gov. Nicholls St.) is open weekends.

SOUVENIRS Among the city's unique souvenirs are pralines (thin, hardened sugar-and-pecan patties), Creole and Cajun spices, packaged-to-go seafood, and packaged mixes of local dishes. Regional cookbooks, Mardi Gras masks, posters, and memorabilia are hot tickets; so are jazz records and parasols.

OUTDOOR ACTIVITIES AND SPORTS

BIKING Bikers wheel around the French Quarter, City Park, and Audubon Park. Rentals are available at **Bicycle Michael's** (618 Frenchmen St., tel. 504/945–9505).

BOATING You can go canoeing on your own or with a guide deep into the former hideouts of pirates in the Barataria Unit of the **Jean Lafitte National Historical Park** (about an hour's drive from New Orleans near Lafitte, tel. 504/589–2330 or 504/589–2636), an area of beautiful coastal wetlands.

■ BOWLING ■ **Don Carter's All Star Lanes** (3640 Williams Blvd., Kenner, tel. 504/443–5353) is a full-service, modern facility. While the more vintage **Mid-City Lanes Rock 'n' Bowl** (4133 Carrollton Ave., tel. 504/482–3133) may not appeal to serious bowlers, it's the most rocking bowling alley in the South, where bowlers dance to live music as a glitter ball revolves above.

■ HIKING AND RUNNING ■ The Barataria Unit of **Jean Lafitte National Historical Park** (tel. 504/589–2330) has about 8 miles of trails that explore Louisiana's Delta Wetlands and important archaeological sites. On tours into the murky reaches of the bayous and swamps, you'll get a gander at gators, egrets, nutria, and such. Self-guided walking tours along raised, wooden platforms are available free of charge. **Audubon Park** has a 2-mile jogging path, with exercise stations, and the Mississippi River levee and City Park are also popular.

■ TENNIS ■ **Audubon Park** (tel. 504/895–1042) has 10 courts, located at the back off Tchoupitoulas Street. **City Park** (Victory Ave., tel. 504/483–9383) has 36 lighted courts.

ENTERTAINMENT

The sound of music almost drowns out all other art forms in New Orleans. This isn't a big-ticket theater, ballet, or opera town, but it's the best place in the world to hear Dixieland and traditional jazz, R&B, Cajun, zydeco, honky-tonk, and rock and roll out of Bourbon Street's clubs, as well as in hangouts in Uptown, Mid-City, the Warehouse District, and the Faubourg Marigny. The most complete daily music calendar is broadcast every two hours, beginning at 11:30 AM, on WWOZ, 90.7 FM. Also see

"Lagniappe" (the Friday entertainment section of the *Times-Picayune*), *Gambit,* a free weekly newspaper, and *OffBeat,* a free music monthly.

■ DIXIELAND AND JAZZ ■ Trumpeter Al Hirt has returned to Bourbon Street to **Al Hirt's Place** (501 Bourbon St., tel. 504/568–0501). Pete Fountain plays Dixieland-style licorice stick in his own nightclub in the **Hilton Hotel** (2 Poydras St., tel. 504/523–4374). Creole dining accompanies traditional jazz at the stately **Palm Court Jazz Cafe** (1204 Decatur St., tel. 504/525–0200). For Dixieland and traditional jazz, head for **Preservation Hall** (726 St. Peter St., tel. 504/523–8939). **Snug Harbor** (626 Frenchmen St., tel. 504/949–0696) is the place for contemporary jazz, including regular appearances by members of the famous Marsalis family.

■ ROCK AND BLUES ■ Blues is the mood at the **Absinthe Bar** (400 Bourbon St., tel. 504/525–8108). The **House of Blues** (225 Decatur St., tel. 504/529–2583) features big-name acts passing through town. Rock rules in the Warehouse District at **Howlin' Wolf** (828 S. Peters St., tel. 504/523–2551). **Jimmy's** (8200 Willow St., tel. 504/861–8200) has an eclectic schedule that ranges from rock to reggae to R&B. **Tipitina's** (501 Napoleon Ave., tel. 504/895–8477) offers alternative rock fare, along with Cajun dancing on Sunday evenings.

■ ZYDECO AND CAJUN ■ Zydeco bands from rural Louisiana are the draw Sunday nights at the **Maple Leaf Bar** (8316 Oak St., tel. 504/866–5323). Cajun dance lessons are offered nightly at **Michaul's** (840 St. Charles Ave., tel. 504/522–5517). The zydeco scene is in full swing on Wednesday and Thursday nights at the ever-popular **Mid-City Lanes Rock 'n' Bowl** (4133 Carrollton Ave., tel. 504/482–3133). **Mulate's** (201 Julia St., tel. 504/522–1492) is a Cajun restaurant with a well-traveled dance floor.

Newport
Rhode Island

Updated by Katherine Imbrie

Perched gloriously on the southern tip of Aquidneck Island and bounded on three sides by water, Newport, Rhode Island, is one of the great sailing cities of the world and the host to world-class jazz, blues, and classical music festivals.

Its first age of prosperity was in the late 1700s, when it was a major port city, on a par with Boston and New York. Many homes and shops built in that era still stand in the Point and Historic Hill sections of the city—tidy, compact areas of brick, clapboard, and narrow streets.

In the 19th century, Newport became a summer playground for the wealthiest families in America, who built monuments to themselves, their wealth, and the Gilded Age in America. Each new home constructed on Bellevue Avenue was grander than the one built just before it, until Cornelius Vanderbilt II attained the acme of extravagance with the luxurious Breakers.

Newport on a summer afternoon can be exasperating, its streets jammed with visitors and the traffic slowed by the procession of air-conditioned sightseeing buses. Yet the quality of Newport's arts festivals persuades many people to brave the crowds. And when the crowds and opulence become oppressive, one can always escape to the small but beautifully situated beaches in and around the city.

ESSENTIAL INFORMATION

WHEN TO GO Newport's weather usually remains pleasant well into November, with October temperatures averaging 69°. Winters do tend to be damp and chilly. Spring comes a bit later on the coast than inland, but by May, temperatures average 59°. Newport, like all of New England, is at its best in the fall, when the crowds of summer thin out considerably. Rates at hotels are generally 30% lower from October through May.

FESTIVALS AND SEASONAL EVENTS Mid-July: **Newport Music Festival** brings together celebrated musicians for a two-week schedule of morning, afternoon, and evening concerts in Newport mansions (tel. 401/846–1133). **Lite Beer Hall of Fame Championship** and **Virginia Slims Hall of Fame Invitational** matches take place on grass courts at the International Tennis Hall of Fame at the Newport Casino (tel. 401/849–6053). **Early-Aug.:** Newport Folk Festival at Fort Adams State Park is the nation's premier folk festival (tel. 401/847–3700). **Mid-Aug.:** The **JVC Jazz Festival** brings renowned performers to Fort Adams State Park (tel. 401/847–3700).

TOURIST OFFICES **Newport County Convention and Visitors Bureau** and **Gateway Information Center** (23 America's Cup Ave., Newport 02840, tel. 401/849–8048 or 800/326–6030).

EMERGENCIES **Police:** tel. 911 or 401/847–1212. **Fire** and **ambulance:** tel. 911 or 401/846–2211. **Hospital:** Newport Hospital (Friendship St., tel. 401/846–6400). **Pharmacy:** Douglas Drug (7 E. Main Rd., Middletown, tel. 401/849–4600).

NEWPORT

TO
NEWPORT
STATE
AIRPORT

*Miantonomi
Memorial
Park*

Admiral   Kalbfus Rd.

*Coasters
Harbor
Island*

Newport Bridge

138

N

Garfield St.

Van Zandt Ave.

Broadway

Common
Burial
Ground

Warner St.

*Rose
Island*

Hunter House

Friends
Meeting
House

W·L·H
House

Friends Ave.

Norman
Bird Sanctuary,
Sachuest Point
National Wildlife
Refuge

Washington
Sq.

Touro
St.

Catherine St.

Brick Market Museum

Touro Synagogue

Church
St.

Old Beach Rd.

Easton
Beach

*Goat
Island*

Memorial   Blvd.

Cliff
Walk
(Begins)

International Tennis
Hall of Fame and
Tennis Museum

Spring St.

Museum of
Yachting

*King Park
and Beach*

The
Elms

Bellevue Ave.

*Fort Adams
State Park*

Wellington Ave.

Webster

St.

Ochre

Thames St.

Halidon Ave.

Fort Adams Rd.

Victoria Ave.

Pt.

The
Breakers

Ave.

Wickham Rd.

Ridge   Rd.

Moorland Rd.

Harrison

Rd.

Hazard   Rd.

Bellevue Ave.

Rosecliff

Brenton

Castle
Ave.

Ocean   Ave.

Marble House

Winans
Ave.

Harrison Ave.

Ocean
Drive

Cliff
Walk
(Ends)

Ocean   Ave.

*Gooseberry
Island*

*Brenton Point
State Park*

0   1 mile

0   1 km

ARRIVING AND DEPARTING

BY PLANE The nearest airport to Newport is **Theodore Francis Green State Airport** (tel. 401/737–4000), with scheduled daily flights by six major U.S. airlines and additional service by regional carriers. The **Newport Shuttle** (tel. 401/846–2500) runs a frequent shuttle service ($15) between Theodore Francis Green Airport and the visitors bureau downtown, as well as the major hotels; some Newport hotels provide free airport shuttle service to guests.

BY CAR If you're coming from the south, exit I–95 at the town of Wyoming and follow Route 138 east across the Jamestown Bridge and Newport Bridge into Newport. If you're coming from the north, take Route 24 south to Route 114 or Route 138.

BY BUS **Rhode Island Public Transit Authority** (tel. 401/847–0209) links Newport and Providence, where there are connections to New York, Boston, and other major northeastern cities.

BY FERRY Ferries leave Providence for Newport from the **India Street Pier** (tel. 203/442–7891).

GETTING AROUND

BY CAR A car can be a liability in summer, when traffic thickens on the city's narrow one-way streets. You can leave your car at the 350-car parking lot at the Gateway Information Center (23 America's Cup Ave.). Each of the Newport mansions has a parking lot.

BY BUS **Rhode Island Public Transit Authority** (tel. 401/847–0209) provides Newport area bus service.

REST STOPS The Gateway Information Center has public rest rooms; other convenient facilities are at the Seaman's Institute on Bowen's Wharf; the Harbor Center on Thames Street; and behind Burger King near the Mary Street Municipal Parking lot.

GUIDED TOURS For a small fee, the **Newport Historical Society** (82 Touro St., tel. 401/

846–0813) offers walking tours of historic Newport by fully trained guides, June 15 through September 30. **Old Colony & Newport Railway** (19 America's Cup Ave., tel. 401/624–6951) follows a route along Narragansett Bay from Newport with a stop at Portsmouth's Green Animals Topiary Gardens; the 18-mile round-trip takes a little over three hours. The *Spirit of Newport* (tel. 401/849–3575) gives one-hour minicruises of Newport Harbor and Narragansett Bay, departing from the Newport Harbor Hotel at 49 America's Cup Avenue every 90 minutes. **Viking Bus Tours of Newport** (Brick Market, tel. 401/847–6921) runs air-conditioned buses departing from the Gateway Information Center.

EXPLORING

COLONIAL NEWPORT To get a sense of how Newport has changed through the centuries, walk the city's narrow streets to view Colonial-era houses and shops clustered around the harbor.

The **Common Burial Ground,** on Farewell Street, offers interesting examples of Colonial stone carving and a large section of pre-Revolution African-American graves.

The **Friends Meeting House,** a short distance northwest of the Brick Market, was built in 1699, which makes it the oldest Quaker Meeting House in America. Note the wide-planked floors, simple benches, balcony, and medieval beam ceiling. *29 Farewell St., tel. 401/846–0813 (by appointment only). Open June–Aug., Mon.–Sat. Admission charged.*

Hunter House on Washington Street is a Colonial home (1748) with a carved pineapple over the doorway. Notice the elliptical arch in the central hall and, in the northeast parlor, the cherubs carved over the cupboard. *54 Washington St., tel. 401/847–1000. Open Apr.–Oct., daily. Admission charged.*

Museum of Newport History at The Brick Market. On display in this fully restored 1760 building—which previously served as a market house, a theater, and town hall—is an engaging exhibit on Newport's history from 1636 to the present, including artifacts, furniture, and more. *Thames St. at Washington Sq., tel. 401/846–0813. Open year-round. Admission charged.*

Touro Synagogue is the oldest surviving synagogue in the United States, dedicated in 1763. Simple on the outside but elaborate within, it combines ornate Georgian decoration with requirements of the Jewish ritual. *85 Touro St., tel. 401/847–4794. Open late Apr.–early Sept., Sun.–Fri.; early Sept.–late Apr., Sun. and by appointment. Calling in advance is recommended.*

Wanton-Lyman-Hazard House, built about 1675, is Newport's oldest surviving residence. A site of the Stamp Act riot in 1765, the house is an excellent example of early architecture and is furnished with authentic period pieces. *17 Broadway, tel. 401/846–0813. Open June 15–Sept. 1, Thurs.–Sun. Admission charged.*

BELLEVUE AVENUE MANSIONS To explore the grand structures along Bellevue Avenue in the southern section of the city, it makes sense to drive (or ride a bicycle) from house to house, since the distances between them are considerable. You'll have plenty of walking to do inside the mansions and through the grounds!

Six of the Newport mansions are maintained by the **Preservation Society of Newport County** (tel. 401/847–1000). A combination ticket—available at any of the properties—gives you a discount on individual admission prices. Each mansion provides a guided tour that lasts about one hour. Most are open daily from April to October.

Proceeding south along Bellevue Avenue, you can visit **The Elms,** with its handsome formal gardens; **Rosecliff,** modeled after the Grand Trianon at Versailles; and **Marble House,** with its grand Corinthian columns supporting an immense portico.

The Breakers, which you reach by turning left off Bellevue Avenue onto Victoria Avenue and continuing to Ochre Point Avenue, is a sumptuous, 70-room, limestone-sheathed palace. Among its marvels are a gold-ceilinged music room, rose alabaster pillars in the dining room, and a porch with a mosaic ceiling. *Ochre Point Ave., tel. 401/847–1000. Open Apr.–Oct., daily. Admission charged.*

MUSEUMS The **International Tennis Hall of Fame** and the **Tennis Museum** are housed in the magnificent **Newport Casino,** a Stanford White building near the start of Bellevue Avenue. The museum features photographs and other tennis memorabilia. The first National Tennis Championships were held here in 1881. *Newport Casino, 194 Bellevue Ave., tel. 401/846–4567. Open daily. Admission charged.*

The **Museum of Yachting,** at the end of the point in Fort Adams State Park, has galleries of pictures of yachts, mansions, and America's Cup races. *Ft. Adams, tel. 401/847–1018. Open mid-May–Oct., daily. Admission charged.*

THE NATURAL WORLD At the 450-acre **Norman Bird Sanctuary** (tel. 401/846–2577), about 2 miles east of the city of Newport on Third Beach Road, you can hike along ridges of "pudding stone," conglomerate rocks that were stretched by the pressure of the earth and then exposed by the action of the glaciers. Hanging Rock, the most scenic pudding-stone ridge, gives you a good view of the ocean. Other ridges in the sanctuary are dikes of lava that cooled before reaching the surface.

Norman Sanctuary and the adjoining **Sachuest Point National Wildlife Refuge** (tel. 401/847–5511) on Sachuest Point Road in Middletown are the best places for bird-watching. Spring and fall bring scores of songbird species, while snowy owls and sharp-shinned and red-tailed hawks may be seen in fall and winter.

HOTELS AND INNS

Newport lodgings can be expensive. Hotels in Newport range from Victorian bed-and-breakfasts with oak paneling, fireplaces, and marble-topped dressers to spanking-new hotels on the harbor. Few B&Bs are inside the mansion district, but several are located on its fringes. Rates are generally 30% lower off-season (October through May). Price categories for double occupancy, excluding 12% tax, are Very Expensive, $145–$325; Expensive, $100–$145; Moderate, $85–$100; and Inexpensive, under $85.

VERY EXPENSIVE **Cliffside Inn.** Near Newport's Cliff Walk and downtown, this 1880 Victorian home on a quiet, tree-lined street offers a somewhat formal atmosphere with light and airy rooms, most with hot tubs and fireplaces. *2 Seaview Ave., 02840, tel. 401/ 847–1811, fax 401/848–5850. 13 rooms, each with private bath. Porch, eating area, hot breakfast included. AE, D, DC, MC, V.*

Francis Malbone House. The design of this elegant brick 1760 house is attributed to Peter Harrison, the architect who also created the Touro Synagogue and the Redwood Library. Beautifully restored and conveniently located at the quieter end of Thames Street close to Newport Harbor, the inn has nine large guest rooms which face either the inn's lovely back garden or the harbor across the street. *392 Thames St., 02840, tel. 401/ 846–0392, fax 401/848–5956. 9 rooms, each with private bath. Hot breakfast included. AE, MC, V.*

EXPENSIVE **Ivy Lodge.** This large Victorian home with a wraparound porch is a splurge, but worth it for the lavish appointments, including a 33-foot Gothic paneled oak entry, a huge brick fireplace, and spacious rooms. *12 Clay St., 02840, tel. 401/849–6865. 8 rooms with private bath. Breakfast buffet included. AE, MC, V.*

Victorian Ladies. You'll find Victorian antiques and good soundproofing at this bed-and-breakfast, located on one of Newport's main thoroughfares and within walking distance of shops. *63 Memorial Blvd., 02840, tel. and fax 401/849–9960. 11 rooms with private bath. Air-conditioning, off-street parking. Breakfast included. MC, V.*

MODERATE-EXPENSIVE **Admiral Farragut Inn.** This pale yellow clapboard inn, in the center of Colonial Newport, features Shaker-style pencil-post beds and handmade spreads along with such modern amenities as telephones and air-conditioning. *31 Clarke St., 02840, tel. 401/848–8000 or 800/343–2863, fax 401/846–4289. 9 rooms with bath. Full breakfast included, sitting room, off-street parking. No children. AE, MC, V.*

Brinley Victorian Inn. Situated within walking distance of mansions and the harbor, this inn has two parlors, a library, a courtyard, and lots of Victorian lace and chintz. *23 Brinley St., 02840, tel. 401/849–7645. 17 rooms, 13 with bath. Continental breakfast included, off-street parking. MC, V.*

MODERATE **Inn at Castle Hill.** Perched on an oceanside cliff 3 miles from the center of Newport and close to the Bellevue mansions and Ocean Drive, this rambling inn was built as a summer home in 1874 and still retains its Victorian character. The inn may appear a bit shabby, but that's part of its authentic charm for the many loyal repeat guests who appreciate unsurpassed ocean views and the private beach. *Ocean Dr., 02840, tel. 401/849–3800. 10 rooms, 7 with private bath. Continental breakfast; restaurant in season. AE, MC, V.*

Sanford–Covell Villa Marina. Located on the waterfront in Newport's historic Point section, this intimate and elegant inn was built in 1869. Among the house's distinctive features is a classic Victorian wraparound veranda with white wicker furniture where guests can sit and sip while surveying a beautifully landscaped heated saltwater pool overlooking the harbor. *72 Washington St., 02840, tel. 401/847–0206. 6 double rooms, 3 with shared baths. Continental breakfast and afternoon refreshments. No credit cards.*

INEXPENSIVE-MODERATE **Commodore Perry Inn.** This property, with eight cozy rooms located above the Red Parrot restaurant, is a bargain for Colonial Newport, although it's not really an inn (it lacks a common room or dining area). *348 Thames St., 02840, tel.*

401/848–8000 or 800/343–2863, fax 401/ 848–8006. 8 rooms with private bath. AE, MC, V.

MOTELS

MODERATE **Best Western Mainstay** (151 Admiral Kalbfus Rd., 02840, tel. 401/849–9880 or 800/528–1234, fax 401/849–4391). 113 rooms; restaurant, pool. **Comfort Inn of Newport** (936 W. Main Rd., Middletown 02840, tel. 401/846–7600 or 800/556–6464, fax 401/849–6919). 162 rooms; restaurant, pool, free shuttle to Newport. **Harbor Base Pineapple Inn** (372 Coddington Hwy., 02840, tel. 401/847–2600, fax 401/847–5230). 48 rooms. **Motel 6** (249 J. T. Connell Hwy., 02840, tel. 401/848–0600). 79 rooms.

DINING

Traditional Rhode Island fare such as johnnycakes (corn cakes cooked on a griddle) and quahogs (the native clam, pronounced KO-hog) served in soups and pies turn up on Newport menus. Italian and Portuguese immigrants serve their cuisine in friendly neighborhood restaurants. Newport restaurants tend to be rather casual and informal. Price categories per person, excluding 7% tax, service, and drinks, are Expensive, $25–$50; Moderate, $15–$25; and Inexpensive, under $15.

EXPENSIVE **Black Pearl.** At this popular waterfront restaurant with a nautical decor, diners choose between the casual tavern and the very formal Commodore's Room. The emphasis is on seafood served in inventive ways. *Bannister's Wharf, tel. 401/846–5264. AE, MC, V.*

Clarke Cooke House. Formal dining is on the upper level, where a green-latticework deck overlooks the bustle of Newport Harbor. The menu is sophisticated Tuscan, with a similar but less expensive menu downstairs. *Bannister's Wharf, tel. 401/849–2900. AE, MC, V.*

White Horse Tavern. Believed to be the nation's oldest operating tavern, the White Horse offers a setting conducive to intimate dining. Traditional entrées such as beef Wellington are served along with some more exotic choices such as honey-and-cinnamon roast duckling. *Marlborough and Farewell Sts., tel. 401/849–3600. AE, MC, V.*

MODERATE-EXPENSIVE **Scales & Shells.** Check the blackboard menu for seafood specials prepared with zest over a wood grill. Lobster *fra diavolo* and mesquite-grilled shrimp are especially good. Informally stylish, this place gets busy on summer evenings, so it's best to go early. *527 Thames St., tel. 401/846–3474. No reservations. No lunch. No credit cards.*

MODERATE **Anthony's Seafood & Shore Dinner Hall.** Families flock to this large, light room with panoramic views of Newport Harbor to enjoy local seafood and lobster. *Lower Thames St. at Waites Wharf, tel. 401/848–5058. MC, V.*

Brick Alley Pub. Low ceilings, small tables, plants, and American memorabilia give this place a friendly atmosphere. An extensive menu includes fresh fish, chowder, steaks, pasta and some Mexican dishes. *140 Thames St., tel. 401/849–6334. AE, D, DC, MC, V.*

Ocean Coffee Roasters. This popular restaurant does a brisk business in Italian specialties as well as homemade muffins, sandwiches, and fresh-roasted coffee. *22 Washington Sq., tel. 401/846–6060. MC, V.*

Salas'. Pastas, lobster, clams, and corn-on-the-cob are the principal fare at this lively, good-natured, waterfront dining spot. *341 Thames St., tel. 401/846–8772. AE, V.*

INEXPENSIVE **Franklin Spa.** This neighborhood luncheonette is a good place for a quick sandwich or more substantial omelet or stew. *229 Spring St., tel. 401/847–3540. No credit cards.*

SHOPPING

Newport is not a city for bargain hunting. Its specialties include antiques, traditional clothing, and marine supplies. Many of Newport's arts and antiques shops can be found on Thames Street or near the waterfront. The Brick Market area—between Thames Street and America's Cup Avenue—has more than 50 shops.

ANTIQUES **Aardvark Antiques** (475 Thames St., tel. 401/849-7233) specializes in architectural antiques, lawn ornaments, stained glass, and lighting fixtures. The **Old Fashion Shop** (38 Pelham St., tel. 401/847-2692) sells American furniture and accessories, including china, quilts, and glass.

ARTS AND CRAFTS The **Liberty Tree** (104 Spring St., tel. 401/847-5925) has contemporary folk art, furniture, carvings, and paintings. **Thames Glass** (688 Thames St., tel. 401/846-0576) sells delicate and dramatic blown-glass gifts, hand-blown on the premises.

FLAGS **Ebenezer Flagg Company** (corner of Spring and Touro Sts., tel. 401/846-1891) offers a large selection of flags, banners, and wind socks.

MARINE ITEMS **JT's Ship Chandlery** (364 Thames St., tel. 401/846-7256) is a major supplier of marine hardware, equipment, and clothing.

OUTDOOR ACTIVITIES

BEACHES **Easton's Beach** (Memorial Blvd.), also known as First Beach, is popular with families, teens, and visitors for its carousel and view of Cliff Walk. It has both changing rooms and food concessions. **Second Beach** (Hanging Rock Rd., Middletown), just east of Easton's Beach, is the largest and most attractive beach in Newport County, with changing rooms and food concessions. It tends to be a bit quieter than Easton's. **Fort Adams State Park** (Ocean Dr.), a very small beach with a picnic area and lifeguards during the summer, has beautiful views of Newport Harbor. Scuba divers like the clear, deep water, but there are no changing rooms.

BIKING Bellevue Avenue, which is fairly flat, shaded, and studded with Newport's grandest mansions, makes a good and not too taxing bike route. **Ten Speed Spokes** (18 Elm St., tel. 401/847-5609) has bikes. **Fun Rentals of Newport** (1 Commercial Wharf, tel. 401/846-4374) has mopeds and more.

BOATING Charter fishing boats depart daily, spring–fall. For information, check with the **Convention & Visitors Bureau** (tel. 401/849-8048 or 800/326-6030). The tall ship *Providence* (Box 76, 02840, tel. 401/846-1776), a replica of a 1776 merchant vessel, takes passengers on three-hour sails on Narragansett Bay several weekends during the summer and fall. **Oldport Marine Services** (Sayer's Wharf, tel. 401/847-9109) offers harbor tours, yacht charters, and rides on a harbor ferry. **Sight Sailing of Newport** (Bowen's Wharf, tel. 401/849-3333) organizes two-hour sailing tours of Newport Harbor in a six-passenger sailboat and sailing instruction for beginners.

WALKING The 3-mile **Cliff Walk** begins at Easton's Beach and runs along Newport's cliffs, offering a breathtaking view of the Atlantic Ocean and many Newport mansions.

ENTERTAINMENT

To sample Newport's lively nightclub scene, just stroll down Thames Street after dark and listen for the music. For a classy bar with a view of the action, try the **Candy Store in the Clarke Cooke House** (Bannister's Wharf, tel. 401/849-2900). **One Pelham East** (270 Thames St., tel. 401/847-9460) draws a young crowd for progressive rock, as does **Thames St. Station** (337 America's Cup Ave., tel. 401/849-9480). The **Red Parrot** (348 Thames St., tel. 401/847-3140) has jazz Thursday, Friday, and Sunday evenings.

New York City
New York

Updated by Jonathan Landreth

ew York is the ultimate in big-city vacation destinations. Its undefinable aura and remarkable energy have something to do with being in the big league, where everybody's watching and keeping score. You can sit down in a restaurant, and at the next table you might spot a celebrity. Even if you don't see someone you recognize, you always feel you just might.

Many people think of New York as expensive, unfriendly, and dirty, if not downright dangerous. New Yorkers may seem hurried and brusque, but they will often gladly come to your aid if you're lost—so don't hesitate to ask for directions. Crime and violence, seldom as random as rumor suggests, can be avoided. The littered sidewalks and slimy gutters that are so much a part of the city's identity coexist with some of the most glittering stores, restaurants, and nightspots on earth. Expensive? Yes, as a rule. But inexpensive restaurants and modestly priced tickets are abundant. And much that you come here to experience won't cost you a thing.

New York is home to some of the world's great museums, a scintillating arts scene, superb shopping and restaurants, and some of the world's most stunning architecture: "New York" and "skyline" are virtually synonymous. Its attractions, such as the Statue of Liberty, Times Square, and the Empire State Building, though situated in Manhattan, belong to the world. Yet what truly sets it apart from several other world capitals is its varied population; the motley faces in its crowds reveal a global pedigree that you rarely encounter. This teeming spectacle, together with the city's vitality and culture, makes New York an essential destination for those who love to travel.

ESSENTIAL INFORMATION

WHEN TO GO The most pleasant times to visit are fall, when cultural activities are in full swing and temperatures range from 50° to 70°, and spring, with plentiful rainfall and temperatures usually ranging from 40° to 70°. In winter, although there's an occasional bone-chilling day, temperatures don't usually drop below the mid-20s. Summer is probably the most unpleasant time of year, with hot and humid days sometimes reaching the mid-90s. With the exception of regular closing days and a few major holidays, the city's museums are open year-round.

FESTIVALS AND SEASONAL EVENTS New Year's Eve kicks off with fireworks from all quarters and rowdy crowds in Times Square. In late January or early February, **Chinese New Year** in Chinatown crackles with firecrackers while feasting celebrants crowd the restaurants. The **St. Patrick's Day Parade,** one of dozens of ethnic processions down 5th Avenue, is a lively, often rowdy, bash. In mid-September, the **Feast of San Gennaro** (tel. 212/226–9546) fills the streets of Little Italy. Macy's **Thanksgiving Day Parade** attracts huge crowds with its giant balloons and floats. The **Christmas season** is particularly beautiful, with animated windows at Lord & Taylor and Saks Fifth Avenue, the New York City Ballet's Nutcracker performances (tel. 212/870–5570), and Radio City Music Hall's Christmas Spectacular (tel. 212/247–4777).

Columbia University ▪ W.116th St.   E.116th St.   Randall's Island

Morningside Park   E.110th St.   Ward's Island

UPPER WEST SIDE   UPPER EAST SIDE

Central Park   Museum Mile

Hudson River

W.86th St.   E.86th St.

Metropolitan Museum of Art ▪   E.79th St.

American Museum of Natural History   E.72nd St.

QUEENS

W.72nd St.   E.65th St.

Lincoln Center   Central Park Zoo   E.59th St.   Queensboro Bridge

W.57th St. Museum of Modern Art   E.57th St.

Rockefeller Center   Grand Central Terminal   United Nations Headquarters

Port Authority Bus Terminal   Times Square   Queens-Midtown Tunnel

Lincoln Tunnel

W.42nd St.   E.42nd St.

MIDTOWN   Empire State Building

Javits Convention Center   W.34th St.

Madison Square Garden/ Penn Station   W.23rd St.   E.23rd St.

CHELSEA   GRAMERCY

W.14th St.   E.14th St.

NEW JERSEY

GREENWICH VILLAGE   EAST VILLAGE

Washington Square Park

W. Houston St.   E. Houston St.   Williamsburg Bridge

Holland Tunnel   SOHO   LITTLE ITALY

Canal St.

TRIBECA   CHINA TOWN   Manhattan Bridge

Chambers St.   Brooklyn Bridge

World Financial Center   South Street Seaport   BROOKLYN

World Trade Center   New York Stock Exchange

LOWER MANHATTAN

MANHATTAN

Statue of Liberty   Ellis Island   Battery Park

0   440 yards
0   400 meters

Brooklyn-Battery Tunnel   Staten Island Ferry Terminal

Henry Hudson Pkwy.   Riverside Dr.   Broadway   Amsterdam Ave.   Central Park West   Columbus Ave.   West End Ave.   East River Dr.   Roosevelt Island   York Ave.   Park Ave.

11th Ave.   10th Ave.   9th Ave.   8th Ave.   7th Ave.   5th Ave.   3rd Ave.   1st Ave.   Franklin D. Roosevelt Drive   East River

Ave. of the Americas   Broadway   Madison Ave.   Lexington Ave.   2nd Ave.   Ave. C

West Side Hwy.   West St.   Broadway   E. Broadway

9A

248

BARGAINS Several museums have pay-what-you-wish policies every day, including the Metropolitan Museum of Art, the American Museum of Natural History, the Museum of the City of New York (*see* Exploring, *below*), and the Museum of Television and Radio (25 W. 52nd St., tel. 212/621–6600); the same policy applies at the Museum of Modern Art and the Whitney Museum of American Art (*see* Exploring, *below*) on Thursday evening. On Tuesday evening, admission is free to several other museums on Museum Mile (*see* Exploring, *below*).

To save on theater tickets, pay half price at the Theater Development Fund's TKTS booths in Duffy Square at 47th Street and Broadway or at 2 World Trade Center; music and dance events have a similar setup at the Bryant Park Music and Dance Half-Price Ticket Booth (42nd St. at 6th Ave., tel. 212/382–2323).

TOURIST OFFICE New York Convention and Visitors Bureau (2 Columbus Circle, New York City 10019, tel. 212/397–8222).

EMERGENCIES Police, fire, or ambulance: Dial 911. **Hospitals:** St. Luke's-Roosevelt (9th Ave. at 58th St., tel. 212/523–6800) and St. Vincent's (7th Ave. at 12th St., tel. 212/604–7997) have emergency rooms with 24-hour service. **Doctors:** Doctors on Call (tel. 212/737–2333) makes house calls. **Dentists:** Emergency Dental Service (tel. 212/679–3966; 212/679–4172 after 8 PM) makes referrals. **Pharmacies:** In residential neighborhoods, many stay open until 11 PM; check the Yellow Pages in your hotel; Kaufman's (Lexington Ave. at 50th St., tel. 212/755–2266) is pricey but open 24 hours year-round.

ARRIVING AND DEPARTING

BY PLANE Virtually all major airlines serve **La Guardia Airport** and **John F. Kennedy (JFK) International Airport,** both located in the borough of Queens, or **Newark International Airport** in nearby northern New Jersey.

Between the Airports and Manhattan: Taxis are available at airport taxi stands. In clear traffic, the ride to midtown will cost $25–$35 from La Guardia or Newark and $35–$45 from JFK, plus tip and up to $3 in tolls. Barring any traffic problems, the trip from La Guardia should take 30–45 minutes; from JFK, an hour; and from Newark, 40–50 minutes.

A number of bus companies operate between the airports and midtown Manhattan; travel time is about the same as for taxis. **Carey Airport Express** (tel. 718/632–0500) serves Grand Central Terminal and major hotels from La Guardia ($10) and JFK ($13). **Gray Line Air Shuttle Minibuses** (tel. 212/757–6840) serves major hotels from La Guardia ($13), from JFK ($16), and from Newark ($18). The **New Jersey Transit Airport Express** (tel. 201/762–5100) operates from Newark ($7) to the Port Authority Bus Terminal. **Olympia Airport Express** (tel. 212/964–6233) goes to Grand Central Terminal from Newark ($7).

Subway service is easily accessible only from JFK. A free shuttle provides transportation from the airport to the Howard Beach station, where you can catch the A line into Manhattan. The whole trip will take 1½–2 hours.

BY CAR The Lincoln Tunnel (I–495), Holland Tunnel, and the George Washington Bridge (I–95) connect Manhattan with the New Jersey Turnpike system and points west. The Lincoln Tunnel is most convenient to midtown sites. From New England, take I–95 to the Bruckner Expressway (I–278), cross the Triborough Bridge and head south on FDR Drive. Tolls apply to all crossings.

BY TRAIN Amtrak (tel. 800/872–7245) operates lines on the Boston–Washington corridor and to Chicago and Montreal. Trains arrive at Penn Station (7th Ave. and 33rd St.).

BY BUS Numerous national and regional bus lines serve the huge **Port Authority Terminal** (8th Ave. and 42nd St., tel. 212/564–8484 for carriers and schedules).

GETTING AROUND

Above 14th Street, city thoroughfares form a grid, with 5th Avenue dividing east from west. Numbered streets are straight lines running east–west; the broad avenues, from 1st to 12th, run north–south. Below 14th Street, in the oldest portion of the city, the situation is chaotic; streets may be aligned with the shoreline or twist along the route of an 18th-century cow path. Your stay will be simplified if you start out with a good map.

BY CAR Gridlocked traffic, cutthroat motorists, and scarce on-street parking make driving in Manhattan a nightmare. Travelers are advised to leave their cars at home. If you must drive to New York and plan to spend a few days, rent a car and drop it off in Manhattan; parking your own car in a lot will be very expensive.

BY SUBWAY New York's 24-hour, 230-mile subway system is usually the fastest way to get around and costs a good deal less than cabs; for route information, call 718/330–1234. Tokens, required for entry and sold at each station, cost $1.50. Buy several at once to cut token-booth waits. Subway maps, free from token booths, are usually posted near booths and in each car, but not necessarily on the platforms. Crime on the subway has been on the decline for a number of years, and you can further reduce your chances of running into trouble if you use the same common sense below ground as above— keep an eye on your valuables, don't wander around alone or late at night, and stand near other passengers on platforms and in cars.

BY BUS Their slow pace makes buses great for sightseeing but infuriating when you're in a rush. The fare, $1.50 per ride, must be paid by token or in exact change (no bills or pennies); ask for a free transfer when boarding to change to an intersecting route. Service is around the clock but infrequent late at night. Routes and schedules are sometimes posted at key stops. For maps, stop at the Convention and Visitors Bureau (tel. 212/397–8222).

BY TAXI Taxis are usually easy to hail on the street or at hotels. A lighted center panel on top signals that the cab is available; a dark panel indicates the cab is already taken; and a lit center panel surrounded by lit off-duty lights means, as you might suspect, that the cab is off duty. The fare schedule is posted inside each cab and on the driver's door; drivers expect 15% tips. Expect to pay $6– $10 to go between Midtown and Greenwich Village or Midtown and the Upper East or West sides.

REST STOPS The cleanest rest rooms tend to be in atriums of public spaces, or in department stores, hotels, and museums.

GUIDED TOURS **Orientation:** The best way to get oriented is to circumnavigate Manhattan; the Circle Line (Pier 83, W. 42nd St., tel. 212/563–3200) provides three-hour cruises that reveal the city in its splendor. By bus, the basics are covered by **Gray Line** (tel. 212/397–2600) and **Short Line** (tel. 212/ 736–4700).

Special Interest: Guided walking tours covering historic and other special-interest topics offer fascinating looks at offbeat parts of New York. Sponsors include the **Municipal Art Society** (tel. 212/935–3960 or 212/ 894–4974); **Sidewalks of New York** (tel. 212/517–0201); the **Parks Department's Urban Park Rangers** (tel. 212/427–4040); and **Penny Sightseeing** (tel. 212/410–0080), whose walks focus on Harlem. Most walks take place on weekends and cost $5–$20 per participant.

EXPLORING

DOWNTOWN **Chinatown.** Home to half the city's 300,000 Chinese, this neighborhood is exotic to the core—especially narrow, twisting Mott Street, crowded with pedestrians at all hours and crammed with souvenir shops and good, inexpensive restaurants. Don't miss Kam Man (200 Canal St., tel. 212/571–0330), a supermarket whose stock ranges from fresh chicken feet to 100 kinds of noodles.

Greenwich Village. Originally a rural outpost, "the Village" has long been home to writers and artists. Despite high rents, its shabby one-of-a-kind shops, cafés, arts groups, and large student population still make it feel bohemian. Eat in one of its warm, cozy restaurants and take a stroll that beguiles at every turn; try St. Luke's Place (between Hudson Street and 7th Avenue) and 10th Street (especially between 5th and 6th avenues), and look in on charming MacDougal Alley, Washington Mews, and Grove Court.

Lower Manhattan. Long central to the city's wealth, this compact area mixes fine ornate old buildings with modern office towers fronted by masterpieces of modern sculpture. The eastern edge of Lower Manhattan is bordered by **South Street Seaport** (centered on Fulton St., between Water St. and East River, tel. 212/748–8600), a complex that mixes a half-dozen small museum buildings (open daily; admission charged) showcasing the days of clipper ships with scores of shops. Lower Manhattan is where you'll find Wall Street, the spiritual center of New York's financial industry; right around the corner is the **New York Stock Exchange** (20 Broad St., tel. 212/656–5168; free tours on weekdays only). The western edge of Lower Manhattan is anchored by the **World Trade Center** (tel. 212/435–4170 or 212/435–7397; Observation Deck admission charged), with New York's two tallest buildings. West of the World Trade Center, and across West Street and the West Side Highway, is the splendid **World Financial Center,** whose soaring Winter Garden atrium offers handsome (if pricey) shops, a range of moderate-to-expensive restaurants, and free concerts (tel. 212/945–0505 for schedules). The World Financial Center is a part of **Battery Park City,** an ambitious commercial-residential development; its idyllic, Hudson River's–edge Esplanade is one of Manhattan's most refreshing corners.

SoHo. Manhattan's postmodern chic pervades the still-gritty downtown streets of this former wasteland, now home to a distinctive mix of artists and Wall Streeters, lofts and galleries, and minimalist shops and restaurants. Gallery-lined West Broadway (parallel to and four blocks west of Broadway) is the main drag.

MIDTOWN **Empire State Building.** King Kong's Art Deco playground may no longer be the world's tallest skyscraper, but it's certainly one of the best loved. There are two observation decks, and except in cloudy weather, the New York panorama is superb at either, both by day and by night. *5th Ave. at 34th St., Midtown, tel. 212/736–3100. Open daily. Admission charged.*

Museum of Modern Art. A bright and airy six-story structure built around a walled sculpture garden, this celebrated institution documents all the important movements of art since 1880. Its collection embraces not only painting and sculpture but photography, architecture, decorative arts, drawings, prints, illustrated books, and films. *11 W. 53rd St., Midtown, tel. 212/708–9400. Open Thurs.–Tues. Admission charged.*

Rockefeller Center. This 22-acre complex of limestone buildings linked by shop-lined underground passageways is a city in its own right. **Radio City Music Hall** (6th Ave. at 50th St., tel. 212/247–4777) may be New York's most famous theater, and the central plaza's golden Prometheus statue is one of New York's most famous sights. The center's tallest tower, the 70-story GE Building (home of NBC-TV), has an information desk with tour brochures. Across 5th Avenue, between 51st and 52nd streets, don't miss grand St. Patrick's Cathedral. Rockefeller Center is located between 47th and 52nd streets, from 5th Avenue to 7th Avenue.

Times Square. At the intersection of Broadway, 7th Avenue, and 42nd Street, this is the heart of the Theater District, aswarm with pickpockets, porn fans, prostitutes, and destitutes. A good way to experience the lyricism of its squalor is to queue for half-price theater tickets at the TKTS booth (*see* Bargains, *above*), where you'll find affable crowds on line. Keep your eyes open: Ambitious redevelopment will soon make history of this scene.

United Nations Headquarters. On a lush 18 acres by the East River, this complex is comprised of the slablike 550-foot-high Secretariat Building, the domed General Assembly Building, and a delightful sculpture-dotted rose garden. Enter the General Assembly Building at the 47th Street door and take a tour or attend a session for free (tickets available in the lobby—first-come, first-served). *1st Ave. between 42nd and 48th Sts., Midtown, tel. 212/963-7713. Open daily. Tour admission charged.*

UPTOWN **American Museum of Natural History.** With a collection of more than 36 million artifacts, this museum displays something for every interest, from dinosaur skeletons to animal-habitat dioramas to the 563-carat Star of India sapphire. *Central Park W at 79th St., Upper West Side, tel. 212/769-5100. Open daily. Donations requested.*

Central Park. This 843-acre triumph of landscape architecture gives New Yorkers a great green refuge from city concrete. For a 1¼-mile nibble of its flavor, enter at 77th Street and Central Park West, stroll southward along the lake curve east to the Esplanade, then turn south under its immense arching elms. Cross the road at the end of the Esplanade, still heading south, and leave the park at Central Park South. Note: Though crime is usually low here, stay away after dark and avoid deserted areas by day. The optimal times to visit are Saturday and Sunday afternoons, when every acre is teeming with a social microcosm of New Yorkers at play.

Metropolitan Museum of Art. The Western Hemisphere's largest art museum has a permanent international collection of some 3 million works, including the world's most comprehensive collection of American art, a collection of European work unequaled outside Europe, and world-renowned collections of ancient Greek, Roman, Asian, and Egyptian art. *5th Ave. at 82nd St., Upper East Side, tel. 212/535-7710. Open Tues.-Sun. Donations requested.*

Museum Mile. Once known as Millionaire's Row, the stretch of 5th Avenue between 79th and 104th streets is home to many fine cultural institutions, often housed in the industrialists' gorgeous former mansions. Besides the Metropolitan Museum of Art (*see above*), there's the **Guggenheim Museum** (at 88th St., tel. 212/360-3500), in an assertive Frank Lloyd Wright rotunda; the **Cooper-Hewitt Museum** (at 91st St., tel. 212/860-6898), where Andrew Carnegie's grand but comfortable mansion shows off decorative arts; the **International Center of Photography** (at 94th St., tel. 212/860-1777); and the memorabilia-packed **Museum of the City of New York** (at 103rd St., tel. 212/534-1672). The **Whitney Museum of American Art** (Madison Ave. at 75th St., tel. 212/570-3676) is nearby in a minimalist granite vault designed by Marcel Breuer. *Open Tues.-Sun. except Whitney Museum, open Wed.-Sun. Admission charged (free Tues. eve. except Museum of the City of New York; Whitney Museum free Thurs. eve.).*

EXCURSIONS FROM MANHATTAN **Ellis Island.** Some 17 million men, women, and children were processed by this former federal immigration facility between 1892 and 1954. Now restored, it offers an evocative look at the first American experience of the ancestors of more than 40% of today's U.S. citizens. The boat trip to the island begins near Castle Clinton in Battery Park. *Tel. 212/363-3200. Open daily. Admission charged for boat trip; Immigration Museum free.*

Staten Island Ferry. It's still the best deal in town: a half-hour ride across New York Harbor and back with great views of the Manhattan skyline and the Statue of Liberty for just 50¢. Pass up the new low-slung craft in favor of big old-timers with benches in the open air.

Statue of Liberty. France's gift to America retains the power to impress. Arrive early to avoid a three-hour wait for the elevator to the viewing platform; from there, trek 12 stories up through the statue's body to the crown. Ferries depart near Castle Clinton, Battery Park. *Tel. 212/363-3200. Open daily. Ferry: fare charged; statue: admission free.*

HOTELS AND INNS

Although most of New York's hotels are expensive, you can still book a clean, acceptable double room in several properties without wreaking havoc with your travel budget. Reputable discount booking firms such as **Express Hotel Reservations** (tel. 800/356–1123) offer 20%–30% savings; cheaper weekend rates are available at most Manhattan properties.

Bed-and-breakfast lodging may cost less and let you mingle with local residents; contact reservation services such as **Bed and Breakfast Network of New York** (130 Barrow St., 10014, tel. 212/645–8134), **City Lights Bed and Breakfast, Ltd.** (Box 20355, Cherokee Station, 10021, tel. 212/737–7049, fax 212/535–2755), **New World Bed and Breakfast** (150 5th Ave., Suite 711, 10011, tel. 212/675–5600 or 800/443–3800), and **Urban Ventures** (306 W. 38th St., 10018, tel. 212/594–5650).

Price categories for double occupancy, excluding 18¼% tax plus $2 occupancy tax, are Expensive, $150–$210; Moderate, $100–$150; and Inexpensive, $75–$100.

MIDTOWN EAST **Doral Inn.** For its Lexington Avenue location, this hotel is a good value, with modestly decorated, cheerful rooms, and a fitness center that includes squash courts and a sauna. *541 Lexington Ave. (at E. 50th St.), 10022, tel. 212/755–1200 or 800/223–5823, fax 212/319–8344. 652 rooms. 2 restaurants, fitness center, self-service laundry. AE, DC, MC, V. Moderate–Expensive.*

Helmsley Middletowne. Although this low-key, residential-style money-saver has no restaurant or room service, it does offer oversize rooms or suites with homey traditional decor and pantries, plus a location near many restaurants. *148 E. 48th St., 10017, tel. 212/755–3000 or 800/221–4982, fax 212/832–0261. 190 rooms. AE, D, DC, MC, V. Moderate.*

MIDTOWN WEST **Algonquin.** This genteel landmark's drawing-room atmosphere and burnished wood lobby have made it a favorite of literati; rooms have Victorian-style furnishings, but everything else, from phones to plumbing, has been updated. *59 W. 44th St., 10036, tel. 212/840–6800 or 800/548–0345, fax 212/944–1419. 165 rooms. 2 restaurants, 2 lounges, free weekend parking. AE, D, DC, MC, V. Moderate–Expensive.*

Chatwal Inns. Small but attractive, immaculate, and gently priced rooms are offered at these five midtown properties: the Best Western Woodward (210 W. 55th St.), the President (234 W. 48th St.), the Quality Inn Midtown (157 W. 47th St.), the Chatwal Inn (132 W. 45th St.), the Aberdeen (17 W. 32nd St.), and the Hojo Inn (429 Park Ave. S, between 29th and 30th Sts.). *Tel. 800/826–4667. Restaurants and lounges, depending on the property. Continental breakfast included in some rates. AE, D, DC, MC, V. Inexpensive–Expensive.*

Days Hotel. This property features pleasant, upgraded rooms and reasonable daily garage rates, while the outdoor rooftop swimming pool makes this a good bet for families during the summer. *790 8th Ave. (at W. 48th St.), 10019, tel. 212/581–7000 or 800/325–2525, fax 212/974–0291. 366 rooms. Restaurant, lounge, pool. AE, D, DC, MC, V. Inexpensive–Moderate.*

Hotel Iroquois. Near the venerable Algonquin and the trendy Royalton, this unprepossessing establishment has a good location and presentable rooms, but curt service and shabby hallways. *49 W. 44th St., 10036, tel. 212/840–3080 or 800/332–7220 outside NY, fax 212/398–1754. 135 rooms. AE, DC, MC, V. Inexpensive.*

Milford Plaza. Though rooms are small and the neighborhood can be seedy, this giant is conveniently located in the heart of the theater district; security appears to be tight in its bright public areas. *270 W. 45th St., 10036, tel. 212/869–3600 or 800/221–2690, fax 212/944–8357. 1,300 rooms. 2 restaurants. AE, D, DC, MC, V. Moderate.*

Paramount. One of the city's best budget buys, the Paramount has trendy public areas, chic (if offbeat) furnishings in the smallish bedrooms, and baths with ultramodern touches like conical steel sinks. *235 W. 46th St., 10019, tel. 212/764–5500 or 800/225–7474, fax 212/354–5237. 601 rooms. Restaurant, bar, take-out food shop, fitness center, playroom, VCRs in rooms. AE, D, DC, MC, V. Moderate–Expensive.*

Wellington Hotel. Small but clean and cheery rooms at reasonable prices attract budget-conscious Europeans to this large, old-fashioned property with a reassuringly bright lobby. *871 7th Ave. (at W. 55th St.), 10019, tel. 212/247–3900 or 800/652–1212 outside NY, fax 212/581–1719. 700 rooms. Restaurant. AE, DC, MC, V. Inexpensive.*

Wyndham. This genteel treasure opposite the posh Plaza Hotel offers some of Manhattan's most spacious quarters, furnished with fresh print bedspreads, comfortable chairs, and decorator wall coverings; suites, fitted with antiques, are only slightly pricier. The lobby is unusually secure, since a doorman controls access around the clock via an "in" buzzer. *42 W. 58th St., 10019, tel. 212/753–3500 or 800/257–1111, fax 212/754–5638. 204 rooms. Restaurant, lounge. AE, DC, MC, V. Moderate.*

UPPER EAST SIDE **Pickwick Arms.** A well-lit, marble-clad lobby, friendly staff, and renovated rooms furnished in white bamboo make this an acceptable option in a neighborhood full of pleasant restaurants. *230 E. 51st St., 10022, tel. 212/355–0300 or 800/742–5945 outside NY, fax 212/755–5029. 385 rooms. AE, DC, MC, V. Inexpensive.*

UPPER WEST SIDE **Broadway American.** This stylish residence hotel is one of the city's true bargains. The least expensive rooms share baths, though most rooms come with private facilities. The decor is basic and modern; the neighborhood is bustling. *2178 Broadway, 10024, tel. 212/362–1100, fax 212/787–9521. 400 rooms. Restaurant. AE, DC, MC, V. Inexpensive.*

Excelsior. A great location across from the American Museum of Natural History, coupled with clean rooms, relatively new furnishings, and a helpful staff, make this a find. *45 W. 81st St., 10024, tel. 212/362–9200 or 800/368–4575, fax 212/721–2994. 150 rooms. Coffee shop, kitchenettes in suites. AE, MC, V. Inexpensive.*

DINING

New York's restaurant scene is staggering not just for the number of restaurants—some 17,000 in all—but also for the variety of cuisines they celebrate and the quality of meals they serve. Reservations are always a good idea. Look into prix-fixe menus, or visit at lunchtime or for weekend brunch, when you can still experience the kitchen's flair—but at lower prices. Price categories per person, excluding 8¼% tax, service, and drinks, are Expensive, over $30; Moderate, $20–$30; and Inexpensive, under $20.

SOHO **Cupping Room Café.** In this mellow spot, exposed brick, a potbellied stove, and an antique bar set the scene for homey breakfasts and innovative American meals. *359 W. Broadway, tel. 212/925–2898. AE, DC, MC, V. Moderate.*

SoHo Kitchen. Soaring ceilings halo giant artwork at this chic hangout, and a well-groomed crowd congregates for good music, pasta and pizzas, and the stunning selection of 100 wines by the glass. *103 Greene St., tel. 212/925–1866. AE, DC, MC, V. Inexpensive.*

Spring Street Natural Restaurant. Hanging plants, huge windows, ceiling fans, and a colorful crowd make this a pleasant spot for light and vegetarian fare sparked with herbs and Asian flavorings. *62 Spring St., tel. 212/966–0290. AE, DC, MC, V. Inexpensive.*

CHINATOWN AND LITTLE ITALY **Benito's II.** This Little Italy charmer with exposed brick walls, a dark wood ceiling, and small tables offers substantial Italian fare that's often pungently laced with garlic. *163 Mulberry St., tel. 212/226–9012. No credit cards. Inexpensive–Moderate.*

Nice Restaurant. By day, this well-turned-out Chinese giant does well with the small dumplings known as dim sum that you pay for by the plateful; by night, try one of the larger entrées—such as soy-flavored squab and seasoned chicken. *35 E. Broadway, tel. 212/406–9510. AE. Inexpensive.*

Wong Kee. This clean, bright, uncluttered Chinese restaurant is on one of the busiest, most interesting streets in Chinatown. The "custard chicken" earns its name by being exquisitely tender. *113 Mott St., tel. 212/226–9018. No credit cards. Inexpensive.*

EAST VILLAGE **Japonica.** Excellent sushi highlights a menu of out-of-the-ordinary Japanese fare at this modest but attractive favorite with decor that changes with the seasons. *100 University Pl., tel. 212/243–7752. AE. Inexpensive–Moderate.*

John's of 12th Street. In this vintage hole-in-the-wall, candles stuck in raffia-wrapped Chianti bottles throw flickering light on age-darkened walls, while companionable crowds of old and young gather for southern Italian fare. *302 E. 12th St., tel. 212/475–9531. No credit cards. Inexpensive.*

Passage to India. Sixth Street between 1st and 2nd avenues is packed wall-to-wall with Indian restaurants, and Passage to India is one of the best, serving delicious curries and 14 types of fresh-baked Indian breads. *308 E. 6th St., tel. 212/529–5770. AE, DC, MC, V. Inexpensive.*

WEST VILLAGE **Anglers & Writers Salon de Thé.** At this charming tearoom, it's hard to resist the delicious baked goods; the lively sandwiches, pastas, and antipasto platters are delicious, too. *420 Hudson St., tel. 212/675–0810. No credit cards. Inexpensive.*

Black Sheep. The quintessential cozy little Village restaurant, this nook with exposed brick walls and rustic wood tables serves five-course prix-fixe dinners with Continental flair. Sunday brunches draw enthusiastic crowds. *344 W. 11th St., tel. 212/242–1010. AE (cash only at brunch). Moderate–Expensive.*

Jane Street Seafood Café. This fish house consistently delights with sea-fresh fare, sometimes grilled and sometimes sauced,

always accompanied by crunchy, zingy cole-slaw. *31 8th Ave., tel. 212/242–0003. AE, D, DC, MC, V. Moderate–Expensive.*

Provence. With its yellow walls and bouquets of dried flowers, this gutsy Provençal restaurant is as pleasant in winter as in summer, when tables sprout in its stone-fountained garden. *38 MacDougal St., tel. 212/475–7500. AE. Moderate–Expensive.*

GRAMERCY PARK AND UNION SQUARE **Friend of a Farmer.** At this countrified charmer on quiet Irving Place, homey, rustic fare predominates—lively salads, apple butter-and-cheddar omelets, and sweets from the restaurant's own ovens. *77 Irving Pl., tel. 212/477–2188. AE, DC, MC, V. Inexpensive.*

Union Square Café. Light, innovative cooking that's never too far-out, a lively wine list, and well-mannered service make this smart, animated room a good value for the money. *21 E. 16th St., tel. 212/243–4020. Jacket and tie. AE, DC, MC, V. Expensive.*

CHELSEA **Lola.** Boisterous and seductive, this chic, convivial room mixes the South with the Caribbean and a bit of France to great effect, particularly at Sunday's gospel brunches. *30 W. 22nd St., tel. 212/675–6700. Jacket and tie. AE, MC, V. Moderate–Expensive.*

Twigs. This sleek little Italian café, all marble and brass, is a neighborhood standby for pastas and individual pizzas with well-blistered crusts and unusual toppings. *196 8th Ave., tel. 212/633–6735. AE, MC, V. Inexpensive.*

MIDTOWN EAST **Christine's.** This diner with glass-topped cloths on crowded tables serves robust soups and other tasty Polish-American fare at extremely gentle prices. *344 Lexington Ave., tel. 212/953–1920. AE, DC, MC, V. Inexpensive.*

Dock's. This giant, high-ceilinged fish house is not only one of the neighborhood's better-looking eateries but also one of the city's best and least costly seafood specialists. *633 3rd Ave., tel. 212/986–8080. AE, DC, MC, V. Moderate–Expensive.*

Les Halles. Recalling the Gauloise-smoky joints where Parisians once congregated for onion soup, this bistro purveys hearty French fare. *411 Park Ave. S, tel. 212/679–4111. AE, DC, MC, V. Moderate.*

MIDTOWN WEST **Bangkok Cuisine.** Eighth Avenue in the 50s is awash with Thai restaurants, and this one is among the best, with highly recommended steamed fish and crispy *mee krob* noodles on the menu. *885 8th Ave., tel. 212/581–6370. AE, MC, V. Inexpensive.*

Carnegie Deli. Delis are a colorful feature of the New York culinary scene, and this one, founded in 1934, serves sandwiches that are mile-high (no wonder there are usually lines outside). *854 7th Ave., tel. 212/757–2245. No credit cards. Inexpensive.*

La Bonne Soupe. Red-checked cloths cover wobbly tables at this pleasant old standby for light meals—and some of the tastiest soups in town. *48 W. 55th St., tel. 212/586–7650. AE, MC, V. Inexpensive.*

Restaurant Row. This Theater District landmark—46th Street between 8th and 9th avenues—is known for dining spots where the food is just fine and waiters know how to get you to the show on time. For basic pub fare at all hours and low prices, try the Joe Allen pub (326 W. 46th St., tel. 212/581–6464; MC, V; Inexpensive). For celebrity-watching, Italian food, and higher tabs, book at bright, casual Orso (322 W. 46th St., tel. 212/489–7212; MC, V; Moderate). For old-fashioned French food and a patronne who welcomes every diner, you want the refreshingly unchanged Crêpe Suzette (363 W. 46th St., tel. 212/581–9717; AE, DC, MC, V; Moderate).

Russian Samovar. Good grills and Russian specialties soothe theater folk in this snug, unprepossessing little dining room with long banquettes and well-spaced tables. *256 W. 52nd St., tel. 212/757–0168. AE, MC, V. Moderate.*

UPPER EAST SIDE **Olio.** With its simple decor, this boîte is not much to look at, but unusual Italian dishes such as lobster ravioli couple with gentle prices to create a standout. *788 Lexington Ave., tel. 212/308–3552. AE, DC. Inexpensive.*

Pamir. This tiny, dimly lit Afghan restaurant hung with rugs and shawls is aromatic with the spices of its cuisine, which crosses Indian and Middle Eastern fare. Try the kebabs and rice pilaws. *1437 2nd Ave., tel. 212/734–3791. MC, V. Moderate.*

Serendipity 3. Moviegoers and models, families and singles have made this ice-cream parlor–café–general store a longtime favorite for pastas, pizzas, sandwiches—and ice-cream sundaes worth a splurge. *225 E. 60th St., tel. 212/838–3531. AE, D, DC, MC, V. Inexpensive.*

Table d'Hote. One of New York's smallest eateries, this cozy spot is convenient to Museum Mile and serves well-prepared American-Continental fare at excellent prices. *44 E. 92nd St., tel. 212/348–8125. AE, MC, V. Moderate.*

LINCOLN CENTER/UPPER WEST SIDE **Café Luxembourg.** In this hip favorite, a sophisticated, good-natured staff offers brasserie standbys spiced with light nouvelle American ideas in a Paris bistro setting. *200 W. 70th St., tel. 212/873–7411. AE, DC, MC, V. Moderate–Expensive.*

Ollie's. The decor is basic, but regulars swear by the dumplings, noodles, and grilled shrimp at this crowded uptown Chinese dining spot. *2957 Broadway, tel. 212/932–3300. AE, MC, V. Inexpensive.*

Popover. While the teddy-bear decor is a bit precious, this café's huge, puffy popovers, served with a variety of toppings and fillings, delight one and all; soups, sandwiches, salads, and omelets are also available. *551 Amsterdam Ave., tel. 212/595–8555. AE, MC, V. Inexpensive.*

Vince & Eddie's. Brick walls, a sprinkling of antiques, oilcloth-covered tables, and a fireplace set the mood for hearty French American fare. *70 W. 68th St., tel. 212/721–0068. AE, D, DC, MC, V. Moderate.*

SHOPPING

New York shopping is theater, architecture, and people-watching rolled into one. Big stores and small ones, one-of-a-kinds and chains present an overwhelming array, from no-holds-barred bargains to the finest (and priciest) in the world.

MAJOR SHOPPING DISTRICTS New York's shops are collected in neighborhoods rather than malls. Hordes of New Yorkers turn out for genial browsing when the weather is fine.

South Street Seaport, downtown Manhattan's lively open-air museum and restaurant-retail complex, sprinkles one-of-a-kind boutiques amid upscale, nationally known chains.

The **Lower East Side,** once home to millions of Jewish immigrants, may look down-at-heels and unsavory. But as New Yorkers' bargain beat, it's a thriving retail center. Narrow, unprepossessing Orchard Street, its spine, is crammed with hole-in-the-wall clothing stores; Grand Street (off Orchard St., south of Delancey St.) is chockablock with linens, towels, and other items for the home. Shops close for the Jewish Sabbath on Friday afternoon and all day Saturday; on Sundays, uptowners appear in droves.

SoHo mixes major art galleries and fashionable clothing and housewares stores; despite high prices, it warrants a look. Landmarks include the gourmet food emporium Dean & DeLuca (Broadway at Prince St., tel. 212/431–1691). Many stores here close on Monday.

Herald Square, where 34th Street and 6th Avenue intersect, is a bastion of reasonable prices. Giant Macy's (tel. 212/695–4400) department store is the linchpin. Immediately south, the Manhattan Mall makes for wonderful browsing with its spate of moderately priced stores.

Fifth and Madison avenues reveal Manhattan's most cosmopolitan facade. Along 5th Avenue from Central Park South to Rockefeller Center, you'll pass the famous F.A.O. Schwarz (at 58th St., tel. 212/644–9400) toy emporium and Bergdorf Goodman (at 58th St., tel. 212/753–7300). Moving south, there's Tiffany & Co. jewelers (at 57th St., tel. 212/755–8000), brass-and-marble Trump Tower (at 56th St.), Steuben glassware (at 55th St., tel. 212/752–1441), Cartier jewelers (at 52nd St., tel. 212/753–0111), and Saks Fifth Avenue (at 50th St., tel. 212/753–4000). Glittering as this all is, Madison Avenue from 57th Street to 86th Street is even more posh with its crowd of luxurious designer boutiques and superlative antiques stores-cum-museums.

Columbus Avenue, between 66th and 86th streets on the Upper West Side, has its own spate of glitzy shops—mostly modern in design, upscale but not top-of-the-line. Browsing is good any day, particularly since the shops are interspersed with moderately priced cafés and restaurants. If you're shopping for gifts for youngsters, don't miss Penny Whistle Toys (Columbus Ave. at 81st St., tel. 212/873–9090).

DEPARTMENT STORES Quality merchandise is expensive everywhere, and New York's department stores are no exception. What you can expect here is a much wider selection, particularly in current styles and at the higher price levels. Both **Bloomingdale's** (Lexington Ave. between 59th and 60th Sts., tel. 212/705–2000) and **Macy's** (Herald Sq., Broadway at 34th St., tel. 212/695–4400) are huge and overwhelming, but both have good markdowns. If you want to see what's hot and trendy in men's and women's clothing and precious, one-of-a-kind gifts, visit **Barneys New York** (7th Ave. at 17th St., tel. 212/593–7800; Madison Ave. at 60th St., tel. 212/826–8900). Though markdowns are more than generous, some of the usual prices will make your head spin, despite the exquisite quality. The taste level is equally high at **Saks Fifth Avenue** (5th Ave. between 50th and 51st Sts., tel. 212/753–4000), embodying the spirit of service and style with which it opened in 1926. **Henri Bendel** (712 5th Ave. at 56th St., tel. 212/247–1100) is stylish and sophisticated—with prices to match.

ANTIQUES Manhattan's antiques markets and shops offer everything from museum-quality wares to the wacky and eminently affordable. To see the former, browse along Madison Avenue north of 57th Street and 47th Street east of 5th Avenue. For the latter, stop at the **Manhattan Art & Antiques Center** (1050 2nd Ave., tel. 212/355–4400), with 100-plus dealers, and don't miss the outdoor weekend **Annex Antiques Fair and Flea Market** (6th Ave. at 26th St., tel. 212/243–5343).

SPECIALTY SHOPS Whether you fancy state-of-the-art cameras or architecture books, Manhattan has a specialist shop in the field. A few stand out.

Books: Gotham Book Mart (41 W. 47th St., tel. 212/719–4448) is an oasis for those who truly love to read. Whodunit lovers love the Mysterious Bookshop (129 W. 56th St., tel. 212/765–0900). Try the Strand (828 Broadway, tel. 212/473–1452), Manhattan's biggest used-book store, for secondhand titles and discounted reviewers' copies.

Cameras and Electronics: For price and selection, it's hard to do better than at 47th Street Photo (67 W. 47th St. and other locations, tel. 212/921–1287).

Menswear: Brooks Brothers (Madison Ave. at 44th St., tel. 212/682–8800) is America's temple of the traditional; you'll pay for all that hand-tailoring. For discounts on traditional as well as contemporary styles, try Moe Ginsburg (162 5th Ave., tel. 212/242–3482) and Syms (42 Trinity Pl., tel. 212/797–1199; cash only).

Women's Clothing: Bargain mavens pilgrim to the flagship Loehmann's (236th and Broadway, tel. 718/543–6420), located in a safe enclave in the Bronx. They also visit S&W (165 W. 26th St., tel. 212/924–6656) for discounts and Encore (1132 Madison Ave., tel. 212/879–2850), a resale shop where top-of-the-line designs go for secondhand prices.

OUTDOOR ACTIVITIES

BIKING Bikes are easily rented at bike stores such as **AAA Bikes** (in Central Park's Loeb Boathouse, near E. 72nd St., tel. 212/861–4137), **Metro Bicycles** (1311 Lexington Ave. at 88th St., tel. 212/427–4450), and **West Side Bikes** (231 W. 96th St., tel. 212/663–7531).

TENNIS Fans jam the 24 public clay courts in **Central Park** (mid-park near 96th St., tel. 212/280–0206); since space is tight, call ahead to find out when it will be easiest to get a court.

WALKING AND JOGGING Central Park is the favorite destination of the city's cyclists, joggers, race walkers, strollers, and roller skaters. For jogging and walking, prime circuits are the Reservoir (1.58 miles) and the park roads (up to 6 miles), which are closed to vehicular traffic 10 AM–3 PM and 7–10 PM weekdays, and from 7 PM Friday to 6 AM Monday on weekends. To run the Reservoir, enter on 5th Avenue at 90th Street. To join a group run, contact the **New York Road Runners Club** (9 E. 89th St., tel. 212/860–4455).

ENTERTAINMENT

Tickets are often modestly priced or available at half price (*see* Bargains, *above*). To find out what's on, top sources are the *New York Times* (particularly Friday's "Weekend" and Sunday's "Arts & Leisure" sections), the *Village Voice* (particularly for the downtown scene), "Goings On About Town" in the *New Yorker,* and the "Cue" listings in *New York* magazine.

BALLET AND DANCE The **New York City Ballet** (tel. 212/870–5500) and **American Ballet Theatre** (tel. 212/477–3030) perform at Lincoln Center. Touring ballet and modern troupes often appear at **City Center** (131 W. 55th St., tel. 212/581–7907). Smaller groups perform at the **Joyce Theater** (8th Ave. at 19th St., tel. 212/242–0800) and the **Dance Theater Workshop** (219 W. 19th St., tel. 212/691–6500).

CONCERTS The New York Philharmonic's season runs from September through May at **Avery Fisher Hall** (tel. 212/875–5030) in Lincoln Center. There's always something on at **Carnegie Hall** (7th Ave. at 57th St., tel. 212/247–7800), whose acoustics are excellent even in the budget seats up high.

FILM The diversity of New York's film offerings—major releases, classics, foreign offerings, and independent flicks—amazes most visitors almost as much as the $8 ticket prices and absence of bargain matinees. For first-run film information, call **Movie Phone** (tel. 212/777–3456) from a touch-tone phone. The **Film Forum** (209 W. Houston St., tel. 212/727–8110), the **Quad Cinema** (34 W. 13th St., tel. 212/255–8800), and the **Walter Reed Theatre** (at Lincoln Center, 65th St. and Broadway, tel. 212/875–5600) offer small new films and revivals and still only charge $7.50 a ticket. In addition, there are programs at the **American Museum of the Moving Image** (35th Ave. at 36th St., Queens, tel. 718/784–0077), a major film museum, and at the **Museum of Modern Art** (11 W. 53rd St., tel. 212/708–9480), home of a world-renowned film archive.

JAZZ AND CABARET Sunday jazz brunches are a lively and inexpensive way to hear hot sounds at such clubs as the **Blue Note** (131 W. 3rd St., tel. 212/475–8592), which may well be the jazz capital of the world. **Red Blazer Too** (349 W. 46th St., tel. 212/262–3112) has '20s, Dixieland, and swing, and **Sweet Basil** (88 7th Ave. S, tel. 212/242–1785) ranges from swing to fusion. For cabaret, visit the venerable **Oak Room** at the Algonquin Hotel (59 W. 44th St., tel. 212/840–6800), or the **Café Carlyle** at the classy Carlyle Hotel (35 E. 76th St., tel. 212/744–1600).

OPERA The **New York City Opera** (tel. 212/870–5570; July–Nov.) is lively and relatively affordable, but if you love opera, you won't want to miss the **Metropolitan Opera** (tel. 212/799–3100; Sept.–Apr.), where every production is a lavish spectacle. To save at the Met, buy standing room (on sale Sunday for the coming week).

SPECTATOR SPORTS Major-league baseball season stars the Yankees at **Yankee Stadium** (E. 161st St. at River Ave., the Bronx, tel. 718/293–6000) and the Mets at **Shea Stadium** (Flushing Meadows–Corona Park, Queens, tel. 718/507–8499). Both venues are easily accessible by subway. **Madison Square Garden** (tel. 212/465–6000), centrally located in midtown, hosts New York Rangers hockey action (Oct.–Apr.) and New York Knicks basketball (Nov.–Apr.).

THEATER Broadway is synonymous with New York theater, but even half-price tickets are pricey (*see* Bargains, *above*), so don't overlook Off- and Off-Off-Broadway shows, where tickets run $8–$35 per person. Downtown's **Public Theater** (425 Lafayette St., tel. 212/260–2400) is a landmark; its first-come, first-served Quiktix scheme cuts your cost further. Another good bet is the collection of small theaters known as **Theatre Row,** located on the downtown side of 42nd St. between 9th and 10th avenues; buy tickets at the joint box office, **Ticket Central** (416 W. 42nd St., tel. 212/279–4200).

Niagara Falls
New York and Ontario, Canada

Updated by Jeremy Braddock

ynics have had their field day with Niagara Falls, calling it everything from "water on the rocks" to "the second major disappointment of American married life" (Oscar Wilde). Others have been more positive. Charles Dickens wrote: "I seemed to be lifted from the earth and to be looking into Heaven. Niagara was at once stamped upon my heart, an image of beauty, to remain there changeless and indelible." The falls were more dramatically immortalized by Hollywood in 1953, when Marilyn Monroe, as a steamy siren, lured her jealous husband down to the crashing cascades in the film *Niagara.*

Part of the longest unfortified border in the world, the falls are actually three cataracts: the American and Bridal Veil falls, in New York State, and the Horseshoe Falls in Ontario, Canada. There may be taller cataracts in Africa, South America, and even elsewhere in New York State, but in terms of sheer volume of water—more than 700,000 gallons per second in the summer—Niagara is unsurpassed in the world. The falls are responsible for the invention of alternating electric current, and they run one of the world's largest hydroelectric developments. And it really is all that water, on its way from four of the Great Lakes—Superior, Michigan, Huron, and Erie—to the fifth, Ontario, that makes Niagara the most famous and accessible waterfall in the world.

As with many other geographic features, Niagara's origins are glacial. More than 10,000 years before the first inscription "My Parents Visited Niagara Falls and All They Got Me Was This Lousy T-Shirt," the glaciers receded, diverting the waters of Lake Erie northward into Lake Ontario.

The malls, amusement parks, and tacky souvenir shops that surround the falls today attest to years as a major tourist attraction; on the New York side is America's oldest state park. Despite the local tourist industry's unyielding and rather garish effort to accommodate hoards of visitors, the beauty of the falls remains undaunted.

ESSENTIAL INFORMATION

WHEN TO GO High season runs from Memorial Day through Labor Day, during which time most cultural activities take place and the falls' boat rides are operating. Consequently, tourists abound and hotel prices are highest. Summer temperatures range from 75° to 85°, with occasional light rainfall. The area near the falls is always misty, which in the summertime is rather refreshing. Very hot, humid days are infrequent. Winter temperatures create ice-covered tree branches and rocks that reflect and sparkle. The railings and bridges can become almost crystalline.

FESTIVALS AND SPECIAL EVENTS From the Saturday after Thanksgiving to the Sunday after New Year's on the U.S. side and through mid-February on the Canadian side, the falls and surrounding area are aglow with various light shows for the spectacular **Festival of Lights.** Sophisticated indoor and outdoor light displays and entertainment take place in downtown Niagara. Even the brink of the falls is lit up.

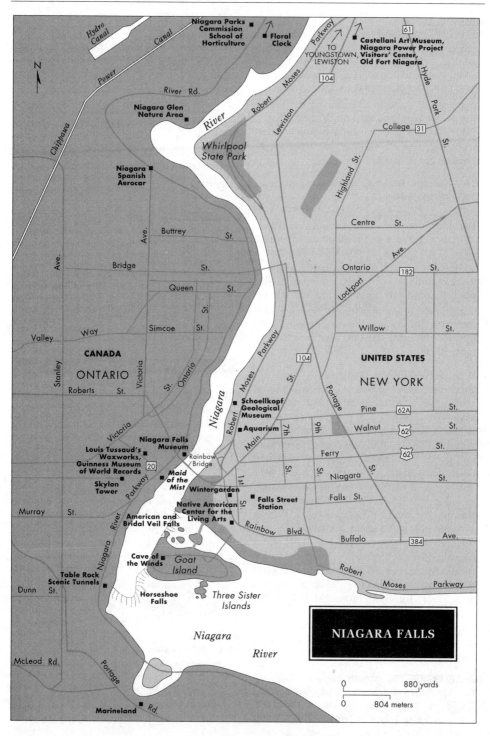

Hydro Canal

Canal

Power

N

Chippawa

Niagara Parks
Commission
School of
Horticulture

Floral
Clock

Parkway

Robert Moses

Lewiston

TO
YOUNGSTOWN,
LEWISTON

104

Castellani Art Museum,
Niagara Power Project
Visitors' Center,
Old Fort Niagara

61

Hyde Park St.

River Rd.

College 31

Niagara Glen
Nature Area

River

Whirlpool
State Park

Highland St.

Niagara
Spanish
Aerocar

Ave.

Buttrey St.

Centre St.

Bridge St.

Ontario 182 St.

Ave.

Lockport

Queen St.

St.

Way

Simcoe St.

Willow St.

Valley

Parkway

Ave.

CANADA

Stanley

ONTARIO

Roberts St.

Victoria

St.

Ontario

Niagara

104

Robert Moses

St.

UNITED STATES

NEW YORK

Portage

Pine 62A St.

Schoellkopf
Geological
Museum

Walnut 62 St.

Victoria

Niagara Falls
Museum

Aquarium

7th

9th

St.

St.

62 St.

Louis Tussaud's
Waxworks,
Guinness Museum
of World Records

20

Rainbow
Bridge

Main

Ferry

St.

St.

Niagara

Maid
of the
Mist

Wintergarden

1st St.

Falls St.

St.

Skylon
Tower

Native American
Center for the
Living Arts

Falls Street
Station

Parkway

River

American and
Bridal Veil Falls

Rainbow Blvd.

Buffalo 384 Ave.

Murray St.

Robert

Cave of
the Winds

Goat
Island

Table Rock
Scenic Tunnels

Moses Parkway

Dunn St.

Niagara

Horseshoe
Falls

Three Sister
Islands

Niagara River

McLeod Rd.

Portage

Rd.

Marineland

NIAGARA FALLS

0 — 880 yards

0 — 804 meters

BARGAINS If you plan to visit the majority of the Niagara Reservation State Park attractions, the **Masterpass coupon book** ($15 adults, $10 children ages 6–12) grants free admission to the six major New York State park attractions. Sold mid-May–October, the pass can be purchased at Niagara Reservation parking booths and Visitor Center, Grand Island Official Information Center, and designated locations in the Niagara Frontier State Parks.

The **Niagara Parks Commission** (tel. 905/356–2241) operates the People Mover buses in Niagara Falls, Ontario. The People Mover is a "loop" transportation system that allows tourists to get on and off all day at any of 12 stops along the Niagara Parkway. The cost is $3 for adults and $1.50 for children ages 6–12. Children under six ride free. Sightseers traveling by auto pay $8, which includes parking and a People Mover ticket for everyone in the car. People Mover buses operate mid-May–mid-October from 9 AM until 11 PM.

It is possible to be reimbursed for taxes on goods purchased in Canada, including hotel room charges totaling more than $100, so save your receipts. The provincial sales tax is 8% in Ontario, and the Government Service Tax (GST) is 7%. The cost of your room and goods purchased can be combined to reach the C$100 minimum. Pick up your rebate forms at hotels or duty-free shops, or order them from Visitors Rebate Program (Revenue Canada, Customs and Excise, Visitors Rebate Program, Ottawa K1A 1J5, tel. 613/991–3346 or 800/668–4748 from Canada). For the provincial and room tax form, contact the Retail Sales Branch (Ontario Provincial Treasury, 2300 Young St., 10th Floor, Toronto, Ontario M4P 1H6, tel. 416/487–1361). The process of getting reimbursed is rather long and complicated, but for those spending lots of Canadian dollars, it may be worth the trouble.

TOURIST OFFICES American Side: Niagara County Tourism (Niagara and Hawley Sts., Lockport, NY 14094, tel. 800/338–7890), **Niagara Falls Tourism Information Center** (4th and Niagara Sts., Niagara Falls, NY 14303, tel. 716/285–2400), **Niagara Falls Convention & Visitors Bureau** (310 4th St., Niagara Falls, NY 14303, tel. 800/421–5223 or 716/285–8711 for touch-tone 24-hr recorded message).

Canadian Side: Niagara Parks Commission (7400 Portage Rd., Niagara Falls, Ontario L2E 6X8, tel. 905/356–2241 or 800/263–2558 for tour information); **Ontario Tourism Information Bureau** (5355 Stanley Ave. at Highway 420, Niagara Falls, Ontario L2E 7C2, tel. 905/358–3221 or 800/668–2746).

EMERGENCIES **Police, fire,** and **ambulance:** Dial 911. **Hospitals:** Niagara Falls Medical Center (621 10th St., Niagara Falls, NY 14302, tel. 716/278–4000) and Mount St. Mary's Hospital (5300 Military Rd., Lewiston, NY 14092, tel. 716/297–4800). Greater Niagara General Hospital (5546 Portage Rd., Niagara Falls, Ontario L2E 6X2, tel. 905/358–0171).

ARRIVING AND DEPARTING

BY PLANE Greater Buffalo International Airport (tel. 716/632–3115) is the primary point of entry by air for Niagara Falls. Many charter tours, however, fly into **Niagara Falls International Airport** (tel. 716/297–4494).

Public buses operated by **Niagara Falls Metro Bus** (tel. 716/285–9319) run between the Buffalo and Niagara airports and downtown Niagara Falls. The bus ride to Niagara Falls from Buffalo International Airport requires a brief stopover in downtown Buffalo and costs about $2. Bus fare from Niagara International Airport costs about $1. Taxi service to Niagara Falls costs approximately $30.

BY TRAIN On the American side, there's an **Amtrak** station (tel. 716/285–4224; for reservations call 800/872–7245) just beyond downtown Niagara Falls, at the end of 27th Street off Lockport Rd., one block east of Hyde Park Blvd. Taxi fare from the station to the falls is about $6. On the Canadian side, the Amtrak station (4267 Bridge St., tel. 905/357–1644) is within walking distance of the falls in downtown Niagara Falls, Ontario.

BY BUS On the American side, a **Greyhound Lines** (tel. 800/231–2222) station is located at the Visitor Information Center next to the convention center at 4th and Niagara streets. On the Canadian side, the bus station (4555 Erie Ave., tel. 905/357–2133) is a hub for the Canada Coach, Empire Trailway, Gray Coach, Greyhound, and Peter Pan lines.

BY CAR Access from the east and south is primarily via I–90, the New York State Thruway. The expressway spur, I–190, leads from 1–90 at Buffalo, across Grand Island to the Robert Moses Parkway into Niagara Falls. Approaches from the west are via a number of highways in Canada, including the Queen Elizabeth Way (QEW), with three bridges funneling traffic stateside.

GETTING AROUND

To avoid bridge traffic caused by Canadian shoppers invading the malls on weekends, travel to Canada in the morning and return home in the late afternoon or evening.

BY PUBLIC TRANSPORTATION AND VIEWMOBILE

In Niagara Falls, New York, a **Metro Bus system** (tel. 716/285–9319) serves the Greater Niagara Falls area. The Niagara Reservation State Park operates the **Viewmobile,** a 40-minute guided trolley (train on wheels) ride that circles Goat Island (tel. 716/278–1770), making five stops.

In Niagara Falls, Ontario, the **Niagara Transit bus system** (tel. 905/356–1179) operates the Niagara Falls Shuttles. A shuttle ticket allows all-day transfers to and from various sites around downtown Niagara Falls, Ontario. The **Niagara Parks Commission** (tel. 905/356–2241) operates the People Mover buses (*see* Bargains, *above*).

ON FOOT All downtown Niagara Falls, New York, attractions are within a 10- to 15-minute walk. After exploring the American

side you can even walk across the Rainbow Bridge into Canada. Most of the Canadian attractions, however, are a 20- to 30-minute walk; so for most visitors, riding the People Mover is preferable, after you've finished exploring Queen Victoria Park.

BY BICYCLE Bicycles are a very practical way to get around, and can be rented on the Canadian side at **Cupolos** (tel. 905/356–4850) on Ferry Street, near the corner of Stanley Avenue.

BY TAXI La Salle Dispatch Service (tel. 716/284–8833) is the most convenient taxi to the downtown Niagara Falls, New York, area. In Niagara Falls, Ontario, call **Niagara Taxi** (tel. 905/357–4000). A taxi ride from the Rainbow Bridge to the Floral Clock, 6 miles north, costs C$15–C$16.

The **5-0 Taxi Service** (tel. 905/358–3232) also operates a specially equipped van for tourists traveling with wheelchairs.

GUIDED TOURS Double Deck Tours (tel. 905/295–3051) offers a six-hour Niagara River Sightseeing package tour of the Canadian side; tickets are available at the Table Rock House, in the Victoria Park Restaurant, or at the bottom of Clifton Hill. The **Niagara Glen Horticultural Department** (tel. 905/356–2241), located 4 miles due north of the falls, runs free guided geological hikes down all the paths of the river to the bottom. **Rainbow Helicopters, Inc.** (tel. 716/284–2800) departs from the downtown heliport on the New York side of the falls for a seven-minute flight over the falls and Canada. The **Schoellkopf Geological Museum** (Niagara Reservation, Box 1132, Niagara Falls, NY 14303-0132, tel. 716/278–1780) runs free guided geological walks on Goat Island; schedules are available by mail with a SASE.

EXPLORING

Although the grandeur of the falls will undoubtedly be the highlight of your trip, the surrounding area is worth discovering. The Niagara River forms the Canadian–U.S. border; the land north of the falls on both sides of the river is comprised primarily of orchards and vineyards. Stateside is the historic community of Lewiston. Farther north, where the river opens into Lake Ontario, are the scenic villages of Youngstown on the U.S. side and Niagara-on-the-Lake on the Canadian side, each about a 20-minute drive from the falls. The latter is replete with many inns, restaurants, and shops, and is the site of the famous Shaw Festival (see Theater, below).

If the experience of the falls themselves isn't dramatic enough for you, you can always go to the movies. Big-screen films of the falls are screened on both sides of the border (see below).

THE AMERICAN SIDE Many of the following attractions offer free admission to holders of the Masterpass coupon book (see Bargains, above).

Aquarium of Niagara Falls. The world's first inland oceanarium, with over 2,000 aquatic creatures, has hourly dolphin, sea lion, and electric eel shows, an outdoor seal and sea lion pool, and interactive Great Lakes fish displays. *701 Whirlpool St., tel. 716/285–3575. Open daily. Admission charged.*

Castellani Art Museum. Located in the center of the Niagara University Campus, this 23,000-square-foot, $3.5 million facility houses both rotating exhibitions and an impressive permanent collection of over 3,000 works of art, including impressive works by Roy Lichtenstein, Jasper Johns, Louise Nevelson, Cindy Sherman, Picasso prints and ceramics, and some pre-Columbian sculptures. Most were donated from the private collection of Armand J. Castellani, the museum's founder. Follow signs for the university north of the falls on Route 104. *Tel. 716/286–8200. Call for hrs or to make appointments. Admission free.*

Cave of the Winds. Get as close as you can to touching the falls by following wooden walkways to within 25 feet of the base. Thin, yellow, plastic rain slickers are provided. *Trip starts on Goat Island, tel. 716/278–1730.*

Open mid-May–mid-Oct., daily. Admission charged; free with Masterpass.

Festival Theatre at the Visitor Center presents Niagara Wonders, a sensational view of the falls in a 70mm, 20-minute film, with six-channel digital sound. *Prospect St. at Niagara St., tel. 716/278–1792. Open daily. Admission charged; group rates available.*

Goat Island. Part of the state park, the island offers the closest possible views of the American falls and the upper rapids; it's one of the best spots to begin your tour of Niagara. There are excellent hiking and biking trails and some guided geological walks are offered. Hop on the Viewmobile sightseeing trains for an overview of each park attraction. The 40-minute tour includes a close-up view of the falls; Cave of the Winds, Schoellkopf Museum, Aquarium, and Three Sisters Island. *Goat Island, tel. 716/278–1700. Hrs vary seasonally. Admission charged.*

Maid of the Mist. Theodore Roosevelt considered this ride "the only way to fully realize the Grandeur of the Great Falls of Niagara." It can be boarded on either the American or Canadian side. The captain expertly guides the boat past the base of the American and Bridal Veil falls and almost into the thunderous deluge of the Horseshoe Falls. *Niagara River at the base of falls, tel. 716/284–8897. Open daily in season. Admission charged; free with Masterpass.*

Native American Center for the Living Arts. Built in the shape of a turtle, the Iroquois symbol of the Earth, the center is just a couple hundred feet from the brink of the falls. It houses a museum and an art gallery focusing on Native American culture and art. Iroquois dance performances are held during the summer season; during the first week of May, the Center also hosts a powwow, a Native American festival of traditional dancing, arts, and culture. If you need a break, there's a gift shop and restaurant on the premises. *25 Rainbow Blvd., tel. 716/284–2427. Closed Mon. Oct.–Apr. Admission charged.*

Niagara Power Project Visitors' Center. The hydroelectric power project has a video, displays, hands-on exhibits, and computer games explaining how water generates electricity and highlighting the importance and history of Niagara in this effort. *5777 Lewiston Rd., Lewiston, NY 14092, tel. 716/285–3211. Open daily. Admission free.*

Old Fort Niagara. This fort on the Historic trail in Youngstown has been occupied by the French, British, and Americans. The original stone buildings have been preserved in their pre-Revolutionary state. There are musket demonstrations May through October and crafts and seasonal archaeological digs. Special summer events include historical encampments on site. *Take Robert Moses Pkwy. north for 14 mi (about a 20-min ride) to Youngstown, tel. 716/745–7611. Open daily. Admission charged.*

Schoellkopf Geological Museum. For insight into the interesting geological history of the falls, visit this museum in Niagara Reservation State Park. A geological garden and nature trail are on the grounds. *Take 1st exit off Robert Moses Pkwy. north of downtown, tel. 716/278–1780. Open Memorial Day–Labor Day, daily 9:30–7; Labor Day–Memorial Day, Thurs.–Sun. 10–5. Admission charged; free with Masterpass.*

THE CANADIAN SIDE Most bus and boat tours begin at Clifton Hill, and many of the better attractions are located near the falls and northeast of the Skylon Tower. Attractions beyond Clifton Hill are best visited by automobile.

Floral Clock. Six miles north of the falls along River Road, the clock is one of the largest blooming clocks in the world, made up of nearly 15,000 plants. It keeps accurate time, and chimes ring every quarter hour. *14004 Niagara Pkwy., tel. 905/357–2411. Open daily. Admission free.*

Guinness Museum of World Records. Contained here are hundreds of exhibits that made it into the famous record book. *4943 Clifton Hill, tel. 905/356–2299. Open daily. Admission charged.*

Louis Tussaud's Waxworks. Life-size reproductions of the most famous and infamous

people, from Bach and Cleopatra to Elvis and Prince Charles, are here in historically accurate costumes and settings. *4915 Clifton Hill, tel. 905/374–6601. Open daily. Admission charged.*

Marineland. The 4,500-seat aqua theater has a large troupe of performing sea lions, harbor seals, and dolphins, as well as two killer whales. The wildlife display includes a herd of buffalo, bears, and over 400 deer to be pet and fed. There are rides for all ages, including the world's largest steel roller coaster. *1 mi south of falls, follow signs along pkwy., tel. 905/356–9565. Open Apr.–Oct., daily. Admission charged.*

Niagara Falls IMAX Theatre and Daredevil Adventure. This theater boasts that it shows the "biggest show in Niagara"; indeed, the 45-minute film *Niagara: Miracles, Myths, and Magic* is shown on Canada's largest movie screen and is accompanied by six-channel Dolby sound. A separate exhibit displays interesting information and paraphernalia (including boats, barrels, and filmed footage) relating to attempts over the years by various daredevils to take the plunge over the falls. *6170 Buchanan Ave., Niagara Falls, Ontario, tel. 905/374–4629. Open daily. Admission charged.*

Niagara Falls Museum. Located at the Rainbow Bridge, housed here is everything from schlock to quality—the Daredevil Hall of Fame, dinosaurs, and a collection of authentic Egyptian mummies. There are also Indian artifacts and zoological and geological exhibits. *5651 River Rd., tel. 905/356–2151. Open daily. Admission charged.*

Niagara Glen. Free guided tours are given by a naturalist four times daily Thursday through Monday (between July and August) down a nature trail to the river's edge, where there are picnic tables. *Niagara River Pkwy., tel. 905/356–2241.*

Niagara Spanish Aerocar. This cable car transports you over the Niagara Gorge and back on an 1,800-foot-long cable. *River Rd., 2½ mi north of falls, tel. 905/354–5711, 800/263–2558 for group tours. Open Apr.–*

Oct., daily; off-season, when weather permits. Admission charged.

Niagara Parks Commission Botanical Gardens. Four miles north of the falls along the Niagara Parkway are 100 acres of lush gardens. All plants are labeled, so you can do a self-guided tour. Ask any questions of the gardeners, most of whom are students. *2565 Niagara River Pkwy., tel. 905/356–8554. Open daily. Admission free.*

Skylon Tower. Amusements, entertainment, and shops are in the tower, as well as an indoor-outdoor observation deck and a revolving restaurant. The view is particularly beautiful at night, when the falls are illuminated. *5200 Robinson St., tel. 905/356–2651. Open daily. Admission charged.*

Table Rock Scenic Tunnels. Raincoats are provided for the fish-eye view of the Canadian Horseshoe Falls and the Niagara River through three tunnels cut into the rock. Tours begin at the Table Rock House in Queen Victoria Park. *Tel. 905/358–3268. Open daily. Admission charged.*

THE NATURAL WORLD From mid-March to the first two weeks in April almost every type of migratory bird in the Northeast—all types of waterfowl, gulls, songbirds, even nesting bald eagles—can be spotted in the Niagara Falls area.

Tanawanda Wildlife Management Area and Iroquois National Wildlife Refuge, about 45 minutes southeast of the falls, is one of the finest bird-watching sanctuaries in the country. *From Rte. 31 take Rte. 77 to Refuge Headquarters on Casey Rd., tel. 716/948–5445. Open mid-Mar.–May, daily.*

HOTELS AND INNS

Hotels and motels in the Niagara Falls area fall primarily into two categories: major chains and lower-priced properties. For a unique experience, you may want to stay in a quaint bed-and-breakfast, but check prices beforehand. Those with fireplaces and complete amenities can cost as much as a luxury

hotel. **Rainbow Hospitality** (504 Amherst St., Buffalo, NY 14207, tel. 716/874–8797) is a bed-and-breakfast reservation service that represents member B&Bs in Buffalo, Niagara Falls, and Canada. **Niagara Region Bed-and-Breakfasts** (4917 River Rd., Niagara Falls, Ontario L2E 3G5, tel. 905/358–8988) represents over 30 member B&Bs in Niagara Falls, Canada. Many very good bed-and-breakfasts do not belong to these systems; for a complete listing, check with the convention and visitors bureaus in both New York and Ontario.

Price categories for double occupancy, excluding tax (5% in Ontario, 10% in New York State for bills under $100 and 15% for bills over $100), are Expensive, over $70; Moderate, $50–$70; and Inexpensive, under $50.

AMERICAN SIDE **Bel-Aire Motel.** Although 4½ miles from the falls, this small, clean motel is a terrific bargain. *9470 Niagara Falls Blvd., U.S. 62, tel. 716/297–2250. 25 rooms. Heated pool. AE, DC, MC, V. Inexpensive.*

Coachman Motel. Just three blocks from the falls, the Coachman is one of the best values within walking distance. *523 3rd St., 14301, tel. 716/285–2295, fax 716/285–6811. 18 rooms. Refrigerators. AE, D, DC, MC, V. Inexpensive.*

Comfort Inn–The Pointe. This is the closest hotel to the falls, and many of the rooms enjoy a view of them. It is attached to the Pointe Retail Complex, so the international eateries and gift shops found here are all added conveniences. *1 Prospect Pointe, 14303, tel. 716/284–6835, fax 716/284–5177. 120 rooms. Restaurant, bar, comedy club, some rooms with hot tubs. AE, MC, V. Moderate–Expensive.*

Days Inn–Falls View. The marble in the lobby and the cathedral ceilings recall the '20s, when this was the only hotel in Niagara. It is spacious and moderately priced, and just steps away from the falls. *201 Rainbow Blvd., 14303, tel. 716/285–9321, fax 716/285–2539. 200 rooms. Restaurant,* lounge. AE, D, DC, MC, V. Moderate–Expensive.

Holiday Motel. Located 3 miles east of the falls, the rooms are clean, quiet, and comfortable. *6650 Niagara Falls Blvd., tel. 716/283–8974. 17 rooms. Air-conditioning, cable TV, heated pool, picnic tables. AE, MC, V. Inexpensive–Moderate.*

Inn at the Falls. Located 1,200 feet from the brink of the falls, the inn has views of both the falls and the downtown district and is conveniently attached to the Wintergarden atrium shopping mall. *240 Rainbow Blvd., 14303, tel. 716/282–1212, fax 716/282–1216. 217 rooms. Restaurant, bar, banquet room, indoor pool, no-smoking rooms. AE, D, DC, MC, V. Moderate–Expensive.*

Plaza Court Motel. The Plaza Court is a good value, is attached to Plaza Court Campgrounds, and is close to the falls. *7680 Niagara Falls Blvd., 14304, tel. 716/283–2638. 10 rooms. Outdoor pool. AE, D, MC, V. Inexpensive.*

Portage House. Located 7 miles north of the falls, the Portage House is at the entrance to ArtPark and is right in the heart of historic Lewiston. All 21 rooms have two double beds and are done in soft, muted tones. Free morning coffee is offered in the lobby. There are no phones in individual rooms. *280 Portage Rd., Lewiston 14092, tel. 716/754–8295. 21 rooms. AE, MC, V. Inexpensive.*

Radisson Hotel–Niagara Falls. Just two blocks from the falls and connected to the Rainbow Factory Outlet Mall by an enclosed walkway, this hotel is the largest in the area. Special honeymoon, second honeymoon, and Festival of Lights packages are available. *3rd and Old Falls Sts., 14303, tel. 716/285–3361, fax 716/285–3900. 401 rooms. Restaurant, indoor heated pool. AE, DC, MC, V. Expensive.*

Ramada Inn. This motel is new and squeaky-clean, just four blocks from the falls. The rooms are spacious and tastefully decorated with bleached oak furniture. *219 4th St. at Rainbow Blvd., 14303, tel. 716/282–1734, fax 716/282–1881. 114 rooms. Restaurant, sou-venir shop, coin laundry, valet service. AE, D, DC, MC, V. Inexpensive–Moderate.*

CANADIAN SIDE Alpine Motel. Set back from the road, the Alpine is small, quiet, and has two rooms with two double beds for families. *7742 Lundy's La., Niagara Falls, Ontario L2H 1H4, tel. 905/356–7016. 10 rooms. Heated outdoor pool, refrigerators, patio, nearby golf. AE, MC, V. Inexpensive.*

The Americana. Set on 25 acres of grounds, this motel's extensive exercise facilities make it one of the nicer moderately priced motels on the strip. *8444 Lundy's La., Niagara Falls, Ontario L2H 1H4, tel. 905/356–8444, fax 905/356–8576. 120 rooms. Restaurant, lounge, coffee shop, indoor and outdoor pools, exercise room, sauna, basketball court, tennis court, squash court, picnic area. AE, D, DC, MC, V. Moderate.*

Fiddler's Green. The Fiddler's has pleasantly decorated rooms and offers four efficiency units with refrigerator, stove, and cooking-dining utensils (for a small deposit). Also available are 12 miniefficiencies and two suites with whirlpools. *7720 Lundy's La., Niagara Falls, Ontario L2H 1H4, tel. 905/358–9833, fax 905/358–3090. 94 rooms. Indoor and outdoor pools. AE, MC, V. Inexpensive.*

Space Motel. Venturi would admire this motor court, which is designed in a Jetsonian mode. The Space Motel is also a terrific value—nearly every one of the large, clean rooms has a refrigerator, and the spacious grounds boast a playground and barbecue facilities. *8618 Lundy's La., Niagara Falls, Ontario L2H 1H4, tel. 905/356–3216, fax 905/354–8157. 33 rooms; 3 family units. Heated pool, patios. AE, D, DC, MC, V. Inexpensive.*

Surfside Inn. The Surfside's rooms are each individually decorated with brass beds and antique furnishings. Rooms with water beds and hot tubs are available. There's a lake across the street in King's Bridge Park. *3665 Macklem St., Niagara Falls, Ontario L2G 6C8, tel. 905/295–4354, fax 905/295–4374. 32 rooms; 8 suites. Closed Jan.–Feb. AE, DC, MC, V. Inexpensive–Moderate.*

DINING

Scattered among the well-represented fast-food chains in Niagara are several respectable restaurants. The ethnic restaurants, particularly Italian, are very good. You can also find excellent Continental cuisine. Casual dress is acceptable in the establishments listed, and reservations are not necessary.

While the American dollar is a bit more than the Canadian dollar, keep in mind that Canadian restaurants tend to be a little more expensive than their American counterparts. Price categories per person, excluding tax (7% in New York State, 15% in Ontario), service, and drinks, are Moderate, $15–$25, and Inexpensive, under $15.

AMERICAN SIDE **Apple Granny.** Right on the main strip in town and near ArtPark, Apple Granny's offers basic American fare—burgers and fries, steaks, and hearty meat-and-potato plates. *433 Center St., Lewiston, tel. 716/754–2028. AE, D, DC, MC, V. Inexpensive.*

Como. The largest and one of the best Italian-American restaurants in Niagara Falls is known especially for its homemade pastas. The steak, Italian veal, and seafood dishes are also good. Every Friday a seafood special is served. *2220 Pine Ave., Niagara Falls, tel. 716/285–9341. AE, MC, V. Moderate.*

Fortunas. Owned by the same family that owns the Goose's Roost and Como, Fortunas has attracted area residents since 1945. The Italian home cooking includes all the old favorites in a warm, bustling environment. *827 19th St., Niagara Falls, tel. 716/282–2252. AE, D, MC, V. Closed Mon.–Tues. Inexpensive.*

Goose's Roost. Right by the bus terminal, the Roost specializes in Italian food, but the menu is extensive and varied. The casual mood belies the chandeliers and the mirrors on the ceilings. *343 4th St. at Niagara St., Niagara Falls, tel. 716/282–6255. AE, D, MC, V. Inexpensive.*

La Casa Cardenas. This casual and inexpensive Mexican restaurant is appropriately bustling and festive. The walls are bright red and covered with murals and Mexican trinkets. The menu also offers Californian selections, and any of the menu items can be ordered without meat. *921 Main St., Niagara Falls, tel. 716/282–0231. AE, D, MC, V. Inexpensive.*

Pete's Market House. This family restaurant serves hearty basics—steak, lobster, veal—in a warm, lively environment. The lines are long, the portions are huge, and the prices are pleasantly low. *1701 Pine Ave., Niagara Falls, tel. 716/282–7225. No credit cards. Moderate.*

CANADIAN SIDE **Casa D'Oro.** The Italian menu combines the basics with more elaborate dishes in opulent surroundings. Specialties include prime rib, sole basilica (flavored with lime juice, paprika, and basil), and pasta primavera. The adjoining nightclub and bar has nightly dancing. *5875 Victoria Ave., tel. 905/356–5646. AE, DC, MC, V. Moderate.*

Falls Manor Restaurant. This "country casual" spot serves a combination of British and American cuisine on big pine tables. In addition to meat dishes, you can have roast chicken or fish-and-chips. Try the seafood bisque and delicious roast chicken. *7104 Lundy's La., tel. 905/358–3211. AE, D, DC MC, V. Inexpensive.*

Michael's Inn. The large, glass-enclosed open-hearth barbecue allows you to watch the chef prepare your meal. The menu specializes in Continental cuisine, with fresh fish daily. *5599 River Rd., tel. 905/354–2727. AE, DC, MC, V. Moderate.*

Millery Dining Room. The Millery prides itself on the variety and authenticity of its menu. Dishes include prime rib, chicken, pasta, seafood, and salads. The cathedral ceilings, the fireplace, and the old wood tables make for a warm atmosphere. *Old Stone Inn, 5425 Robinson St., tel. 905/357–1234. AE, D, DC, MC, V. Moderate.*

Table Rock Restaurant. Here at the brink of the falls, the spacious Table Rock Restaurant offers a spectacular view of the falls. The prices on the Continental menu are fixed by the Canadian government. *Just yards from Horseshoe Falls, tel. 905/354–3631. AE, MC, V. Inexpensive.*

Victoria Park Cafe and Dining Room. Right in the park is a comfortable indoor dining area and an outdoor terrace overlooking the Victoria Park gardens and the falls. The cafeteria offers soups, salads, pasta dishes, hot food, and sandwiches. The restaurant offers seasonal features, a summer luncheon buffet, and Sunday brunch. *Queen Victoria Park, 6345 Niagara Pkwy., tel. 905/356–2217. Closed mid-Oct.–early May. AE, MC, V. Inexpensive.*

SHOPPING

Between 15 million and 18 million visitors come to Niagara Falls annually, and according to a recent survey, the second most popular activity—next to visiting the falls—is shopping. Niagara factory outlets offer up to 70% off retail prices on top-quality manufacturers' goods, including fine china and dinnerware, books, apparel, shoes, jewelry, and accessories. The outlets are easy to reach by foot or car and group tours are available.

Rainbow Center Factory Outlet is a one-block walk from the falls. *302 Rainbow Blvd., Niagara Falls, NY 14303, tel. 716/285–9758 or 716/285–5525.*

Factory Outlet Mall has more than 90 stores and is just 7 miles from the falls. *1900 Military Rd, Niagara Falls, NY 14304, tel. 716/297–2022.*

Pyramid Place, on the Canadian side of the falls and just steps from the Skylon Tower, contains specialty retail stores and a number of unusual museums. There's an impressive Elvis Presley memorabilia museum (no phone; admission charged) and the Brian

McFarlane Hockey Museum (tel. 905/354–7760; admission charged), a hands-on exhibit established by Canada's most celebrated hockey announcer. *5400 Robinson St., Niagara Falls, Ontario L2G 2A6.*

ENTERTAINMENT

Call the Niagara Falls Convention and Visitors Bureau (tel. 716/285–8711) for a list of special events, activities, and performances.

ArtPark. The only U.S. state park devoted to the visual and performing arts, this 2,300-seat open-air amphitheater (with an additional 1,500 seats on the lawn) boasts first-quality opera, musicals, dance, and concerts. From late May to Labor Day free arts activities—demonstrations, participatory art workshops by artists, craftspeople, and performers—are held throughout the park. *Tel. 716/754–9001 in season, 716/745–3377 off-season. Call 800/659–7275 for Buffalo Philharmonic tickets.*

Oh Canada Eh?! This 2½-hour dinner show in the Pyramid Place mall (*see* Shopping, *above*) features hearty food and spirited versions of more than 40 Canadian songs, all in a whimsical tribute to Canadian culture. Your flat fee pays for dinner and entertainment. *5400 Robinson St., Niagara Falls, Ontario L2G 2A6, tel. 905/374–1995. Admission charged; group rates available.*

Shaw Festival. Held just 12 miles north of Niagara Falls, this world-renowned theater festival features the works of George Bernard Shaw and his contemporaries in three theaters. The festival runs from April to November and includes nine plays. Take the scenic Niagara Parkway and follow clearly marked signs for Niagara-on-the-Lake north of the falls. Once in town, the festival venues are easily found on the left. *Tel. 905/468–2172. Open Tues.–Sun. Admission charged.*

The Outer Banks

North Carolina

Updated by Susan Ladd

North Carolina's Outer Banks comprise a series of barrier islands that curve 130 miles from the Virginia state line southward past Morehead City. For centuries a threat to shipping despite an extensive network of lighthouses and lifesaving stations, the area is called the Graveyard of the Atlantic. More than 400 years ago, a colony of English settlers on Roanoke Island disappeared without a trace. Their story is told annually in an outdoor drama, The Lost Colony, presented in the Waterside Theater. The coves and inlets of the islands offered seclusion to pirates, and the notorious Blackbeard lived and died here. For many years the Outer Banks remained isolated, home only to a few fishing families, whose descendants still speak with Elizabethan accents. Today, the islands, linked by bridges and ferries, are popular with visitors, who come in large numbers during the long summers mostly for the magnificent beaches. Crowds are reduced during the mild spring and fall. Much of the area is within the Cape Hatteras and Cape Lookout national seashores; the largest towns on the islands are Manteo, Kill Devil Hills (sites of the Wright brothers' flight), and Nags Head.

ESSENTIAL INFORMATION

WHEN TO GO Weather on the Outer Banks is relatively mild year-round, with an average temperature of 62°. In summer, when the mercury climbs as high as 87°, rates are at their peak, and ferry reservations are a must. August and September are the peak season for hurricanes and tropical storms, but authorities estimate that the probability of a hurricane striking the area is less than 15% per year. Spring and fall are breezy, balmy, and less crowded; many hotels and motels offer off-season rates September to May. On cooler winter days the thermometer can drop to the mid-30s or even below freezing. "Nor'easters" are common during the colder months of the year.

BARGAINS Cape Hatteras National Seashore is the best bargain around. Not only are the beaches and scenery free, but there are festivals, lighthouses, and shipwrecks. Free activities in summer range from puppet shows to nature walks and campfire programs (tel. 919/473–2111). No admission is charged at Jockey's Ridge State Park, Nags Head Woods Preserve, Fort Raleigh, Pea Island National Wildlife Refuge, Chicamacomico Lifesaving Station, or Cape Hatteras Lighthouse.

TOURIST OFFICES **Cape Hatteras National Seashore** (Rte. 1, Box 675, Manteo 27954, tel. 919/473–2111). **Dare County Tourist Bureau** (Box 399, Manteo 27954, tel. 919/473–2138 or 800/446–6262). **Division of Travel and Tourism** (430 N. Salisbury St., Raleigh 27611, tel. 919/733–4171 or 800/847–4862 [VISITNC]).

EMERGENCIES **Police, fire,** and **ambulance:** Dial 911. The **Outer Banks Medical Center** at Nags Head (tel. 919/441–7111) is open 24 hours a day.

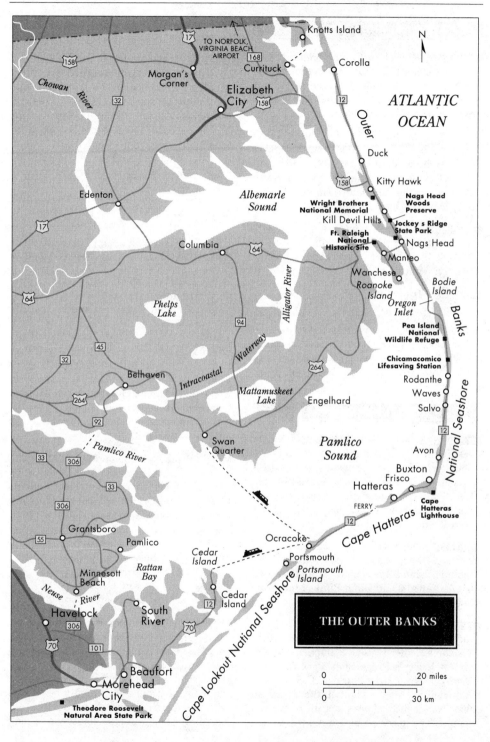

THE OUTER BANKS

ARRIVING AND DEPARTING

BY PLANE The closest commercial airport is the **Norfolk (Virginia) International Airport** (tel. 804/857–3340), served by American, Continental, Delta, and USAir. Rental cars are available in the terminal.

BY CAR U.S. 158 links the Outer Banks with Norfolk and other places north. U.S. 64 and 264 are western routes. Toll ferries connect Ocracoke to Cedar Island and Swan Quarter on the mainland. There is a free ferry between Ocracoke and Hatteras Island.

BY TRAIN Amtrak (tel. 800/872–7245) serves Newport News (Virginia) and, by Amtrak bus, Norfolk and Virginia Beach. You can rent cars in all three locations.

BY BUS Trailways (tel. 800/531–5332) serves Elizabeth City and Norfolk, Virginia.

BY BOAT Seagoing visitors traveling the Intracoastal Waterway may dock at Elizabeth City, Manteo, Ocracoke, Beaufort, and other ports, where cars can be rented.

GETTING AROUND

BY CAR A car is the most practical way to get around on the Outer Banks. You can get detailed road maps that also list ferry schedules from the Dare County Tourist Bureau (*see* Tourist Offices, *above*). The main north–south road (U.S. 158/Route 12) has convenient mileposts (MP).

BY TAXI Beach Cabs (tel. 919/441–2500) offers 24-hour service. Other companies include **Island Limousine and Taxi** (tel. 919/441–8803) and **Outer Banks Limousine Service** (tel. 919/261–3133).

REST STOPS There are rest rooms and picnic shelters at Dare County Aycock Brown Welcome Center (U.S. 158 Bypass, MP 1.5) and at Jockey's Ridge State Park (MP 12). Dare County Tourist Bureau (U.S. 64 and Budleigh St., Manteo) and all the Cape Hatteras National Seashore's facilities have rest rooms. The ferry stops on Cedar Island, Ocracoke, and Hatteras have rest rooms that are open year-round.

GUIDED TOURS Aerial tours are offered by **Kitty Hawk Aero Tours** (First Flight Airstrip, Kill Devil Kills, tel. 919/441–4460) and **Southeast Air Tours** (Dare Co. Airport, Manteo, tel. 919/473–1566). **Water Works** (MP 16.5, Whalebone Junction, tel. 919/441–8875) offers airboat tours and dolphin-watching excursions. Tour the sounds and estuaries with **Kayak EcoTours** (Kitty Hawk Kites, Nags Head, tel. 919/441–4124) or **Wilderness Canoeing** (Manns Harbor, tel. 919/473–3270).

EXPLORING

Bodie, Hatteras, and Ocracoke islands (from north to south) are linked to each other and to the mainland by bridges and ferries. You can drive the Outer Banks down U.S. 158/Route 12 in a day, but allow plenty of time in summer to wait for the ferries. For reservations, call 800/293–3779 (BY-FERRY) for departures from Cedar Island, Ocracoke, or Swan Quarter. A "ghost fleet" map, available at the Wright Brothers National Memorial, is helpful in locating the sites of shipwrecks.

Wright Brothers National Memorial, a granite monument that resembles the tail of an airplane, sits atop a 90-foot dune as a tribute to Wilbur and Orville Wright, the two Ohio bicycle mechanics who took to the air on December 17, 1903. You can see a replica of the *Flyer,* explore marked historic trails and exhibits, and hear an informative talk by a National Park Service ranger. *U.S. 158 Bypass, MP 8.5, Kill Devil Hills, tel. 919/441–7430. Open daily. Admission charged.*

Nags Head Woods Preserve, shielded from the salt-laden breezes by a ridge of high, ancient dunes, is a glorious 1,400-acre maritime forest. The preserve nurtures a diverse range of plant and animal species—including many that are not normally associated with the harsh environment of a barrier island. Tour this unique forest via several nature trails. *West Ocean Acres Dr., off Rte. 158 near MP 9, Kill Devil Hills, tel. 919/441–2525. Open Tues.–Thurs. and Sat. in summer; weekdays in winter; Tues.–Thurs. in fall and spring. Admission free.*

Jockey's Ridge State Park, containing the tallest sand dune in the eastern United States, is a popular spot for hang gliding, kite flying, hiking, picnics, and photography. There is a 1½-mile self-guided nature trail with 14 stations and a natural-history museum, with guided tours on request. *U.S. 158 Bypass, MP 12, tel. 919/441–7132. Open daily. Admission free.*

The **Elizabethan Gardens,** created by the Garden Club of North Carolina in memory of Elizabeth I and the early colonists, has easy walking trails amid profuse period plantings and antique statuary. *Off U.S. 64/264 on north end of Roanoke Island, tel. 919/473–3234. Open Mar.–Nov., daily; Dec.–Jan., weekdays. Admission charged.*

Fort Raleigh National Historic Site is a reconstruction of what is thought to be the first colonists' fort. An orientation film and guided tour explain its significance. The Thomas Hariot Nature Trail leads to an outlook on Roanoke Sound. *Off U.S. 64/264, Roanoke Island, tel. 919/473–5772. Open daily. Admission free.*

The Lost Colony, America's oldest outdoor drama, dating to 1937, reenacts the story of the Outer Banks' first colonists, who disappeared mysteriously in 1591. *Waterside Amphitheater, Roanoke Island, tel. 919/473–3414 or 800/488–5012. Open mid-June–late Aug., Sun.–Fri. Admission charged.*

North Carolina Aquarium. You can see sharks and wetland creatures, enjoy hands-on and interactive exhibits, like the "touch tank," and take behind-the-scenes tours and trips to coastal habitats. *Airport Rd., Roanoke Island, tel. 919/473–3493. Open daily. Admission charged.*

Elizabeth II State Historic Site. There's a little something for everyone here: a visitor center, museum, multimedia program, and a full-size floating replica of a 16th-century sailing ship, the Elizabeth II. You can also meet park workers portraying—in dress, speech, and attitude—haggard mariners and Elizabethan-era colonists. *Manteo waterfront, tel. 919/473–1144. Open Nov.–Mar., Tues.–Sun; Apr.–Oct., daily. Admission charged.*

Pea Island National Wildlife Refuge is a 6,000-acre haven for more than 265 species of birds, with observation platforms, dunes, marsh, beach, man-made habitats, and nature trails. *Rte. 12, between Oregon Inlet and Rodanthe, tel. 919/473–1131. Open Apr.–Nov., weekdays 8–4. Admission free.*

Chicamacomico Lifesaving Station, a few miles south of Pea Island, is a museum dedicated to the 24 lifesaving stations that once lined the Outer Banks. *Rte. 12, Rodanthe, tel. 919/987–2203. Open May–Oct., Tues., Thurs., and Sat. Admission free.*

Cape Hatteras Lighthouse, at 208 feet, is the tallest in America. Recent renovations allow visitors once again to climb the circular stairs to the top for fine views of the Atlantic. *The Visitor Center, Buxton, tel. 919/995–4474. Open daily. Admission free.*

Ocracoke Island, a small oasis of restaurants, motels, shops, and a visitor center (tel. 919/928–6711) has a quaint charm about it. The picturesque harbor, with the Ocracoke Lighthouse in the background, is where the pirate Blackbeard met his demise in 1718. Ferries make several trips a day from Ocracoke to Swan Quarter and Cedar Island on the mainland.

THE NATURAL WORLD Look for deer, rabbits, foxes, lizards, and various birds along the nature trail in Jockey's Ridge State Park. Walk through the rich environment of a maritime forest at the Nags Head Woods Preserve. The Pea Island National Wildlife Refuge is home to numerous species of wading, shore, and upland birds; large concentrations of snow geese winter there. You often see egrets, blue herons, and pelicans on the causeway connecting Bodie and Roanoke islands. Catch sight of a pod of porpoises working the surf while checking the beach for shells and interesting things. Wild ponies live near the Corolla Lighthouse, on Ocracoke Island, and on Shackleford Banks in the Cape Lookout National Seashore.

HOTELS AND INNS

Weathered beach cottages, condos, and motels line the beach at Nags Head and Kill Devil Hills. There are laid-back lodges and motels in Ocracoke, and motels and bed-and-breakfasts in Manteo and the Albemarle region. Hundreds of cottages and condos are available through local real-estate agencies; try **Sun Realty** (tel. 800/334–4745) or **Resort Realty** (tel. 800/345–3522). Camping information can be obtained from the **National Park Service** (tel. 919/473–2111). High-season price categories for double occupancy, excluding 10% tax, are Moderate, $60–$100, and Inexpensive, under $60.

MODERATE **Berkeley Center Country Inn.** Secluded by trees on spacious, well-maintained grounds near the ferry dock, this former corporate retreat resembles a lifesaving station and is furnished with mixed antiques and reproductions. *Rte. 12, Box 220, Ocracoke 27960, tel. 919/928–5911. 9 rooms. Free Continental breakfast. No credit cards. Closed Nov.–Mar.*

Comfort Inn–Hatteras Island. Probably the prettiest chain hotel you'll ever see, the gray-shingled building with lookout tower is patterned after the lifesaving stations that dot the coast. It's within walking distance of restaurants, shops, and the beach. *Rte. 12, Box 1089, Buxton 27920, tel. 919/995–6100 or 800/432–1441. 60 rooms. Free continental breakfast, outdoor pool. AE, D, DC, MC, V.*

Island Inn and Dining Room. The inn's best rooms (in the third-floor Crow's Nest), with panoramic views, have been redone, and the dining room's island cuisine features wonderful crab cakes and hush puppies. *Rte. 12, Box 9, Ocracoke 27960, tel. 919/928–4351. 35 rooms. Heated outdoor pool. D, MC, V.*

Quality Inn John Yancey. A mainstay on the Outer Banks for years, the John Yancey has

been newly redecorated and offers eight different room styles. It's convenient to Wright Brothers Memorial and Jockeys Ridge State Park. *MP 10, Box 1625, Nags Head 27959, tel. 919/441–7141 or 800/367–5941. 107 rooms. Refrigerators, pool, sundeck, children under 12 free. AE, D, DC, MC, V.*

INEXPENSIVE **C. W. Pugh's Bed & Breakfast.** Enjoy the comforts of a beautiful old beach house, surrounded by live oaks and the ocean, in the fishing village of Wanchese, on Roanoke Island. *Box 427, Wanchese 27981, tel. 919/473–5466. 2 rooms. Full breakfast. AE, D, DC, MC, V. Open Mar.–Oct.*

Scarborough Inn. Heirloom beds and family antiques fill the simple rooms at the Scarborough, a quiet inn lined with wide porches and only minutes away from Manteo's attractions. *Box 1310, Manteo 27954, tel. 919/473–3979. 12 rooms, 4 in annex. Refrigerators, coffeemakers. AE, DC, MC, V.*

MOTELS

MODERATE **Anchorage Inn and Marina** (Rte. 12, Ocracoke, tel. 919/928–1581). 41 rooms; complimentary breakfast, pool, marina. **Blue Heron Motel** (6811 S. Virginia Dare Trail, Nags Head 27959, tel. 919/441–7447). 19 rooms, 11 efficiencies; heated indoor pool with spa, outdoor pool. **Cape Hatteras Motel** (Box 339, Buxton 27920, tel. 919/995–5611). 6 rooms, 7 efficiencies, 21 apartments; pool with heated spa, refrigerator, microwave, coffeemaker. **Elizabethan Inn** (Box 549, Manteo 27954, tel. 919/473–2101 or 800/346–2466). 100 rooms; restaurant, indoor/outdoor pools, health club, sauna, whirlpool, racquetball, picnic area, and room refrigerators. **Outer Banks Motel** (Rte. 12, Box 428, Buxton 27920, tel. 919/995–5601, fax 919/995–5082). 9 rooms, 7 efficiencies, 20 cottages; refrigerators, microwaves, coffeemakers, decks or porches. **Sea Foam Motel** (MP 16.5, 7111 S. Virginia Dare Trail, Nags Head 27959, tel. 919/441–7320, fax 919/441–7324). 29 rooms, 18 efficiencies, 2 cottages, 1 apartment; room refrigerators, microwaves, pool, shuffleboard.

INEXPENSIVE **Nettlewood Motel** (MP 7, Box 367, Kill Devil Hills 27948, tel. 919/441–5039). 22 rooms, 16 efficiencies, 4 condos; refrigerators, outdoor pool. **Olde London Inn** (MP 12, Box 637, Nags Head 27959, tel. 919/441–7115). 21 rooms, 49 efficiencies; refrigerators, laundry. **Salvo Inn Motel** (Box 37, Salvo 27972, tel. 919/987–2240). 9 rooms, 7 efficiencies, 3 cottages. **Sea Sound Motel** (Rte. 12, Rodanthe 27968, tel. 919/987–2224). 6 rooms, 5 efficiencies; pool. **See Sea Motel** (MP 9, Box 75, Kill Devil Hills 27948, tel. 919/441–7321). 11 rooms, 5 efficiencies, 1 cottage; refrigerator, outdoor pool, laundry.

DINING

The Outer Banks has a wide variety of dining opportunities, from fast food to fancy. Fresh seafood is abundant and comes broiled, grilled, poached, battered and deep-fried, blackened, or sauced. Price categories per person, excluding 5% tax, service, and drinks, are Expensive, $15–$25; Moderate, $8–$15; and Inexpensive, under $8.

EXPENSIVE **Owens' Restaurant.** Owens has been serving first-rate seafood—from fish-and-chips to grilled bass—for more than 40 years in an old Nags Head–style shingled cottage. *Rte. 12, MP 17, Nags Head, tel. 919/441–7309. AE, DC, MC, V. Closed Jan.–Mar. No lunch.*

Sanderling Inn and Restaurant. Fresh ingredients and a deft hand are evident in the Continental and southern dishes served at Sanderling. The restaurant is housed in a restored lifesaving station and retains its soaring ceilings and natural wood wainscoting. *5 mi north of Duck on Rte. 12, tel. 919/261–4111. AE, D, MC, V.*

MODERATE **Clara's Seafood Grill.** Grilled seafood and burgers are standard fare at this art deco–style eatery overlooking the Manteo waterfront. *Downtown Manteo, tel. 919/473–1727. MC, V.*

Dunes Restaurant. This busy family-style restaurant is known for its large helpings of seafood, steak, and chicken, and its equally generous and inexpensive breakfast. *U.S. 158 Bypass, MP 16.5, Nags Head, tel. 919/441–1600. D, MC, V.*

Etheridge's Seafood Restaurant. The fish, lobster, bass, tuna or whatever's freshest—comes straight from local boats to the kitchen of this popular family-owned restaurant. *U.S. 158 Bypass, MP 9.5, Kill Devil Hills, tel. 919/441–2645. MC, V. Closed Nov.–Feb.*

Lance's Seafood Bar & Market. It's hard to miss the hot pink building that houses Lance's. While you're dining on steamed or raw seafood and putting the shells through the hole in the table, you can contemplate the restaurant's nostalgic fishing and hunting memorabilia. *U.S. 158 Bypass, MP 14, Nags Head, tel. 919/441–7501. AE, MC, V.*

Sands Seafood Restaurant. One of the best seafood restaurants on the beach offers prime rib and shrimp combos for the same price many places would charge for the shrimp alone. This is where the locals come for fresh seafood. *U.S. 158, MP 10, Nags Head, tel. 919/441–1649. MC, V.*

Tides Restaurant. Whether you've come for breakfast or a seafood dinner, you'll likely rub elbows with locals rather than tourists at this casual eatery on Hatteras Island. *Rte. 12, Buxton, tel. 919/995–5988. MC, V.*

Waves Edge. Dine overlooking Pamlico Sound on mesquite-grilled seafood, beef, or chicken—specialties of the house at this open-air restaurant on Hatteras Island. *Rte. 12, Waves, tel. 919/987–2100. D, MC, V.*

INEXPENSIVE **Sam & Omies.** This stoically weathered restaurant will cook your (cleaned) fresh catch or serve you one of theirs. If fish makes you queasy, don't miss the Sam & Omies' hearty breakfasts. *7228 Virginia Dare Trail, tel. 919/441–7366. MC, V.*

SHOPPING

Antiques shops carry many nautical items, while numerous specialty shops cover all of the needs of the beachgoer and souvenir hunter. Culture vultures can also pursue the work of local artists at a number of art galleries. Long before Christmas stores were a fad, the **Christmas Shop and Island Gallery** (U.S. 64, Manteo) was an institution on the Outer Banks. Outlet shopping can be found at the **Soundings Factory Stores** at MP 16.5. Some of the most beautiful and unusual kites, as well as hang gliders and supplies, are found at **Kitty Hawk Kites** (MP 13, tel. 919/441–4124).

OUTDOOR ACTIVITIES

BEACHES The 70 miles of unspoiled beaches in Cape Hatteras National Seashore are ideal for all water activities, but you should swim only where there are lifeguard stations—Cape Hatteras and Ocracoke; in commercial areas, lifeguards are stationed near motels and hotels. Beach volleyball is the game of choice for landlubbers. Surfers practice their trade along the length of the Banks, while divers concentrate on the wrecks. Fishing from the beach and piers is popular. Hang gliding lessons are available from **Kitty Hawk Kites** (*see* Shopping, *above*).

BICYCLING The pamphlet "Bicycling on the Outer Banks" is available from the Dare County Tourist Bureau (*see* Tourist Offices, *above*). The best areas for the casual cyclist are Ocracoke and Manteo, which has a new bike that bisects the island parallel to U.S. 64. Many hotels and inns have bicycles for their guests; rentals are available from **Ocean Atlantic Rentals, Inc.** at Nags Head (Beach Rd., MP 10, tel. 919/441–7823), Duck (tel. 919/261–4346), Corolla (tel. 919/453–2440), Waves (tel. 919/987–2492), and Avon (tel. 919/995–5868). Reservations can be made by calling 800/635–9559.

BOATING AND SAILING There are 10 marinas along the Intracoastal—among them **Pirate's Cove Yacht Club** (tel. 919/473–3906) at Manteo, **Oregon Inlet Fishing Center** (tel. 919/441–6301), **Hatteras Harbor Marina** (tel. 919/986–2166), and the **Park Service Docks** (tel. 919/928–5111) in Ocracoke. Check with **Nags Head Watersports** (MP 17, tel. 919/480–2236) or **Kitty Hawk Sports** (MP 13, tel. 919/441–9200) for all types of boat rentals and lessons. Sea kayaking and windsurfing on the sounds are very popular activities.

FISHING Blue and channel bass, sea mullet, trout, flounder, spot, croaker, tuna, dolphin, marlin, king mackerel, and billfish abound. Fall is the best time to fish from the eight ocean fishing piers between Kitty Hawk and Cape Hatteras—from certain bridges and causeways, and by surf-casting all along the beach. You can charter boats for Gulf Stream fishing trips from **Hatteras Harbor Marina** (tel. 800/676–4939), **Oregon Inlet Fishing Center** (tel. 800/272–5199), or the **Pirate Cove Yacht Club** (tel. 800/367–4728). Inland, there is good freshwater fishing for largemouth bass, white and yellow perch, and catfish. Freshwater licenses can be bought locally or over the phone (with a credit card) from the **North Carolina Wildlife Commission** (tel. 919/715–4091).

HIKING/WALKING You can take a self-guided walking tour of Manteo, following the map available at **Manteo Booksellers** (105 Sir Walter St., tel. 919/473–1221), or hike for miles and miles on the uncrowded beaches and on marked trails in Jockey's Ridge State Park, Nags Head Woods Preserve, the Wright Brothers Memorial, and Fort Raleigh.

ENTERTAINMENT

NIGHTLIFE Many of the nightspots feature bands on weekends and certain midweek nights. For high-energy dance music, head to the attic at **Woody's** (Pirates Quay Shopping Center, MP 11, Nags Head, tel. 919/441–4881). For laughs, there's the **Comedy Club at the Carolinian** (Rte. 12, MP 10.5, Nags Head, tel. 919/441–7171).

Pennsylvania Dutch Country
Pennsylvania

Updated by Rathe Miller

he plain and fancy live side by side in Lancaster County, some 65 miles west of Philadelphia—an area more popularly known as Pennsylvania Dutch Country. The county is home to the nation's largest population of Plain people (Amish, Mennonite, and Brethren), descendants of German and Swiss immigrants who came to the area to escape persecution; they have thrived over the years while maintaining their own cuisine, language, and traditions. Tourists come here mainly to observe the Old Order Amish, who cling to a centuries-old way of life. These conservative people shun the amenities of modern civilization, such as electricity and cars, preferring to use kerosene or gas lamps, and to drive horse-drawn carriages. They also reject military service and Social Security benefits. Ironically, in turning their backs on the modern world, they have attracted its attention.

The Amish, however, are far from the only reason to visit this county. Along with the commercialism and the kitsch that have sprung up to cater to the tourist trade, you'll also discover much charm along the tranquil country lanes dotted with picture-perfect farms. You can also take a stroll past 18th-century buildings in lovely small towns; ride a bicycle, steam train, or horse-drawn buggy through the countryside; hike along the Susquehanna River; or sleep overnight in a caboose or an historic inn.

ESSENTIAL INFORMATION

WHEN TO GO "Changeable" best describes Lancaster's weather. Temperatures can range from 58° to 96° in summer and from 0° to 70° in winter. July just beats August as the hottest and most humid month, with temperatures ranging from an average high of 86° to an average low of 65°; December sees average highs of 40°, and lows of 24°. On summer weekends, you'll find the main arteries, shops, and restaurants crowded with busloads of visitors. The same is true in October, when tourists come for the fall foliage. September, winter, and early spring are less crowded times, with good views of rolling farmland. Although many restaurants, shops, and farmers markets are closed on Sunday, commercial attractions remain open.

BARGAINS Festivals, quilt and farm-equipment auctions, flea markets, and chicken-corn soup or ox-roast suppers are frequently staged to raise money for the volunteer fire company crews and attract large numbers of Amish people. The events offer good, cheap, home-cooked foods and inexpensive entertainment. The Pennsylvania Dutch Convention & Visitors Bureau publishes a calendar of these almost weekly events. The Visitors Bureau's (*see* Tourist Offices, *below*) "Free Map and Visitor's Guide" contains coupons with savings on dining, lodging, and admissions. Another free map with discount coupons comes from Amish Country Tours (*see* Guided Tours, *below*).

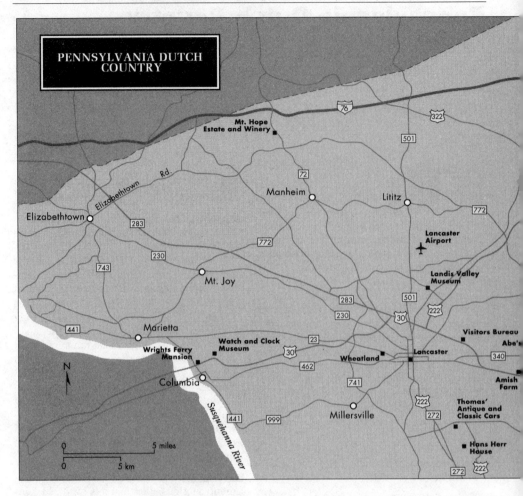

PENNSYLVANIA DUTCH COUNTRY

TOURIST OFFICES Pennsylvania Dutch Convention & Visitors Bureau (Dept. 2201, 501 Greenfield Rd., Lancaster 17601, tel. 717/299–8901 or 800/735–2629). **Mennonite Information Center** (2209 Millstream Rd., Lancaster 17602, tel. 717/299–0954). **Intercourse Information Center** (3546 Old Philadelphia Pike, Intercourse 17534, tel. 717/768–3882). **Susquehanna Heritage Tourist & Information Center** (Box 510, 5th and Linden Sts., Columbia 17512, tel. 717/684–5249).

EMERGENCIES Police, fire, and **ambulance:** Dial 911. **Hospitals:** Community Hospital of Lancaster (1100 E. Orange St., tel. 717/397–

3711). Lancaster General Hospital (555 N. Duke St., tel. 717/299–5511). St. Joseph's Hospital (250 College Ave., tel. 717/291–8211). **Doctors:** Lancaster City and County Medical Society (tel. 717/393–9588) gives referrals. **Pharmacy:** CVS (1507 Lititz Pike, tel. 717/399–8762) is open 24 hours.

ARRIVING AND DEPARTING

BY PLANE Philadelphia International Airport (tel. 215/937–6937), 65 miles east of Lancaster, has scheduled daily flights by major carriers. **Lancaster Municipal Airport** (contact USAir Express at 717/948–5400) is

Philadelphia's 30th Street Station to Lancaster's Amtrak station at 53 McGovern Avenue.

BY BUS **Capital Trailways** (tel. 800/444–2877) has two runs daily from Philadelphia to the R&S Bus Terminal (22 W. Clay St., Lancaster). The ride takes two hours.

GETTING AROUND

BY CAR AND RV Because the area's attractions are spread out, a car is essential for touring. The main east–west arteries are U.S. 30 and Route 340; U.S. 222 is the main north–south route. You can pick up Route 772 where it intersects U.S. 30 near the town of Gap and follow it westward through towns like Intercourse and Mount Joy. Parking is plentiful and free at all attractions.

BY TAXI **Yellow Cab** (tel. 717/397–8108) is based in the city of Lancaster; the average crosstown fare is $5–$6. **Lancaster County Taxi** (tel. 717/626–8294) mainly serves the towns of Ephrata, Manheim, and Lititz.

REST STOPS Public rest rooms can be found at the Pennsylvania Dutch Information Center, located at the Greenfield Road exit off U.S. 30; the Downtown Visitors Information Center, in the heart of Lancaster at South Queen and Vine streets; the Mennonite Information Center, on Millstream Road off U.S. 30; and at the Rockvale Square Factory Outlet Village, at the intersection of U.S. 30 and Route 896.

GUIDED TOURS **Amish Country Tours** (Rte. 340, between Bird-in-Hand and Intercourse, tel. 717/768–8400 or 800/441–3505) has a variety of bus and minivan tours of the area, such as the popular Amish farmlands trip.

Abe's Buggy Rides (Rte. 340, ½ mi east of Rte. 896, no phone) and **Ed's Buggy Rides** (Rte. 896, 1½ mi south of U.S. 30, Strasburg, tel. 717/687–0360) offer horse-drawn carriage rides along scenic back roads.

The **Historic Lancaster Walking Tour** (Downtown Visitors Center, tel. 717/392–1776) is a 90-minute stroll through this

7 miles north of the city, and **Harrisburg International Airport** (tel. 717/948–3900) is 30 miles northwest of the city.

BY CAR From Philadelphia, take the Schuylkill Expressway (I–76) west to the Pennsylvania Turnpike. Lancaster County attractions are accessible from Exits 20, 21, and 22. From Exit 22, you can follow scenic Route 23 to Lancaster. You can also follow U.S. 30 west (Lancaster Pike) from Philadelphia to Lancaster County. Allow about 1½ hours for either route.

BY TRAIN **Amtrak** (tel. 800/872–7245) has frequent train service (80 minutes) from charming old city, conducted by guides in period costume.

EXPLORING

The **People's Place**, situated in Intercourse on Route 340 in eastern Lancaster County, provides an introduction to the Amish, Mennonite, and Hutterite peoples; a slide show features close-up shots of Amish life and sensitive narration. *Tel. 717/768–7171. Open Mon.–Sat. Admission charged.*

Intercourse (on Route 340) is a good starting point for exploring the country roads. Many Amish farms, distinguished by windmills and green blinds, are clustered in the area between Intercourse and **New Holland** (on Route 23). Drive along back roads, visit the roadside stands, and stop at the farms selling quilts, wooden toys, homemade root beer, or new potatoes.

The **Amish Farm and House** and the **Amish Village** both offer guided tours through an authentically furnished re-creation of an Amish home. At the Farm and House, a self-guided tour continues through cultivated fields, animal pens, and a museum. At the Village, an operating smokehouse, a blacksmith shop, and a one-room schoolhouse built by Amish craftsmen are open for inspection. *Amish House: U.S. 30, Lancaster, tel. 717/394–6185. Open daily. Admission charged. Amish Village: Rte. 896, Strasburg, tel. 717/687–8511. Open Apr.–Nov., daily. Admission charged.*

Strasburg (reached by driving south from U.S. 30 or Route 340 on Route 896 and turning left on Route 741) is a town devoted to the railroad. The **Strasburg Rail Road** (tel. 717/687–7522; open Apr.–Oct., daily; Nov.–Mar. weekends, except 1st 2 weekends in Jan.) provides a scenic 9-mile round-trip excursion from Strasburg to Paradise on a rolling antique with a turn-of-the-century iron steam locomotive. Strasburg also has the **Railroad Museum of Pennsylvania** (tel. 717/687–8628; open May–Oct., daily; Nov.–Apr., Tues.–Sun.), housing colossal historic engines and railroad cars. The **Toy Train Museum** (tel. 717/687–8976; open May–Oct., daily; Apr. and Nov.–mid-Dec., weekends) displays antique and 20th-century model trains. The **Choo Choo Barn** (tel. 717/687–7911; open Apr.–Dec.) has a 1,700-square-foot exhibit of Lancaster County in miniature. If you fancy fancy cars, the **Gast Classic Motorcars Museum** (Rte. 896, Strasburg, tel. 717/687–9500; admission charged) has a changing display of more than 50 antique, classic, sports, and celebrity vehicles. *Admission charged at all Strasburg attractions.*

Lancaster, at the intersection of U.S. 30 and U.S. 222, is the nation's oldest inland city, dating from 1710. The best way to see its blocks of quaint row houses is on foot. The **Central Market** (open Tues., Fri., and Sat.) at King and Queen streets is one of the oldest covered markets in the country. Nearby, Old City Hall, reborn as the **Heritage Center Museum** (tel. 717/299–6440; open Tues.–Sat; donation requested), shows the works of Lancaster County artisans and craftsmen.

Wheatland (1½ miles west of Lancaster) was the home of the only president from Pennsylvania—James Buchanan. The restored 1828 Federal mansion contains much of the 15th president's original furnishings. *1120 Marietta Ave. (Rte. 23), tel. 717/392–8721. Open Apr.–mid-Dec., daily, with guided tours. Admission charged.*

The **Hans Herr House** (reached by following U.S. 222 5 miles south from Lancaster and turning right onto Hans Herr Drive), a former Mennonite meeting place, is an outstanding example of medieval German architectural styles and the oldest structure in the county, dating from 1719. *1849 Hans Herr Dr., Willow St., tel. 717/464–4438. Open Apr.–Nov., Mon.–Sat. Admission charged.*

Landis Valley Museum (2½ miles north of U.S. 30 on Oregon Pike or Route 272) is an outdoor museum devoted to Pennsylvania German rural life and folk culture before 1900. *2451 Kissel Hill Rd., tel. 717/569–0401. Open Apr.–Oct., Tues.–Sun. Admission charged.*

Ephrata Cloister (10 miles north of the museum on Route 322), established in 1732, once housed a self-sufficient community of German Pietists who lived an ascetic life of work, study, and prayer. Guides lead tours of three restored buildings; visitors can tour the stable, print shop, and crafts shop by themselves. *Rte. 322 east of junction with Rte. 272, Ephrata, tel. 717/733–6600. Open daily. Admission charged.*

Lititz (west of Ephrata at the intersection of Routes 501 and 772) was founded by Moravians who settled here to do missionary work among the Indians. Its tree-shaded main street is lined with 18th-century cottages and specialty shops selling antiques, crafts, clothing, and gifts. Pick up a Historical Foundation walking-tour brochure at the **General Sutter Inn** (Main St. and Rte. 501). You can twist a pretzel at the **Julius Sturgis Pretzel House** (219 E. Main St.), the nation's oldest pretzel bakery.

HOTELS AND INNS

In Lancaster County, you can sleep under the stars at one of the many campgrounds or under a lace canopy at a historic country inn. The Pennsylvania Dutch Convention and Visitors Bureau (tel. 717/299–8901 or 800/735–2629) has free brochures listing bed-and-breakfasts.

A number of families, many of them Mennonite, open their farmhouses to visitors and allow them to observe, and even participate in, day-to-day farm life. Accommodations are simple, comfortable, and inexpensive, ranging in price from $25 to $45. Make reservations weeks in advance; most farms are heavily booked during the summer. Some recommended farms include **Jonde Lane Farm** (1103 Auction Rd., Manheim 17545, tel. 717/665–4231), **Rocky Acre Farm** (1020 Pinkerton Rd., Mount Joy 17552, tel. 717/653–4449), and **Verdant View Farm** (429 Strasburg Rd., Paradise 17562, tel. 717/687–7353). Contact the Pennsylvania Dutch Convention and Visitors Bureau or the Men-

nonite Information Center (*see* Tourist Offices, *above*) for more information.

Hotels charge peak rates from Memorial Day to Labor Day; you can expect about a 25% drop in spring and fall, and up to a 50% reduction in winter. Price categories for double occupancy, excluding 6% tax, are Expensive, $85–$100; Moderate, $65–$85; and Inexpensive, under $65.

BIRD-IN-HAND **Village Inn of Bird-in-Hand.** This Victorian-style country inn, updated with down-filled bedding and cable TV, offers a free two-hour tour of the area. *Box 253, 2695 Old Philadelphia Pike, 17505, tel. 717/293–8369 or 800/914–2473. 11 rooms, including 2 suites with hot tubs. Continental breakfast, access to pool and tennis courts. AE, D, MC, V. Moderate–Expensive.*

CHURCHTOWN **Churchtown Inn.** A 1735 fieldstone mansion, between Morgantown and New Holland, is presided over by warm-spirited innkeepers who serve up a five-course breakfast (included). *2100 Main St. (Rte. 23), Navron 17555, tel. 717/445–7794 or 800/637–4446. 8 rooms, carriage house. Children over 12 welcome. MC, V. Inexpensive–Expensive.*

EPHRATA **Inns at Doneckers.** Light, airy rooms and French country antiques distinguish the guest rooms in a collection of properties from the 18th century to the 1920s. *318–24 N. State St., 17522, tel. 717/738–9502. 40 rooms. Continental breakfast included. AE, D, DC, MC, V. Inexpensive–Expensive.*

LANCASTER **King's Cottage.** This elegant Spanish mansion has been transformed into a cozy B&B featuring antiques and a goldfish pond. Accommodations include full breakfast and afternoon tea. *1049 E. King St., 17602, tel. 717/397–1017 or 800/747–8717. 10 rooms. Children over 12 welcome. D, MC, V. Moderate–Expensive.*

Willow Valley Family Resort. A mom-and-pop operation that blossomed into a sprawling, stylish family resort, this Mennonite-owned property (there's no liquor served) offers the most personal attention and the best rates of the area's large resorts. *2416 Willow Street Pike, 17602, tel. 717/464–2711 or 800/444–1714, fax 717/464–4784. 353 rooms. 2 restaurants, 3 pools, lighted tennis courts, 9-hole golf course. AE, D, DC, MC, V. Expensive.*

LITITZ **General Sutter Inn.** The oldest continuously occupied inn in the state (circa 1764) is a Victoriana-lover's dream. *14 E. Main St. (Corner of Rtes. 501 and 772), 17543, tel. 717/626–2115, fax 717/626–0992. 10 rooms, 2 suites. Dining room, coffee shop, tavern. AE, D, MC, V. Moderate–Expensive.*

Swiss Woods. Nestled on the edge of the woods overlooking Speedwell Forge Lake, this sublime Swiss-style chalet offers goosedown comforters and a hearty breakfast. *500 Blantz Rd., 17543, tel. 717/627–3358 or 800/594–8018, fax 717/627–3483. 6 rooms, 2 with hot tubs, 1 suite. Biking, fishing, hiking, canoeing. No smoking. D, MC, V. Moderate–Expensive.*

MOUNT JOY **Cameron Estate Inn.** This grand Federal mansion provides large guest rooms with canopy beds, Oriental rugs, and working fireplaces (in seven rooms); a lovely porch overlooks the 15 wooded acres. *Donegal Springs Rd., 17552, tel. 717/653–1773, fax 717/653–9432. 18 rooms. Restaurant, Continental breakfast included, pool, tennis courts nearby. AE, D, DC, MC, V. Moderate–Expensive.*

STRASBURG **Historic Strasburg Inn.** This sprawling, 58-acre Colonial-style property represents one of the best values in the heart of the Dutch Country. Rooms are modern and simple, but the restaurant and tavern recall 18th-century America. *Rte. 896 (Historic Dr.), 17579, tel. 717/687–7691 or 800/872–0201. 103 rooms. Restaurant, tavern, outdoor pool, bicycles, volleyball. AE, D, DC, MC, V. Moderate–Expensive.*

Strasburg Village Inn. Outside, guests relax on the old-fashioned porch overlooking Main Street; inside the lure is elegant Williamsburg-style furnishings and canopy or four-poster beds. *1 W. Main St., 17579, tel. 717/687–0900 or 800/541–1055. 11 rooms. Full or Continental breakfast included. AE, D, MC, V. Moderate–Expensive.*

MOTELS

MODERATE **Bird-in-Hand Family Inn** (Box 402, 2740 Old Philadelphia Pike, Bird-in-Hand 17505, tel. 717/768–8271 or 800/537–2535). 100 rooms; restaurant, pools, tennis courts. **Hilton Garden Inn** (101 Granite Run Dr., intersection of U.S. 30 and 272, Lancaster 17601, tel. 717/560–0880 or 800/445–8667). 156 rooms; restaurant, pool, fitness center. **1722 Motor Lodge** (1722 Old Philadelphia Pike, Lancaster 17602, tel. 717/397–4791). 21 rooms, Continental breakfast included.

INEXPENSIVE **Red Caboose Motel** (303 Paradise La. off Rte. 741, Strasburg 17579, tel. 717/687–6646). 40 railroad cabooses converted into rooms; restaurant, playground, buggy rides. **Smoketown Motor Lodge** (190 E. Brook Rd., Rte. 896, Smoketown 17576, tel. 717/397–6944). 17 rooms; Continental breakfast included. **Spruce Lane Motor Lodge** (2439 Old Philadelphia Pike, Box 241, Smoketown 17602, tel. 717/393–1991 or 800/446–4901). 12 rooms; tennis courts, basketball.

CAMPGROUNDS

Camping is very popular in summer and fall months; book your stay several months in advance. The Pennsylvania Dutch Convention and Visitors Bureau (tel. 717/299–8901 or 800/735–2629) lists about 30 campgrounds in their "Free Map & Visitor's Guide." Here are three of the best.

Mill Bridge Village and Campresort. Close to major attractions and attached to a restored 18th-century village, these campgrounds aren't too scenic, but they offer enjoyable summer activities, such as free buggy rides. *Box 86 (½ mi south of U.S. 30 on Ronks Rd.), Strasburg 17579, tel. 717/687–*

8181 or 800/645–2744. 113 RV and tent sites; showers, bathrooms, snack shop, fishing stream. AE, D, MC, V.

Muddy Run Park. Lovely campgrounds with nature walks and bird-watching are set among 700 acres of woodland and rolling fields that surround a 100-acre lake. *172 Bethesda Church Rd. W, Holtwood 17532, tel. 717/284–4325. 163 trailer and tent sites; showers, bathrooms, laundry facilities, LP gas available, charcoal grills, playground, general store, snack bar, boating, fishing. No credit cards.*

Spring Gulch Resort Campground. This glorious setting has shaded sites, cottages, a farmhouse, and a lodge to rent; there's swimming, miniature golf, tennis and volleyball courts, fishing, and other weekend activities. *475 Lynch Rd. (Rte. 897 between Rtes. 340 and 322), New Holland 17557, tel. 717/ 354–3100 or 800/255–5744. 400 RV and tent sites; showers, bathrooms, LP gas available. D, MC, V.*

DINING

German-influenced Pennsylvania Dutch meals are hearty feasts prepared with local farm ingredients. To sample regional fare, try a family-style restaurant. Diners may sit with up to a dozen people, and a set menu of food is placed on the table in bowls that are passed around. The dishes include fried chicken, grilled ham, roast beef, dried corn, buttered noodles, mashed potatoes, bread, pepper cabbage, desserts, and beverages. Price categories per person, excluding 6% tax, service, and drinks, are Moderate, $15–$25, and Inexpensive, under $15.

BIRD-IN-HAND **Bird-in-Hand Family Restaurant.** This casual, diner-style restaurant serves hearty, home-cooked regional favorites such as chicken-corn soup. No liquor is served. *2760 Old Philadelphia Pike, tel. 717/ 768–8266. MC, V. Closed Sun. Inexpensive.*

EPHRATA **Nav Jiwan International Tea Room.** The name is Hindi for "new life," and they offer a lunch menu representing a dif-

ferent ethnic cuisine each week; dinner is served on Friday nights only. *240 N. Reading Rd. (Rte. 272), tel. 717/738–1101. MC, V. Inexpensive.*

Restaurant at Doneckers. A light-fare menu of classic and country French cuisine is served amid Colonial antiques in the Hearthside Café—a budget alternative to the much pricier formal menu. *333 N. State St., tel. 717/738–9501. AE, D, DC, MC, V. Moderate–Expensive.*

INTERCOURSE **Stoltzfus Farm Restaurant.** Homemade Pennsylvania Dutch foods, including meats butchered right on the farm, are served family style in this small country farmhouse. *Rte. 772 (½ mi east of Rte. 340), tel. 717/768–8156. MC, V. Closed Dec.–Mar. Inexpensive.*

LANCASTER **Market Fare.** In this cozy dining room with big armchairs and fine art, an American menu of steaks, seafood, and veal is served with homemade soups and fresh-baked breads. A menu of lighter choices is available, as is a menu for children. *Market and Grant Sts. across from Central Market, tel. 717/299–7090. AE, D, DC, MC, V. Moderate.*

MOUNT JOY **Bube's Brewery.** The only intact, pre-Prohibition U.S. brewery houses three first-rate restaurants (the brewery, however, no longer produces spirits): the casual Bottling Works for drinks and light meals; Alois's for more formal six-course dinners; and The Catacombs, where steaks and seafood are served in aging cellars 43 feet below ground. *102 N. Market St., tel. 717/653– 2056. AE, D, MC, V. Moderate.*

Groff's Farm. At this famous restored 1756 farmhouse, well-prepared Mennonite farm fare is served à la carte or family style to your private table. A rooftop deck has added alfresco dining to the Groff's award-winning restaurant. *650 Pinkerton Rd., tel. 717/653– 2048. AE, D, DC, MC, V. Moderate.*

RONKS **Miller's Smorgasbord.** One of the few local restaurants open Sundays, Miller's is known for its lavish buffets, including a sensational breakfast spread and a good sampling of Pennsylvania Dutch foods. *2811 Lincoln Hwy. E, tel. 717/687-6621 or 800/669-3568. AE, D, MC, V. Moderate.*

SMOKETOWN **Good 'N Plenty.** An Amish farmhouse has been remodeled into a bustling, family-style restaurant seating more than 600 for festive dining on tasty, home-cooked foods. *Rte. 896 (½ mi off U.S. 30), tel. 717/394-7111. MC, V. Inexpensive.*

SHOPPING

FACTORY OUTLETS A number of factory outlets line U.S. 30 near Route 896; at the intersection is **Rockvale Square Factory Outlet Village** (tel. 717/293-9595), the largest outlet center in Lancaster, with 120 stores and counting. The newest addition to outlet row is the designer **MillStream Factory Shops** (tel. 717/392-7202), with 52 outlets including Ann Taylor and Brooks Brothers.

FARMERS MARKETS AND ANTIQUES FAIRS On Sundays, antiques hunters flock to the huge antiques malls (Renninger's, Barr's, Black Angus) located on Route 272 between Adamstown and Denver, 1 mile west of Pennsylvania Turnpike Exit 21. The best farmer's markets are the **Central Market** in Lancaster (*see* Exploring, *above*), **Bird-in-Hand Farmers Market** (Rte. 340, Bird-in-Hand, tel. 717/393-9674), **Farmers Market at Doneckers** (100 N. State St., Ephrata, tel. 717/738-9555), and the **Green Dragon Farmers Market and Auction** (N. State St., Ephrata, tel. 717/738-1117; open Fri.), a traditional agricultural market with livestock auctions, food stalls, and a flea market.

SPECIALTY SHOPS The **Weathervane Shop** (Landis Valley Museum, 2451 Kissel Hill Rd., Lancaster, tel. 717/569-9312) carries handmade local crafts. For antique quilts, try **Pandora's** (Rte. 340, just east of U.S. 30, Lancaster, tel. 717/299-5305) or **Witmer Quilt Shop** (1070 W. Main St., New Holland, tel. 717/656-9526). The **Artworks at Doneckers** is a marketplace of 40 artists' galleries and studios (100 N. State St., Ephrata, tel. 717/738-9503).

OUTDOOR ACTIVITIES

BALLOONING The **Great Adventure Balloon Club** offers a bird's-eye view of Pennsylvania Dutch Country. You help inflate the balloon, maneuver the controls, and after a one-hour flight, land the craft in a farmer's field. *Lancaster, tel. 717/397-3623. Reservations required.*

BIKING The gently rolling back roads are ideal for bicycling. The **Pennsylvania Department of Transportation** (tel. 717/787-7350) publishes a state bicycling resource directory covering touring, mountain biking, racing, and bike clubs.

HIKING If you travel as far west in Lancaster County as Mount Joy, Marietta or Columbia, you should take the time to hike along the Susquehanna River. At **Chickies County Park** (Rte. 441 midway between Marietta and Columbia), a short path from the parking area leads to a bare rock outcropping with commanding views of the river as it snakes through the valley. **Lake Aldred** (tel. 717/284-2278) has 39 miles of hiking trails ranging from the mile-long Pequea Creek Nature Trail (for the novice) to the 15-mile-long section of the Conestoga Trail (for the more experienced). **Susquehannock State Park** (south of Rte. 372) and **Muddy Run Recreation Park** (Rte. 372 between Rte. 272 and the Susquehanna River) also have marked hiking trails.

Philadelphia
Pennsylvania

Updated by Rathe Miller

hey no longer roll up the sidewalks at night in Philadelphia: An entertainment boom, a restaurant renaissance, and a cultural revival have helped transform the birthplace of the nation into a city of superlatives. It has the world's largest municipal park, one of the best public collections of art in the United States, the widest variety of urban architecture in America, and the highest concentration of institutions of higher learning in the country.

Philadelphia extends north, south, and west from downtown into more than 100 neighborhoods covering 130 square miles. Center City, the popular name for the museums, business, and historic districts, radiates from City Hall. The Benjamin Franklin Parkway breaks the rigid grid pattern by leading diagonally out of downtown into Fairmount Park, which straddles the Schuylkill River and the Wissahickon Creek for 10 miles. If you stay at a downtown hotel, you can easily take in most of the city's major attractions on a two- or three-day visit.

ESSENTIAL INFORMATION

WHEN TO GO Although each of the four seasons brings distinct and pleasurable features to life in Philadelphia, late spring and early fall are the best times to visit. Philadelphia can be uncomfortably hot and humid in the summer, with temperatures ranging from 62° to 85°, and freezing cold in winter, when snowfalls average 21 inches and the temperature ranges from 26° to 49°. In the fall and spring, the atmosphere as well as the climate are comfortable and welcoming, with temperatures ranging from 50° to 76°.

FESTIVALS AND SEASONAL EVENTS **Jan. 1:** The Mummers Parade is an all-day event with 30,000 sequined and feathered paraders and musicians marching north up Broad Street to City Hall. **Mar.:** The Philadelphia Flower Show is the nation's largest indoor flower show, featuring acres of landscapes, flowers, and other exhibits. **Apr.–May:** Philadelphia Open House is a two-week period during which selected private homes, gardens, and historic buildings open their doors to the public. **July:** The Welcome America! Festival celebrates the nation's birth with several days of parades, hot-air-balloon races, ceremonies at Independence Hall, and a grand fireworks display. **Sept.:** Super Sunday turns the Benjamin Franklin Parkway into Philadelphia's biggest block party with food, entertainment, rides, and hundreds of exhibit booths. **Thanksgiving:** Thanksgiving Day Parade features thousands of marchers, floats, and local personalities. **Dec.:** Christmas festivities include the Pennsylvania Ballet's heartwarming rendition of *The Nutcracker* at Philadelphia's Academy of Music. **New Year's Eve:** Philly welcomes the new year with fireworks set to music over the Delaware River at Penn's Landing. Check with the Philadelphia Convention and Visitors Bureau (*see* Tourist Offices, *below*) for information relating to these and other events.

BARGAINS Philadelphia's number-one tourist attraction, **Independence National Historical Park** (tel. 215/597–8974), is also its number-one bargain. All the sites within the

PHILADELPHIA

George St.
Vineyard St.
Ridge Ave.
Poplar St.
Parrish St.
Parrish St.
Corinthian Ave.
27th St.
26th St.
25th St.
24th St.
23rd St.
Brown St.
North St.
Clay St.
Broad Street Subway
Aspen St.
Fairmount Ave.
Wallace St.
Mt. Vernon St.
19th St.
Green St.
Brandywine St.
Spring Garden St.
Philadelphia
Museum of Art
Hamilton St.
Buttonwood St.
Buttonwood St.
18th St.
Benjamin Franklin Parkway
Schuylkill River
Rodin
Museum
Callowhill
St.
Broad St.
17th St.
Ridge Ave.
76
30
676
30
Free Lilbrary
of Philadelphia
Vine St.
10th St.
Logan
Circle
Franklin Institute
Science Museum
and Fels Planetarium
23rd St.
Cathedral of
Saints Peter
and Paul
Race St.
Pennsylvania Convention Ce
Reading Terminal Market
Academy
of Natural
Sciences
Cherry St.
19th St.
Pennsylvania
Academy of the
Fine Arts
N
Arch St.
30th St.
Station
Airport Train (R1)
Suburban
Station
Filbert St.
Mar
Stat
J. F. Kennedy Blvd.
Market-Frankford Subway
30th St.
Subway-Surface
Market St.
City Hall
Broad St.
Ludlow St.
Chestnut St.
21st St.
Sansom St.
13th St.
11th St.
Sar
TO
AIRPORT
Walnut St.
20th St.
Rittenhouse
Square
16th St.
Juniper St.
Locust St.
Locust St.
76
Spruce St.
19th St.
17th St.
15th St.
Broad Street Subway
Quince St.
Schuylkill River
24th St.
25th St.
Pine St.
12th St.
Lombard St.
South St.
Bridge St.
22nd St.
Bainbridge St.
Fitzwater S
Grays Ferry Ave.
23rd St.
Pemberton St.
Fitzwater St.
Catharine St.
Christian S
0   440 yards
Webster St.
TO VETERANS
STADIUM,
SPECTRUM
0   400 meters
Christian St.
Carpenter St.

country's "most historic square mile" are free. For a free fun ride and a great view, take the City Hall elevator up to the observation deck at the foot of **William Penn's statue** (tel. 215/686–1776). And in Fairmount Park, **Boathouse Row** consists of 11 architecturally varied 19th-century buildings, home to the 13 rowing clubs dubbed the "Schuylkill Navy." The view of the houses from the west side of the river is splendid—especially at night, when they're outlined with hundreds of small lights.

Tickets to hear the world-famous **Philadelphia Orchestra** at the Academy of Music can cost around $50, but lawn seating is free for concerts under the stars during the orchestra's summer season at the Mann Music Center (tel. 215/878–7707 or 215/567–0707).

The **Philadelphia Museum of Art** (tel. 215/763–8100), one of the world's great museums, is free Sundays 10 AM–1 PM. The **Pennsylvania Academy of the Fine Arts** is free on Wednesdays 5:30–7:30 PM (tel. 215/972–7600).

You can save up to 50% on some theater tickets and other events at UpStages, the ticket booth at the **Philadelphia Arts Bank** (tel. 215/893–1145).

For fresh, cheap eats and an experience in itself, wander around the **Reading Terminal Market** (tel. 215/922–2317) and sample from the more than 80 stalls, lunch counters, and restaurants. You can get a taste of Philadelphia's most expensive restaurant, Le Bec-Fin (dinners cost $100), for under $15 at its downstairs bistro.

TOURIST OFFICES Philadelphia Visitors Center (16th St. and John F. Kennedy Blvd., 19102, tel. 215/636–1666 or 800/537–7676). **Philadelphia Convention and Visitors Bureau** (1515 Market St., Suite 2020, 19102, tel. 215/636–3300). **National Park Service Visitor Center** (3rd and Chestnut Sts., tel. 215/597–8974), for info on Independence National Historical Park.

EMERGENCIES Police, fire, and ambulance: Dial 911. **Hospitals:** Pennsylvania Hospital (8th and Spruce Sts., tel. 215/829–3358) is closest to the historic district; near City Hall is Hahnemann University Hospital (Broad and Vine Sts., tel. 215/448–7963). **Doctors:** For referrals, call the Philadelphia County Medical Society (tel. 215/563–5343). **Dentists:** For referrals, call the Philadelphia County Dental Society (tel. 215/925–6050). **Pharmacies:** The downtown pharmacy with the longest hours is Corson's Pharmacy (15th and Spruce Sts., tel. 215/735–1386); CVS Pharmacy (10th and Reed Sts., tel. 215/ 465–2130) in South Philadelphia is open 24 hours.

ARRIVING AND DEPARTING

BY PLANE **Philadelphia International Airport** (tel. 215/492–3181) is located in the southwestern part of the city, 8 miles from downtown.

Between The Airport And Downtown: The Airport Express train is an easy and relatively cheap way to travel between the airport and downtown. The downtown stops are 30th Street Station (30th and Market Sts.), Suburban Station (16th St. and John F. Kennedy Blvd.), and Market East Station (10th and Market Sts.). It runs every 30 minutes from 6:10 AM to 12:10 AM. The trip takes 20 minutes and costs $5.

Taxis line up at every exit door of the terminals. The 20-minute trip into town will cost about $20, plus tip, varying slightly in heavier traffic. A few steps from the taxis are the "limos" (vans, not limousines). At about $8 per person, limos are cheaper, but service is less frequent and they stop only at certain hotels and downtown points.

BY BUS **Greyhound Lines** (tel. 800/231–2222) operates out of a terminal at 10th and Filbert streets, just north of the Market Street East commuter rail station.

GETTING AROUND

ON FOOT Foot power is the best way to see downtown Philadelphia. William Penn laid out his original city—today's compact 2-square-mile downtown—in a simple grid pattern with numbered streets starting with Front Street near the Delaware River and running west to 26th Street near the Schuylkill River. City Hall at Broad (14th Street) and Market streets is thought of as the center of town. Divide your sightseeing between the historic district and the riverfront on the east, and the museum-Parkway area on the west.

BY CAR You don't need a car to see Philadelphia. Parking is difficult and expensive downtown. Illegally parked cars are ticketed and towed. If you do have a car with you, leave it in the hotel garage and travel around downtown by public transportation or on foot.

BY BUS Philadelphia has a good network of buses, trolleys, and subways. A day pass entitles you to unlimited rides within a 24-hour period on all **Southeastern Pennsylvania Transportation Authority** (SEPTA; tel. 215/580–7800) buses, streetcars, subways, and elevated lines in the city, plus one ride on any regional rail line, including the Airport Express train. Call for fare and route information.

BY TRAIN Commuter trains are your best bet for reaching outlying destinations such as Germantown, Chestnut Hill, Merion Station (site of the Barnes Foundation), and other suburbs. Call SEPTA (tel. 215/580–7800) for route information.

BY TAXI Cabs are plentiful downtown during the day. It's harder to get one at night, though they can usually be found at the hotels, train stations, and along Broad Street or South Street. A 10%–15% tip is standard. The main cab companies are **Yellow** (tel. 215/922–8400), **United Cab** (tel. 215/238–9500), and **Quaker City Cab** (tel. 215/728–8000).

REST STOPS You don't have to pay over $200 a night to enjoy the elegance and comfort of one of Philadelphia's luxury hotels—just visit the lobby. The Rittenhouse (210 W. Rittenhouse Sq.), the Four Seasons (18th and the Parkway), and the Sheraton–Society Hill (2nd and Walnut Sts.) are the three best for lobby lounging—and the bathrooms are terrific.

Good public lavatories can be found at Borders Bookstore (1727 Walnut St.), Free Library (Rittenhouse Sq. W), Visitors Center (3rd St. below Chestnut St.), and Wanamaker's Department Store (13th and Market Sts.).

GUIDED TOURS Boating: Sightseeing cruises on the Delaware River are offered by the **Spirit of Philadelphia** (tel. 215/923–1419) and **Liberty Belle II** (tel. 215/629–1131).

Orientation: Philadelphia has no orientation tours per se, but **Gray Line Tours** (tel. 215/569–3666) has full-size bus tours of the historic and cultural areas. **Old Town Trolley** (tel. 215/928–8687) gives a two-hour tour in a Victorian-style trolley bus of the downtown area and Fairmount Park, with unlimited on-offs.

Walking: Audio Walk and Tour (tel. 215/925–1234) offers go-at-your-own-pace tours of the historic area, with cassette and tape player for rent and an accompanying map. Theme tours from the **Foundation for Architecture Tours** (tel. 215/569–3187) focus on architecture but touch on the history and development of each area covered.

EXPLORING

HISTORIC DISTRICT The National Park Service administers **Independence National Historical Park** and calls it "the most historic square mile in America." The first eight sights are located in the park area. All have free admission and the same telephone number (tel. 215/597–8974).

Start your tour at the **Visitor Center** (3rd and Chestnut Sts.). The park rangers behind the counter will answer your questions and supply maps and brochures. Catch the 28-minute movie, *Independence,* dramatizing the events surrounding the birth of the nation.

Directly across 3rd Street is the **First Bank of the United States** (3rd and Chestnut Sts.). The carving on the pediment is one of the few remaining examples of 18th-century wood carving. Next to the bank is a wrought-iron gateway topped by an eagle. Pass through it and you step out of modern-day Philadelphia and into Colonial America.

At the gateway begins a redbrick path that leads past a dozen important historic buildings. **Carpenter's Hall** (320 Chestnut St.) is where the first Continental Congress convened in 1774 and addressed a declaration of rights and grievances to King George III. Next door is the **New Hall Military Museum,** which depicts highlights of the Revolutionary War and displays weapons, uniforms, and medals dating from 1775 to 1815.

As you continue west and cross 5th Street, you'll arrive at **Independence Square,** where on July 8, 1776, the Declaration of Independence was first read in public. A few more steps and you're at **Independence Hall** (Chestnut St. between 5th and 6th Sts.) where on July 4, 1776, the Declaration of Independence was adopted; in 1778, the Articles of Confederation was signed; and in 1787, the Constitution was formally adopted. Tours start from the east wing (Old City Hall) and last about 35 minutes.

One block north of Independence Hall is Philadelphia's best-known symbol, the **Liberty Bell** (Market St. between 5th and 6th Sts.). For now, you're still allowed to touch the 2,080-pound bell and read its biblical inscription: "Proclaim liberty throughout all the land unto all the inhabitants thereof." Rangers will tell you stories about the bell, including the tale of its famous crack. After hours, you can still see the bell in its glass-enclosed pavilion and press a button on the outside wall to hear a recorded account of its history.

Five blocks to the east is the Delaware River and **Penn's Landing**—the spot where William Penn stepped ashore in 1682—now a 37-acre park. Attractions here include the new **Independence Seaport Museum** (tel. 215/925–5439) with interactive exhibits that kids love;

the **USS Olympia** (tel. 215/922–1898), Commodore George Dewey's flagship at the battle of Manila in the Spanish-American War; and the **USS Becuna** (tel. 215/922–1898), a World War II "search and destroy" submarine. *Open daily. Park admission free. Admission charged for museum and ships.*

Other sites you'll be walking near on this tour include **Christ Church** (2nd St. above Market St., tel. 215/922–1695; open daily; admission free), where 15 signers of the Declaration worshiped; **Elfreth's Alley** (off Front and 2nd Sts. between Arch and Race Sts., tel. 215/574–0560), the oldest continuously occupied street in America; **Betsy Ross House** (239 Arch St., tel. 215/627–5343; open Tues.–Sun.; admission free); the **United States Mint** (5th and Arch Sts., tel. 215/597–7350; open Mon.–Sat.; admission free); and the **Graff House** (7th and Market Sts., tel. 215/597–8974; open daily; admission free), where Thomas Jefferson wrote the Declaration of Independence.

CENTER CITY AND BENJAMIN FRANKLIN PARKWAY

Stroll west down Market Street, turn right on 12th Street, and walk one block north to the **Pennsylvania Convention Center** (12th and Arch Sts., tel. 215/418–4700). This $522 million brick-and-granite complex opened in 1993, with a main exhibit hall that could swallow up seven football fields. You can sneak a peek at the best part—the magnificently restored Reading Terminal Train Shed—by crossing the skybridge from the third floor of the Philadelphia Marriott next door.

Walk west two blocks to Broad Street to the **Pennsylvania Academy of the Fine Arts.** This architecturally extravagant building (designed by Philadelphian Frank Furness) is the oldest art institution in the United States (founded in 1804) and houses a collection that ranges from Winslow Homer to Andrew Wyeth to Red Grooms. *Broad and Cherry Sts., tel. 215/972–7600. Open daily. Admission charged.*

Head west on Cherry Street for two blocks to the **Benjamin Franklin Parkway,** which angles across the city's grid system from City

Hall to Fairmount Park. This 250-foot-wide boulevard, inspired by Paris's Champs-Elysées, is adorned with fountains, statues, trees, and flags of every country.

Walk northwest one block to **Logan Circle,** where you'll see the beautiful **Swann Fountain.** Cross Logan Circle to the south for the **Academy of Natural Sciences** (19th St. and Benjamin Franklin Pkwy., tel. 215/299–1020; open daily; admission charged), America's first museum of natural history, founded in 1812. On the east side of Logan Circle is the **Cathedral of Saints Peter and Paul** (18th and Race Sts., tel. 215/561–1313; open daily; admission free), the basilica of the Archdiocese of Philadelphia. On the north side is the **Free Library of Philadelphia** (19th St. and Benjamin Franklin Pkwy., tel. 215/686–5322; open daily; admission free), a Greek Revival building housing over 1 million volumes.

On the west side is the **Franklin Institute Science Museum.** The Institute is actually four major attractions, including the Science Center, the Fels Planetarium, and the $72 million Mandell Center and Omniverse Theater with its 79-foot domed screen. *20th St. and Benjamin Franklin Pkwy., tel. 215/448–1200. Open daily. Admission charged.*

Go two blocks farther up the Parkway to the **Rodin Museum,** a jewel box of a museum housing the best collection of Auguste Rodin's works outside of France. Even if you don't go in, walk up to the door and marvel at the 21-foot sculpture *The Gates of Hell. 22nd St. and Benjamin Franklin Pkwy., tel. 215/586–6026. Open Tues.–Sun. Donations requested.*

Crowning the top of the Parkway is Philadelphia's cultural triumph, the **Philadelphia Museum of Art.** Walk or run up the 99 steps, made famous in the movie *Rocky,* to the massive Greek temple–style building, covering 10 acres, with 200 galleries and over 300,000 works. *26th St. and Benjamin Franklin Pkwy., tel. 215/763–8100. Open Tues.–Sun. Admission charged.*

And finally, just over the city line at Merion Station (Montgomery County) is one of the great collections of paintings in the world. The **Barnes Foundation** contains more than 1,000 works—including 175 Renoirs, 66 Cézannes, 65 Matisses, and numerous works by van Gogh, Rousseau, Degas, El Greco, and many others. The museum reopened in 1995 after a two-year renovation. User-friendly improvements include a gift shop, catalogue, CD-ROM, and an audio-tour system. Take the Main Line Local commuter train to Merion Station, and it's a pleasant 10-minute walk east from the station. *300 Latch's La., Merion Station, tel. 610/667–0290. Call for hrs. Admission charged.*

HOTELS AND INNS

Although the number of rooms—13,120—is small for a city of nearly a million and a half, the 1,200-room Marriott that opened in 1995 boosted the room count substantially. For the time being, hotel reservations are advised. Most of the hotels in downtown Philadelphia are located in three areas: the main shopping and theater district that encompasses a few blocks on either side of Broad Street, near Walnut Street; the Parkway-museum area that runs along the Benjamin Franklin Parkway from 16th Street to the Philadelphia Museum of Art; and the historic district on the east side of downtown that centers on Independence Hall and the Liberty Bell and extends to the Delaware River.

Price categories for double occupancy, excluding 12% tax, are Expensive, over $100; Moderate, $60–$100; and Inexpensive, under $60.

EXPENSIVE The **Barclay.** Rittenhouse Square (Philadelphia's poshest downtown park) is right outside your door when you stay in this elegant 1929 hotel with four-poster or canopied beds. *Rittenhouse Sq. E, 19103, tel. 215/545–0300 or 800/421–6662, fax 215/545–2896. 105 rooms. Restaurant, lobby lounge with jazz pianist, concierge. AE, D, DC, MC, V.*

Holiday Inn–Independence Mall. As the name indicates, the location is most conve-nient to the historic district (it's around the corner from the Liberty Bell). Colonial furni-ture, including poster beds and wing chairs, adds to the appeal of this family-oriented hotel. *4th and Arch Sts., 19106, tel. 215/923–8660 or 800/465–4329, fax 215/923–4633. 364 rooms. Restaurant, outdoor pool, gift shop. AE, D, DC, MC, V.*

Holiday Inn–Midtown. This 1964-vintage hotel has spacious rooms decorated with prints of Philadelphia scenes or floral motifs; it also has an excellent central loca-tion in the theater and shopping district. *1305 Walnut St., 19107, tel. 215/735–9300 or 800/465–4329. 166 rooms. Restaurant, lounge, outdoor pool, no-smoking rooms. AE, D, DC, MC, V.*

The Warwick. Guests stay in spacious rooms decorated in "English country-style" and mix in the bright, busy lobby with those who live in the apartments that make up half of the rooms in this stylish hotel. Capricco, the European-style café, serves desserts and espresso until the wee hours. *17th and Locust Sts., 19103, tel. 215/735–6000 or 800/523–4210, fax 215/790–7766. 153 rooms. Restaurant, bar, business center, weekend theater package. AE, DC, MC, V.*

MODERATE **Clarion Suites.** Because of the slightly out-of-the-way location in China-town, you get suite accommodations (with kitchen, some with exposed brick, and over-head wooden beams) at hotel-room prices in this historically certified building that was once a rocking-chair factory. *1010 Race St., 19107, tel. 215/922–1730 or 800/628–8932, fax 215/922–6258. 96 suites. Buffet breakfast included, discount parking. AE, D, DC, MC, V.*

Comfort Inn at Penn's Landing. The location has more noise than charm (tucked between the Benjamin Franklin Bridge, Delaware Avenue, and I–95), but this 10-story hotel, opened in 1987, gives fine basic rooms and service at a good price. *100 N. Delaware Ave., 19106, tel. 215/627–7900 or 800/228–5150, fax 215/238–0809. 185 rooms. Conti-nental deluxe breakfast included, lobby lounge, free parking. AE, D, DC, MC, V.*

Shippen Way Inn. Two adjacent 18th-century houses have been turned into a Colonial-style inn. Most rooms have original exposed wooden beams, wide plank floors, and antiques. *416–18 Bainbridge St., tel. 215/627–7266 or 800/245–4873, fax 215/ 271–2690. 9 rooms. Full breakfast, living room with TV and fireplace, courtyard. AE, MC, V.*

Society Hill Hotel. This 1832 former longshoremen's house is one of the smallest hotels in the city. All 12 of the rooms are uniquely furnished with antiques and brass beds. *301 Chestnut St., 19106, tel. 215/925– 1394, fax 215/925–3780. 12 rooms, including 6 suites. Restaurant, piano bar, outdoor café. AE, DC, MC, V.*

Thomas Bond House. This 1769, four-story house in the heart of Old City, has been faithfully restored with 18th-century features, from the molding and wall sconces to the marble fireplaces and four-poster beds. *129 S. 2nd St., 19106, tel. 215/923–8523 or 800/ 845–2663, fax 215/923–8504. 12 rooms, including 2 suites. Parlor, complimentary wine and cheese. AE, D, DC, MC, V.*

■■INEXPENSIVE■■ Bed-and-breakfasts are often a less expensive alternative to hotels. Most operate under the auspices of central booking agencies that screen and match guests and homes.

Bed and Breakfast Connections/Philadelphia has a selection of more than 100 host homes that includes a Colonial town house, an English Tudor mansion in Chestnut Hill, and an 18th-century farmhouse on the Main Line. Prices range from $35 to $125. *Box 21, Devon 19333, tel. 610/687–3565 or 800/ 448–3619. AE, MC, V.*

DINING

Since the "restaurant renaissance" of the early 1970s, Philadelphia has become a first-class restaurant city. There is no specific Philadelphia cuisine—unless you count soft pretzels, cheese steaks, hoagies, and Tastykakes.

All restaurant locations listed as Center City are within a 10-minute walk from Broad and Walnut streets. Society Hill and Old City are in the Historic District of downtown near the Delaware River. Price categories per person, excluding 6% tax, service, and drinks, are Moderate, $15–$25, and Inexpensive, under $15.

■■MODERATE■■ **Carolina's.** Cobb salad (a flaky tortilla shell stuffed with chicken, avocado, bleu cheese, black olives, tomato, and romaine lettuce) is one of the popular dishes at this Center City favorite, offering good-size portions from a large menu of sandwiches, pastas, and a dozen entrées. *261 S. 20th St., near Rittenhouse Sq., tel. 215/545– 1000. AE, D, DC, MC. V.*

Downey's. There's Irish memorabilia on the walls, Irish stew on the menu, and always a lively crowd on hand at this popular South Street bar and restaurant. *Front and South Sts., Society Hill, tel. 215/629–0525. AE, D, DC, MC, V.*

Middle East. This Old City favorite is as well known for its sultan's-palace decor and belly dancers as for its first-rate menu—filled with dishes from Lebanon and other Middle Eastern countries. *126 Chestnut St., Old City, tel. 215/922–1003. AE, D, DC, MC, V.*

Sansom Street Oyster House. This unpretentious place, with the family collection of oyster plates lining the walls, serves some of Philly's best raw oysters, plus clams, fish, shellfish, and grilled and blackened dishes. *1516 Sansom St., Center City, tel. 215/567– 7683. AE, D, DC, MC, V.*

Tequila's. This is the place to go in Philadelphia for Mexican food: From the lemon-based seviche (a favorite is the lobster stuffed with pineapple) to the crepes with goat's milk syrup for dessert, Tequila's puts a creative twist on authentic Mexican dishes. *1511 Locust St., Center City, tel. 215/546– 0181. AE, DC, MC, V.*

Victor Cafe. If you like northern Italian cuisine—and if you love opera—the Victor Cafe offers a changing menu of pastas and grilled meats, plus operatic waiters and waitresses who burst into song at regular intervals. *1303 Dickinson St., South Philadelphia, tel. 215/468–3040. AE, DC, MC, V.*

White Dog Café. *The* restaurant in West Philadelphia serves excellent regional cuisine with the finest local products. University of Pennsylvania students and professors crowd around the lively bar and in the Victorian piano lounge. *3420 Sansom St., tel. 215/386–9224. AE, DC, MC, V.*

INEXPENSIVE **Chef Theodore.** Here's the best Greek food in town, and lots of it. Try the bargain-priced *meze*—a combination plate of eight delicacies, including marinated octopus and stuffed grape leaves. *1100 S. Delaware Ave., South Philadelphia, tel. 215/271–6800. AE, DC, MC, V.*

Joe's Peking Duck. Philadelphia's Chinatown has more than 50 restaurants, and this is the best—friendly atmosphere, plain decor, and great food. *925 Race St., Chinatown, tel. 215/922–3277. No credit cards.*

Melrose Diner. This classic Philadelphia diner serves nothing elaborate but offers top-quality diner meals—creamed chipped beef, breaded shrimp, apple pie with vanilla sauce—at bargain prices. It's also open 24 hours. *1501 Snyder Ave., tel. 215/467–6644. No credit cards.*

Reading Terminal Market. If you're hungry and not sure what you want to eat, this is the place. A one-square-block market with more than 80 food shops, stalls, and lunch counters gives you a choice of Chinese, Greek, Mexican, Japanese, Italian, Pennsylvania Dutch, seafood, soul food, and hoagies. *12th and Arch Sts., Center City, tel. 215/922–2317.*

Van's Garden. This is the least expensive Asian restaurant in Philadelphia—a variety of traditional noodle dishes topped with barbecued pork or beef can be had for less than $5—yet the food is definitely first-rate. *121 N. 11th St., Chinatown, tel. 215/923–2439. No credit cards.*

SHOPPING

Philadelphia has a wide array of stores and shopping areas. It has an upscale shopping district centered on 17th and Walnut streets, a jewelers' row (Sansom St., between 7th and 8th Sts.), an antiques row (Pine St., between 9th and 12th Sts.), and three enclosed downtown shopping malls (*see Malls, below*).

DEPARTMENT STORES **Strawbridge and Clothier** (8th and Markets Sts., tel. 215/629–6000) founded in 1868, is still operated by the Clothier and Strawbridge families and is the only independent regional department store left in the country.

MAIN SHOPPING DISTRICTS **South Street.** From Front Street to 9th Street you'll find more than 300 unusual stores—new-wave and high-fashion clothing, New Age books, avant-garde art galleries, and 100 restaurants. There's great window-shopping and people-watching, especially in the evenings.

Walnut Street. The leading shopping area is Walnut Street between Broad Street and Rittenhouse Square, and the intersecting streets just north and south. These blocks are filled with boutiques, art galleries, jewelers, fine-clothing stores, and many other shops. **Borders Book Shop** (1727 Walnut St., tel. 215/568–7400) is the biggest, best, and friendliest bookstore in town, complete with espresso bar.

MALLS The **Gallery at Market East** (Market St. from 8th to 11th Sts., tel. 215/925–7162) is America's first enclosed downtown shopping mall. The four-level, glass-roofed structure contains 160 shops and restaurants and two department stores—Strawbridge and Clothier (tel. 215/629–6000) and JCPenney (tel. 215/238–9100). The **Shops at Liberty Place** (17th and Chestnut Sts., tel. 215/851–9000) houses 70 shops and a food court placed around two levels of a circular 90-foot glass atrium.

SOUVENIR AND GIFT SHOPS The bookstore–gift shop at the **Visitor Center** (3rd and Chestnut Sts., tel. 215/597–8974) specializes in items related to Colonial Philadelphia and the Revolution. **Destination Philadelphia** (Bourse Bldg., 21 S. 5th St., tel. 215/440–0233) is a clothing store where every item bears some form of Philadelphia logo or design.

OUTDOOR ACTIVITIES

BIKING A treat for bikers is to ride out on the east side of the Schuylkill River, cross Falls Bridge, and return on the west side of the river. The scenic 8.2-mile loop has no hills and takes about an hour of casual pedaling.

GOLF Philadelphia has six city golf courses open to the public. The most difficult is **Cobbs Creek** (7800 Landsdowne Ave., tel. 215/877–8707) and the shortest is **Walnut Lane** (Walnut La. and Henry Ave., tel. 215/482–3370). Try to call a few days ahead to reserve tee times.

JOGGING AND HIKING The best locale for jogging and hiking is Forbidden Drive in the Wissahickon Valley in Fairmount Park, with more than 5 miles through a beautiful forested gorge, with no automobile traffic allowed.

ENTERTAINMENT

BALLET AND DANCE The **Pennsylvania Ballet** (tel. 215/551–7000) dances at the Academy of Music from October to June. Philadanco, **Philadelphia Dance Company** (tel. 215/387–8200), performs modern dance at the Annenberg Center (3680 Walnut St., tel. 215/898–6791) and other locations.

CONCERTS The world-renowned Philadelphia Orchestra performs at the **Academy of Music** (Broad and Locust Sts., tel. 215/893–1900) from September to May and at the **Mann Music Center** (W. Fairmount Park, tel. 215/878–7707) in the summer. The **Curtis Institute of Music** (1726 Locust St., tel. 215/893–5261) presents free student recitals every Monday, Wednesday, and Friday of the school year.

FILM The **Ritz Five** (214 Walnut St., tel. 215/925–7900) and **Ritz at the Bourse** (4th St. north of Chestnut St., tel. 215/440–1181) are the finest movie theaters in town for avant-garde and foreign films.

SPECTATOR SPORTS The major league holds home games in the sports complex at Broad Street and Pattison Avenue. The **Phillies** (tel. 215/463–1000) baseball team and the **Eagles** (tel. 215/463–5500) football team play at Veterans Stadium. The **76ers** (tel. 215/339–7676) basketball team and the **Flyers** (tel. 215/755–9700) hockey team play at the Spectrum. The **CoreStates Pro Cycling Championship** (tel. 215/636–1666) races along Philadelphia streets every June, and the **U.S. Pro Indoor Tennis Championships** (tel. 215/336–3600) are held each February.

THEATER The **Forrest Theater** (1114 Walnut St., tel. 215/923–1515) has major Broadway productions. The **Walnut Street Theater** (9th and Walnut Sts., tel. 215/574–3550) has comedies, musicals, and dramas in an auditorium where almost every seat is a good one. The **Wilma Theater** (2030 Sansom St., tel. 215/963–0345) is a smaller theater that has gained critical acclaim for its innovative work.

Rocky Mountain National Park
Colorado

Updated by Janet Lee

ithin a single hour's drive, you ascend from 7,800 feet, at park headquarters, to 12,183 feet at the apex of Trail Ridge Road. Sweeping vistas from atop this vantage, the highest continuous paved road in the United States, take in the high-country lakes and meadows flushed with wildflowers, rushing mountain streams, and cool, dense forests of lodgepole pines and blue spruce that lie below. Above are snow-dusted peaks that seem to float in the sky, small glaciers, patches of blue Colorado columbine, and finally, a fragile, treeless ecosystem of alpine tundra seldom found outside the Arctic. Rocky Mountain National Park in Colorado isn't a pretty passage; it's a moment of grandeur.

Today, the visitor can see evidence of the park's long (1.8 billion years) and varied past. Scientists estimate that 530 million years ago the park was covered by water, which eventually receded and left tropical plains inhabited by dinosaurs. Erupting volcanoes came next—violent uplifts that created the Rocky Mountains. The glaciers that followed left the park as it looks now, full of valleys and peaks carved by ice.

With 355 miles of hiking trails, trail rides, bus tours, rock-climbing, golf courses, bike routes, fishing, and fine dining, the region delights both mountain explorers and those to whom roughing it is staying at an elegant country hotel. In Rocky, as the locals call it, you won't feel that you're just visiting the mountains; you'll be living up in the sky, too.

ESSENTIAL INFORMATION

WHEN TO GO The great advantage of traveling to Rocky in the summertime is that conditions are gentle and you can see and hike through much more of the park. The drawback is the people; they are everywhere, and so are their cars, trucks, and RVs. Summer is, however, the best time to drive across the 45-mile Trail Ridge Road; the road closes with the first heavy snowfall—sometime between the end of September and mid-October—and does not reopen until Memorial Day. The best time to come here is early fall—after the crush of people and cars has gone and before the cold weather sets in—although some parts of Rocky remain crowded into the leaf-gazing season in early fall. In wintertime, the east slope of the park at lower elevations is usually free of snow, but higher up there are blizzards and impassable drifts.

Due to the altitude, weather in the park is very changeable. Most of the improved campgrounds are below 9,400 feet, and conditions there are usually better than at higher elevations (on Trail Ridge Road it can snow even in July). Spring comes late, but by May much of the snow has melted and the wildflowers are in bloom. Summer days often reach into the 70s or 80s but drop into the 40s at night. July is the warmest month, with frequent late-day showers. August is the wettest period. September sees rain and snow, with temperatures in the 70s in the daytime and falling into the 30s at night. October is colder and snowier, particularly on the west side, but November's snowfall is usually light, and skiing is not yet satisfactory. December and Jan-

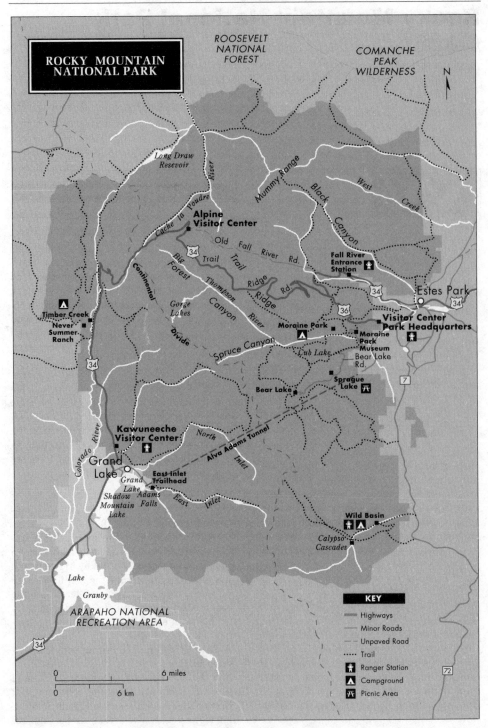

ROCKY MOUNTAIN NATIONAL PARK

ROOSEVELT NATIONAL FOREST

COMANCHE PEAK WILDERNESS

N

Long Draw Resevoir

Cache la Poudre River

Mummy Range

Black Canyon

West Creek

Alpine Visitor Center

Old Fall River Rd.

Fall River Trail

Fall River Entrance Station

Big Forest

Thompson River

Ridge Rd.

Estes Park

Continental

Gorge Lakes

Canyon

Moraine Park

Visitor Center Park Headquarters

Divide

Spruce Canyon

Cub Lake

Moraine Park Museum

Bear Lake Rd.

Colorado River

Sprague Lake

Timber Creek Never Summer Ranch

Bear Lake

Kawuneeche Visitor Center

North Inlet

Alva Adams Tunnel

Grand Lake

Grand Lake

East Inlet Trailhead

Adams Falls

East Inlet

Shadow Mountain Lake

Wild Basin

Calypso Cascades

Lake Granby

ARAPAHO NATIONAL RECREATION AREA

KEY

Highways
Minor Roads
Unpaved Road
Trail
Ranger Station
Campground
Picnic Area

uary are cold, and at high elevations the windchill factor can be nasty. For the park's recorded weather forecast, call 970/586–1333.

TOURIST OFFICES **Park Headquarters** (Superintendent, Rocky Mountain National Park, Estes Park 80517-8397, tel. 970/586–1206). **Estes Park Chamber of Commerce** (500 Big Thompson Ave., Estes Park 80517, tel. 800/443–7837).

EMERGENCIES **Police, fire,** and **ambulance:** Dial 911. **Doctors:** Estes Park Medical Center (555 Prospect Ave., Estes Park, tel. 970/586–2317).

ARRIVING AND DEPARTING

BY PLANE The nearest airport is **Denver International Airport** (tel. 303/342–2000) in Denver, 75 miles southeast of the park. In summertime, allow two hours to drive from the airport to Rocky—the roads are generally two-lane and traffic can be heavy.

BY CAR From the east the best way to reach the park is on U.S. 34 or U.S. 36. Inside the park, U.S. 34 becomes Trail Ridge Road, which carries you across the Continental Divide and into Grand Lake. If you want to come in on the western, more scenic side of Rocky but you're in Denver, take I–70 to U.S. 40 and turn north. Just past Granby go north on U.S. 34 toward the park. Grand Lake is about 100 miles northwest of Denver.

BY TRAIN **Amtrak** (tel. 800/872–7245) trains from around the country stop at Union Station in Denver, but there is no train service to Estes Park or Grand Lake.

BY BUS **Charles Tour and Travel** (tel. 970/586–5151) operates charter buses between Denver and Estes Park year-round. Tickets are around $30, and the bus drops you off at your lodging. Charles Tour and Travel also offers tour packages through the park.

GETTING AROUND

ON FOOT The sweeping vistas are stupendous from inside an automobile or bus but even better when you leave your car and take a hike. Small trails are plentiful in every direction.

BY BUS In the summertime, a free shuttle bus runs daily from the Glacier Basin parking lot to Bear Lake. Buses leave every half hour from 8 AM to 9:30 AM and approximately every 12–15 minutes from 9:30 AM to 5:30 PM. From mid-August to the end of September it runs only on weekends.

BY CAR Since Rocky has only three paved roads, the driving options are limited.

REST STOPS Rocky has many public rest rooms at rest stops along Trail Ridge Road, at the Longs Peak campground, and at the visitor centers at Rocky's eastern and western entrances.

GUIDED TOURS Free ranger-led tours covering different aspects and areas of the park are offered regularly. One of the best tours is "Rocky after Dark," in which a ranger leads visitors into the park after sundown to observe the animals' nocturnal habits. Tundra walks are also recommended, but they are rigorous, involving two to three hours of hiking at high altitudes. *High Country Headlines,* a free publication found at the park's visitor centers and ranger stations, has a listing of tours with meeting times and places.

EXPLORING

Trail Ridge Road is the main paved road cutting through the park. In normal summer traffic, Trail Ridge Road is about a two-hour drive from the west to the east side. There are many gradual climbs and turnoffs, and the grade does not exceed 7°.

Begin your tour at the **Kawuneeche Visitor Center** on U.S. 34 at the west entrance to the park, and watch the 22-minute film on Rocky. The center also has exhibits, maps, and booklets on virtually every aspect of the park. *Tel. 970/586–2371. Open daily. Admission free.*

Backtrack on U.S. 34 to Grand Lake and make a left on West Portal Road to reach the

East Inlet Trailhead. From here, it's a pleasant ³⁄₁₀-mile walk to **Adams Falls,** an excellent spot for a picnic.

Head back up U.S. 34 past the Kawuneeche Visitor Center. About 7½ miles up the road on the west side is a turnoff called **Never Summer Ranch,** a working ranch in the early 1900s. From the road it's a short walk to the ranch. *Tel. 970/586–1206. Open June 15–Labor Day, daily. Admission free.*

Continue along U.S. 34 to the **Alpine Visitor Center.** Nearby is Trail Ridge Store, the only snack bar in the park and a good place to stop for lunch. After eating, attend one of the ranger-led programs at the center. Then take Trail Ridge Road back toward Estes Park. *Open daily, except when Trail Ridge Rd. is closed (mid-Oct.–Memorial Day). Admission free.*

Old Fall River Road runs for 9 miles, from Horseshoe Park west to Fall River Pass. The original road crossing the mountains, Old Fall River Road, is one-way and uphill and features a gravel surface and many switchbacks. For the best one-day driving tour, drive up the road to the Alpine Visitor Center.

Along the 9.2-mile **Bear Lake Road,** the **Moraine Park Museum** houses natural-history exhibits, including a depiction of the process of glaciation in the area. Adjacent to the museum is another building that can be viewed from a distance—the **William Allen White Cabin,** named after the famous Kansas journalist who wrote here during the summers. Visiting artisans now use the cabin in the warm months, so it's not open to the public. *Museum: tel. 970/586–1206. Open May–Sept., daily. Admission free.*

The road leading west off Bear Lake Road, across from the museum, leads to the **Cub Lake area.** The 4.6-mile (round-trip) trek is a moderate one, providing the best hiking experience for one day.

Farther down Bear Lake Road, stop at Sprague Lake and walk the half mile around it. At the end of Bear Lake Road is Bear Lake, a good place to spot magpies. The half-mile walk to Nymph Lake is relatively even, with only a 225-foot climb in elevation.

THE NATURAL WORLD The park's ecosystem has great variety: 66 species of mammals, 260 species of birds, and 900 species of plants. A few black bears remain in Rocky. Mountain lions and bobcats are seldom seen. Bighorn sheep are a more common sight, especially along Big Thompson Canyon. Moose have been spied in the willows of the Kawuneeche Valley. In autumn, herds of elk wander down to lower elevations and are most often visible at early morning or evening. The beavers usually work at night. Squirrels, chipmunks, and marmots are seen everywhere. Some people find these small mammals cute, but they can carry rabies and should not be befriended or fed.

Broad-tailed hummingbirds, woodpeckers, peregrine falcons, mountain jays, Steller's jays, and scores of other birds add color to the park. The white-tailed ptarmigan—pure white in its winter feathers—spends the year on the alpine tundra. At visitor centers and park information booths, employees will tell you the best sites for bird-watching. Vegetation includes such wildflowers as the wood lily, the wild iris, and the yellow lady's slipper orchid.

HOTELS AND INNS

There are no hotels within Rocky itself, but the surrounding area offers a range of everything from upscale hotels and resorts to bed-and-breakfasts, cabins by the river, vacation homes and condominiums, and guest ranches. The Estes Park area alone has nearly 75 different overnight options, and Grand Lake offers numerous other possibilities. For a complete guide to accommodations in Estes Park, call the Chamber of Commerce Lodging Referral Service at 970/586–4431 or 800/443–7837. Price categories for double occupancy, excluding 7% tax, are Expensive, over $100; Moderate, $50–$100; and Inexpensive, under $50.

ESTES PARK **Aspen Lodge.** Located 8 miles south of Estes Park on Highway 7, the "ultimate family resort" has your pick of family reunion packages. Whether you stay in the main lodge or in an adjoining cabin, the decor is rugged alpine all the way. *6120 Hwy. 7, 80517, tel. and fax 970/586–8133 or tel. 800/332–6867. 36 rooms, 23 cabins. Meals included in summer, 3-night weekend stay required. Pool, sauna, hot tub. AE, D, DC, MC, V. Expensive.*

Estes Park Center/YMCA of the Rockies. Cabins on this huge, bucolic property have kitchens with stoves and refrigerators; some cabins have fireplaces. *2515 Tunnel Rd., 80511-2800, tel. 970/586–3341, fax 970/ 586–6078. 200 cabins. Restaurant, library, museum. No credit cards. Inexpensive– Moderate.*

Riversong Bed and Breakfast. The bedrooms in this elegant, romantic hideaway feature antique furniture and fireplaces. Some even have sunken bathtubs. *Box 1910, 80517, tel. 970/586–4666. 9 rooms with bath. MC, V. Expensive.*

Stanley Hotel. The classiest of the local hotels, The Stanley features both 19th-century elegance and modern conveniences. The hotel exterior is of old-fashioned, white-painted wood; the guest rooms, continually renovated and redone to their original 19th-century decor, match the exquisite public rooms. The hotel was just purchased and although nobody is sure what will happen, locals are confident that the new owners will be making much-needed improvements. *333 Wonderview, Box 1767, 80517, tel. 970/586–3371 or 800/762–5437, fax 970/586–3673. 90 rooms. Heated outdoor pool, hot tub, tennis courts. AE, D, MC, V. Expensive.*

Telemark Resort. Located just west of Estes Park, this resort borders the Big Thompson River. Its rustic cabins have screened-in porches and fireplaces. *Box 100R, 80517, tel. 970/586–4343 or 800/669–0650. 20 cottages. AE, MC, V. Moderate.*

Trappers Inn. Just three blocks from downtown Estes Park, this quiet, squeaky-clean motel has fishing just across the road in Fall River. *Box 487, 80517, tel. 970/586–2833. 20 rooms. AE, MC, V. Inexpensive–Moderate.*

Tyrol Motor Inn. All units have picture windows and panoramic views of the mountains. *Box 1409, 80517, tel. 970/586–3382, fax 970/586–5941. 53 rooms. Heated pool, hot tub, sauna. AE, D, MC, V. Moderate.*

Whispering Pines Cottages. Located among the pines and alongside the Big Thompson River, these cottages give you the chance to hook a trout from your deck or patio. *Box 877 AC, 80517, tel. 970/586–5258. 15 cottages. Fully equipped kitchens, outside grills. D, MC, V. Moderate.*

GRAND LAKE **Grand Lake Lodge.** Built of lodgepole pine in 1919, this lodge is known as Colorado's favorite front porch because of the view of both Grand Lake and Shadow Mountain Lake. *Box 569, 80447, tel. 970/ 627–3967, fax 970/627–9495, or off-season tel. 303/759–5848, fax 303/759–3179. 66 cabins. Restaurant, swimming pool, horse rental, playground. AE, D, MC, V. Moderate.*

Lemmon Lodge. This Grand Lake favorite on the banks of the lake itself offers seclusion, a sandy beach, and a private dock for those who bring along their boats. *Box 514, 80447, tel. 970/627–3314 in summer, tel. and fax 970/595–3733 in winter. 24 cabins for 4–12 people. MC, V. Open Memorial Day–mid-Oct. Moderate–Expensive.*

Shadowcliff Lodge. This Grand Lake retreat offers privacy and spectacular views, and with one double bed and two bunk beds in each room, it's perfect for large groups. *Box 658, 80447, tel. 970/627–9220. 13-room lodge and 7-room lodge, all with shared bath, and 3 cabins. No credit cards. Inexpensive.*

CAMPGROUNDS

Rocky has five designated drive-in campgrounds. During the summer, reservations are required at Moraine Park and Glacier Basin, but Longs Peak, Timber Creek, and Aspenglen have first-come, first-served policies. Longs Peak allows tents only; the others accommodate RVs. Most of the park's 562 RV spaces are paved. There are no gas hookups; bottled LP gas is available at the campgrounds.

From June to September, camping at the five park campgrounds is limited to seven days (three days at Longs Peak). Advance reservations can be made through **MISTIX** (tel. 800/365–2267). Camping fees vary with the season; additionally, if water is unavailable, camping is free.

If you are planning an overnight trek into the backcountry, you must have a permit. These can be picked up at Park Headquarters and at the Kawuneeche Visitor Center. To obtain a permit in advance, contact the **Superintendent of Park Headquarters** (Rocky Mountain National Park, Estes Park 80517–8397, tel. 970/586–1206). Reservations made by telephone for a permit should be made before June 1.

Outside the park, Estes Park has private camping facilities, and there are many sites near Grand Lake in the **Arapaho National Recreation Area** (Box 10, Granby 80446, tel. 970/887–3331).

DINING

With nearly 100 different dining options in and around Estes Park and Grand Lake, you can sample everything from Mexican fare to Cajun, French, and Chinese cuisines. Many restaurants offer not only fine cuisine but great views of Rocky. Price categories per person, excluding 7% tax, service, and drinks, are Expensive, over $15; Moderate, $10–$15; and Inexpensive, under $10.

ESTES PARK **Big Horn Restaurant.** Its breakfast has been voted the best in Estes Park, but its steaks make it a popular lunch and dinner spot as well. *401 W. Elkhorn Ave., tel. 970/586–2792. No credit cards. Moderate.*

Dunraven Grille at the Stanley Hotel. If you want to splurge, this restaurant offers excellent trout and filet mignon in an elegant resort setting. *333 Wonderview, tel. 970/586–3371. AE, D, DC, MC, V. Moderate–Expensive.*

Dunraven Inn. This local favorite features homemade Italian cooking, a dark interior, and walls pasted with autographed dollar bills. *2470 Hwy. 66, tel. 970/586–6409. D, MC, V. Moderate.*

Fawn Brook Inn. This romantic, secluded restaurant is a local favorite for elegant dining in an informal, relaxed atmosphere. The kitchen prides itself on its veal, lamb, and duck. *15 mi south of Estes Park on Hwy. 7, tel. 303/747–2556. AE, MC, V. Expensive.*

La Casa. This Mexican-Cajun restaurant on Estes Park's main street has a cozy back room with broad picture windows; frame your face in sunshine and take in the beauty of La Casa's outdoor garden. *222 E. Elkhorn Ave., tel. 970/586–2807. AE, D, DC, MC, V. Inexpensive–Moderate.*

Molly B's. The atmosphere here is homespun and friendly, and the menu offers fresh seafood, crepes, steaks, vegetarian dishes, and homemade desserts. *200 Moraine Ave., tel. 970/586–2766. AE, MC, V. Moderate.*

Mountain Home Cafe. Estes Park is full of good breakfast spots, but the Swedish pancakes, potato pancakes, and waffles are truly exceptional. *Upper Stanley Village Shopping Center, 1 block from downtown, tel. 970/586–6624. D, MC, V. Inexpensive.*

GRAND LAKE **Grand Lake Lodge Restaurant.** This restaurant offers a wonderful view of Grand Lake as well as numerous mesquite-grilled specialties, such as grilled chicken glazed with honey or grilled beef brushed with tangy barbecue sauce. *Off U.S. 34 north of Grand Lake, tel. 970/627–3967. AE, D, MC, V. Moderate.*

Mountain Inn. After a long day exploring in the park, relax in the casual atmosphere, enjoy the friendly service, and savor the family-style menu, especially the fried chicken. *612 Grand Ave., tel. 970/627–3385. AE, MC, V. Inexpensive.*

OUTDOOR ACTIVITIES

BIKING Biking is the best in the early morning, before the roads are overrun with cars. The roads don't have much shoulder to accommodate the mountain bicyclist, and there are no bike paths. Rentals are not available in the park, but you can rent bicycles in Estes Park from **Colorado Bicycling Adventures** (184 E. Elkhorn Ave., tel. 970/586–4241).

BOATING There is no motorized boating inside the park. Nearly all of the lakes within Rocky are accessible only by hiking in, so you must carry your inflatable boating gear with you. (Not even inflatable boats are allowed on Bear Lake.) Lily Lake, at the eastern boundary of the park west of Twin Sisters, is right by the road and good for boating. Sprague Lake is also a good choice for boating, and it's an easy walk in. Fan Lake is recommended, but it's smaller.

FISHING Inside Rocky, you'll need a Colorado fishing license, and special regulations apply within the park. In some areas, you must release the fish you have caught. The town of Grand Lake is known for its fishing; big brown trout, 20-pound mackinaw, and modest kokanee salmon are regularly pulled from these waters. With Grand Lake itself, Lake Granby, Shadow Mountain Lake, and the nearby Colorado River, an angler can keep busy. Fishing licenses can be purchased in Estes Park at **Scot's Sporting Goods** (870 Moraine Ave., U.S. 36, tel. 970/586–2877).

GOLF The **Grand Lake Golf Course** (tel. 970/627–8008) offers outstanding views and moderate greens fees. The **Estes Park Golf Course** (tel. 970/586–8146), just south of downtown on Highway 7, is shorter but more challenging. **Lake Estes Executive Course** (tel. 970/586–8176) has nine holes.

HORSEBACK RIDING **Glacier Creek Stables** (tel. 970/586–3244), near Sprague Lake, and **Moraine Park Stables** (tel. 970/586–2327) offer two-hour rides for about $30. Other trips last for up to eight hours.

SKIING **Never Summer Mountain Sports** (tel. 970/627–8008) in Grand Lake rents backcountry skis for $12. On Rocky's east side, the summer trail at Bear Lake is the point of departure for many winter activities. On the west side of the park is the Tonahutu Creek Trail. Leave your car at the Kawuneeche Visitor Center and ski east from the parking lot. Skiers should always beware of high winds (up to 100 miles per hour) and avalanches.

SWIMMING Rocky's streams and lakes, fed by melting snow, are always cold. The **Lake Estes Marina** (1770 Big Thompson Ave., tel. 970/586–2011) rents wet suits. The **YMCA** (tel. 970/586–3341) just outside Estes Park has a swimming pool. The **Estes Park Aquatic Center** (tel. 970/586–2340) has an indoor pool.

WATER SPORTS The park's rivers are generally too shallow for rafting, and the main location for water sports is not inside the park but at Grand Lake or in the nearby **Arapaho National Recreation Area** (Box 10, Granby 80446, tel. 970/887–3331).

San Antonio and Austin
Texas

Updated by Mark Potok

sk Texans to name the state's most charming city, and they will inevitably pick San Antonio, which has a historic setting that never fails to impress visitors with its easy grace. Here Mexican traditions can be most readily felt, tempered by the influence of the German immigrants who settled in the nearby Hill Country. Although the city's namesake river may be an impediment to highway engineers, its twisting way has given San Antonio a priceless gift: *Paseo del Rio,* or the River Walk. Sequestered 20 feet below street level, this natural waterway winds through the middle of the downtown business district; it's laced over with stone arches, bordered by a subtropical terrain of lush plants, cypress trees, and flowers. All of San Antonio comes here to dine, shop, and meet friends.

If San Antonio is the most soothing of Texas cities, Austin is surely the most mellow. North on I–35 about 80 miles, this city is the seat of Texas government as well as home to the University of Texas. Austin has always been a progressive college town, and today it is testament to the efforts of environmentalists, with numerous parks and lakes that are used year-round by scullers and pleasure boaters. If sociology is more your style than outdoor life, the city will delight you with its mix of university students, aging hippies, musicians, and Texas politicians. Austin also serves as the heart of the Texas music industry and is justly famous for its 6th Street nightclubs and other venues; such musicians as Willie Nelson and Lyle Lovett sometimes stop in.

ESSENTIAL INFORMATION

WHEN TO GO Central Texas summers are hot, usually in the 90s and sometimes more than 100°. Fortunately, the humidity in San Antonio and Austin is not as suffocating as on the coast. Weatherwise, spring and fall are most comfortable, with average daytime temperatures in the 70s. A spring trip offers the additional attraction of wildflower season. Although winter can be chancy, with occasional cold snaps and rain, daytime temperatures in the 50s are more like it.

FESTIVALS AND SPECIAL EVENTS San Antonio heralds the arrival of spring with its biggest celebration of the year, the century-old **Fiesta San Antonio** (tel. 210/227–5191), 10 days of parades, street fairs, festivals, art shows, sporting events, and elegant social balls. Held in April, Fiesta's dates vary each year but always include San Jacinto Day, April 21, commemorating the 1836 date when Texas defeated Mexico to win its freedom as an independent nation. Christmas is absolutely magical (and crowded), with a month of holiday celebrations, including the **Holiday River Festival** that illuminates the trees and bridges along the River Walk from the night after Thanksgiving until New Year's Eve. Thousands of candles glow softly inside paper bags and line the River Walk during **Fiesta de Las Luminarias** (Festival of Lights), held the first three weekends in December. The poignant **Las Posadas** (The Inns), a reenactment of the Holy Family's search for an inn, winds along the River Walk the second Sunday of December.

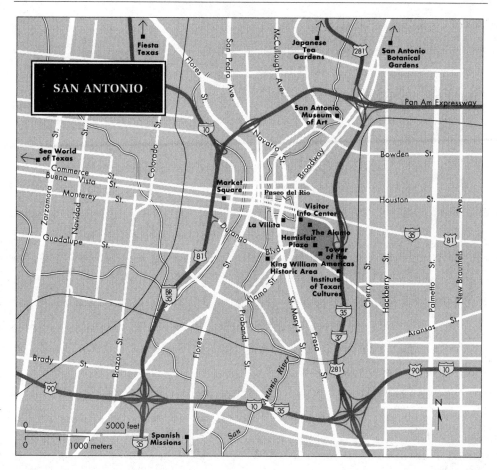

BARGAINS San Antonio offers many free attractions. During the city's many fiestas, you're likely to find free entertainment, such as mariachi bands, dancers, and street entertainers, especially in Market Square and on the River Walk.

Austin's bargains include free tours of the State Capitol, the Governor's Mansion, and the Lyndon Baines Johnson Library. The University of Texas schedules concerts, recitals, and speakers throughout the year; tickets are often free or cost just a few dollars. Free concerts and dance performances are plentiful in Zilker Park and at Auditorium Shores along Town Lake, especially during the summer.

TOURIST OFFICES **San Antonio Convention & Visitors Bureau** (121 Alamo Plaza, Box 2277, San Antonio 78298, tel. 210/270–8700 or 800/447–3372, fax 210/270–8782). **Austin Convention and Visitors Bureau** (201 E. 2nd St., Austin 78701, tel. 512/474–5171 or 800/888–8287), or stop by **Austin Visitor Information** (201-B E. 2nd St., Austin 78701, tel. 512/478–0098). For a free Texas State Travel Guide, write: **Texas Department of Transportation** (Travel and Information Division, Box 5064, Austin 78763, tel. 800/452–9292).

EMERGENCIES **Police, fire,** and **ambulance:** Dial 911. **Hospitals:** In San Antonio, the Alamo City Medical Group Clinic (408

Navarro St., tel. 210/271–1841) and Santa Rosa Health Care Corp. (519 W. Houston St., tel. 210/228–2011), and in Austin, the emergency room at Brackenridge Hospital (601 E. 15th St., tel. 512/476–6461) are open 24 hours for medical emergencies.

ARRIVING AND DEPARTING

BY PLANE San Antonio International Airport (tel. 210/821–3411) has two terminals hosting a dozen or so airlines. Ground transportation to downtown takes about 15 minutes when traffic is normal, and an average cab fare is about $12, plus tip. **Star Shuttle** (tel. 210/366–3183) offers 24-hour service

from the airport and serves major downtown hotels ($6 one-way; 24 hrs advance reservation recommended). If you rent a car, take U.S. 281 south (McAllister Freeway) from the airport to downtown.

Austin's main airport is the **Robert Mueller Municipal Airport** (tel. 512/472–3321). A cab ride from the airport to downtown (5 miles) is about $7, plus tip. If you rent a car, take I–35 south from the airport to downtown. No airport shuttle service is available. Many of the larger hotels offer courtesy van service to and from the airport.

BY CAR San Antonio has interstate highways leading into it from every direction, including I–10 (from Houston) and I–35 (from Austin and Dallas); major highways pass through or nearby the central downtown area. The city is surrounded by Loop 410, which bypasses some, but not all, traffic.

Austin's major north–south arteries include I–35 to the east, and, to the west, Loop 360 (also known as Capital of Texas Highway) and MoPac Expressway (Loop 1).

BY TRAIN **Amtrak** (tel. 800/872–7245) serves both Austin and San Antonio.

BY BUS **Greyhound Lines** (tel. 800/231–2222) and **Kerrville Bus Company** (tel. 512/389–0319) serve both San Antonio and Austin.

GETTING AROUND

SAN ANTONIO The best way to enjoy the city is on foot. Should you tire, **VIA Metropolitan Transit Service** (112 W. Soledad St., tel. 210/227–2020) has 94 regular bus routes and four trolley routes downtown. A Day Tripper Pass allows you to ride the VIA system all day; this includes the VIA Vistas Cultural Route, which stops at more than a dozen museums and other attractions, including the historic missions. Express routes are also available from downtown to Sea World and Fiesta Texas.

AUSTIN The 6th Street cabaret district and the University of Texas campus can be explored on foot, but otherwise Austin is better seen by car. The city has a regular city bus system, **Capital Metro** (tel. 512/474–1200), which runs a number of routes as well as the free Armadillo Express downtown trolley buses between the University of Texas, Capitol complex, and convention center.

REST STOPS There's a gas station at practically every city intersection and virtually every freeway interchange, and all of them have rest rooms.

GUIDED TOURS San Antonio tour companies offer shopping trips to Mexico, nature hikes at various state parks, and tours of historic sites. **Gray Line** (tel. 210/226–1706 or 800/472–9546, fax 210/226–2515) schedules daily bus tours around the city.

In Austin, **Gray Line** (tel. 512/345–6789) covers the basic sights. **Around Austin** (tel. 512/345–6552) provides personalized tours of the city and can arrange a weekend Hill Country tour. The **Lone Star Riverboat** (tel. 512/327–1388) takes passengers on a 90-minute cruise of Town Lake (March–October).

EXPLORING

SAN ANTONIO Downtown San Antonio is a tourist mecca. Have breakfast at one of the restaurants on Paseo del Rio, and you'll be within minutes of many places you will want to visit. You will also want to browse along Commerce Street, Houston Street, and Alamo Plaza.

The Alamo. This former mission was established in 1718 by Spanish Franciscan friars, but it's remembered for the 1836 battle in which Lt. Col. William B. Travis, Davy Crockett, Jim Bowie, and more than 180 other Texans died fighting Mexico's General Antonio Lopez de Santa Anna. The Alamo became the symbol of Texas's fight for independence from Mexico, and 46 days after the massacre there, Santa Anna himself was captured and the Republic of Texas came into being. The adobe chapel looks much the same today as it did 150 years ago. The plaza out front tends to be a busy meeting place. *300 Alamo Plaza, tel. 210/225–1391. Open daily. Admission free. No hats, cameras, or video-recording devices inside.*

Fiesta Texas. Situated in an abandoned quarry at the base of sheer, 100-foot-tall limestone cliffs, this musical theme park managed by Opryland celebrates the state's diverse cultures with four entertainment theme areas—Hispanic, German, Old West, and 1950s rock and roll. Thrill seekers venture aboard the Rattler, billed as the world's tallest and fastest wooden roller coaster, for the ride of their lives. *17000 I–10 West at Loop 1604, tel. 210/697–5443. Open Mar.–Memorial Day and Labor Day–Nov., weekends; Memorial Day–Labor Day, daily. Admission charged (children under 3 free).*

HemisFair Park. The site of the 1968 World's Fair is now home to the 750-foot-tall Tower of the Americas. The waterfall-filled park also features the Institute of Texan Cultures, a museum providing a fascinating, hands-on interpretation of Texas history and folk culture. The institute hosts the annual Texas Folklife Festival the first weekend of August. *Open daily. Admission free. Institute: 801 S. Bowie St., tel. 210/558–2300. Open Tues.–Sun. Donations accepted.*

Japanese Tea Gardens. Goldfish-stocked ponds, pebble pathways, and outstanding floral displays make this a relaxing spot. *3800 N. St. Mary's St., tel. 210/734–0816. Open daily. Admission free.*

King William Historic Area. In the late 1800s, the 25-block King William District on the south bank of the San Antonio River was the most elegant residential area in the city. Today, many of the stately mansions have been restored and about a dozen operate as bed-and-breakfast inns. A map for a self-guided walking tour is available from the **San Antonio Conservation Society** (107 King William St., tel. 210/224–6163).

La Villita. Located right on the River Walk, this mid-18th-century Texas settlement and the city's original town site has been restored, with the houses and buildings providing spaces for artists and craftsmen. You can watch glassblowers, boot makers, painters, and jewelers, or dine at one of its three restaurants. *418 Villita at the River Walk, tel. 210/207–8610. Open daily. Admission free.*

Paseo del Rio (River Walk). Locals as well as visitors are drawn to this special 2½-mile promenade with European-style sidewalk cafés, specialty boutiques, and nightclubs—all fronted by cobblestone paths. At one narrow bend in the river, the Arneson River Theatre is carved right into the riverbank so

that spectators can applaud shows being staged across the river. Extensions to the original WPA-built walkway lead to Rivercenter Festival Marketplace and to the San Antonio Convention Center.

San Antonio Botanical Gardens and Lucile Halsell Conservatory. This 38-acre garden blooms year-round with a profusion of colorful, thematic planting areas. You can "Walk Through Texas," discovering the state's native flora, or visit the Biblical Garden filled with fig trees, date palms, and other plant life mentioned in the Bible. The conservatory's futuristic-style glass pavilions re-create environments from around the world for some 2,000 different plants. *555 Funston Pl. at N. New Braunfels, tel. 210/821–5115. Open Tues.–Sun. Admission charged.*

San Antonio Museum of Art. The collections, housed in the former Lone Star Brewing Company's castlelike building, range from pre-Columbian treasures and Mexican folk art to American masterpieces and antiquities from ancient Greece, Rome, and Egypt. *200 W. Jones Ave., tel. 210/829–7282. Open daily. Admission charged.*

Sea World of Texas. The largest marine-life theme park in the world features water rides, a beach and wave pool, daily shows, and exhibits devoted to killer whales, penguins, walruses, dolphins, sea lions, and other aquatic life. *10500 Sea World Dr. at intersection of Ellison Dr. and Westover Hills Blvd. off Texas Hwy. 151, tel. 210/523–3611 or 800/527–4757. Open June–Labor Day, daily; Mar.–May and Sept.–Dec. 1., weekends only. Admission charged (children under 3 free).*

Spanish Missions. San Antonio's debt to the Spanish crown can be seen at five Franciscan missions established in the early 18th century. Except for the Alamo, the missions still serve active parishes. The best way to see the missions is aboard VIA's Vistas Cultural route, as the Mission Trail road signs are difficult to follow. The largest and best-restored building is Mission San Jose, where a mariachi mass is held at noon every Sunday. *San Jose: 6539 San Jose Dr. at Mission Rd., tel. 210/229–4770. Open daily. Admission free.*

AUSTIN You need not rush to see everything in Austin. A favorite pastime here is spending a lazy afternoon at a spring-fed swimming hole, sipping a cool beverage.

Governor's Mansion. Since 1856 this elegant Greek Revival mansion has housed the Texas head of state. Each governor and his or her family have left their unique mark on the house, and you'll hear plenty of entertaining anecdotes on the short guided tour (weekdays; tours leave every 20 minutes from the mansion's front gate). *1010 Colorado St., tel. 512/463–5518. Call for hrs. Admission free.*

Hill Country. West of Austin and San Antonio, the Hill Country area has many little 19th-century German towns and runs from Dimebox and Flatonia to Fredricksburg and New Braunfels. These towns are known for their delightful country inns, old-fashioned restaurants, antiques shops, wurst makers, dude ranches, and many festivals. In Johnson City, the Lyndon B. Johnson National Historical Park includes the former president's boyhood home, a visitor center, the Johnson Ranch, and Texas White House. The Hill Country is popular among nature lovers and outdoorsmen, with a chain of seven Highland Lakes that wind for 150 miles. If you only have time for a quick look at the scenery, get on Loop 360 (Capital of Texas Highway) from South Lamar Boulevard or MoPac (Loop 1), and head north. Loop 360 swings around the west side of Austin, allowing views of violet-colored hills. Loop 360 runs into Loop 1 south for the return to downtown.

Hill Country Flyer. All aboard on restored steam engine No. 786 for a half-day, weekend-only excursion between Cedar Park (30 miles north of downtown Austin) and Burnet. The journey—in vintage coaches—and the roar of the powerful engine returns riders to a nostalgic bygone era. *Depot in Cedar Park, just north of FM 1431 and U.S. 183 North, tel. 512/477–8468; for tickets,* *tel. 512/477–6060. Reservations required. Admission charged.*

Laguna Gloria Art Museum. The collection here includes works by regional and nationally known artists and photographers. Be sure to stroll the lovely landscaped grounds facing Lake Austin. *3809 W. 35th St., tel. 512/458–8191. Open Tues.–Sun. Admission charged.*

Lyndon Baines Johnson Library. Located on the University of Texas campus, this presidential library houses more than 36 million personal and official documents as well as historical and cultural exhibits. *2313 Red River St. near E. 23rd St., tel. 512/482–5279. Open daily. Admission free.*

National Wildflower Research Center. Founded by Lady Bird Johnson, this is the only institution in the country dedicated exclusively to conserving and promoting the use of native plants in North America. It reopened in the Hill Country in 1995 after a $10 million renovation, and now these lush gardens sprawl over 42 acres and amid 10 typically Texan limestone buildings. *4801 LaCrosse Ave., tel. 512/292–4200. Open weekdays with extended weekend hrs in spring. Admission free.*

State Capitol Building. This grand Renaissance Revival structure is the largest U.S. state capitol, actually 9 feet taller than the national Capitol building in Washington, D.C. Austin's capitol features 7 miles of exquisite wainscoting, 500 doors, and 900 windows. An underground expansion added another 650,000 square feet to the original building, and a major outside renovation brought new luster to its reddish exterior. You can take a free tour or guide yourself around with a free pamphlet, "Texas Capitol Guide," available at the visitors desk. *11th St. and Congress Ave., tel. 512/463–0063. Open daily. Admission free.*

Umlauf Sculpture Garden. More than 100 sculptures by internationally known artist Charles Umlauf are exhibited in a small museum and throughout the site's landscaped gardens, set overlooking Zilker Park.

605 Robert E. Lee Rd. (off Barton Springs Rd.), tel. 512/445–5582. Open Thurs.–Sun. Admission charged.

Wineries. The hills and lakes in this part of Texas create the perfect environment for grapevines. Among the wineries in the area open to visitors are Fall Creek (Tow, near Llano, tel. 512/476–4477), Bell Mountain/ Oberhellmann Vineyards (Fredericksburg, tel. 210/685–3297), Hill Country Cellars (Cedar Park, tel. 512/259–2000), and Slaughter-Leftwich Vineyards (Austin, on Lake Travis, tel. 512/266–3331). Hours of operation change according to the season, so call ahead. For a free wine-country tour guide, contact the **Texas Department of Agriculture** (Box 12847, Austin 78711, tel. 512/463–7624).

THE NATURAL WORLD **Bats.** The world's largest urban bat colony—750,000 Mexican free-tailed bats—hangs out beneath Austin's Congress Avenue Bridge April through October. It's become popular to find a spot just before dusk and watch their dramatic departures against the setting sun. The best vantage spots are from the hike-and-bike trail by the bridge or from the patio of Shoreline Grill restaurant.

Caves. The rugged hills near San Antonio and Austin are honeycombed with more than 2,500 caves, most of them wild and undeveloped. One of the most striking is Natural Bridge Caverns, where formations continue to form from constant water activity. 8 mi west of Natural Bridge Caverns Exit off I-35, tel. 210/651–6101. Open daily. Admission charged.

Colorado River Lakes. In Central Texas, the Colorado River forms a 150-mile chain of lakes that run from Burnet County to Austin. Along the Highland Lakes you can find great fishing, spectacular scenery, and an endless array of water recreation. At Lake Buchanan, the Vanishing Texas River Cruise ventures through miles of backwater wilderness for scenic views of towering limestone cliffs, beautiful waterfalls, and majestic eagles in flight during the winter. Vanishing Texas River Cruise, RR 2341 (3½ mi northwest of Burnet), tel. 512/756–6986. Daily cruises. Admission charged.

McKinney Falls State Park. Seven miles southeast of Austin, this park features tree-lined Onion Creek and its two waterfalls. The park has good bird-watching, campgrounds, shady picnic areas, and playgrounds as well as 19th-century ruins scattered along the 1.7 miles of winding shoreline. Swimming is not allowed in the swimming hole when the bacteria count is high; call the park's hot line (tel. 512/243–0848) for the latest water conditions. Scenic Rd., 2 mi west of U.S. 183, tel. 512/243–1643. Open daily. Admission charged.

HOTELS AND INNS

San Antonio accommodates visitors with numerous historic hotels and a wide range of bed-and-breakfast inns. In Austin, several downtown hotels border Town Lake, where frequent outdoor concerts add to the ambience. Both cities have fancier modern hotels and chain motels. Make your reservations well in advance: One of the nation's top convention destinations, San Antonio's rooms always seem to be booked to capacity, and Austin is packed with alumni during the University of Texas football season.

The reservation service **Bed & Breakfast Hosts of San Antonio** (tel. 210/824–8036, fax 210/824–9926) lists nearly 50 bed-and-breakfast properties in the San Antonio area, with more than a dozen in the historic King William District.

Price categories for double occupancy, excluding 8% tax, are Expensive, $90–$140; Moderate, $70–$90; and Inexpensive, under $70. Rates are subject to a 15% total tax in San Antonio, 13% in Austin.

SAN ANTONIO **Hyatt Regency Hill Country Resort.** Located directly across the highway from Sea World, this 200-acre resort is a destination in itself. Settled on the site of a historic Texas ranch, it spreads across rolling Hill Country terrain. Among the amenities is a 950-foot-long Ramblin' River for tubing. *9800 Resort Dr. (off Hwy. 151), 78251, tel. 210/647–1234 or 800/233–1234, fax 210/ 681–9681. 500 rooms, 46 suites. Restaurant, pool, tennis, golf, health club, jogging and biking trails. AE, D, MC, V. Expensive.*

La Mansion del Rio. This Spanish Colonial hotel, built in 1852 as a private boys' school, overlooks the Paseo del Rio and has a graceful, Old World charm that captures the ambience of the city. *112 College St., 78205, tel. 210/225–2581 or 800/531–7208, fax 210/ 226–0389. 337 rooms, 11 suites. Restaurants, entertainment, pool. AE, D, DC, MC, V. Expensive.*

Menger Hotel and Motor Inn. Ask for one of the Texana-furnished rooms in the original wing of the city's oldest hotel, located directly across the alley from the Alamo. Be sure to visit the famous Menger Bar, where Teddy Roosevelt recruited his Rough Riders in 1898. *204 Alamo Plaza, 78205, tel. 210/ 223–4361 or 800/345–9285, fax 210/228– 0022. 320 rooms, 18 suites. Restaurant, entertainment, pool, health club. AE, D, DC, MC, V. Moderate–Expensive.*

Ramada Emily Morgan Hotel. The triangular shape of this Art Deco gem makes it one of the most distinctive buildings on the city's skyline. Located next door to the Alamo, the hotel is convenient to the River Walk and other downtown attractions. *705 E. Houston St., 78205, tel. 210/225–8486 or 800/824–6674. 177 rooms, 1 suite. Restaurant, pool, health club. AE, D, DC, MC, V. Expensive.*

AUSTIN **Doubletree Guest Suites.** This modern high-rise hotel is conveniently located downtown; many of the one- and two-bedroom suites have views of the Capitol, two blocks away. *303 W. 15th St., 78701, tel. 512/478–7000 or 800/222–8733. 189 suites. Restaurant, lounge, pool. AE, D, DC, MC, V. Expensive.*

Driskill Hotel. Since opening on Christmas Eve 1885, the grande dame of Austin hotels has been the gathering spot for politicians and other big-name decision makers. Reno-vations completed in 1995 restored the original beauty of the Driskill's lavish lobby and rooms. *604 Brazos St. (at 6th St.), 78701, tel. 512/474–5911 or 800/527–2008, fax 512/ 474–2214. 178 rooms. Restaurant, entertainment. AE, D, DC, MC, V. Moderate– Expensive.*

Fairview. This early 20th-century Colonial Revival mansion offers guest rooms, all with private baths, in either the main or adjoining carriage house. Overlooking a quiet, tree-lined street, the main house with its massive white columns and delightful Victorian furnishings makes for a wonderful weekend getaway. *1304 Newning Ave. (near South Congress and Riverside Dr.), 78704, tel. 512/ 444–4746. 3 rooms, 3 suites, 2 with kitchenettes. Full breakfast included. AE, DC, MC, V. Moderate–Expensive.*

MOTELS

The following motels are all in the Inexpensive category.

SAN ANTONIO **Drury Inn/Airport** (143 N.E. Loop 410, 78216, tel. 210/366–4300 or 800/ 325–8300, fax 210/366–4300). 125 rooms, 12 suites; pool. **Hampton Inn/Airport** (8818 Jones Maltsberger, 78216, tel. 210/366–1800 or 800/426–7866, fax 210/366–1800). 121 rooms; pool. **Holiday Inn Downtown/Market Square** (318 W. Durango St., 78204, tel. 210/225–3211 or 800/422–2419, fax 210/ 225–1125). 318 rooms, 2 suites; restaurant, pool. **La Quinta Convention Center** (1001 E. Commerce St., 78205, tel. 210/222–9181 or 800/531–5900, fax 210/228–9816). 140 rooms; pool. **La Quinta Market Square** (900 Dolorosa, 78207, tel. 210/271–0001 or 800/ 531–5900, fax 210/228–0663). 124 rooms, 2 suites; pool. **Rodeway Inn Fiesta Park** (19793 I–10 W, 78257, tel. 210/698–3991 or 800/424–4777). 76 rooms, 1 suite; restaurant, pool.

AUSTIN **Capitol Motor Inn** (2525 S. I–35, 78741, tel. 512/441–0143). 80 rooms; Continental breakfast included, pool. **Drury Inns** (919 E. Koenig La., 78751, tel. 512/454–

1144 or 800/325–8300). 137 rooms; breakfast served, pool. **Holiday Inn–Austin Town Lake** (20 N. I–35, 78701, tel. 512/472–8211 or 800/465–4329, fax 512/472–4636). 321 rooms; restaurant, pool, health club. **La Quinta Inn** (5812 I–35 N, 78751, tel. 512/459–4381 or 800/531–5900, fax 512/452–3917). 59 rooms; pool. **Quality Inn Airport** (909 E. Koenig La., 78751, tel. 512/452–4200 or 800/228–5151, fax 512/452–4200). 91 rooms; breakfast served, pool.

DINING

When in Texas, dine as Texans do, and that usually means eating Mexican. Both San Antonio and Austin have hundreds of Tex-Mex restaurants. Despite the Texas tradition of eating beef, you'll easily find restaurants that also serve salads, light pastas, seafood, and fresh vegetables. Price categories per person, excluding sales tax, service, and drinks, are Moderate, $15–$25, and Inexpensive, under $15.

SAN ANTONIO **Boudro's on the River.** On the River Walk, this sidewalk café serves seafood and southwestern food, such as crab and shrimp tamales, pecan-grilled fish, and its trademark corn pudding. *421 E. Commerce St., tel. 210/224–8484. AE, DC, MC, V. Moderate.*

Cappy's. Changing exhibits by local artists add to the refreshing atmosphere of this Broadway landmark. The menu offers a varied selection of pasta dishes and mesquite-grilled fish, along with such tempting desserts as apple pie with butter-rum sauce and chocolate cake served warm and topped with Bluebell ice cream. *5011 Broadway, tel. 210/828–9669. AE, DC, MC, V. Inexpensive–Moderate.*

La Margarita. This restaurant receives credit for introducing the world to fajitas— grilled steak served with peppers and onions in a flour tortilla. Eat outdoors and watch the Market Square action or dine indoors (which is only slightly less frenetic) at the Cortez family's popular Tex-Mex

cantina. *120 Produce Row in Market Sq., tel. 210/227–7140. AE, DC, MC, V. Inexpensive–Moderate.*

L'Etoile. While children are welcomed at this upscale French venue, they don't distract from a pleasurable evening out, as the restaurant provides baby-sitting next door. You can't go wrong with the delectably creamy lobster bisque or the veal, roast lamb, and grilled fish entrées. *6106 Broadway, tel. 210/826–4551. AE, DC, MC, V. Moderate.*

Rio Rio Cantina. A lively, youthful atmosphere and generous servings of mole (a chili- and chocolate-based sauce) chicken, enchiladas *suiza*, and other traditional Mexican dishes make this one of the best Tex-Mex choices on the River Walk. *421 E. Commerce St., tel. 210/226–8462. AE, D, DC, MC, V. Inexpensive.*

AUSTIN **Chuy's Hula Hut.** Mix together a little Polynesian, Caribbean, and Mexican, and you've got the Hula Hut, an eclectic eatery along the shores of Lake Austin just west of downtown. Order an appetizer of tapas (small samplings) or a *pu-pu* platter large enough to feed two. A popular choice at Chuy's is the Polynesian *pescado* platter, with coconut fried shrimp, grilled salmon fillet, and shrimp *flautas* with orange-mustard sauce. *3625 Lake Austin Blvd., tel. 512/476–4852. AE, D, DC, MC, V. Inexpensive.*

Fonda San Miguel. Like a lush garden from a Mexican villa, the dining room makes a beautiful setting for dining on seviche, chicken in mole, fish coated with *achiote* (a reddish, earthy-tasting seed), and other Mexican specialties. *2330 W. North Loop, tel. 512/459–4121. AE, D, DC, MC, V. Moderate.*

Mezzaluna. This trendy spot near downtown specializes in contemporary Italian cuisine— goat-cheese fritters, sautéed shrimp with smoked tomato-basil sauce, veal scaloppine, and the chef's signature dish, smoked-chicken lasagna. *310 Colorado St., tel. 512/472–6770. AE, DC, MC, V. Moderate.*

Salt Lick. For a taste of true Texan barbecue, head about 25 miles southwest of downtown

Austin to Driftwood and the Salt Lick. Ribs, brisket, sausage, and chicken cook slowly over an open pit and are served family style with all the trimmings. There's no air-conditioning, but fans and the shade of huge oak trees help to cool the place. If you want a cold beer to wash down the barbecue, bring your own—the Salt Lick is in a dry county. *FM 1826 (off U.S. Hwy. 290 West), tel. 512/858–4959. No credit cards. Open Wed.– Sun. Inexpensive.*

Shoreline Grill. With a spectacular view of Town Lake, diners find the cuisine to be as inviting as the scenery. The regional menu borrows heavily from the Creole cooking of neighboring Louisiana; try the Shoreline's blackened fish specialties, crab cakes with remoulade sauce, or the carmelized crème brûlée. Steak lovers should try the prime rib, slowly roasted on the grill. *98 San Jacinto Blvd., tel. 512/477–3300. AE, D, DC, MC, V. Moderate.*

Threadgills. In this converted old service station, the late Kenneth Threadgill, a yodeler and music lover, created an Austin legend when he began inviting his friends over to play music (among those aspiring musicians was a University of Texas student named Janis Joplin). The restaurant also enjoys a reputation for its good home-style cooking. Some say the chicken-fried steaks are the best in town. *6416 N. Lamar, tel. 512/ 451–5440. MC, V. Inexpensive.*

SHOPPING

SAN ANTONIO San Antonio's **Market Square** (514 W. Commerce St., tel. 210/207–8600) offers shops, restaurants, and a farmers' market where you can buy dried-chili wreaths or fresh-made tortillas. El Mercado at the square is a large indoor shopping area, with stalls selling wrought iron, pottery, and Mexican dresses.

The newest extension of the River Walk leads to **Rivercenter** (849 E. Commerce St., tel. 210/225–0000), an entertainment, hotel, and shopping complex, anchored by the lux-

urious Marriott Rivercenter and Dillard's department store. Small specialty boutiques, along with national retail chains rise along three levels. An IMAX Theatre (483 Rivercenter Mall, tel. 210/225–4629 or 800/354–4629) shows *Alamo: The Price of Freedom* on a six-story screen.

AUSTIN Austin's distinctive shopping district is **The Drag,** which means Guadalupe Street from Martin Luther King Boulevard to 26th Street across from the University of Texas campus. On the busiest part of Guadalupe Street, you'll find **Bevo's Book Store** (2304 Guadalupe St., tel. 512/476–7642), the university's souvenir store. The **People's Renaissance Market** (W. 23rd and Guadalupe Sts.), an open-air bazaar, is always busy.

Elsewhere in Austin, visit **Bluebonnet Markets** (310 Neches, tel. 512/476–3484), where about a dozen artisans ply their mostly Texana handicrafts under one roof. The **Travis County Farmers' Market** (6701 Burnet Rd., tel. 512/454–1002) features fresh produce and crafts. For upscale shopping, The **Arboretum** (10000 Research Blvd. and Great Hills Trail, tel. 512/338–4437) features a number of boutiques, art galleries, Simon David gourmet grocery store, and Amy's Ice Cream.

FACTORY OUTLETS The area between San Antonio and Austin is a bargain hunter's mecca. In New Braunfels, the **Mill Store Plaza** (I–35 North, exit 189, tel. 210/620–6806), anchored by WestPoint Pepperell, features more than 50 name-brand factory stores where shoppers save 20% to 70% off retail prices. The **San Marcos Factory Shops** (tel. 512/396–2200) offers discount prices at several hundred showrooms, which include Donna Karan, Guess, Brooks Brothers, and Mikasa. The center is located at I–35 and Center Point Road, via Exit 200, in San Marcos.

OUTDOOR ACTIVITIES

BIKING Austin's scenic back roads offer gently rolling hills and tempting diversions, from tucked-away waterfalls to country antique emporia to barbecue joints. Loop 360 provides a grueling workout, while the hike-and-bike trail around Town Lake is more leisurely. The **Bicycle Sport Shop** (1426 Toomey Rd., tel. 512/477–3472) rents bikes.

CANOEING AND RAFTING You can canoe on any of the lakes in and around Austin. Within the city, rent a canoe by the hour or day at **Zilker Park Boat Rentals** (2000 Barton Springs Rd., tel. 512/478–3852). Serious adventurers go to New Braunfels and the neighboring village of Gruene (pronounced "Green"), where they pick up a raft, canoe, or tube from **Rockin' "R" River Rides** (1405 Gruene Rd., tel. 800/553–5628) to float down the Guadalupe River.

GOLF In San Antonio, **Mission del Lago** (1250 Mission Grande, tel. 210/627–2522), **Brackenridge** (2315 Ave. B, tel. 210/226–5612), and **Cedar Creek** (8250 Vista Colina, tel. 210/695–5050) are recommended 18-hole golf courses. In Austin, check out **Jimmy Clay Municipal Golf Course** (5400 Jimmy Clay, east of I–35 at Stassney La., tel. 512/444–0999), or championship courses at **Circle C Golf Club** (11511 FM 1826, tel. 512/288–4297) and **River Place** (4207 River Place Blvd., off FM 2222 West, tel. 512/346–6784).

JOGGING AND WALKING Austin has 20 miles of hike-and-bike trails. The most popular is the 8½-mile trail that runs along the north and south shores of Town Lake.

SWIMMING Austin's favorite swimming hole is the naturally spring-fed Barton Springs in **Zilker Park** (Barton Springs Rd. between Robert E. Lee and Loop 1, tel. 512/476–9044); a 997-foot-long pool has chilly waters (a constant 68°).

ENTERTAINMENT

MUSIC If you like a lively music scene, Austin's 6th Street district is world-famous, with some two dozen nightclubs and music halls clustered within a few blocks. Else-

where in town, traditional country fans flock to the **Broken Spoke** (3201 S. Lamar Blvd., tel. 512/442–6189). For blues, try **Antone's** (2915 Guadalupe St., tel. 512/474–5314). Jazz lovers enjoy **Top of the Marc** (618 W. 6th St., tel. 512/472–9849), an upscale nightspot upstairs from Katz's Deli. **Symphony Square** (E. 11th and Red River Sts., tel. 512/476–6090), on the banks of Waller Creek, is home to the Austin Symphony and other music groups. A traditional gathering spot for politicians (a must on presidential campaign stops) and University of Texas alumni, **Scholz Garten** (1607 San Jacinto St., tel. 512/477–4171) is one of the best places in town to hear good Texas music from the likes of Asleep at the Wheel, Gary P. Nunn, or Jerry Jeff Walker. The **Backyard** (13101 Hwy. 71 West, tel. 512/263–4146) primarily books national touring acts for its 25,000-square-foot natural amphitheater where massive oak trees, a creek, and a waterfall provide the backdrop.

NIGHTLIFE The River Walk is a good place to sample San Antonio's fine restaurants and sometimes rowdy nightlife. Topping the list of fun places is **Dick's Last Resort** (River level, Navarro St. Bldg., 406 Navarro St., tel. 210/224–0026), with Dixieland jazz and would-be comedians doubling as waiters. The **Landing** (Hyatt Regency river level, 123 Losoya and River Walk, tel. 210/222–1234) is home to Jim Cullum's Jazz Band. Sing-alongs keep the atmosphere boisterous at **Durty Nelly's** (Hilton Palacio del Rio river level, 200 Alamo and River Walk, tel. 210/222–1400).

SPECTATOR SPORTS The **San Antonio Spurs** (tel. 210/554–7787) play basketball November through April at the Alamodome, a 65,000-seat sports arena located downtown just east of I–35.

THEATER The **Majestic Theatre** (212 E. Houston St., tel. 210/226–3333), built in 1929 and renovated in the late 1980s, is home to the San Antonio Symphony and the most popular venue for touring Broadway shows and concerts.

San Diego
California

Updated by Jane Onstott

ach year San Diego, California, absorbs thousands of visitors who are drawn by the climate: sunny, dry, and warm nearly year-round. Sunshine and crisp ocean air give San Diego—a city where snow falls maybe *once* a decade—the trappings of a temperate, tropical paradise: oases of lazy palms, sheltered bays fringed by golden pampas grass, and far-ranging parklands blossoming with brilliant bougainvillea, jasmine, ice plant, and birds of paradise. Ask San Diegans what they enjoy most, but don't be surprised by the consistency of their response: communing with sea and sand on one of the city's long, powdery beaches, maybe swimming, maybe napping, maybe watching the whales, seals, and dolphins swim offshore.

Visitors can run, bike, and walk for hours down the city's wide, lively streets or along coastal paths planned for the city's seemingly endless supply of fit, well-tanned denizens. Or you can drive by Mission Bay, a 4,600-acre aquatic park, where dozens of colorful, intricate kites fly over hundreds of picnickers lounging in the sun. Downtown you can wander the crowded streets and soak up the colorful lunchtime scene: mimes and musicians hamming it up for the parade of sailors, shoppers, and skateboarders. For a real San Diego experience, blend in with the masses streaming from steel-and-glass office towers to grab a quick lunch at the fanciful Horton Plaza shopping center, which serves as San Diego's de facto city center, with theaters, restaurants, and endless shops.

San Diego has always been recognized as an environmental utopia—reflected in everything from the city's unique modern architecture to its miles of immaculate public beaches. The city is a hodgepodge in the best sense due to its mix of military personnel and beach bums, immigrants and gays. Today, San Diego retains its sense of a western frontier as it develops into a major cosmopolitan centerpiece for the nation.

ESSENTIAL INFORMATION

WHEN TO GO San Diego's climate is as close to perfection as one can imagine, with an average annual high temperature of 70°, an average annual low of 55°, and an average annual rainfall of less than 10 inches. The 70 miles of coastline becomes foggy during June. The ocean water doesn't warm up until August, when it hits the high 60s. Hot Santa Ana winds whip the trees in the fall, but that's about as extreme as the weather gets. As far as San Diegans are concerned, September is their town's best month: The water is still warm and the beaches are blessedly empty.

BARGAINS Mimes, jugglers, magicians, and musicians perform for free in Balboa Park, and an endless stream of skateboarders, roller skaters, and bicyclists show off along the beaches and bays. Seaport Village is another great spot for impromptu performances.

The San Diego Symphony gives free evening concerts June through August at Seaport Vil-

SAN DIEGO

lage, complete with fireworks. Sea World also has fireworks on summer nights—Mission Bay and Ocean Beach are the best spots from which to watch them. Navy ships docked downtown are sometimes open for free tours.

Balboa Park's museums offer free admission on Tuesdays on a rotating basis; the Information Center (temporarily housed in the Plaza de Panama, in front of the Museum of Art, tel. 619/239–0512) has a posted list. The Information Center also sells the "Passport to Balboa Park," with coupons and reduced rates for admission to the museums. Free organ concerts take place in the Organ Pavilion on Sunday afternoons, and a variety of choral groups and bands perform here for free on summer evenings.

TOURIST OFFICES International Information Center (Horton Plaza, corner of 1st Ave. and F St., San Diego 92101, tel. 619/236–1212). **Mission Bay Visitor Information** (2688 E. Mission Bay Dr., San Diego 92109, tel. 619/276–8200).

EMERGENCIES Police, fire, and ambulance: Dial 911. **Hospitals:** UCSD Medical Center (200 W. Arbor St., tel. 619/543–6400) and Mercy Hospital (4077 5th Ave., tel. 619/260–7000) have emergency rooms with 24-hour service. **Doctors:** The San Diego County Medical Society (tel. 619/565–8161) has a referral service, as do all the major hospitals. **Dentists:** Referral Service (tel. 800/917–6453). **Pharmacies:** The large chains—Longs, Sav-On, and Thrifty—stay open until 9 PM; Hillcrest Pharmacy (tel. 619/297–3993) delivers throughout the county.

ARRIVING AND DEPARTING

BY PLANE Most major airlines serve **San Diego International Airport** (tel. 619/231–5220), also known as Lindbergh Field, 3 miles northwest of downtown. San Diego Transit (tel. 619/233–3004) runs Bus 2 between the airport and downtown, where you can transfer to another bus or a trolley; the fare is $1.50, including transfer. Many hotels also have airport shuttle services. A taxi from the airport to a downtown hotel is $7–$8. Taxis are lined up across the street from the baggage claim areas.

BY CAR I–5 runs south from Los Angeles (actually, from Washington State) to San Diego and is the fastest route to the coastal towns and downtown; Route 1 (the Pacific Coast Highway) travels through the coastal towns and is a more scenic, and congested, route. I–805 is the inland north–south route. I–8 travels west from Arizona and ends at the Pacific Ocean in Ocean Beach.

BY BUS Greyhound Lines (tel. 619/239–9321 or 800/231–2222) operates frequent daily service between San Diego's downtown terminal (120 W. Broadway) and Los Angeles, with connections to other U.S. cities.

BY TRAIN Amtrak (tel. 800/872–7245) makes eight trips daily between San Diego and Los Angeles.

GETTING AROUND

San Diego attractions are spread out, and public transportation among them is less than satisfactory. If you travel by bus, visit attractions that are close to one another; for example, visit downtown and Balboa Park, or Sea World and Mission Bay, on the same day. Or take the Old Town Trolley (*see* Guided Tours, *below*).

BY CAR I–5 connects most of the beach towns, Old Town, downtown, and Balboa Park. Harbor Drive is a beautiful route along downtown's waterfront, Mission Bay Drive and Ingraham Street pass by most of the Mission Bay Park's popular areas, and Mission Boulevard is a must if you want to see the classic southern California beach scene. Scenic drives are marked by road signs with pictures of seagulls or flowers. The nicest ones go through La Jolla and Point Loma.

Several parking lots around the downtown Embarcadero and Seaport Village charge $3–$5 a day. Parking meters cost 50¢ an hour and are usually good for two hours; don't bother running back to the meter to throw in more change—the space is good for two hours only, and you'll be ticketed if you stay longer (even if there's money in the meter). The lots at Balboa Park and the beach areas are free. From May through Labor Day, parking spots at most beaches are scarce; be prepared to cruise side streets if you arrive after 11 AM.

BY BUS The San Diego Transit Information Line (tel. 619/233–3004); weekdays 5:30 AM–8:25 PM, weekends 8–5) has operators who will help you plan your route. The **Transit Store** (449 Broadway, tel. 619/234–1060) sells the Day Tripper Pass, a $5 investment good for a day of unlimited travel on buses, ferry, and the trolley. A four-day pass is $15.

BY TROLLEY The bright-red electric San Diego Trolley travels along the waterfront in downtown to the Tijuana border and to El Cajon in East San Diego County. The fare is $1–$2 each way, and tickets can be purchased at vending machines at the trolley stops; exact change is required at many machines. The trolley runs approximately every 15 minutes from 5 AM to 1 AM.

BY TAXI Rates vary according to the company. Radio-dispatched cab companies include **Coronado Cab Co.** (tel. 619/435–6211), **Yellow Cab** (tel. 619/234–6161), and **Orange Cab** (tel. 619/291–3333). Cabs rarely cruise the streets; except at the airport, bus, or train stations, call for a cab.

REST STOPS Public rest rooms are available downtown, at the beaches and Mission Bay, and in tourist areas such as Old Town and Balboa Park. Freeways have rest stops on long stretches between outposts of civilization.

GUIDED TOURS One of the best ways to see the city is on the **Old Town Trolley** (tel. 619/298–8687). Open-air, trackless trolleys are used for the 30-mile, two-hour, narrated city tour. You can get off the trolley at any of the 10 stops and continue the tour later in the day. The fare is around $20 for adults;

kids, less than half. Tours begin at 9 AM. This is a great way to see the sights without a car. The last tour of the day is 5–7 PM, with no stops.

EXPLORING

You could easily spend a week and not see all that San Diego has to offer, but you can hit the highlights in about three days. For culture, architecture, shopping, and a quick survey of the top sights, stick to downtown or Old Town, Balboa Park's museums, and the San Diego Zoo. For a more relaxing vacation of swimming, fishing, and sunbathing, stay in Mission Bay or one of the beach towns and make side trips to other attractions.

Balboa Park, with its Spanish-Moorish buildings, gardens, and museums clustered along El Prado (the central walkway), is San Diego's cultural center. Its most outstanding museums are the **San Diego Museum of Art** (tel. 619/232–7931), highlighting American painting, Asian arts and sculpture, Italian renaissance, and Spanish baroque; the **Museum of Photographic Arts** (tel. 619/239–5262), with varying shows from photographic greats and unknowns; and the **Reuben H. Fleet Space Theater and Science Center** (tel. 619/238–1233), with an Omnimax theater and hands-on science exhibits—great for kids! Many are open daily and charge admission; some are closed Monday. Also in the park is the Botanical Building (next to the Lily Pond), the anthropology- and history-oriented Museum of Man, and the Simon Edison Center for Performing Arts.

Cabrillo National Monument, a park at the very tip of Point Loma, commemorates the first European discovery of San Diego in 1542. The view of the Navy and civilian vessels in the harbor is spectacular, and in January or February you might even glimpse a whale spouting during the gray whales' winter migration. *Cabrillo Dr., tel. 619/557–5450. Open daily. Admission charged.*

Coronado's 2.2-mile-long Coronado Bridge looks magnificent as you cross San Diego Bay on the Coronado Ferry—which sails from downtown. The ferry docks at the Old Ferry Landing, where there is a collection of specialty shops and restaurants. From here, tour buses or a trackless trolley proceed to the **Hotel Del Coronado** (1500 Orange Ave., tel. 619/435–6611), a huge gingerbread palace with cupolas, terraces, towers, and the grandest lobby in town.

The **Embarcadero** (waterfront), an array of restaurants and cruise-ship piers lining Harbor Drive downtown, is a great place to walk. Begin at the B Street Pier, where cruise ships dock, passengers embark on harbor excursions, and the **Coronado Ferry** (1306 N. Harbor Dr., tel. 619/234–4111) and the **Maritime Museum** (B St. Pier, tel. 619/234–9153)—a collection of historic vessels—have their headquarters. The Embarcadero's pedestrian path curves by Navy vessels and parklands to **Seaport Village** (tel. 619/235–4013), at Harbor Drive and Market Street. Wander through the shops and landscaped grounds of this 14-acre shopping, dining, and entertainment center that has become the cornerstone of the waterfront. Call for recorded information about magicians, mimes, music, and more happenings at Seaport Village. Continuing south along the waterfront you'll see the mirrored towers of the San Diego Marriott Hotel and Marina and the San Diego Convention Center. The Convention Center has an imaginative design that juts out over the water like a sailing vessel. Climb the center's back stairs for a smashing view across the bay.

The **Gaslamp Quarter,** a 16-block national historic district in downtown, contains restored Victorian buildings from the late 19th century. Some interesting structures are the **William Heath Davis House** (410 Island Ave.), the headquarters of the Gaslamp Quarter Association, and the **Horton Grand Hotel** (311 Island Ave.) across the street. The **Gaslamp Foundation** (tel. 619/233–5227 or 619/233–4691) gives 1½-hour guided walks of the historic Gaslamp Quarter, downtown, on Saturday at 11 AM; call for recorded events information.

Horton Plaza (4th Ave. and Broadway, downtown, tel. 619/238–1596), a large, colorful, modern shopping plaza with a tiled dome and a copper roof, houses several tiers of shops, restaurants, and theaters overlooking a central courtyard. If you drive to the plaza, purchase at least a candy bar to have your parking stub validated for three hours of free parking.

La Jolla, often called the Monte Carlo of California, is the address of San Diego's wealthiest and most prestigious residents. Its natural highlight is Ellen Browning Scripps Park and the La Jolla Cove. Towering palms line the sidewalk from the cove's small beach (where divers and snorkelers congregate at the underwater preserve) for about a mile south to the Children's Pool, a safe, protected bay. Prospect and Girard streets are fun for people-watching and window-shopping. The **San Diego Museum of Contemporary Art,** located here, has imaginative exhibits of painting, sculpture, and furnishings by modern artists. *700 Prospect St., tel. 619/454–3541. Closed Mon. Admission charged.*

Mission Bay, a 4,600-acre aquatic park, is San Diego's best biking, running, walking, and picnicking spot. Its **Visitor Information Center** (2688 E. Mission Bay Dr., tel. 619/276–8200) is stocked with information on all of San Diego's attractions.

Old Town best illustrates San Diego's Spanish and Mexican history and heritage. Clustered around Old Town Plaza (where art shows are often held), in Old Town San Diego Historical Park, the houses date back to San Diego's earliest settlements, in the early 1800s. **Old Town's Visitor Center**—at press time, it was in the process of moving from the Robinson-Rose House (San Diego Ave. at Mason St.) to the McCoy House, behind it—has maps for a walking tour; free guided tours are offered daily at 2 PM. At the north end of the park, the **Bazaar del Mundo** is a colorful shopping and restaurant complex with a Mexican flavor. Surrey bicycles can be rented daily at **Old Town Surrey** (2505 San Diego Ave., tel. 619/296–7010) for an easygoing tour of Old Town's shops and historic places. Presidio Park, at Presidio Drive and Taylor Street, overlooks Old Town and Mission Valley, and is a nice place for a family picnic. Also here is the **Junipero Serra Museum** (tel. 619/297–3258; closed Mon.; admission charged).

San Diego Zoo, Balboa Park's most heavily visited attraction, has more than 4,000 animals and 6,000 plant species. The newest exhibit is Hippo Beach, a "bioclimatically correct" enclosure where you can see the hippos both above and below the water. Several new one-hour walking tours are now available, as are bus tours with unlimited day access. *Zoo Way at Park Blvd., tel. 619/234–3153. Open daily. Admission charged.*

Sea World, in Mission Bay, is the world's largest marine-life park. You have to be a big fan of sea creatures to spring for the nearly $30 admission fee for adults (not to mention $5 for parking), but if you love penguins, killer whales, sharks, and sea lions, it's worth it. Come early and spend the whole day here—when you need a rest, let the kids run rampant on 2 acres of play equipment at the new Shamu's Happy Harbor. The park closes at 6 PM except during the summer, when it remains open until 11 PM. *Sea World Dr., tel. 619/226–3901. Open daily. Admission charged.*

HOTELS AND INNS

Because public transportation is less than efficient, it's best to stay near the things you most want to see and do. New restaurants and hotels are springing up all the time in downtown to serve the convention center; if you stay here, you'll be near the boats in the bay, downtown's dining and shopping scene, and Balboa Park. San Diego's traditional hotel zone is Mission Valley's Hotel Circle, where chain hotels and motels crowd both sides of I–8. Hotel Circle is convenient if you have a car (all the major freeways intersect here), but it's a terrible spot if you don't, and it has no natural beauty whatsoever. Several budget hotels and motels have opened in Old Town along I–5, with good freeway access. Mission Bay and Pacific Beach along the coast have a few budget hotels, as does La Jolla, although for the most part lodging in La Jolla is more expensive. Stay in Coronado if you want to relax, walk through charming neighborhoods, and go to the beach, but keep in mind that it's removed from San Diego's other attractions.

Ask about specials, weekday rates, packages, and discounts for senior citizens and retired military personnel. Hotel rates are higher during the summer and at Christmas and Easter. Price categories for double occupancy, excluding 10½% tax, are Moderate, $60–$100, and Inexpensive, under $60.

CORONADO **Coronado Motor Inn.** This spotless and peaceful motel is about 10 blocks from Coronado's main attractions. *266 Orange Ave., 92118, tel. 619/435–4121 or 800/598–6624, fax 619/435–6296. 24 rooms. Pool, parking, refrigerators. AE, MC, V. Inexpensive.*

DOWNTOWN **Grosvenor Inn.** Recently remodeled and with reasonably priced full- and half-kitchen suites, this pleasant alternative to the larger chain hotels is relatively close to all downtown attractions. *810 Ash St., 92101, tel. 800/232–1212 or 619/233–8826, fax 619/544–0134. 54 rooms. Pool, hot tub. AE, D, DC, MC, V. Inexpensive.*

Holiday Inn Harborview. This round high-rise (built in 1969) on the northern outskirts of downtown offers standard Holiday Inn–quality rooms with spectacular views. *1617 1st Ave., 92101, tel. 619/239–6171 or 800/366–3164, fax 619/233–6228. 202 rooms. Restaurant, lounge, pool. AE, D, DC, MC, V. Moderate.*

Hotel Churchill. The interior of this hotel, built in 1915, resembles that of an English castle. Rooms with a shared bath are downright cheap, and even those with a private bath are a super bargain; weekly and monthly rentals are available. *827 C St., 92101, tel. 619/234–5186. 88 rooms. MC, V. Inexpensive.*

LA JOLLA **La Jolla Cove Motel.** This popular motel overlooks the famous La Jolla Cove beach and has studios and suites (some with spacious oceanfront balconies) at the lowest rates in the area. Exercise buffs can work out next door at the La Jolla Athletic Club. *1155 Coast Blvd., 92037, tel. 619/459–2621 or 800/248–2683, fax 619/454–3522. 116 rooms. Pool, hot tub, parking. AE, D, DC, MC, V. Moderate.*

La Jolla Palms Inn. This modest motel, with fairly large rooms done in green, blue, and beige, is in a quiet neighborhood south of downtown La Jolla, within walking distance of good beaches and restaurants. *6705 La Jolla Blvd., 92037, tel. 619/454–7101. 58 rooms. Restaurant, pool, hot tub, complimentary Continental breakfast. AE, MC, V. Inexpensive–Moderate.*

MISSION BAY/BEACHES **Dana Inn & Marina.** This sprawling low rise, near Sea World and some of Mission Bay's best biking trails, has on-site rentals of marine and sports equipment, including kayaks, sailboats, wave runners, bikes, and in-line skates. *1710 W. Mission Bay Dr., 92109, tel. 619/222–6440 or 800/445–3339, fax 619/222–5916. 196 rooms. Restaurant, pool, marina, sports equipment rentals, tennis courts, Sea World shuttle. AE, D, DC, MC, V. Moderate.*

Mission Bay Motel. The streets around this motel swarm night and day with beach revelers, so it's not peaceful but it is close to both the water and the action. *4221 Mission Blvd., 92109, tel. 619/483–6440. 50 rooms. Pool. D, MC, V. Inexpensive–Moderate.*

Surfer Motor Lodge. The neighborhood is noisy but fun, and the ocean view from this high-rise is wonderful. *711 Pacific Beach Dr., 92109, tel. 619/483–7070 or 800/787–3373, fax 619/274–1670. 52 rooms. Restaurant, pool, refrigerators. AE, DC, MC, V. Moderate.*

OLD TOWN/MISSION VALLEY/HOTEL CIRCLE **Best Western Seven Seas Lodge.** One of the better values in Hotel Circle, this hotel is within walking distance of Fashion Valley Shopping Center, Mission Valley's major bus stop. *411 Hotel Circle S, 92108, tel. 619/291–1300 or 800/328–1618, fax 619/291–*

6933. 309 rooms. Restaurant, coffee shop, game room, pool, 2 spas. AE, D, DC, MC, V. Moderate.

King's Inn. This sprawling, motel-like two-story complex is located in the heart of Mission Valley. *1333 Hotel Circle S, 92108, tel. 619/297–2231, fax 619/296–5255. 140 rooms. Coffee shop, restaurant, pool, whirlpool. AE, D, DC, MC, V. Inexpensive–Moderate.*

Padre Trails Inn. This low-key '50s-era motel, just southwest of Mission Valley, is within walking distance of Old Town. *4200 Taylor St., 92110, tel. 619/297–3291. 100 rooms. Restaurant, lounge, pool. AE, MC, V. Inexpensive.*

Vacation Inn. Palm trees punctuate the courtyards and patios of this adobe-look, three-story hotel in Old Town's center, one block east of Highway 5. Rooms have microwaves, refrigerators, and coffeemakers. *3900 Old Town Ave., 92110, tel. 619/299–7400, 800/451–9846, fax 619/299–1619. 125 rooms. Pool, whirlpool, Continental breakfast, parking. AE, D, DC, MC, V. Inexpensive.*

CAMPGROUNDS

Campland on the Bay. Located right on the sand, this bayside campground has a kids' game room, an 18-hole golf course, and full-service RV hookups. Sailboats, paddle boats, bikes, and other equipment is available for rent. *2211 Pacific Beach Dr., 92109, tel. 800/422–9386 or 619/581–4260, fax 619/581–4206. 640 tent-RV sites; beach, 2 heated pools, whirlpool, marina, playground, rec room, boat ramp, dock, coin laundry, dump station, flush toilets. MC, V.*

San Elijo State Beach. There's plenty of sun and sand for everyone at this campground, right on the ocean just south of Encinitis, close to surf shops, health-food stores, and civilization in general. RVs are permitted, but no hookups. *Hwy. 101 in Cardiff-by-the-Sea, tel. 619/753–5091; reservations, MISTIX, tel. 800/444–7275. 170 sites; showers, laundry facilities, store. No credit cards.*

Silver Strand State Beach. This beautiful beach, established in 1932, is a great place for surf fishing and clam digging. The campground accommodates cars and self-contained recreational vehicles. *5000 Hwy. 75 (Silver Strand Blvd. at Coronado Bay Rd.), 92108, tel. 619/435–5184. 122 sites; rest rooms, showers, fire rings. No credit cards.*

MOTELS

MODERATE **Howard Johnson's** (1430 7th Ave., 92101, tel. 619/696–0911). 136 rooms; coffee shop, pool, exercise room. **Super 8 of Mission Bay** (4540 Mission Bay Dr., 92109, tel. 619/274–7888, fax 619/234–9416). 117 rooms; pool.

INEXPENSIVE **Super 8 Bay View** (1835 Columbia St., 92101, tel. 619/544–0164). 101 rooms; Continental breakfast, parking. **Travelodge Balboa Park** (840 Ash St., 92101, tel. 619/234–8277). 28 rooms; off-site restaurant and pool.

DINING

Mexican food is everywhere in San Diego. Take-out stands—try one of the countless Roberto's, Royberto's, Rigoberto's, or Alberto's—are delicious and cheap. Most of San Diego's inexpensive restaurants have some Mexican items on their menus; other bargains are Greek and Japanese restaurants.

Seafood is abundant, though more expensive than you might think. Fresh lobster from local waters is available from October to March, fresh abalone from March to October. Good values can be found for shark (which tastes much like swordfish but is half the price), dorado (also called mahimahi), halibut, yellowtail, and fresh yellowfin and albacore tuna. Other local specialties are avocados and fresh citrus.

Price categories per person, excluding 7% tax, service, and drinks, are Moderate, $10–$15, and Inexpensive, under $10.

BEACHES **Cafe Athena.** Everything in this pretty, airy Greek restaurant is simply delicious. You can make an interesting meal of the many dips and appetizers, or try the cream of roasted eggplant soup, chicken souvlaki, or the swordfish brochettes. Meals area a wonderful value for the money, and take-out is available. *1846 Garnet Ave., Pacific Beach, tel. 619/274–1140. MC, V. Moderate.*

Point Loma Seafoods. Don't miss this fish market and take-out restaurant with sublime crab-salad sandwiches, seviche, and seafood cocktails; seating is at a premium in the glassed-in dining areas. *2805 Emerson St., Point Loma, tel. 619/223–1109. No credit cards. No dinner. Inexpensive.*

Rusty Pelican. This seafood chain is one of the most consistent on the Mission Beach Boardwalk; popular dishes include the mustard-crusted salmon and mahimahi fillet in African barbecue sauce. Budget-priced early-bird dinners make it easier to enjoy the second-story view of the sunset over the Pacific. A second location is in Mission Valley. *4325 Ocean Blvd., tel. 619/274–3474; 5010 Mission Center Rd., tel. 619/291–6974. AE, D, MC, V. Moderate.*

Souplantation. Diners at this all-you-can-eat salad bar fill their plates with fresh vegetables and marinated salads, their bowls with chili and several varieties of soups, and more plates still with fresh fruit, muffins, pizza, and soft-serve ice cream—all for one low price. *3960 W. Point Loma Blvd., near Sports Arena, tel. 619/222–7404. D, DC, MC, V. Inexpensive.*

DOWNTOWN **Fish Market.** Choose the oyster bar, the sushi bar, or restaurant seating at this spacious and noisy fish house (with free parking after 6 PM) on the waterfront, great for mesquite-grilled fish and pasta dishes. *750 N. Harbor Dr., tel. 619/232–3474. AE, D, DC, MC, V. Moderate.*

Greek Town. Baked lemon chicken, bountiful salads, and hunks of baked moussaka make this family-run restaurant perfect for casual lunches or dinner with friends. *431 E St., tel. 619/232–0461. AE, MC, V. Closed Sun. Inexpensive–Moderate.*

Panda Inn. Often voted the best Chinese restaurant in San Diego, this elegant dining spot offers low-priced Szechuan vegetable dishes and outdoor seating; if you can splurge, try the Peking duck. *506 Horton Plaza, tel. 619/233–7800. AE, D, DC, MC, V. Moderate.*

Sushi Deli. This very casual restaurant—with two downtown locations (the newer one is called Sushi Deli Too)—is probably the greatest bargain in town. Try the California rolls, the teriyaki chicken platter, or any of the reasonably priced sushi combinations. Both locations are closed between lunch and dinner, from 2 PM to 5 PM. *828 Broadway, tel. 619/231–9597; 339 W. Broadway, tel. 619/233–3072. MC, V. Closed Sun. No lunch Sat. Inexpensive–Moderate.*

LA JOLLA **Alfonso's.** The oldest sidewalk café in La Jolla serves an outstanding carne asada burrito and a large tostada salad. *1251 Prospect St., tel. 619/454–2232. AE, D, DC, MC, V. Moderate.*

Sammy's California Woodfired Pizza. For a taste of southern California, stop here for grilled Jamaican jerk chicken salad, Thai shrimp, and more than 20 versions of gourmet pizza (with such exotic toppings as goat cheese and sun-dried tomatoes). *702 Pearl St., tel. 619/456–5222. AE, DC, MC, V. Moderate.*

MISSION VALLEY/HOTEL CIRCLE **Adam's Steak and Eggs/Albie's Beef Inn.** Generous American and Mexican breakfasts, with such hard-to-find delicacies as grits and corn fritters, are served up by friendly waitresses at Adam's. Next door, Albie's takes over at noon, proffering top sirloin steaks and other American favorites. *1201 Hotel Circle S, tel. 619/291–1103. AE, D, DC, MC, V. Closed Sat. between lunch and dinner. Breakfast only Sun. Inexpensive–Moderate.*

Trophy's Sports Grill. Kids will like the special menu, and parents will appreciate the reasonable prices, large portions, and congenial atmosphere of this lively sports bar and restaurant. Some of the best-loved lunch and dinner items are the mesquite-grilled burgers and wood-fire pizzas. *7510 Hazard Center Dr., Suite 215, tel. 619/296–9600. MC, V. Inexpensive–Moderate.*

OLD TOWN **Old Town Mexican Café.** This large restaurant is as popular with San Diegans as with tourists. Try the savory *carnitas* (marinated pork served with cilantro, onions, rice, beans, and delicious fresh tortillas). You can watch the señoras slap the dough around in the open-air kitchen while you wait. *2489 San Diego Ave., tel. 619/297–4330. AE, D, MC, V. Inexpensive–Moderate.*

SHOPPING

SHOPPING DISTRICTS **Coronado:** The Old Ferry Landing (1201 1st St., tel. 619/435–8895) is a small shop and restaurant complex. **Downtown:** Horton Plaza (4th Ave. and Broadway, tel. 619/239–8180) and Seaport Village (Harbor Dr. at Market St., tel. 619/235–4014) house shops and restaurants amid a festive atmosphere. **Hotel Circle:** Fashion Valley Shopping Center (452 Fashion Valley Rd., Mission Valley, tel. 619/688–9113) and Mission Valley Center (1640 Camino del Rio N, Mission Valley, tel. 619/296–6375) are sprawling, outdoor malls, great for people-watching and getting a sense of southern California style. **La Jolla:** University Towne Centre (4545 La Jolla Village Dr., tel. 619/546–8858) is an open-air village featuring department stores, specialty shops, sportswear chains, restaurants, and cinemas. **Old Town:** The Bazaar del Mundo (2754 Calhoun St., Old Town, tel. 619/296–3161), a group of shops specializing in high-quality jewelry, fabrics, housewares, gifts, and books, is built around a Mexican courtyard with brightly colored flowers and squawking parrots.

DEPARTMENT STORES Department-store chains with branches at the malls are **The Broadway** (at Fashion Valley, Horton Plaza, and University Towne Centre), **Robinsons–May Company** (at Mission Valley, Fashion Valley, and University Towne Center), and **Nordstrom** (at Fashion Valley, University Towne Centre, and Horton Plaza). Other department stores are **Neiman Marcus** (Fashion Valley, tel. 619/692–9100) and **Saks** (Fashion Valley Center, tel. 619/260–0030). For bargains, try **Nordstrom Rack** (824 Camino del Rio N, tel. 619/296–0143), where discards from Nordstrom's larger stores are sold at great reductions.

OUTDOOR ACTIVITIES

BEACHES Public city beaches—Coronado Beach, Ocean Beach, Mission Beach, Pacific Beach, and La Jolla Shores—have lifeguards (in summer), rest rooms, and fire rings. Silver Strand State Beach (between Imperial Beach and Coronado) is a state park with RV camping facilities. Torrey Pines State Beach (North of La Jolla, ½ mile south of Carmel Valley Road) is also a state park, but without camping facilities. The beach lies under sandstone cliffs topped by treasured Torrey pine trees and hiking trails. The beaches at Mission Bay are best for sunbathing and boating; there have been problems with water pollution—look for signs warning you to stay out of the water. La Jolla Cove is an underwater nature preserve perfect for snorkeling and diving; Scripps Canyon and Black's Beach (an unofficial nude beach which requires a trek down crumbly cliffs) are also excellent for diving.

BIKING The Embarcadero, the Silver Strand in Coronado, and Mission Bay are popular biking areas. Call **Bikeways Map** (tel. 619/231–2453) for a free map of San Diego's extensive network of bike trails. Bicycle helmets are common, and children are required by law to wear helmets.

For rentals, contact **Bikes and Beyond** (1201 1st St. at Ferry Landing, Coronado, tel. 619/435–7180), **Hamel's** (704 Ventura Pl., Mission Beach, tel. 619/488–5050), or **Rent-A-Bike** (127 E. Island St., downtown, tel. 619/232–4700).

FISHING You don't need a license to fish from the piers in Ocean Beach and Imperial Beach, but you do need one (available at all bait-and-tackle shops) for fishing from the shoreline (the Silver Strand is a good spot). Full-day deep-sea fishing trips for tuna, marlin, dorado, and halibut (depending on the season) are offered April through October by **Fisherman's Landing** (tel. 619/221–8500) and **Seaforth** (tel. 619/224–3383). Freshwater fishing is available at several stocked lakes in East San Diego County. For general information about area lakes, call 619/465–3474.

GOLF Popular public golf courses are **Balboa Park Municipal Golf Course** (Golf Course Dr., tel. 619/570–1234), **Coronado Golf Course** (2000 Visalia Rd., Coronado, tel. 619/435–3121), **Mission Bay Golf Resort** (2702 N. Mission Bay Dr., tel. 619/490–3370), an executive-length course, and **Torrey Pines Golf Course** (11480 N. Torrey Pines Rd., La Jolla, tel. 619/570–1234).

JOGGING AND WALKING Popular areas for long runs or walks include the Embarcadero (waterfront) downtown, all of Mission Bay, the Mission Beach boardwalk (which gets very crowded on weekends), Balboa Park, and most beaches at low tide.

TENNIS Public courts are available at **Morley Field** (tel. 619/295–9278) in Balboa Park, **Robb Field** (tel. 619/226–3407) in Ocean Beach, and the **La Jolla Recreation Center** (tel. 619/552–1658; courts available on a first-come, first-served basis only).

ENTERTAINMENT

SPECTATOR SPORTS The San Diego Padres play baseball April through September for the National League West at **San Diego Jack Murphy Stadium** (9449 Friar's Rd., tel. 619/ 280–4636). The San Diego Chargers (tel. 619/280–2111) take over the stadium for the National Football League August through December. The Barracudas Roller Hockey team (tel. 619/683–7655) tear up the **San Diego Sports Arena** (3500 Sports Arena Blvd., tel. 619/224–4176) June–August; the Sockers play indoor soccer there June–September.

THEATER San Diego has become a theater town, with acclaimed productions at the Old Globe Theatre at **Simon Edison Centre for the Performing Arts** (Balboa Park, tel. 619/239–2255), the **San Diego Repertory Theatre** (Lyceum Theatre, 79 Horton Plaza, tel. 619/235–8025), the **Gaslamp Quarter Theatre** (playhouse: 547 4th Ave., tel. 619/ 234–9583; showcase: 444 4th Ave., tel. 619/ 232–9608), and several smaller theater company venues. Half-price tickets are available on the day of the performance from **TIMES ARTS TIX** (28 Horton Plaza, downtown, tel. 619/238–3810). Tickets are also available here for the San Diego Symphony, the opera, and other cultural events.

San Francisco
California

Updated by Mark Evans and Paul Williams

Bordered by the Pacific Ocean, the Golden Gate Strait, and San Francisco Bay, San Francisco encompasses only about 46 square miles. But it is packed with sights: the majestic Golden Gate and San Francisco–Oakland bridges; the hills and steep streets with cable cars rattling up and down; and exuberant architecture, including pastel-colored Victorian houses, stately mansions, and ultramodern downtown high-rises. Its temperate climate nurtures lush vegetation, and its restaurants are some of the best in the country.

Never a small town, San Francisco went from a settlement of cabins and tents to an instant metropolis during the 1840s gold rush. Since then, this port city has attracted generations of immigrants from around the world, including European, Asian, and Latin American countries. This unusually large number of residents with ties to other cultures flavors the cuisine, commerce, and tenor of the place; it also encourages a tolerance for diversity in customs, beliefs, and lifestyles. As a result, the city's neighborhoods are self-aware and retain strong cultural, political, and ethnic identities. Russian bakeries can still be found in the Richmond District, Irish bars dot the streets of Noe Valley, and taquerias send their enticing smells through the Mission District.

San Francisco's steep hills are notorious, but they do provide spectacular vistas all over town—the crests of the city's seven main hills offer variations on a theme of astounding beauty. From the top of Telegraph Hill you might see jewel-like Angel Island glittering in the sun or the clouds rolling in to cover the bay in a blanket of fog.

ESSENTIAL INFORMATION

WHEN TO GO Any time of the year is the right time to visit San Francisco. Its temperate marine climate is characterized by winters that rarely reach the freezing point, with average maximum and minimum temperatures in January at 55° and 41°. Summers are cooler than visitors might expect, with average maximum and minimum temperatures in July of 69° and 51°. Fog usually rolls in from the ocean during summer mornings (and evenings), normally clearing by midmorning. The city's residents most enjoy September, October, and November, when the weather is relatively warm, the fog has usually dispelled, and tour buses have thinned out. Spring has highs in the 60s and lows in the mid-40s.

FESTIVALS AND SPECIAL EVENTS **Chinese New Year** celebrations run for a week in February and culminate with the Golden Dragon Parade through downtown and Chinatown. In April, the **Cherry Blossom Festival**, a presentation of Japanese culture, includes a parade in Japantown. **Carnaval**, held in May or June in the Mission District, includes a parade, a street festival, and a costume contest. The **Lesbian, Gay, and Bisexual Freedom Day Parade** takes up most of Market Street for an entire day in June and is usually as entertaining as it is long. In September, the **San Francisco Blues Festival** takes place on the Great Meadow in Fort Mason. Check the San Francisco Convention and

Visitors Bureau (*see* Tourist Offices, *below*) for information relating to these and other events.

BARGAINS Many of San Francisco's favorite attractions are free, including a walk across the **Golden Gate Bridge,** a visit to the **Wells Fargo History Museum,** and the view from **Coit Tower** (*see* Exploring, *below*). Admission to the **San Francisco Cable Car Museum** (Washington and Mason Sts.), where you can examine the winding machinery designed to make the motorless cars navigate the city's streets, is also free.

Free summer concerts take place in the Golden Gate Park Music Concourse (tel. 415/666–7107) and on summer Sundays in Stern Grove amphitheater (tel. 415/666–7107) on Sloat Boulevard. **Half-price tickets** to many stage shows go on sale at 11 AM Tuesday–Saturday at the TIX booth (tel. 415/433–7827) on the Stockton Street side of Union Square, between Geary and Post streets.

Good areas for inexpensive dining are North Beach, Chinatown, and Clement Street between 2nd and 14th avenues. Inexpensive souvenirs are available in the Fisherman's Wharf area.

TOURIST OFFICES San Francisco Convention and Visitors Bureau (201 3rd St., Suite 900, 94103, tel. 415/391–2001 or 415/391–2000) has a Visitors' Information Center on the lower level at Hallidie Plaza, at Market and Powell streets, that is open daily.

EMERGENCIES Police, fire, and ambulance: Dial 911. **Hospitals:** San Francisco General Hospital (1001 Potrero Ave., tel. 415/206–8000) and University of California Medical Center (505 Parnassus Ave., tel. 415/476–1000) have 24-hour emergency rooms. **Doctors:** Medical Society Referral Service (tel. 415/561–0853).

ARRIVING AND DEPARTING

BY PLANE Most U.S. and international airlines serve the city's major airport, **San Francisco International Airport** (tel. 415/761–0800), which is located about 15 miles south of the city, between Highway 101 and San Francisco Bay. Allow a half-hour driving time from downtown.

Between the Airport and Downtown: Taxis will cost $25–$30 for the half-hour trip from the airport to downtown. **SFO Airporter** (tel. 415/495–8404) provides bus service between the airport and many downtown hotels; **Supershuttle** (airport tel. 415/871–7800, city tel. 415/558–8500) offers van service between the airport and any destination within San Francisco. Both of these companies charge $10–$20.

BY TRAIN Amtrak (tel. 800/872–7245) trains stop at the Oakland Depot (245 2nd St.); from there, buses will take you across the Bay Bridge to the Transbay Terminal in San Francisco.

BY BUS Greyhound Lines (tel. 800/231–2222) serves the city from the Transbay Terminal (1st and Mission Sts.).

GETTING AROUND

Because the city is relatively compact and parking can be expensive and difficult to find, you will probably want to explore on foot or by public transportation as much as possible. You may not need a car at all, except perhaps for exploring the Presidio, the Golden Gate Bridge and Golden Gate Park, the Cliff House, or out-of-town destinations.

BY BUS, TROLLEY, AND STREETCAR The San Francisco Municipal Railway, or **Muni** (tel. 415/673–6864), operates the city's transit systems. Diesel and electric trolley buses serve most of the routes on city streets. The Muni Metro trains run underground along Market Street from the Embarcadero westward, then aboveground into the neighborhoods. Exact change is required (bills and tokens may be used on some lines) and free transfers are available. Take advantage of Muni's Passport ($6 a day, $10 for three days), which works on all buses, cable cars, and the Muni Metro rail system.

SAN FRANCISCO

0 —— 1 mile
0 —— 1 km

Golden Gate Bridge

Fort Point

TO MUIR WOODS SAUSALITO

Marina Green

Marina

MARINA

Bay St.

Palace of Fine Arts

Lomb

Baker Beach

The Presidio

PACIFIC HEIGHTS

Divisadero St.

Sacramento

California

Pin

Bus

JA

TO

Presidio Ave.

Geary St.

Steiner St.

Palace of the Legion of Honor

Phelan Beach

Lake St.

Lands End

Lincoln Park

SEACLIFF

Clement St.

8th Ave.

Arguello Blvd.

Geary Blvd.

Cliff House

43rd Ave.

34th Ave.

25th Ave.

19th Ave.

Balboa St.

Turk Blvd.

Masonic Ave.

Golden Gate Ave.

RICHMOND

Fulton St.

M.H. de Young Memorial Museum

Asian Art Museum

Fell St.

Conservatory

HAIGHT-ASHBURY

WE

AD

Golden Gate Park

Kennedy Dr.

Middle Dr.

California Academy of Science

Strybing Arboretum

Japanese Tea Garden

Stanyan St.

Buena Vista Park

Clayton St.

Castro St.

Lincoln Way

Judah St.

28th St.

Funston Ave.

7th Ave.

Market St.

CAST

Lawton St.

Clarendon Ave.

NO

VAL

Noriega St.

Ortega St.

19th Ave.

Twin Peaks

SUNSET

41st Ave.

Sunset Blvd.

Quintara St.

14th Ave.

Dewey Blvd.

Diamond St.

McCoppin Square

Taraval St.

Larsen Park

Vicente St.

Mt. Davidson

Dr.

Yerba Buena Ave.

Miramar Ave.

Bosworth St.

Stern Grove

Portola

Monterey Blvd.

Monterey Blvd.

280

San Francisco Zoo

Sloat Blvd.

STONESTOWN

Ocean Ave.

Balboa Park

San Jose Ave.

Alemany Blvd.

Skyline Blvd.

Harding Park

Lake Merced

Lake Merced Blvd.

Font Blvd.

San Francisco State Univ.

Junipero Serra Blvd.

Holloway Ave.

Garfield St.

Great Highway

BY CABLE CAR San Francisco's rolling land-marks have been clattering up and down the hills since 1873; today a ride on a cable car can be just as exciting as a theme-park thrill ride. Two lines begin at Powell and Market streets: The Powell–Hyde line (No. 60), the most spectacular ride, ends up near Ghi-rardelli Square, while the Powell–Mason line (No. 59) terminates near Fisherman's Wharf. To avoid crowds and long waits in line, try the scenic California Street line (No. 61) that runs from Market and Drumm streets to Van Ness Avenue. Tickets are sold from machines at cable-car terminals and the Nob Hill intersection. Exact change is required. *Tel. 415/673–6864. Tickets: $2.*

BY CAR A car is not a necessity for getting around San Francisco. Driving is a challenge because of the city's hills, many one-way streets, and heavy daytime traffic. Parking is also a problem; downtown parking lots are often full and always expensive. Note that maps of the city that have not been updated since the 1989 earthquake are out of date: The Embarcadero freeway between I–80 (the Bay Bridge approach) and Broadway was demolished in 1991, and traffic returned to street level along the Embarcadero. Highway 101 south freeway access is available at Oak Street; exits and entrances beyond that have been demolished.

BY SUBWAY Bay Area Rapid Transit trains, known as **BART** (tel. 415/788–2278) travel under San Francisco Bay from Market Street stations to Oakland, Berkeley, and other East Bay cities.

BY TAXI Since San Francisco is geographi-cally compact, taxis may be a good and affordable option. Hailing a passing cab is usually possible only downtown and in the Civic Center area, so you may need to phone ahead or use the nearest hotel taxi stand to grab a taxi. Major cab companies include **Yellow** (tel. 415/626–2345) and **Veteran's** (tel. 415/552–1300).

REST STOPS Although the city maintains few public bathrooms, you can find accessi-ble rest rooms at the shopping complexes on the Northern Waterfront, at the San Francisco Public Library in the Civic Center, and downtown at major department stores and hotels.

GUIDED TOURS **Orientation: Golden Gate Tours** (tel. 415/788–5775) offers van and bus tours in and around the city; senior-citizen discounts are available. The **Gray Line** (tel. 415/558–9400) uses double-decker buses for tours of the city and beyond. The **Great Pacific Tour** (tel. 415/626–4499) provides 13-passenger vans for sightseeing in the area.

Walking: City Guides (tel. 415/557–4266) conducts free city walking tours, lasting 1–1½ hours. The **Friends of Recreation and Parks** (tel. 415/221–1311) offers free, guided 1½- to two-hour walking tours of Golden Gate Park May–October.

EXPLORING

Few cities in the world pack so much diversity into so little space as San Francisco does. Though most of San Francisco's attractions are located in the northeastern quarter of the city, the outlying neighborhoods provide their own kinds of entertainment. The city's legendary hills may slow you down a bit, but steps replace sidewalks on the steepest slopes, and the views from the top of the streets are breathtaking. (And, of course, it's only uphill halfway.) The San Francisco Municipal Railway's Street and Transit Map, available at newsstands and bookstores, charts all the city routes.

THE BAY AND ALCATRAZ A ferry ride on San Francisco Bay provides a fresh perspective of the city's skyline, the East Bay, and Marin County. The least expensive trip is on one of the Golden Gate ferries (tel. 415/923–2000), leaving from the Ferry Building at the foot of Market Street to Sausalito. Red and White Fleet (Piers 41 and 43½ on Fisherman's Wharf, tel. 415/546–2628 or 415/546–2700) offers a variety of bay cruises, including a ride under the Golden Gate Bridge; it also provides service to **Alcatraz Island,** where National Park Service guides lead excellent

tours of the isle's infamous prison, now partly in ruins, which closed in 1963. (Dress warmly and wear comfortable shoes for the tour.) Advance reservations are recommended for the Alcatraz trip (tel. 415/546–2628).

CHINATOWN The largest Chinese settlement outside Asia, this neighborhood was established in the 1850s and now extends from the dragon-crowned gateway spanning Grant Avenue at Bush Street north to Broadway. Grant and Stockton streets may get crowded, but they have bountiful food markets, bakeries, restaurants, and souvenir shops, as well as pagoda roofs and Chinese street signs. A walk along Waverly Place (which parallels Grant Avenue from Sacramento to Washington streets) will give you a sense of Chinatown's past.

The **Chinese Cultural Center** offers art exhibitions and, on Saturday, neighborhood walking tours (fee charged). *750 Kearny St., in Holiday Inn, tel. 415/986–1822. Open Tues.–Sun. Admission free.*

CIVIC CENTER This area incorporates adjoining cultural institutions in an impressive building complex. The French Renaissance-style **City Hall** (filling the block bounded by Van Ness Avenue and Polk, Grove, and McAllister streets) dominates the area, with its dome higher than the Capitol's in Washington, D.C. Completed in 1915, City Hall was gradually surrounded by other civic buildings: the opulent **War Memorial Opera House** (Van Ness Ave. at Grove St.); the **Veterans' Building** (Van Ness Ave. and McAllister St.); the **Public Library** (McAllister and Larkin Sts.), with a third-floor history museum; and the glass-fronted **Davies Symphony Hall** (Van Ness Ave. and Grove St.). Nearby the Civic Center is a row of art galleries, crafts shops, and cafés on Hayes Street (between Franklin and Gough streets). *Library museum: tel. 415/557–4567. Open Tues.–Sun. Admission free. Symphony Hall and Opera House tour information, tel. 415/552–8338.*

FINANCIAL DISTRICT Once called "Wall Street West," this area, which bustles during weekdays, runs north along Montgomery Street from Market Street. You might want to begin your walk at the grand **Sheraton Palace Hotel** (2 New Montgomery St., tel. 415/392–8600) with its elegant Garden Court restaurant and the famous "Pied Piper of Hamlin," a Maxfield Parish painting commissioned by the hotel in 1909. Architectural highlights in the area include the **Mills Building** (220 Montgomery St.), which survived the 1906 earthquake; the Gothic-style **Russ Building** (235 Montgomery); and the **Pacific Stock Exchange** (Pine and Sansome Sts.). The 853-foot **Transamerica Pyramid** (Montgomery and Clay Sts.) has a free observation area on the 27th floor (open weekdays) and a relaxing redwood grove on its east side.

The **Federal Reserve Bank of San Francisco** hosts an exhibit, "The World of Economics," and offers free tours with reservations in advance. *101 Market St., tel. 415/974–3252. Open Mon.–Thurs. Admission free.*

The **Wells Fargo Bank History Museum** displays gold nuggets, original Western art, a bandit's mementos, and an 1850s red stagecoach. *420 Montgomery St., tel. 415/396–2619. Open weekdays, except bank holidays. Admission free.*

FISHERMAN'S WHARF AND THE NORTHERN WATERFRONT You'll see more tourists and souvenir stands than fishing boats along the Wharf (Piers 43–47 at Taylor and Jefferson Sts.), but a stroll here can be rewarding as you pass by numerous seafood restaurants, craftsmen selling their wares, and street performers. East of the Wharf looms **Pier 39,** which includes a mall with shops, eateries, and free entertainment. South of the Wharf is **The Cannery** (Leavenworth and Beach Sts.), a three-story structure packed with shops and cafés. Another block west on Beach Street stands **Ghirardelli Square,** a charming complex of renovated 19th-century brick factory buildings with unusual gift shops, galleries, and restaurants.

Across the street from the Ghirardelli complex, the **National Maritime Museum** offers exhibits relating to maritime history and a collection of historic boats and ships at the **Hyde Street Pier.** *Aquatic Park at the foot of Polk St. (Pier is 2 blocks east), tel. 415/556–3002. Open daily. Admission charged to Pier.*

GOLDEN GATE BRIDGE, FORT POINT, AND THE PRESIDIO Built in the late 1930s, the **Golden Gate Bridge** is a 2-mile, Art Deco–style orange suspension bridge that connects the city to Marin County. A city Muni bus (No. 28) reaches the toll plaza on the San Francisco side, where there is also a parking lot for motorists. Though it can often be foggy and windy during the free walk across the bridge (warm clothing is needed), you'll have unparalleled views of the Bay Area on the east and west walkways and on the Marin side.

Below the toll plaza, down a path and stairs (also accessible by car from Long Avenue) is the handsome **Fort Point** (tel. 415/556–1693; open Wed.–Sun.; admission free), built in the 1850s to protect the city during the Civil War from sea invaders; the site is now a military museum with a superb bay view from the top floor. From here, hardy walkers may elect to stroll about 3½ miles along the **Golden Gate Promenade** to **Fort Mason** and the Northern Waterfront area (*see above*).

The bridge is situated just north of the **Presidio,** a former army base that was transferred to civilian use in 1994. Now a park, it has more than 1,500 acres of hills, woods, and picnic sites that also allow walking and jogging. *Main entrance: Lombard and Lyon Sts. tel. 415/556–0865. Open daily. Admission free.*

GOLDEN GATE PARK Developed from sand dunes and weeds at the end of the 19th century, this park encompasses 1,000 acres of greenery, lakes, playgrounds, and museums stretching from Stanyan Street in the Haight–Ashbury neighborhood west to the Pacific Ocean. Joggers, bicyclists, skaters, and picnickers flock here, and lawns and benches are available for relaxing.

Just beyond the park's western edge, where the Great Highway meets Point Lobos Avenue, is the Cliff House, a historic restaurant complex overlooking the Pacific and Seal Rocks. All of the attractions below are in the eastern half of the park. Although most visitors visit the park by car, Muni buses also provide service from downtown. To reach the park by public transportation, take the Muni 21–Hayes or 5–Fulton bus westbound at downtown Market Street to 10th Avenue, and walk south into the park.

California Academy of Sciences. This excellent attraction contains a natural-history museum, a planetarium, and the Steinhart Aquarium, which has a dramatic 100,000-gallon tank housing 14,000 creatures. *Golden Gate Park, tel. 415/750–7145. Open daily. Admission charged. Free 1st Wed. of month.*

Conservatory of Flowers. This Victorian structure, the park's oldest building, is an ornate copy of London's Kew Gardens greenhouse; it houses a tropical garden and many rare flowers. *Tel. 415/666–7017. Open daily. Admission charged.*

Japanese Tea Garden. The serene grounds of this garden are landscaped with small ponds, flowering shrubs, and a teahouse. *Tel. 415/666–7017. Open daily. Admission charged.*

M. H. de Young Memorial Museum and the Asian Art Museum. One of the West Coast's best art museums, the de Young features American art, with special collections of painting, sculpture, textiles, and decorative arts from Colonial times through the 20th century. It also has a fine shop and a pleasant café. The de Young adjoins the Asian Art Museum, with more than 10,000 sculptures, paintings, and ceramics. *Golden Gate Park. de Young Museum: tel. 415/863–3330. Asian Art Museum: tel. 415/668–8921. Open Wed.–Sun. One admission charge allows entrance to both museums. Free 1st Wed. of month.*

MISSION DOLORES Begun in 1782, this adobe building, the 6th of 21 missions founded by the Franciscans, has a small museum and an adjacent cemetery with more than 5,000 Indian graves. For public transportation, take

the Muni Metro J–Church car to 16th Street. *Dolores and 16th Sts., tel. 415/621–8203. Open daily. Admission charged.*

MUIR WOODS NATIONAL MONUMENT Located 17 miles northwest of San Francisco, this 550-acre park contains majestic redwood groves. Some trees are nearly 250 feet tall and 1,000 years old. The weather is usually cool and often wet. By car, take Highway 101 north to the Mill Valley–Muir Woods Exit; note that traffic into the park can be heavy during summer, so this is one excursion worth taking by bus. For Golden Gate Transit bus information, call 415/332–6600; for Gray Line bus tour information, call 415/558–9400.

NOB HILL A cable-car ride, or steep hike, up Powell Street from Union Square, this neighborhood was once the site of the estates belonging to the city's most prominent 19th-century robber barons; it is still home to many of the city's elite. The Gothic **Grace Cathedral** (1051 Taylor St.), the city seat of the Episcopal Church, is notable for its gilded bronze doors. Other landmarks in the area are the regal **Fairmont Hotel** (California and Mason Sts.), with its flamboyant red, black, and gold lobby, and the stately **Mark Hopkins Hotel** across the street. For a relaxing stop, visit the well-kept **Huntington Park** (California and Mason Sts.). From Nob Hill, you can hop on a Hyde Street cable car and ride to Lombard Street for a stroll down the brick-paved and flower-lined "crookedest street in the world," which leads to North Beach (*see below*).

NORTH BEACH, TELEGRAPH HILL, AND COIT TOWER Centered around Washington Square Park at Powell and Union streets and also around Columbus Avenue north of Broadway, this easygoing neighborhood, originally settled by Italians during the gold-rush era, has several reasonably priced Italian restaurants, and a few other ethnic dining spots as well. A few highlights include **Panelli Brothers** (1419 Stockton St.), opened in 1934, and **Molinari's** (373 Columbus Ave.), two popular delicatessens, and **Caffe Puccini** (411 Columbus Ave.) for cappuccino and pastries. Farther south of these cafés is **City Lights Bookstore** (261 Columbus Ave.), a landmark from the 1950s bohemian years with a fine book selection for browsing.

From Washington Square, you can proceed to **Coit Tower,** a legacy of eccentric millionaire Lillie Hitchcock Coit, on the crest of Telegraph Hill; here you'll have unparalleled views of the neighborhood, the bay, and downtown. The east end of Lombard Street continues uphill to Coit Tower, but there can be a long waiting line for the small parking lot. If you don't have a car, you can reach Coit Tower from North Beach by walking up Grant Avenue and following the steps to the right on Filbert Street, or taking the Muni 39–Coit bus from Washington Square. The most memorable way down from the tower is along the Filbert Street steps that pass wooded gardens and Victorian cottages from Montgomery Street east to the base of the hill. *Tel. 415/362–0808. Open daily. Admission charged.*

PALACE OF FINE ARTS Reconstructed in the 1960s, this rose-colored Roman Classic–style structure with massive columns, a great rotunda, and a swan-filled lagoon is the sole survivor of a 1915 exposition. The interior houses the first-rate Exploratorium, a popular hands-on science museum with 600 exhibits. *Baker and Beach Sts., the Marina, tel. 415/563–7337. Open Labor Day–Memorial Day, Tues.–Sun.; Memorial Day–Labor Day, daily. Admission charged.*

SAUSALITO This hillside town on a sheltered site along San Francisco Bay in Marin County is filled with shops, cafés, and seafood restaurants; its views across the bay to San Francisco, however, are the prime attractions. By car, cross the Golden Gate Bridge and take Highway 101 north to the Sausalito exit. The ferry ride from the Embarcadero is more enjoyable than the drive. *Golden Gate Ferry, tel. 415/923–2000. Red and White Fleet, tel. 415/546–2628 or 415/546–2700.*

UNION SQUARE Bounded by Geary, Stockton, Sutter, and Powell streets, this area, the heart of downtown, has been San Francisco's retail center for more than a century. Here you'll find the city's finest department stores and boutiques. About 40 hotels are situated within three blocks of the square, and the downtown theater district is also nearby. The square itself, planted with palms and flowers, attracts a mixed crowd. The biggest retail stores around the square include **Macy's** (Stockton and O'Farrell Sts., tel. 415/397–3333), **Neiman Marcus** (150 Stockton St., tel. 415/362–3900), and **Saks Fifth Avenue** (384 Post St., tel. 415/986–4300). A short walk from the square are the more reasonably priced **Emporium** (Market St. near Powell St., tel. 415/764–2222) department store with a complete stock of clothing and home furnishings; and the upscale **San Francisco Shopping Centre** at Powell and Market streets, which is topped by **Nordstrom** (tel. 415/243–8500), with designer clothing and first-rate service. The following are worth a visit: the ornate atrium from the old City of Paris department store installed within Neiman Marcus; **Gump's** (135 Post St., tel. 415/982–1616), the elegant importer; the only San Francisco building designed by Frank Lloyd Wright (140 Maiden La., just east of the square); the glass-roofed **Crocker Galleria** (Post and Kearny Sts.), with 50 shops, restaurants, and services; and the art galleries upstairs in buildings around the intersection of Grant and Sutter streets.

YERBA BUENA GARDENS AND THE SOUTH OF MARKET ARTS DISTRICT This fast-growing and thriving area south of Market Street and the Civic Center is a testimony to San Francisco's appreciation for modern art media.

Ansel Adams Center for Photography. Dedicated to creative photography, this museum has five galleries, one of which displays work by noted landscape photographer Ansel Adams, who is best known for his images of Yosemite. *250 4th St., tel. 415/495–7000. Open Tues.–Sun. Admission charged.*

San Francisco Museum of Modern Art. Swiss architect Mario Botta's Modernist design for the city's newest museum is as much of a masterpiece as the works it exhibits. Besides displays of the comprehensive permanent collection of 20th-century art—highlights include pieces by Matisse, Klee, Picasso, O'Keeffe, Pollock, and Frieda Kahlo—galleries are devoted to traveling exhibitions and a film and video series. *151 3rd St., tel. 415/357–4000. Open Tues.–Sun. Admission charged.*

Yerba Buena Gardens. This urban park, home to a stunning waterfall and memorial to Dr. Martin Luther King, Jr., offers spectacular cityscape views. The **Center for the Arts at Yerba Buena Gardens** has three galleries dedicated to modern multicultural art and also hosts dance, theater, and film exhibitions. *3rd St., between Mission and Howard, tel. 415/978–2787. Open Tues.–Sun. Admission charged.*

HOTELS AND INNS

The construction and restoration of plush grand hotels in San Francisco has been matched by the extensive transformation of smaller properties into distinctive, European-style lodgings that offer warm personal service—often at half the price of the expensive hotels. The city also has a good selection of bed-and-breakfasts, often located in Victorian-style structures. Many of the city's budget accommodations are found a block or two west of Union Square and around the Civic Center, though some are also located in the downtown area alongside the pricier establishments. Because of the city's year-round appeal, few hotels offer off-season rates. Most motels are located along Lombard Street between Van Ness Avenue and the Golden Gate Bridge approach.

Reservation services include **San Francisco Reservations** (22 2nd St., 4th Floor, 94105, tel. 415/227–1500 or 800/667–1550). You can save money by staying in private homes and apartments, available by contacting **Bed & Breakfast San Francisco** (Box 420009, 94142, tel. 415/931–3083, fax 415/921–2273) and **Bed & Breakfast International San Francisco** (Box 282910, 94128-2910, tel.

415/696–1690 or 800/872–4500, fax 415/696–1699).

Price categories for double occupancy, excluding 12% tax, are Expensive, $110–$175; Moderate, $75–$110; and Inexpensive, under $75.

CIVIC CENTER **Hotel Richelieu.** The Richelieu's rooms acquired new beds, furniture, and carpeting in an extensive 1995 renovation that helped re-create a Victorian-style atmosphere. The hotel is convenient to public transportation. *1050 Van Ness Ave., 94109, tel. 415/673–4711 or 800/227–3608, fax 415/673–9362. 150 rooms. No-smoking rooms, 24-hr restaurant adjacent. AE, DC, MC, V. Moderate.*

Pensione San Francisco. This European-style hotel offers smartly decorated rooms and lobby areas, plus excellent facilities (but no in-room TVs), at bargain prices. *1668 Market St., 94102, tel. 415/864–1271 or 800/886–1271. 36 rooms with shared bath. Concierge. AE, MC, V. Inexpensive.*

FISHERMAN'S WHARF **Columbus Motor Inn.** This attractive motel between North Beach and Fisherman's Wharf has airy rooms with bay windows and two-bedroom suites that are ideal for families. *1075 Columbus Ave., 94133, tel. 415/885–1492. 45 rooms. No-smoking rooms, cable TV, parking. AE, DC, MC, V. Moderate.*

LOMBARD STREET/MARINA DISTRICT **Cow Hollow Motor Inn.** This large, modern motel balances clean rooms with a convenient Marina area location only four blocks from the bay. *2190 Lombard St., 94123, tel. 415/921–5800, fax 415/922–8515. 129 rooms. Restaurant, access to health club, fully equipped kitchens. AE, DC, MC, V. Moderate.*

Marina Inn. Dainty flowered wallpaper, poster beds, and pine furniture give the rooms here an English-country air. *3110 Octavia St. at Lombard St., 94123, tel. 415/928–1000, fax 415/928–5909. 40 rooms. AE, MC, V. Moderate.*

Town House Motel. This appealing two-story wood-and-stucco motel is one of the best values on Lombard Street. *1650 Lombard St., 94123, tel. 415/885–5163 or 800/255–1516, fax 415/771–9889. 24 rooms. Parking, TV with 24-hr movie channel, shuttle from airport. AE, DC, MC, V. Inexpensive–Moderate.*

Vagabond Inn. The Vagabond offers comfortable B&B accommodations at motel prices. Breakfast is served in a cozy central sitting room, and turned-down beds and chocolate greet guests at the end of each day. *2550 Van Ness Ave. near Lombard St., 94109, tel. 415/776–7500 or 800/522–1555. 132 rooms. Continental breakfast included, restaurant, valet and laundry service, kitchens. AE, DC, MC, V. Moderate.*

NOB HILL **Mark Hopkins Inter-Continental.** The epitome of luxurious San Francisco, this historic and prestigious hotel is the best choice for serious pampering. For unbeatable panoramic views, visit the Top of the Mark, *the* rooftop lounge in San Francisco since 1939. *1 Nob Hill, 94108, tel. 415/392–3434 or 800/327–0200, fax 415/421–3302. 390 rooms. Valet and laundry service, 24-hr room service, world-class lounge, restaurant, fitness room, limousine service, concierge. AE, DC, MC, V. Expensive.*

PACIFIC HEIGHTS **The Majestic.** This elegant and romantic hotel is a wonderful way to experience the gracious and old-style charm of San Francisco. Beautiful antiques fill the lobby, and all of the rooms feature four-poster canopied beds. It's conveniently situated near cafés, stores, and public transportation. *1500 Sutter St., 94109, tel. 415/441–1100 or 800/ 869–8966, fax 415/673–7331. 59 rooms. Valet and laundry service, valet parking, concierge, restaurant-bar, complimentary Continental breakfast and evening cordials. AE, DC, MC, V. Expensive.*

UNION SQUARE/DOWNTOWN **Adelaide Inn.** Although the bedspreads and drapes may not always match, this cozy bargain offers clean rooms, an amiable staff, and complimentary Continental breakfast. *5 Isadora Duncan Ct., off Taylor St. between Geary and Post Sts., 94102, tel. 415/441–2474. 16 rooms with shared bath. MC, V. Inexpensive.*

Amsterdam. This European-style B&B has clean, bright rooms looking out from a prim Victorian building and is a good value for its location between Union Square and Nob Hill. *749 Taylor St., 94108, tel. 415/673– 3277 or 800/637–3444, fax 415/673–0453. 32 rooms, 5 with shared bath. Breakfast included, cable TV, some kitchens. AE, MC, V. Inexpensive.*

Bedford. Cheerful floral prints and canopy beds dominate the rooms in this stylishly renovated 17-story hotel, four blocks from Union Square. *761 Post St., 94109, tel. 415/ 673–6040 or 800/227–5642; in CA, 800/ 652–1889; fax 415/563–6739. 144 rooms. Restaurant, complimentary wine in afternoon, laundry service. AE, DC, MC, V. Moderate.*

Beresford Arms. Built in 1910 and full of Old World charm, the Beresford earns high marks for the complimentary wine and cheese served afternoons in the grand lobby. Standard rooms have queen-size beds and small refrigerators, while the suites with whirlpool baths and full kitchens are perfect for families. *701 Post St., 94109, tel. 415/ 673–2600 or 800/533–6533, fax 415/474– 0449. 96 rooms. Valet and laundry service. AE, DC, MC, V. Moderate.*

Cartwright. Antiques, fresh flowers, and afternoon tea add to the distinctive surroundings of this friendly, family-owned hotel just off Union Square; rooms feature brass or wood-carved beds and refrigerators. *524 Sutter St., 94102, tel. 415/421–2865 or 800/227–3844, fax 415/421–2865. 114 rooms. Restaurant, concierge, valet and laundry service. AE, DC, MC, V. Moderate.*

Chancellor Hotel. This venerable hotel near the cable-car line has been attracting a loyal clientele since it was built in 1914; the rooms are elegantly decorated with cherry-wood furniture. *433 Powell St., 94102, tel. 415/362–2004 or 800/428–4748, fax 415/ 362–1403. 140 rooms, 6 suites. Restaurant, lounge. AE, DC, MC, V. Moderate.*

Grant Plaza. This bargain-priced hotel at the entrance of Chinatown has small but clean rooms with plain, whitewashed furniture and a lovely stained-glass dome on the sixth floor. *465 Grant Ave., 94108, tel. 415/434–3883 or 800/472–6899, fax 415/434–3886. 72 rooms. AE, MC, V. Inexpensive.*

Holiday Inn Union Square. Cable cars stop outside the front doors of this sleek and tasteful 30-story hotel, which also offers great views. Large, well-appointed rooms and many services are some of the benefits of a 1993 renovation. *480 Sutter St., 94108, tel. 415/398–8900 or 800/243–1135, fax 415/989–8823. 400 rooms. Fitness room, roof-top lounge, valet and laundry service, bellman, gift shop, room service. AE, DC, MC, V. Expensive.*

King George. Built to welcome visitors to the 1915 Panama Pacific International Exposition, this elegantly refurbished Georgian-style hotel in the theater district has a quaint tearoom. *334 Mason St., 94102, tel. 415/781–5050 or 800/288–6005, fax 415/391–6976. 140 rooms. Bellman, 24-hr room service, special package rates. AE, DC, MC, V. Moderate–Expensive.*

Ramada Inn. Cheerfully decorated rooms with refrigerators, an attentive staff, and a location just two blocks from Union Square make this hotel a good choice. *345 Taylor St., 94102, tel. 415/673–2332 or 800/227–4074; in CA, 800/622–0873; fax 415/398–0733. 116 rooms. Restaurant, lobby bar, valet and laundry service, sundeck, special package rates. AE, DC, MC, V. Moderate.*

Pickwick Howard Johnson. This Gothic-style brick hotel is only a half block from the elegant San Francisco Shopping Centre. *85 5th St., 94103, tel. 415/421–7500 or 800/227–3282, fax 415/243–8066. 190 rooms. Restaurant, lounge, valet and laundry service, special package rates. AE, DC, MC, V. Inexpensive–Moderate.*

York Hotel. This carefully renovated hotel located between Union Square and the Polk Street shopping area boasts its own cabaret—the stylish Plush Room—and complimentary breakfast. *940 Sutter St., 94109, tel. 415/885–6800 or 800/808–9675, fax 415/885–*

2115. 96 rooms. Fitness center, limousine service, complimentary wine in afternoon. AE, DC, MC, V. Moderate–Expensive.

MOTELS

MODERATE **Bel Aire Travelodge** (3201 Steiner St., 94123, tel. 415/921–5162 or 800/255–3050). 32 rooms; parking. **Central Travelodge S.F.** (1707 Market St., 94103, tel. 415/621–6775 or 800/255–3050). 84 rooms; coffee shop, parking, valet and laundry service. **Days Inn near the Wharf** (2358 Lombard St., 94123, tel. 415/922–2010 or 800/325–2525, fax 415/563–7958). 22 rooms; parking. **Valu Inn by Nendels** (900 Franklin St., 94109, tel. 415/885–6865 or 800/843–4021; in CA, 800/223–9626; fax 415/474–1652). 59 rooms; parking, health club.

DINING

So seriously do San Franciscans take their food that the city is said to have more restaurants per capita than any city in the nation. The Bay Area's signature "California cuisine," invented at Chez Panisse in Berkeley, emphasizes lightly grilled fish and poultry and fresh seasonal produce from nearby farms. Vegetarian food is available in almost every restaurant, even in the Mission District's smallest family-run Mexican eatery. Visitors may eat well here without straining their budgets. Price categories per person, excluding 8½% tax, service, and drinks, are Expensive, over $25; Moderate, $15–$25; and Inexpensive, under $15.

CIVIC CENTER **Max's Opera Cafe.** At this lively, cheerful restaurant in an upscale condo complex, deli sandwiches, salads, and grilled fish and chicken are served by singing waiters. *601 Van Ness Ave., tel. 415/771–7300. AE, MC, V. Inexpensive–Moderate.*

Stars Café. Stars Café is affiliated with the adjacent, upscale Stars restaurant, but lacks the exorbitant prices; for the moment, the Café is also one of the city's hippest eateries.

The never-dull menu adds a healthy, exotic edge to its soups, gourmet salads, and fresh pastas. *555 Golden Gate Ave. in Civic Center, tel. 415/861–4344. AE, MC, V. Inexpensive.*

Vicolo. This downtown restaurant is perfect for lunch or a light dinner and is conveniently located near the Opera House and Symphony Hall. Besides the crisp salad selections, the menu features cornmeal-crust pizzas with some very imaginative (and *very* California) toppings. *201 Ivy St. off Franklin St., tel. 415/863–2382. No credit cards. Inexpensive.*

Zuni Cafe Grill. Zuni's Italian–Mediterranean menu and its vibrant atmosphere pack in diverse and eclectic crowds from morning to late evening. Grilled fish and chicken and fresh oysters are among the specialties, and even the hamburgers have an Italian accent: They're served on herbed focaccia buns. Be sure to arrive early for a drink at the bar, where San Franciscans go to see and be seen. *1658 Market St., just west of Civic Center, tel. 415/552–2522. AE, MC, V. Moderate.*

EMBARCADERO **Ciao.** Light, contemporary Italian food is served in a bright high-tech setting accented by bronze and chrome. Specialties include squid-ink half-moon pasta stuffed with white fish in a shrimp sauce, osso buco (veal roast), and *crespelle all' aragosta* (crepes with lobster in a lobster sauce). *230 Jackson St., north of Financial District, tel. 415/982–9500. AE, DC, MC, V. Moderate.*

Harbor Village. This beautifully designed branch of a Hong Kong restaurant, with antiques and teak furnishings, prepares subtly seasoned Cantonese cuisine, dim sum lunches, and fresh seafood from the restaurant's own tanks. *Embarcadero Center 4, Sacramento and Drumm Sts., tel. 415/781–8833. AE, MC, V. Moderate.*

Splendido's. Mediterranean cooking is the focus at this stylish dining spot. Specialties include shellfish soup and warm goat-cheese-and-ratatouille salad; for tamer gourmets there are hearty homemade soups and pizzas

topped with fresh vegetables. *Embarcadero 4, Sacramento and Drumm Sts., tel. 415/986–3222. AE, DC, MC, V. Moderate.*

FINANCIAL DISTRICT **Palio D'Asti.** This vibrant, upbeat Italian trattoria specializes in antipasti and gourmet pizzas from its wood-burning oven. Entrées combine the methods of traditional Italian cooking with California cuisine; pastas often have an emphasis on seafood. *640 Sacramento St., tel. 415/395–9800. AE, DC, MC, V. Moderate.*

FISHERMAN'S WHARF AND THE NORTHERN WATERFRONT **Alioto's No. 8.** A San Francisco tradition since 1925, the oldest restaurant on Fisherman's Wharf offers a charming atmosphere with a view of the boat basin and the Golden Gate Bridge. The restaurant specializes in local seafood; dishes feature such fresh, flavorful local catches as salmon and swordfish. *8 Fisherman's Wharf, tel. 415/673–0183. AE, DC, MC, V. Moderate.*

JAPANTOWN **Mifune.** This amiable café in the Japan Center specializes in the Japanese version of fast food: wheat or buckwheat noodles in steaming broth, with egg, seafood, and vegetable toppings. Tempura and grilled entrées are also available. *1737 Post St., near Fillmore St., tel. 415/922–0337. AE, DC, MC, V. Inexpensive.*

MARINA **Greens at Fort Mason.** Even resolute carnivores enjoy the wide range of creative vegetarian dishes at this celebrated dining spot; homemade breads and desserts are as exceptional as the bay views. *Building A, Fort Mason, Marina Blvd. at Laguna St., tel. 415/771–6222. MC, V. Moderate–Expensive.*

Scott's Seafood Grill and Bar. This pleasant restaurant has made its reputation on fresh fish—usually about a dozen choices—simply but delicately prepared. Try to arrive by 6:30 PM. *2400 Lombard St., tel. 415/563–8988 (also at Embarcadero 3, Sacramento and Davis Sts., tel. 415/981–0622). AE, DC, MC, V. Moderate.*

MIDTOWN **Golden Turtle.** This popular Vietnamese café has an extensive menu, including stir-fried and heart-healthy steamed dishes and a variety of salads and first-course vegetables. *2211 Van Ness Ave., near Broadway, tel. 415/441–4419. AE, MC, V. Inexpensive.*

NORTH BEACH **Capp's Corner.** This is one of the last of North Beach's family-style Italian restaurants—the sort of place where diners sit at long Formica tables and feast on serious servings of soup, salad, roast chicken, and pasta. *1600 Powell St., tel. 415/989–2589. AE, DC, MC, V. Inexpensive.*

North Beach Pizza. This pizza restaurant has been a San Francisco favorite for years. Unpretentious and bustling, it serves a variety of imaginative and delicious entrées, including pasta, poultry, barbecue, sandwiches, and of course its award-winning pizza. Service is very friendly, and prices are reasonable. *1499 Grant Ave., at Union St., tel. 415/433–2444 (also at 1310 Grant Ave., near Vallejo St., tel. 415/433–2444). AE, DC, MC, V. Inexpensive.*

PACIFIC HEIGHTS **Café Majestic.** The cozy and romantic restaurant in the Majestic Hotel offers fine dining. Specialties include rack of lamb, tender steaks, and roast chicken. *1500 Sutter St., at Gough St., tel. 415/776–6400. AE, DC, MC, V. Expensive.*

SOUTH OF MARKET **Chevy's.** This big, boisterous Mexican establishment stakes its reputation on using the freshest ingredients and sauces and offers a good selection of grilled chicken and fish dishes in addition to more traditional Mexican creations. *4th and Howard Sts., near Moscone Convention Center, tel. 415/543–8060. MC, V. Inexpensive.*

UNION SQUARE/DOWNTOWN **Bentley's Oyster Bar & Restaurant.** The bustling bar here serves 12 different types of oysters, while the quiet dining room upstairs offers grilled fish in a variety of creative sauces, as well as crab cakes and New Orleans–style gumbo. There's live piano music during the week and live jazz on Friday and Saturday nights downstairs in the bar. *185 Sutter St., tel. 415/989–6895. AE, DC, MC, V. Moderate.*

City of Paris. This art-nouveau bistro is convenient to the theater district and features spit-roasted chicken, duck confit, and wonderful hamburgers. *101 Shannon Alley, at the Shannon Court Hotel, tel. 415/441–4442. AE, MC, V. Inexpensive–Moderate.*

Fog City Diner. This sleek and upscale diner has an outdoor patio. A varied menu includes American-style classics and fresh shellfish. *1300 Battery St., tel. 415/982–2000. AE, DC, MC, V. Moderate.*

Les Joulins. This friendly, unpretentious French bistro near Union Square serves a fresh salad of the day, as well as daily specials of fish, shellfish, chicken, and pasta. *44 Ellis St., near Stockton St., tel. 415/397–5397. AE, DC, MC, V. Moderate.*

Salmagundi. The soups and fresh salads change daily at this no-nonsense downtown cafeteria, which also prepares sandwiches. *442 Geary St., tel. 415/441–0894. No credit cards. Inexpensive.*

Souper Salad. Imaginative salads and hearty soups are the highlights at this comfortable café on the lower level of the San Francisco Shopping Centre. *865 Market St., tel. 415/777–9922. No credit cards. Inexpensive.*

SHOPPING

SHOPPING DISTRICTS Between Gough and Fillmore streets and south of the Marina and Fort Mason, **Union Street** shines with contemporary apparel, jewelry, and antiques shops; more antiques can be found on **Sacramento Street** near Presidio Avenue. Under one roof, the **Japan Center** (Geary and Post Sts.) in Japantown is usually uncrowded; it has crafts and houseware shops, where you can find antique kimonos, tansu chests, and fine porcelains. Once the nation's hippie headquarters, the **Haight Street** area, stretching from Central Avenue to Stanyan Street, now features vintage fashions from the '40s and '50s, Mexican art, and collectibles. Nearby **Castro Street** is the focus of the city's gay and lesbian communities; stores along the lively avenue feature crafts, health foods, clothes, and some very interesting clothing accessories.

Downtown's Union Square is flanked by the city's best department stores and expensive boutiques. Chinatown has a seemingly endless choice of shops selling Chinese silks and jewelry, toy trinkets, pottery, baskets, and groceries. North Beach offers small clothing stores, antiques shops, or eccentric specialty shops. Fisherman's Wharf and the Northern Waterfront have Pier 39, the Anchorage, Ghirardelli Square, and The Cannery, four renovated complexes full of shops, restaurants, and outdoor entertainment. For more information on these neighborhoods, *see* Exploring, *above.*

SPECIALTY ITEMS San Francisco's famous sourdough bread will be fresher and probably less costly from a North Beach bakery or neighborhood grocery store than from the airport gift shop. (The most authentic loaf is wrapped in a paper bag, not plastic.)

For a variety of chocolate gifts, try the **Ghirardelli Chocolate Shop** (900 North Point, Ghirardelli Sq., tel. 415/474–3938) and the downtown shop **Ghirardelli Chocolate** (44 Stockton St. at Union Sq., tel. 415/397–3615).

The city is known for Asian imports, and everything from trinkets to silk brocade can be found in Chinatown and Japantown. **Cost Plus** (Taylor St. between Beach and Bay Sts., tel. 415/885–5100) near Fisherman's Wharf is a good place to buy inexpensive imported gifts.

Specialized books about San Francisco and the Bay Area can be found at the **National Maritime Museum and Hyde Street Pier** (Aquatic Park, tel. 415/556–3002) and at the **City Lights Bookstore** (261 Columbus Ave., tel. 415/362–8193) in North Beach.

OUTDOOR ACTIVITIES

BIKING Bike routes in **Golden Gate Park** (tel. 415/666–7201; *see also* Exploring, *above*) include one route through the park to Lake Merced and another from the south end of the city to the Golden Gate Bridge. Many bike-rental shops are located on Stanyan Street across from Golden Gate Park; major streets in the park are closed to cars on Sunday.

BOATING **Stow Lake** (tel. 415/752–0347; open daily) in Golden Gate Park has rowboat, pedal boat, and small electric boat rentals.

FISHING Fishing boats leave from Fisherman's Wharf for salmon outside the bay or striped bass and giant sturgeon within the bay. Licenses can be bought at sporting-goods stores. Temporary licenses are available on charters and from **Lovely Martha Sport Fishing** (tel. 415/871–4445) and **Wacky Jacky** (tel. 415/586–9800).

GOLF The city maintains three easily accessible golf courses: the 18-hole **Lincoln Park** (34th Ave. and Clement St., tel. 415/221–9911), the nine-hole **Golden Gate Park** (47th and Fulton Sts., tel. 415/751–8987), and the 18-hole **Harding Park** (Lake Merced and Skyline Blvds., tel. 415/664–4690) on the city's western edge.

TENNIS The **San Francisco Recreation and Park Department** (tel. 415/753–7101 or 415/753–7001) maintains 130 free tennis courts throughout the city, including some in Golden Gate Park and Mission Dolores Park.

ENTERTAINMENT

CONCERTS The city has an extensive year-round concert schedule; check the "Datebook" section of the Sunday San Francisco *Examiner* and *Chronicle* for details. **San Francisco Symphony** (Davies Symphony Hall, Van Ness Ave. at Grove St., tel. 415/431–5400) performs September–May; the Symphony also presents pops concerts in July, at modest prices.

DANCE **San Francisco Ballet** (War Memorial Opera House, Van Ness Ave. at Grove St., tel. 415/703–9400) performs *The Nutcracker* in December, and classic ballets and more contemporary works February–May.

FILM First-run theaters are scattered throughout the city but concentrated along

Van Ness Avenue north of the Civic Center. The **Castro Theater** (429 Castro St. near Market St., tel. 415/621–6120), the city's last remaining movie palace from the 1920s, has an extensive schedule of classic revivals.

SKYLINE LOUNGES **Carnelian Room** (top of the Bank of America Bldg., 555 California St., tel. 415/433–7500) has dinner or cocktails on the 52nd floor. **Sherlock Holmes, Esq.** (Holiday Inn Union Square, Sutter and Powell Sts., tel. 415/398–8900) offers piano music and reasonably priced drinks on the 30th floor. **Top of the Mark** (Mark Hopkins Hotel, California and Mason Sts., tel. 415/ 392–3434) has fabulous views on the 19th floor.

SPECTATOR SPORTS Baseball's **San Francisco Giants** play spring and summer at Candlestick Park (tel. 415/467–8000), and the Oakland A's play at the **Oakland Coliseum** (tel. 510/638–0500). The **Golden State Warriors** play basketball at the Oakland Coliseum Arena (tel. 510/638–6300) October– April. Football's **San Francisco 49ers** (tel. 415/468–2249) appear at Candlestick Park, and the newly returned **Oakland Raiders** appear at Oakland Coliseum.

Santa Fe and Taos

New Mexico

Updated by Daniel Gibson

ith crisp, clear air and bright, sunny weather, Santa Fe—and Taos, its trendy satellite 60 miles to the north—couldn't be more welcoming. These two New Mexican towns are both situated at an invigorating altitude of more than 7,000 feet.

Both Santa Fe, founded around 1608, and Taos, where the Coronado Expedition pushed north in 1598, echo with reminders of the early days of Spanish colonization. The predominance of adobe architecture in these communities testifies to the unique intermingling of Spain's Moorish heritage and the Pueblo Indian culture of northern New Mexico. Even today, the populations of Santa Fe (60,000) and Taos (4,500) come predominately from three separate cultures—Native American, Spanish, and Anglo (a term used in New Mexico to designate people of European, non-Spanish descent).

This combination of a stunning location, dramatic landscapes, and a rich historical and cultural background have lured artists and writers for centuries. Visitors to these towns can appreciate streets filled with art galleries and outstanding museums; shops showcasing the finest Native American, Hispano, and contemporary arts and crafts; restaurants offering distinctive regional cuisine; and hotels—both elegant and simple—decorated with regional handmade, hand-painted furnishings that have inspired "Santa Fe" and "Taos" decorative trends throughout the United States.

ESSENTIAL INFORMATION

WHEN TO GO Santa Fe and Taos have fairly mild climates, though severe cold can be encountered in midwinter, with occasional snowfall from November to May. The winter ski season attracts plenty of visitors from Thanksgiving to Easter. Average daily winter minimum and maximum temperatures in Santa Fe fall between 19° and 45°, but the thermometer sometimes reads as low as 0°. The summer is a pleasant time to visit, but in July and August the area becomes crowded with tourists. Average daily minimum and maximum temperatures range from the mid-50s to the 90s. The sun is often intense because of the high altitude, but low humidity makes high temperatures bearable. Even when days are warm, evenings can become chilly or cold. Spring and fall are less crowded times for tourists. Average temperatures in the area range from 35° to 70° in the spring; 28° to 70° in the fall.

FESTIVALS AND SEASONAL EVENTS **New Year's Day:** For Indian New Year's celebrations, there's a Turtle Dance at the Taos Pueblo. **May:** Taos Spring Arts Celebration runs for three weeks. **Early July:** Rodeo De Santa Fe provides a taste of the Old West with cattle shows and roping contests. **Late July:** Spanish Market is held on the Santa Fe Plaza during the last weekend in July, with Hispano arts and crafts. Late **Aug.:** Indian Market, held the third weekend of the month on the Santa Fe Plaza, is the world's greatest showcase of Native American arts and crafts. **Early Sept:** Las Fiestas de Santa Fe, begin-

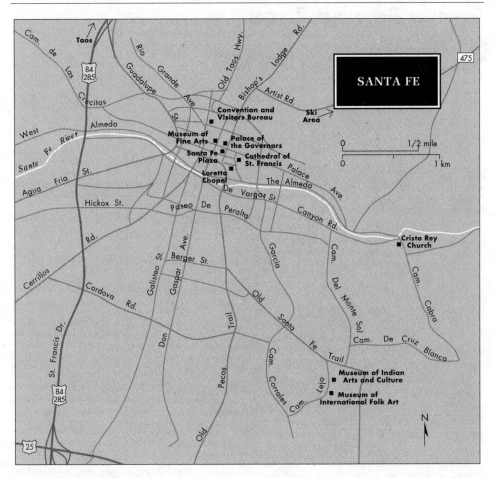

ning on the first Friday after Labor Day, celebrates the reconquest of Santa Fe in 1692, with parades, dancing, and fireworks. **October:** Cooler temperatures usher in the annual Wool Festival at Kit Carson Park in Taos, and the Harvest Festival at Las Golindrinas living museum in La Cienega near Santa Fe. **Christmas:** Christmas Eve in Santa Fe is festive, with carols at the Palace of the Governors and farolitos and luminarias (minibonfires) burning throughout the city. Christmas Day Indian dances take place at the Taos Pueblo.

BARGAINS Santa Fe Summerscene is a series of free concerts, dance performances, and storytelling sessions on the Santa Fe Plaza (June–Aug.). **Shakespeare in Santa Fe** presents the Bard's classics at the John Meem Library courtyard, St. John's College (tel. 505/982–2910; July and Aug.). Entrance to the Indian pueblos outside of Santa Fe, with ceremonial dances and crafts shops, is free, excluding occasional fees charged for parking and camera permits.

TOURIST OFFICES Santa Fe Convention & Visitors Bureau (201 W. Marcy St., Box 909, Santa Fe 87504, tel. 505/984–6760 or 800/777–2489, fax 505/984–7769). **Taos County Chamber of Commerce** (1139 Paseo del Pueblo Sur, Drawer I, Taos 87571, tel. 505/758–3873 or 800/732–8267, fax 505/758–

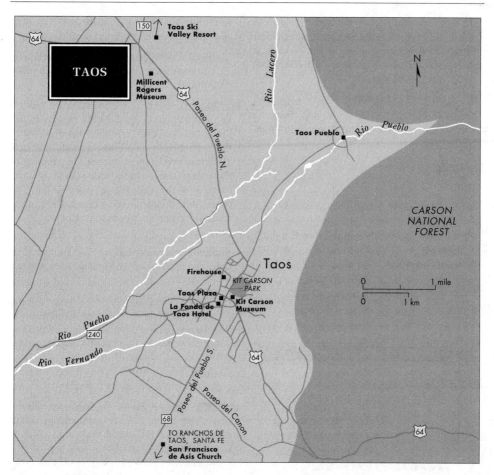

3872). **New Mexico Tourism Department** (491 Old Santa Fe Trail, Santa Fe 87503, tel. 800/545–2040). **Indian Pueblo Cultural Center** (2401 12th St. NW, Albuquerque 87102, tel. 505/843–7270).

EMERGENCIES Santa Fe: **Police, fire,** and **ambulance:** Dial 911. **Hospitals:** St. Vincent Hospital (455 St. Michaels Dr., tel. 505/983–3361). **Doctors:** Lovelace Urgent Care Centers (901 W. Alameda, tel. 505/986–3666; 440 St. Michaels Dr., tel. 505/986–3556).

Taos: **Police:** tel. 505/758–4656. **Fire:** tel. 505/758–3386. **Ambulance:** tel. 911. **Hospi-** tals: Holy Cross Hospital (Paseo del Pueblo Sur, tel. 505/758–8883).

ARRIVING AND DEPARTING

BY PLANE To reach Santa Fe and Taos, you fly into **Albuquerque International Airport** (tel. 505/842–4366), which is 65 miles southwest of Santa Fe and 130 miles south of Taos. Charter flights in and out of Santa Fe and Taos from Albuquerque can be arranged.

BY CAR Because of the spectacular scenery, you may wish to rent a car and drive from the airport to your destination. From the Albuquerque airport, I–25 north goes directly to Santa Fe; from there, U.S. 84/285 goes north to Espanola, where you get on NM 68 to Taos (65 miles); all the major car-rental services have desks at the airport.

Santa Fe is less than a day's drive from several metropolitan areas via I–25 (from El Paso, TX; Denver, CO) and I–40 (from Oklahoma City; Flagstaff, AZ).

BY BUS Greyhound Lines (tel. 800/231–2222) provides buses between Albuquerque and Santa Fe and Taos. **Shuttlejack** (tel. 505/982–4311 or 800/452–2665) offers bus service between Albuquerque and Santa Fe. Taos-based **Faust's Transportation** (tel. 505/758–3410) and **Pride of Taos** (tel. 505/758–8340) make airport pickups.

BY TRAIN Amtrak (tel. 800/872–7245) serves the area via the village of Lamy, 17 miles from Santa Fe.

GETTING AROUND

SANTA FE Downtown Santa Fe is easily explored by foot, with the majority of its museums, galleries, shops, and restaurants located within a comfortable radius of the famous Santa Fe Plaza. You'll need a car, bus, or taxi for the city's outer reaches, and you may want a lift for the 2-mile trip from the plaza to the base of Canyon Road.

By Bus: Santa Fe Trails (tel. 505/984–6730) operates seven bus routes from Sheridan Avenue in downtown Santa Fe (one block west of the Plaza and the Museum of Fine Arts) to various points throughout the city. Schedules can be obtained at the public library (145 Washington Ave.) and some downtown hotels.

By Car: Santa Fe's main thoroughfares are St. Francis Drive, St. Michael's Drive, and Cerrillos Road (which connects with Route 14 and I–25 from Albuquerque). Paseo de Peralta encircles most of downtown Santa Fe with the central historic plaza sandwiched between San Francisco Street and Palace Avenue. Local car-rental services include

Avis (tel. 505/982–4361), **Budget** (tel. 505/984–8028), and **Hertz** (tel. 505/982–1844).

By Taxi: Citywide taxi service is available via **Capital City Cab Company** (tel. 505/438–0000).

TAOS Like Santa Fe, Taos radiates around its famous plaza, and a walk through downtown can take only a few minutes. Many of the top restaurants, stores, and galleries are all on or within the immediate vicinity of the plaza. Taos's main streets are Paseo del Pueblo Norte and Paseo del Pueblo Sur, which skirts historic Taos Plaza. Bent Street and Kit Carson Road are the principal shopping areas.

By Car: Local car-rental services include **Dollar** (tel. 505/758–9501) and **Friday Motors** (tel. 505/758–2252).

By Taxi: The **Pride of Taos** (next to the Chamber of Commerce office on Paseo del Pueblo Sur, tel. 505/758–8340 or 800/273–8340) provides taxi service to various points within town. **Faust Tours** (tel. 505/758–3410) offers radio-dispatched taxis to ski areas and other points in the vicinity.

REST STOPS In Santa Fe there are public rest rooms in the Sweeny Convention Center (201 W. Marcy St.) about 2½ blocks north of the plaza. In Taos, there are public rest rooms in Kit Carson Park (just off Paseo del Pueblo Norte), several blocks north of the Taos Plaza. In addition, Santa Fe and Taos are adequately supplied with rest rooms in restaurants, hotels, museums, galleries, and even supermarkets—although they are normally for patrons' use only. During festivals or citywide celebrations, portable facilities are made available.

GUIDED TOURS Santa Fe: Gray Line of Santa Fe (1330 Hickox St., tel. 505/983–9491) features a variety of orientation tours. **Afoot in Santa Fe** (211 Old Santa Fe Trail, tel. 505/983–3701) offers walking tours with resident guides that provide a close-up look at the city. **Recursos** (826 Camino de Monte Rey, tel. 505/982–9301) provides educational tours centered around pueblos, history, culture, and nature. **Santa Fe Detours** (La Fonda

Hotel Lobby, 100 E. San Francisco St., tel. 505/983–6565) has city walks, minibus tours, trail rides, and rafting. **Art Tours of Santa Fe** (310 E. Marcy St., tel. 505/988–3527) specializes in art-related trips.

Taos: Pride of Taos Tours (Box 5271, tel. 505/758–8340 or 800/273–8340) provides trolley tours of Taos highlights. **Taos Historic Walking Tours** (Box 8, El Prado 87529, tel. 505/758–4020) covers all of the historically famous homes and sites.

EXPLORING

SANTA FE Santa Fe Plaza is the best place for a get-acquainted stroll of the city. First laid out around 1608, this area was formerly a bullring, the site of fiestas and fandangos, and the actual "End of the Santa Fe Trail." Today the plaza still remains the heart of the city, lined with a wide selection of shops, art galleries, restaurants, and museums.

The **Palace of the Governors,** the oldest public building in the United States, borders the north side of the plaza on Palace Avenue. Built in Pueblo style at the same time that the plaza was designed, it has been a New Mexican history museum since 1913. *100 W. Palace Ave., tel. 505/827–6483. Open Mar.–Dec., daily; Jan.–Feb., Tues.–Sun. Admission charged.*

The **Museum of Fine Arts** is across the street from the Palace of the Governors on the corner of Palace and Lincoln avenues. Its outstanding 8,000-piece permanent collection concentrates on regional artists, such as Georgia O'Keeffe and Indian and Hispano masters. *107 Palace Ave., tel. 505/827–4455. Open Mar.–Dec., daily; Jan.–Feb., Tues.–Sun. Admission charged.*

The **Cathedral of St. Francis,** a block east of the plaza, was built in 1869 by French architects in a French Romanesque style. Italian stonemasons added the finishing touches. It was founded by Santa Fe's first archbishop, French-born Jean Baptiste Lamy, who inspired Willa Cather's novel *Death Comes for*

the Archbishop. *131 Cathedral Pl., tel. 505/982–5619. Open daily. Admission free.*

Loretto Chapel is next to the Inn at Loretto behind the landmark La Fonda Hotel. This handsome 1873 structure is known for the 20-foot "Miraculous Staircase" that leads to the choir loft, built by an itinerant carpenter who some believe was St. Joseph himself. *208 Old Santa Fe Trail, tel. 505/984–7971. Open daily. Admission charged.*

The **Museum of International Folk Art** is perched on a hillside 2 miles from the plaza and near the southeastern edge of the city. The museum's main attraction is the Girard wing, containing thousands of examples of colorful folk-art creations from around the world, with miniature dioramas, religious imagery, and Mexican patios. The Hispanic Heritage wing is also worth a visit. *706 Camino Lejo, tel. 505/827–6350. Open Mar.–Dec., daily; Jan.–Feb., Tues.–Sun. Admission charged.*

The **Museum of Indian Arts and Culture,** located next door, focuses on the history and contemporary culture of the state's Pueblo, Navajo, and Apache Indians. *710 Camino Lejo, tel. 505/827–6344. Open Mar.–Dec., daily; Jan.–Feb., Tues.–Sun. Admission charged.*

Canyon Road is reached by bearing right from the St. Francis Cathedral to the end of Cathedral Place, turning left on Alameda Street, and then right onto Paseo de Peralta. Canyon Road is now one of the city's most fashionable streets, lined with many art galleries, shops, and restaurants. A shopping complex at the lower end (225 Canyon Rd.) provides parking and rest rooms for customers only.

Cristo Rey Church (Christ the King Church), at the corner of Upper Canyon Road (1½ miles from the plaza), was constructed in 1939 to commemorate the 400th anniversary of Coronado's exploration of the Southwest. Built the old-fashioned way, with parishioners making the mud-and-straw bricks themselves, this is the largest adobe structure in the United States. *1107 Cristo Rey, tel. 505/983–8528. Open daily. Admission free.*

TAOS While the **Taos Plaza** does not possess the grace and dignity of Santa Fe's plaza, it has its own small-town charm. The Spanish established the community around the Taos Plaza in 1617, and it remains a center of town life today, with assorted shops, galleries, and restaurants.

La Fonda de Taos Hotel, on the south side of the Plaza, has its own eccentric charm and houses erotic paintings by D. H. Lawrence in the manager's office. The paintings were once banned in London but are hardly scandalous by today's standards. *S. Plaza, tel. 505/758–2211.*

The **Kit Carson Museum,** located near the main intersection of town, just off the plaza, is the former home of the famous mountain man, trapper, and scout. Carson purchased the 12-room adobe building in 1843 as a wedding gift for his young bride. *East Kit Carson Rd., tel. 505/758–0505. Open daily. Admission charged.*

Taos Pueblo, one of the Southwest's top attractions, is situated about 2 miles north of town. The largest existing multistoried pueblo structure in the United States, it has been continuously inhabited for centuries. Within its mud-and-straw walls, the Indian way of life has changed little over time. The site can get very crowded during summer weekends. *Off Rte. 3, tel. 505/758–1028. Open daily, except during a funeral or religious ceremony. Admission free. Charge for parking and camera permits.*

San Francisco de Asis Church lies 4 miles south of Taos in a Spanish Colonial ranching and farming community. This early 18th-century monumental adobe masterpiece had a new exterior mud finish applied by community volunteers in 1979. The rectory contains the painting *Shadow of the Cross,* in which the cross on Christ's shoulder appears only at night. *Ranchos de Taos, tel. 505/ 758–2754. Open daily. Admission free.*

The **Millicent Rogers Museum** (4 miles north of the plaza) contains more than 5,000 marvelous pieces of Native American and Hispanic art. *1504 Museum Rd., tel. 505/ 758–2462. Open daily. Admission charged.*

THE NATURAL WORLD **Wheeler Peak Wilderness Area,** to the east of Taos, is named after the state's highest peak. It is most easily accessed via NM 150. **Pecos Wilderness Area**—223,333 acres of high mountains, forests, and meadows at the end of the Rocky Mountain chain—runs between Santa Fe and Taos. The Bureau of Land Management (BLM) also operates several scenic areas along the Rio Grande Gorge. For information on camping, contact the **Santa Fe National Forest Office** (tel. 505/988–6940), the **BLM's Taos office** (224 Cruz Alta, tel. 505/758–8851), or the **Carson National Forest** (tel. 505/758–6200). Forest maps are available for less than $5.

HOTELS AND INNS

Santa Fe and Taos are popular destinations for travelers interested in culture, history, and stunning scenery. In recent years, room prices have escalated steadily. Low-season hotel rates fluctuate considerably from place to place, but they are generally in effect from the beginning of November until the end of April (excluding the Thanksgiving and Christmas holidays). Price categories for double occupancy, excluding 10% tax, are Expensive, over $125; Moderate, $60–$125; and Inexpensive, under $60.

SANTA FE **Alexander's Inn.** This 1903 American Craftsman house exudes all the charm of an old country inn, with country-style wooden furnishings, lots of open space, and a generous Continental breakfast. *529 E. Palace Ave., 87501, tel. 505/986–1431, fax 505/982–8572. 7 rooms. MC, V. Moderate–Expensive.*

Hotel Santa Fe. This three-story hotel near downtown is operated by the Picuris Pueblo Indians and offers rooms and suites decorated in the traditional Southwestern style, with local handmade furniture and Native American paintings. Many of the arresting bronzes throughout the hotel are by renowned Apache sculptor Allan Houser. *1501 Paseo de Peralta, 87501, tel. 505/982–1200 or 800/825–9876, fax 505/984–2211. 40 rooms, 91 suites. Bar, breakfast buffet. AE, D, DC, MC, V. Moderate–Expensive.*

Inn of the Animal Tracks. Three blocks east of the plaza, this 90-year-old, restored Pueblo-style home has beamed ceilings, hardwood floors, handcrafted furniture, and fireplaces. Full breakfast and afternoon repast are served. *707 Paseo de Peralta, 87504, tel. 505/988–1546. 5 double rooms. AE, D, MC, V. Moderate.*

Inn of the Governors. This Territorial-style hotel has long been popular with families. It is right downtown and alongside the Rio Santa Fe. *234 Don Gaspar, 87501, tel. 505/982–4333, fax 505/989–9141. 100 rooms, including several suites. Pool, patio, restaurant, bar. AE, DC, MC, V. Moderate–Expensive.*

Preston House. This 1886 Queen Anne house, a rarity in a city of adobe structures, is tucked away in a quiet garden setting not far from the plaza. *106 Faithway St., 87501, tel. 505/982–3465. 15 rooms. AE, MC, V. Moderate–Expensive.*

Pueblo Bonito B&B Inn. This century-old adobe compound retains a Southwest Pueblo design throughout; all rooms have fireplaces. *138 W. Manhattan St., 87501, tel. 505/984–8001, fax 505/984–3155. 11 rooms, 7 suites. MC, V. Moderate.*

Territorial Inn. Creature comforts are a high priority in this elegant 100-year-old, two-story stone and adobe structure. The stylish decor is Victorian throughout, and Continental breakfast, afternoon treats, and brandy nightcaps are offered. *215 Washington Ave., 87501, tel. 505/989–7737, fax 505/986–9212. 10 rooms. MC, V. Moderate–Expensive.*

TAOS **Don Fernando de Taos Holiday Inn.** One mile south of the plaza, this 1989 hotel is built in a distinct Pueblo-style design, with rooms grouped around central courtyards. *1005 Paseo del Pueblo Sur, Drawer V, 87571, tel. 505/758–4444, fax 505/758–*

0055. 126 rooms. Restaurant, bar, pool. AE, D, MC, V. Moderate.

El Monte Lodge. Nestled among cottonwoods in a quiet residential area just east of the plaza, this lodge has been in business for more than 50 years, and its owners, George and Pat Schumacher, know the area well. *317 Kit Carson Rd., Box 22, 87571, tel. 505/758–3171 or 800/828–8267, fax 505/758–7244. 23 rooms AE, DC, MC, V. Moderate.*

Hotel La Fonda de Taos. This historic lodging on the plaza is a bit run-down, but it has a certain offbeat appeal. Cinema buffs take note: Rudolph Valentino once stayed here. *Taos Plaza, Box 1447, 87571, tel. 505/758–2211 or 800/833–2211. 24 rooms. AE, MC, V. Moderate.*

Inn on the Rio. This colorful inn, lovingly converted from a motel by a former owner, features a heated pool, free mountain bikes, and a trout stream rushing past the property. *Kit Carson Rd., Box 6612, 87571, tel. 505/758–7199. 12 rooms. D, MC, V. Inexpensive.*

Old Taos Guesthouse. This 7.5 acre tract, nestled amid a grove of old trees on a hill overlooking Taos, offers seclusion and lovely grounds, while the 150-year-old main home exudes northern New Mexico charm. *1028 Witt Rd., tel. 505/758–5448. 8 rooms, each with private entrance and bath. Continental breakfast. MC, V. Inexpensive–Moderate.*

Sagebrush Inn. One of the Southwest's classic lodgings since its opening in 1919, the Sagebrush is notable for its massive lobby fireplace, Navajo textiles, and leather easy chairs. Painter Georgia O'Keeffe resided here for several summers. *1508 Paseo del Pueblo Sur, tel. 505/758–2254 or 800/428–3626, fax 505/758–5077. 100 rooms, including several suites. AE, D, DC, MC, V. Moderate–Expensive.*

MOTELS

The following motels fall in the Inexpensive price category (suites may be more).

SANTA FE Budget Inn of Santa Fe (725 Cerrillos Rd., 87501, tel. 505/982–5952, fax 505/984–8879). 160 rooms; pool. **El Rey** (1862 Cerrillos Rd., 87501, tel. 505/982–1841, fax 505/989–9249). 86 rooms, including 14 suites. **Motel 6** (3695 Cerrillos Rd., 87501, tel. 505/471–4140, fax 505/474–4370). 121 rooms; pool. **Super 8 Motel** (3358 Cerrillos Rd., 87501, tel. 505/471–8811 or 800/843–1991, fax 505/471–3239). 59 rooms.

TAOS Quality Inn (1043 Paseo del Pueblo Sur, tel. 505/758–2200, fax 505/758–9009). 99 rooms; pool, hot tub. **Taos Super 8 Motel** (1347 Paseo del Pueblo Sur, tel. 505/758–1088). 50 rooms. For those who don't mind sacrificing homey atmosphere and a high level of cleanliness, the **Taos Motel** has some of the least expensive rooms in Taos (1799 Paseo del Pueblo Sur, tel. 505/758–2524 or 800/323–6009). 28 rooms; senior-citizen discounts.

CAMPGROUNDS

SANTA FE Hyde State Park (12 mi north of town on NM 475, tel. 505/983–7175), **KOA** (Old Las Vegas Hwy., tel. 505/982–1419), **Los Campos RV Park** (3574 Cerrillos Rd., tel. 505/473–1949), and **Rancheros de Santa Fe Camping Park** (Old Las Vegas Hwy., tel. 505/466–3482).

TAOS Orilla Verde Recreation Area (BLM, Santa Cruz Rd., 10 mi south of Taos along NM 570, tel. 505/758–8851) is along the banks of the Rio Grande. **Taos Valley RV Park & Campground** (2½ mi south of the plaza just off Paseo del Pueblo Sur at Estes Rd., tel. 505/758–4469 or 800/999–7571). Both are open spring through autumn.

DINING

Santa Fe and Taos cuisine is like no other: a delicious and extraordinary mixture of Pueblo Indian, Spanish colonial, Mexican, and American frontier cooking, all steeped and bubbled over the centuries. Spanish recipes were adapted generations ago for local ingredients—chiles (as chilies are spelled in the Southwest), corn, pork, beans, honey, apples, piñon nuts, and squash—and have remained much the same ever since. Chiles contain an entire storehouse of vitamins and minerals, and are loaded with vitamin C, while corn tortillas provide protein and calcium. Besides the ever-popular New Mexican hangouts, the area has numerous ethnic, health-food, and vegetarian restaurants. A number of restaurants now serve buffalo stew, steaks, and burgers for those allergic to beef or on low-cholesterol diets. Price categories per person, excluding 5.8% tax, service and drinks, are Expensive, over $25; Moderate, $15–$25; and Inexpensive, under $15.

SANTA FE Cafe Pasqual's. Only a block from the plaza, this cozy, informal restaurant serves regional specialties and breakfast all day for sleepyheads. People sometimes stand in line outside, lured by thoughts of a *chorizo* burrito (sausage, scrambled eggs, home fries, and scallions wrapped in a flour tortilla). *121 Don Gaspar Ave., tel. 505/983–9340. AE, MC, V. Moderate.*

Coyote Cafe. Restaurateur Mark Miller is known internationally for the innovative menu (it changes seasonally) he created for this eye-popping downtown establishment. *132 W. Water St., tel. 505/983–1615. AE, D, DC, MC, V. Expensive.*

Dave's Not Here. Santa Fe has few good, cheap places to eat: This is among the best. It has excellent chili *relleños* (whole green chiles stuffed with cheese and then fried) and tasty burgers. *1115 Hickox St., tel. 505/983–7060. No credit cards. Closed Sun. Inexpensive.*

El Nido. This Santa Fe institution has been serving fine prime rib, succulent cuts of salmon and swordfish, and regional New Mexican specialties in its intimate, firelit rooms for over 50 years. *Bishops Lodge Rd. (exit at Tesuque on NM 285 North), tel. 505/988–4340. MC, V. Moderate.*

Guadalupe Cafe. Even the most demanding diners will not be disappointed with the portions and the quality of the fare at this casual northern New Mexican establishment. *313 Guadalupe, tel. 505/982–9762. D, MC, V. Inexpensive.*

La Tertulia. The lofty waiting room is reason enough to visit La Tertulia, housed in a converted 19th-century convent highlighted with pieces of Spanish colonial art. The creative New Mexican menu also features the excellent house sangria. *416 Agua Fria, tel. 505/988–2769. AE, D, DC, MC, V. Closed Mon. Moderate.*

Maria's New Mexico Kitchen. You can see fresh tortillas being made right in from of your eyes at this landmark restaurant, in business for over 40 years. Great margaritas, plus typical local favorites: homemade tamales, relleños, blue-corn tamales, green chili stew, and sizzling fajitas. *555 W. Cordova Rd., tel. 505/983–7929. AE, D, DC, MC, V. Inexpensive.*

Ore House on the Plaza. The Ore House has a perfect location, with a heated cocktail balcony overlooking Santa Fe's main plaza. Salmon, swordfish, and lobster are all artfully prepared, and margaritas come in 64 flavors. *50 Lincoln Ave., tel. 505/983–8687. AE, D, DC, MC, V. Moderate.*

Shohko-Cafe. At this popular Japanese-Chinese restaurant, you can sample tempura, sushi, sukiyaki, and teriyaki, alongside vegetarian and seafood specials. *321 Johnson St. at Guadalupe, tel. 505/983–7288. AE, D, MC, V. Moderate.*

Tecolote Cafe. If you love brunch, come here for superb *huevos rancheros* (eggs served on a tortilla, with hot sauce and refried beans). The atmosphere at this breakfast-and-lunch eatery is casual. *1203 Cerrillos Rd., tel. 505/988–1362. AE, D, MC, V. Closed Mon. No dinner. Inexpensive.*

TAOS **Amigos Natural Grocery and Juice Bar.** With a health-food store in front, you'll find this natural-food café and juice bar in the rear a delight. *325 Paseo del Pueblo Sur, tel. 505/758–8493. No credit cards. Inexpensive.*

Apple Tree. One of Taos' most popular dining spots for lunch and dinner, this restaurant gives New Mexican dishes a gourmet twist. It also has one of the state's best wine lists. *123 Bent St., tel. 505/758–1900. DC, MC, V. Inexpensive–Moderate.*

Bent Street Deli and Cafe. Simple and unpretentious, this is the place for you if you're yearning for a good sandwich or a vegetarian, fresh fish, or pasta dinner entrée; deli food, cappuccino, soups, and salads are also available. *120 Bent St., tel. 505/758–5787. MC, V. Inexpensive–Moderate.*

Casa de Valdez. Two and a half miles south of the plaza, this restaurant, in a rustic A-frame building, specializes in hickory-smoke barbecue and regional cuisine. *1401 Paseo del Pueblo Sur, tel. 505/758–8777. AE, D, MC, V. Closed Wed. Inexpensive–Moderate.*

Chile Connection. Housed in a sprawling ranch-style adobe building with a large patio offering stunning mountain views, this dining spot serves up blue-corn enchiladas, homemade salsa, buffalo steaks, fajitas, and outstanding margaritas. *Mile Marker 1, Ski Valley Rd., tel. 505/776–8787. AE, D, DC, MC, V. Inexpensive–Moderate.*

El Taoseño. What this eatery lacks in sophistication it makes up for in its ample portions and down-home New Mexican food. Locals swear by it. *817 Paseo del Pueblo Sur, tel. 505/758–4142. MC, V. Inexpensive.*

Lambert's. This elegant small restaurant serves up creative American and regionally influenced cuisine. Its lamb and fresh fish are especially notable. Lunch is served seasonally. *309 Paseo del Pueblo Sur, tel. 505/758–1009. AE, DC, MC, V. Moderate.*

Michael's Kitchen. This family-run coffee shop and bakery specializes in both American and local dishes, and offers plenty of choices—over 15 types of pancakes and 25 types of sandwiches alone. *304 Paseo del Pueblo Norte, tel. 505/758–4178. AE, MC, V. Inexpensive.*

SHOPPING

SANTA FE Santa Fe may strike newcomers as one massive mall, with stores and shopping nooks sprouting up in the least likely of places. The downtown district offers a mix of shops, galleries, restaurants within a five-block radius of the plaza. Under the shaded portals of the Palace of the Governors (*see* Exploring, *above*), local Indian vendors display their wares. Items are all handmade or hand-strung in Indian households; silver jewelry is either sterling or coin silver; all metal jewelry bears the maker's mark, registered with the Museum of New Mexico. Canyon Road is another notable and historic shopping destination. At the southwest perimeter of the downtown core, the Guadalupe neighborhood is great for shopping, strolling, or relaxing at a sidewalk café. The local museums each have a gift shop carrying original folk-art pieces, fine-art reproductions, postcards, posters, books, and T-shirts.

Shops: Act 2 (410-B Old Santa Fe Trail, tel. 505/983–8585) carries vintage and modern clothing. **Artesanos** (222 Galisteo St., tel. 505/983–1743) is a large showroom for Mexican crafts. **Kachina House and Gallery** (236 Delgado Rd., tel. 505/982–8415) features an incomparable collection of authentic Hopi kachina dolls and Navajo arts and crafts. **Old Santa Fe Trail Books** (613 Old Santa Fe Trail, tel. 505/988–8878) is a bookstore, bar, and café. **Sanbusco Outfitters** (550 Montezuma Ave., tel. 505/988–1664) and **Santa Fe Western Mercantile** (6820 Cerrillos Rd., tel. 505/471–3655) have complete lines of western wear.

Art Galleries: Copeland Rutherford Fine Arts (403 Canyon Rd., tel. 505/983–1588) has an excellent cross section of regional up-and-coming artists and a large sculpture garden. **Gerald Peters Gallery** (439 Camino del Monte Sol, tel. 505/988–8961) carries original work by Georgia O'Keeffe and other leading regional painters.

Flea Markets: Trader Jack's Flea Market (7 mi north of Santa Fe on U.S. 84/285; look for Santa Fe Opera next door), draws up to 400 dealers and thousands of buyers on warm-weather weekends.

TAOS The main concentration of shops is directly on or just off the historic central plaza. That includes the John Dunn boardwalk on Bent Street, running parallel to the plaza on the north, and Kit Carson Road, extending east off the northeast corner.

El Rincon (114 Kit Carson Rd., tel. 505/758–9188) is the oldest trading post in Taos. **Navajo Gallery** (210 Ledoux St., tel. 505/758–3250) is home base for the prolific local painter, R. C. Gorman. The **Taos Book Shop** (122 Kit Carson Rd., tel. 505/758–3733) is the oldest bookstore in New Mexico. The **Tony Reyna's Indian Shop** (Taos Pueblo, tel. 505/758–3835), founded in 1950, carries authentic Indian arts and crafts.

OUTDOOR ACTIVITIES

FISHING The following are noted for trout fishing: the Rio Chama northwest of Santa Fe off U.S. 84; the Rio Grande, between Velarde and the Colorado border off NM 68; Abiquiu Lake, 40 miles northwest of Santa Fe; Heron Lake, 23 miles southwest of Chama via U.S. 64/84 and NM 95; and Lake Nambe, just north of Santa Fe off NM 4. For additional information, contact the **Game and Fish Department** (Villagra Bldg., 408 Galisteo St., Santa Fe 87503, tel. 800/275–3474).

GOLF Santa Fe: **Cochiti Lake Golf Course** (5200 Cochiti Hwy., Cochiti Lake, tel. 505/465–2239), **Quail Run** (Old Pecos Trail, tel. 505/986–2235), and **Santa Fe Country Club** (Airport Rd., tel. 505/471–0601).

Taos: **Angel Fire Country Club** (22 mi east of Taos on NM 484, tel. 505/377–6401 and **Taos Country Club** (Ranchos de Taos, tel. 505/758–7300).

HORSEBACK RIDING Santa Fe: **Circle S Stables** (Pecos, tel. 505/757–6821), **Bar C Bar** (tel. 505/471–3331), **Galarosa Stables** (Galisteo, tel. 505/983–6565), **Pool Wells** (tel. 505/852–2013).

Taos: Taos Indian Horse Ranch (on Taos Pueblo, tel. 505/758–3212 or 800/659–3210).

RIVER RAFTING The following companies offer river trips on the Rio Chama above Abiquiu, on the middle Rio Grande near Santa Fe, and on the upper Rio Grande near Taos: **Los Rios River Runners** (Ski Area Rd., Taos, tel. 505/983–6565 or 800/544–1181, fax 505/776–1842), **New Wave Rafting Company** (107 Washington Ave., Santa Fe, tel. 505/984–1444), **Rio Grande River Tours** (Pilar, NM 68, tel. 800/525–4966), and **Kokopelli Rafting** (Santa Fe, tel. 800/879–9035).

SKIING The ski season in Santa Fe and Taos runs from Thanksgiving through Easter. The **Santa Fe Ski Area** (tel. 505/982–4429 or Santa Fe Central Reservations, tel. 800/982–7669) has a 1,650-foot vertical drop, 40 trails, six lifts, and several restaurants.

The combination of Taos Ski Valley and the ski areas of Angel Fire, Red River, Ski Rio, and Sipapu makes Taos one of the premier ski destinations in the country. **Taos Ski Valley** (tel. 505/776–2291) alone boasts a 2,600-foot vertical drop, 71 runs, 11 lifts, lodging for 1,000 guests, and many restaurants. It also receives phenomenal snowfall. For queries and reservations, contact **Taos Valley Resort Association** (Box 85, Taos Ski Valley 87525, tel. 505/776–2233 or 800/776–1111).

The **New Mexico Tourism and Travel Division** offers a free packet of ski information (tel. 800/545–2040), and during the season current snow-condition information is available by calling 505/984–0606. For cross-country skiing information, contact the national forest offices (*see* the Natural World *in* Exploring, *above.*

ENTERTAINMENT

SANTA FE Horse Racing: The **Santa Fe Downs** (off I–25, 6 mins west of town, tel.

505/471–3311) attracts nearly a quarter-million spectators June through Labor Day.

Music: The acclaimed **Santa Fe Opera** performs July through August in a spectacular indoor-outdoor amphitheater (U.S. 84/285, 7 mi north of Santa Fe, tel. 505/982–3855). The **Santa Fe Symphony Orchestra** appears September through May at the **Sweeny Center** (Marcy and Grant Sts., tel. 505/983–3530). The internationally renowned **Santa Fe Chamber Music Festival** holds concerts July–August in the lovely **St. Francis Auditorium** (tel. 505/983–2075).

Theater: Greer Garson Theater (College of Santa Fe, St. Michael's Dr., tel. 505/473–6511) stages comedies, dramas, and musicals. Other local companies include the **Santa Fe Community Theater** (142 E. de Vargas, tel. 505/988–4262), **Southwest Children's Theater** (tel. 505/984–3055), **Madrid Melodrama** (Madrid, tel. 505/473–0743), and **Shakespeare in Santa Fe** (tel. 505/982–2910).

TAOS Music: The **Taos Community Auditorium** (145 Paseo del Pueblo Norte, tel. 505/758–4677) offers modern dance, drama, concerts, and movies. **Taos Chamber Music Festival** (tel. 505/776–2388) presents concerts June–August in town and at the **Hotel St. Bernard** (Taos Ski Valley, tel. 505/776–2251). **Music from Angel Fire** (tel. 505/758–4667) is a classical and chamber music series featuring international artists (mid-August–September) in Taos and Angel Fire.

The **Sagebrush Inn** (1508 Paseo del Pueblo Sur, tel. 505/758–2254) offers live entertainment—mostly of the country-and-western variety—nightly in its spacious lobby lounge. During the ski season, the **Thunderbird Lodge** (tel. 505/776–2280) and other lodges at Taos Ski Valley provide live music.

Savannah and the Golden Isles
Georgia

Updated by Carol and Dan Thalimer

Savannah and the Golden Isles. . . . The very sound of these words conjures up misty images of mint juleps, live oaks dripping with Spanish moss, handsome mansions, and life lived at a leisurely southern pace. The mint juleps are still there, along with the moss and the mansion and the easygoing ways, but these popular destinations have their own up-to-date surprises.

On February 12, 1733, the English general James Edward Oglethorpe and 120 colonists arrived at Yamacraw Bluff on the Savannah River to found the 13th and last colony in the New World. As the port city grew, Scots, Huguenots, Germans, Salzburgers, Sephardic Jews from Spain and Portugal, Moravians, Italians, Swiss, Welsh, and Irish all arrived, creating in a rich gumbo the diverse mixture of cultures that shaped the city's character. Today, in the historic district, a wealth of restored mansions and other landmark buildings survive, many open to the public.

An hour south of the city begins the chain of Golden Isles: a string of lush, subtropical barrier islands meandering down the coast to the Florida border. Here, Indian relics have been found that date from about 2500 BC. English settlers who came to farm cleared the low-lying land and grew prosperous off cotton. In the early 20th century, Rockefellers, Morgans, Pulitzers, and Astors maintained vacation homes on Jekyll Island.

From the causeways and bridges leading to Jekyll Island, Sea Island, and St. Simons Island, you'll see a sea of flat, marshy grassland, but the islands are punctuated by stands of pines and live oaks (so called because the nondeciduous trees are green, or "live," all winter). One drives along roads shaded by oaks hung with Spanish moss. Cumberland Island is a National Seashore reached by ferry from St. Marys, and Little St. Simons Island is a privately owned retreat with a guest lodge. Each island, shaped by its history and ecology, has a character all its own.

ESSENTIAL INFORMATION

WHEN TO GO Mild weather prevails here year-round; temperatures remain in the mid-50s during late fall and early winter and only occasionally fall below freezing. The thermometer climbs to the mid-60s and 70s by March, rising throughout April and into May, to hit 80° through most of June. Summer is typically humid, with temperatures in the high 80s and mid-90s. The hurricane season stretches from mid-August through most of September. Spring and early summer and fall are ideal times to come: Both Savannah and the Golden Isles are less crowded, the weather is at its best, and the mosquitoes are relatively inactive (they increase as summer progresses). Mid-spring and early fall are good times to catch lower lodging prices. If you are bothered by crowds, avoid Savannah around St. Patrick's Day—the city annually holds one of the country's largest outdoor bashes.

FESTIVALS AND SEASONAL EVENTS **Feb.:** Georgia Heritage Celebration in Savannah is a 12-day festival of the performing arts as well as arts and crafts. **Early Mar.:** Savannah's St.

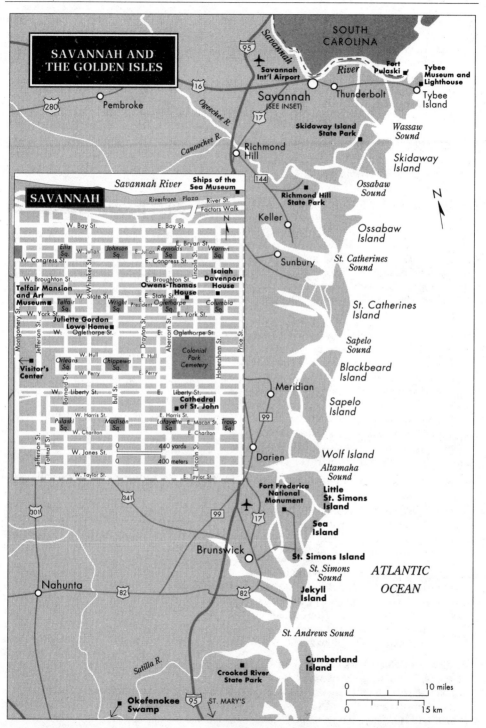

SOUTH CAROLINA

Savannah River

95

Savannah Int'l Airport

Fort Pulaski

Tybee Museum and Lighthouse

Savannah (SEE INSET)

Thunderbolt

Tybee Island

16

280

Pembroke

Ogeechee R.

17

Skidaway Island State Park

Wassaw Sound

Canoochee R.

Richmond Hill

Skidaway Island

144

Richmond Hill State Park

Ossabaw Sound

Keller

Ossabaw Island

N

SAVANNAH

Savannah River

Ships of the Sea Museum

Riverfront Plaza

River St.

Factors Walk

Sunbury

St. Catherines Sound

W. Bay St.

E. Bay St.

N

Ellis Sq.

W. Julian

Johnson Sq.

E. Julian

Reynolds Sq.

Warren Sq.

St. Catherines Island

W. Congress St.

E. Bryan St.

E. Congress St.

W. Broughton St.

Isaiah Davenport House

Telfair Mansion and Art Museum

Owens-Thomas House

E. Broughton St.

Sapelo Sound

W. State St.

E. State St.

Telfair Sq.

Wright Sq.

President

Oglethorpe Sq.

Columbia Sq.

Blackbeard Island

Juliette Gordon Lowe Home

W. York St.

E. York St.

Oglethorpe St.

Oglethorpe St.

Sapelo Island

Visitor's Center

W. Hull

E. Hull

Orleans Sq.

Chippewa Sq.

Colonial Park Cemetery

Meridian

W. Perry

E. Perry

99

W. Liberty St.

E. Liberty St.

Cathedral of St. John

Pulaski Sq.

Madison Sq.

Lafayette Sq.

E. Macon St.

Troup Sq.

Wolf Island

W. Harris St.

E. Harris St.

W. Charlton

E. Charlton

Darien

Altamaha Sound

W. Jones St.

0   440 yards

0   400 meters

Little St. Simons Island

W. Taylor St.

E. Taylor St.

Fort Frederica National Monument

Sea Island

341

99

17

St. Simons Island

301

Brunswick

St. Simons Island

St. Simons Sound

ATLANTIC OCEAN

Nahunta

82

82

Jekyll Island

St. Andrews Sound

Satilla R.

Cumberland Island

Crooked River State Park

Okefenokee Swamp

95

ST. MARY'S

0   10 miles

0   15 km

Patrick's Day celebration kicks off with a midmorning parade through downtown, and other events take place along the riverfront and on the streets and squares. **Apr.:** The Savannah Seafood Festival allows you to sample tasty native specialties like lowcountry shrimp boil, oyster roasts, and seafood casseroles. **June:** Country by the Sea draws large crowds to the beach on Tybee Island. **Aug.:** Beach Music Festival on Jekyll Island is a "shaggin' in the sand" blowout that attracts large crowds. Sea Island Festival, held on St. Simons Island, is a regional cultural event at the pier, highlighted by the acclaimed Sea Island Singers and the art and crafts for sale at the booths of local artists and artisans. **Dec.:** Jekyll's Christmas Island begins on the first weekend and continues throughout the month. Historic houses, decorated for the holidays, are open for tours. Savannah also has a wealth of Christmas activities.

BARGAINS Free concerts by various music groups are held in Savannah's Johnson Square in summer on Wednesday and Friday from 11:30 AM to 1:30 PM. Seafood is a regional bargain. Discounted clothing, athletic equipment, housewares, luggage, books, and shoes are found at factory outlets and shopping centers. Bargain rates at local hotels and motels are usually in effect from late September to mid-February.

Fleets of shrimp boats troll up and down the coastal waterways, and dockside distributors and small businesses buy and sell all types of seafood directly off the boats. It is even possible to collect oysters, net crabs, and catch your own shrimp along the shoreline.

TOURIST OFFICES **Greater Savannah Area Convention and Visitors Bureau** (222 W. Oglethorpe Ave., Savannah 31499, tel. 912/944-0456 or 800/444-2427). **Savannah Visitors Center** (301 Martin Luther King, Jr. Blvd., Savannah 31499, tel. 912/944-0455).

Brunswick–Golden Isles Chamber of Commerce (4 Glynn Ave., Brunswick 31520, tel. 912/265-0620). **Jekyll Island Convention and Visitors Bureau** (Box 13186, Jekyll Island 31520, tel. 912/635-3400 or 800/841-6586;

in GA, 800/342-1042). **St. Simons Island Chamber of Commerce** (530-B Beachview Dr., Neptune Park, St. Simons Island 31522, tel. 912/638-9014 or 800/525-8678).

EMERGENCIES **State Police:** Brunswick (tel. 912/265-6050), Jekyll Island (tel. 912/635-2303), or Savannah (tel. 912/651-3000). **Hospitals:** Savannah Candler Hospital (5353 Reynolds St., tel. 912/692-6000). **Doctors:** Glynn County Walk-in Clinic (3400 Parkwood Dr., Brunswick, tel. 912/267-7600).

ARRIVING AND DEPARTING

BY PLANE **Savannah International Airport** (tel. 912/964-0514), 10 miles west of town, is served by American, Delta, Northwest, United, and USAir. McCall's Limousine Service (tel. 912/966-5364 or 800/673-9365) runs a shuttle van service between the airport and the city ($15 one-way, $25 round-trip).

For the Golden Isles, **Glynco Jetport** (tel. 912/265-2070), 6 miles north of Brunswick, is served daily by Atlantic Southeast Airline (tel. 404/765-2000), whose flights connect with Delta in Atlanta. You can also fly into Savannah or Jacksonville International Airport in Jacksonville, Florida, both an hour away, and make the commute into the area by car or shuttle.

BY CAR The north–south I–95 and east–west I–16 intersect just outside Savannah. I–16 leads into Savannah and dead-ends downtown. Follow I–95 south to the Golden Isles. U.S. 17, the Coastal Highway, also runs from Savannah to the Golden Isles and is more scenic.

BY TRAIN The **Amtrak** (tel. 800/872-7245) *Palmetto, Silver Meteor,* and *Silver Star* lines serve Savannah, arriving at a station (2611 Seaboard Coastline Dr., tel. 912/234-2611) 7 miles west of the historic district. Hotels run shuttle service to downtown, and taxis are plentiful.

BY BUS **Greyhound Lines** (tel. 800/231-2222) serves both Savannah and Brunswick daily.

GETTING AROUND

BY CAR Although the sights of Savannah can be seen on walking tours, a car is a necessity in this southern corner of Georgia. You can locate points of interest on display maps and pick up driving maps in the Chamber of Commerce offices and the Savannah Visitors Center.

REST STOPS Most restaurants, convenience stores, shops, and roadside markets in this area allow the public to use their rest rooms. The Savannah Visitors Center has public rest rooms. A boardwalk with gazebos and benches facing the Savannah River runs along the River Street area. Fort Pulaski has a visitor center with rest rooms as well as picnic areas. Welcome centers with rest rooms and travel information are on I–95 between Exits 8 and 9 south of Savannah, at the start of the F. J. Torras Causeway, on the causeway leading to Jekyll Island, and at the Neptune Park area on St. Simons's south end, which also has shaded picnic tables. More public rest rooms are in the bathhouses dotting the Jekyll Island shore.

GUIDED TOURS **Carriage Tours of Savannah** (tel. 912/236–6756 or 800/442–5933) runs modestly priced daytime horse-and-buggy tours from City Market, Madison Square, the Hyatt Regency Hotel, and the Savannah Visitors Center. **Classic Historic Tours** (tel. 912/354–7913) offers bus and trolley city tours as well as evening candlelight tours. **Gray Line of Savannah/Landmark Tours** (tel. 912/234–8687) conducts short, informative tours of the historic and Victorian districts and makes four-hour low-country excursions outside the city to stately mansions, a historic fishing village and plantation, and a notable Savannah cemetery. **Multicultural Heritage Tour** (tel. 912/233–2027), operated by the Greater Savannah Black Tourism Network, offers three walking or driving tours that highlight significant sites linked to the area's rich black history. **Sea Island Boat Tours** (tel. 912/638–3611, ext. 5202, or 912/638–9354) offers daily two-hour tours of the marshes, narrated by a trained naturalist;

tours depart from the fishing dock in the morning and afternoon. **Tours by BJ** (tel. 912/233–2335) presents twilight strolls through the historic area that concentrate on Savannah's many ghosts.

EXPLORING

SAVANNAH The city's high points can be seen in a fast-paced two days, though the seductive powers of its 22 lushly landscaped squares and cobblestone streets, draped in the shade of 200-year-old live oaks, might compel you to spend a leisurely week. History and architecture buffs can occupy themselves touring the many period houses in town, while others will contentedly cruise the spirited River Street area, a renovated warehouse district where Dixieland music wafts across a nine-block stretch of boutiques and taverns.

Cathedral of St. John the Baptist. Two blocks south from the historic Colonial Park Cemetery, this French Gothic building with impressive pointed arches is Georgia's oldest Roman Catholic church (1874); it faces Lafayette Square and its graceful fountain. *222 E. Harris St., tel. 912/233–4709. Open daily.*

Fort Pulaski. This restored fort 15 miles outside Savannah is a must for Civil War buffs. Operated by the National Park Service, it is complete with moats, drawbridges, massive ramparts, and towering walls. *U.S. 80, tel. 912/786–5787. Open daily. Admission charged.*

Green-Meldrim House. Located on Madison Square and used as the Parish House of St. John's Church, this house is considered to be the finest Gothic Revival mansion in Savannah. It is noted for its ornate ironwork porch that wraps around three sides of the house as well as for superior interior architectural details. *14 W. Macon St., tel. 912/233–3845. Closed Mon., Wed., Sun. Donations accepted.*

Isaiah Davenport House. This stately house, just a short walk south on Abercorn Street from Reynolds Square, is one of the city's finest examples of Georgian architecture. It is furnished with Chippendale, Hepplewhite, and Sheraton antiques. *324 E. State St., tel. 912/236–8097. Tours on the ½ hr. Closed Thurs. Admission charged.*

Juliette Gordon Lowe Home. Completed in 1821, this Regency-style mansion is the birthplace of Juliette Gordon Lowe, who founded the Girl Scouts of America in 1912. The home is filled with original Gordon family furnishings and is noted for its large Tuscan-style columns and decorative plasterwork. *142 Bull St., tel. 912/233–4501. Closed Wed. Admission charged.*

Owens-Thomas House. This was the first Regency mansion the English architect William Jay built in the city. Constructed of local materials, including tabby (a mixture of lime, sand, and ground oyster shell used in the 17th and 18th centuries), it was a showcase house, where the Marquis de Lafayette delivered his farewell speech in 1825. *124 Abercorn St., tel. 912/233–9743. Closed Mon. Admission charged.*

Ships of the Sea Museum. A large collection of maritime memorabilia is housed here, including models of sailing ships, steamships, nuclear vessels, and Christopher Columbus's *Niña, Pinta,* and *Santa Maria. 503 E. River St., tel. 912/232–1511. Open daily. Admission charged.*

Telfair Mansion and Art Museum. The South's oldest public art museum is housed in another William Jay masterpiece. There are American, French, and German Impressionist paintings; a collection of works by Kahlil Gibran; and Regency furniture and decorations in three period rooms. *121 Barnard St., tel. 912/232–1177. Closed Mon. Admission charged.*

Tybee Museum and Lighthouse. Outside Savannah, 3 miles beyond Fort Pulaski (*see above*), is Georgia's oldest lighthouse, which dates from 1773. The ocean view from the 145-foot-high deck is well worth the climb. The museum is devoted to the history of the surrounding four-state area. *30 Meddin Dr., tel. 912/786–4077. Closed Tues. Admission charged.*

THE GOLDEN ISLES Though Georgia's coast is strung with islands along its entire length, many of them are undeveloped and not open to the public. Of the islands where visitors can stay, Jekyll, Sea Island, and St. Simons are accessible by car from Brunswick; Cumberland Island National Seashore, by ferry from St. Marys; and Little St. Simons, by launch from St. Simons.

Cumberland Island. Largely undeveloped, Cumberland is a natural sanctuary for wild horses, deer, bobcats, and stressed-out vacationers. Remote expanses of sun-drenched beaches and sand dunes make it ideal for day trips and camping. The island has no transportation, nothing to buy, and all trash must be packed back to the mainland. Contact the National Park Service for ferry reservations and schedules and for camping information. *Cumberland Island National Seashore, Box 806, St. Marys 31588, tel. 912/882–4335.*

Jekyll Island. A vast playground flanked by the Intracoastal Waterway and the Atlantic, this island offers 63 holes of golf, 10 miles of beach, fishing, tennis, biking, and walking. Between 1886 and 1942, America's rich and famous wintered here, and today the **Jekyll Island Club Historic Landmark District** contains many of their brick, shingle, and tabby mansions. Tours of the district and buildings are conducted in open-air trolleys. *Exit 6, across causeway, tel. 912/635–2236. Tours daily. Admission charged.*

St. Simons Island. As wide and as long as Manhattan, St. Simons has 14,000 year-round residents and is the most developed of these islands. Its southern tip is rimmed by beaches, and a network of bike paths extends through the surrounding marshland and onto the island. Visit **Fort Frederica,** a national monument that was built in the 1730s by the English to protect against a Spanish invasion from Florida; the fort's tabby ruins and many building foundations still stand. *St. Simons Island, tel. 912/638–3639. Open daily. Admission charged.*

Little St. Simons. This small, privately owned island has three (very expensive) lodges for overnight guests. Day trips by boat from St. Simons include a naturalist-led tour of the secluded island, lunch, and swimming. *Tour: tel. 912/638–7472. $70 per person (limited space). Tues., Thurs., Sat. only.*

Sea Island. Linked by bridge to St. Simons, Sea Island has been the domain of the Cloister (tel. 912/638–3611), a famous hotel and resort, since 1928. The public is free to admire the hotel grounds, drive by the houses along Sea Island Drive, use the golf course (space permitting), and dine in the main dining room by reservation.

THE NATURAL WORLD The marshes, beaches, and wooded thickets of the coastal islands support a vast network of wildlife. In the early morning and evening hours, rabbits are easy to spot along roadsides. Predawn low tides in spring are the prime time to walk any of the area's beaches to watch female turtles crawl ashore to lay their eggs. Twilight draws deer, raccoons, armadillos, and owls out of their hiding places.

On beach walks, you'll see quick-footed sandpipers running along the water's edge and seagulls and pairs of pelicans flying low across the ocean's surface. Regal egrets and herons stalk the marshes, while schools of dolphins and lone alligators swim the waterways. Ghost crabs are frequently seen at night during low tides, scurrying above the waterline.

The stands of majestic live oaks are heavily draped in Spanish moss. Palms of all sizes—from clumps of fan-shaped palmetto undergrowth to manicured rows of magnificent date palms—are also native to the area.

HOTELS AND INNS

Savannah has a diverse selection of charming accommodations steeped in history as well as more affordable hotels and chain motels outside the historic districts on main thoroughfares. Brunswick, St. Simons Island, Sea Island, and Jekyll Island offer both value and luxury. Price categories for double occupancy, excluding 6% sales and 5% hotel tax, are Expensive, $90–$120; Moderate, $50–$90; and Inexpensive, under $50.

SAVANNAH **Ballastone Inn.** Genteel elegance reminiscent of the Old South pervades this 1850s brick town house in the historic district, with rooms painted in authentic Savannah colors and furnished with rice-carved four-poster and canopy beds. *14 E. Oglethorpe Ave., 31401, tel. 912/236–1484 or 800/822–4553, fax 912/236–4626. 18 rooms, 6 suites. Continental breakfast included, fresh fruit, library, landscaped courtyard, tennis, golf. AE, MC, V. Expensive.*

Comer House. The polished pine floors, spacious rooms, sweeping verandas, and walled garden of this four-story Victorian have the same elegance they displayed when Confederate president Jefferson Davis spent a week here. *2 E. Taylor St., 31401, tel. 912/234–2923 or 800/262–4667. 2 rooms. Continental breakfast included. No credit cards. Moderate.*

East Bay Inn. This charming restored cotton warehouse is located on the doorstep of Savannah's waterfront district. Antiques-filled rooms include poster rice beds or brass beds, and you can enjoy evening cordials in the parlor. *225 E. Bay St., 31401, tel. 912/238–1225 or 800/500–1225, fax 912/232–2709. 28 rooms. Continental breakfast included, on-site restaurant (no lunch weekends; no dinner Sun.–Tues.), free parking. AE, D, DC, MC, V. Expensive.*

Eliza Thompson House. Nestled in a peaceful residential area in the historic district, this lovely Federal-style inn offers a full breakfast and afternoon wine and cheese in a beautiful garden courtyard. Rooms are decorated with period antiques, reproductions, and poster beds. *5 W. Jones St., 31401, tel. 912/236–3620 or 800/348–9378, fax 912/238–1920. 25 rooms. Breakfast included, afternoon wine and cheese. AE, MC, V. Expensive.*

The Gastonian. You'll step back in time when you enter these two houses, where finely crafted details, well-kept Savannah antiques, working fireplaces, and southern hospitality create an intimate atmosphere. *220 E. Gaston St., 31401, tel. 912/232–2869 or 800/322–6603, fax 912/232–0710. 13 rooms. Hot tub on sundeck, whirlpool baths, off-street parking. AE, MC, V. Expensive.*

Olde Harbour Inn. Built in 1892, the three-story building overlooking the Savannah River and River Street, was originally the offices, warehouse, and shipping center of the Tide Water Oil Company. Today an all-suite property, each guest accommodation has a fully equipped kitchen, living-dining room, and a bedroom or sleeping loft. *508 E. Factors Walk, 31401, tel. 912/234–4100 or 800/553–6533, fax 912/233–5979. 24 suites. Continental breakfast, afternoon wine and cheese. AE, D, DC, MC, V. Expensive.*

BRUNSWICK AND THE GOLDEN ISLES

Brunswick Manor–Major Downing House. High tea is an afternoon tradition in this restored Victorian (circa 1886), furnished with antiques, that overlooks a square in the Old Towne district. *825 Egmont St., Brunswick 31520, tel. 912/265–6889. 4 rooms, 2 suites. 2 guest kitchenettes. Continental breakfast and afternoon tea included, boat charters available. MC, V. Moderate.*

Clarion-Buccaneer. This centrally located oceanfront motel offers more amenities (including kitchenettes and private balconies and patios), at a better price than most of the island's other motels. *85 S. Beachview Dr., Jekyll Island 31527, tel. 912/635–2261 or 800/253–5955, fax 912/635–3230. 206 rooms, 3 suites. Restaurant, pool, whirlpool, playground, tennis court, paddle-tennis court. AE, D, DC, MC, V. Moderate.*

The Cloister. Georgia's only five-star, five-diamond property, the Mediterranean-style Cloister has been welcoming presidents, potentates, and ordinary folks since 1928. A complete resort with meals and activities included in the nightly rate, the hotel offers complete spa services, a beach club, golf, skeet and trap shooting, tennis, horseback riding, fishing, and sailing. Theme weekends are devoted to special interests such as bridge, gourmet cooking, fine wines, big bands, and ballroom dancing. *1 Hudson Pl., St. Simons Island 31522, tel. 912/638–3611 or 800/732–4752, fax 912/638–5153. 262 rooms, 28 suites, 14 villas. 3 restaurants, 4 lounges, 3 pools, 15 shops. MC, V. Expensive.*

Greyfield Inn. Cumberland Island is home to this charming inn built by the Carnegies in 1901. Wide, airy porches surround the majestic southern-style mansion, which, combined with the island's natural beauty, provides an ideal getaway. *8 N. 2nd St. or Box 900, Fernandina Beach, FL 32035, tel. 904/261–6408. 11 rooms. Rates include meals, boat transportation to island, outings with naturalist guide, bicycles. MC, V. Expensive.*

Jekyll Inn. The two-level villas perched on the edge of the ocean have balconies and patios that give beachcombers direct access to their rooms. *975 N. Beachview Dr., Jekyll Island 31527, tel. 912/635–2531 or 800/736–1046, fax 912/635–2332. 188 guest rooms, 74 town-house villas with kitchens. Restaurant, lobby bar, cocktail lounge, pool. AE, D, DC, MC, V. Expensive.*

Jekyll Island Club Hotel. This turreted building, built by 19th-century financiers as a private retreat, is now a Radisson Resort property that offers turn-of-the-century elegance in a charming, updated historic setting. *371 Riverview Dr., Jekyll Island 31527, tel. 912/635–2600, fax 912/635–2818. 134 rooms, 15 suites, 8 with whirlpools. 2 restaurants, pool, croquet court, gift shops, tennis. AE, D, DC, MC, V. Expensive.*

King & Prince. St. Simons's premier resort has sprung up around a turreted, castlelike structure, which contains some of its guest rooms; housekeeping villas are in contemporary tiered buildings adjoining it. *102 Arnold Dr., St. Simons Island 31522, tel. 912/638–3631 or 800/342–0212, fax 912/634–1720. 125 rooms, 48 2- and 3-bedroom villas. Restaurant, indoor-outdoor pool, tennis, bike and sailboat rentals, gift shop. AE, D, DC, MC, V. Expensive.*

Little St. Simons. This 10,000 acre-private island makes an ideal informal island hideaway—perfect for couples and family reunions. Twelve rooms divided among four cottages accommodate only 24 guests at a time. Seven miles of unspoiled beach and abundant wildlife more than make up for the lack of radio, TV, and newspapers. All meals and activities are included in the nightly rate. *Box 1078, St. Simons Island 31522, tel. 912/638–7472, fax 912/634–1811. 12 rooms. Dining room, honor bar, pool, boating, fishing, horseback riding. MC, V. Expensive.*

Queens Court. In the heart of St. Simons's quaint village area, within walking distance of shops, restaurants, nightlife, and beaches, this small motel is a very good bargain. *437 Kings Way, St. Simons Island 31522, tel. 912/638–8459. 18 rooms, 9 with kitchenettes; 4 suites. Pool. MC, V. Inexpensive–Moderate.*

Rose Manor Guest House. Restored in the style of an English manor house, this circa-1890 Victorian bungalow offers the charm of formal gardens and rooms with Victorian furniture and antique linens. *1108 Richmond St., Brunswick 31520, tel. 912/267–6369. 4 guest rooms, 2 with shared bath, 2 suites. Airport shuttle service. No credit cards. Inexpensive–Expensive.*

Sea Gate Inn. At this orange-and-white *U*-shape motel, constructed with a '30s-modern Jetsons flair, you can stay in beachfront or poolside rooms or suites with private balconies. *1014 Ocean Blvd., St. Simons Island 31522, tel. 912/638–8661 or 800/562–8812, fax 912/638–4932. 48 rooms, 17 with kitchenettes; 2 suites. Pool. AE, MC, V. Moderate–Expensive.*

Shipwatch Oceanfront Condominiums. Stay a day or a month in these well-established units with a nautical look and porthole windows, in one of the island's quieter residential neighborhoods. *1524 Wood Ave., St. Simons Island 31522, tel. 912/638–5450 or 800/627–6850, fax 912/638–2983. 42 2-bedroom, 2-bath units. MC, V. Expensive.*

MOTELS

EXPENSIVE Glynn Place Mall Suites Hotel (500 Mall Blvd., Brunswick 31522, tel. 912/264–6100 or 800/432–3229, fax 912/267–1615). 130 suites; restaurant, lounge, pool, health club, shuttle service.

MODERATE Best Western–Savannah Riverfront Inn (412 W. Bay St., Savannah 31401, tel. 912/233–1011, fax 912/234–3963). 142 rooms; restaurant, pool, shuttle service. **Clubhouse Inn** (6800 Abercorn, Savannah 31405, tel. 912/356–1234, fax 912/352–2828). 122 rooms, 16 suites; full hot breakfast, pool, kitchenettes. **Comfort Inn** (5308 New Jesup Hwy., Brunswick 31525, tel. 912/264–6540 or 800/551–7591, fax 912/264–9296). 118 rooms; restaurant, pool, lounge. **Days Inn–Historic District** (201 W. Bay St., Savannah 31401, tel. 912/236–4440, fax 912/232–2725). 195 rooms, 58 suites; restaurant, pool, fitness facilities, shuttle service, kitchenettes. **Days Inn–St. Simons** (1701 Frederica Rd., St. Simons Island 31522, tel. 912/634–0660, fax 912/638–7115). 101 rooms; microwaves, refrigerators. **La Quinta Motor Inn** (6805 Abercorn St., Savannah 31405, tel. 912/355–3004, fax 912/355–0134). 154 rooms; pool, shuttle service. **Westin–Downtown** (231 W. Boundary St., Savannah 31401, tel. 912/232–3200, fax 912/232–3200). 172 rooms; restaurant, pool, lounge.

INEXPENSIVE Days Inn–Abercorn (11750 Abercorn St., Savannah 31419, tel. 912/927–7720, fax 912/925–8424). 114 rooms; Continental breakfast included, hot tub. **Hampton Inn Hotel** (201 Stephenson Ave., Savannah 31405, tel. 912/355–4100, fax 912/356–5385). 129 rooms; Continental breakfast included, pool. **Super 8 Motel** (472 New Jesup Hwy., Brunswick 31525, tel. 912/264–8800). 62 rooms.

CAMPGROUNDS

Camping facilities in this area are extremely limited, though there's an occasional chain-operated KOA Kampground and mobile-home park where recreational vehicles can find hookups. The Golden Isles has two popular campgrounds connected to national and regional parks that are in more pleasant settings.

Blythe Island Campground. This medium-size, waterfront facility outside Brunswick is isolated in a natural setting among oaks and pine trees. The maximum stay is 14 nights from Memorial Day to Labor Day. *6616 Blythe Island Hwy., Brunswick 31525, tel. 912/261–3805 or 800/343–7855, fax 912/261–3806. 40 RV sites with full hookups, 30 with water and electric connections, 27 tent sites; showers, toilets, laundry, cable TV, picnic tables, barbecue areas. Reservations by phone or mail. MC, V.*

Jekyll Island Campground. Just off the ocean on 18 shady acres, this campground is a few minutes' walk from an uncrowded beach and a bicycle ride to four golf courses, tennis, and the historic district. Maximum stay is 14 nights, March–Labor Day. *1187 Riverview Dr., Jekyll Island 31527, tel. 912/635–3021. 80 RV sites with full hookups, 64 with water and electric connections, 76 tent sites; picnic tables, showers, toilets, laundry, store. Reservations by phone or mail. D, MC, V.*

Skidaway Island State Park. Located 8 miles southeast of Savannah, this 533-acre barrier island is comprised of marshlands and estuaries and offers a wide variety of activities. *Skidaway Island State Park, Savannah 31411, tel. 912/598–2300. 88 combination tent and trailer sites with water and electrical hookups; picnic tables, grills, 4 comfort stations providing hot showers, flush toilets, electrical outlets, automatic laundry. AE, D, MC, V.*

DINING

People come to the coast for the freshly caught shrimp, fish, crabs, and oysters. Although seafood is still served deep-fried or with heavy cream sauce, growing health concerns have brought more broiled, boiled, and lightly sautéed dishes to the menus of even the established restaurants. Price categories per person, excluding 6% tax, service, and drinks, are Moderate, $15–$25, and Inexpensive, under $15.

SAVANNAH **Crystal Beer Parlor.** Located in the historic district, this casual and longtime Savannah favorite is famous for its crab stew, shrimp salad, and "Crystalburger"

served with thick french fries. *301 W. Jones St., tel. 912/232–1153. No reservations. AE, D, MC, V. Inexpensive–Moderate.*

Elizabeth on 37th. An elegant mansion with old-Savannah decor in the historic district is where Elizabeth Terry, one of the city's top chefs, prepares delicately sauced seafood dishes and a variety of meats. *105 E. 37th St., tel. 912/236–5547. Reservations advised. AE, D, MC, V. No lunch. Moderate.*

45 South. This popular south-side eatery serves a range of well-prepared dishes acclaimed by local critics—from grilled swordfish to breast of duck to pork tenderloin—in a stylish, up-to-date setting with glass and mirrors. *20 E. Broad St., tel. 912/233–1881. Reservations advised. AE, D, DC, MC, V. No lunch. Moderate.*

Huey's. This riverfront New Orleans–style bistro serves authentic regional specialties, including heaping plates of red beans and rice, and fresh sugar-dusted beignets. *115 E. River St., tel. 912/234–7385. No reservations. AE, D, MC, V. Inexpensive.*

Mrs. Wilkes Boarding House. The fine, family-style, southern fare served in this understated basement restaurant has attracted the likes of David Brinkley and Charles Kuralt. Come early and expect to wait in line. *107 W. Jones St., tel. 912/232–5997. No reservations. No credit cards. Closed weekends. No dinner. Inexpensive.*

Pearl's Elegant Pelican. There's a nautical theme to the decor of this restaurant in the historic district, which specializes in boiled, fried, or steamed seafood served family style. *152 Montgomery St., tel. 912/352–8221. No reservations. AE, D, DC, MC, V. No lunch. Inexpensive.*

Pirates' House. Located in the same building as 45 South (*see above*), this local dining legend with a piratical flair emphasizes all types of seafood—shrimp, fish, crab, and oysters—and serves more than 40 different desserts. *20 E. Broad St., tel. 912/233–5757. Reservations advised. AE, D, DC, MC, V. Inexpensive–Moderate.*

Seashell House. This no-frills establishment on the road to Skidaway Island serves all types of seafood dishes, including a tasty low-country boil and a first-rate seafood platter. *3111 Skidaway Rd., tel. 912/352–8116. AE, D, MC, V. No lunch. Inexpensive.*

GOLDEN ISLES **Alfonza's Olde Plantation Supper Club.** Seafood, superb steaks, and fried chicken are served by friendly waiters and waitresses in a low-key, come-as-you-are atmosphere. *Harrington La., St. Simons Island, tel. 912/638–9883. Reservations advised. D, DC, MC, V. No lunch. Moderate.*

Bennie's Red Barn. A converted barn with massive stone fireplace and balcony seating lends a clublike atmosphere to this long-standing restaurant that specializes in seafood and steaks. *5514 Frederica Rd., St. Simons Island, tel. 912/638–2844. Reservations advised. MC, V. No lunch. Moderate.*

Blanche's Courtyard. With an intimate courtyard shaded by a 300-year-old live oak and interior decor described as Bayou Victorian, Blanche's exudes a New Orleans atmosphere that's complemented by live jazz performances on Saturday nights. The specialty of the house is broiled fish, and *Southern Living* has characterized their steaks as "best in the islands." *440 Ocean Blvd., St. Simons Island, tel. 912/638–3030. Reservations advised. AE, DC, MC, V. No lunch. Moderate.*

Crabdaddy's. Freshly grilled, blackened, or steamed seafood are the house specialty of this fun and informal restaurant a few blocks from the beach. *1217 Ocean Blvd., St. Simons Island, tel. 912/634–1120. No reservations. MC, V. No lunch. Inexpensive–Moderate.*

Crab Trap. This popular restaurant's rustic nautical theme and informal atmosphere complement a straightforward selection of broiled and fried seafood. *1209 Ocean Blvd., St. Simons Island, tel. 912/638–3552. No reservations. MC, V. No lunch. Inexpensive.*

Kyoto Restaurant. The evening's entertainment begins as table-side chefs cook your meal to order in this sleek, contemporary restaurant done in black with polished wood. *224 Retreat Rd., St. Simons Island, tel. 912/638–0885. AE, DC, MC, V. No lunch. Moderate.*

Latitude 31. Surrounded by nautical decor, diners can choose from seafood, pasta, and beef dishes while enjoying a waterfront view. *1 Pier Rd., Jekyll Island, tel. 912/635–3800. Reservations advised. MC, V. No lunch. Inexpensive.*

Mullet Bay. Wide verandas provide outside dining at this upbeat eatery on St. Simons. The informal menu offers burgers, sandwiches, seafood, and pasta dishes. *500 Ocean Blvd., St. Simons Island, tel. 912/634–9977. No reservations. AE, D, DC, MC, V. Inexpensive.*

Spanky's. A trendy restaurant and bar, this popular spot serves pizza, salads, and sandwiches. No alcohol is served on Sunday. *1200 Glynn Ave., St. Simons Island, tel. 912/638–0918. No reservations. AE, D, MC, V. Inexpensive.*

SHOPPING

Souvenir shops in Savannah and the Golden Isles sell T-shirts and beachwear. In the nine cobblestone blocks of River Street along the Savannah River, you can find everything from pottery to paintings. Several antiques shops are just above this level off Bay Street, and there are more in the historic district. Two major suburban malls house a wide variety of regional and national chains, such as Belk's and Abercrombie & Fitch. Frederica Road on St. Simons Island is lined with fine clothing stores and gift shops; beachwear, gift, and souvenir stores thrive in the small commercial district in St. Simons village.

OUTDOOR ACTIVITIES

BEACHES Although natives rarely swim between September and March, the water temperatures remain relatively warm much longer. Some hardy souls swim as late as January. Tybee Island, 18 miles east of downtown Savannah, has wide-open stretches of public beaches, and all the beach areas rimming St. Simons and Jekyll islands are easily accessible.

BIKING St. Simons Island and Jekyll Island offer miles and miles of flat, well-paved biking trails, and their wide beaches are actually hard enough to bike on. The trail over the elevated bridges and across stretches of the F. J. Torras Causeway is more challenging. Contact the **Chamber of Commerce** (Brunswick, tel. 912/265–0620) for information about daily or weekly bike rentals.

BOATING AND SAILING All these coastal areas offer both sailboat and powerboat rentals. Try **Barry's Beach Service** (St. Simons Island, tel. 912/638–8053) for sailboats, **Captain Jeanne** (St. Simons Island, tel. 912/638–3611, ext. 5202) for charters with a captain, or **Taylor's Fish Camp** (St. Simons Island, tel. 912/638–7690) for captained or bareboat charters.

FISHING The **Georgia Department of Natural Resources** (1 Conservation Way, Brunswick 31520, tel. 912/264–7218) is the best source for current information on fishing regulations. Fishing charters operate out of St. Simons Island and Jekyll Island.

GOLF This is a golfer's paradise. The mild climate makes it a year-round sport, and there's a wide selection of challenging public and resort-operated courses to choose from. Contact local chambers of commerce for more information (*see* Tourist Offices, *above*).

WALKING In Savannah's Forsyth Park, oak trees generously shade a network of trails through the 20 lushly groomed acres. Tybee Island's wide beaches and seashore vistas make it another favorite walking spot. The flat beaches rimming St. Simons and Jekyll islands are ideal for jogging and walking, and there's an extensive system of paved paths that connects inland areas to the coastal islands over bridges and causeways.

ENTERTAINMENT

CONCERTS Local and traveling productions of theatrical, musical, and dance events are held at the **Savannah Civic Center** (Liberty and Montgomery Sts., Savannah, tel. 912/651–6550 or 912/651–6556 for ticket information).

DANCE **Ballet South** (201 Varn Dr., Savannah, tel. 912/354–3899), the city's resident classical dance company, appears at the Savannah Civic Center and other theaters.

MUSIC The **Savannah Symphony Orchestra** (225 Abercorn St., Savannah, tel. 912/236–9536) maintains an annual performance schedule. **Coastal Jazz Association** (224 W. Congress St., Savannah, tel. 912/232–2222) puts on concerts by local and national artists in and around the historic district.

THEATER **Island Players** (Neptune Park, St. Simons Island, tel. 912/638–3031) presents musicals and plays from January through June and children's plays in summer.

The **Jekyll Island Musical Theater Festival** (tel. 912/635–4060) presents outdoor musicals performed by professional actors from June through mid-August in the amphitheater of Jekyll Island.

Seattle
Washington

Updated by Loralee Wenger

eattle is defined by water. There's no use denying the city's damp weather, or the fact that its skies are cloudy for much of the year. Residents of Seattle don't tan—goes the joke—they rust.

But Seattle is also defined by a different kind of water. A variety of rivers, lakes, and canals bisect steep hills, creating a series of distinctive areas along the water's edge, where fishing boats and floating homes, swank yacht clubs and waterfront restaurants exist side by side.

Seattle's wet climate tends to foster an easygoing, indoor lifestyle. Overcast days and long winter nights help make the city a haven for moviegoers and book readers (per-capita book purchases are among the highest in the country). At the same time, Seattleites are serious about the outdoors—whether it's hiking in the Cascade Mountains to the east, the Olympics to the west, or strolling in the city's extensive park system (designed by Frederick Law Olmsted, creator of New York City's Central Park).

The city is also defined by its people; the half million in the city proper and the 2.75 million in the surrounding Puget Sound region are a diversified bunch. Seattle has long had an active Asian and Asian-American population, and also includes well-established communities of Scandinavians, African-Americans, Jews, Native Americans, Hispanics, and other ethnic groups.

Shedding it's sleepy-town image, Seattle has been one of the fastest-growing cities in the United States and an important Pacific Rim seaport. The town that Sir Thomas Beacham once described as a "cultural wasteland" now has all the artistic trappings of a full-blown big city, with ad agencies and artists' co-ops, symphonies and ballet companies. Locals may berate this wet and misty city, but there's plenty of reasons why Seattle consistently ranks high on lists of the country's best places in which to live.

ESSENTIAL INFORMATION

WHEN TO GO Seattleites may gripe about the weather, but with raincoats and umbrellas, they have adapted to this damp, gray climate where it rains 37–39 inches per year. In any season, several days of overcast and light showers are not unusual. Spring, with showers mixed with sunshine, and temperatures in the high 50s to low 60s, brings beautiful garden displays. Summer daytime temperatures are generally in the 70s, but there is usually a week of extremely hot weather, when temperatures hit the high 80s or low 90s. Even on those days, evening temperatures cool to the point where a sweater may be necessary. Fall may be the best time to visit—summer crowds are gone and blue skies and sunshine often persist, with temperatures in the 60s. The average temperature in January is 38°—freezing temperatures are rare, with only two or three snowfalls a season.

FESTIVALS AND SEASONAL EVENTS The **Folklife Festival** on Memorial Day weekend showcases some of the region's best folk singers, jugglers, and bands, along with crafts and food vendors at the Seattle Center.

Seafair (tel. 206/728–0123), held from late July to early August, salutes Seattle's marine heritage with a parade in downtown and hydroplane races on Lake Washington near Seward Park. **Bumbershoot** packs the four days of Labor Day weekend with music, including classical, blues, reggae, zydeco, and popular performances at Seattle Center.

BARGAINS Seattle's greatest asset—its spectacular scenery—is free. Another visual treat is the **Pike Place Market** (1st Ave. at Pike St.), where vendors hawk fresh seafood and produce, and craftspeople offer their wares. Just across the street at Victor Steinbreuck Park, you can picnic, listen to street musicians, and watch ferries crossing Puget Sound.

Seattle's **Out to Lunch summer concert series** (tel. 206/623–0340) runs from mid-June to early September every weekday at noon in various spots downtown.

The **Seattle Art Museum** (100 University St., tel. 206/654–3100) has a free day at the beginning of each month. The **Elliott Bay Book Company** (101 S. Main St., tel. 206/624–6600) hosts lectures and readings by authors of local and international acclaim. Most are free, but phone ahead to be sure.

Ticket/Ticket (401 Broadway E, 2nd Floor in the Broadway Market, tel. 206/324–2744) sells half-price tickets (cash only) for most theater, music, and dance events on the day of the performance. Prices for movies that have just left downtown theaters are affordable at less than ⅓ the regular price at the **Crest Cinema** (16505 5th Ave. NE, tel. 206/363–6338).

The **Pavilion Outlet Mall** (17100 Southcenter Pkwy., tel. 206/575–8090) just south of Southcenter Mall in Tukwila has a number of stores with discounted merchandise.

TOURIST OFFICES The **Seattle/King County Convention and Visitors Bureau** (800 Convention Pl., Seattle 98101, tel. 206/461–5840), at the I–5 end of Pike Street, can provide you with maps and information about lodging, restaurants, and attractions throughout the city.

EMERGENCIES Police, fire, and **ambulance:** Dial 911. **Hospitals:** Area hospitals with emergency rooms include Harborview Medical Center (325 9th Ave., tel. 206/223–3074) and Virginia Mason Hospital (925 Seneca St., tel. 206/624–1144).

ARRIVING AND DEPARTING

BY PLANE Seattle-Tacoma International Airport (Sea-Tac) is 20 miles from downtown Seattle and is served by most major U.S. and international airlines. Allow 30–45 minutes' driving time to or from downtown.

Between the Airport and Downtown. Visitors can take **Gray Line Airport Express** (tel. 206/626–6088) buses from 6:10 AM to 11:45 PM, with departures every 20–30 minutes depending on the location of your hotel; the fare is $8–$15. **Super Shuttle** (tel. 206/622–1424) offers service to and from the airport; fares are $18–$25.

BY CAR I–5 enters Seattle from the north and south, I–90 from the east.

BY BUS Seattle is served by **Greyhound** (tel. 800/231–2222) from its 8th Avenue and Stewart Street depot.

BY TRAIN **Amtrak** (303 S. Jackson St., tel. 800/872–7245) provides rail transportation from Seattle. In 1995, after a 14-year suspension, the Seattle–Vancouver, British Columbia, train route (about four hours in duration) was reestablished.

GETTING AROUND

BY BUS **Metropolitan Transit** (821 2nd Ave., tel. 206/553–3000) provides a free-ride service in the downtown waterfront area from 5 AM to 7 PM. Fares to other destinations range from $1 to $2, depending on the zone and time of day.

BY MONORAIL The **Monorail** (tel. 206/684–7200), built for the 1962 World's Fair, makes the three-minute trip from between Westlake Center and the Seattle Center every 15 minutes. Hours are Sunday–Thursday 9–9 and Friday and Saturday 9 AM–midnight. The fare is less than $1.

BY TAXI Major companies are **Farwest** (tel. 206/622–1717) and **Yellow Cab** (tel. 206/622–6500).

BY TROLLEY Waterfront trolleys (tel. 206/553–3000) run from Pier 70 into Pioneer Square. Fares are around $1, slightly more during the morning and evening rush hours.

REST STOPS Good for putting your feet up are atriums such as the one inside Columbia Center Court or Westlake Mall. The cleanest rest rooms are in these indoor centers and in department stores.

GUIDED TOURS Orientation: From Pier 55, **Argosy Tours** (Pier 55, Suite 201, 98101, tel. 206/623–1445) offers one-hour tours exploring Elliott Bay and the Port of Seattle.

Special Interest: Tillicum Village (Pier 55–56, tel. 206/443–1244) sails from Pier 55–56 across Puget Sound to Blake Island for a four-hour experience of traditional Northwest Indian life, including a dinner of steamed clams and salmon and the Dance of the Wind performance. **Underground Tours** (610 1st Ave., tel. 206/682–4646 for reservations or 206/682–1511 for information) offers a 90-minute walking tour of the belowground sections of Pioneer Square with tongue-in-cheek narration.

Self-Guided: "A Directory of Seattle's Public Art," an illustrated brochure by the **Seattle Arts Commission** (221 1st Ave. W, Suite 100, tel. 206/684–7171) is available by sending a self-addressed envelope of at least 8 by 10 inches with $1 in postage. The brochure describes walks and drives to see more than 256 innovative works of art in public places.

EXPLORING

INTERNATIONAL DISTRICT The population of the International District, located south and east of the Kingdome, is split three ways between people of Chinese, Filipino, and other Asian descent. The district began as a haven for Chinese workers after they finished the Transcontinental Railroad; it contains many Chinese, Japanese, and Korean restaurants as well as herbalists, massage parlors, acupuncturists, and about 30 private clubs for gambling and socializing. **Uwajimaya** (519 6th Ave. S, tel. 206/624–6248), possibly the largest Japanese store on the West Coast, stocks china, gifts, fabrics, housewares, and a complete supermarket with an array of Asian foods.

KINGDOME Seattle's covered stadium is the home of the Seattle Seahawks NFL team and the Seattle Mariners baseball team. The 650-foot-diameter stadium was built in 1976 and has the world's largest self-supporting roof, which is 250 feet high. If you're interested in the inner workings, take the one-hour guided tour. *201 S. King St., tel. 206/296–3111. Open hrs vary. Admission charged.*

MUSEUM OF FLIGHT The Red Barn, the original Boeing airplane factory, houses an exhibit on the history of aviation. The Great Gallery, a dramatic structure designed by Seattle architect Ibsen Nelson, contains more than 20 airplanes—suspended from the ceiling and on the ground—dating back to the Wright brothers. *9404 E. Marginal Way S, tel. 206/764–5720. Open daily. Admission charged.*

PIKE PLACE MARKET This Seattle institution began in 1907 when the city issued permits to farmers allowing them to sell produce from their wagons parked at Pike Place. In 1911, the city built stalls that were allotted to the farmers on a daily basis. Urban renewal almost killed the market, but city voters led by the late architect Victor Steinbreuck rallied and voted it to be a historical asset. Many of the buildings have been restored, and the project is connected by stairs and an elevator to the waterfront. You can still purchase fresh seafood (which can be packed in dry ice for your flight home), produce, cheese, Northwest wines, bulk spices, tea, coffee, and arts and crafts. *1st Ave. at Pike St., tel. 206/682–7453. Open daily. Admission free.*

PIONEER SQUARE To get a sense of how Seattle has changed through the years, take a look at the old section of the city with its cobblestone streets and brick buildings. Start at Pioneer Park (Yesler Way and 1st Ave. S), the site of Seattle's original business district. In 1889, a fire destroyed many of the wood-frame buildings in the area, but the industrious residents and businesspeople rebuilt them with brick and mortar. The term "Skid Row" originated here, when timber was logged off the hill and sent to the city's sawmill. The skid road was made of small logs laid down and greased so the freshly cut timber could slide down to the mill. With the Klondike gold rush, this area became populated with saloons and brothels and the old pioneering area deteriorated. Eventually drunks and bums hung out on Skid Road, and the term changed to Skid Row.

Today, Pioneer Square encompasses about 18 blocks and includes restaurants, bars, shops, the city's largest concentration of art galleries (*see* Shopping, *below*), and the **Klondike Gold Rush National Historical Park,** with a center showing film presentations, permanent exhibits, and summer gold-panning demonstrations. *117 S. Main St., tel. 206/553–7220. Open daily. Admission free.*

SEATTLE AQUARIUM Sea otters and seals swim and dive in their pools, and the "State of the Sound" exhibit shows aquatic life and the ecology of Puget Sound. Just next door is the **Omnidome Film Experience,** which showcases large-scale OMNIMAX films such as the one showing the eruption of Mt. St. Helens. *Pier 59. Aquarium: tel. 206/386–4320; Omnidome: tel. 206/622–1868. Open daily. Admission charged.*

SEATTLE CENTER This 74-acre complex built for the 1962 Seattle World's Fair includes an amusement park, theaters, the Coliseum, exhibition halls, museums, shops, and the city's most famous landmark, the **Space Needle,** with its lounge, restaurants (tel. 206/443–2100 or 800/937–9582), and observation deck. The 605-foot-tall spire is visible from almost anywhere in the downtown area. The observation deck offers an impressive view of the city.

UNIVERSITY OF WASHINGTON Some 33,500 students attend the university, which was founded in 1861. On the northwestern corner of the beautifully landscaped campus is the **Burke Museum** (17th Ave. NE and N.E. 45th St., tel. 206/543–5590; open daily; donation requested), Washington's natural-history and anthropological museum. Nearby, the **Henry Art Gallery** (15th Ave. NE and N.E. 41st St., tel. 206/543–2280; admission charged) displays paintings from the 19th and 20th centuries, textiles, and traveling exhibits; the gallery was closed at press time but was scheduled to reopen in early 1997.

Washington Park Arboretum, just south of the campus, offers self-guided walking tours of its lush grounds. A visitor center at the north end of the park is open to instruct you on the species of flora and fauna you'll see here. *2300 Arboretum Dr. E, tel. 206/543–8800. Open daily. Admission charged.*

WOODLAND PARK ZOO Many of the animals are free to roam their section of a total of 92 acres. The African Savanna, the Elephant Forest, and the Tropical Rain Forest are popular features. *N. 59th St. and Frement Ave., tel. 206/684–4800. Open daily. Admission charged.*

MT. RAINIER NATIONAL PARK Just 85 miles southeast of Seattle is **Mt. Rainier National Park.** At 14,411 feet, Mt. Rainier is the fifth-highest mountain in the lower 48 states. In addition to the mountain with its glaciers and ice caves, the park includes some 400 square miles of wilderness, 300 miles of hiking trails, cross-country skiing trails, lakes and rivers for fishing, and camping facilities. At Paradise, the **Henry M. Jackson Visitor's Center,** the starting point for many hikes, has exhibits, films, and a 360-degree view of the summit and surrounding peaks. At 6,400 feet, the **Sunrise Visitor's Center** is the highest point accessible by car at Rainier. *To reach Mt. Rainier from Seattle, follow I–5, Hwy. 7, and Hwy. 706 south and east or Hwy. 410 east and south. Henry M. Jackson Visitor's Center: tel. 360/569–2211. Jackson is open Memorial Day–Labor Day, daily; Sunrise is open July 4th weekend–Labor Day, daily.*

HOTELS AND INNS

Downtown hotels are the most convenient, and most expensive. More economical are accommodations near the Seattle Center, where you can board the monorail for the short trip downtown. For recommendations regarding bed-and-breakfast accommodations, contact the **Washington State Bed & Breakfast Guild** (tel. 509/548–6224) or **Pacific Bed & Breakfast Agency** (tel. 206/784–0539). Price categories for double occupancy, excluding 15.2% tax, are Expensive, over $120; Moderate, $90–$120; and Inexpensive, under $90.

DOWNTOWN **Inn at Virginia Mason.** Located east of the I–5 freeway from downtown, this midsize inn has attractively decorated rooms and ample parking. *1006 Spring St., 98104, tel. 206/583–6453. 77 rooms, 2 suites. Restaurant. MC, V. Inexpensive–Moderate.*

Mayflower Park Hotel. Brass fixtures and antiques give a muted Oriental feel to this pleasant older hotel, built in 1927. Although it is quieter than most modern downtown hotels, its guest rooms are somewhat smaller. *405 Olive Way, 98101, tel. 206/623–8700, fax 206/382–6997. 153 rooms, 20 suites; no-smoking rooms available. Restaurant, lounge, access to health club. AE, DC, MC, V. Moderate–Expensive.*

Pacific Plaza. Built in 1928, this ideally located downtown hotel reflects its original character, with rooms and furnishings reminiscent of the '20s and '30s. Guest rooms are sized adequately for couples but not for families. *400 Spring St., 98104, tel. 206/623–3900 or 800/426–1165, fax 206/623–2059. 160 rooms. Continental breakfast included, 2 restaurants. AE, DC, MC, V. Inexpensive.*

Seattle YMCA. These downtown rooms are clean and plainly furnished with a bed, phone, desk, and lamp. Four people can sleep in each dorm unit. *909 4th Ave., 98104, tel. 206/382–5000. 198 units. Pool, health club. MC, V. Inexpensive.*

West Coast Camlin Hotel. This 1926 hotel–motor inn is on the edge of downtown but close to the convention center. It features spacious rooms slightly blemished by the noisy heating system. Rooms ending with 10 are best because they have windows on three sides. *1619 9th Ave., 98101, tel. 206/682–0100 or 800/426–0670, fax 206/682–7415. 132 rooms, 4 suites. Restaurant, lounge, outdoor pool. AE, D, DC, MC, V. Moderate.*

SEATTLE CENTER **Seattle Inn.** Just a couple of blocks from the Seattle Center and the monorail (which provides easy access to downtown), this 1960s-vintage motel has appealing, but not fancy, decor. *225 Aurora Ave. N, 98107, tel. 206/728–7666. 160 rooms, no-smoking rooms available. Indoor pool, whirlpool, parking. AE, MC, V. Inexpensive.*

Sixth Avenue Inn. This small but comfortable motor hotel, built in the 1960s, is a few blocks between downtown and the Seattle Center. Suitable for families, the property has unexceptional but well-maintained decor and color schemes. *2000 6th Ave., 98121, tel. 206/441–8300, fax 206/441–9903. 166 rooms, no-smoking rooms available. Restaurant, lounge. AE, DC, MC, V. Moderate.*

NORTH END **Meany Tower Hotel.** Built in 1931 and completely remodeled several times, this pleasant hotel, just a few blocks from the University of Washington, has retained much of its old-fashioned charm; the rooms on the upper floors have views of Lake Washington and Lake Union. *4507 Brooklyn Ave. NE, 98105, tel. 206/634–2000, fax 206/634–2000. 155 rooms; no-smoking rooms available. Restaurant, lounge. AE, DC, MC, V. Moderate.*

University Plaza Hotel. This is a full-service motor hotel on the west side of I–5 from the University of Washington. Rooms are spacious and pleasantly decorated with teak furniture; rooms near the freeway can be noisy. *400 N.E. 45th St., 98105, tel. 206/634–0100, fax 206/633–2743. 135 rooms; no-smoking rooms available. Restaurant, lounge, outside heated pool, fitness room, beauty parlor. AE, D, DC, MC, V. Moderate.*

SEATTLE-TACOMA AIRPORT **Holiday Inn Sea-Tac.** The atrium lobby of this hotel, built in 1970, has an attractive garden room that's convenient for meeting people. Guest rooms are spacious, and the Top of the Inn revolving-view restaurant features singing waiters. *17338 Pacific Hwy. S, 98188, tel. 206/248–1000 or 800/465–4329, fax 206/242–7089. 260 rooms. Restaurant, coffee shop, lounge, indoor pool, whirlpool, health club. AE, DC, MC, V. Moderate.*

Seattle Marriott. The Marriott is surprisingly luxurious for being so far away from downtown. Built in 1981, the hotel features a five-story-high, 20,000-square-foot tropical atrium. *3201 S. 176th St., 98188, tel. 206/241–2000, fax 206/248–0789. 459 rooms; no-smoking rooms available. Restaurant, 2 whirlpools, health club, game room, concierge service, airport shuttle. AE, D, DC, MC, V. Moderate-Expensive.*

MOTELS

MODERATE **Black Angus Motor Inn** (12245 Aurora Ave. N, 98133, tel. 206/363–3035). 53 rooms; restaurant, lounge, coffee shop, pool, no-smoking rooms. **University Inn** (4140 Roosevelt Way NE, 98105, tel. 206/632–5055). 102 rooms; outdoor pool, complimentary coffee and newspapers.

INEXPENSIVE **Commodore Motor Hotel** (2013 2nd Ave., 98121, tel. 206/448–8868). 100 rooms; downtown location. **Max-Ivor Motel** (6188 4th Ave. S, 98108, tel. 206/762–8194). 42 rooms; restaurant next door. **Nendels Valu Inn** (2106 5th Ave., 98121, tel. 800/547–0106). 68 rooms.

DINING

Dining in Seattle means many things. One of them is seafood—salmon, halibut, crab, shrimp, you name it. Another is dining with outstanding views—Elliott Bay in downtown, the Olympic Mountains and Shilshole Bay to the west, and Lake Washington and the Cascade Mountains to the east. Great ethnic restaurants are also in good supply; try Chinese, Thai, Vietnamese, and East

Indian establishments. Price categories per person, excluding 8.2% tax, service, and drinks, are Moderate, $15–$25, and Inexpensive, under $15.

MODERATE **Cafe Sport.** This Pike Place Market restaurant serves a variety of cuisines—one day it may be Italian, another it may be Thai—but whatever it is, the food is excellent and the portions are hearty. *2020 Western Ave., tel. 206/443–6000. AE, DC, MC, V.*

Chau's Chinese Restaurant. This small, plain place on the edge of Chinatown serves great seafood and specials as an alternative to the standard Cantonese fare. *310 4th Ave. S, tel. 206/621–0006. MC, V.*

Cucina! Cucina! Enjoy basic Italian fare— lightly sauced pasta and seafood dishes and one-person pizzas—in the restaurant or on the large deck overlooking Lake Union. *901 Fairview Ave. N, tel. 206/447–2782. AE, MC, V.*

Han II. This upscale Korean restaurant serves great lunch specials and classic Korean barbecue, all prepared on gas burners at your table and accompanied by a troop of side dishes and dipping sauces. *409 Maynard Ave. S, tel. 206/587–0464. MC, V.*

Kells. This traditional Irish pub is tucked into an old brick building along the Pike Place Market. The menu is simple but satisfying—choose from Irish stew, leg of lamb, and meat pies, and wash it all down with a pint of Guinness. On some nights there's live Irish music. *1916 Post Alley, tel. 206/728– 1916. MC, V.*

Linyen. This comfortable restaurant offers a new, light style of Cantonese food. Most nights you'll find clams in black-bean sauce, spicy chicken, and fresh fish on the blackboard menu of specials. *424 7th Ave. S, tel. 206/622–8181. AE, DC, MC, V.*

Salvatore Ristorante Italiano. You may have to wait at this small place, but most people believe it's worth it when they taste the individual pizzas, pasta dishes, or one of the meat and fish courses chalked onto the blackboard above the kitchen window. *6100 Roosevelt Way NE, tel. 206/527–9301. MC, V.*

Takara. Sushi and sashimi are the hallmarks of this popular, classical Japanese restaurant. The salmon teriyaki is superb, as is the steamed black cod. *1501 Western Ave., tel. 206/682–8609. AE, MC, V.*

Wild Ginger. This restaurant's specialty is Pacific Rim cookery—primarily tasty and eclectic Asian fare—including southern Chinese, Vietnamese, Thai, and Malaysian dishes. *1400 Western Ave., tel. 206/623– 4450. AE, D, DC, MC, V.*

INEXPENSIVE **A. Jay's Eatery.** Good sandwiches, omelets, and soups are served at this deli that lets you linger over coffee. *2619 1st Ave., tel. 206/441–1511. AE, MC, V.*

Bahn Thai. Because of the variety of dishes and the quality of the preparations, the Bahn Thai is still one of the best and most popular Thai places in Seattle, but it can get noisy in the evening. *409 Roy St., tel. 206/283–0444. AE, DC, MC, V.*

El Puerco Lloron. There's a pink awning and a pig outside this steel-and-glass building, and fresh, handmade tortillas with great texture and flavorful fillings inside. *Pike Place Market Hillclimb, 1501 Western Ave., tel. 206/624–0541. AE, MC, V.*

Hien Vuong. An unpretentious place that serves up great Vietnamese food, making it one of the best lunch places in town. *502 S. King St., tel. 206/624–2611. No credit cards.*

Sunlight Cafe. The Sunlight Cafe draws an easygoing crowd for its steady and flavorful vegetarian dishes, such as hearty soups, stirfried vegetables with a yogurt-cheese sauce, and bountiful vegetable salads with sesametahini dressing. *6403 Roosevelt Way NE, tel. 206/522–9060. No credit cards.*

Three Girls Bakery. This tiny, 13-seat lunch counter behind a Pike Place Market bakery serves good sandwiches, soups, chili, and great bread—try the sourdough. *1514 Pike Pl., tel. 206/622–1045. No credit cards.*

SHOPPING

With fresh and natural ingredients in abundance, Seattleites are excited to share the bounty. They do so by offering smoked salmon, jams, jellies, honey, and syrups made from fresh, local ingredients. Artists and photographers make good use of the splendid scenery all around the region and offer their creations for sale through galleries and the Pike Place Market.

MALLS **Westlake Center** (400 Pine St., tel. 206/467–1600) lies in the middle of downtown Seattle. The three-story steel-and-glass building contains 80 shops as well as covered walkways to Seattle's two major department stores, Nordstrom's and The Bon. **Northgate Mall** (I–5 and Northgate Way, tel. 206/362–4777), located 10 miles north of downtown, encompasses 118 shops, including Nordstrom's, The Bon, Lamonts, and JCPenney.

ANTIQUES Seattle's antiques shops offer everything from expensive, high-quality pieces to the wacky, way-out, and eminently affordable. To see the former, browse at **David Reed Weatherford** (133 14th Ave. E, tel. 206/329–6533), specializing in 17th- and 18th-century English, French, and Oriental pieces. **Pioneer Square Mall** features 85 stalls of antique glassware, jewelry, and furniture (602 1st Ave. S, tel. 206/624–1164). **Antique Importers** (640 Alaskan Way, tel. 206/628–8905) offers 14,000 square feet of pieces from Victoriana to Art Deco and specializes in stained-glass windows.

SPECIALTY SHOPS **Books:** Elliott Bay Book Company (101 S. Main St., tel. 206/624–6600) is a great place for browsing, especially for children's, Northwest, and travel books. The University Book Store (4326 University Way NE, tel. 206/634–3400) is among the largest general bookstores in the country. **Crafts, Souvenirs, Toys: Pike Place Market** (*see* Exploring, *above*). **Menswear:** For discounted men's clothing, go to the Men's Wearhouse (1404 4th Ave. at Union St., tel. 206/622–00570). **Women's Clothing:** For supreme bargains, visit Loehmann's (3620

128th St. SE, Bellevue, tel. 206/641–7596) just across the I–90 bridge from Seattle.

OUTDOOR ACTIVITIES

BIKING The Burke-Gilman Trail is a city-maintained trail extending 12.1 miles from Lake Washington nearly to Salmon Bay. Myrtle Edwards Park, north of Pier 70, has a two-lane path for jogging and cycling. Bikes can be rented at **Gregg's Greenlake Cycle** (7007 Woodlawn Ave. NE, tel. 206/523–1822).

FISHING There are good spots for fishing on Lake Washington, Green Lake, and Lake Union, and there are several fishing piers along the Elliott Bay waterfront. **Ballard Salmon Charter** (tel. 206/789–6202) is one of the many Seattle-based charter companies that offer trips for catching salmon, rock cod, flounder, and sea bass. **A Spot Tail Salmon Guide** (tel. 206/283–6680) offers charter fishing trips.

GOLF There are almost 50 public golf courses in the Seattle area. Among the most popular municipally run courses are **Jackson Park** (100 N.E. 135th St., tel. 206/363–4747) and **Jefferson Park** (4101 Beacon Ave. S, tel. 206/762–4513).

HIKING Lincoln Park in West Seattle or Discovery Park in the Magnolia area both have inspiring walks along the beach or up on the bluff, with fabulous views of the Olympic Mountains, ferries, and sea life.

JOGGING Green Lake is a favorite destination for cyclists, joggers, race walkers, strollers, and roller skaters. Several outlets along the east side offer skate and cycle rentals. Other good areas for jogging and walking are the Burke-Gilman Trail, around the reservoir at Volunteer Park, and at Myrtle Edwards Park, north of the waterfront.

SKIING Snoqualmie Pass in the Cascade Mountains, about an hour's drive east of Seattle on I–90, has a number of fine resorts offering downhill and cross-country skiing trails. Among them: **Alpental, Ski Acres, Snoqualmie Summit** (for all areas: 3010 77th St. SE, Mercer Island 98040, tel. 206/232–8182).

TENNIS There are public tennis courts in many parks around the Seattle area. For information, contact the **King County Parks Division** (tel. 206/296–4258).

ENTERTAINMENT

The Weekly has detailed arts, movie, and music reviews; it hits the newsstands every Wednesday. You can order tickets by phone from **Ticketmaster** (tel. 206/628–0888) or **Ticket/Ticket** (401 Broadway E, in the Broadway Market, tel. 206/324–2744), which sells half-price tickets for cash only for most theater, music, and dance events on the day of the performance.

BARS Bars with waterfront views include **Pescatore** (5300 34th Ave. NW, tel. 206/784–1733), **Ray's Boathouse** (6049 Seaview Ave. NW, tel. 206/789–3770), and **Anthony's Home Port** (6135 Seaview Ave. W, tel. 206/783–0780) at Shilshole Bay.

CONCERTS **Seattle Symphony** (Opera House at Seattle Center, tel. 206/443–4747) continues to uphold its long tradition of excellence. Most live rock and country-western concerts are held at the **Paramount Theater** (901 Pine St., tel. 206/682–1414), which was renovated at a cost of $31 million and reopened in early 1995, and the **Moore Theater** (1932 2nd Ave., tel. 206/443–1744), both elegant former movie-music halls.

DANCE **Pacific Northwest Ballet** (Opera House at Seattle Center, tel. 206/292–2787) is the city's resident company. **Meany Hall for the Performing Arts** (University of Washington campus, tel. 206/543–4880) presents important national and international companies with an emphasis on modern and jazz dance.

DINNER SHOWS **Dimitriou's Jazz Alley** (2033 6th Ave., tel. 206/441–9729) is a downtown club with nationally known, high-quality performers and dinner service.

OPERA **Seattle Opera** (Opera House at Seattle Center, Mercer St. at 3rd Ave., tel. 206/443–4711) is a world-class opera company, considered to be one of the top organizations in the country.

SPECTATOR SPORTS The **Seattle Mariners** (Kingdome, 201 S. King St., tel. 206/628–3555) play baseball April through early October. The **Seattle SuperSonics** basketball team (Seattle Center Coliseum, 1st Ave. N, tel. 206/281–5850) plays October through April. The NFL **Seahawks** (Kingdome, 201 S. King St., tel. 206/827–9777) play August through December.

THEATER **Seattle Repertory Theater** (Bagley Wright Theater at Seattle Center, 155 Mercer St., tel. 206/443–2222) presents a variety of high-quality programming from classics to new plays October–May. **Intiman Theater** (Playhouse at Seattle Center, 2nd and Mercer Sts., tel. 206/626–0782) presents classic world drama in an intimate, high-quality setting May–November. The **Fifth Avenue Musical Theater Company** (Fifth Avenue Theater, 1308 5th Ave., tel. 206/625–1418) is a resident professional troupe that mounts four lavish musicals October–May each year.

Sequoia and Kings Canyon National Parks
California

Updated by Marty Olmstead

When famed naturalist John Muir first laid eyes on this region of the Sierra, he called it a sublime wilderness. Contemporary visitors to California's Sequoia and Kings Canyon national parks still walk awed among the silent giants—the sequoias, the earth's largest living things—and they still marvel at the deep granite canyons and the snowcapped peaks. The two parks share a boundary and are administered as one park. They now encompass 1,300 square miles that are rivaled only by Yosemite National Park, to the north, in terms of rugged Sierra beauty. The topography runs from foothill chaparrals in the west, to the Giant Sequoia belt at 5,000 to 7,000 feet, to the towering peaks of the Great Western Divide; 14,494-foot Mt. Whitney, the highest point in the contiguous United States, is the crown jewel of the east side.

Today 2 million people visit the parks annually. They come to wile away peaceful hours on uncrowded trails, or to trek into the rugged grandeur of the backcountry. But there was a time, beginning in the 1860s, when people came to these timberlands to cut trees, and in some places the scars are still evident. By 1890, however, the area's beauty was officially recognized and the destruction was put in check by the establishment of Sequoia National Park, the country's second national park. In 1940 the adjacent General Grant Park was expanded to include the South Fork Kings River and renamed Kings Canyon National Park.

Most of the major attractions in both parks can be reached by automobile, but the major-

ity of acreage is without roads. If you expect to simply drive through, you will probably be disappointed: The panoramic views and striking geological features found in other national parks exist here, but they are less accessible. If you want to explore these parks, you will have to hike; and you'll have 900 miles of trails from which to choose.

ESSENTIAL INFORMATION

WHEN TO GO During the summer months, daytime highs usually run from the 70s to low 80s in the middle elevations, where the park's most popular attractions are located. The lower elevations often experience temperatures above 100°. Overnight lows average 46° to 53°. Visitors should bear in mind that summer thundershowers are not uncommon, and that the weather can change quickly in the mountains.

In winter, temperatures usually range from the low 20s to mid-40s, with overnight lows down into the single digits. Much of the area is covered with a deep blanket of snow from December to May. The roads to Giant Forest and Grant's Grove and the Generals Highway, which connects the two areas, are open year-round but are subject to closures or chain restrictions because of snowfall.

The best times to visit the parks are during late spring and early fall, when the temperatures are still moderate and the crowds thin. The parks draw their heaviest crowds during the month of August and over holiday weekends. Summer visitors should remember that they will be approaching the park

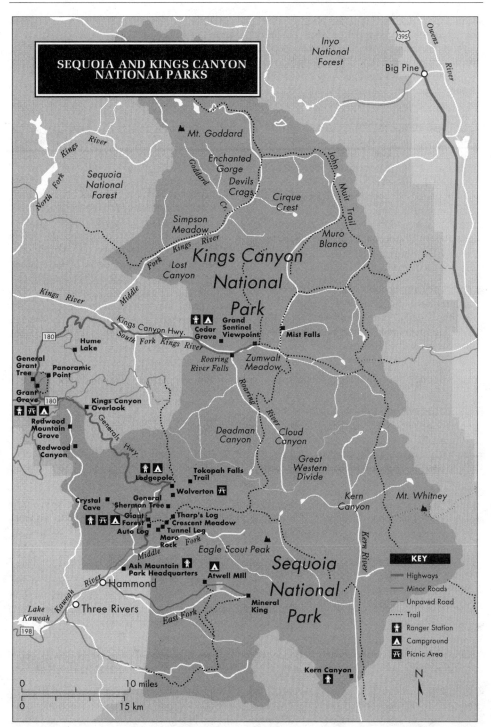

SEQUOIA AND KINGS CANYON
NATIONAL PARKS

Big Pine

Inyo
National
Forest

Owens River

395

Mt. Goddard

Kings River

North Fork

Sequoia
National
Forest

Goddard Cr.

Enchanted
Gorge
Devils
Crags

Cirque
Crest

John Muir Trail

Simpson
Meadow

Middle Fork Kings River

Kings Canyon

National

Park

Lost
Canyon

Muro
Blanco

Kings River

Middle

Kings Canyon Hwy.

South Fork Kings River

Cedar
Grove

Grand
Sentinel
Viewpoint

Mist Falls

180

Hume
Lake

General
Grant
Tree

Panoramic
Point

Roaring
River Falls

Zumwalt
Meadow

Grant
Grove

180

Kings Canyon
Overlook

Roaring River

Redwood
Mountain
Grove

Generals Hwy.

Deadman
Canyon

Cloud
Canyon

Redwood
Canyon

Great
Western
Divide

Lodgepole

Tokopah Falls
Trail

Wolverton

Kern
Canyon

Mt. Whitney

Crystal
Cave

General
Sherman Tree

Giant
Forest

Tharp's Log
Crescent Meadow

Auto Log

Tunnel Log

Maro
Rock

Kaweah Fork

Eagle Scout Peak

Middle

Sequoia

Kern River

KEY

Ash Mountain
Park Headquarters

Atwell Mill

National

Highways
Minor Roads
Unpaved Road
Trail
Ranger Station
Campground
Picnic Area

Hammond

Kaweah River

Three Rivers

Mineral
King

Park

Lake
Kaweah

198

East Fork

Kern Canyon

N

0   10 miles

0   15 km

from the west, across the San Joaquin Valley, where temperatures often exceed 100° from late May through early September. In May, June, September, and October, lodging rates within the park are reduced by about 20%; from November through April, they are reduced by more than 30%.

FESTIVALS AND SEASONAL EVENTS The **Jazz Affair,** held in the town of Three Rivers in April, is mostly swing jazz, held at several locations, with shuttle buses between sites. The **Red Bud Festival,** in Three Rivers, is a two-day arts and crafts festival in early May. The **Woodlake Rodeo,** held in Woodlake in May, is a weekend event that draws large crowds. On **Christmas,** carolers gather at the base of the General Grant Tree, the Nation's official Christmas tree.

TOURIST OFFICES **Park Headquarters** (Superintendent, Sequoia and Kings Canyon National Parks, Three Rivers 93271, tel. 209/565–3134). **Fresno Visitor and Convention Bureau** (808 M St., Fresno 93721, tel. 209/233–0836). **Visalia Chamber of Commerce** (720 West Mineral King, Visalia 93291, tel. 209/734–5876).

EMERGENCIES For **police, fire,** and **ambulance:** Dial 911.

ARRIVING AND DEPARTING

BY PLANE Sequoia and Kings Canyon national parks are serviced by the **Fresno Airport** (tel. 209/498–4700), located 5 miles from downtown Fresno and 55 miles from Grant Grove. At the **Visalia Airport** (tel. 209/738–3201), commercial passengers may arrive on American Eagle (tel. 800/433–7300), which makes connections in Los Angeles and San Jose.

BY CAR OR RV Only two roads lead into the parks and both approach from the west: Highway 180 from Fresno and Highway 198 from Visalia.

BY TRAIN Amtrak (tel. 800/872–7245) has stations in Fresno and Hanford, which is located 15 miles from Visalia. A shuttle bus

(included in the fare) takes train passengers from Hanford to Visalia.

BY BUS Both Fresno and Visalia are served by **Greyhound Lines** (tel. 800/231–2222), with buses that come in from San Francisco and Los Angeles.

GETTING AROUND

BY CAR Highway 180 from Fresno passes through the peninsula-like Grant Grove in the southwestern section of Kings Canyon, travels north through the national forest, reenters the park as the Kings Canyon Highway, then dead-ends. Highway 198 travels 59 miles from Visalia, entering Sequoia from the southwest at Ash Mountain. The Generals Highway connects the two highways, thereby linking the two parks. No roads enter the parks from the east. Vehicles longer than 22 feet are strongly advised to enter the park via Highway 180. Be warned that the National Park Service is currently in the midst of a long-term road-improvement program: Sporadic delays are a possibility for the next few years. At park entrances visitors are given a free informational brochure, which includes a map of the parks. You must carry chains at all times.

BY BUS An hourly shuttle connects Lodgepole to Moro Rock by way of Giant Forest in summer.

REST STOPS Approaching the park on Highway 198, Kaweah Lake, located 5 miles west of Three Rivers, offers boating, swimming, fishing, picnic facilities, camping, and public rest rooms.

GUIDED TOURS All-day guided tours of the park are available only through private tour companies. Call **Park Headquarters** (tel. 209/565–3134) for information.

EXPLORING

There are three centers of interest in the two parks: In Kings Canyon, there is the eponymous river and its surrounding Cedar Grove, and there is Grant Grove; in Sequoia, most people flock to the Giant Forest. From early May through October all the roads in the parks are normally open, providing access to some spectacular scenery. But the nature of these parks is best appreciated by including at least a few short walks in your tour. If you have only one or two days and want to see all three of these areas, it is best to stay in Grant Grove, which is a one-hour drive from both Cedar Grove and Giant Forest (along the Generals Highway). If you do not plan on extensive hikes, two or three days is ample time to acquaint yourself with these two parks.

The **Lodgepole Visitor Center** (Sequoia) or the **Grant Grove Visitor Center** (Kings Canyon), located at the parks' entrances, are excellent places to begin a visit. Exhibits and audiovisual programs provide a natural and cultural history of the parks, from their geological development to man's impact. Rangers are on duty to answer questions, and a large selection of printed materials is available.

From the Lodgepole Visitor Center, backtrack on General's Highway just under 4 miles to the **General Sherman Tree,** the largest living tree in the world. A sequoia slab nearby illustrates the big trees' dependence on fire for their existence. Nearby, the easy, 2-mile Congress Trail is a paved loop through the heart of the sequoia forest that takes one to three hours to complete.

Next, head farther south and turn off on the **Moro Rock–Crescent Meadow Road,** a 3-mile spur road that begins at the Cedar Grove Village and explores the southwest portion of the Giant Forest. The road is closed in winter, when it may be used as a ski trail, and is not recommended for RVs or trailers any time of the year. Among the odd attractions on this road is the **Auto Log,** a fallen giant sequoia on top of which you can drive your car, and the **Tunnel Log,** a sequoia that you drive through (there is a bypass for larger vehicles). Make the effort to climb the steep, ¼-mile staircase to the summit of **Moro Rock,** a large granite dome that

offers excellent views of the Great Western Divide and the western half of Sequoia National Park. About 100 yards from the end of the road is **Crescent Meadow,** John Muir's "gem of the Sierra," where brilliant wildflowers bloom in midsummer. Many trails begin here, including the 1-mile route to **Tharp's Log** (a home built in a fallen tree) and the High Sierra trail, which runs 71 miles to the summit of Mt. Whitney.

In summer you can take a 45-minute walking tour through **Crystal Cave** (admission charged) every day from 10 AM to 3 PM on the half hour. The marble cavern is full of stalagmites and stalactites. Bring a sweater, as the temperatures are in the 50s. It is at least a 45-minute drive from Giant Forest Village to the parking lot, and it will take you an additional 15 minutes to walk to the cave entrance. No trailers, RVs, or buses are allowed on Crystal Cave Road, which has a weight limit of 6,000 pounds.

The **Kings Canyon Highway** winds alongside the powerful Kings River, below the towering granite cliffs and past the tumbling waterfalls of a canyon John Muir called a rival to Yosemite. One mile east past the Cedar Grove Village turnoff is a turnoff allowing a wonderful vista of the glacial past of the *U*-shape canyon, everything from the valley floor to where the forks in the Kings River come together. Four miles farther along is the Grand Sentinel Viewpoint, where you will see the 3,500-foot tall granite monolith and some of the most interesting rock formations in the canyon. The drive takes about one hour each way. Take Highway 190 east from Grant Grove.

Back on Generals Highway, head north to Grant Grove and the **General Grant Tree,** the third-largest living tree in the world, believed to have been standing for 2,000 years. A designated National Shrine, it is the Nation's Christmas Tree and the only living memorial to American soldiers who have died while fighting for the United States in its wars. To reach the tree, take the short trail, which also passes the historic Gamlin Cabin, a cabin built in 1867, and the Fallen

Monarch, a hollowed, fallen giant sequoia early explorers used for shelter. This trail begins 1 mile northwest of the Grant Grove Visitor Center.

Nearby, a steep and narrow spur road (not recommended for trailers and RVs) heads east through the visitor center parking lot, curves left around the meadow, splits to the right, and leads 2.3 miles to **Panoramic Point**. A ¼-mile walk from the parking lot, the viewpoint offers a spectacular vista of the High Sierra. You can see from Mt. Goddard in northern Kings Canyon Park to Eagle Scout Peak in Sequoia Park. Unfortunately, Mt. Whitney can't be seen from the west side of the park because of the height of the Great Western Divide. The Park Ridge Trail, a 4-mile round-trip, begins here.

About 8 miles southeast of Grant Grove on Generals Highway, there is another turnoff. This one is unpaved and bumpy; it dead-ends after about 2 miles at Redwood Saddle, where you'll find the trailhead to **Redwood Canyon**. Here there are miles of trails leading through the world's largest grove of the world's tallest tree. Take in the cascades and quiet pools of Redwood Creek on a short walk, day hike, or overnight backpacking trip.

The sandy **Mist Falls Trail** follows the glaciated South Fork Canyon through forest and chaparral, past several rapids and cascades, to one of the largest waterfalls in the two parks. This 8-mile round-trip hike is relatively flat but climbs 600 feet in the last mile. It takes four to five hours to complete. The trailhead is at Road's End, 5½ miles east of the Cedar Grove Village turnoff.

HOTELS AND INNS

All of the parks' lodges and cabins are open during the summer months, but in winter only those in Giant Forest and Grant Grove remain open. A variety of accommodations are offered at Giant Forest and Grant Grove, from rustic cabins without baths to a deluxe motel. From November through April, excluding holiday periods, low-season rates are in effect, resulting in savings of 20%–30%.

All of the lodging facilities within the park are operated by Sequoia Guest Services, an authorized concessionaire of the National Park Service, and each of the areas has a simple, inexpensive restaurant. Most of the accommodations do not have formal names; when calling for reservations, describe the room using the guidelines below. For information and reservations, contact **Sequoia Guest Services** (Box 789, Three Rivers 93271, tel. 209/561–3314, fax 203/561–3135). Price categories for double occupancy, excluding 16½% tax, are Expensive, over $85; Moderate, $50–$85; and Inexpensive, under $50. All hotels accept MasterCard and Visa.

INSIDE THE PARK **Giant Forest.** The deluxe motel (Expensive) is the finest accommodation available in the park, with two queen-size beds, carpeted floors, and private showers. There are no low-season rates available. There are a variety of family cabins (Moderate): a cozy cabin with two double beds and carpeted floors; two rooms with bed space for six and carpeting; or smaller units with one double and one single bed and wood floors. All have private tub or shower bath. There is a standard motel (Moderate–Expensive) with simple, comfortable rooms with two double beds, carpeted floors, private tub-shower bath, and a large picture window. Some special motel units have an outdoor balcony. There are very rustic cabins (Inexpensive) that don't have baths, and some do not have electricity, in which case kerosene lamps are provided. Some have woodstoves for cooking (utensils not included) and tent roofs. All are closed in the winter.

Grant Grove. The most luxurious accommodations here are carpeted cabins with private bath, electric wall heaters, and twin-size beds. Most of these units, however, are in twos, and the adjoining walls are a little thin. Other cabins are even simpler, with woodstoves providing heat and kerosene lamps providing light. A central rest room and shower facility is nearby. *Inexpensive–Moderate.*

CEDAR GROVE **Cedar Grove Motel.** This is a small, 18-room motel-lodge, with rooms featuring two queen-size beds, carpeted floors, private showers, and air-conditioning. Open late May through September; rooms should be booked well in advance. *Moderate.*

STONY CREEK **Stony Creek Motel.** Open late May to September, the quiet motel-lodge here is actually on national forest land between Grant Grove and Giant Forest. The rooms are carpeted and have private showers. *Moderate.*

MOTELS

The following accommodations are outside the park perimeter.

MODERATE **Best Western** (40105 Sierra Dr., Three Rivers 93271, tel. 209/561–4119). 44 rooms; pool, spa. **Buckeye Tree Lodge** (46000 Sierra Dr., Three Rivers 93271, tel. 209/561–5900). 12 rooms, all with view of river; close to park. **Lazy J Motel** (39625 Sierra Dr., Three Rivers 93271, tel. 209/561–4449). 12 small cabins, 6 kitchenettes; swimming pool, river access, recommended for families.

CAMPGROUNDS

Staying in a campground is by far the most economical way to stay in Sequoia/Kings national parks. Campgrounds are located near each of the major centers, and most have all the basic facilities; prices range from $5 to $15. Those planning to camp should note the various seasonal temperatures and be prepared for precipitation at any time of the year. The only campground offering reservations is Lodgepole in **Sequoia National Park** (tel. 800/365–2267). All other campgrounds are on a first-come, first-served basis, and they often fill by Friday afternoon in July and August. More information on campgrounds is available through the **Park Superintendent** (Sequoia and Kings National Parks, Three Rivers 93271, tel. 209/565–3134).

KINGS CANYON **Cedar Grove Area. Sentinel, Moraine,** and **Sheep Creek** have a total of 314 sites, with immediate access to the views and trails of Kings Canyon and the Kings River. *Showers, bathrooms, coin laundry, picnic tables, store, pay phone, short-order food service, service station. Closed mid-Oct.–mid-May.*

Grant Grove Area. Azalea (114 sites), **Sunset** (119 sites), and **Crystal Springs** (66 sites)— with a total of 299 sites—are all situated among the giant sequoias and close to restaurants and stores. These areas draw a lot of families. *Pay showers, bathrooms, store, phones, restaurant, service station, dump station in Azalea.*

SEQUOIA **Foothills Area. Potwisha, Buckeye Flat,** and **South Fork** are in the 2,100-to 3,600-foot elevation area, located within a half-hour's drive of the Giant Forest, and have a total of 85 sites. Buckeye Flat and South Fork are not recommended for RVs or trailers, and Potwisha has a sanitary disposal station. South Fork tends to draw an older crowd and remains fairly quiet, largely because of its isolated location. *Potwisha: bathrooms and phone. Buckeye Flat: bathrooms. South Fork: pit latrines. Buckeye Flat open mid-Apr.–mid-Oct.; South Fork open mid-May–Oct.*

Giant Forest/Lodgepole Area. Dorst and **Lodgepole** campgrounds are located 12 miles north of Giant Forest Village, at an elevation of 6,800 feet. Together they have 468 campsites. Lodgepole is located within a half mile of the visitor center and a 10-minute drive from the shops and restaurants in the Giant Forest Village. *Lodgepole: Limited facilities and no fees after heavy snow accumulates. Bathrooms, coin laundry, dump station, store, phone service station. Dorst: Bathrooms, picnic tables, phone. Open Memorial Day–Labor Day.*

Mineral King Area. Atwell Mill (21 sites) and **Cold Springs** (40 sites) are located about 20 miles up a steep and very curvy road from the Generals Highway. The road is not recommended for trailers or RVs, and trailers are not permitted in the campgrounds. These are the quietest, most remote campgrounds, and they offer easy access to a number of hiking and backpacking trails. Campground elevations are 6,650 feet to 7,500 feet. *Pit latrines, phones. At Silver City Resort (2 mi away) there are pay showers and restaurant (gas and ice not always available). Open Memorial Day–mid-Oct.*

DINING

Each of the major areas within the park has only one restaurant, serving breakfast, lunch, and dinner. These are simple, no-frills eateries where basic American fare is well prepared and prices are reasonable. All of the restaurants within the parks are managed by **Guest Services** (Giant Forest, Box A, Sequoia National Park 93262, tel. 209/565–3381). There are several restaurants on the way in or out of the park that are worth a visit. Price categories per person, excluding 6½% tax, service, and drinks, are Moderate, $15–$25, and Inexpensive, under $15. All restaurants within the parks accept MasterCard and Visa.

WITHIN THE PARK **Cedar Grove Cafe.** As in many fast-food restaurants, patrons here order their food at a counter and then carry it to a table themselves. The limited menu includes hamburgers, hot dogs, and sandwiches for lunch and dinner; eggs and toast for breakfast. *Open when snow melts–Labor Day. Inexpensive.*

Giant Forest Lodge Dining Room. This is the fanciest restaurant in the two parks, with table cloths, soft lighting, and a quiet atmosphere. The dinner menu features soups, salads, chicken, and fish. *Open when snow melts–mid-Oct. No lunch. Sun. brunch. Moderate.*

Grant Grove Restaurant. This spacious restaurant serves up American fare for breakfast, lunch, and dinner. Among the tasty specials is a delicious red snapper in lemon-mush-

room sauce. Chef's salad, fruit platters, and several other fish dishes are also offered. *Inexpensive.*

Lodgepole Delicatessen. For a quick lunch or dinner try this deli for hot and cold sandwiches, hamburgers, pizza, and other short-order items. *Open when snow melts–mid-Oct. Inexpensive.*

Stony Creek Restaurant. At this sit-down coffee shop you can have eggs and toast in the morning, sandwiches for lunch, and burgers for dinner. The menu is similar to that of the coffee shop in Grant Grove. *Open when snow melts–Labor Day. Inexpensive.*

Village Cafeteria in Giant Forest. Breakfast, lunch, and dinner are served in a cafeteria-style setting, with dishes such as fish, chicken, and vegetable stir-fry for the health-conscious. *Inexpensive.*

OUTSIDE THE PARK **Clingan's Junction Restaurant.** If you're anywhere near this place when you get hungry, make the drive. For breakfast you'll be treated to omelets or strawberry waffles with potatoes; at lunch try the turkey-breast sandwich with mushrooms. Dinner might start with homemade soup and fresh-baked breads. *35591 E. Kings Canyon Hwy. (Hwy. 180), Clingan's Junction, tel. 209/338–2559. AE, MC, V. Inexpensive.*

Noisy Water. Yet another casual establishment, the Noisy Water is named for the North Fork Kaweah River, which flows within view of the restaurant's large windows. *41775 Sierra Dr., Three Rivers, tel. 209/561–4517. AE, MC, V. Inexpensive–Moderate.*

Staff of Life. The sunny atmosphere in this local hangout allows the many indoor plants to flourish. Lunch, served from 11 AM to 4 PM, includes soups, salads, and sandwiches, ranging from roast beef to vegetarian. Try the yogurt smoothies for dessert. *41651 Sierra Dr., Three Rivers, tel. 209/561–4937. AE, MC, V. Inexpensive.*

White Horse Inn. Locals consider this the finest dining in town. Filled with antiques and bedecked with draperies and mirrors, the White Horse retains an English atmosphere. The house special is prime rib. Other choices are teriyaki chicken, the fresh fish, or duck à la Montmorency, which is half of a roasted duck in a cherry sauce. *42975 Sierra Dr., Three Rivers, tel. 209/561–4185. AE, D, MC, V. Closed Mon.–Tues. Moderate.*

OUTDOOR ACTIVITIES

CROSS-COUNTRY SKIING There are cross-country touring centers and marked trails at **Giant Forest** (tel. 209/565–3435) and **Grant Grove** (tel. 209/335–2314). Qualified instructors, lessons, and rentals (touring and backcountry skis and snowshoes) are available. The centers operate weekdays 9 AM–5 PM, weekends and holidays 8 AM–6 PM.

FISHING There is a limited amount of trout fishing available in the parks' creeks and rivers from late April through mid-November, primarily in the Kings and Kaweah rivers. A California fishing license is required for persons 16 and older, and anglers should check the state and park fishing regulations for special closures and restrictions. Licenses and fishing tackle are available in Lodgepole, Stony Creek, Grant Grove, and Cedar Grove.

HORSEBACK RIDING A number of private operators offer everything from one-hour trips to full-service, multiday pack trips into the backcountry. Popular one-day destinations are Mist Falls and Upper Bubb's Creek. Horseback rides are available through **Cedar Grove Pack Station** (tel. 209/565–3464), **Grant Grove Stables** (tel. 209/335–2374), **Mineral King Pack Station** (tel. 209/561–4142), or **Wolverton Pack Station** (tel. 209/565–3445).

SNOWSHOE WALKS Naturalist-guided snowshoe walks are offered on weekends and holidays, as conditions permit (usually mid-Dec.–mid-Mar.). It is recommended that you make reservations through the **visitor centers** (tel. 209/335–2315 in Grant Grove; 209/565–3341, ext. 631 in Giant Forest/Lodgepole).

WALKING AND HIKING The most popular trails within the parks are well marked and well maintained. Walkers should remember that at many times of the year, snow and ice can make for treacherous footing on the trails. In each of the areas, a variety of trail options allows walkers and hikers to pick the length of their walks. The Redwood Canyon trail offers miles of easy walking through the world's largest grove of redwoods; the Buena Vista Peak trail provides an overview of the high Sierra; the Congress Trail is a 2-mile stroll on a paved loop trail through the heart of the Sequoia Forest; the Hazelwood Nature trail is a 1-mile loop featuring trailside information about sequoias and man's impact on them; the Crescent Meadow trail has an excellent midsummer wildflower show; the Trail for All People is a paved trail that forms a ⅔-mile loop around Round Meadow. Information on longer, more strenuous trails is available at the parks' visitor centers.

ENTERTAINMENT

During the summer months, evening campfire programs are held at many of the parks' campgrounds. In winter, programs are held at the Lodgepole Visitor Center, the Beetle Rock Center, and the Grant Grove Visitor Center on Fridays and Saturdays. Additional programs are sometimes offered during holidays. A full schedule of evening programs is published in the *Sequoia Bark,* the free park newspaper handed to each visitor at the entrance gates. The program schedules are also posted on visitor-center bulletin boards.

Shenandoah Valley and Charlottesville
Virginia

Updated by Dale Leatherman

 lanting southwesterly through Virginia between the gentle Blue Ridge and the rugged Appalachian Mountains is the lush Shenandoah Valley. Once the route blazed by European settlers from the coastal colonies into Kentucky, it was long covered with wheat and cornfields, but now its green acres offer more diversity. Today, the valley is sought out by travelers for its picturesque Skyline Drive and Blue Ridge Parkway, its colorful old towns founded by Germans and Scotch-Irish, its early crafts, and its old inns and eating places.

East of the valley—over well-traveled Afton Mountain in the Blue Ridge chain—lies Thomas Jefferson's hometown of Charlottesville, site of the University of Virginia. That city and the valley fit neatly into Virginia's most popular tourist package: a triangular tour beginning in Washington, D.C., and continuing to Williamsburg, Richmond, Charlottesville, Lexington, and then back to D.C. through the valley and the northern Virginia horse country.

Three towns of unusual interest in upcountry Virginia are Lexington, where Lee and Jackson lie buried near educational institutions they served; Winchester, where Washington embarked in youth on his military career; and Staunton, Woodrow Wilson's birthplace. Other highlights are Natural Bridge; the hunt country around Warrenton and Middleburg, where foxhunts, races, and horse shows enliven weekends; and Abingdon, near the southwest tip of the state, with its famous Barter Theater and music festivals.

ESSENTIAL INFORMATION

WHEN TO GO June, July, and August are the best months to visit, because temperatures average in the upper 70s to mid-80s. October is also a favorite with many valley visitors, when turning leaves brighten the lowlands with red and yellow. May and June are blooming time for mountain laurel and rhododendron, which illumine upland hills with their pink-white blossoms. In addition, April is Garden Month in Virginia, and local garden tours are a highlight of this cool and often rainy month.

BARGAINS The biggest bargain in the region is the Blue Ridge Parkway, the Park Service's free scenic skyway through part of Virginia's mountains. The 469-mile parkway connects the Shenandoah National Park in Virginia with the Great Smoky Mountains National Park in North Carolina and Tennessee. Virginia's 216-mile section begins near Waynesboro at Rockfish Gap, at the southern end of the Skyline Drive. Also free is historic Goshen Pass, a picturesque upland river gorge near Lexington and Staunton. Free admittance to grounds and historic buildings is offered by Washington and Lee University, Virginia Military Institute, and the University of Virginia. Also free to visitors is the Cyrus McCormick Farm and Workshop at Steele's Tavern, where the McCormick reaper was invented. Numerous Charlottesville and Shenandoah Valley wineries offer free wine tasting; contact the local chambers of commerce and visitor information centers (*see* Tourist Offices, *below*) for advance information on local wineries.

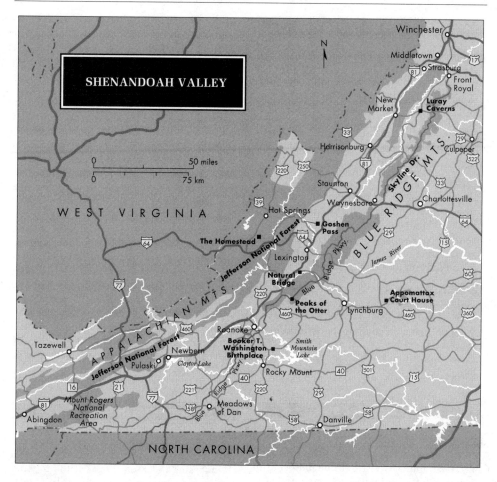

SHENANDOAH VALLEY

50 miles

75 km

WEST VIRGINIA

Winchester
Middletown
Strasburg
Front Royal
New Market
Luray Caverns
Harrisonburg
Culpeper
Staunton
Waynesboro
Charlottesville
Hot Springs
Goshen Pass
Lexington
BLUE RIDGE MTS.
Skyline Dr.
Blue Ridge Pkwy.
James River
Natural Bridge
Appomattox Court House
Peaks of the Otter
Lynchburg
The Homestead
Jefferson National Forest
APPALACHIAN MTS.
Roanoke
Tazewell
Newbern
Booker T. Washington Birthplace
Smith Mountain Lake
Pulaski
Claytor Lake
Rocky Mount
Jefferson National Forest
Mount Rogers National Recreation Area
Abingdon
Meadows of Dan
Danville
NORTH CAROLINA

TOURIST OFFICES **Augusta-Staunton-Waynesboro Travel Information Center** (Richmond Rd. [Rte. 250] at I–81, Exit 222, Staunton 24401, tel. 540/332–3972). **Charlottesville-Albemarle Convention and Visitors' Bureau** (Box 161, Charlottesville 22902, tel. 804/977–1783). **Lexington Visitor Center** (102 E. Washington St., Lexington 24450, tel. 540/463–3777). **Roanoke Valley Convention and Visitors' Bureau** (114 Market St., Box 1710, 24088, tel. 540/342–6025 or 800/635–5535). **Shenandoah Valley Tourist Information Center** (off I–81 at Exit 67, Box 1040, New Market 22844, tel. 540/740–3132). In addition, the Rockfish Gap Visitor Information Center,

located just off I–64 at the intersection of the Skyline Drive and Blue Ridge Parkway on Afton Mountain, is staffed by some very knowledgeable volunteers.

EMERGENCIES **Police, fire,** and **ambulance:** Dial 911. In Shenandoah National Park, dial 540/999–2227 or 800/732–0911; on Blue Ridge Parkway, 800/727–5928. **Hospitals:** In Charlottesville, emergency rooms are at Martha Jefferson Hospital (459 Locust Ave., tel. 804/982–7150) and the University of Virginia Hospital (Jefferson Park Ave., tel. 804/924–2231). Both are open 24 hours. In Lexington, phone 540/463–2112 for the police or rescue squad.

ARRIVING AND DEPARTING

BY PLANE Frequent service to northern Virginia by major airlines is available through Washington National and Dulles International airports, Roanoke Municipal Airport, and Charlottesville-Albemarle Airport.

BY BUS Greyhound Lines (tel. 800/231–2222) serves Abingdon, Charlottesville, Lexington, Roanoke, and Staunton.

BY CAR The valley is served by I–81 from the north, I–66 from Washington, D.C., I–64 from the eastern part of Virginia and from the west, and by I–77, which runs north–south through the southwest tip of the valley. Virginia offers a **weather and road-condition information line** (tel. 800/367–7623).

BY TRAIN Amtrak (tel. 800/872–7245) stops daily at Charlottesville on its New York–New Orleans run and also has service three days a week at Staunton and at Charlottesville en route between New York and Chicago. The same train stops at Clifton Forge for the Homestead.

GETTING AROUND

BY CAR The easiest way to visit the Shenandoah Valley and Charlottesville is by car. I–81 and U.S. 11 run through the entire valley, intertwined with each other and connecting with I–64 at Staunton and at Lexington. A car is needed in Charlottesville and, of course, to take the scenic Skyline Drive and connecting Blue Ridge Parkway.

REST STOPS There are rest rooms at Fairfield Information Center, on I–81 southbound in Rockbridge County, near Lexington; at Buchanan Information Center on I–81 southbound near Buchanan; at Harrisonburg Information Center on I–81 northbound near Harrisonburg; at the picnic area off I–81 at the Cyrus McCormick Birthplace Farm at Steele's Tavern; and at the Thomas Jefferson Visitors Center off I–64 at Route 20 South.

GUIDED TOURS Washington and Lee University at Lexington offers a free guided tour of Lee Chapel, where Lee is buried and portraits of founders are shown. The **Virginia Military Institute** (tel. 540/464–7326) at Lexington runs free guided tours daily from September till June; during the summer, tours are offered weekdays. The **Lexington Carriage Company** (tel. 540/463–3777 or 540/463–5647) will take you around town in a horse-drawn carriage for 50 minutes, April to October. A walking-tour brochure is available at the **Lexington Visitor Center** (tel. 540/463–3777). The **Historic Staunton Foundation** (tel. 540/885–7676) offers free one-hour guided tours of the town on Saturday mornings, Memorial Day through October, departing from the Woodrow Wilson Birthplace (24 N. Coalter St.). A brochure is available for a self-guided tour. The **University of Virginia at Charlottesville** (tel. 804/924–3239 or 804/924–7969) gives five free guided tours daily (at 10 and 11 AM and 2, 3, and 4 PM) of the Rotunda and Lawn. A map of the university—plus parking and general information—is available at the university of Virginia Visitor Information Center/Police Station (tel. 804/924–7969).

EXPLORING

It's helpful to think of Virginia's Shenandoah Valley as a carrot-shaped region with Winchester and Front Royal at the top and Abingdon close to its bottom. One side is delineated by the mountaintop Skyline Drive and Blue Ridge Parkway, which run in splendor along the heights from Front Royal southwesterly into North Carolina. Paralleling the mountains is I–81, which follows the valley bottom from the Maryland border into Tennessee, tracing the route blazed long ago by European settlers. In the 18th century, it was called the Great Wagon Road, while a western branch from Roanoke was the Wilderness Road, made famous by Daniel Boone.

Present-day visitors may combine both the Skyline Drive–Blue Ridge Parkway and I–81 in their circuit of the valley, enjoying both nature and history. The parkways, designed for taking in the scenery at a leisurely pace, have two lanes and 35 mph (Skyline Drive) and 45 mph (Blue Ridge Parkway) speed limits that are strictly enforced. On weekends in good weather, traffic can be abominable, so be warned. We cover the valley's highlights from north to south.

About 10 miles south of the south West Virginia line on I-81 is **Winchester,** gateway city to the Shenandoah Valley, center of apple production. Founded in 1732 and still full of Colonial buildings, the city has always been an important intersection. Washington worked as a surveyor here (his office is now a museum), and during the Civil War, the town changed hands 72 times.

Shenandoah National Park is the upland mountain empire surrounding the 105-mile **Skyline Drive.** It offers hundreds of miles of hiking trails, including part of the Appalachian Trail, plus campgrounds and trout fishing in white-water streams. Pick up *Shenandoah Overlook,* a free newspaper, when you enter the park. (For information, call 540/999–3483, 540/999–2266, or 800/828–1140.)

Luray Caverns are the largest of the valley's spectacular lighted caves. Underground rock formations are illumined to eerie effect. A "Stalacpipe Organ" made of stalactites is played from a keyboard. A one-hour tour starts every 20 minutes. *West of Rte. 211 from Skyline Dr. at Luray, tel. 540/743–6551. Open daily; hrs vary by season. Admission charged.*

New Market, on I-81 not far from the parkway, is the site of a Civil War battle in which teenage Virginia Military Institute cadets fought Union soldiers. It is today the New Market Battlefield Historical Park and the Hall of Valor Civil War Museum. *I-81 at New Market, tel. 540/740–3101. Open daily. Admission charged.*

Staunton, pronounced "Stanton," is the seat of once-huge Augusta County, which originally included all of West Virginia, Kentucky, Ohio, and Indiana. Here, in the now-restored Woodrow Wilson House, the 28th president was born in 1856. *18–24 N. Coalter St., tel. 540/885–0897. Open daily. Admission charged.*

Just outside town is the **Museum of American Frontier Culture,** with re-created working farms from Northern Ireland, England, Germany, and upland Virginia. *1250 Richmond Rd. off I-81 at Exit 222, tel. 540/332–7850. Open daily. Admission charged.*

Charlottesville lies just outside the Shenandoah Valley in rolling and beautiful Albemarle County. Here, at **Monticello,** Jefferson's mountaintop home and avocation, one can get a clear picture of the third president. Stop at the Thomas Jefferson Visitors Center just off I-64 at Route 20S for a free movie, permanent exhibition, bathroom facilities, gift shops, information and tickets for Monticello, Ash Lawn-Highland, and Michie Tavern. *Rte. 53 (off Rte. 20), 2 mi southeast of Charlottesville, tel. 804/984–9822. Open daily. Admission charged.*

Jefferson's idyllic **University of Virginia** can be seen on free tours, starting at the Rotunda (tel. 804/924–1019). Nearby is **Ash Lawn,** onetime farm of James Monroe, which survives as a plantation house and arts center. *Rte. 795 (off Rte. 53), 2 mi past Monticello, tel. 804/293–9539. Open daily. Admission charged.*

Blue Ridge Parkway, free to all users, is a mountaintop scenic drive (and a national park) that diverges from Skyline Drive. From the majestic mountaintop of Afton, it curves gracefully for 469 miles southwest into North Carolina and Tennessee. Its 5,000-acre **Peaks of Otter Area** (tel. 540/586–4357) near Roanoke has a campground, visitor center, self-guided trail, summer interpretive programs, camp store, and a nice lakeside lodge, plus a section of the Appalachian Trail. *For parkway information, call 704/298–0398 or 704/271–4779.*

Goshen Pass is a picturesque 3-mile scenic drive that follows the white-water Maury River through the Allegheny Mountains. The Pass lies along Route 39, which branches westward from I–81 and I–64 just north of Lexington. The route leads into Bath County, a mountainous recreational oasis and spa area where you'll find Warm Springs, Bolar Springs, and Hot Springs, site of the 15,000-acre **Homestead** (tel. 800/838–1766), the country's oldest resort, known for its old-fashioned luxury and its golf courses, bridle paths, and hiking trails.

Lexington is a must for travelers with an interest in history. A center of early Scotch-Irish settlement in the valley, it is the home of **Washington and Lee University.** Endowed by George Washington and presided over by Robert E. Lee, W & L is the sixth-oldest college in the nation. Visit its ancient colonnaded campus and its Lee Chapel and Museum. *Tel. 540/463–8400. Open daily. Admission free.*

Next door is **Virginia Military Institute,** founded in 1839. The **VMI Museum** contains much about Stonewall Jackson, who taught there. *Tel. 540/464–7232. Open daily. Admission free.*

On the VMI grounds is the **George C. Marshall Museum,** honoring the Nobel Prize–winning alumnus who was U.S. chief of staff in World War II and designer of the Marshall Plan for European economic recovery after the war. *Tel. 540/463–7103. Open daily. Admission free.*

The **Stonewall Jackson House,** near the two schools, is preserved much as he left it to serve the Confederate army in 1861. *8 E. Washington St., tel. 540/463–2552. Open daily. Admission charged.*

Natural Bridge, 15 miles south of Lexington on I–81, is a world-famous arch 215 feet high and 90 feet long, carved out of Rockbridge County limestone by Cedar Creek below and once owned by Thomas Jefferson. *I–81 to Exit 49 or 50, tel. 540/291–2121. Open daily. Admission charged.*

Roanoke is a modern railroad center 54 miles south of Lexington. It is also a center of educational institutions and of three museums and an art gallery, the **Arts Museum of Western Virginia** (tel. 540/342–5760; admission free), which chiefly shows works of regional artists. The **Science Museum of Western Virginia** (tel. 540/342–5710; admission charged) displays natural history and includes a planetarium and children's exhibits. The **Roanoke Valley Historical Society** (tel. 540/342–5770; admission free) displays relics of Virginia Indians, from whose name for wampum the word "Roanoke" comes.

The **Virginia Museum of Transportation** in Roanoke is devoted to trains. *303 Norfolk Ave., tel. 540/342–5670. Open daily. Admission charged.*

Rocky Mount, 20 miles southeast of Roanoke, is Booker T. Washington's birthplace, now a national monument. Born in slavery, the brilliant educator and writer became an early leader of blacks and slaves, consultant to presidents, and founder of Tuskegee Institute in Alabama. *Rte. 116S to Burnt Chimney, then 6 mi east on Rte. 122N, tel. 540/721–2094. Open daily. Admission charged.*

Abingdon, near the North Carolina border, is a cultural crossroads in the wilderness, with the famous Barter Theater (*see* Entertainment, *below*), the Virginia Highlands Festival (when 150,000 people come for the music, crafts exhibits, and antiques displays), and the Burley Tobacco Festival, whose stars are country-music performers and farm animals.

THE NATURAL WORLD The forested empires of federal park lands in the valley provide cover for many animals, birds, and plants. These holdings include not only Shenandoah National Park and Blue Ridge Parkway but also George Washington National Forest and Jefferson National Forest. Though the eastern buffalo no longer survives in these uplands, black bear and wildcats are common in the woods, and bald eagles not unknown. Even more visible are white-tailed deer, woodchucks, squirrels, foxes, rabbits, hawks, doves, owls, and songbirds. The region is noted for its concentration of geological phenomena, including Natural Bridge, the cascading riverbed of Goshen Pass, the many natural caverns, and mountain ranges varying in age from the ancient Blue Ridge to the more recent and rugged Appalachians. A brochure is available on all the **Virginia State Parks** (tel. 800/786–1712).

HOTELS AND INNS

The scale of hotels in the Shenandoah Valley is small, like the valley towns themselves, except Roanoke. Motel chains offering standard amenities have one- or two-story structures close to exits in the towns along I–81, and a few old family-owned hotels and many bed-and-breakfasts survive, especially in college towns like Charlottesville, Staunton, and Lexington. For information and bed-and-breakfast reservations, contact **Guesthouses, Bed & Breakfast, Inc.** (Box 5737, Charlottesville, VA 22905, tel. 804/979–7264), a reservation service for the Charlottesville area. **Virginia Bed and Breakfast Inns** (Box 791, Orange, VA 22960, tel. 540/672–0870) or **Blue Ridge Bed & Breakfast Reservation Service** (Rock & Rills, Rte. 2, Box 3895, Berryville, VA 22611, tel. 540/955–1246) provides the same service up and down the Shenandoah Valley.

Price categories for double occupancy, excluding 4½% sales tax, are Expensive, over $95; Moderate, $60–$95; and Inexpensive, under $60.

ABINGDON **Alpine Motel.** At this small, upland motel with pleasant, simple decor, you get a good view of Mount Rogers, Virginia's highest peak. The Barter Theater is nearby. *882 E. Main St., 24210, tel. 540/628–3178. 19 rooms. AE, D, MC, V. Moderate.*

Martha Washington Inn. Built in 1832 by General Francis Preston, this exclusive inn across from the Barter Theater is an elegant testimony to Virginia's aristocratic past. The inn underwent an $8 million renovation in 1985. Rooms are furnished with antiques and some have fireplaces, hot tubs, and steam showers. *150 W. Main St., 24210, tel. 540/628–3161 or 800/533–1014, fax 540/628–8885. 61 rooms and 15 suites. AE, D, DC, MC, V. Expensive.*

CHARLOTTESVILLE **Boar's Head Inn.** Located 2 miles outside town on Route 250 West, this quiet resort features both rooms and suites with simple but elegant furnishings, mostly antiques. Efficiencies, suites, and rooms with king- and queen-size beds are available. Hot-air-balloon rides and foot hunts are two of the inn's unique offerings. *Rte. 250 W, Box 5307, 22905, tel. 804/296–2181 or 800/476–1988, fax 804/972–6024. 173 rooms and 11 suites. AE, D, DC, MC, V. Expensive.*

English Inn. This convenient motel has a three-story atrium lobby with cascading plants and a bed-and-breakfast friendliness. *2000 Morton Dr. (junction of U.S. 29 and Rte. 250 bypass), 22901, tel. 804/971–9900 or 800/786–5400, fax 804/977–8008. 88 rooms and suites. Restaurant, indoor pool, sauna, exercise equipment. AE, D, DC, MC, V. Moderate.*

Omni Charlottesville. This hotel is located on the Downtown Mall, at the center of town and near a variety of shops and restaurants. The decor is a mixture of Colonial and modern, but don't expect too much Old World charm from this chain offering. *235 W. Main St., 22901, tel. 804/971–5500 or 800/843–6664, fax 804/979–4456. 208 rooms and 3 suites. AE, DC, MC, V. Expensive.*

Osceola Mill Country Inn. At the Mill you'll find warm, friendly, unpretentious accommodations just off the Blue Ridge Parkway, about 15 miles outside Charlottesville at milepost 27 on Virginia Route 56. This country inn was once part of the McCormick Farm, where the McCormick reaper was invented, and the Victorian Farmhouse, Mill, and the Old Mill Store (a private honeymoon cottage) still offer a unique, pleasantly rural lodging experience. *Rte. 56, Steele's Tavern 24476, tel. and fax 540/377–6455, tel. 800/242–7352. 12 rooms, 1 cottage. Continental breakfast included. MC, V. Expensive.*

HOT SPRINGS **The Homestead.** Founded in 1891 at the source of natural mineral springs, the Homestead is the oldest and certainly one of the most luxurious resorts in the United States. All rooms are decorated elegantly with fine antiques and country memorabilia. As for facilities, the Homestead cannot be beat. *U.S. 220, Hot Springs*

24445, tel. 540/839–1766 or 800/838–1766, fax 540/839–7670. 521 rooms, including 75 suites. 7 restaurants, tennis courts, 9 ski slopes, 3 18-hole golf courses, indoor-outdoor pools, spa, riding trails, fishing. AE, MC, V. Expensive.

Roseloe Motel. This family-run hostelry has excellent views of Warm Springs Valley and is located near the Warm Springs pools. Rte. 2, Box 590, 24445, tel. 540/839–5373. 14 rooms, some with kitchenette. AE, DC, MC, V. Inexpensive.

LEXINGTON **Days Inn–Keydet–General Motel.** This one-story brick establishment, perched on a suburban hill, is a favorite with alumni of Lexington's famed schools. Rte. 60W outside town, 24450, tel. 540/463–2143 or 800/325–2525, fax 540/463–2143. 53 rooms. Restaurant, wet bars, refrigerators in some rooms. Pets permitted. AE, D, DC, MC, V. Moderate.

MEADOWS OF DAN **Rocky Knob Cabins.** These refreshingly simple rustic cabins just off Blue Ridge Parkway have kitchens but no private baths. Milepost 174, Rte. 1, Box 5, 24120, tel. 540/593–3503. 7 cabins. AE, MC, V. Open Memorial Day–Labor Day. Inexpensive.

MIDDLETOWN **Wayside Inn.** Once called Wilkerson's Tavern on the Black Bear Trail, it has a string of first-floor taprooms and dining rooms and is furnished with antiques and Victoriana. 7783 Main St. (junction of I–81 and U.S. 11), 22645, tel. 540/869–1797, fax 540/869–6038. 24 rooms and suites. Restaurant. AE, D, DC, MC, V. Moderate.

NATURAL BRIDGE **Natural Bridge Resort and Conference Center.** Close to the bridge, this resort hostelry with old-fashioned decor and food offers good views of the Blue Ridge from porches and rocking chairs. Exits 175 and 180 off I–81, Box 57, 24578, tel. 540/ 291–2121 or 800/533–1410, fax 540/291– 1896. 180 rooms. Restaurant, lounge, deli-snack bar, pool, tennis courts, walking trails, indoor miniature golf course. AE, D, DC, MC, V. Moderate.

PEAKS OF OTTER **Peaks of Otter Lodge.** This rustic, modern hotel is known for its cuisine and moderate prices. The elevated site offers a rare view of the Blue Ridge, Abbott Lake, and the valley. Milepost 86, Blue Ridge Pkwy., north of Roanoke (Box 489, Bedford 24533), tel. 540/586–1081 or 800/542–5927 in VA, fax 540/586–4420. 62 rooms. Restaurant, coffee shop, bar. MC, V. Moderate.

ROANOKE **Radisson Patrick Henry Hotel.** Renovated in 1991, this 1925 landmark is centrally located in Roanoke's downtown district and within walking distance of many sights. Oriental rugs, white-marble floors, and antique furniture create quite a presence in this beautiful old building. All of the guest rooms are large and include sitting areas as well as kitchenettes. 617 S. Jefferson St., 24011, tel. 540/345–8811, fax 540/342–9908. 100 rooms with kitchenettes. AE, MC, V. Expensive.

STAUNTON **Belle Grae Inn.** Built in 1870, this restored Victorian mansion offers 14 uniquely decorated rooms with rocking chairs and canopied or brass beds. Complimentary breakfast and afternoon teas are served. 515 W. Frederick St., 24401, tel. 540/ 886–5151, fax 540/886–6641. 14 rooms. No children under 14. AE, DC, MC, V. Moderate.

Frederick House. Five restored houses dating from 1810 form this inn in the historic downtown. All rooms are furnished with antiques, and a pub and restaurant are adjoining. Smoking is not allowed. 28 N. New St., 24401, tel. 540/885–4220 or 800/ 334–5575. 14 rooms. Full breakfast included. AE, D, DC, MC, V. Moderate.

MOTELS

MODERATE **Boxwood Bed and Breakfast** (Rte. 847, Harrisonburg 22801, tel. 540/867– 5772). 4 rooms; no smoking. **Budget Host Inn** (Rte. 2, Box 78, Woodstock 22664, tel. 540/459–4086). 43 rooms; restaurant, pool, pets allowed. **Comfort Inn–Stephens City** (I–81 at Exit 78, Stephens City 22655, tel. 540/869–6500 or 800/228–5150). 59 rooms;

Continental breakfast included, whirlpool baths. **Hampton Inn–Harrisonburg** (Rte. 33E on University Blvd., 22801, tel. 540/432–1111 or 800/426–7866). 126 rooms; Continental breakfast included. **Hampton Inn–Winchester** (west of town on U.S. 50 at 1655 Apple Blossom Dr., Winchester 22601, tel. 540/667–8011 or 800/426–7866). 103 rooms; Continental breakfast included, pool, elevators. **Holiday Inn Golf and Conference Center** (I–81 at Exit 58, Woodrow Wilson Pkwy., Staunton 24401, tel. 540/248–6020 or 800/932–9061). 112 rooms; restaurant, golf and tennis privileges at country club. **Holiday Inn–Staunton** (I–81 at Exit 58, Staunton 24401, tel. 540/248–6020 or 800/465–4329). 100 rooms; restaurant and lounge. **Hotel Strasburg** (I–81 at Exit 74, 201 Holliday St., Strasburg 22657, tel. 540/465–9191 or 800/348–8327). 21 rooms; whirlpool baths.

INEXPENSIVE **Battlefield Motel** (I–81 at Exit 67, New Market 22844, tel. 540/740–3105 or 800/296–6835). 14 rooms; free coffee, basketball court. **Blue Ridge Motor Lodge** (I–81 at Exit 67, New Market 22844, tel. 540/740–8088 or 800/545–8776). 18 rooms; free coffee, playground, basketball. **Bond's Motel** (I–81 at Exit 79, Winchester 22601, tel. 540/667–8881). 16 rooms; free coffee. **Cardinal Motel** (U.S. 211, Luray 22835, tel. 540/743–5010). 12 rooms. **Center City Motel** (I–81 at Exit 2, Front Royal 22630, tel. 540/635–4050). 18 rooms. **Echo Village Motel** (I–81 at Exit 79, Winchester 22601, tel. 540/869–1900). 66 rooms. **New Market Battlefield Days Inn** (I–81 at Exit 67, New Market 22844, tel. 540/740–4100 or 800/325–2525). 86 rooms. **Shenandoah Motel** (I–81 at Exit 76, Front Royal 22630, tel. 540/635–3181). 32 rooms. **Travelodge of Winchester** (I–81 at Exit 80, Winchester 22601, tel. 540/665–1685 or 800/255–3050). 149 rooms; free coffee, doughnuts.

CAMPGROUNDS

The two national parks and two national forests in the valley offer many opportunities for camping, as does Mount Rogers National Recreation Area in the southwest tip of the state. Fees at these public campgrounds range from free to $15.

Shenandoah National Park (tel. 540/999–2266) has three campgrounds with showers, flush toilets, and coin laundries, but no hookups at Big Meadows (MP 51 on the Skyline Drive; reservations), and at Lewis Mountain (MP 57.5) and Loft Mountain (MP 79.5), both first-come, first-served. **Blue Ridge Parkway** (tel. 540/857–2213) has four campgrounds in Virginia (Otter Creek, MP 60.9; Peaks of Otter, MP 86; Roanoke Mountain, MP 120.4; and Rocky Knob, MP 169), all first-come, first-served primitive sites with flush toilets and dumping stations but no showers or hookups. **George Washington National Forest** (tel. 540/564–8300) has 21 campgrounds, five of which take reservations. Facilities range from primitive sites with pit latrines to some that have showers and bathrooms, to a few with electrical hookups. **Jefferson National Forest** (tel. 540/265–6054) has 16 campgrounds in its six districts, some primitive, some with bathrooms and showers, but no hookups. **Mount Rogers National Recreational Area** (part of the Jefferson National Forest, tel. 540/783–5196) has six campgrounds, all with flush toilets, some with showers, none with hookups.

Many privately owned campgrounds are also scattered throughout the region; information is available from the **Virginia Division of Tourism** (tel. 202/659–5523). Try **Yogi Bear's Jellystone Park Camp–Resort** (Rte. 1, Box 275, Charlottesville 29943, tel. 540/456–6409 or 800/558–2954), located off Route 250 between Charlottesville and Waynesboro at the base of Afton Mountain. Fees for one of its 120 wooded and creek-side campsites, including hookups, are $18–$25.

DINING

The ethnic roots of upland Virginia go back not only to England but also to Scotland and Germany, and the fare is apt to have a hearty Germanic flavor. Fresh, homemade rolls and

German pancakes are popular, along with sauerkraut, sauerbraten, cottage cheese, and pastries made from local apples, peaches, and berries. Another favorite is shoofly pie, which got its name from its resemblance to cauliflower, or *choufleur,* the French word used in Alsace. The valley is also known for its locally cured hams and bacon. Virginia is one of the half-dozen leading wine producers of the nation. Wineries abound, especially in Albemarle County, around Charlottesville. Dinner price categories per person, excluding 4½% tax (plus any local tax), service, and drinks, are Expensive, over $25; Moderate, $15–$25; and Inexpensive, under $15.

ABINGDON **The Tavern.** Built in 1779, this cozy restaurant was a hospital in the Civil War. The menu includes rainbow trout from nearby waters. *222 E. Main St., tel. 540/628–1118. MC, V. Moderate–Expensive.*

CHARLOTTESVILLE **Blue Ridge Brewery.** This casual restaurant smells like a brewery because it is one. Its home brews are named for various mountain peaks, and provide a fine accompaniment for dishes such as bourbon steak, smoked trout wontons, and Thai pork chops. *709 W. Main St., tel. 804/977–0017. A, MC, V. Moderate.*

C & O Restaurant. Don't let the boarded-up storefront with the old Pepsi sign fool you. Downstairs is a lively bistro, upstairs a more formal dining room (jacket and tie required). C & O features excellent regional French cuisine and has a wine list with over 300 varieties. *515 E. Water St., tel. 804/971–7044. Reservations advised. MC, V. Expensive.*

Martha's Cafe. Try the crab cakes, enchiladas, or vegetarian entrées at this local favorite near the University of Virginia. The shaded outdoor café is open from midspring to late fall, and two dining rooms are open all year. *11 Elliewood Ave., tel. 804/971–7530. V. Inexpensive.*

Southern Culture. There's a true mix of styles and influences at Southern Culture—everything from Tex-Mex to Cajun, Creole, and just plain southern. Try such delicacies as Cajun baby cakes—shrimp and scallops blended with spicy jalapeño peppers—before moving on to a substantial plate of Louisiana short stacks. The atmosphere here is reminiscent of the Florida Keys in the late '40s. *633 W. Main St., tel. 804/979–1990. MC, V. Moderate.*

LEXINGTON **Willson Walker House.** American cuisine is served in a handsome old house of the Jefferson period that's a favorite site for entertaining out-of-towners. *30 N. Maine St., tel. 540/463–3020. AE, MC, V. Closed Sun.–Mon. Moderate.*

MIDDLETOWN **Wayside Inn Dining Room.** This 18th-century inn in a village near Winchester is a survivor from George Washington's day, furnished in antiques. It serves such favorites as spoon bread, smothered chicken, and peanut soup. *7783 Main St., tel. 540/869–1797. AE, D, DC, MC, V. Moderate.*

PEAKS OF OTTER **Peaks of Otter Lodge.** This elevated inn near Roanoke and the Blue Ridge Parkway is celebrated for its Friday night seafood buffet and Sunday country buffet. *MP 86, Blue Ridge Pkwy. north of Roanoke, Bedford, tel. 540/586–1081 or 800/542–5927 in VA. AE, D, DC, MC, V. Moderate.*

ROANOKE **The Library.** This Continental restaurant with quiet, refined decor is known for its superbly prepared seafood dishes. If you're looking for a formal eatery in Roanoke—jackets are required for men— you've just found it. *3117 Franklin Rd. SW (Piccadilly Sq. shopping center), tel. 540/985–0811. AE, DC, MC, V. Closed Sun. No lunch. Expensive.*

STAUNTON **Italia at 23 Beverly.** Formerly a men's clothing store and hot dog haven, this unique restaurant in Staunton's historic district is decorated with the work of local artists and features modern American cuisine—mostly pastas and grilled meats. The wine cellar is stocked with over 120 Virginia varieties. *23 Beverly St., tel. 540/885–0102. AE, D, MC, V. Moderate.*

Rowe's Family Restaurant. This is a country place that has been in the same family since 1947. Its entrées include chicken and Virginia ham; the breads are home-baked. *I-81* *at Exit 57, tel. 540/886–1833. D, MC, V. Inexpensive.*

WARM SPRINGS **Waterwheel Restaurant.** This former gristmill dates from 1700 and contains a fine French and regional restaurant with a refreshing mix of haute cuisine and old favorites. *Grist Mill Sq., tel. 540/ 839–2231. MC, V. Closed Sun.–Mon. No lunch. Moderate–Expensive.*

SHOPPING

There are numerous discount outlets throughout the valley. The **Waynesboro Village Factory Outlet** (tel. 540/949–5000) at Waynesboro includes Liz Claiborne, London Fog, and Royal Doulton porcelain among its 40 exhibitors. The **Aileen Factory Outlet** (tel. 540/459–3711) at Woodstock handles first-grade women's wear. For crafts and collectibles, try the amusing Tuttle and Spice General Store near New Market. The **P. Buckley Moss Museum** (tel. 540/949–6473), at Waynesboro, sells prints by the popular local artist. At Front Royal, the **Maple Leaf** (tel. 540/636–9984) offers antiques, quilts, collectibles, folk art, and crafts. The **Strasburg Emporium** (tel. 540/465–3711), a center for 55 dealers who sell under one roof, calls itself Virginia's largest antiques center; it's in Strasburg, near Front Royal. More sophisticated antiques are found in shops in Winchester, Charlottesville, and Roanoke.

OUTDOOR ACTIVITIES

BIKING All parks and forests in the valley permit biking, with some restrictions as to use on walking trails, and separate biking trails are not usually designated. Steep grades and rough surfaces make mountain bikes desirable.

BOATING AND CANOEING One of the few water resorts in the valley is Smith's Mountain Lake, 45 miles southeast of Roanoke, where guests enjoy boating, sailing, fishing, and land sports. **Bernard's Landing** (Monita, VA 24121, tel. 540/721–8870 or 800/572–2048)

also rents housekeeping cottages, town houses, and condos. The **Smith Mountain Lake State Park** (on the north shore, tel. 540/ 297–6066) has a beach, boat rentals, and the like. Other recreational waterways are **Claytor Lake** (tel. 540/674–5492), a state park south of Radford, and crystal-clear Lake Moomaw in George Washington National Forest, near Covington. **Douthat State Park** (tel. 540/862–7200) in nearby Clifton Forge has a 50-acre lake for swimming, trout fishing, and boating, plus hiking trails and campsites.

You can rent a canoe to negotiate the valley's cascading streams at **Front Royal Canoe** (Rte. 340 near Front Royal, tel. 540/635–5440), **Downriver Canoe Company** (Rte. 613 near Front Royal, tel. 540/635–5526), **Shenandoah River Outfitters** (Rte. 684 near Luray, tel. 540/743–4159), **James River Basin Canoe Livery** (Rte. 4, Box 125, Lexington 24450, tel. 540/261–7334), and **James River Runners** (Rte. 4, Box 106, Scottsville 24590, tel. 804/ 286–2338).

FISHING Several freshwater species are caught in the 500-mile trout streams in Jefferson National Forest and in 50 other streams. Be sure to obtain a five-day Virginia fishing license, available April through mid-October at concession stands along Skyline Drive and at sportsmen's shops.

GOLF Among golf courses open to the public are the 27-hole **Shenandoah Valley Golf Club** (tel. 540/636–4653) and the 36-hole **Bowling Green Golf Club** (tel. 540/635–2024) on U.S. 522 in Front Royal; the **Homestead** (tel. 540/839–1766 or 800/838–1766) in Hot Springs, with three 18-hole courses; **Caverns Country Club Resort** (Rte. 211 in Luray, tel. 540/743–7111), whose course is along a river; and **Greene Hills Golf Club** (Rte. 33 in Stanardsville, tel. 804/985–7328). **Wintergreen** (tel. 804/325–2200 or 800/325–2200) in Nellysford has two courses, one in the mountains and one in the valley.

HIKING The famous Appalachian Trail runs through part of this area, and more than 500 miles of trails exist in Shenandoah National Park alone. They are shown in a guidebook available at the visitor centers at mileposts 4.6 and 51 on the Skyline Drive. There are others on the Blue Ridge Parkway, in Woods Creek Park, and Chessie Nature Trail (the latter two in and near Lexington). For a list, write the **Virginia Department of Conservation and Recreation** (203 Governor St., Richmond 23219).

HORSEBACK RIDING On the Skyline Drive, guided trail rides leave Shenandoah National Park's **Skyland Lodge** (tel. 540/999–2210) several times daily for one- to 2½-hour outings. **Virginia Mountain Outfitters** (tel. 540/261–1910) in Buena Vista offers a variety of half-day and multiday rides in the Blue Ridge and Allegheny Mountains. Horse shows and other competitions are held year-round at the **Virginia Horse Center** (tel. 540/463–2194), Lexington. The **Homestead** (tel. 540/839–1766 or 800/838–1766) in Hot Springs also has extensive riding trails.

SKIING Winter sports are popular at such upland Virginia sites as **Wintergreen** (tel. 800/325–2200) in Nelson County, the **Homestead** (tel. 540/839–1766 or 800/838–1766) in Hot Springs, **Bryce Mountain Resort** (tel. 540/856–2121) in Bayse, and **Massanutten Mountain Resort** (tel. 540/289–9441), off Route 33 in McGaheysville. All offer ski weekend packages.

TENNIS The **Homestead** (tel. 540/839–1766 or 800/838–1766) in Hot Springs has 19 courts, including one all-weather; **Wintergreen** (tel. 804/325–2200 or 800/325–2200) in Nellysford has 25 outdoor courts. Four courts are available to the public at **Caverns Country Club Resort** (Rte. 211, in Luray, tel. 540/743–7111). Many other hostelries have courts, as do most major towns, especially those with colleges or universities.

ENTERTAINMENT

CONCERTS Frequent musical events are offered by such sponsors as **Shenandoah College and Conservatory** (tel. 540/678–1299) at Winchester, **Ash Lawn-Highland Professional Opera Company** (tel. 804/293–4500) in Charlottesville, **Shenandoah Valley Music Festival** (tel. 540/459–3396) near Harrisonburg, and the **Garth Newell musicians** (tel. 540/839–5018) at Warm Springs. A partial listing is available from the **Virginia Division of Tourism** (202 N. 9th St., Richmond 23219, tel. 804/768–4484 or 800/847–4882).

THEATER The **Barter Theater** (tel. 540/628–3991 or 800/368–3240), one of America's leading professional companies, produces frequent plays at its theater in Abingdon. Nearby in Lexington, the popular **LimeKiln Theater** (tel. 540/463–3074) revives memories of valley history with its *Stonewall Country* and other dramas. At Roanoke, **Mill Mountain Theater** (tel. 540/342–5740) performs throughout the year. For a listing, contact the **Virginia Division of Tourism** (202 N. 9th St., Richmond 23219, tel. 804/786–4484 or 800/847–4882).

The Texas Gulf Coast

Texas

Updated by Mark Potok

T he Texas Gulf Coast has almost a thousand miles of sawtooth shoreline made up of barrier islands, river deltas, and bays. Some of its towns and villages have been developed as tourist resorts, primarily at the northern and southern ends of Padre Island. But by far the largest part of the coast is preserved as wetlands by state and federal edict, with large estuary tracts set aside for reptiles, mammals, and migratory birds.

The Gulf of Mexico is the common link among the coast's cities and towns, yet visitors who look beyond the obvious find many differences as they explore the Texas coast. There's Galveston, a sand barrier island that was once the home of Karankawa Indians and later grew into a prosperous shipping port (at one time it was the second-wealthiest city in the United States); the laid-back fishing village of Port Aransas; the artists' colony of Rockport; and at the state's far southern tip, South Padre Island, the sea-and-sand mecca for thousands of spring breakers, and the neighboring Rio Grande Valley, winter home to thousands of Canadians and Midwesterners.

Resort-hoppers should know that Galveston, Corpus Christi, and South Padre Island have all become more cosmopolitan in recent years and are blooming with high-rise condos. Even so, none has quite outgrown the feeling of being a simple beach town, kind to budgets. Everywhere along the coast there are funky oyster bars, docks where you can see the "mosquito" fleet (so called because shrimp boats with their nets up look like giant mosquitoes), deep-sea fishing boats for charter, and inexpensive lodging.

Texans are famous for driving fast and talking slow. Here on the coast, far from the madding crowds of Dallas and Houston, life is leisurely and very casual. Folks strictly adhere to the motto "living on island time." So, meander gently here and leave schedules and deadlines at home.

ESSENTIAL INFORMATION

WHEN TO GO The humidity is so high all along the Texas coast that winters can be occasionally chilly (in Galveston temperatures sometimes hover in the 40s, though mid-50s is usually the average daily temperature), while the summers are muggy, usually in the high 80s. The temperate seasons, fall and spring, with average Galveston temperatures around 80° and 69°, respectively, are the most reliable, although many winter Texans contend that winter down in the Rio Grande Valley, with its average of 63°, is just about perfect. Travelers should keep in mind that Brownsville's summer heat can be unbearable, but the town is pleasant to visit in the winter. Hurricane season runs from June through September; storms are tracked well in advance of their landfall, giving coastal residents plenty of time to clear out. Bird-watching is usually best from early November through mid-March during the winter migration, but weather conditions may vary. Deep-sea fishing is excellent year-round.

BARGAINS In Galveston, take a free ride on the **Bolivar Ferry** (tel. 409/763-2386); the

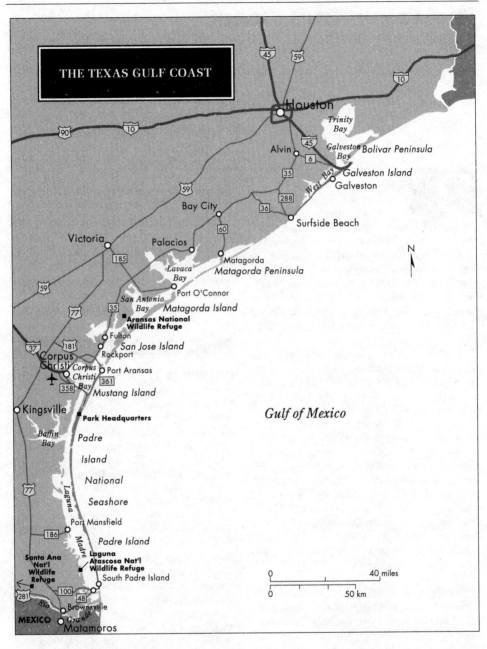

THE TEXAS GULF COAST

ride is a great way to see dolphins during the day or view a full moon at night. To catch the ferry, take the Seawall east to Ferry Road until it ends. For offbeat shopping bargains in Galveston, try **Colonel Bubbie's** (2202 Strand, tel. 409/762–7397), a surplus store of military gear (no guns or ammunition) from around the world. **Hendley Market** (2010 Strand, tel. 409/762–2610) offers offbeat gift items, including antique postcards and maps, old linens and lace, and folk-art treasures. The Old Peanut Butter Warehouse is chock-full of antique furniture, depression glass, vintage jewelry, and a pantry offering homemade peanut butter.

You shouldn't leave south Texas without driving across the Mexican border for a day of shopping. Brownsville's sister city is Mexico's Matamoros, and you can cross the border easily via the bridge in downtown Brownsville. However, it is advisable to take a cab across the border rather than walking or driving your own vehicle. Also use common sense and don't venture away from the crowd or into deserted areas alone. As long as you stay within 25 miles of the border, you don't need a passport, visa, or other papers. The shopping markets and curio shops are popular for their Mexican embroidered clothing, jewelry, handicrafts, footwear, furniture, and guayaberas, a traditional men's shirt worn in south Texas. If spirited bargaining in the markets is not your style, you may want to shop at the government-run Centro Artesanal in Matamoros, where the prices are fixed and the quality is high.

TOURIST OFFICES Brownsville Convention and Visitors Bureau (650 FM 802, Brownsville 78523, tel. 210/546–3721 or 800/626–2639, fax 210/546–3972). **Corpus Christi Area Convention and Tourist Bureau** (1201 N. Shoreline Dr., Corpus Christi 78403, tel. 512/881–1888 or 800/678–6232, fax 512/887–9023). **Galveston Island Convention and Visitors Bureau** (2106 Seawall Blvd., Galveston 77550, tel. 409/763–4311 or 800/351–4237; in TX, 800/351–4236; fax 409/765–8611). **Port Aransas Chamber of Commerce** (421 W. Cotter St., Port Aransas 78373, tel. 512/749–5919 or 800/452–6278, fax 512/749–4672). **Rockport-Fulton Area Chamber of Commerce** (Box 1055, Rockport 78382, tel. 512/729–6445 or 800/242–0071; in TX, 800/826–6441). **South Padre Island Convention and Visitors Bureau** (600 Padre Blvd., South Padre Island 78597, tel. 210/761–6433 or 800/343–2368, fax 210/761–9462). For information on **Padre Island National Seashore,** contact the National Park Service (9405 Padre Island Dr., Corpus Christi 78418, tel. 512/937–2621).

EMERGENCIES Police, fire, and **ambulance:** Dial 911. **Hospitals:** AMI Brownsville Medical Center (1040 W. Jefferson St., Brownsville, tel. 210/544–1400) has a 24-hour emergency room. In Galveston, there is a 24-hour emergency room at the University of Texas Medical Branch (6th St. and the Strand, tel. 409/772–1521).

ARRIVING AND DEPARTING

BY PLANE Galveston is not served by any major airlines, so plan to fly into either of Houston's two airports. **Intercontinental Airport** (tel. 713/230–3000), the larger of the two, is in the far north of Houston, about 1½–2 hours from Galveston, depending on traffic; the more manageable **Hobby Airport** (tel. 713/643–4597) is on the south side of the city and about an hour from the island. Call the **Galveston Limousine Service** (tel. 409/740–5466) for a pickup, or your Galveston hotel may have a courtesy car. Be sure to call ahead to make arrangements so you are not left stranded.

Corpus Christi and the Rio Grande Valley (which includes the Brownsville and South Padre Island areas) are both served by a number of airlines, although lower-priced Southwest Airlines is the most frequent flyer between Texas cities. For more information, call **Corpus Christi International Airport** (tel. 512/289–2675) or **Valley International Airport** (tel. 210/430–8600) at Harlingen.

BY CAR There is no coastal highway as such along the Gulf Coast, so plan on detours to see some of the smaller seaside towns. From Galveston, take County Road 3005 out of the west end of the island and cross over the toll bridge to the mainland at Surfside Beach. Pick your way over to Highway 35, then follow it south along the coast to Corpus Christi. It's a well-maintained road that offers plenty of local color and frequently winds along the coast. U.S. 77, which runs from just north of Rockport south to Brownsville, is a straight shot, but about 20 miles inland from the sea.

GETTING AROUND

Given the large distances involved, a car is the most practical way to travel the Texas Coast. RV centers dot the coast, especially down near the border (most RV parks rent hookups by the night, week, or month). Pleasure boaters also have safe access with the many marinas and protected waterways along the coast.

The Galveston Island trolley runs daily from the beachfront to the Strand. A motorized trolley connects Corpus Christi's major hotels to the Bayfront, and the Tide, a brightly painted bus, takes you from downtown to the aquarium and beaches. A water taxi also shuttles passengers from downtown to Corpus Christi Beach. On South Padre Island, the WAVE coastline trolley daily runs up and down the island's main street, Padre Boulevard.

REST STOPS The coast's many service stations are usually reliable rest stops, and many are noted by highway signs. In the cities, towns, and wildlife refuges, the visitor centers (see Tourist Offices, above; The Natural World, below) offer dependable facilities.

GUIDED TOURS Galveston: The **Galveston Historical Foundation** (2016 Strand, tel. 409/765–7834) offers tours of the area. **Island Tours Unlimited** (tel. 409/762–8605) arranges custom tours. The **Colonel** (tel. 409/740–7797), a Victorian-style paddle-wheel boat, offers day and dinner cruises. **Treasure Island Tour Train** (tel. 409/765–9564) provides a 90-minute tour around the city; board the train at Moody Center (Seawall Blvd. at 21st St.).

Aransas National Wildlife Refuge: While in the Rockport area, you can view the celebrated whooping cranes that winter in the Aransas National Wildlife Refuge. Four boats leave from Rockport Harbor and carry up to 250 passengers each to visit the nesting grounds every day. Reservations should be made at least a day in advance with the vessels **Captain Ted's** (tel. 800/338–4551), **New Pelican** (tel. 512/729–8448), or **Pisces** (tel. 800/245–9324).

Corpus Christi: You can view the city from the water on the 265-passenger **Flagship** (tel. 512/884–1693); it docks at the Peoples Street marina.

South Padre Island: At Sea Ranch Marina, all kinds of boats are available for hire, including three that specialize in two-hour narrated cruises with, hopefully, bottlenose dolphins frolicking in the waters around you. For information, call the **South Padre Convention and Visitor's Bureau** (tel. 210/761–6433) or just stroll to the marina and take your pick.

Brownsville: Historic trolley tours depart from **Brownsville Convention Center** twice daily, Thursday–Saturday (tel. 210/546–3721).

EXPLORING

Following are the main attractions along the coast from north to south.

GALVESTON Texas is a state of large landscapes, best explored by car, but historical Galveston can be easily explored on foot. Start on the waterfront at **Pier 21.** A 7-acre harbor development along Pier 21 includes retail shops, restaurants, a hotel, and the **Pier 21 Theatre,** which shows The Great Storm, a documentary about the 1900 hurricane that nearly wiped Galveston off the map. Nearby, the **Elissa,** an 1877 three-masted iron barque, has been restored as an operational sailing ship and is part of the adjacent **Texas Seaport Museum,** which has historical exhibits of 19th-century Galveston and observation decks. Pier 21, 1 block off the Strand, tel. 409/763–1877. Open daily. Admission charged.

The **Railroad Museum,** housed in an Art Deco station on the Strand near the Elissa, re-creates a people-filled train station lobby with lifelike statuary. It also features an extensive collection of vintage railroad cars. *The Strand at 25th St., tel. 409/765–5700. Open daily. Admission charged.*

Several blocks of the **Strand Historic District** between the *Elissa* and Railroad Museum are lined with fine, old, 19th-century iron-fronted buildings, once part of a financial hub known as the "Wall Street of the Southwest." Most have been restored and today house boutiques, restaurants, bars, art galleries, and several manufacturers' outlet stores.

The **East End Historical District,** six blocks from the Strand, is a 40-block area between 19th and 11th streets and Broadway to Market Street; here you'll find examples of Greek Revival, Gothic, Victorian, and other architectural styles of the last century. A free brochure available at the Strand Visitor Center (2016 Strand, tel. 409/765–7834) has a map that suggests a walking tour of the district. A companion audio tour (fee charged) is also available. Several grand homes, such as **Aston Villa** (2328 Broadway, tel. 409/762–3933; admission charged) and the **Bishop's Palace** (1402 Broadway; tel. 409/762–2475; admission charged) are open daily. Others, privately owned, are open only for the semiannual home tours in early May and early December.

Moody Gardens, a 142-acre property landscaped with some 20,000 plants and trees, creates a lush environment for the 10-story Rainforest Pyramid, a white-sand beach and lagoon, an IMAX theater, and an exotic animal petting zoo. *1 Hope Blvd., tel. 409/744–4673 or 800/582–4673. Open daily. Admission charged.*

ROCKPORT-FULTON These two small towns are the jumping-off point for viewing the whooping cranes and exploring the Aransas National Wildlife Refuge (*see* Guided Tours, *above*; the Natural World, *below*). Rockport is also known as an artists' colony, and you'll find seascape paintings for sale in galleries, such as the **Estelle Stair Gallery,** along Austin Street. The **Rockport Arts Center**

(902 Navigation Circle, tel. 512/729–5519; admission free) also features changing exhibits from local artists. The town has a good beach—Rockport Beach Park—as well as excellent deep-sea game fishing. Just off Highway 35 between Rockport and Fulton sits the **Fulton Mansion** (Henderson St. and Fulton Beach Rd., tel. 512/729–0386; admission charged), a beautifully restored French Second Empire mansion built in 1874.

CORPUS CHRISTI The gleaming white Philip Johnson–designed **Art Museum of South Texas** has collections of pre-Columbian figures and modern painting; it stands at the Corpus Christi–side entrance to the ship channel turning basin. *1902 N. Shoreline Dr., tel. 512/884–3844. Open Tues.–Sun. Admission charged.*

Directly across the channel is the **Texas State Aquarium,** which showcases more than 250 species of aquatic life from the Gulf of Mexico. *2710 N. Shoreline Dr. (Corpus Christi Beach), tel. 512/881–1200 or 800/477–4853. Open daily. Admission charged.*

Docked next door to the aquarium is the **USS *Lexington*,** a naval aircraft carrier nicknamed the "Blue Ghost" during World War II, when it served in the South Pacific. It now houses a floating naval museum. *Corpus Christi Beach, tel. 512/888–4873. Open daily. Admission charged.*

The **Corpus Christi Museum of Science & History** features an exceptional exhibit with artifacts and sunken treasures from a Spanish galleon that wrecked on Padre Island in 1554. *1900 N. Chaparrel St., tel. 512/883–2862. Open daily. Admission charged.*

Following the quincentennial celebration of Columbus's visit to the Americas, the **Columbus Fleet**—authentic reproductions of the *Niña, Pinta,* and *Santa Maria*—is now permanently anchored at Cargo Dock 1, adjacent to Corpus Christi Museum. *1901 N. Chaparrel St., tel. 512/883–2863. Open daily. Admission charged.*

Corpus Christi offers some of the best water sports on the coast, from windsurfing to fishing to skiing. Either stay on the mainland and enjoy the protected bay beaches (including Corpus Christi Beach, McGee Beach, and Cole Park) or take the causeway over to Padre Island's Malaquite Beach or Mustang Island State Park. A number of concessions along the seawall and marina offer other recreational activities, such as three-wheeled surreys and water trikes.

BROWNSVILLE Aviation history takes flight at the **Confederate Air Force's Rio Grande Valley Wing Museum,** where hangars at Brownsville International Airport shelter vintage World War II aircraft and combat memorabilia. The CAF stages air shows in early March and late October. *922 Minnesota St., Brownsville Airport, tel. 210/ 541–8585. Open daily. Admission charged.*

The Audubon Society's 32-acre **Sabal Palm Grove Sanctuary** welcomes bird-watchers to explore one of the last remaining Sabal palm woodlands in the region. Bobcats, coyotes, and the endangered ocelot are also found here. *Southmost Rd. on Rabb Plantation south of Brownsville, tel. 210/541–8034. Open Nov.–Apr., Thurs.–Mon.; May–Oct., weekends. Admission charged.*

Gladys Porter Zoo, rated as one of the 10 best zoos in the nation, has more than 1,750 uncaged mammals, birds, and reptiles, many of them among the world's rarest endangered species. *500 Ringgold, tel. 210/ 546–2177. Open daily. Admission charged.*

Few American visitors leave Brownsville without going over the bridge into Matamoros, Mexico, to shop (*see* Bargains, *above*).

SOUTH PADRE ISLAND At **Sea Turtle Incorporated** the endearing Ila Loetscher, recognized worldwide for her campaign to save the endangered Ridley sea turtle, stages Turtle Lady Shows each Tuesday and Saturday morning. *5805 Gulf Blvd., tel. 210/761–2544. Admission charged.*

THE NATURAL WORLD Positioned at the convergence of two major flyways, the Texas Coast is well known for its bird sanctuaries. In the Rio Grande Valley, both Santa Ana and Laguna Atascosa, known for their many rare animals and birds, offer self-guided auto tours, miles of walking trails, and several photography blinds.

Just 3 degrees north of the Tropic of Cancer, **Santa Ana** is a 2,000-acre remnant of a subtropical forest where you can view many plants and animals seldom seen anywhere else in the country. Located on a bend of the Rio Grande River, the junglelike refuge is famous for more than 300 documented species of birds, many of Mexican origin. *South and east of McAllen off U.S. 281 along Military Hwy., tel. 210/787–3079. Open daily to pedestrians, dawn–dusk; tour road open to vehicles weekdays. Guided tram runs in winter. Admission free.*

The **Laguna Atascosa** wildlife refuge contains 46,000 acres, composed of coastal prairies, salt flats, and brushlands, that attract large flocks of waterfowl. Javelina, white-tailed deer, and alligators are also among the inhabitants. *On coast just north of Port Isabel, off FM 106, tel. 210/748–3607. Open daily. Admission charged.*

The 54,829-acre **Aransas National Wildlife Refuge,** crisscrossed with hiking trails and roads for cars, is home to whooping cranes from mid-October to late March (*see* Guided Tours, *above,* for information on boat tours). The area also features some 500 species of waterfowl, songbirds, and hummingbirds as well as wild boars, alligators, bobcats, wolves, and deer. *38 mi north of Rockport near Hwy. 35, tel. 512/286–3559. Open daily. Admission charged.*

Padre Island National Seashore is a protected, primitive area where you can hike, camp, and collect shells. (Remember that there is no potable water in the area for 110 miles, so bring your own.) From the tops of some sand dunes, you can look at the Gulf of Mexico to the east and the Laguna Madre to the west. You can tour the pristine barrier island in a four-wheel-drive vehicle, but first consult with park rangers about tides and weather conditions. *From I–37 in Corpus Christi, take Hwy. 358 to Park Rd. 22, which leads to Malaquite Beach visitor center (tel. 512/949–8068), with informative rangers. Open daily. Admission charged.*

HOTELS AND INNS

Bed-and-breakfasts have caught on in Texas in recent years and are good alternatives to the chain motels if you're on a tight budget. In Galveston, one good choice is the moderately priced **Gilded Thistle** (1805 Broadway, tel. 409/763–0194). Galveston has the greatest variety of accommodations, but prices run a little higher here than farther south. Condos are also available for short-term leases. Any local chamber of commerce (*see* Tourist Offices, *above*) can steer you toward a real-estate agent eager to send you listings and brochures.

Most Texas cities levy a hefty local room tax, which can raise your tariff rather dramatically. At most coastal properties, rates double during spring break (late-February–mid-March); summer rates average 30% higher than winter rates. Price categories for double occupancy, excluding 8% tax, are Expensive, $90–$140; Moderate, $70–$90; and Inexpensive, under $70.

BROWNSVILLE **Holiday Inn Fort Brown.** This lovely motor inn, surrounded by a *resaca* (lagoon) with tropical gardens and waterfalls, has a great location—you can walk to Mexico. *1900 E. Elizabeth St., 78520, tel. 210/546–2201 or 800/465–4329. 278 rooms, 12 suites. Restaurant, pool, tennis. AE, D, DC, MC, V. Moderate.*

Rancho Viejo Resort. One of south Texas's most stunning resorts is also a golfer's paradise, with two 18-hole courses; choose between one of the Spanish-style villas right on the golf course or a room in the main lodge. *6 mi north of Brownsville on Expressway 77/83 (Box 3918), 78520, tel. 210/350–4000 or 800/531–7400. 58 rooms, 31 suites with kitchenettes. Restaurant, pool, tennis. AE, DC, MC, V. Moderate–Expensive.*

CORPUS CHRISTI **Best Western Sandy Shores.** Ask for a room facing the gulf at this pleasant, beachside, high-rise hotel near the Texas State Aquarium. *3200 Surfside, 78403, tel. 512/883–7456 or 800/242–5814, fax 512/883–1437. 252 rooms, 7 suites.*

Restaurant, pool, gift shop, kite museum. AE, D, DC, MC, V. Inexpensive–Moderate.

Corpus Christi Marriott Bayfront. Overlooking the bay and sitting across the street from People's Street T-head, this luxurious hotel is convenient to all downtown attractions. *900 N. Shoreline Blvd., 78401, tel. 512/887–1600 or 800/874–4585, fax 512/887–6715. 450 rooms, 28 suites. Restaurant, indoor and outdoor pool, health club. AE, D, DC, MC, V. Expensive.*

GALVESTON **Harbor House.** The anchor attraction of a waterfront development, this comfortable but plain inn is settled into a former steamship terminal and features nautical-theme decor. The inn's greatest asset may be its waterfront views. *Pier 21, No. 28, 77550, tel. 409/763–3321 or 800/874–3721, fax 409/765–6421. 42 rooms, 3 suites. Restaurant. AE, DC, MC, V. Expensive.*

Hotel Galvez. This 1911 Spanish-style stucco hotel, across from the Gulf of Mexico, hosts many celebrities and places visitors in the middle of the beachfront action. *2024 Seawall Blvd., 77550, tel. 409/765–7721 or 800/392–4285, fax 409/765–7721, ext. 667. 225 rooms, 3 suites. Restaurant, 2 pools, room service, guest membership in Galveston Country Club. AE, D, DC, MC, V. Moderate–Expensive.*

Tremont House. A soaring atrium lobby, white-lace linens on the beds, a fine restaurant, and a convenient Strand location make this elegant restoration of a 19th-century mercantile building one of the city's most popular hotels. *2300 Ship's Mechanic Row, 77550, tel. 409/763–0300 or 800/874–2300, fax 409/763–1539. 117 rooms, 9 suites. Dining room, room service, concierge, gift shop, limo, passes to Galveston Racquet Club. AE, DC, MC, V. Expensive.*

Victorian Inn. Located in the East End Historical District near the Strand, Galveston's first bed-and-breakfast, an Italian-Victorian beauty, features antique furnishings throughout. *511 17th St., 77550, tel. 409/762–3235. 4 rooms, 1 suite. AE, DC, MC, V. Moderate.*

PORT ARANSAS **Port Royal.** A destination in itself, this condominium resort on Mustang Island gives guests the option of lounging on the beach, just outside your door, or on the banks of the largest lagoon in Texas. *Hwy. 361, Box 336, 78373, tel. 512/749–5011 or 800/242–1034, fax 512/749–6399. 170 rental units. Restaurant, pool, tennis courts, convenience store, gift shop. AE, D, DC, MC, V. Expensive.*

Tarpon Inn. Circled with long porches fitted with rockers, this Hemingwayesque hotel, built in 1886 and on the National Register of Historic Places, appeals to anglers out to catch big game fish. Creatures of comfort note: Despite recent renovations, rooms do not have televisions or phones. *200 E. Cotter St. (Box 8), 78373, tel. 512/749–5555 or 800/ 365–6784. 22 rooms, 2 suites. Nearby restaurant, free parking. AE, MC, V. Inexpensive.*

ROCKPORT-FULTON **Sandollar Resort.** Bird-watchers and fishermen alike flock to this relaxed bargain motel nestled amid live oak trees on a hill overlooking the sea. *Fulton Beach Rd. at Hwy. 35, Box 30, 78382, tel. 512/729–2381. 27 rooms, some with kitch-enettes; 2 suites. Restaurant, pool, RV spaces, marina. MC, V. Inexpensive.*

SOUTH PADRE ISLAND **Bahia Mar Resort.** One of the first hotel-condo developments on the island, this beachfront property offers wonderful views of the water and access to miles of pristine beach. *6300 Padre Island Blvd., 78597, tel. 210/761–1343 or 800/292–7502, fax 210/761–6287. 200 rooms, 20 suites, 50 condominium units. Restaurant, pool, night-club, tennis courts, putting green, gift shop. AE, D, DC, MC, V. Moderate–Expensive.*

Sheraton Fiesta Beach Resort. Every room has an ocean view at this beautiful 12-story resort, with lavish landscaping and an inviting beach. *310 Padre Island Blvd., 78597, tel. 210/761–6551 or 800/222–4010, fax 210/ 761–6570. 200 rooms, 50 suites. Restaurant, pool, gift shop, water sports. AE, D, DC, MC, V. Expensive.*

MOTELS

MODERATE **Holiday Inn on the Beach** (5002 Seawall Blvd., Galveston 77550, tel. 409/ 740–3581 or 800/465–4329). 178 rooms; restaurant, gift shop, pool, ocean view. **Ramada Inn** (600 Strand, Galveston 77550, tel. 409/765–5544 or 800/228–2828). 232 rooms; restaurant, water view.

INEXPENSIVE **Comfort Inn** (2300 Seawall Blvd., Galveston 77550, tel. 409/762–1166). 124 rooms; pool. **Days Inn Corpus Christi** (901 Navigation, Corpus Christi 78408, adjacent to Corpus Christi Greyhound Racetrack, tel. 512/888–8599 or 800/233–3297). 121 rooms; restaurant, pool. **Days Inn Rockport** (1212 Laurel, Rockport 78382, tel. 512/729–6379 or 800/325–2525). 25 rooms, 5 suites; pool. **Gaido's Seaside Inn** (3800 Seawall Blvd., Galveston 77550, tel. 409/762–9625). 108 rooms; pool, restaurant. **Howard Johnson** (1945 N. Expressway, Brownsville 78520, tel. 210/546–4591). 159 rooms, 3 suites; restaurant, pool. **La Quinta Motor Inn** (55 Sam Perl Blvd., Brownsville 78520, tel. 210/546–0381). 137 rooms, 6 suites; restaurant, pool. **Sandcastle** (200 W. Kingfish, South Padre Island 78597, tel. 210/761–1321 or 800/221–5218). 50 condo units; kitchens, pool, fishing, boat slips. **Sea Shell Inn** (202 Kleberg Pl., Corpus Christi 78402, tel. 512/888–5391). 26 rooms; pool, beach. **Travelers Inn** (6805 S. Padre Island Dr. at Nile Dr., Corpus Christi 78412, tel. 512/992–9222 or 800/663–8300). 119 rooms, 3 suites; pool.

DINING

The trinity of Texas cuisine is Tex-Mex, chicken-fried steak, and barbecue—all delicious, hearty foods. However, fresh seafood contributes a fourth, lighter component to the regional cooking. The Gulf of Mexico boasts some of the most fertile fishing grounds in the world, yielding black drum, yellowfin tuna, gulf mahimahi, flounder, snapper, grouper, redfish, swordfish, and pompano. The coast's warm waters also yield sweet shrimp, blue crabs (excellent barbecued), and mild-flavored oysters. You will find the Tex-Mex food down around Brownsville especially good. Price categories per person, excluding 8% tax, service, and drinks, are Moderate, $15–$25, and Inexpensive, under $15.

BROWNSVILLE **Los Camperos.** Strolling mariachi bands add to the festive atmosphere of this Mexican-style steak house that offers steak *al carbón* (grilled) along with enchiladas, fajitas, and other Tex-Mex favorites. *1442 International Blvd., tel. 210/546–8172. AE, MC, V. Inexpensive.*

Palm Court. The relaxed setting and tropical foliage blend well with the health-minded menu, but even serious epicureans will not be disappointed by the shrimp crepes, lasagna, terrific soups, and fresh daily specials. *2235 Boca Chica Blvd., tel. 210/542–3575. AE, MC, V. Inexpensive.*

CORPUS CHRISTI **Elmo's City Diner & Oyster Bar.** This '50s-style diner offers Coastal Bend delicacies, such as King Ranch chicken, guacamole, oysters-on-the-half-shell, and home-style hamburgers. *622 N. Water St., tel. 512/883–1643. AE, D, DC, MC, V. Inexpensive–Moderate.*

La Pesca. This casual place features fresh seafood cooked with a Mexican flair, plus homemade breads and desserts. *701 N. Water St., tel. 512/887–4558. AE, D, DC, MC, V. Moderate.*

The Lighthouse. An easy walk from the downtown hotels, this marina restaurant offers a dramatic bay view along with seafood, pasta, and chicken. *Lawrence St. T-head, tel. 512/883–3982. AE, D, DC, MC, V. Moderate.*

Rusty's. What's a trip to the beach without a thick, juicy "cheeseburger in paradise"? These are the best around. *1645 Airline Rd., tel. 512/993–5000. AE, MC, V. Inexpensive.*

Water Street Oyster Bar. Amberjack steaks are grilled to perfection at this former garage turned restaurant; original brick walls and the concrete floor add to the lively atmosphere of this landmark eatery. House specialties include oysters and shrimp *en brochette* (wrapped in bacon, skewered and grilled) and blackened redfish. *309 N. Water St., tel. 512/881–9448. AE, DC, MC, V. Moderate.*

GALVESTON **Benno's on the Beach.** Cajun-inspired seafood, including rich peppery crawfish étouffée, red beans and rice, and blackened oysters, are served in this open-air beachside shack. *1200 Seawall Blvd., tel. 409/762–4621. MC, V. Inexpensive.*

El Nopalito. Locals come to this colorful, ramshackle favorite for a cheap and funky Mexican breakfast and heaping platters at lunch. *614 42nd St. between Church St. and Broadway Ave., tel. 409/763–9815. No credit cards. No dinner. Inexpensive.*

Gaido's. This granddaddy of seafood houses in Galveston, known all over Texas for its changing menu, offers crabs, oysters, shrimp, and snapper, each prepared a dozen ways. *3828 Seawall Blvd., tel. 409/762–9625. AE, MC, V. Moderate.*

Hill's Pier 19. Gumbo, oyster po'boys, and seafood are the standards at this dockside salty dog; eat outside at picnic tables where you can watch freighters, tugboats, and shrimp boats. *20th St. at the wharves, tel. 409/763–7087. AE, DC, MC, V. Inexpensive.*

Mallory's Wharf. This popular restaurant at the Harbor House hotel offers delectable variations on traditional seafood specialties—try the blackened shrimp, chicken-fried catfish, or the house specialty, Wharf Chowder. *Pier 21, tel. 409/763–3321. AE, DC, MC, V. Moderate.*

The Wentletrap. The beautiful three-story Renaissance Revival restoration, Continental food, and gracious service all make dining here special; try the salads at lunch and the seafood at dinner. *2301 Strand, tel. 409/765–5545. AE, DC, MC, V. Moderate.*

PADRE ISLAND **Snoopy's Pier.** You can fill up on fried fish, shrimp, or oysters at this breezy, seaside café. Start with an order of crabmeat-stuffed jalapeños. Dine outside and watch the brown pelicans soar over the waves. *13313 S. Padre Island Dr., tel. 512/949–8815. No credit cards. Inexpensive.*

PORT ARANSAS **Quarterdeck.** From the Quarterdeck you can watch fishing boats unload the catch of the day, only to find it reappear later on your own menu—grilled, fried, broiled, or stuffed. *914 Tarpon, Fisherman's Wharf, tel. 512/749–4449. AE, MC, V. Moderate.*

Seafood & Spaghetti Works. While the building may resemble a spaceship gone off course, it's the delicious seafood and pasta dishes that draw diners back again and again for giant grilled shrimp, wonderful pasta dishes, and scrumptious desserts such as Butterfinger cheesecake. *709 Alister St., tel. 512/749–5666. AE, DC, MC, V. Moderate.*

ROCKPORT-FULTON **Boiling Pot.** Shrimp, crabs, corn-on-the-cob, and potatoes are all boiled together, Cajun style, and served right on the butcher-paper-covered tables at this lively dining spot. *Fulton Beach Rd. at Palmetto, tel. 512/729–6972. AE, D, MC, V. Inexpensive–Moderate.*

SOUTH PADRE ISLAND **Rovan's Restaurant and Bakery.** The lines are long, but the service is quick, the prices cheap, and the food plentiful at this popular homespun spot. Breakfast is served all day, and locals give Rovan's barbecued ribs a serious thumbs-up. Many locals also swear by the home-baked goods. *5300 Padre Blvd., tel. 210/761–6972. No credit cards. Closed Tues. Inexpensive.*

OUTDOOR ACTIVITIES

BEACHES The 110-mile-long Padre Island has the best beaches in Texas, most of them protected as National Seashore, largely undeveloped and accessible only by four-wheel-drive vehicles. Malaquite Beach at the northern tip and South Padre Island to the south offer scenic stretches of beach. Other exceptional beaches include Mustang Island,

the barrier island that protects Corpus Christi Bay and extends north from Padre Island to Port Aransas; Galveston's East Beach, the least eroded of Galveston's beaches; and Bolivar Peninsula, north of Galveston Island and accessible by ferry. Many Texas beaches are still relatively primitive, although some offer amenities. In Galveston, for example, Apffel Park has a pavilion with showers, a snack bar, and rest rooms.

FISHING You can charter a boat for a day of deep-sea fishing in almost any port along the coast. Most charters go out about 40 miles for kingfish, dorado, bluefish, shark, Spanish mackerel, tuna, wahoo, and barracuda. In Galveston, contact **Aqua Safari Charters** (tel. 409/935–4646 or 800/759–4547). In Port Aransas, contact **Fisherman's Wharf** (tel. 512/749–5760), specializing in offshore and party boats. **Woody's Sports Center** (tel. 512/749–5252) offers offshore, bay and bay party boats. **Deep Sea Headquarters** (tel. 512/749–5597) is another Port Aransas fishing charter service. The *Capt. Clark* (tel. 512/884–4369) departs from People Street T-head three times daily in Corpus Christi.

You will also find piers and jetties all along the coast. Most, but not all, are free. In Port Aransas, the Horace Caldwell fishing pier jets 1,240 feet into the Gulf of Mexico and permits anglers to hook tarpon, shark, and many other species. In addition, excellent surf fishing is found along the public beaches, especially at the north end of South Padre Island between Andy Bowie Park and the Mansfield jetties, and at San Luis Pass on the western tip of Galveston Island. If you plan to fish or gather oysters, check locally to make sure there is no red tide and that the waters are unpolluted.

A Texas fishing license is required for fishing persons aged 17 to 65, regardless of your state of residence. A special, three-day saltwater-sport fishing license is also available. Licenses may be purchased at most bait camps, sporting-goods and tackle stores, and convenience stores. For more information, contact the **Texas Parks and Wildlife Department** (tel. 800/792–1112).

GOLF The **Galveston Island Municipal Golf Course** (tel. 409/744–2366) has 18 holes and a large clubhouse. **Galveston Country Club at Pirates Beach** (tel. 409/737–2776 or 409/737–2040) is a private facility, but area hotels offer guest membership privileges. Corpus Christi and the Valley also have many fine golf courses, including the **Rancho Viejo Country Club** (tel. 210/350–4000), north of Brownsville, with its two 18-hole courses.

HIKING The wildlife refuges and Padre Island National Seashore offer extensive trail systems and self-guided walking tours (*see* The Natural World, *above*).

SHELLING San Jose Island, or St. Jo to the locals, is a beachcomber's paradise. Uninhabited and accessible from the mainland only by ferry from Port Aransas, its secluded beaches sprawl for miles. Fall and winter are the best times for finding perfect, unbroken sand dollars and other fragile treasures that wash ashore. **Woody's Boat Basin** (114 Cotter St., Port Aransas, tel. 512/749–5252) has daily boat trips to St. Jo; don't forget your ice chest (lots of ice and cold drinks), picnic basket, umbrella, towels, fishing tackle, and sunscreen. There are no rest rooms or potable water on the island, and little shade.

WINDSURFING Windsurfers rank Corpus Christi as one of the top sailing spots in the country because of its constant strong winds (the average wind velocity is 12 mph). Colorful sails dot the waters most every day of the year beneath the **JFK Causeway** and at **Bird Island Basin** on Padre Island. Lessons and rentals are available from **Wind & Wave** (10721 S. Padre Island Dr., Corpus Christi, tel. 512/937–9283).

Walt Disney World and the Orlando Area

Florida

Updated by Marianne Camas

Orlando, a high-profile city of fast growth in central Florida, is the number-one tourist destination in the United States, attracting more than 13 million visitors annually. Most of these visitors come to enjoy the whimsical pleasures of Walt Disney World, a lush, clean resort of 27,400 acres that is twice the size of Manhattan. When most people imagine Disney World, they usually think of the Magic Kingdom, which encompasses only 98 acres, but in actuality there is much more. In addition to two other theme parks—Epcot and Disney–MGM Studios—some 2,500 acres are occupied by hotels and villa complexes, each with its own theme and each equipped with recreational facilities.

From the gardens full of birds and butterflies, bamboo thickets, and topiary statues, to the lakes thrumming with motorboats and the shops brimming over with treasures and trinkets, every detail is as highly polished as the best Disney film. You can relax, stop fighting the battles of the real world, and let yourself be seduced by the pleasantness of it all. As you take a heart-stopping ride through Magic Kingdom's Space Mountain galaxy or inspect the rose gardens in the shadow of Epcot Center's Canadian pavilion or gasp at the laser pyrotechnics of the IllumiNations fireworks, the pleasure of the moment is enough.

If you find that you and Mickey Mouse need a short vacation from each other, there are plenty of other recreational options in the Orlando area; many of the attractions outside Disney World are equally enjoyable (including Universal Studios Florida and Sea World) and sometimes less crowded and less expensive. The city itself has retained its charming parklike atmosphere, with homes near spring-fed lakes and the smell of orange blossoms and citrus trees in the air.

ESSENTIAL INFORMATION

WHEN TO GO December, January, and February offer the best weather, when the humidity disappears and the daily temperature averages in the low 70s. It can get quite cool when the sun goes down. Count on hot and humid weather from April through October, with a daily shower usually late in the afternoon. Average daily maximum temperatures are in the 80s in April and October and in the 90s from May to September.

The most crowded time of the year to visit is from Christmas through New Year's Day. The parks are also packed around Easter. Memorial Day weekend is not only crowded, but temperatures can be quite high. Other inadvisable times to visit are from mid-June through mid-August, Thanksgiving weekend, the week of Washington's Birthday in mid-February, and the weeks of college spring break in late March. The rest of the year is generally hassle-free, particularly from early September until just before Thanksgiving. The best time of all is from just after the Thanksgiving weekend until the beginning of the Christmas holidays. Another excellent time is from early January through the first week of February. If you come here during summer, late August is best.

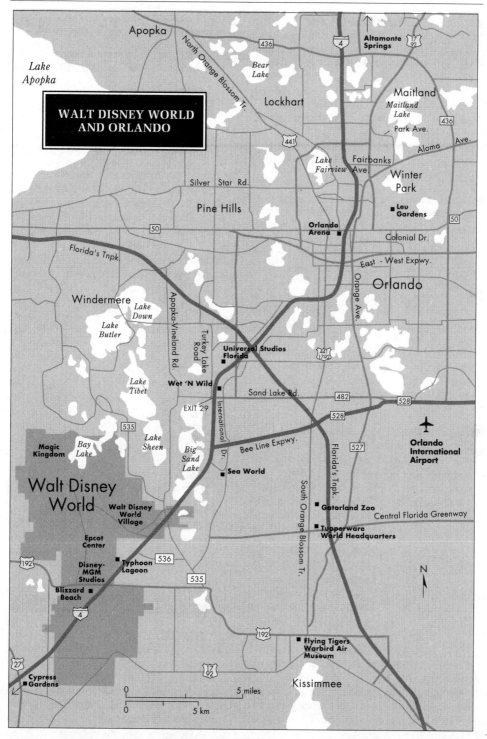

WALT DISNEY WORLD
AND ORLANDO

Apopka

Lake
Apopka

North Orange Blossom Tr.

436

I 4

Altamonte
Springs

17
92

Bear
Lake

Lockhart

Maitland

Maitland
Lake

441

Park Ave.

436

Aloma Ave.

Lake
Fairview

Fairbanks
Ave.

Winter
Park

Silver Star Rd.

Pine Hills

Leu
Gardens

50

50

Orlando
Arena

Colonial Dr.

Florida's Tnpk.

East - West Expwy.

Windermere

Lake
Down

Apopka-Vineland Rd.

Orange Ave.

Orlando

Lake
Butler

Turkey Lake Road

Universal Studios
Florida

441
1792

Lake
Tibet

Wet 'N Wild

Sand Lake Rd.

482

528

EXIT 29

International Dr.

528

535

Lake
Sheen

Big
Sand
Lake

Bee Line Expwy.

527

Orlando
International
Airport

Magic
Kingdom

Bay
Lake

Sea World

Florida's Tnpk.

Walt Disney
World

Walt Disney
World
Village

South Orange Blossom Tr.

Gatorland Zoo

Central Florida Greenway

Tupperware
World Headquarters

Epcot
Center

192

Disney-
MGM
Studios

Typhoon
Lagoon

536

535

Blizzard
Beach

4

N

27

192

Flying Tigers
Warbird Air
Museum

92

Cypress
Gardens

Kissimmee

0   5 miles

0   5 km

FESTIVALS AND SPECIAL EVENTS **Jan. 1:** The Comp USA Florida Citrus Bowl Football Classic matches two national college football powers. **Early Feb.:** Walt Disney World Village Wine Festival includes the participation of 60 U.S. wineries. **Mid-Mar.:** Winter Park Sidewalk Art Festival draws art enthusiasts to chic Park Avenue. **Mid-Oct.:** Disney World Classic is played at golf courses at Lake Buena Vista. **Mid-Nov.:** Light Up Orlando is a street party downtown with live entertainment.

BARGAINS For no admission charge, visit **Spaceport USA** (Kennedy Space Center, about 50 mi east of Orlando, tel. 407/452–2121; open daily except on launch days), with a Museum of Space History and an Astronauts Memorial. **Leu Botanical Gardens** (1730 N. Forest Ave., Orlando, tel. 407/246–2620; open daily) offers 57 acres of fragrant flora—including rose gardens and a floral clock—and plentiful sitting areas for a nominal fee. **Belz Factory Outlet World** (5401 W. Oakridge Rd. at north end of International Dr., tel. 407/352–9600) has more than 160 outlet stores. Several Orlando-area restaurants have reduced-priced menus before 6 PM.

TOURIST OFFICES **Walt Disney World** (Box 10040, Lake Buena Vista 32830, tel. 407/824–4321). For Disney World information and brochures, go to any Disney theme park ticket window or call; lines are open daily 8 AM–9 PM. **Orlando Visitor Information Center** (8445 International Dr. in Mercado Mediterranean Village, tel. 407/363–5871).

EMERGENCIES **Police, fire,** and **ambulance:** Dial 911. **Hospitals:** Orlando Regional Medical Center/Sand Lake Hospital (9400 Turkey Lake Rd., tel. 407/351–8500). **Doctors:** Centra Care (6001 Vineland Rd., 1 block west of Kirkman Rd., tel. 407/351–6682). Buena Vista Walk-In Medical Center (adjacent to Walt Disney World Village entrance on Rte. 535, tel. 407/828–3434). **Pharmacies:** Eckerd Drugs (908 Lee Rd., Orlando, tel. 407/644–6908) and Walgreens (4578 S. Kirkman Rd., Orlando, tel. 407/293–8389) have 24-hour pharmacies.

ARRIVING AND DEPARTING

BY PLANE Served by several major U.S. airlines, **Orlando International Airport** (tel. 407/825–2001), located on the southeast edge of town, is only minutes from the main attractions. Disney World and Universal Studios information booths are at the airport; tickets and maps are available to save you time from standing in line at the parks.

Between the Airport and Hotels. If you're driving a rental car from the airport and your lodging is on International Drive or around Disney World, take the Beeline Expressway (Route 528) west. The Beeline also hooks up with I–4 if you need to head into downtown Orlando. Several shuttle and limousine services at the airport offer regularly scheduled service to and from all major hotels (about $13 adults, $8 for children): Mears Transportation Group (tel. 407/423–5566), Town & Country Limo (tel. 407/828–3035), and First Class Limousine (tel. 407/862–2277). Taxis are the quickest way to travel from the airport. They cost about $35 plus tip from the airport to hotels on U.S. 192 or around Disney World; about $25 plus tip to International Drive hotels.

BY CAR I–4 and the Florida Turnpike are the main thoroughfares into Orlando.

BY BUS **Greyhound Lines** (tel. 800/231–2222) has a west-side terminal at 555 North John Young Parkway.

BY TRAIN **Amtrak** (tel. 800/872–7245) has stops in Winter Park (150 Morse Blvd.), in Orlando (1400 Sligh Blvd.), and, 20 minutes later, in Kissimmee (416 Pleasant St.).

GETTING AROUND

WALT DISNEY WORLD If you're staying at Disney World, the best way to get around is by bus; rarely will you have to wait more than 20 minutes for one. On-site hotels have schedules. Disney World also has a monorail and a water-based transportation system. Transportation is free for those staying at a

Walt Disney World Village hotel and for those with a three-park ticket. Otherwise, a ticket for unlimited transportation costs $2.50 a day.

ORLANDO **By Bus.** The colorfully painted LYNX buses of the **Tri-County Transit Authority** (tel. 407/841–8240) public buses are an inexpensive way to get around Orlando.

By Car. The most important artery in the Orlando area is I–4, which ties everything together. On this road, remember that when the signs say east you are often going north, and when the signs say west, you are often going south. International Drive (Exits 28, 29, and 30B from I–4), another main road, has several major hotels, restaurants, attractions, and shopping centers. The other major highway, U.S. 192, also known as Irlo Bronson Memorial Highway, cuts across I–4 at Exits 25A and 25B. This highway goes through the Kissimmee area and crosses Walt Disney World property, taking you to the Magic Kingdom's main entrance.

By Taxi. Call **Yellow Cab Co.** (tel. 407/699–9999) or **Town and Country Cab** (tel. 407/828–3035).

REST STOPS All the major attractions provide maps that clearly mark rest rooms. The major shopping areas and malls also offer clean rest rooms. Public bathrooms in the downtown Orlando area are ample. The Church Street Station Exchange, with shops and restaurants, offers public rest rooms. A public rest room and concession area is available at Lake Eola, near the band shell. Lake Ivanhoe Park (off I–4 at Orange Ave. and Midway Dr.) offers a public rest area.

GUIDED TOURS **Walt Disney World:** The Keys to the Kingdom is a 3½- to four-hour guided orientation tour. Tours leave from City Hall on Main Street in the Magic Kingdom daily between 9:15 and 9:30 AM and are on a first-come, first-served basis. Included are visits to some of the "backstage" zones—the parade staging area and parts of the underground "Tunnel," including the wardrobe area. The minimum age for children is 10,

and they pay the adult rate. In Epcot, there are several behind-the scenes tours that can be booked up to three weeks in advance (tel. 407/560–6150).

Boat: Scenic Boat Tours (312 Morse Blvd., Winter Park, tel. 407/644–4056) offers relaxing cruises past large lakeside homes and Rollins College.

EXPLORING

Walt Disney World is open daily, with longer hours in the summer and during holidays; call 407/824–4321 for the latest information on admission prices and hours. The best time to be at the parks is first thing in the morning (until 11) and in the evening.

A visit to WDW is not particularly cheap. A one-day ticket that allows a single day's admission to one of the three main theme parks (Disney–MGM Studios Theme Park, Epcot, and the Magic Kingdom) costs around $41 for adults and $33 for children under 10—and prices go up $1–$2 annually. Prices at other area theme parks, such as Universal Studios and Sea World, are comparable. WDW does offer a variety of multiday passes, and if you plan to spend at least three days, they are worth investigating. The **Four-Day Value Pass** (around $133 for adults, $104 for children) allows admission to each of the three parks on any three days. You can then visit one of the parks again on one more day. You cannot visit more than one park on one day. There is a way to avoid this restriction: the **Four-Day Park Hopper** (around $147 for adults, $117 for children) a personalized photo ID pass that allows unlimited visits to the three parks on any four days. The **Five-Day World Hopper** is also a photo ID; it includes unlimited visits to the three theme parks over five days, plus seven days' admission to WDW's minor parks—Pleasure Island, Typhoon Lagoon, River Country, Blizzard Beach, and Discovery Island.

DISNEY-MGM STUDIOS THEME PARK This park transports visitors behind the scenes and in front of the cameras at a working movie and television studio reminiscent of '30s and '40s Hollywood. The park can be seen in one day. Begin with the **Great Movie Ride,** as it often opens before the other attractions do. If there are thrill-seekers in your group, head first instead to the **Twilight Zone Tower of Terror,** where long lines form early. Then visit the **Magic of Disney Animation** because lines get long and most of the artists leave by 5 PM. The **Backstage Studio Tour** takes you on a tram ride through the back lot, and then guided walking tours explain the creation of special effects.

The best attractions are **Star Tours,** a breathtaking simulated ride into space (which isn't recommended for those who are prone to motion sickness or have back problems, heart conditions, and other physical limitations) and the **Indiana Jones Epic Stunt Spectacular,** in which performers, with the help of audience volunteers, re-create action scenes from the movie *Raiders of the Lost Ark.* Other attractions include the **Monster Sound Show,** a humorous lesson on sound effects; and **Jim Henson's Muppet Vision 3D,** which combines a 3-D movie with live action and Audio-Animatronics.

EPCOT CENTER This park was designed more for thoughtful adults (and curious children) than for a thrill-seeking crowd; for many adults, it is the most enjoyable part of Disney World. Although Epcot stands for Experimental Prototype Community of Tomorrow, the park is filled with attractions that more often explain past and present. Epcot is divided almost equally into two distinct areas: **Future World,** where pavilions focus on discoveries and the fascinations of science; and **World Showcase,** with 10 foreign countries represented by recreations of famous landmarks, typical crafts and foods, and a staff of natives.

To minimize your time in lines, go left through the breezeway past Innoventions attractions as fast as you can before the crowd catches up to you. Then leave Future World and work your way clockwise around the 40-acre lagoon in World Showcase. Din-

ner and early evening hours are the less crowded times in either section.

In Future World, many of the attractions involve rides. Hands down, the most popular is now **Honey, I Shrunk the Audience,** a hilarious 3D showcase with terrific in-theater special effects. Another popular place to visit is **Wonders of Life,** with Cranium Command, a delightful stage and film presentation about the brain of a teenage boy; The Making of Me, a movie on reproduction, pregnancy, and birth; and Body Wars, a simulated ride through the body's immune system. Other impressive attractions are **Universe of Energy,** which teaches you about the origins of energy and takes you to a world of dinosaurs; **Journey into Imagination,** a combination 3-D rock video, family fun ride, and hands-on play area, and **The Land,** with a boat ride through a greenhouse of the future. The two buildings that house **Innoventions** have a split personality. **Innoventions West** is hugely popular with preteens; it features an enormous display of Sega toys and games and an eight-car Formula One Grand Prix race in which you get to drive a full-size car through a turn-filled course that's projected onto a huge screen in front of each vehicle. **Innoventions East** features a selection of products for the home of the not-too-distant future.

The World Showcase features pavilions devoted to the native food, entertainment, and wares of 11 countries. Among the highlights are **Mexico,** devoted to the country's major tourist spots and involving a boat ride; **Norway,** with a ride back in time in a small Viking vessel; and **China,** with a fascinating film that reveals the country's glorious landscapes. The **American Adventure** is a 30-minute Audio-Animatronics show, hosted by figures representing Benjamin Franklin and Mark Twain.

MAGIC KINGDOM When people think of Disney World, it's this park that sparks their imagination. There are nearly 50 major attractions in seven imaginary lands spread across 98 acres, but most of the rides are geared for younger children. Town Square's City Hall has an information desk.

The young at heart may enjoy the **WDW Railroad,** a 14-minute ride around the park's perimeter; **Pirates of the Caribbean,** a visit to pirate strongholds, in Adventureland; and the **Haunted Mansion** in Liberty Square. Those with a penchant for thrills will enjoy Frontierland's **Splash Mountain,** a suped-up log-flume ride with it's five-story plunge climax, and Tomorrowland's **Space Mountain,** a turbulent roller-coaster ride in the dark. Lines are shortest in the evening.

WDW WATER PARKS **Blizzard Beach** (tel. 407/ 560–3400), the newest Disney water park, is themed as a ski resort where all the snow has melted into water. **Typhoon Lagoon** (tel. 407/560–4141) is a lushly landscaped, 50-acre aquatic entertainment complex at Walt Disney World with a saltwater pool containing a coral reef and Caribbean sea creatures, including baby sharks. **River Country,** the first WDW water park, is smaller and in some ways has more charm than its glitzier successors. *All 3 parks open daily 10–5, 9–8 in summer. Admission charged; River Country admission sold separately from combined, all-day Typhoon Lagoon–Blizzard Beach ticket.*

ORLANDO AREA **Cypress Gardens.** Central Florida's oldest continuously running attraction, the Gardens contain some 8,000 varieties of perennial plants and flowers. A popular waterskiing show features high-speed stunts along Lake Eloise. You can also attend shows with alligators and birds. *From Disney World take I-4 west to U.S. 27S exit; follow signs to Winter Haven; at Waverly, turn right on Rte. 540 to the Gardens. Tel. 813/ 324–2111 or 800/237–4826; in FL, 800/282– 2123. Open daily. Admission charged.*

Flying Tigers Warbird Air Museum. This former aircraft restoration facility is now a museum of World War II planes with souvenirs, models, and memorabilia. *231 Hoagland Blvd., Kissimmee, tel. 407/933–1942. Open daily. Admission charged.*

Gatorland Zoo. This unusual attraction houses more than 400 alligators and 40 crocodiles swimming in a lake. The zoo contains other reptiles, in addition to monkeys, farm animals, and even a tapir. *14501 S. Orange Blossom Trail, Kissimmee, tel. 407/ 855–5496. Open daily. Admission charged.*

Ripley's Believe It or Not Museum. There's antiques, oddities, miniatures, disasters, and more in the Orlando version of this worldwide exhibition museum. *8201 International Dr., Orlando, tel. 407/363–4418. Open daily. Admission charged.*

Sea World of Florida. This aquatic park can be seen in one day. The star is Shamu, the killer whale who performs in a tank containing 5 million gallons of water. Other top attractions include "Hotel Clyde and Seamore," starring otters and walruses, and "Terrors of the Deep," which takes you through the middle of a shark tank. The complex also includes petting and feeding pools, a dolphin and whale show, a 400-foot revolving observation tower, and a nightly Polynesian luau dinner show. New attractions include "Wild Arctic," an exhibit of polar bears, beluga whales, and walrus that includes a simulated helicopter ride to the North Pole, "Manatees, the Last Generation," and "Shamu's Happy Harbor." *7007 Sea World Dr., Orlando, tel. 407/351–3600 or 800/327–2424; in FL, 800/432–1178. Open daily. Admission charged.*

Splendid China. A relative newcomer to the attraction scene, this park contains 60-plus replicas of China's greatest man-made and natural landmarks, among them the Imperial Palace, the Great Wall, and the rock formations of the Stone Forest. Daily live entertainment, a children's area, and the requisite shops and restaurants are also offered. *3000 Splendid China Blvd., Kissimmee, tel. 407/ 397–8800 or 800/244–6226. Open daily. Admission charged.*

Universal Studios Florida. The largest motion picture and television studio outside Hollywood makes learning fun with movie-theme attractions and more than 40 restaurants and shops. A walking tour takes you to more than 50 locations created for films. The main big rides include "Earthquake—The Big One," "E.T.'s Adventure," "Kongfrontation," and "Jaws." The best flight-simulator in central Florida, "Back to the Future" takes you on an amusing simulated ride through various time periods. The most entertaining attraction may be "The Funtastic World of Hanna-Barbera," featuring Yogi Bear and the Flintstones. A show is always in production at the Nickelodeon Production Center. *Get off I-4 at Exit 29 and follow signs or take Exit 30B and go north on Kirkman Rd., 1000 Universal Studios Plaza, Orlando, tel. 407/ 363–8000. Open daily. Admission charged.*

Wet 'n Wild. At this popular aquatic park you can swim, slide, and play water sports with plenty of lifeguards on duty. *6200 International Dr., Orlando, tel. 407/351– 3200. Open mid-Feb.–Dec., daily. Admission charged.*

HOTELS AND INNS

With more than 80,000 hotel rooms, Orlando leads the country in accommodations. You won't have trouble finding an inexpensive room (with prices even lower during the off-season, Sept.–mid-Dec.), but don't expect much more than a color TV and a pool. You'll be surprised at the number and quality of amenities if you spend a few extra dollars.

If you're planning a vacation centered around Disney World, you'll need to choose between convenience and cost. Although Disney World has relatively few inexpensive lodgings, staying here means you won't need to drive; transportation within Disney World is free, quick, and efficient. You can leave the parks when they get crowded, return to your hotel for a nap or a swim, and head back to the parks in the evening when things are quieter. You can also make advance reservations at Epcot restaurants and save on entrance fees. Properties outside of Disney World, however, are usually less pricey, and many of them offer inexpensive shuttles to the parks. Off Disney property, the two main roadways flanking the parks—International Drive to the north and U.S. 192 to the south—have numerous affordable accommodations.

Price categories for double occupancy, excluding 9% tax, are Expensive, over $125; Moderate, $75–$125; and Inexpensive, under $75.

DISNEY-OWNED HOTELS These hotels may be booked through the **Walt Disney World Central Reservations Office** (Box 10100, Suite 300, Lake Buena Vista 32830, tel. 407/934– 7639). Reservations should be made several months in advance, and for the best rooms, during high season, a year in advance. You should also check with **Delta Airlines** (tel. 800/221–1212), which has many rooms allotted to its travel packages. Several hotels and attractions offer discounts of up to 40% from September to mid-December. For land packages, including admission tickets, car rentals, and hotels, contact **Walt Disney Travel Company** (1675 Buena Vista Dr., Lake Buena Vista 32830, tel. 407/828–3255). Land-air packages can be booked through **Disney Reservation Service** (tel. 800/828– 0228). Following are the best bargains among the Disney-owned hotels.

All-Star Resorts. This huge complex, which contains two hotels—All-Star Music Resort and the All-Star Sports Resort—is the most inexpensive on Disney property. It's a bit out of the way from many of the attractions, except Blizzard Beach, but there's continuous free bus service to wherever in the World you want to go. Kids love its oversize replicas of musical instruments and sports equipment. *3,840 rooms. Food courts, shops, 4 pools. AE, MC, V. Inexpensive–Moderate.*

Caribbean Beach Resort. This cheerful, tropical-theme property has five two-story buildings on a 42-acre lake with access to foot and bike paths for exercise. *2,112 rooms. Counter-service restaurants, shops, pools, baby-sitting, marina. AE, MC, V. Moderate.*

Disney's Village Resort. This is a good value if you plan to visit with a larger group; a one-bedroom villa with a study, for instance, has a fully equipped kitchen and sleeps five. *39 1-bedroom and 151 2-bedroom villas, 316 Club Suites, 60 3-bedroom villas, 4 Grand Vista Suites. Dining area, 5 pools, biking, 3 tennis courts. AE, MC, V. Expensive.*

Dixie Landings Resort. Connected to Port Orleans Resort by winding paths, this resort has four plantation structures surrounded by formal gardens. *2,048 rooms. 2 dining areas, shops, 3 pools. AE, MC, V. Moderate.*

Fort Wilderness. Campers stay amid 730 acres of woodland and streams along Bay Lake at the northern edge of Disney World. You can choose between a campsite with electrical outlets and a picnic table or a trailer home with a kitchen, full bath, color TV, telephone, and daily housekeeping. *407 trailers; 785 campsites. 2 pools, 2 tennis courts, biking and jogging paths, fishing, marina, horseback riding. AE, MC, V. Trailers: Expensive; campsites: Inexpensive.*

Port Orleans Resort. With cobblestone streets, courtyards, and intricate railings, this hotel reminds you of the French Quarter in New Orleans. *1,008 rooms. 2 dining areas, shops, 3 pools, playground, arcades. AE, MC, V. Moderate.*

HOTEL PLAZA This area on Disney property consists of seven independently owned hotels that offer free transportation, use of the golf and tennis facilities, and advance Epcot restaurant reservations. The following hotels offer good deals for the price:

Buena Vista Palace. This upscale property features comfortable all-suite accommodations. *Hotel Plaza Blvd., Lake Buena Vista 32830, tel. 407/827–2727 or 800/327–2990. 1,028 rooms and suites. 9 restaurants and lounges, 3 pools, health club, game room, summer kid's program. AE, DC, MC, V. Moderate–Expensive.*

Grosvenor Resort. This attractive hotel, renovated in British Colonial style, has brightly decorated rooms and recreational facilities geared toward the active life. *1850 Hotel Plaza Blvd., Lake Buena Vista 32830, tel. 407/828–4444 or 800/624–4109. 629 rooms. 2 pools, 2 tennis courts. AE, DC, MC, V. Moderate.*

INTERNATIONAL DRIVE **Days Inn East of Universal Studios.** This is the best bargain next to Universal Studios Florida, with clean rooms and an on-site, 24-hour restaurant.

5827 Caravan Ct., Orlando 32819, tel. 407/351–3800. 262 rooms. Pool, restaurant, in-room safes. AE, D, MC, V. Inexpensive.

Days Inn Orlando Lakeside. The motel fronts busy Sand Lake Road, just off I–4 and International Drive, but the other side is on tranquil Spring Lake, providing ample recreation. *7335 Sand Lake Rd., Orlando 32819, tel. 407/351–1900 or 800/777–3297. 695 rooms. 3 pools, beach, shuttle service. AE, D, MC, V. Inexpensive.*

Embassy Suites International Drive South. This all-suite hotel has a southern flavor with hanging lamps, ceiling fans, tropical gardens, and complimentary breakfasts. *8978 International Dr., Orlando 32819, tel. 407/352–1400 or 800/433–7275. 245 suites. Pool, whirlpool, sauna, room refrigerators and microwaves. AE, DC, MC, V. Moderate.*

Gateway Inn. This property offers helpful service, affordable rooms, and a free shuttle to major attractions. *7050 Kirkman Rd., Orlando 32819, tel. 407/351–2000 or 800/327–3808; in FL, 800/432–1179; fax 407/363–1835. 354 rooms. Restaurant, 2 pools, playground, pets allowed. AE, D, MC, V. Inexpensive.*

Orlando Heritage Inn. If you're looking for charm, try this Victorian-style inn, complete with reproduction turn-of-the-century furnishings, French windows and brass lamps, and genuine 19th-century antiques. *9861 International Dr., Orlando 32819, tel. 407/352–0008 or 800/447–1890. 150 rooms. Pool, shuttle. AE, D, MC, V. Moderate.*

Radisson Barcelo Hotel. The best rooms face the pool at this large, modern hotel with outstanding athletic facilities, including an Olympic-size pool. *8444 International Dr., Orlando 33819, tel. 407/345–0505 or 800/333–3333. 300 rooms. 2 pools, Nautilus center, tennis, racquetball, aerobics classes, access to golf country club. AE, DC, MC, V. Moderate.*

U.S. 192 **HoJo Inn Main Gate East.** Clean, courteous, and convenient to sights, this simple motel is for people who don't demand many extras other than a color TV and a heated pool. *6051 W. Irlo Bronson Memorial Hwy., Kissimmee 34746, tel. 407/ 396–1748 or 800/288–4678. 367 rooms. Pool, game room. AE, D, MC, V. Inexpensive.*

Radisson Inn Maingate. Right near Disney World's main entrance, this sleek, modern building has cheerful rooms and large bathrooms. *7501 W. Irlo Bronson Memorial Hwy., Kissimmee 34746, tel. 407/396–1400 or 800/ 333–3333. 580 rooms. Restaurant, deli, pool with whirlpool and bar, game room, 2 tennis courts, jogging trail. AE, DC, MC, V. Moderate.*

Ramada Resort Maingate at the Parkway. The hotel offers large rooms and lushly landscaped grounds. *2900 Parkway Blvd., Kissimmee 34746, tel. 407/396–7000, 800/ 634–4774, or 800/272–6232. 716 rooms. Restaurants, deli, shops, swimming pool, 3 tennis courts, jogging. AE, DC, MC, V. Moderate.*

Residence Inn by Marriott. This property facing a lake consists of a row of four-unit town houses with full kitchens, private entrances, and complimentary Continental breakfast and grocery-shopping service. *4786 W. Irlo Bronson Memorial Hwy., Kissimmee 34746, tel. 407/396–2056 or 800/468–3027; in FL, 800/648–7408. 160 units. Pool, water sports, fishing, picnic area. AE, DC, MC, V. Moderate–Expensive.*

Sheraton Lakeside Inn. This 25-acre lakeside complex consists of 15 two-story buildings that offer many recreational activities, including free paddleboats. *7769 W. Irlo Bronson Memorial Hwy., Kissimmee 34746, tel. 407/239–7919 or 800/848–0801. 653 rooms. 3 pools, 2 children's pools, 4 tennis courts, miniature golf, game rooms, playground. AE, DC, MC, V. Moderate.*

Wilson World. Rooms are larger than those in most U.S. 192 motels, and there's a sandy beach and a lake in the back of the property. *7491 W. Irlo Bronson Memorial Hwy., Kissimmee 34746, tel. 407/396–6000 or 800/669– 6753. 442 rooms. Restaurant, 2 pools. AE, D, MC, V. Moderate.*

MOTELS

MODERATE **Clarion Plaza Hotel** (9700 International Dr., Orlando 32819, tel. 407/352– 9700 or 800/366–9700). 810 rooms; 2 restaurants, pool. **Comfort Inn at Lake Buena Vista** (8442 Palm Pkwy., Lake Buena Vista 32830, tel. 407/239–7300 or 800/999–7300). 640 rooms; restaurant, 2 pools, shuttle. **Courtyard by Marriott Airport** (7155 Frontage Rd., Orlando 32812, tel. 407/240–7200). 149 rooms; pool, airport bus. **Holiday Inn Sunspree Resort Lake Buena Vista** (13351 Rte. 535, Lake Buena Vista 32830, tel. 407/239– 4500 or 800/465–4329). 507 rooms; pool, shuttle. **Travelodge Maingate West** (7785 W. Irlo Bronson Memorial Hwy., Kissimmee 34746, tel. 407/396–1828 or 800/322–3056). 199 rooms; restaurant, pool, shuttle.

INEXPENSIVE **Cedar Lakeside Inn** (4960 W. Irlo Bronson Memorial Hwy., Kissimmee 34741, tel. 407/396–1376 or 800/327–0072). 200 rooms; beach, pool, whirlpool, some kitchenettes. **Quality Inn International** (7600 International Dr., Orlando 32819, tel. 407/ 351–1600 or 800/825–7600). 787 rooms; restaurant, pets allowed. **Quality Inn Plaza International** (9000 International Dr., Orlando 32819, tel. 407/345–8585 or 800/999– 8585). 1,020 rooms; 3 pools.

DINING

When you visit central Florida, do as the locals do: Put on casual cotton clothes and find a place serving fresh seafood dishes, such as stone crabs, Apalachicola oysters, Florida lobsters, conch chowder, or pompano (a mild white fish). In recent years, a number of small, good ethnic restaurants have opened in the area. Because the area caters to numerous cost-conscious tourists, many restaurants offer early-bird specials before 6 PM. Price categories per person, excluding 6% tax, service, and drinks, are Moderate, $20–$30, and Inexpensive, under $20.

DISNEY-MGM STUDIOS **Commissary.** This counter-service restaurant features low-fat foods, such as marinated chicken-breast sandwiches served with cucumber salad or fresh fruit or stir-fried chicken and vegetables with rice and nuts. *AE, MC, V. Inexpensive.*

50's Prime Time Cafe. Club sandwiches, turkey burgers, and mashed potatoes are served on Fiesta Ware or old-time TV dinner trays as old TV shows are telecast around the restaurant. Guests at a Disney-owned hotel can make reservations one to two days in advance (tel. 407/828–4000), or make reservations as soon as you enter the park. *AE, MC, V. Moderate.*

Sunset Ranch Market. This outdoor eatery features hot dogs and fresh fruit. *No credit cards. Inexpensive.*

EPCOT CENTER World Showcase in Epcot Center offers some of the finest dining in the entire Orlando area. The top-of-the-line places, such as those in the French, Italian, and Japanese pavilions, can be pricey; you can often save money by having lunch here and grabbing dinner elsewhere. Guests at a Disney-owned hotel or at Hotel Plaza can make reservations the day before (tel. 407/ 828–4000). Other visitors will need to go to Epcot when it opens and go straight to a WorldKey computer to make reservations.

Biergarten. Visitors dine on hearty German fare at long communal tables and are served by waitresses in typical Bavarian garb while an oompah band plays. *AE, MC, V. Moderate.*

Marrakesh. Try the national dish of Morocco, couscous, served with garden vegetables, as belly dancers and a three-piece Moroccan band set the mood. *AE, MC, V. Moderate.*

Mitsukoshi. At the Japanese pavilion, you can sample meat and fish cooked on a grill or try tempura shrimp at the Tempura Kiku dining room, with a great view of the lagoon. *AE, MC, V. Moderate.*

Restaurant Akershus. Norway's tradition of seafood and cold-meat dishes is highlighted at the Norway pavilion restaurant's *koldtbord*, or Norwegian buffet. *AE, MC, V. Moderate.*

Rose and Crown. This friendly British offering, on the lagoon, serves simple pub fare such as fish-and-chips. *AE, MC, V. Moderate.*

San Angel Inn. This lush tropical restaurant serves unusual Mexican specialties. *AE, MC, V. Moderate.*

MAGIC KINGDOM Two good, inexpensive choices in the Magic Kingdom are **Pinocchio's Village House** in Fantasyland and **Aunty Gravity's** in Tomorrowland. Both large restaurants are only a tad better than a fast-food joint, but they offer some healthful choices, such as salads, soups, and turkey burgers.

ORLANDO AREA **Basil's.** Come here for quickly prepared innovative American cuisine, including chicken and seafood entrées, and admire the artful desserts. *1009 W. Irlo Bronson Memorial Hwy., Kissimmee, tel. 407/846–1116. AE, MC, V. Moderate.*

Beeline Diner. A '50s diner in the Peabody Hotel, open 24 hours, offers old tunes on the jukebox and salads, sandwiches, and griddle foods. *9801 International Dr., Orlando, tel. 407/352–4000. AE, DC, MC, V. Moderate.*

Border Cantina. This pink-walled Tex-Mex on trendy Park Avenue serves scrumptious chicken fajitas. *329 S. Park Ave., Winter Park, tel. 407/740–7227. AE, MC, V. Inexpensive.*

Donato's Italian Market. Large, friendly, and informal, this place has better-than-average pizza, vegetable calzone, and large salads. *5159 International Dr., tel. 407/363–5959. AE, MC, V. Inexpensive.*

Le Coq au Vin. The atmosphere here is mobile-home-modern, but the traditional French cuisine is first-class and fairly priced. House specialties include fresh rainbow trout, roast Long Island duck with green peppercorns, and homemade chicken-liver pâté. *4800 S. Orange Ave., Orlando, tel. 407/851–6980. AE, DC, MC, V. Moderate.*

Ming Court. This elegant Chinese restaurant overlooking a pond and floating gardens serves excellent jumbo shrimp in lobster sauce; also try the grilled chicken stuffed with nuts. *9188 International Dr., Orlando, tel. 407/351–9988. AE, DC, MC, V. Moderate.*

Pebbles. A local eatery with an eclectic menu ranging from light bites to rack of lamb. Salads and soups are particularly good, as are the daily specials. *17 W. Church St., Orlando, tel. 407/839–0892; The Crossroads, Lake Buena Vista, tel. 407/827–1111; 25416 Aloma Ave., Winter Park, tel. 407/678–7001. AE, MC, V. Moderate.*

Phoenician. Inexperienced with Middle Eastern food? The best bet is to order a tableful of appetizers (*meza*) and sample as many as possible. Otherwise try the hummus, *baba ghanouj,* or the *lebneh* dishes. *7600 Dr. Phillips Blvd. in the Marketplace, Orlando, tel. 407/345–1001. AE, MC, V. Inexpensive.*

Pizzeria Uno. It's a chain, but when the pizza tastes this good, you can't hold that against it. *5 Church St., Orlando, tel. 407/839–1800; The Crossroads, Lake Buena Vista, tel. 407/827–1212. AE, MC, V. Inexpensive.*

Ran-Getsu. A creative menu distinguishes this Japanese restaurant, complete with carp-filled pond and decorative gardens, and even a staple like sukiyaki is special. *8400 International Dr., Orlando, tel. 407/345–0044. AE, MC, V. Moderate.*

Rolando's. Cuban cuisine is a Florida staple, and the drive away from tourist-oriented areas is worth it to try Rolando's excellent, spicy black-bean soup and chicken with yellow rice. *870 E. State Rd. 436, Casselberry, tel. 407/767–9677. MC, V. Inexpensive.*

SHOPPING

WALT DISNEY WORLD **Disney–MGM:** Sid Cahuenga's One-of-a-Kind at the main entrance carries movie posters, autographed pictures, and original costumes once worn by film stars. Animation Gallery, at the end of the Animation Tour, sells original Disney animation cels, books, and more. **Epcot:** You can do one-stop souvenir shopping at Future World's Centorium. **Magic Kingdom:** Monogrammed mouse ears can be found at The Chapeau on Main Street or at The Mad Hatter in Fantasyland, which is usually less crowded. The Frontier Trading Post sells western-style gifts.

MALLS **Altamonte Mall** is ½ mile east of I–4 on Route 436 (451 Altamonte Ave., Altamonte Springs, tel. 407/830–4400). **Florida Mall** is 4½ miles east of I–4 and International Dr. (8001 S. Orange Blossom Trail, Orlando, tel. 407/851–6255).

SHOPPING VILLAGES **Church Street Exchange** (Church Street Station, 129 W. Church St., tel. 407/422–2434) is a Victorian-theme "festival marketplace" filled with more than 50 specialty shops. **Disney Village Marketplace** (Lake Buena Vista, tel. 407/282–3058) features Mickey's Character Shop, the world's largest Disney merchandise store, and shops selling art, fashions, and crafts. **The Marketplace** (7600 Dr. Phillips Blvd., Orlando, tel. 407/345–8668) has a 24-hour Gooding's supermarket, pharmacy, post office, and one-hour film processor. **Mercado Mediterranean Village** (8445 International Dr., tel. 407/345–9337) houses more than 50 gift shops and an international food court. **Old Town** (5770 Irlo Bronson Memorial Hwy., Kissimmee, tel. 407/396–4888), east of I–4, has 70 shops, an Elvis Presley museum, an antique carousel, and an ice-cream parlor. **Park Avenue** in Winter Park is an upscale shopping district with restaurants, bookshops, galleries, and boutiques.

OUTDOOR ACTIVITIES

BEACHES The closest beaches are those at Cocoa Beach about 50 minutes away; about 100 miles of sandy beaches are accessible to the public between Ormond Beach and Sebastian Inlet. **Canaveral National Seashore** (tel. 407/867–2805), just east of New Smyrna Beach on Route A1A, is a 57,000-acre park that is home to more than 250 kinds of birds and animals. A self-guided hiking trail leads to the top of an Indian shell midden at Turtle Mound, where picnic tables are available. Free brochures and maps are available at the Visitor Center on Route A1A.

BIKING The most scenic bike riding in Orlando is on Disney World property, along roads that take you past forests, lakes, golf courses, and Disney's wooded resort villas and campgrounds. Bikes are available for rent at **Caribbean Beach Resort** (tel. 407/934–3400), **Fort Wilderness Bike Barn** (tel. 407/824–2742), and **Walt Disney World Village Villa Center** (tel. 407/827–1100).

FISHING Fort Wilderness Campground (tel. 407/824–2900) in Disney World is the starting point for fishing trips, with a boat, equipment, and a guide for up to five anglers.

GOLF Golfpac (417 Whooping Loop, Altamonte Springs, tel. 407/260–2288) packages golf vacations and prearranges tee times at more than 30 courses around Orlando. Walt Disney World's championship courses—the site of a PGA tournament in the fall—are among the busiest and most expensive in the region. At public courses, you pay for what you get. Outside Disney World, try **Hunter's Creek Golf Course** (14401 Sports Club Way, tel. 407/240–4653) and **MetroWest Country Club** (2100 S. Hiawassee Rd., tel. 407/297–0052).

HORSEBACK RIDING Grand Cypress Equestrian Center (tel. 407/239–4608) offers private lessons, with novice and advanced trails. **Fort Wilderness Campground Resort** (tel. 407/824–2832) in Disney World offers tame trail rides through backwoods and along lakesides.

TENNIS At Walt Disney World, courts are free for guests, but you must make reservations, except at Fort Wilderness. You'll find courts at **Disney Inn** (tel. 407/824–1469), the **Village Clubhouse** (tel. 407/828–3741), **Fort Wilderness Campground** (tel. 407/824–3578), **Contemporary Resort** (tel. 407/824–3578), **Grand Floridian** (tel. 407/824–2438), **Yacht and Beach Club** (tel. 407/934–7000), **Swan** (tel. 407/934–3000), and **Dolphin** (tel. 407/934–4000). Also try **Orange Lake Country Club** (8505 west U.S. 192, Kissimmee, tel. 407/239–2255) and **Orlando Tennis Center** (649 W. Livingston St., tel. 407/246–2162).

WALKING/JOGGING Walt Disney World has several scenic walking and jogging trails.

Pick up trail maps at any Disney resort. **Fort Wilderness** (tel. 407/824–2900) has a 2.3-mile course with fresh air and woods, and **Caribbean Beach Resort** has a ¼-mile trail. Park Avenue in Winter Park is a mile walk of shops, museums, and restaurants, and there's an hour-long walk around Lake Eola in downtown Orlando.

WATER SPORTS At Walt Disney World, marinas at Caribbean Beach Resort, Contemporary Resort, Fort Wilderness, Polynesian Village, Grand Floridian, Disney's Yacht and Beach Club, Port Orleans, and Disney World Shopping Village rent Sunfish, catamarans, motorpowered pontoon boats, pedal boats, and tiny two-passenger water sprites. Polynesian Village marina and Fort Wilderness rent canoes. For waterskiing reservations, call 407/824–1000. **Orange Lake Water Sports** (8505 W. U.S. Hwy. 192, Kissimmee, tel. 407/239–4444) has waterskiing and waverunners on a private lake next to Disney World.

ENTERTAINMENT

WALT DISNEY WORLD Evening entertainment includes the **Polynesian Revue** (Polynesian Village Resort, tel. 407/934–7639), **Hoop-Dee-Doo Revue** (Fort Wilderness Resort, tel. 407/934–7639) with a western messhall setting; and **Pleasure Island** (tel. 407/934–7781), an entertainment complex with nightclubs, restaurants, shopping, 10 movie theaters, and fireworks. Don't miss Epcot's grand finale, **IllumiNations,** a brilliant laser and fireworks show held every night along the shores of the lagoon before the park closes.

Pleasure Island. Six clubs with everything from hot rock and cool country to crazed comedy and astounding adventure. "New Year's Eve" fireworks go off every night. *Tel. 407/824–4321. Admission charged.*

ORLANDO AREA Church Street Station (129 W. Church St., Orlando, tel. 407/422–2434; admission charged) is a very popular downtown entertainment complex, with old-fashioned saloons, turn-of-the-century memorabilia, dance halls, dining rooms, and shopping arcades.

Dinner Shows: Arabian Nights (6225 W. Irlo Bronson Memorial Hwy., Kissimmee, tel. 407/239–9223 or 800/553–6116) has performing horses. **Wild Bill's Wild West Dinner Show** in Fort Liberty (5260 W. Irlo Bronson Memorial Hwy., Kissimmee, tel. 407/351–5151 or 800/883–8181) has a country-western motif. **King Henry's Feast** (8984 International Dr., Orlando, tel. 407/351–5151 or 800/883–8181) is a 16th-century celebration. **Capone's Dinner and Show** (4740 W. Irlo Bronson Memorial Hwy. Kissimmee, tel. 407/397–2378) is a return to the days of gangland Chicago. Dinner is an unlimited buffet that's heavy on the pasta. **Mark Two** (3376 Edgewater Dr., Orlando, tel. 407/843–6275 or 800/726–6275) is a dinner theater producing live Broadway shows. **Mardi Gras** (8445 International Dr., Orlando, tel. 407/351–5151 or 800/883–8181) is a New Orleans–style cabaret.

Spectator Sports: Orlando Magic play basketball October–April at the Orlando Arena (1 Magic Pl., Orlando, tel. 407/839–3900). During spring training in March, you can watch baseball's **Houston Astros** at Osceola County Stadium (Kissimmee, tel. 407/933–5500), and the **Kansas City Royals** play at Baseball City (less than 30 minutes from Disney World, at the intersection of I–4 and U.S. 27, tel. 813/424–2424).

Theater: Bob Carr Performing Arts Centre (401 Livingston St., Orlando, tel. 407/849–2020) presents performances of ballet, modern dance, classical music, opera, and theater.

Washington, D.C.

Updated by Bruce Walker

ecause many of us spent our childhoods in dreary classrooms learning about checks and balances and the three branches of the federal government, it's easy to think of Washington as little more than a civics book come to life. But that would be missing the rest of the curriculum. Washington is a science book, too, home to the Smithsonian Institution and 14 of its world-class museums. It's a coffee-table art book, with galleries holding some of the most beloved and historic works from America and beyond. And when the bell rings for recess, there's still plenty to do, from sampling creative ethnic cuisine in this melting-pot capital to frolicking on the lush banks of the Potomac.

And guess what? You own the school. If you mutter every April 15 when signing your name to an income-tax check, then you should come to town to see your tax dollars at work. Washington—from the organized free-for-all called Congress to the peaceful and contemplative Lincoln Memorial—truly is every American's city.

Don't let the politicians spoil Washington for you. Even native Washingtonians—and don't be fooled, there is such a thing—get fed up with their antics from time to time. But remember, those responsible for political high jinks don't come *from* Washington, they come *to* Washington. And once you visit, you'll see why.

ESSENTIAL INFORMATION

WHEN TO GO Washington was once a hardship posting for diplomats from certain European countries. And indeed the city's hot, humid summers can seem malarial. The average maximum temperature in August is 86°, but from June to September, heat waves can push the thermometer above 95°. Winters are less extreme (January's average high is 47°), but one or two snowstorms a year seem to paralyze the city. Spring and fall, however, are delightful.

You'll find cheaper hotel rates in winter and during the long summer recess (check with your local legislative office; the recess takes place at a different time each summer). Fall is when you'll find the city's museums and galleries the least crowded.

FESTIVALS AND SEASONAL EVENTS **Feb.:** Black History Month is celebrated at sites around the city. **Late Mar.–early Apr.:** The National Cherry Blossom Festival celebrates the Japanese cherry trees that ring the Tidal Basin (though the festival almost never coincides with the trees' peak bloom). **Late June–early July:** The Festival of American Folklife on the Mall features music, food, and arts and crafts of various cultures. **July 4:** The Fourth of July offers a band concert and fireworks on the Mall. **Mid-Dec.:** The National Christmas Tree Lighting and Pageant starts the holiday season, as the president lights the tree.

BARGAINS Washington is not cheap; however, many of its best-known sights are. All the memorials in the city, from the Jefferson to the Vietnam Veterans, are free of charge.

If you know well ahead of time that you'd like to visit some of Washington's federal sites, contact your senator or representative and get the special free tickets that allow you to wait in lines slightly shorter than

those many of your fellow citizens will be standing in. Visitors with disabilities are entitled to go to the head of all lines when touring federal buildings and monuments.

The National Building Museum hosts free lunchtime concerts the fourth Wednesday of the month. There are free classical concerts in the National Gallery of Art West Building on Sunday evenings from October to June. The Sylvan Theater on the Washington Monument grounds is the site of military concerts from mid-June to August. You can get obstructed-view tickets to National Symphony Orchestra performances in the Kennedy Center Concert Hall for $6.

Half-price, day-of-performance theater tickets are available at TicketPlace (Lisner Auditorium, 730 21st St. NW, tel. 202/842–5387). The National Theatre (1321 Pennsylvania Ave. NW, tel. 202/783–3372) hosts a wide-ranging free-performance series each Monday night during much of the year.

TOURIST OFFICES Washington, D.C., Convention & Visitors Association (1212 New York Ave. NW, Washington, DC 20005, tel. 202/789–7000). **Dial-A-Park** (tel. 202/619–7275) is a recording of events at Park Service attractions around Washington.

EMERGENCIES Police, fire, and ambulance: Dial 911. **Hospitals:** There's an emergency room at George Washington University Hospital (901 23rd St. NW, tel. 202/994–3211). **Doctors and Dentists:** Prologue (tel. 202/362–8677) runs a physician and dentist referral. The DC Dental Society (tel. 202/547–7615) refers dentists. **Pharmacies:** CVS Pharmacy operates two 24-hour pharmacies (14th St. and Thomas Circle NW, tel. 202/628–0720; 7 Dupont Circle NW, tel. 202/785–1466).

ARRIVING AND DEPARTING

BY PLANE Three airports serve the Washington area: **National Airport** (tel. 703/419–8000), 4 miles south of downtown in Virginia; **Dulles International Airport** (tel. 703/661–2700), 26 miles west of the city; and **Baltimore–Washington International**

Airport (BWI; tel. 410/859–7100), about 30 miles northeast of Washington in Maryland.

From the Airport by Bus: National and Dulles airports are served by the buses of Washington Flyer (tel. 703/685–1400). Buses stop at numerous hotels as well as at a downtown terminal at 1517 K Street Northwest. The service runs daily from around 5:30 AM to 9:30 PM, with buses leaving roughly every half hour. The ride from National to downtown takes 20 minutes and costs around $10. From Dulles, it's less than $20 for the hour-long ride. The BWI SuperShuttle (tel. 800/809–7080) serves BWI with buses that leave roughly every hour from 6 AM to midnight for the 1517 K Street Northwest terminal with a stop in Greenbelt, Maryland. The hour-long ride costs about $15.

From the Airport by Subway: If you are arriving at Washington National Airport, don't have much to carry, and are staying at a hotel near a subway stop, it makes sense to take the Metro downtown. The ride takes about 20 minutes and costs between $1 and $1.50, depending on the time of day.

From the Airport by Train: Free shuttle bus service is provided between BWI airport terminals and the airport's train station, where Amtrak (tel. 800/872–7245) and Maryland Rail Commuter Service (MARC; tel. 800/325–7245) trains stop. Trains depart BWI for Washington's Union Station from around 6 AM to midnight—but call for details. The cost for the 40-minute ride is $10 on an Amtrak train, $5 on a MARC train. MARC trains run weekdays only from 5:30 AM to 8:30 PM.

From the Airport by Taxi: Taxis queue in front of the terminals at all three airports. If you're traveling alone, expect to pay about $15 to get from National Airport to downtown; from Dulles, $45; from BWI, $50. Big D.C. cab companies include **Diamond** (tel. 202/387–6200) and **Capitol** (tel. 202/546–2400).

BY CAR I–95 runs north and south and skirts Washington as part of the Beltway, the six- to eight-lane highway that encircles the city. Major routes for entering the city include I–395 from the south to the 14th Street Bridge and 14th Street; I–270 from the northwest to I–495 and Connecticut Avenue or 16th Street into the city; and I–66 from the southwest across the Theodore Roosevelt Bridge to Constitution Avenue. (*Note:* I–66 has weekday rush-hour high-occupancy vehicle [HOV] restrictions. From 6:30 to 9 AM, cars traveling eastbound inside the Beltway must have at least three people in them. A similar restriction applies westbound from 4 to 6:30 PM.) A more scenic route is joining the George Washington Parkway off I–495 in Virginia and following it east along the Potomac and then across the Arlington Memorial Bridge and past the Lincoln Memorial.

BY TRAIN More than 80 trains a day arrive at **Washington's Union Station** (50 Massachusetts Ave. NE, tel. 800/872–7245).

BY BUS Washington is a major terminal for **Greyhound Lines** (1005 1st St. NE, tel. 800/231–2222 or 202/289–5160).

GETTING AROUND

The District of Columbia is arranged, said Pierre L'Enfant, the Frenchman who designed it in 1791, "like a chessboard overlaid with a wagon wheel." Streets run north–south and east–west in a grid pattern; avenues—most named after states—run diagonally, connecting the various traffic circles scattered throughout the city. The District is divided into four sections: northwest, northeast, southwest, and southeast; the Capitol Building serves as the center of the north–south and east–west axes. North Capitol and South Capitol streets divide the city into east and west; the Mall and East Capitol Street divide the city into north and south. Streets that run north to south are numbered; those that extend east to west are lettered (until the letters run out, at which point alphabetical names are used: Adams, Belmont, and so forth). Make sure you have a destination's complete address, including quadrant (there are *four* 4th and D intersections in Washington: one each in Northwest, Northeast, Southwest, and Southeast). Bring a good map, too.

BY BUS OR SUBWAY Subway trains run weekdays 5:30 AM–midnight, weekends 8 AM–midnight. The base price is a bit more than $1, but your actual fare depends on the time of day and distance traveled. You can buy your ticket at the computerized Farecard machines in each station. They take change as well as crisp bills up to twenties. A pass is available that gives you one day of unlimited subway travel all day on weekends and holidays (except July 4), and after 9:30 AM on weekdays. Passes are available at Metro Sales Outlets (including the Metro Center station) and at many hotels.

Transfers, good for two hours, are available on buses and in Metro stations. Bus-to-bus transfers are accepted at designated Metrobus transfer points. Rail-to-bus transfers must be picked up before boarding the train. There may be a transfer charge when boarding the bus.

For general subway and bus travel information, call 202/637–7000. A helpful brochure—"All about the Metro System"—is available by calling the travel information number or writing to **Office of Marketing, WMATA** (600 5th St. NW, Room 6-G, Washington, DC 20001).

BY CAR A car can be a drawback in Washington. Traffic is horrendous, especially at rush hours, and driving is confusing, with many lanes and some entire streets changing direction suddenly at different times of day. Parking is also an adventure: at a premium and expensive (private lots downtown charge as much as $4 an hour and up to $13 a day). Since its major attractions—especially those on the Mall—are within easy walking distance of one another, see the city on foot and take the Metro to out-of-town sights such as Old Town Alexandria and Arlington National Cemetery.

If you do drive downtown, note that there is free, two-hour parking around the Mall on Madison and Jefferson drives. You can park free—in some spots all day—in parking

areas south of the Lincoln Memorial on Ohio Drive and West Basin Drive in West Potomac Park and off Ohio Drive near the Jefferson Memorial. Both areas fill quickly.

Some peculiar Washington traffic idiosyncrasies: Traffic lights often hang down at the sides of intersections, not directly above them. Cars entering a traffic circle must yield to those already in it.

BY TAXI Taxis in the District are not metered, operating instead on a curious zone system. There is a basic single rate for traveling within one zone (around $3.50), with additional charges of $1–$2 applied for each of the following: additional passengers; traveling during the 4–6:30 PM rush hour; calling for a radio-dispatched cab; and/or having bulky suitcases or requiring personal services. A typical nonrush-hour ride for two from, say, Union Station to the National Gallery of Art, would be about $4.50, excluding tip.

REST STOPS All Smithsonian Institution museums have free, clean, and safe public rest rooms. Metro stations don't have any.

GUIDED TOURS **Tourmobile** (tel. 202/554–7950) buses provide several narrated tours. One stops at 18 historic sites and museums between the Capitol and Arlington National Cemetery, arriving at each site every 20 minutes. Other tours go to Mount Vernon or the Frederick Douglass Home. The 90-minute, 18-stop **Old Town Trolley tour** (tel. 301/985–3020) takes in the main downtown sights and also ventures into Georgetown and Upper Northwest. Passengers on both tours can get on and off as often as they like. The **Gray Line Tour** (tel. 301/386–8300) offers a number of tours ranging from four hours (the Washington tour) to two days long (trips to nearby sites like Colonial Williamsburg); the four-hour tour of Washington, Embassy Row, and Arlington National Cemetery leaves Union Station at 8:30 AM and 2 PM.

The **Smithsonian's Associate Program** (tel. 202/357–3030) frequently sponsors weekend bus and walking tours of Washington's most interesting neighborhoods and sights. The

National Building Museum (tel. 202/272–2448) hosts tours with an architectural or construction bent. **Scandal Tours** (tel. 202/783–7212) snakes past locales like Gary Hart's Capitol Hill town house and, of course, the Watergate. "Datebook" in the *Washington Post*'s Thursday "Home" section often lists other tours.

EXPLORING

You can say you've "done" Washington if you've walked from the Capitol Building to the Lincoln Memorial and visited the museums and monuments in between. The Mall is the city's tourist core and it's the place most visitors head for first. Spend a few days sampling its many offerings, then venture beyond the federal enclave and see the other side of the city. The sections below outline the Mall's highlights. Sights farther afield follow.

MUSEUMS It would be easy to spend a week on the Mall, where nine of the Smithsonian museums are located, with other attractions nearby. Smithsonian museums are free, and are open seven days a week from 10 AM to 5:30 PM (some stay open later during the summer).

For help sorting out Mall exhibits and activities, stop at the Smithsonian Castle's high-tech information center, or in summer, visit the information kiosks along the Mall. *Smithsonian Castle: 1000 Jefferson Dr. SW, tel. 202/357–2700. Open daily. Admission free.*

Near the Smithsonian Castle, the **Freer** (Jefferson Dr. at 12th St. SW, tel. 202/357–4880) and the **Sackler Gallery** (1050 Independence Ave. SW, tel. 202/357–4880) display Asian art; the **National Museum of African Art** (950 Independence Ave. SW, tel. 202/357–4600) is the premiere museum in the country that is exclusively dedicated to artifacts from sub-Saharan Africa.

The **United States Holocaust Memorial Museum,** a block away from the Freer, opened in 1993. This museum's exhibits, public spaces, and architecture reflect and memorialize the tragedy, horror, and heroism that accompanied the Nazi's campaign of murder and genocide. The very moving displays unfold chronologically from 1933 to 1945. *100 Raoul Wallenberg Pl. SW, 20024, tel. 202/488–0400. Open daily. Admission free but ticket reservations required.*

The **National Air and Space Museum** is the most-visited museum in Washington, with displays that follow aviation from its early days (the plane the Wright brothers flew) to its heady days (Charles Lindbergh's *Spirit of St. Louis*) to its extraterrestrial days (a backup model of the Skylab and a piece of moon rock). Films dealing with flight are shown on an IMAX screen that is so big (five stories high!), it might make you airsick. *Jefferson Dr. and 6th St. SW, tel. 202/357–2700. Open daily. Admission free.*

The **National Gallery of Art,** directly north from the Air and Space Museum, is a beautiful John Russell Pope–designed building that contains one of the most impressive art collections in the world. The soaring, angular East Building—across 4th Street Northwest—generally shows more modern works and is home to changing exhibits. *Madison Dr. and 4th St. NW, tel. 202/737–4215. Open daily. Admission free.*

The **National Museum of Natural History** lies west of the National Gallery. This is a museum's museum, with more than 120 million objects in its research collection. Highlights include dinosaur bones, plant and animal specimens, a living coral reef, the Insect Zoo, and the supposedly cursed Hope Diamond. *Madison St. between 9th and 12th Sts. NW, tel. 202/357–2700. Open daily. Admission free.*

Before you move on, stop at the **U.S. Botanic Garden** for a restful pause from Washington's multitude of sights. The oldest botanical garden in America—its first greenhouse was constructed in 1842—is at the Mall's east end, near the Capitol. Permanent exhibits include New and Old World cacti and a Dinosaur Garden featuring prehistoric plants, and there are beautiful seasonal shows such as the annual

Christmas poinsettia display. *1st St. and Maryland Ave. SW, tel. 202/225–8333. Open daily. Admission free.*

GOVERNMENT BUILDINGS The governing of the country takes place in the massive, block-long buildings that surround the Mall. Many popular sites offer free daily tours, though in the summer you'll need to line up early for free tickets—usually at 8:30 AM. At federal buildings and monuments, people with disabilities are entitled to go to the head of the line.

The **United States Capitol** provides the best example of democracy in action that Washington has to offer. Its attractions aren't only political, though, since the building contains some of the finest art in town, including Constantino Brumidi's *Apotheosis of Washington* in the center of the Capitol dome and the lovingly restored Old Senate Chamber. To get a quick, free tour, join the line that forms in the Rotunda. To watch senators and representatives speechifying in their respective chambers, get a pass for the visitor's gallery from the offices of your senators or representative. However, committee meetings, where much of the real wrangling goes on, can be more interesting than watching the action in the main chambers; the *Washington Post*'s "Today in Congress" section lists what committees are in session and where. Ride the subway that runs beneath Capitol Hill's streets, connecting the Capitol Building to the various House and Senate office blocks where the committees meet. *East end of Mall, tel. 202/224–3121. Open daily. Admission free.*

From the Capitol walk west on Independence to 7th St., then continue four blocks north to the **National Archives.** The Declaration of Independence, Bill of Rights, and Constitution are displayed in the Archives in a bulletproof case and bathed in protective green light and helium gas. Researchers can study immigrant documents, military records, government papers, and millions of other items stored here, while casual visitors can enjoy changing exhibits related to American history. *Constitution Ave. between 7th and 9th Sts. NW, tel. 202/501–5000. Open daily. Admission free.*

Head west four blocks on Constitution Avenue and turn north on 15th Street for two blocks. On the left is the **White House,** home to every U.S. president since John Adams. Stop at the new White House Visitor Center in the north end of the Commerce Department at 1450 Pennsylvania Avenue Northwest for tour tickets. *1600 Pennsylvania Ave. NW, tel. 202/456–7041. Open Tues.–Sat. Admission free.*

MONUMENTS Washington's elegant, stately monuments are largely gathered at the western end of the Mall. The **Washington Monument** punctuates the city like a huge exclamation point. Finished in 1884, the 555-foot obelisk is the tallest masonry structure in the world. An elevator takes visitors to the top for a view unmatched in this largely horizontal city. The monument is open until 11:45 PM during the summer. Walk-down tours are available on weekends if you want to walk down the 898 steps. *Constitution Ave. at 15th St. NW, tel. 202/426–6840. Open daily. Admission free.*

South of the monument, on the banks of the Tidal Basin, is the John Russell Pope–designed **Jefferson Memorial,** dedicated in 1943. A 19-foot statue of the third president stands in a rotunda inscribed with his writings. *Tidal Basin, South bank, tel. 202/426–6821. Open daily. Admission free.*

A 10-minute walk away, across the Inlet Bridge and down West Basin and Ohio drives, is the **Lincoln Memorial,** considered by many to be the most inspiring monument in the city. The modified Greek temple, designed by Henry Bacon and completed in 1922, contains Daniel Chester French's peaceful statue of the 16th president. *West end of Mall, tel. 202/426–6895. Open daily. Admission free.*

Northeast of the Lincoln Memorial, nestled in the ground past a grove of trees, is what has fast become one of the most visited sights in Washington, the **Vietnam Veterans Memorial.** The gentle black granite *V* is inscribed with the names of the more than 58,000 Americans who died in the Vietnam War. *23rd St. and Constitution Ave. NW, tel. 202/634–1568. Open daily. Admission free.*

OTHER ATTRACTIONS Here are some of Washington's other top attractions, a few of which you can venture to on foot from the Mall. You'll want to take the Metro or drive to those that are farther away.

Arlington National Cemetery. More than 200,000 graves are spread out over these 612 acres of rolling Virginia hills, confiscated from Robert E. Lee during the Civil War. John F. Kennedy, Jacqueline Kennedy Onassis, and Robert Kennedy are buried here, as are the remains of the unknown soldiers from past American conflicts. *West end of Arlington Memorial Bridge, Arlington, VA, tel. 703/692–0931. Open daily. Admission free.*

Bureau of Engraving and Printing. A 40-minute tour takes visitors past presses that turn out some $40 million a day. Tours run from 9 until 2 (also 4–7:30 during summer). From April through September, tickets are required and are available starting at 8 AM. Sadly, there are no free samples. *14th and C Sts. SW, tel. 202/622–2000. Open daily. Admission free.*

Georgetown. Like Alexandria, Virginia, this community was an active port long before Washington became a city. Today, it's the capital's wealthiest neighborhood, a profusion of Georgian, Federal, and Victorian homes, and center of the best nightlife and shopping in town. The bustling crossroads is M Street and Wisconsin Avenue Northwest. To the south, below M Street, is the tranquil **C&O Canal** (hitch a National Park Service barge ride in warmer months at 1057 Thomas Jefferson St. NW, tel. 202/653–4190). **Fletcher's Boat House,** at the intersection of Reservoir and Canal roads, rents canoes and rowboats for use on the canal and the river (weather permitting). Fletcher's also sells fishing licenses and tackle. To the north, on N Street and above, are expensive homes and estates. One of the loveliest spots in town is **Dumbarton Oaks,** a sprawling property that has 10 acres

of enchanting gardens and a museum housing two galleries: one of pre-Columbian works, another of Byzantine art. *Dumbarton Oaks: 31st and R Sts. NW, tel. 202/338–8278 or 202/342–3200. Gardens open daily; admission charged. Museums open Tues.–Sun.; admission charged.*

Old Town Alexandria. The colorful past of this once bustling Virginia tobacco port is still alive in restored 18th- and 19th-century homes, churches, and taverns. Start your tour at **Ramsay House,** home of the town's first postmaster and lord mayor and today headquarters of the Alexandria Convention & Visitors Bureau (221 King St., tel. 703/838–4200; open daily). Other stops should include **Gadsby's Tavern Museum** (134 N. Royal St., tel. 703/838–4242; open Tues.–Sun.), a center of political and social life in the 18th century; the **boyhood home of Robert E. Lee** (607 Oronoco St., tel. 703/548–8454; open daily, closed Dec. 15–Feb. 1; admission charged), a fine example of a 19th-century Federal-style town house, filled with antique furnishings; and the **Torpedo Factory Arts Center** (105 N. Union St., tel. 703/838–4565; open daily; admission free), a former munitions plant that now serves as studio and gallery space for some 160 professional artists.

The **Phillips Collection.** In 1921, Duncan Phillips turned two rooms of his Georgian Revival home in the fashionable Dupont Circle neighborhood into an art gallery, in the process creating the first permanent museum of modern art in the country. On display are works by such modern masters as Braque, Cezanne, Klee, Matisse, and Renoir as well as by American modernists. *1600 21st St. NW, tel. 202/387–2151. Open Tues.–Sun. Admission charged.*

JUST FOR KIDS The Smithsonian museums put on a host of free children's programs. At the **Arts and Industries Building** (900 Jefferson Dr. SW, tel. 202/357–1500; admission charged), Discovery Theater presents performances for children. The **National Museum of Natural History** (*see above*) features an Insect Zoo, a Discovery Room full of touchable objects from nature, and, of course, the Dinosaur Hall with its fully reconstructed skeletons of prehistoric creatures of land and sea.

The **Capital Children's Museum** has everything to delight children, from bubble demonstrations to a crawl-through maze, plus an animation exhibit. *800 3rd St. NE, tel. 202/543–8600. Open daily. Admission charged.*

The charmingly dilapidated **Glen Echo Park,** in Maryland, features two children's programs hosted by **Adventure Theatre** (tel. 301/320–5331) and the **Puppet Company** (tel. 301/320–6668). *7300 MacArthur Blvd., Glen Echo, MD. Park admission charged.*

The **National Zoological Park** is home to more than 5,500 animals representing some 480 species, including the famously shy giant panda Hsing-Hsing, the only living panda in the United States. The ambitious Amazonia exhibit re-creates a rain-forest ecosystem. *3001 Connecticut Ave. NW, tel. 202/673–4800. Open daily. Admission free.*

The **Washington National Cathedral** offers stone-carving, stained-glass, and other medieval workshops on Saturday mornings all year. *Wisconsin and Massachusetts Aves., tel. 202/537–2934. Donation requested.*

HOTELS AND INNS

The nation's capital has been riding a hotel boom for more than a decade, with 49 new hotels built between 1976 and 1988 alone. That means visitors can expect variety and quantity. (It also means room rates are flexible.) Washington is small enough—and public transportation smooth enough—that you shouldn't feel "out of it" no matter where you stay. Still, Capitol Hill hotels will put you that much closer to federal attractions; hotels in Georgetown or near Dupont Circle will allow you a shorter walk home from restaurants and nightspots. December and January and the stifling months of July and August are when you'll find the best off-season rates.

To find reasonably priced accommodations in small guest houses and private homes, contact either of the following bed-and-breakfast services: **Bed & Breakfast Accommodations, Ltd.** (Box 12011, 20005, tel. 202/328–3510, fax 202/332–3885) or **Bed and Breakfast League/Sweet Dreams and Toast** (Box 9490, 20016, tel. 202/363–7767).

Price categories for double occupancy, excluding 13% room and occupancy ($1.50 a night) tax, are Moderate, $100–$130, and Inexpensive, under $100.

MODERATE **Bellevue Hotel.** Charming and comfortable, this small Capitol Hill hotel is close to Union Station and within six blocks of the Smithsonian museums on the Mall. *15 E St. NW, 20001, tel. 202/638–0900 or 800/327–6667, fax 202/638–5132. 140 rooms. Restaurant, bar, library, free overnight parking. AE, DC, MC, V.*

Georgetown Dutch Inn. Tucked away on a side street in Georgetown near the C&O Canal, this hotel has a homey ambience, guest rooms complete with sofa beds, and walk-in kitchens. *1075 Thomas Jefferson St. NW, 20007, tel. 202/337–0900 or 800/388–2410, fax 202/333–6526. 47 rooms. Access to health club, free parking. AE, DC, MC, V.*

Holiday Inn Capitol Hill. A good value for the budget-minded traveler, this hotel offers a Capitol Hill location with a view of the Capitol dome from some rooms. *415 New Jersey Ave. NW, 20001, tel. 202/638–1616 or 800/638–1116, fax 202/347–1813. 346 rooms. Restaurant, pool, parking. AE, DC, MC, V.*

Latham Hotel. A small, elegant hotel located right in the middle of fashionable Georgetown, the Latham also offers a critically acclaimed restaurant. *3000 M St. NW, 20007, tel. 202/726–5000 or 800/368–5922, fax 202/337–4250. 143 rooms. Restaurant, bar, outdoor pool, health-club access, valet parking. AE, DC, MC, V.*

Radisson Barceló Hotel. Near the bohemian Dupont Circle, this well-appointed hotel boasts some of the largest guest rooms in the city. *2121 P St. NW, 20037, tel. 202/293–3100 or 800/843–6664, fax 202/857–0134. 300* rooms. Restaurant, bar, pool, exercise room, sauna, valet parking. AE, D, DC, MC, V.

INEXPENSIVE **Channel Inn.** An informal waterside establishment south of the Mall on an inlet of the Potomac, the Channel Inn seems far from the city's hub but is convenient to the Waterfront Metro station. 650 Water St. SW, 20024, tel. 202/554–2400 or 800/368–5668, fax 202/863–1164. 100 rooms. Restaurant, bar, coffee shop, pool, free parking. AE, DC, MC, V.

Days Inn Connecticut Avenue. On a wide street away from downtown but near such northwest Washington attractions as the zoo and the cathedral, the Days Inn offers standard hotel furnishings. 4400 Connecticut Ave. NW, 20008, tel. 202/244–5600 or 800/ 952–3060, fax 202/244–6794 155 rooms. AE, D, DC, MC, V.

Hotel Tabard Inn. Located in a set of Victorian town houses on a quiet street not far from Dupont Circle and downtown, this hundred-year-old inn's antiques-filled rooms and gracious service make for an English-style experience. 1739 N St. NW, 20036, tel. 202/785–1277, fax 202/785–6173. 40 rooms, 25 with private bath. Restaurant, no TV in rooms. MC, V.

Howard Johnson Kennedy Center. This eight-story lodge offers reliability, large rooms with refrigerators, and a site near the Kennedy Center and Georgetown. 2601 Virginia Ave. NW, 20037, tel. 202/965–2700 or 800/654–2000, fax 202/965–2700, ext. 7910. 192 rooms. Restaurant, rooftop pool, laundry, valet, free parking for cars (no vans). AE, DC, MC, V.

Kalorama Guest House. Reminiscent of Grandma's house, this quaint, Victorian town house in Adams-Morgan has a relaxed atmosphere and features a complimentary breakfast. A separate annex in Woodley Park is not far from the National Zoo. 1854 Mintwood Pl. NW, 20009, tel. 202/667–6369, fax 202/319–1262. Annex: 2700 Cathedral Ave., tel. 202/328–0860. 55 rooms, 30 with private bath. AE, DC, MC, V.

Normandy Inn. A small, European-style hotel on a quiet street near many embassies, the Normandy offers comfortable rooms and a Continental breakfast. 2118 Wyoming Ave. NW, 20008, tel. 202/483–1350 or 800/424–3729, fax 202/387–8241. 75 rooms. Underground parking. AE, MC, V.

Washington Courtyard by Marriott. This high-rise up the street from Dupont Circle is popular with visitors who can't find rooms at the more expensive Hilton across the street. 1900 Connecticut Ave. NW, 20009, tel. 202/332–9300 or 800/842–4211, fax 202/328–7039. 147 rooms. Restaurant, pool, access to health club. AE, D, DC, MC, V.

Windsor Park Hotel. Near to (but cheaper than) the major convention hotels, the Windsor Park offers small, immaculate rooms and a residential setting a short walk away from Dupont Circle, Embassy Row, and Woodley Park. 2116 Kalorama Rd. NW, 20008, tel. 202/483–7700 or 800/247–3064, fax 202/332–4547. 44 rooms. AE, D, DC, MC, V.

DINING

The District has weathered wave after wave of restaurant trends, from New American to Southwestern, from upscale Italian to postmodern Oriental. Somehow it's survived them all. Of course, some tastes are immune to fads, and Washington's location near the Chesapeake Bay and the Atlantic Ocean means seafood is usually fresh, none more so than the hallowed Chesapeake blue crab.

As for favorite dining neighborhoods, there's a strong Latin and Ethiopian flavor in Adams-Morgan, especially on 18th Street south of Columbia Road. Dupont Circle boasts some of the city's best Italian eateries. Georgetown, around Wisconsin Avenue and M Street, is chockablock with restaurants. And Washington even has a compact Chinatown, centered around 7th and G streets Northwest. Price categories per person, excluding 10% tax, service, and drinks, are Expensive, $25–40; Moderate, $15–$25; and Inexpensive, under $15.

ADAMS-MORGAN **Belmont Kitchen.** On warm spring nights, customers flock to this neighborhood restaurant's outdoor dining area, enjoying upside-down pizzas, grilled fish and meat, and a low-calorie, three-course dinner that's always on the menu. *2400 18th St. NW, tel. 202/667–1200. AE, D, DC, MC, V. Moderate.*

Cities. Periodically this restaurant changes both menu and decor to match the look and taste of such cities as Palermo, Mexico City, and Los Angeles. The chef has been called one of the best in Washington; weekend crowds confirm her popularity. *2424 18th St. NW, tel. 202/328–7194. AE, DC, MC, V. Moderate.*

La Fourchette. It looks the way a bistro should—with an exposed brick wall, tin ceiling, and bentwood chairs—and serves hearty entrées like bouillabaisse, rabbit, and lamb and veal shanks, all at a reasonable price. *2429 18th St. NW, tel. 202/332–3077. AE, DC, MC, V. Moderate.*

Meskerem. Adams-Morgan is a hotbed of Ethiopian restaurants, but none are as distinctive as this exotically decorated spot, where diners sit on cushions and sample *watt* (meat and vegetarian stews) scooped up in spongy *injera* bread. *2434 18th St. NW, tel. 202/462–4100. AE, DC, MC, V. Inexpensive.*

CAPITOL HILL **America.** A lively and attractive bar and restaurant in the soaring main hall of Union Station, America has a menu as broad as its name, from Minnesota scrambled eggs to New Mexico–style pasta. *Union Station, 50 Massachusetts Ave. NE, tel. 202/ 682–9555. AE, DC, MC, V. Moderate.*

American Cafe. With several locations in the area, this is a D.C. success story; the secret is affordable, healthy food—croissant sandwiches, salads, fresh fish—in casual but sophisticated spaces. *277 Massachusetts Ave. NE, tel. 202/547–8500. AE, MC, V. Inexpensive.*

DOWNTOWN **Bombay Palace.** A cosmopolitan setting provides the backdrop for authentic Indian dishes, from mild to scorching, with such entrées as chicken and prawns cooked in a tandoor oven, butter chicken (tandoori chicken in a tomato sauce), and *gosht patiala* (a stew of meat, potatoes, and onions in a ginger sauce). *2020 K St. NW, tel. 202/331–0111. AE, DC, MC, V. Moderate.*

Primi Piatti. An exuberant Roman atmosphere underscores this Washington favorite almost as much as the light and healthful Italian dishes it serves, many of which—including lamb and veal chops and tuna with raisins and pine nuts—are prepared on a wood-burning grill. *2013 I St. NW, tel. 202/ 223–3600. Jacket and tie suggested. AE, DC, MC, V. Moderate.*

DUPONT CIRCLE **Sala Thai.** The chef will honor requests for spicy food but is more interested in flavor than fire, preparing such subtly seasoned dishes as *panang goong* (shrimp in curry-peanut sauce), chicken sautéed with ginger and pineapple, and flounder with a choice of four sauces. *2016 P St. NW, tel. 202/872–1144. AE, DC, MC, V. Inexpensive.*

Skewers. Lamb with eggplant and chicken with roasted peppers are favorites at this avant-garde Middle Eastern restaurant, whose healthful, reasonably priced selections are said to be popular with Ralph Nader. *1633 P St. NW, tel. 202/387–7400. AE, DC, MC, V. Moderate.*

GEORGETOWN **Aditi.** At first glance this two-story dining room seems to be too elegant for a moderately priced Indian restaurant. But the decor is not the only draw: Tandoor and curry dishes, although not aggressively spiced, are expertly prepared. The rice *biryani* entrées are good for lighter appetites, and a few dollars will get you a delicious bread sampler. *3299 M St. NW, tel. 202/625–6825. AE, DC, MC, V. Moderate.*

Austin Grill. A boom in Tex-Mex restaurants includes this bright, lively spot whose mesquite grill turns out fajitas, grilled fish, and cubed beef that goes into some of the best chili in town. *2404 Wisconsin Ave. NW, tel. 202/337–8080. AE, MC, V. Inexpensive.*

Citronelle. There's a wide window here with quite a view of a hectic kitchen in which white-clad chefs steadily turn out deliciously inventive nouvelle cuisine. Your palate will tingle all the way from the gingery abalone carpaccio appetizer through the gravity-free Napoleons with butterscotch sauce. *Latham Hotel, 3000 M St. NW, lower level, tel. 202/ 625–2150. Reservations advised. Jacket and tie advised. AE, MC, V. Expensive.*

Sushi-Ko. Washington's first sushi bar remains one of its best, with a menu that extends beyond raw fish to encompass seafood and vegetable tempuras, fish teriyaki, and udonsuki noodles. *2309 Wisconsin Ave. NW, tel. 202/333–4187. AE, MC, V. Moderate.*

UPPER NORTHWEST **Dancing Crab.** Heaps of spicy, steaming crabs are piled high on the brown-paper-covered tables at this informal uptown spot, where a casual crowd uses wooden mallets to crack the shells of the tasty crustaceans. *4611 Wisconsin Ave. NW, tel. 202/244–1882. AE, DC, MC, V. Moderate.*

SHOPPING

MUSEUM STORES When it comes to shopping, Washington has one unsung gem: the museum gift shop. Washington's museums, especially those of the Smithsonian Institution, offer high-grade selections based on the collections they display. At the National Gallery of Art, you'll find accurate copies of famous works both suitable for framing and suitably framed. You can take home a model of the space shuttle or an astronaut's freeze-dried ice-cream sandwich from the National Air and Space Museum. Handsome handcrafts, ceramics, and glass are plentiful at the Renwick Gallery (Pennsylvania Ave. at 17th St. NW). And for a complete selection of books on America and Americana as well as blues, jazz, and folk music albums released by the Smithsonian, visit the massive store in the National Museum of American History (14th St. and Constitution Ave. NW).

SHOPPING DISTRICTS **Georgetown** is probably Washington's favorite shopping area. The intersection of Wisconsin Avenue and M Street is the hub, and spread out from this nexus, you'll find shops that sell jewelry, antiques, foreign magazines, and designer fashions. The crossroads is also the location of Georgetown Park, a three-level, upscale mall that manages to be both Victorian and modern at the same time.

Dupont Circle, especially Connecticut Avenue north of Massachusetts, has some of the flavor of Georgetown but is a little on the funkier side, with book and record stores as well as shops selling coffee, stationery, clothing, and bric-a-brac.

Eastern Market (7th St. and North Carolina Ave. SE, tel. 202/543–7293), popular with locals, has an outdoor farmers market and, across the street, established specialty shops that will intrigue most bargain hunters.

Around the **Metro Center** metro station are two of the city's biggest department stores: Woodward & Lothrop (11th and F Sts. NW) and Hecht's (12th and G Sts. NW) as well as cut-price, low-quality shops selling everything from wigs to foundation garments. The Shops at National Place (13th and F Sts. NW, tel. 202/783–9090) is a glittering, three-story collection of stores, including the Sharper Image.

Union Station (50 Massachusetts Ave. NE, tel. 202/371–9441) underwent a complete renovation in 1988, transforming it into a massive mall with lots of boutiques and special-interest shops.

DEPARTMENT STORES Both **Hecht's** (12th and G Sts. NW, tel. 202/628–6661) and **Woodward & Lothrop** (11th and F Sts. NW, tel. 202/347–5300) are bright and spacious, with sensible groupings of merchandise that make shopping easy on the eyes and feet. "Woodies" is especially good for clothes in a variety of styles and price ranges.

If you're looking to spend a little more money, three stores near the Maryland border will be happy to accommodate you. **Lord & Taylor** (5255 Western Ave. NW, tel. 202/362–9600), **Nieman Marcus** (Mazza Gallerie, tel. 202/966–9700), and **Saks Fifth Avenue** (5555 Wisconsin Ave., Chevy Chase, tel. 301/657–9000).

OUTDOOR ACTIVITIES

BIKING Cyclists spin their wheels on flat, well-paved bike trails in Rock Creek Park along Rock Creek Parkway and Beach Drive, and around the monuments and into East Potomac Park, southeast of the Tidal Basin. There is a good 3-mile loop around the golf course in East Potomac Park. The entryway is near the Jefferson Memorial; the park is safe in the daytime, but avoid it after dark. There's also scenic biking on the towpath along the C&O Canal in Georgetown and north into Maryland. It's 15 miles on the occasionally rocky packed-earth surface up to Great Falls. For further information, consult the **Potomac Pedalers Touring Club** (tel. 202/363–8687) or the **Washington Area Bicyclist Association** (tel. 202/872–9830).

Rentals: You can rent bikes at **Big Wheel Bikes** (1034 33rd St. NW, Georgetown, tel. 202/337–0254; 315 7th St. SE, tel. 202/543–1600), **Fletcher's Boat Center** (intersection of Reservoir Rd. and Canal St., tel. 202/244–0461), **Metropolis Bikes** (709 8th St. SE, Capitol Hill, tel. 202/543–8900), and **Thompson's Boat House** (Virginia Ave. and Rock Creek Pkwy. behind Kennedy Center, tel. 202/333–4861).

JOGGING AND HIKING Popular routes include looping around the Mall on the gravel walkways between the Lincoln Memorial and the Capitol. You can extend the 4.5-mile run by veering south of the Mall past the Jefferson Memorial and into East Potomac Park. Rock Creek Park has 15 miles of trails. A 4-mile loop starts at P Street in Georgetown and extends to the National Zoo. For information on group runs, call the **D.C. Road Runners Club** (tel. 703/241–0395).

SWIMMING Call the District of Columbia's **Department of Recreation** (tel. 202/576–6436) for information on the six indoor and 19 large outdoor pools it maintains.

TENNIS **Hains Point** (East Potomac Park, tel. 202/554–5962) and the **Washington Tennis Center** (16th and Kennedy Sts. NW, tel. 202/722–5949) each have around two dozen outdoor courts and six indoor courts. Fees are $15–$25 an hour, depending on the season and type of court; call ahead to reserve.

ENTERTAINMENT

You can find just about anything you want at the **Kennedy Center** (New Hampshire Ave. and Rock Creek Pkwy. NW, tel. 202/467–4600 or 800/444–1324). There are five separate performance areas in which you can find anything from repertory film to opera.

Tickets to many performance and sporting events are available through **TicketMaster** (tel. 202/432–7328). For information on various activities, consult the *Washington Post,* the free weekly *City Paper,* and *Washingtonian* magazine.

BALLET AND DANCE The **Washington Ballet** (tel. 202/362–3606) performs works by such masters as George Balanchine and Paul Taylor, mainly at the Kennedy Center.

MUSIC **Classical:** The National Symphony Orchestra's season extends from September through June, with most performances at the Kennedy Center (tel. 202/416–8100). During the Armed Forces Concert Series (June–August) there's free music nightly from military bands at sites around the city; for information call 202/767–5658, 703/696–3718, 202/433–2525, or 202/433–4011. Chamber groups from around the world perform on Sunday afternoons from September through May at the Phillips Collection art gallery (1600 21st St. NW, tel. 202/387–2151). The Smithsonian Institution sponsors performances in the theaters of its various museums (tel. 202/357–2700 or 202/357–3030).

Contemporary: There's frequent jazz and rhythm-and-blues performers at Blues Alley (rear of 1073 Wisconsin Ave. below M St., tel. 202/337–4141), jazz at the One Step Down (2517 Pennsylvania Ave. NW, tel. 202/331–8863), bluegrass at the Birchmere (3901 Mt. Vernon Ave. in Alexandria, tel. 703/549–5919), and alternative rock at the 9:30 Club (930 F St. NW, tel. 202/393–0930).

OPERA The **Washington Opera** (tel. 202/416–7800) presents seven lavish operas at the Kennedy Center during its November-to-March season. Though it usually sells out by subscription, returned tickets are sometimes available. Cheaper, standing-room tickets go on sale each Saturday for the following week's performances. Other operatic choices include **Mount Vernon College** (2100 Foxhall Rd. NW, tel. 202/625–4655), which produces experimental operas in the spring and winter, and the **Summer Opera Theater Company** (Hartke Theater, on Catholic University of America campus in northeast Washington, tel. 202/526–1669) and the two productions it mounts each June and July.

SPECTATOR SPORTS The closest major-league baseball team is the **Baltimore Orioles,** in their Camden Yards home (333 W. Camden St., Baltimore, MD, tel. 410/685–9800); purchase tickets in Washington at the Orioles Baseball Store (914 17th St. NW, tel. 202/296–2473) or from TicketMaster outlets. The USAir Arena in suburban Maryland (1 Harry S. Truman Dr., Landover, MD, tel. 301/350–3400) hosts **Washington Bullets** basketball (September–April) and **Washington Capitals** hockey (October–April). All **Washington Redskins** home football games at RFK Stadium (East Capitol and 22nd Sts. SE, tel. 202/546–2222) have been sold out since 1966 to season ticket holders. Seats to preseason games are usually available, though, and if you're willing to pay dearly, you can get regular season seats from ticket brokers who advertise in the *Washington Post* classifieds.

THEATER **Arena Stage** (6th St. and Maine Ave. SW, tel. 202/488–3300) is one of the country's leading repertory theaters. **Ford's Theatre** (511 10th St. NW, tel. 202/347–4833), the site of Lincoln's assassination, is both a museum (managed by the Park Service) and a functioning theater. The **National Theatre** (1321 Pennsylvania Ave. NW, tel. 202/628–6161) is the oldest in the city and is the home of many pre- and post-Broadway shows. The **Shakespeare Theatre** at the Lansburgh Theatre (450 7th St. NW, tel. 202/393–2700) presents Elizabethan plays from September to May.

Waterton/Glacier International Peace Park
Montana and Alberta, Canada
Updated by Bud Journey

 aterton/Glacier International Peace Park is like the frontier before it was altered by man. Formed of the United States' giant Glacier National Park and Canada's far smaller Waterton Lakes National Park, which meet at the U.S.–Canadian border in northwestern Montana, the area embodies the essence of the Rocky Mountains. Its massive peaks form the backbone of the Continental Divide. The huge ice sheets for which Glacier Park was named have retreated, but the wild terrain they created reveal their power, and the more than four dozen glaciers that remain give a sense of what they were like. Ribbons of pure, clear water streaming from these ice fields eventually flow into three oceans—the Pacific, via the Columbia River; the Atlantic, via the Mississippi; and the Arctic, via the St. Mary River. There are dozens of waterfalls, many large, deep lakes, and scores of smaller ones. Flora is profuse, and the coniferous forests, alpine mountainsides, thickly vegetated stream banks, and green-carpeted meadows provide homes and sustenance for abundant and varied wildlife; Glacier is one of the few parks with substantial numbers of grizzly bears. In Waterton, the rugged alpine scenery gives way to prairie grasslands.

Going-to-the-Sun Road, one of the most dizzying rides in North America, is just one of several scenic routes that showcase these natural wonders and provide access to nature centers and hiking trails that give a more intimate view. Assuring a comfortable stay is a wide variety of accommodations—campgrounds to castlelike hotels, basic diners to fine restaurants. You'll find these just outside the park in communities such as East Glacier Park and West Glacier, and in the small but busy commercial centers within park boundaries: Two Medicine, Apgar, Lake McDonald, Rising Sun, and Many Glacier in Glacier, and Watertown Townsite in Waterton.

ESSENTIAL INFORMATION

WHEN TO GO Most people visit Waterton/Glacier in summer: Weather is warmest, flora freshest, wildlife best distributed, and the glacier-fed streams and waterfalls running full.

Temperatures average in the high 70s and low 80s by day in summer, 45°–50° at night; 20°–30° by day in winter, below zero at night; and 65°–70° by day in spring and fall, 35°–40° at night. However, weather on any day often varies more drastically. It is most consistently stable in early September, when crowds dissipate. It's a good time to visit. High-country winters last at least from September to June.

FESTIVALS AND SPECIAL EVENTS **Late Apr. or early May:** The opening of the Going-to-the-Sun Road, one of Glacier's big annual events, draws spectators as crews plow away tons of snow. **July 1 (Canadian Independence Day)–July 4 (U.S. Independence Day):** Days of Peace and Friendship offers special talks on the International Peace Park theme. **Third weekend in Aug.:** The Beargrass Festival has native dancers, cowboy poetry, storytelling, fiddling, golf, and chili-cooking competitions in Waterton Townsite.

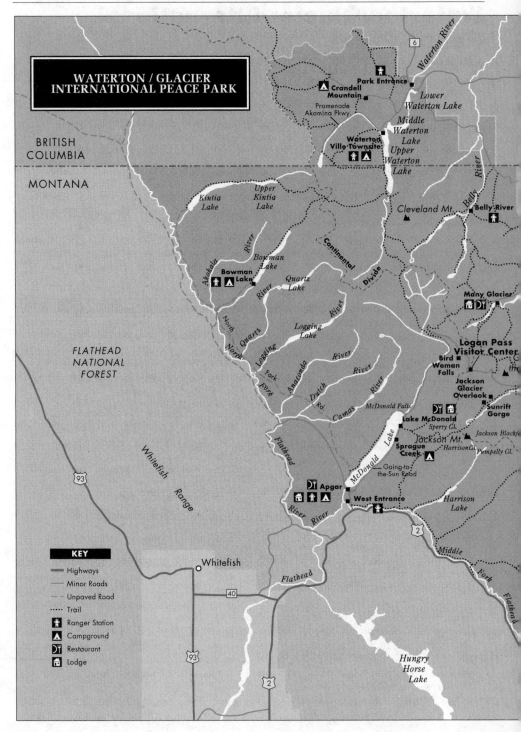

WATERTON / GLACIER
INTERNATIONAL PEACE PARK

BRITISH
COLUMBIA

MONTANA

Park Entrance

Crandell
Mountain

Promenade
Akamina Pkwy

*Lower
Waterton Lake*

*Middle
Waterton
Lake*

Waterton
Ville Townsite

*Upper
Waterton
Lake*

*Kintia
Lake*

*Upper
Kintia
Lake*

Cleveland Mt.

Belly River

Belly

River

Akokala

River

*Bowman
Lake*

Bowman
Lake

*Quartz
Lake*

Continental

Divide

Many Glacier

North

Quartz

River

*Logging
Lake*

Logging

River

Logan Pass
Visitor Center

FLATHEAD
NATIONAL
FOREST

North

Fork

Logging

Fork

Anaconda

River

River

Dutch

Rd.

Bird
Woman
Falls

Jackson
Glacier
Overlook

Sunrift
Gorge

Camas

River

McDonald Falls

Sperry Gl.

Lake McDonald

Jackson Mt.

Jackson Blackfi

Pompelly Gl.

HarrisonGl.

Sprague
Creek

Going-to-
the-Sun Road

Flathead

McDonald Lake

Apgar

West Entrance

*Harrison
Lake*

River

River

*Whitefish
Range*

Whitefish

Flathead

Middle

Fork

Flathead

Hungry
Horse
Lake

KEY

Highways

Minor Roads

Unpaved Road

Trail

Ranger Station

Campground

Restaurant

Lodge

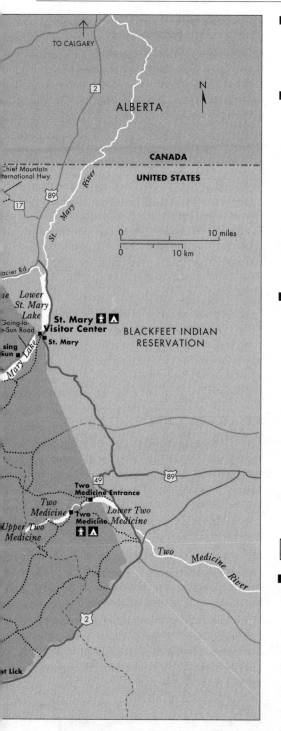

BARGAINS The best activities are always free: hiking, picnicking, fishing, wildlife-watching, naturalist activities. Canada's 7% tax on rooms, meals, and purchases is refundable; inquire at the border.

TOURIST OFFICES **Glacier National Park** (West Glacier 59936, tel. 406/888–5441). **Waterton Lakes National Park** (Waterton Park, Alberta, Canada T0K 2M0, tel. 403/859–2224). **Travel Montana** (Box 200533, Helena 59620-0533, tel. 406/444–2654). **Travel Alberta** (10065 Jasper Ave., Edmonton, Alberta, Canada T5J 0H4, tel. 800/661–8888). **Waterton Park Townsite Chamber of Commerce** (Box 55–6, Waterton Lakes National Park, Alberta, Canada T0K 2M0, tel. 403/859–2203). **Glacier Park, Inc.** (Dial Corporate Center, Phoenix, AZ 85077-0928, tel. 602/207–6000).

EMERGENCIES Stop in at a ranger station or dial 911 for **police, fire,** and **ambulance.** Or, in Glacier, call headquarters (tel. 406/888–5441). In Waterton, phone the emergency number (tel. 403/859–2636), park superintendent (tel. 403/859–2224), or Waterton Royal Canadian Mounted Police Complaint Line (tel. 403/859–2244). **Doctors and Hospitals:** Glacier resources include the Kalispell Regional Hospital, about 30 miles southwest of West Glacier (tel. 406/752–5111). Nearer Waterton, try Cardston, 20 miles west of the north park boundary (hospital, tel. 403/653–4411; clinic, tel. 403/653–3311 or 403/653–3331), or Pincher Creek, 30 miles north of the north park boundary (hospital, tel. 403/627–3333; clinic, tel. 403/627–3321).

ARRIVING AND DEPARTING

BY PLANE The nearest airport to Glacier is **Glacier Park International Airport** (tel. 406/257–5994), 30 miles southwest of the park between Kalispell and Whitefish. **Flathead/Glacier Transportation** (tel. 406/862–7733) runs vans from the airport, charging $35 to West Glacier, on the park's southwest border; $100 to East Glacier Park, just outside the southeast boundary; and $160 to Many Glacier, in the northeast. Fares are for one; you pay $2 per additional passenger.

BY CAR Uncrowded, two-lane U.S. 2 accesses Glacier Park from the east and west. It connects to I–90, which cuts through Butte and Missoula, via I–15 on the east, and U.S. 93 on the west.

BY TRAIN Amtrak (tel. 800/872–7245) stops at West Glacier and East Glacier Park.

GETTING AROUND

BY CAR A car is the best transportation here. Roads are suitable for RVs, though caution is necessary and some vehicle-length restrictions apply. The North Fork Road, Going-to-the-Sun Road, Two Medicine Road, and Many Glacier Road travel deep into the park and access trailheads and points of interest. In winter, these close, and your sole option is U.S. 2, which runs just outside the south boundary, dipping into the park at the Goat Lick and passing the winter game range. In Waterton, Route 5 into Waterton Townsite is the only road that's open all year.

REST STOPS All park campgrounds and picnic areas accessible by car have rest rooms, as do all visitor centers. So do private businesses in Apgar Village, Lake McDonald, Two Medicine, Rising Sun, Swiftcurrent, Many Glacier, and Waterton Townsite. West Glacier, East Glacier Park, St. Mary, and Babb, just outside the Glacier Park boundary, also have rest rooms.

GUIDED TOURS Bus: These can be exciting, especially the tours offered by Glacier Park, Inc. (*see* Tourist Offices, *above*), which uses vintage 1936, rolltop Scarlet Buses.

Narrated Cruises: Especially good are **Waterton Shoreline Cruises** (tel. 403/859–2362), which dock at Waterton Townsite and stop on both sides of the international border, venturing as far south as Goat Haunt. Or you can opt for **Glacier Park Boat Company** (tel. 406/888–5727 or 406/732–4430), 45 minutes to 1½ hours long, on Lake McDonald, Many Glacier, Two Medicine, or St. Mary Lake.

Naturalist Walks: Both parks have many ranger-guided walks. For details, contact park headquarters (*see* Tourist Offices, *above*).

EXPLORING

It is possible to travel through this vast area in a single day. But it's a shame to hurry. And while park roads do showcase abundant scenery, it's important to make time for walks and picnics. Stop at visitor centers at Apgar, St. Mary, Logan Pass, and Waterton Townsite to find out about special programs scheduled during your visit.

NORTH FORK ROAD Narrow and unpaved, North Fork Road is one of the two (along with Two Medicine Road) least-traveled roads in the park. It parallels the North Fork of the Flathead River for 43 miles and leads through lodgepole pine flats and other river-bottom terrain with the forested mountains of the Whitefish Range rising to the west. It also provides access to beautiful Bowman and Kintla lakes, where you'll find campgrounds and good trout fishing (though if you walk into Logging and Quartz lakes, the angling will probably be even better). Driving time is around two hours, excluding stops. You can pick up the road at the stop sign about a mile inside the park's west entrance; make a left turn.

GOING-TO-THE-SUN ROAD Accessible by turning right at the stop sign, Going-to-the-Sun Road is probably the biggest single attraction in Glacier. Literally blasted out of solid rock, this 1930s-era engineering feat climbs to Logan Pass, topping the Continental Divide at 6,664 feet, then drops downhill to St. Mary Lake on the east side. Along the way, it twists through conifer forests, past mountain peaks, and along grassy basins brightly dotted with summer flowers. To complement the breathtaking scenery, there are many opportunities for hikes, walks, and animal-watching both on and off the road.

At rustic Lake McDonald Lodge, named for its location on the park's largest lake, you can have a bite, rent a small boat or canoe, embark on a guided cruise, go for a hike, or take a horseback ride. Beyond there, you can stop to view the McDonald Falls off the left side of the road or the treeless avalanche chutes on the mountainsides above. Bears are often visible there, especially in early summer, and Bird Woman Falls stripes the opposite canyon wall. At the panoramic visitor center atop Logan Pass, you can learn about the local alpine environment, or stroll the 1½-mile trail to Hidden Lake Overlook for a fine view of the deep-blue lake below. Across the road you could hike a short distance along the 35½-mile-long Highline Trail; carved out of a sheer cliff (but negotiable for most visitors), it overlooks a vast portion of southwest Glacier. On the trip down, on the east side of the Continental Divide, there's a vista of bald, 9,642-foot Going-to-the-Sun Mountain; a glimpse of Jackson Glacier looming in a rocky pass; several waterfalls; and intriguing Sunrift Gorge, a miniature canyon just off the road.

The road is 50 miles long and should take about 1½ hours to drive, excluding stops. The last two or three hours before dark are best for the trip—with best lighting for photos, best wildlife-spotting, and smallest crowds.

MANY GLACIER ROAD This road parallels Sherburne Lake along a scrubby forest of lodgepole pines, aspens, and cottonwoods broken by meadows that come alive with flowers in the summer. Many Glacier Road ends in a glacially carved valley surrounded by rugged mountains. Grinnell and Salamander glaciers, once a single ice mass, are clearly visible along the way. Access is from the northeast side of the park, southwest of Babb; the 20-mile road ends at Swiftcurrent, where you can fish, take a boat cruise, ride horseback, have a meal, and camp or check into a motel, then enjoy a ranger campfire talk. There are also good hikes, long and short, including the one to Grinnell Glacier, the largest in the park; the high basin on the north side of the valley is a good place to spot bears, mountain goats, sheep, and other wildlife.

CHIEF MOUNTAIN INTERNATIONAL HIGHWAY This is another one of Waterton/Glacier's great drives. Moving from Glacier northwest to Waterton Townsite then down toward Waterton Lakes, Chief Mountain International Highway begins in the rolling hills at the edge of the prairie and climbs through open fields patched with cottonwoods and aspens, into thick forests—first of deciduous trees, then conifers, mostly lodgepole pine and spruce. Coming down, there's a panorama embracing almost all of Waterton Park and a view of the Lewis Overthrust—600-million-year-old rock that geological movements have thrust over 100-million-year-old rock—where grizzly bears, mountain goats, or other wildlife can often be spotted. To cover the 35 miles between St. Mary and Waterton, allow 1½ hours, excluding stops.

THE NATURAL WORLD You can almost always see goats and other wildlife at the Goat Lick, on the extreme southern tip of Glacier. Bighorn sheep and mule deer are usually present in and around Waterton Townsite. Deer and chipmunks are also easy to see. An astute observer can often pick out elk, black bears and grizzly bears, moose, and coyotes. Bobcats, lynxes, mountain lions, raccoons, foxes, wolverines, and martens are present but less common. Smaller animals include pikas, snowshoe hares, porcupines, beavers, marmots, and other rodents. A small number of bison reside in Waterton, and gray wolves live in both parks. Both parks shelter a wide variety of birds, including songbirds, waterfowl, and such predators as bald eagles and ospreys.

HOTELS AND INNS

Accommodations here range from plain to ornate, but a western-rustic mood prevails, and rates are reasonable, despite the demand. Reserve two months to a year in advance, especially for July and August—you can't count on cancellations. The most distinctive (and most expensive) properties are inside the Peace Park, but you don't have to spend a fortune to enjoy their convenience, since there are several less expensive options. Note: Unless otherwise noted, all properties in the Peace Park are run by Glacier Park, Inc. (*see* Tourist Offices, *above*).

Price categories for double occupancy, excluding tax (4% in Montana, 12% in Canada), are Expensive, $80–$210; Moderate, $50–$80; and Inexpensive, under $50. Note that rates sometimes drop in June, before winter is fully dissipated. Unless otherwise noted, all hotels, inns, and motels are closed from September or October until May or June.

GLACIER **Apgar Village Lodge.** This establishment, built early in this century—one of the few in Glacier Park not run by Glacier Park, Inc.—stands out for its setting among big trees rather than for its somewhat plain, though meticulously clean, accommodations. *Box 398, West Glacier 59936, tel. 406/ 888–5484. 48 units (28 cabins), 26 with kitchenettes. D, MC, V. Open May–Oct. 15. Moderate.*

Glacier Park Lodge. This grand old hotel at East Glacier Park was built in the 1920s with 500- to 800-year-old fir and cedar logs 3 feet in diameter as its main supports. *161 rooms. Restaurant, snack bar, lounge, evening entertainment, heated pool, 9-hole golf course. D, MC, V. Expensive.*

Granite Park Chalet and Sperry Chalet. These popular wilderness chalets, built around the time of World War I from rugged natural materials, are in a class by themselves—and an unforgettable experience— since accommodations are spartan and access is only via a long, steep trail. The chalets, however, are closed for repairs and not expected to reopen until 1997. Call Glacier National Park Headquarters (tel. 406/888–5441) for the latest information.

Lake McDonald Lodge. Set amid the cedars on the south side of the lake of the same name, this old lodge in the Lake McDonald area has a Wild West look to it, in part owing to the animal heads on the lobby walls. *100 rooms. Restaurant, coffee shop, lounge, evening entertainment, gas station, store. D, MC, V. Moderate–Expensive.*

Many Glacier Hotel. The most isolated of the Peace Park's grand hotels, this vintage chalet on Swiftcurrent Lake in northeast Glacier is often considered the most scenic as well. *211 rooms. Restaurant, snack bar, lounge, evening entertainment, gas station. D, MC, V. Expensive.*

Rising Sun Motor Inn. Disregard the barracks-like appearance—the Rising Sun is clean, neat, and conveniently and prettily situated on Going-to-the-Sun Road at mountain-encircled St. Mary Lake. *72 units (25 cabins). Coffee shop, store. D, MC, V. Moderate.*

Swiftcurrent Motor Inn. This motel-and-cabin complex is plain but practical—and its location at the end of Many Glacier Road assures fine views. *88 units (26 cabins, some without bath). Coffee shop, coin laundry, store. D, MC, V. Inexpensive–Moderate.*

Village Motor Inn. This two-story wooden lodge with balconies has a spectacular view of the mountains and the lake out front, where there's a beach—though swimming in such cold water is not for the faint of heart. *36 rooms, 12 with kitchenettes. D, MC, V. Moderate.*

WATERTON **Bayshore Inn.** The L shape of this motel-style establishment, probably the most modern in the Peace Park, matches the shoreline of Upper Waterton Lake and parallels a gravel beach. *Box 38, Waterton Townsite, T0K 2M0, tel. 403/859–2211. 70 rooms (49 facing lake). Restaurant, coffee shop, lounge, hot tub, room service, coin laundry. AE, MC, V (no credit card guarantees for reservations made more than 10 days in advance of stay). Moderate–Expensive.*

Kilmorey Lodge. A year-round, full-service lodge in Waterton Park, this older, two-story structure faces the lake and is surrounded by trees. *Box 100, Waterton Townsite, T0K 2M0, tel. 403/859–2334. 25 rooms. Restaurant, gazebo-café, lounge, room service. AE, DC, MC, V. Moderate.*

Prince of Wales Hotel. This grand establishment at Waterton Townsite, designed like a Swiss chalet, seems old-fashioned but offers a great look at the mountains, especially from the rooms facing south toward Upper Waterton Lake. *86 rooms. Restaurant, tearoom, lounge. D, MC, V. Expensive.*

MOTELS

MODERATE **Aspen-Village Inn** (Box 100, Waterton Townsite, T0K 2M0, tel. 403/859–2255). 50 rooms and cabins, 12 with kitchenettes; Jacuzzi. **Crandell Mountain Lodge** (Box 114, Waterton, T0K 2M0, tel. 403/859–2288). 17 rooms, 8 with kitchenettes. **East Glacier Motel** (Box 93, East Glacier Park 59434, tel. 406/226–5593). 16 rooms and cabins, 11 with kitchenettes. **River Bend Motel** (Box 398, West Glacier 59936, tel. 406/888–5662). 27 rooms and cabins, 5 with kitchenettes; restaurant, store, nearby coin laundry. **St. Mary Lodge Motel** (St. Mary 59417, tel. 406/732–4431 in summer, 208/726–6279 in winter). 76 rooms and creekside or deluxe cabins, 18 kitchenettes; restaurant, lounge, coin laundry. **Vista Motel** (Box 98, West Glacier 59936, tel. 406/888–5311 or 800/831–7101). 26 rooms, 4 with kitchenettes; heated pool.

INEXPENSIVE **Glacier Highland Motel** (Box 397, West Glacier 59936, tel. 406/888–5427). 33 rooms, 2 with kitchenettes. **Jacobson's Cottages** (Box 216, East Glacier Park 59434, tel. 406/226–4422). 12 cabins, 2 with kitchen. **Mountain Pine Motel** (Box 260, East Glacier Park 59434, tel. 406/226–4403). 26 rooms. **Sears Motel and Campground** (Box 275, East Glacier Park 59434, tel. 406/226–4432). 16 rooms, 19 campsites (15 with full RV hookups); Dollar Car Rentals.

CAMPGROUNDS

There are more than a dozen campgrounds as well as several picnic areas in Glacier, and several others in Waterton; they range from busy areas with all services to quiet, rustic spots where you can enjoy a true woodland experience. All campgrounds are first-come, first-served and fill up by early afternoon during July and August. No credit cards are accepted; fees range from $8 to $18, with most sites costing around $10.

In Glacier, none offer utility hookups, and none have showers (available for nominal fee at Rising Sun and Swiftcurrent Motor inns). Waterton campgrounds have more comprehensive facilities. For details, contact park headquarters (*see* Tourist Offices, *above*).

GLACIER **Apgar.** A short walk from Apgar Village and Lake McDonald, this campground is large, busy, and close to many activities and services. *Just inside Glacier's west entrance. 196 sites; bathrooms, dump station, picnic tables, boat access.*

Bowman Lake. Here, off a graveled road at Bowman Lake in northwest Glacier, you'll find a campground that doesn't feel crowded—though it lacks some of the amenities of bigger spots. *At end of Bowman Lake Rd. near Polebridge. 48 sites; picnic tables, boat access.*

Many Glacier. This large, busy campground in a scenic valley in northeast Glacier is the departure point for hikes into the park's northern areas. *At end of Many Glacier Rd. at Swiftcurrent. 117 sites; bathrooms, dump station, picnic tables, boat access.*

Rising Sun. This campground on the north side of Glacier's St. Mary Lake is almost as big and just as busy as Apgar. It offers such water sports as fishing, cruising, and paddling. *Located 5 mi west of Glacier's east entrance. 83 sites; bathrooms, dump station, picnic tables, boat access.*

Two Medicine. Though lacking the facilities you find at Apgar and Rising Sun, this campground on Two Medicine Lake in southeast Glacier is not only scenic but, happily, fills up later than the rest. *At end of Two Medicine Rd., next to Two Medicine Store, 11 mi northwest of East Glacier Park. 99 sites; bathrooms, dump station, picnic tables, boat access.*

WATERTON **Belly River.** This small, wooded campground feels delightfully rustic. *Off Chief Mountain International Hwy., 17½ mi east of Waterton Townsite. 24 hike-in sites; picnic tables, playground.*

Crandell Mountain. The deep-woods location in the center of the park is far from any development. *Off Red Rock Rd., 11 mi from Waterton Townsite. 129 sites; showers, bathrooms, dump station, picnic tables, playground.*

Waterton Townsite. Within walking distance of this large, busy campground, you'll find all the facilities of the town. The tradeoffs for such convenience are occasional crowds and noise. Ask about the waiting list if there's no site available when you arrive. *On south end of Waterton Townsite. 95 sites with hookups, 113 sites without hookups, 30 walk-in sites; showers, bathrooms, dump station, picnic tables, playground.*

DINING

Price categories per person, excluding tax (7% in Canada only), service, or drinks, are Moderate, $13–$25, and Inexpensive, under $13.

GLACIER AND ENVIRONS **Cedar Dining Room.** The straightforward cooking takes second place to the Old West atmosphere at this grand, circa-1914 lodge. *Lake McDonald Lodge off Going-to-the-Sun Rd., tel. 406/888–5431. D, MC, V. Moderate.*

Cedar Tree Deli. The counter here dishes out sandwiches, ice cream, and yogurt to go—and there are picnic tables outside. *Going-to-the-Sun Rd., Apgar Village, tel. 406/888–5232. No credit cards. Inexpensive.*

Eddie's Café. This simple restaurant is a good bet for salads, chicken, rainbow trout, or beef. *Going-to-the-Sun Rd., Apgar Village, tel. 406/888–5361. MC, V. Inexpensive.*

Glacier Park Lodge. A gracious ambience prevails in the dining room of this giant log structure. The menu is strictly western—burgers, steaks, beans, and potatoes. *Rte. 49, East Glacier Park, tel. 406/226–9311. D, MC, V. Moderate.*

Interlaken Lounge. The turn-of-the-century chalet decor—and the fine view of Swiftcurrent Lake just outside—makes a fine backdrop for leisurely, hearty meals of steak, grilled chicken, pasta, and steaming stews.

Many Glacier Hotel, Many Glacier Rd., tel. 406/732–4411, ext. 610. D, MC, V. Moderate.

Snow Goose Grill. For something special, this spot with western flair makes a good alternative to dining in the park. Steaks and pasta are specialties, as is whitefish the restaurant buys from Native Americans who fish nearby St. Mary Lake. *St. Mary Lodge, St. Mary, tel. 406/732–4431. AE, MC, V. Moderate.*

WATERTON AND ENVIRONS **Garden Court.** This room in the spectacular hilltop Prince of Wales château-hotel makes a fine setting for special meals of local favorites—and the view of Waterton Lake out the windows will take your breath away. *Prince of Wales Hotel, Waterton Townsite, tel. 403/859–2231. D, MC, V. Moderate.*

Kootenai Brown. In this dining area of a modern inn overlooking mountain-backed Waterton Lake, the focus is western fare, including salads, chicken, trout, and beef. *Bayshore Inn, Waterton Ave., Waterton Townsite, tel. 403/859–2211. AE, MC, V. Moderate.*

Lamp Post. Light dishes—such as grilled trout and skinless chicken—come as a welcome surprise in an area where heavy, old-fashioned American cooking predominates. *Kilmorey Lodge, Waterton Townsite, tel. 403/859–2334. AE, DC, MC, V. Moderate.*

New Frank's Restaurant. This simple eatery is the only restaurant in the Peace Park where you can get Chinese as well as western fare. *Waterton Ave., Waterton Townsite, tel. 403/859–2240. AE, MC, V. Inexpensive.*

Pearl's. Pearl's, a squeaky-clean soup-and-sandwich deli, is the place for fresh-made sandwiches and pasta. *Windflower Ave., Waterton Townsite, tel. 403/859–2284. MC, V. Inexpensive.*

Zum-M-M's. You can grab some fast food at the counter at this popular local spot—but you'll probably opt for its café or the somewhat fancier dining room, where you'll be treated to classic western cuisine (in other words, chicken, beef, and trout). *Waterton*

Ave., Waterton, tel. 403/859–2388. AE, MC, V. Inexpensive–Moderate.

OUTDOOR ACTIVITIES

BIKING Waterton allows bicycling on designated trails; Red Rock Canyon Road would suit novice pedalers.

CROSS-COUNTRY SKIING Winter enthusiasts appreciate the relatively flat terrain on the North Fork Road and around Lake McDonald in Glacier, and in northern Waterton.

FISHING Local waters shelter ling, northern pike, whitefish, kokanee, grayling, and several types of trout—cutthroat, bull, brook, rainbow, and lake. You can catch fish in virtually all park waters; as elsewhere, the best is the hardest to get to. A license is necessary in Waterton but not Glacier.

GOLF It is not unusual to see moose, elk, deer, bighorn sheep, and other wildlife while playing 18 at Waterton Lakes Golf Course, at **Waterton Townsite** (tel. 403/859–2114; fee charged; reservations advised on weekends). Or try the nine-hole course at **Glacier Park Lodge** (tel. 406/226–9311; fee charged; no reservations) and West Glacier's 18-hole **Glacier View Golf Course** (tel. 406/888–5471; fee charged; reservations advised).

HIKING Roads in the Peace Park provide access to some 850 miles of marked trails that allow for short strolls, rough cross-country treks, and everything in between.

In Glacier, for instance, Going-to-the-Sun Road leads to the ¼-mile-long Trail of the Cedars, which cuts through an ancient cedar and hemlock forest and enters Avalanche Gorge. There you can pick up the 2-mile-long Avalanche Trail to Avalanche Lake, surrounded by Avalanche Basin, a huge natural amphitheater with a half-dozen waterfalls. Farther along, at Logan Pass, the short walk to Hidden Lake Overlook is popular.

Many Glacier Hotel (*see* Hotels and Inns, *above*) is a departure point for day hikes that take in glaciated canyons, steep mountains, profuse flora, and varied wildlife. From Two Medicine, trails head into southeast Glacier, to Paradise Point and Appistoki, and Rockwell Falls, among other sites.

North Fork Road (*see* Exploring, *above*) accesses trails to Logging, Quartz, Rogers, and Trout lakes.

In Waterton, Waterton Townsite is the starting point for several popular hikes: the steep ¾-miler up to Bear's Hump, for a great view of Waterton Townsite, Waterton Lake, and the surrounding mountains; the Lakeshore Hike along Waterton Lake to Boundary Bay (3½ miles away) and Glacier's Goat Haunt (6½ miles away); and the 8-mile round-trip to Alderson Lake. In northwest Waterton, the Snowshoe and Blakiston Valley trails, which skirt the north and south sides of 8,803-foot Anderson Mountain, lead to meadows of wildflowers and sites rich in wildlife, particularly mountain goats. Note: Backcountry-use permits, available at ranger stations, are required for fires and backcountry camping.

HORSEBACK RIDING Look into short jaunts or overnight trips from **Mule Shoe Outfitters** (tel. 406/732–4203 or 406/888–5010), or, in Waterton, **Alpine Stables** (tel. 403/859–2462).

TENNIS Public courts adjoin the Waterton Townsite campground.

WHITE-WATER RAFTING Several West Glacier outfitters stage trips on the pristine Flathead River: **Glacier Raft Company** (tel. 406/888–5454), **Glacier Wilderness Guides** (tel. 406/387–5555 or 800/521–7238), **Great Northern Whitewater** (tel. 406/387–5340 or 800/735–7897), **Wild River Adventures** (tel. 406/387–9453 or 800/826–2724).

The White Mountains
New Hampshire

Updated by Tara Hamilton

Northern New Hampshire claims the highest mountains in New England, the 750,000 acres of White Mountain National Forest, as well as wilderness that stretches north into Canada. It's no wonder that hikers, climbers, and nature lovers flock here every season of the year. New Hampshire's mountains are not only higher than those of neighboring Vermont and Maine, they are more rugged and more challenging to climb and have a more unpredictable climate. Gorges slash through the rock-strewn mountain flanks, rivers rush south down the steep-sided valleys, and storms swirl around the summit of Mt. Washington with a powerful force unknown down below. But the White Mountains offer more than the harsh beauty of wilderness. Motorists can take in some of the region's most spectacular scenery by driving the Kancamagus Scenic Byway. Southeast of the national forest, on the eastern side of the state, North Conway lures shoppers to its miles of factory outlets and off-price designer boutiques. And when the White Mountains are covered with snow, they offer some of the finest and most varied skiing east of the Rockies.

ESSENTIAL INFORMATION

WHEN TO GO Brisk nights are common even in midsummer, though the occasional muggy heat wave does settle over the region in July and August, sending temperatures into the high 80s and low 90s. Autumn, with daytime temperatures ranging from 50° to 70°, comes early. Unless you hunt, avoid the region during hunting season (early November–mid-December). Winters are long and often brutally cold in the mountains (daytime temperatures range from 12° to 34°), but snow is plentiful for skiing. Spring arrives slowly, first bringing mud season from late March to mid-April. Rates at motels and inns are considerably lower in spring, and they drop again after the fall foliage season.

TOURIST OFFICES White Mountains Attractions Association (Box 10, North Woodstock 03262, tel. 603/745–8720 or 800/346–3687 outside NH, fax 603/745–6765), **Mt. Washington Valley Visitors Bureau** (Box 2300VG, North Conway 03860, tel. 603/356–3171 or 800/367–3364), **White Mountain National Forest** (719 N. Main St., Laconia 03246, tel. 603/528–8721).

The **Pinkham Notch Visitor Center** (Rte. 16, Box 298, Gorham, NH 03581, tel. 603/466–2725; open daily 8 AM–10 PM), the northern New England regional office headquarters of the nonprofit Appalachian Mountain Club, is an educational and recreational visitor center. It provides hikers with information on the Appalachian Trail and all other trails maintained by the organization.

You can also contact the **Franconia/Easton/Sugar Hill Chamber of Commerce** (Box D, Franconia, NH 03580, tel. 603/823–5661 or 800/866–3334), **Lincoln/Woodstock Chamber of Commerce** (Rte. 112, Box 358, Lincoln, NH 03251, tel. 603/745–6621 or 800/227–4191 for lodging reservations), **Northern White Mountain Chamber of Commerce** (163 Main St., Box 298, Berlin, NH 03470, tel. 603/

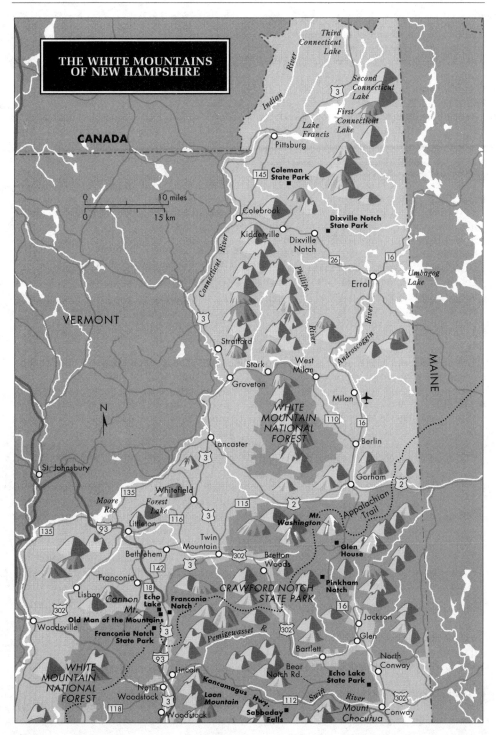

THE WHITE MOUNTAINS
OF NEW HAMPSHIRE

*Third
Connecticut
Lake*

*Second
Connecticut
Lake*

CANADA

*First
Connecticut
Lake*

Indian *River*

*Lake
Francis*

Pittsburg

145
**Coleman
State Park**

0   10 miles
0   15 km

Colebrook

**Dixville Notch
State Park**

Kidderville

Dixville
Notch

26   16

Connecticut River

VERMONT

3

Phillips

Errol

*Umbagog
Lake*

River

Androscoggin River

Stratford

Stark

West
Milan

MAINE

Groveton

*WHITE
MOUNTAIN
NATIONAL
FOREST*

Milan

110   16

Lancaster

Berlin

N

St. Johnsbury

Gorham

2

Whitefield

135

*Moore
Res.*

*Forest
Lake*

116   3

115

2

**Mt.
Washington**

*Appalachian
Trail*

93

Littleton

Twin
Mountain

302

Bretton
Woods

**Glen
House**

135

Bethlehem

Franconia

142

3

**Pinkham
Notch**

16

Lisbon

18
*Cannon
Mt.*

Echo
Lake

**Franconia
Notch**

*CRAWFORD NOTCH
STATE PARK*

Jackson

302

Old Man of the Mountains

Glen

Woodsville

**Franconia Notch
State Park**

3

Pemigewasset R.

302

Bartlett

North
Conway

93

Lincoln

Bear
Notch Rd.

**Echo Lake
State Park**

302

*WHITE
MOUNTAIN
NATIONAL
FOREST*

North
Woodstock

Kancamagus Hwy.

*Loon
Mountain*

112

Swift

River

118

Woodstock

**Sabbaday
Falls**

*Mount
Chocurua*

Conway

752–6060 or 800/992–7480), and **Waterville Valley Region Chamber of Commerce** (Rte. 49, Box 1067, Campton, NH 03223, tel. 603/726–3804 or 800/237–2307) for other area information.

EMERGENCIES **State Police:** (tel. 800/852–3411). **Hospital:** Memorial Hospital (Intervale Rd., North Conway, tel. 603/356–5461).

ARRIVING AND DEPARTING

BY PLANE **Manchester Airport** (tel. 603/624–6556) in southern New Hampshire is the state's principal airport. **Laconia Municipal Airport** (30 mi south of southern boundary of forest, tel. 603/524–5003) has facilities for charters and private planes; **Lebanon Municipal Airport** (35 mi southwest of southern boundary of forest, tel. 603/298–8878) is served by USAir, Northwest, and Delta/Business Express.

You'll need a car to proceed to the White Mountains area, which is accessible from the airport by driving north on I–93.

BY CAR I–93 and Route 3 run north–south from Massachusetts to Quebec, bisecting the White Mountain National Forest at its western end. I–89 links Concord, south of the White Mountains, with central Vermont. Route 16, also running north–south, accesses the eastern portion of the forest, slicing through the Mt. Washington Valley. The Kancamagus Scenic Byway (Route 112) and Route 2 are the east–west thoroughfares that access the southern and northern regions of the national forest, respectively. Route 302 winds through the central portion of the forest in a southeast-to-northwest direction.

The official state map, available free from the Office of Travel and Tourism Development (Box 856, Concord, NH 03302, tel. 603/271–2666), has useful directories for each of the tourist areas.

BY BUS **Greyhound Lines** (tel. 800/231–2222) and its subsidiary, **Vermont Transit Lines** (tel. 603/228–3300 or 800/451–3292),

link the cities of New Hampshire with major cities along the eastern seaboard.

GETTING AROUND

BY CAR I–93 and Route 3 bisect the White Mountain National Forest on their south–north extent between Massachusetts and the Province of Quebec, Canada. On the eastern side of the area, Route 16 is the main artery from the coast, past the Mt. Washington valley and on toward Maine. The Kancamagus Scenic Byway (Route 112) is the east–west thoroughfare through the White Mountain National Forest.

BY BUS **Concord Trailways** (tel. 603/228–3523 or 800/639–3317 in NH).

REST STOPS North Conway at Routes 16 and 302 has a rest area with rest rooms, picnic facilities, and public phones. The visitor center at Lincoln, I–93, Exit 32, has rest rooms.

GUIDED TOURS **Otter Brook Wildlife Programs** (Intervale, tel. 603/356–5045) offers naturalist-led walks in the area to groups of any size. **Raven Interpretive Wildlife Programs** (Conway, tel. 603/447–5796) provides guides who lead bird- and mammal-watching expeditions. The **Appalachian Mountain Club** offers hundreds of educational programs each year, most of them out of the Pinkham Notch Visitor Center (*see* Tourist Offices, *above*). These include day programs covering a wide range of topics, including geology, meteorology, and forest ecology; workshops focusing on outdoor skills, such as backpacking, canoeing, snowshoeing, orienteering, and telemark skiing; and hikes led by skilled guides with extensive knowledge of the natural and cultural history of the White Mountains. For more information, or a catalogue—which makes choosing from its daunting array of guided hikes a bit easier— contact AMC Education Programs (Rte. 16, Box 298, Gorham, NH 03581, tel. 603/466–2721).

Outdoor Bound (Bear Swamp Rd., Montpelier, VT 05602, tel. 800/223–4172) offers a guided hut-to-hut hiking tour in the Presidential Range. **Great Outdoors Hiking and Walking Vacations** (Stonehurst Manor, Box 1937, North Conway, NH 03860, tel. 603/356–3113 or 800/525–9100) caters programs to various ages and abilities. **Hiking Holidays** (Monkton Rd., Bristol, VT 05443, tel. 802/453–4816) offers two- to five-day inn-to-inn tours.

EXPLORING

The White Mountains region is compact enough geographically so that you can drive in a single morning from the discount shopping malls of North Conway to the rugged scenery of the presidential range, the spine of mountains running north from Mt. Jackson to Mt. Madison.

North Conway has a high concentration of hotels, motels, and restaurants, along with discount outlets. Here the **Conway Scenic Railroad** (Main St., tel. 603/356–5251) operates from May to October (admission charged). A steam engine pulls antique coaches, 11 miles in one hour, past forests, cornfields, and rocky rivers. From North Conway, take Route 16/302 north to Glen. If you want to drive up Mt. Washington, continue on Route 16 to Glen House, 16 miles north of Glen.

Mt. Washington, at 6,288 feet the highest mountain in the northeastern United States, has severe weather conditions practically year-round. The two-hour drive up the mountain should be taken with caution, as hairpin turns and sharp drop-offs without guardrails are common; you should use low gear all the way. At the top, the Sherman Adams Summit Building has a museum and glassed-in viewing area. Hired drivers are available at Glen House to take you on a tour up the mountain. You can also hike it or take the Cog Railway at Bretton Woods (*see below*). *Road: Tel. 603/466–3988. Open mid-May–mid-Oct., daily. Toll charged on road.*

Crawford Notch State Park (tel. 603/374–2272), west of Glen past Bartlett on Route 302, is a good place for a picnic and a hike along the well-trodden trails to Arethusa Falls or Silver and Flume cascades. A more strenuous hike is the 1.4-mile trail up Mt. Willard. The trail departs from the Crawford Notch Depot information center on the west side of Route 302.

Bretton Woods, north of the park on Route 302, is a secluded village that was a preferred retreat of wealthy vacationers at the turn of the century who stayed at the sumptuous Mt. Washington Hotel, which still welcomes guests today. The view of the presidential range towering over the immense white structure is memorable.

The **Mt. Washington Cog Railway** is a steam-powered, mountain-climbing railway, operating since 1869. To reach the railway from Bretton Woods, take the marked road 6 miles northeast from Route 302. Don't attempt the 3½-hour round-trip in poor weather. *Rte. 302, Bretton Woods, tel. 603/846–5404 or 800/922–8825, ext. 6, outside NH. Operates May–early Nov., daily, weather permitting. Admission charged. Reservations advised.*

Continue west on Route 302, then pick up Route 3 after Twin Mountain and drive southwest toward Franconia Notch. A short detour north on Route 18 takes you to the town of Franconia, and if you head south for a few miles on Route 116, you'll see signs for Robert Frost's home.

The **Frost Place,** the poet's 1915 home, contains memorabilia and signed editions of his books. *Ridge Rd., Franconia, tel. 603/823–5510. Open July–Aug., Wed.–Mon.; June, weekends; call for hrs during fall foliage season. Admission charged.*

Return to Route 3 and drive south into Franconia Notch. From Route 3 you can pick up the **Franconia Notch State Parkway,** an 8-mile stretch of I–93 that cuts through this popular scenic area.

Echo Lake, off Exit 3 of the parkway, offers a pleasant sandy beach and swimming, fishing, and boating. Visitors have a view of Mt. Lafayette and nearby Cannon Mountain.

The **Cannon Mountain Aerial Tramway,** off Exit 2, lifts you 2,022 feet in five minutes to the 4,200-foot summit of the mountain. *Franconia Notch State Park, tel. 603/823–5563. Open mid-May–mid-Oct., daily; mid-Oct.– mid-May, weekends, weather permitting. Admission charged.*

Old Man of the Mountains (Great Stone Face), the most famous attraction in the Franconia Notch area, lies about ½ mile south of the Cannon Mountain tramway. This natural granite formation in the side of Profile Mountain resembles a flinty-faced old gentleman; it has been immortalized in writings of Nathaniel Hawthorne and Daniel Webster.

The Flume is located off Exit 1 at the southern end of Franconia Notch State Park, south of the Cannon Mountain tramway. At the site of this 800-foot-long natural chasm at the base of Mt. Liberty, visitors make their way along a series of boardwalks and stairways, and they get a view of **Avalanche Falls.** The visitor center offers a historic exhibit about the area and a 20-minute film that serves as an introduction to all the major sights in Franconia Notch State Park. The center also marks the beginning of a 9-mile paved bicycle path through the park that is suitable for walking. *Tel. 603/745–8391. Open mid-May–mid-Oct., daily. Admission charged to the Flume.*

The **Kancamagus Scenic Byway,** a 34-mile stretch interrupted by only one cutoff at Bear Notch Road, takes you through some of the east's most magnificent mountain scenery. It is the state's most popular (and crowded) route for viewing the fall foliage. The road takes you by Loon Mountain and follows the Hancock branch of the Pemigewasset River and the Swift River. About halfway through the drive, keep an eye out for the parking lot and picnic area at Sabbaday Falls. A ½-mile trail takes you to the multilevel cascade that plunges through two potholes and a flume. A few miles east you'll find the beginning of the self-guided Rail and River trail at the Passaconaway Information Center near the Bear Notch Road. About 5 miles farther east, the moderately demanding 2.8-mile Boulder Loop trail begins opposite the Blackberry Crossing campground. The ledges offer good views of Mt. Chocorua and the Swift River valley. The Kancamagus Highway ends at Route 16 in Conway.

THE NATURAL WORLD The Presidential range contains the largest alpine area in the eastern United States and the exposed summits are home to many endangered plant species. Evergreen perennials grow close to the ground and many have leaves that overlap each other or have protective coverings. Many of these tiny alpine plants flower from early spring to midsummer; they are best seen in late June. Look for the five-petaled white diapensia, minuscule pink alpine azalea, white Labrador tea, and pink-magenta Lapland rosebay. The rare mountain avens is common here; the only other place in the world where it is found is on a small island off Nova Scotia. Robbins (dwarf) cinquefoil, a fuzzy plant with yellow flowers, grows only in a small area of the Presidential Range and is one of the rarest species in the United States.

Keep a lookout for moose in marshy, boggy areas along the eastern section of the Kancamagus Scenic Byway. Weighing in at about 1,000 pounds and measuring up to 6 feet at the shoulder, it is the largest animal in the White Mountains. Its gangly grace and unpredictability make sighting one an unforgettable experience. Often spotted at lower elevations and along roadsides in the spring (where they seek food and refuge from the black flies), moose tend to be active at night, making car–moose collisions an increasing problem. Visitors to the area are advised to be extremely cautious around these beasts: Do not approach them—take photographs and view them from a safe distance.

More than 200 species of birds make their warm-weather home in the White Mountains. Watch for gold and purple finch, rose-breasted grosbeak, blackpoll and Canada warbler, scarlet tanager, and wood thrush. At higher elevations, on rock ledges or above the tree line, sightings of broad-winged hawks, great horned owls, and other birds of prey are frequent. Sharp-sighted bird-watchers may also spot bald eagles and peregrine falcons in the region.

HOTELS AND INNS

Resorts, motels, country inns, and bed-and-breakfasts are thick as snowflakes; only during foliage season should you hesitate to travel without reservations. (Getting into a special place requires advance calling in any season.) The following organizations have reservation services: **Lincoln/Woodstock Chamber of Commerce** (tel. 603/745–6621 or 800/227–4191), **White Mountains Attractions** (tel. 603/745–8720 or 800/346–3687), the **Mt. Washington Valley Visitors Bureau** (tel. 603/356–3171 or 800/367–3364), **Country Inns in the White Mountains** (tel. 603/356–9460 or 800/562–1300), and the **Jackson Resort Association** (tel. 800/866–3334). Price categories for double occupancy, excluding 8% tax, are Expensive, $100–$130; Moderate, $70–$100; and Inexpensive, under $70.

BARTLETT **Notchland Inn.** Overlooking the Saco River valley at the entrance to Crawford Notch, this unique, wood-paneled mansion dating from the 19th century features bedrooms furnished with armoires, wing chairs, afghans, and working fireplaces. *Rte. 302, Hart's Location, 03812, tel. 603/374–6131 or 800/866–6131. 9 rooms, 2 suites. Full breakfast included, dining room, pool, hot tub, hiking, cross-country ski trails. AE, MC, V. Moderate.*

BETHLEHEM **The Bells.** This pagoda-shape bed-and-breakfast filled with family heirlooms and choice bits from the owners' antiques shop offers good value on a quiet residential side street. *Strawberry Hill St., 03574, tel. 603/869–2647. 4 rooms with bath. Full breakfast included. MC, V. Inexpensive–Moderate.*

CONWAY **Tanglewood Motel & Cottages.** You can swim or fish in a mountain stream just outside the door of this neat, family-operated, one-floor motel, with rooms in a variety of sizes (some sleep up to six) and two-person cottages with fully equipped kitchens. *Rte. 16, 03818, tel. 603/447–5932. 13 rooms with bath. AE, MC, V. Inexpensive–Moderate.*

EAST MADISON **Purity Spring Resort.** Once a farm and sawmill situated on a private lake, Purity Spring has been run for a century as a four-season, American-plan resort. Whether you choose rooms in the main inn, adjacent lodge, or separate cottages, the decor is sturdy, old-fashioned New England. Skiers note: the King Pine Ski Area is on the property. *Rte. 153, 03849, tel. 603/367–8896 or 800/367–8897. 45 rooms, 35 with bath. Restaurant, private lake, tennis courts, volleyball. MC, V. Moderate.*

FRANCONIA **Franconia Inn.** Many of the rooms have canopy beds at this friendly white-clapboard bed-and-breakfast inn on 117 scenic acres, with access to various sports. *Easton Rd., 03580, tel. 603/823–5542 or 800/473–5299. 31 rooms, 3 suites. Full breakfast included, restaurant, pool, tennis court, cross-country skiing, riding stable, glider field. AE, MC, V. Moderate.*

GLEN **Covered Bridge House.** The second-floor bedrooms at this conveniently located inn—complete with its own authentic 1851 covered bridge—have lace curtains, period furniture, country-style accessories, and a selection of books for rainy-day relaxation. *Box 358, Rte. 302, 03838, tel. 603/383–9109 or 800/232–9109. 5 rooms. Full breakfast included, gift shop, private river beach. AE, MC, V. Inexpensive–Moderate.*

JACKSON **Inn at Thorn Hill.** This casually elegant, romantic hideaway with a main house (designed by Stanford White), a carriage house, and three cottages is convenient to shops, galleries, and sports; it's better suited to couples than families. *Thorn Hill Rd., 03846, tel. 603/383–4242 or 800/289–8990. 14 double rooms, 2 suites, 3 cottages. Full breakfast included, restaurant, pub,* *pool, cross-country ski trails. AE, MC, V. Moderate–Expensive.*

NORTH CONWAY **1785 Inn.** This striking white Colonial inn with blue trim offers mountain views, rooms with country-style furnishings and varied Colonial-to-Victorian antiques, and a prize-winning restaurant. *Box 1785, Rte. 16, 03860, tel. 603/356–9025 or 800/421–1785. 17 rooms, 12 with bath; 1 suite. Full breakfast included, restaurant, room service, pool, cross-country ski trails, tennis courts. AE, D, DC, MC, V. Moderate–Expensive.*

SNOWVILLE **Snowvillage Inn.** Guest rooms furnished with four-posters and working fireplaces, and conservationist innkeepers who lead guided mountain walks with fine lunches, make this complex of three converted buildings an outstanding choice. *Box A-50, Snowville 03849, tel. 603/447–2818 or 800/447–4345. 18 rooms with bath. Restaurant, cross-country trails, tennis. AE, MC, V. Choice of bed-and-breakfast or breakfast and dinner. Moderate–Expensive.*

MOTELS

MODERATE **Briarcliff Motel** (North Conway 03860, tel. 603/356–5584 or 800/338–4291). 29 rooms; pool. **Covered Bridge Motor Lodge** (Box V, Jackson 03846, tel. 603/383–9151 or 800/634–2911). 32 rooms; pool, tennis courts, fishing. **The Lodge at Jackson Village** (Box 593, Jackson Village 03846, tel. 603/383–0999 or 800/233–5634). 32 rooms; pool, tennis courts, room refrigerators. **Swiss Chalets Motel** (RR 1, Box 91, Intervale 03845, tel. 603/356–2232 or 800/831–2727). 36 rooms; pool, cross-country trails.

INEXPENSIVE **School House Motel** (Box 368, North Conway 03860, tel. 603/356–6829 or 800/638–6050). 25 rooms; pool. **Villager Motel** (Box 427, Barlett 03812, tel. 603/374–2742 or 800/334–6988). 18 rooms; pool, rooms available with kitchenettes and fireplaces. **The Will's Inn** (Box 359, Barlett 03812, tel. 603/383–6757 or 800/233–6780). 23 rooms; 9 rooms with kitchenettes.

CAMPGROUNDS

New Hampshire Campground Owners Association (Box 320, Twin Mountain 03595, tel. 603/846–5511) will send a list of all private, state, and national forest campgrounds.

Appalachian Mountain Club runs eight mountain huts, where you can experience the wilderness with a roof over your head and meals prepared for you. The huts vary in size, with most of them sleeping about 40 people, mostly in bunk rooms. All have superb settings alongside the trails of the White Mountain National Forest; you can hike from one hut to the next. The club also runs a rustic yet immaculate lodge with 23 dorm-style rooms and a restaurant adjacent to the Pinkham Notch Visitor Center. Hiking trails start right from the front door! *Rte. 16, Box 298, Gorham 03581, tel. 603/466–2727, fax 603/466–2720. Reservations advised. MC, V.*

White Mountain National Forest (Box 638, Laconia 03247, tel. 603/528–8721) has 22 roadside campgrounds that tend to provide less in the way of such facilities as hot water, showers, and electricity than private campgrounds; most can accommodate small trailers, but offer no hookups. The campgrounds listed below are among the most popular; reservations are taken for portions of Basin, Campton, Blackberry Crossing, Covered Bridge, and Dolly Copp (tel. 800/280–2267) from March through September. For a complete listing of the national forest campgrounds in the White Mountains, contact the forest service (tel. 603/528–8721). Unless noted otherwise, the campgrounds described below are in New Hampshire.

Russell Pond (Tripoli Rd., Campton, 13 mi off I–93, Exit 31) is situated on a particularly scenic pond and offers interpretive nature programs Saturday evening at dusk during the summer; the boat launch and dock are designed for wheelchair access. It has 49 tent sites and 38 trailer sites. Fee: About $15. **Basin** (Rte. 113, 15 mi north of Fryeburg, ME) has 21 sites, fishing, and a boat ramp.

Fee: About $15. **Hancock** (Kancamagus Hwy., 4 mi east of Lincoln) has 56 sites, 35 with trailer space, and was designed for easy access by trailers or RVs. An appealing swimming hole, Upper Lady's Bath, is a five-minute walk downstream from the campground. Fee: About $15 (no reservations taken). **Campton** (2 mi east of the city of Campton on Rte. 49) has 58 sites in an area heavily wooded with towering white pines; it has a playing field and summer interpretive programs, and is the only campground with showers. Vacancies are usually available in the summer season, even on weekends and holidays. Fee: About $15–$20. **Blackberry Crossing** and **Covered Bridge** (Kancamagus Hwy., 6 mi west of Conway) are across the street from each other, and conveniently located for hiking and fishing; Blackberry has 26 sites (fee: about $15), Covered Bridge has 49 sites (fee: about $15). **Dolly Copp** (Rte. 16, 6 mi south of Gorham) is huge—as many as 1,000 people may be camped here at one time. It offers summer interpretive programs and is close to many of the popular hiking areas; there are 176 sites. Fee: About $15.

State Parks in New Hampshire have campgrounds in or near White Mountain National Forest, with fees ranging from $12 to $15 per night. No reservations are accepted: Sites are available on a first-come, first-served basis. Campgrounds are generally set up for tent camping; small trailers are welcome where they fit, but no hookups are provided. Campgrounds are open from mid-May through mid-October, with the exception of Lafayette Campground in Franconia Notch, which is open year-round, although there is no water in winter. Senior citizens get reduced rates Sunday through Thursday. A carry-in, carry-out policy has been established at the state parks: Trash barrels have been removed to provide visitors with a more pristine outdoor experience and to encourage wildlife to remain wild. Contact the **New Hampshire Division of Parks and Recreation** (172 Pembroke Rd., Box 856, Concord, NH 03302, tel. 603/271–3254) for more information about the campgrounds.

DINING

Dining opportunities in the White Mountains range from country inns serving fine dinners in hushed, candlelit dining rooms to simple, easygoing family restaurants specializing in generous portions and cheerful service; diners with special dietary demands will find most establishments sympathetic to their needs. Visitors should be aware that many inns in the area have their own restaurants that are open to nonguests. Only the very special dining rooms require reservations. Price categories per person, excluding 8% tax, service, and drinks, are Moderate, $15–$25, and Inexpensive, under $15.

CONWAY **Darby Field Inn.** Visitors at this delightful, blue-clapboard mountain retreat can dine by candlelight as they sample the eclectic menu, featuring American and Continental cuisines, with attention paid to those seeking low-fat and vegetarian entrées. *Bald Hill, tel. 603/447–2181 or 800/426–4147, fax 603/447–5726. AE, MC, V. Moderate.*

FRANCONIA **Franconia Inn.** The two brothers who own the Franconia Inn devote themselves to pleasing a variety of customers, from families with young children to health-conscious couples who dine on simply prepared veal and chicken dishes. *Easton Rd., tel. 603/823–5542 or 800/473–5299. Reservations advised. AE, MC, V. Moderate.*

GLEN **The Bernerhof.** The dining room with its rubbed wood and flowers has an alpine ambience, and the cooking is primarily classic French, with veal dishes a specialty. *Rte. 302, tel. 603/383–4411. AE, MC, V. Moderate.*

Margaritaville. If you need a break from traditional New England cuisine, you'll find superbly prepared, authentic Mexican food at this appropriately named restaurant, presided over by five friendly sisters. *Rte. 302, tel. 603/383–6556. No credit cards. Inexpensive.*

NORTH CONWAY **Scottish Lion.** You can sample such American-Scottish specialties as hot oatcakes in the cozy dining room of this part bed-and-breakfast inn and part tartan-papered pub, both overlooking meadows and mountains. *Rte. 16, tel. 603/ 356–6381. AE, DC, MC, V. Moderate.*

SNOWVILLE **Snowvillage Inn.** The influence of Austria turns up in the decor of the inn's wood-paneled, mountain-view dining room and in the single-entrée dinners. The kitchen staff happily accommodates diners who request low-cholesterol or vegetarian meals. *Stuart Rd., tel. 603/447–2818 or 800/ 447–4345. Reservations required. AE, MC, V. Moderate.*

SHOPPING

Custom-made hiking boots are the pride of the Mt. Washington Valley, but the area is also known for good family sportswear, especially ski clothes. North Conway has become a shopping mecca for its dense concentration of designer and factory outlets, but the town also offers less frantic specialty stores along Route 16/302, known locally as Main Street.

FACTORY OUTLETS AND MALLS **Mt. Washington Valley Outlet Association** (Box 2264, Conway, tel. 603/447–5295) answers questions about the more than 90 outlets in Mt. Washington Valley. On Route 16 in North Conway, look for names like Anne Klein, Dansk, L. L. Bean, Corning, Reebok, and Ralph Lauren. The **Depot Factory Outlet Stores** (Rte. 112, Lincoln) stock predominantly factory seconds. **Millfront Marketplace, Mill at Loon Mountain** (tel. 603/ 745–2245) is a clutch of specialty stores at the junction of I–93 and the Kancamagus Highway.

OUTDOOR ACTIVITIES

BIKING Loon Mountain and Bretton Woods ski resorts (*see* Skiing, *below*) open their trails and surrounding logging roads to cyclists during the summer months, and also offer bike rentals and repairs. Miles of well-maintained cross-country ski trails in

the Whitaker Woods area are also accessible to mountain bikers. The Bartlett Experimental Forest has various graded dirt roads that lead off Bear Notch Road; the terrain is gentle and ideal for beginners. National Forest Service maps of the extensive trail network open to cyclists on federal land can be purchased at the Pemigewasset and Saco ranger district offices. Also, look for "20 Off-Road and Back-Road Routes in Mt. Washington Valley," a pamphlet available at local sporting goods stores. Mountain bikers should take note that the five wilderness areas—Caribou-Speckled Mountain, Great Gulf, Pemigewasset, Presidential Range/Dry River, and Sandwich Range—are closed to bicycles.

Off-Road Cycling Adventures (Box 2055, North Conway, NH, tel. 603/356–2080) offers guided, half-day mountain-biking excursions in the Mt. Washington Valley. Among the many shops that rent and repair bikes are **Franconia Sport Shop** (Main St., Franconia, NH, tel. 603/823–5241), **The Greasy Wheel** (40 S. Main St., Plymouth, NH, tel. 603/536– 3655), and **Ski Fanatics** (Campton Plaza, Rte. 49, Campton, NH, tel. 603/726–4327).

CANOEING **Saco Bound** (Rte. 302, Center Conway, NH, tel. 603/447–2177 or 603/ 447–3801 for a brochure) specializes in guided family canoe, kayak, and camping trips—and white-water rafting on five rivers—as well as sales and rentals. Also try **Canoe Ring of New England** (Rtes. 16/302, North Conway, NH, tel. 603/356–5280) or **The Ledges** (Rte. 3, Woodstock, VT, tel. 603/ 745–8433) for rentals and shuttles. In the eastern side of the forest, **River Run** (Brownfield Bridge, Rte. 160, Brownfield, ME, tel. 207/452–2500) offers canoe rentals, shuttles, and camping areas for overnight trips.

FISHING The White Mountain National Forest supports 750 miles of streams and 50 freshwater ponds that abound with salmon, northern pike, pickerel, black bass, walleye, and lake, brook, and rainbow trout. For serious trout and salmon fishing, try the Connecticut lakes, though any clear stream in the White Mountains will do, many of which are stocked. The Swift River, flowing in an easterly direction for more than 20 miles along the Kancamagus Scenic Byway, is a popular and easily accessible spot for nabbing trout. Healthy brook and rainbow trout can also be found on the Ellis, Wildcat, and Saco rivers.

For those looking for a quieter angling experience, Big and Little Sawyer ponds—a hike from either the Kancamagus or Route 302—host brook trout, brown bullhead, American smelt, and creek chub. You can angle for chain pickerel, yellow perch, brown bullhead, and white sucker at Elbow Pond, a 1½-mile hike from Route 118 near Woodstock.

State fishing licenses are available from many area sporting goods and general stores or by writing to the **New Hampshire Fish and Game Department** (Rte. 3 N, Box 241, Lancaster, NH 03301, tel. 603/788–3164) or the **Maine Department of Inland Fisheries and Wildlife** (284 State St., Augusta, ME 04333, tel. 207/289–2043). **Twin Mountain Fish and Wildlife Center** (Rte. 3, Twin Mountain, tel. 603/846–5108) and **Warren Wildlife Center** (Rte. 25, Warren, tel. 603/764–8593) both have informative fishing-related displays and information.

HORSEBACK RIDING Guided trail rides through the national forest, as well as hay-wagon and pony rides, are available from the **Waterville Riding Stable** (north end of Waterville Valley, tel. 603/236–4811), **Fields at Attitash** (Rte. 302, Bartlett, tel. 603/374–2368), **Loon Mountain Park** (Kancamagus Hwy., Lincoln, tel. 603/745–8111), and **Nestlenook Farm** (Box Q, Dinsmore Rd., Jackson, tel. 603/383–0845).

HIKING The Appalachian Trail runs across the state and is a popular route for backpackers. Short hikes in Franconia Notch State Park include Artist's Bluff, Lonesome Lake, and the Basin-Cascades Trail. Off the Kancamagus Highway, try the Boulder Loop or Greely Ponds trail or the more challenging Champney Falls and Piper trails to the summit of Mt. Chocorua. Sanguinari Ridge Trail in Dixville

Notch is also a good, fairly easy hike. For further information about hiking, contact the **Appalachian Mountain Club** (Box 298, Pinkham Notch, Gorham 03581, tel. 603/466–2725), **White Mountain National Forest** (719 N. Main St., Laconia 03246, tel. 603/528–8721), and **New England Hiking Holidays-White Mountains** (Box 1648, North Conway 03860, tel. 603/356–9696 or 800/869–0949).

LAMA TREKKING **Snowvillage Inn** (Snowville, tel. 603/447–2818 or 800/447–4345) conducts a guided trip up Foss Mountain. Your elegant picnic will include gourmet food from the inn's kitchen along with champagne. Luckily you don't have to carry the food, the fine china, or the silverware—llamas do that for you. Reservations are required. **White Mountain Llamas at the Stag Hollow Inn** (Jefferson, tel. 603/586–4598) will introduce you to llama trekking, with one- to four-day hikes on beautiful, secluded trails. The hiking trips include picnic foods, but the primary focus is on the surrounding nature.

SKIING **Attitash** (Rte. 302, Barlett 03812, tel. 603/374–2368) has downhill skiing on 22 miles of trails. **Black Mountain** (Rte. 16B, Jackson 03846, tel. 603/383–4490) has primarily easy to middling terrain on a mountain with a 1,100-foot vertical drop. **Bretton Woods** (Rte. 302, Bretton Woods 03575, tel. 603/278–5000) offers both downhill skiing on 26 trails and 62 miles of cross-country ski trails. **Cannon Mountain** (Franconia Notch State Park, Franconia 03580, tel. 603/823–5563) is one of the oldest New England ski areas and still one of the more challenging, with a 2,150-foot vertical drop. **Loon Mountain** (Kancamagus Hwy., Lincoln 03251, tel. 603/745–8111) specializes in wide, straight, and consistent intermediate trails, with 22 miles of cross-country trails. **Mount Cranmore** (Box 1640, North Conway 03860, tel. 603/356–5543) has a range of downhill slopes (mostly for intermediates) and 37 miles of cross-country trails. **Wildcat Mountain** (Pinkham Notch, Rte. 16, Jackson 03846, tel. 603/466–3326) is known for tough expert trails.

Williamsburg
Virginia
Updated by Bruce Walker

f all our surviving Colonial American towns, none is more colorful or historic than Williamsburg, the capital of Virginia in the days of Washington, Jefferson, and Patrick Henry. It sits between the James and the York rivers, astride the busy Virginia Peninsula, preserving the exciting pace of 18th-century America.

The heart of Williamsburg is the mile-long Historic Area that the late John D. Rockefeller, Jr., quietly began buying up in 1926, now restored to its pre-Revolutionary luster. At one end is the College of William and Mary, founded in 1693, and at the other stands the Capitol, seat of the royal governor until 1776. Throughout the town are dozens of historic sites—Colonial homes, crafts shops, and taverns like the Raleigh, where Washington and fellow legislators talked revolt over ale and chicken pie.

Today, trained craftspeople make rifles and wigs and wagon wheels before your eyes. Costumed interpreters bring the Capitol and the Governor's Palace to life, and up and down Duke of Gloucester Street roll horse-drawn carriages as the bell clangs in Bruton Church's tower. Against the Colonial backdrop, reconstructed taverns serve 18th-century food, actors and musicians perform, and militia drills draw crowds to the village greens. Harpsichord concerts are held in the Governor's Palace, folk art is exhibited in the Abby Aldrich Rockefeller Folk Art Center, and 18th-century decorative arts in the DeWitt Wallace Gallery.

A scenic drive, the Colonial Parkway, connects Williamsburg with Jamestown, England's first permanent foothold in the New World, and Yorktown, site of the conclusive battle of the Revolution. Near Williamsburg lie several of the historic James River plantations, well worth a trip.

ESSENTIAL INFORMATION

WHEN TO GO Most visitors to Williamsburg come in July and August, when the temperature is frequently in the 90s. Spring and fall have better weather and fewer people; from January to the end of March and from mid-September through November the crowds are thinnest. The height of spring bloom comes at the end of April, when Virginia celebrates Historic Garden Week and many old homes are opened to the public. Rains sometimes mar June, but in July and August the sun usually shines. Many visitors come for Christmas shopping on Merchants Square in town and at the Williamsburg Pottery and discount malls on Richmond Road.

FESTIVALS AND SPECIAL EVENTS **Feb.:** a five-day Antiques Forum. **Apr.:** a four-day Garden Symposium and Virginia Garden Week. **July–Aug.:** family programs abound and fife-and-drum parades march from the Capitol to Market Square. **Labor Day weekend:** Publick Times—children's songs and dances, militia encampments on Palace Green and Market Square, and old-time horse races. **Oct.:** An Occasion for the Arts (street fair with sales of

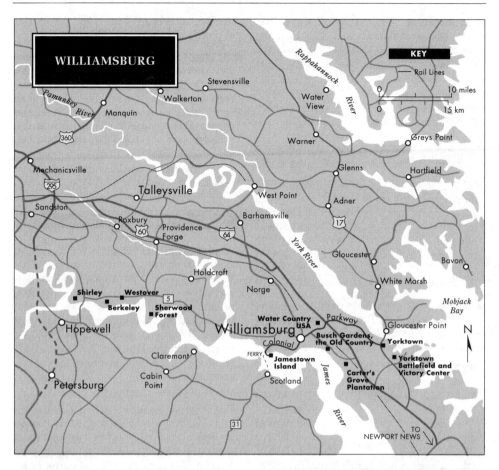

arts and crafts). **Dec.:** The spectacular Grand Illumination, candlelight concerts, caroling, and tree-decoration workshops are some of the many holiday activities.

BARGAINS Frequent free concerts and lectures are held at William and Mary (tel. 804/221–2630), and street theater in the Historic Area takes the form of "character interpreters" dressed as 18th-century citizens who engage visitors in conversation about such "current" events as the infamous stamp tax. Among local wares that are good buys are peanuts from nearby farms, Smithfield and country hams, glassware reproductions from the Jamestown Glasshouse, and reproductions of the salt-glaze and brown-glaze pottery of the early settlers. At Yorktown, the National Park Service's Visitor Center and the battlefields are free. The Jamestown–Scotland Wharf toll ferry (fee charged) will take you on a beautiful 2½-mile crossing of the James River.

TOURIST OFFICES Contact the **Williamsburg Convention and Visitors Bureau** (201 Penniman Rd., Williamsburg 23185, tel. 804/253–0192) for a visitors guide to Williamsburg; the **Visitor Center** (tel. 804/220–7659 or 800/447–8679) for general information and Historic Area hotels and restaurants; and the **Colonial National Historical Park** (tel. 804/898–3400 for Yorktown, and 804/229–1733 for Jamestown).

EMERGENCIES For Williamsburg **police, fire,** and **ambulance:** dial 911. Virginia State Police (tel. 800/582–8350). **Hospital:** Williamsburg Community Hospital (301 Monticello Ave., tel. 804/253–6000). **Pharmacies** are open Monday–Saturday 9–9 and Sunday 11–6; at other times, call the hospital.

ARRIVING AND DEPARTING

BY PLANE Newport News–Williamsburg International Airport (tel. 804/877–0924) is 20 miles from Williamsburg. **Richmond International** (tel. 804/226–3052) and **Norfolk International** (tel. 804/857–3351) are both 50 miles away. All airports are served by taxis and by Carey/VIP & Celebrity Limousines Inc. (tel. 804/220–1616, fax 804/253–1948).

BY CAR Most visitors arrive by car on I–64. Those coming from Richmond may want to take slower-paced Route 5, the John Tyler Highway, past the James River plantations.

BY TRAIN AND BUS Amtrak (tel. 800/872–7245) has train service from Boston, New York, and Washington, D.C. **Greyhound Lines** (468 N. Boundary St., tel. 800/231–2222) connect Williamsburg with all parts of the nation.

GETTING AROUND

Historic Area shuttle buses (free for ticket holders) make nine stops on a constant circuit of the area before returning to the Visitor Center. Williamsburg is best seen on foot and by using these buses, but a car is convenient for visiting outlying sights.

REST STOPS At the Visitor Center; at the ticket center at Duke of Gloucester and Henry streets; behind the Davidson Shop at Duke of Gloucester and Botetourt streets; between the Governor's Palace and the Brush-Everard House on Palace Green; in the Governor's Palace courtyard; between the Capitol and Waller Street; on Francis Street near the Magazine; at the Publick Hospital, DeWitt Wallace Gallery of Decorative Arts, Abby Aldrich

Rockefeller Folk Art Center, and Bassett Hall Visitor Center on Francis Street.

GUIDED TOURS Williamsburg Limousines, Inc. (tel. 804/877–0279) conducts guided tours to Jamestown and Yorktown. It also runs shuttle buses from Williamsburg hotels and motels daily to Jamestown, Yorktown, Busch Gardens, and Carter's Grove plantation. **Historic Air Tours** (tel. 804/253–8185) runs flights over the Colonial settlements, James River plantations, and historic battlefields.

EXPLORING

COLONIAL WILLIAMSBURG People usually go first to the **Visitor Center,** close to I–64, to buy tour passes, make dinner and entertainment reservations, and watch *The Patriot* orientation film (35 minutes). One-day, one-week, and one-year passes cost $25–$30; Bassett Hall admission is included in the $30 pass. Get a copy of the weekly "Visitors Companion," which lists programs and has a good map. To do the town justice, allow at least three days.

Duke of Gloucester Street, the spine of the pedestrian area, extends from the **Wren Building** at William and Mary to the **Capitol.** Both are exquisite buildings, and the Capitol will orient you historically. In between are the **Governor's Palace, Bruton Parish Church,** private houses and gardens, taverns of the period, and the functioning workshops of a wig maker, printer, tailor, wheelwright, silversmith, milliner, and the like. Here you can also see wonderful collections of folk art (at the Abby Aldrich Rockefeller Center) and decorative arts (at the DeWitt Wallace Gallery) as well as the Rockefellers' personal treasures, on view at Bassett Hall.

A day trip west of town along Route 5 will take you to four of the famous James River plantations. If your time is limited, go to Berkeley or Shirley.

JAMESTOWN ISLAND The **Visitor Center** (tel. 804/229–1733) is a National Park Service museum that tells Jamestown's history and the story of John Smith, Pocahontas, and Chief Powhatan in diorama and archaeological exhibits. Nearby is the reconstructed Glasshouse of 1608, where costumed artisans blow glass. Admission to both is included in the park entrance fee (about $10 per car). **Jamestown Settlement** (tel. 804/229–1607), adjoining Jamestown Island, is a 20-acre state park with full-scale replicas of the Jamestown settlers' three ships, *Susan Constant, Godspeed,* and *Discovery*; a reconstruction of a Powhatan Indian village and of the original triangular James Fort; and an indoor museum. *Glasshouse Point. Open daily; closed Dec. 25. (settlement also closed Jan. 1). Admission charged.*

YORKTOWN The **Visitor Center Museum** (tel. 804/898–3400), near the actual 1781 siege lines, depicts on a relief map the siege that forced the British to surrender; it also depicts the Battle of the Capes, in which the French fleet halted British rescue ships. At the **Nelson House** in summer, a historical drama on the life of Thomas Nelson takes place every half hour. The **Yorktown Victory Center,** a state-run museum, focuses on events in the Revolution leading to the siege, with a film, replicas of an encampment and an 18th-century farm site, and an audio exhibit starring six talking plaster figures. *Tel. 804/887–1776. Open daily; closed Jan. 1, Dec. 25. Admission free to Visitor Center; admission charged to Victory Center.*

BUSCH GARDENS An open-air theme park celebrates the popular attractions of Great Britain, France, Germany, and Italy, with amusement-park rides, entertainments and shows, and hearty European food. *3 mi east of town, tel. 804/253–3350. Open mid-May–Labor Day, daily; other times, weekends; closed Nov.–Mar. Admission charged.*

CARTER'S GROVE At the Burwell estate, 5 miles east of town, the house is exhibited as restored in the 1930s by its last private owners. The grounds contain the **Winthrop Rockefeller Archaeological Museum** and remains of Wolstenholme Town, wiped out by Indians in 1622. *Rte. 60 at Grove, tel.*

800/246–2099. Open mid-Mar.–Dec., Tues.–Sun. Admission charged.

SHIRLEY The Colonial home of the Hill and Carter families was visited in the Civil War by Robert E. Lee, whose mother, Anne Carter Lee, lived here. *Rte. 5, in Charles City County, tel. 804/829–5121. Open daily; closed Dec. 25. Admission charged.*

BERKELEY This plantation, settled in early Jamestown days, was later owned by the Harrisons. Benjamin Harrison V, who built much of the present house, signed the Declaration of Independence, served as governor, and fathered President William Henry Harrison. *Rte. 5, Charles City County, tel. 804/829–6018. Open daily; closed Dec. 25. Admission charged.*

SHERWOOD FOREST When John Tyler retired from the presidency in 1845, he enlarged this farmhouse for himself and his new wife and named it for Robin Hood's hideaway. *Rte. 5, Charles City County, tel. 804/829–5377. Open daily; closed Thanksgiving, Dec. 25. Admission charged.*

WESTOVER William Byrd II, founder of Richmond, urbane scholar, and man of the world, built this mansion to be the seat of the Byrd dynasty. *Rte. 5, Charles City County, tel. 804/829–2882. Grounds and garden open daily; closed Jan. 1, Dec. 25. Admission charged.*

MARINER'S MUSEUM Thirty miles east of town is a maritime park created in 1931, whose galleries are crammed with ship models, paintings, historic vessels, and artifacts of the seven seas. *Warwick Blvd. and J. Clyde Morris Blvd., Newport News, tel. 804/595–0368. Open daily; closed Dec. 25. Admission charged.*

WATER COUNTRY USA Although you can't swim in the huge wave pool, a dozen aquatic rides will get you delightfully wet. *Rte. 199 east of town, tel. 804/229–9300. Admission charged. Open Memorial Day–Labor Day, daily; May and early Sept., weekends.*

THE NATURAL WORLD Williamsburg sits in flat tidewater farmland crisscrossed by creeks and punctuated by stands of tall pines. The town is a haven for songbirds, many resisting the urge to migrate because of the year-round bird feeding. Livestock is kept in town pastures, as was done in early times, and visitors are greeted by the sight of browsing horses and dray oxen. Jamestown Island (admission $8 per car), a federal game preserve inhabited by deer, possum, raccoon, rabbits, squirrels, and songbirds, is circuited by a 5-mile nature trail. In the early morning, bird-watchers stand with binoculars along the James, scanning the scene for the abundant wildlife.

HOTELS AND INNS

The most unusual and convenient hostelries—the Williamsburg Inn, the Williamsburg Lodge, Woodlands, and the Governor's Inn—are run by Colonial Williamsburg (tel. 804/229–1000 or 800/447–8679). Bed-and-breakfasts and motels outside the area are less expensive but have less Colonial atmosphere; you'll get even lower prices in Yorktown and Newport News. Price categories for double occupancy, excluding 8½% sales tax, are Expensive, over $95; Moderate, $60–$95; and Inexpensive, under $60.

EXPENSIVE **Liberty Rose Bed and Breakfast.** This pleasant clapboard-and-brick suburban house on wooded grounds has eclectic, romantic decor that combines Victorian with 18th-century antiques and reproductions. *1022 Jamestown Rd., 23185, tel. 804/253–1260. 4 rooms. Full breakfast included. AE, MC, V.*

Williamsburg Inn. This prestigious inn adjacent to the Historic Area is decorated in the elegant Regency style and is known for its impeccable service. *Francis St., 23185, tel. 800/447–8679, fax 804/220–7798. 120 rooms. Dining room, bar, health club with indoor pool, outdoor pool, golf course. AE, MC, V.*

Williamsburg Hospitality House. This convenient, modern hotel within walking distance of the Historic Area has quiet service

and sumptuous decor and offers off-street parking. *415 Richmond Rd., 23185, tel. 804/229–4020 or 800/932–9192, fax 804/220–1560. 309 rooms. Dining room, bar, pool. AE, D, DC, MC, V.*

Williamsburg Lodge. This well-known Early American–style hotel, part of Colonial Williamsburg's Conference Center, is in the Historic Area. *5 S. England St., 23185, tel. 800/447–8679; fax 804/220–7797. 315 rooms. Dining room, bar, exercise club with indoor pool, outdoor pool, bike rentals, golf course. AE, MC, V.*

MODERATE **Applewood Colonial Bed and Breakfast.** This pleasant brick house with Colonial decor, canopy beds, and an apple theme is a fine place for families, within walking distance of the Historic Area. *605 Richmond Rd., 23185, tel. 800/899–2753. 4 rooms. Full candlelit breakfast and afternoon beverages included. MC, V.*

Heritage Inn. This charming and comfortable motel 1 mile from the Historic Area is a three-story building built in the mid-'60s, decorated inside and out in true colonial style. *1324 Richmond Rd., 23185, tel. 804/229–6220 or 800/782–3800, fax 804/229–2774. 54 rooms. Dining room, pool with patio. AE, D, DC, MC, V.*

Williamsburg Woodlands. At this spacious facility adjoining the Visitor Center, some rooms accommodate up to five. Guests dine at the adjacent Woodlands Grill or the Cascades Restaurant. *102 Visitor Center Dr., tel. 800/447–8679, fax 804/220–7788. 311 rooms. 3 outdoor pools, picnic area, fitness trail, tennis courts, golf, miniature golf. AE, D, DC, MC, V.*

INEXPENSIVE-MODERATE **War Hill Inn.** This 1960s colonial, secluded amid pastures and orchards 2 miles from town, is full of family things and Colonial reproductions. *4560 Long Hill Rd., 23188, tel. 804/565–0248 or 800/743–0248. 5 rooms, 2 sleep 4. Full breakfast included. MC, V.*

MOTELS

MODERATE **Budget Host-Governor Spotts-wood** (1508 Richmond Rd., 23185, tel. 804/229–6444 or 800/368–1244, fax 804/253–2410. 80 rooms; pool, playground, coffee in rooms, cable TV. **Carolyn Motor Court** (1446 Richmond Rd., 23185, tel. 804/229–6666 or 800/446–8930, fax 804/220–9917). 65 rooms; coffee shop, pool, cable TV. **Governor's Inn** (506 N. Henry St., 23185, tel. 804/220–7379, fax 804/220–7788). 200 rooms; free bus to Historic Area and Cascades restaurant, pool, Continental breakfast included, pets allowed. **Holiday Inn Express** (119 Bypass Rd., 23185, tel. 804/253–1663, fax 804/220–9117). 132 rooms; pool, Continental breakfast included, cable TV.

INEXPENSIVE **King William Inn** (824 Capitol Landing Rd., 23185, tel. 804/229–4933 or 800/446–1041, fax 804/229–9686). 183 rooms; pool, cable TV. **Quality Inn–Lord Paget** (901 Capitol Landing Rd., tel. 804/229–4444 or 800/537–2438, fax 804/220–9314). 95 rooms; café, pool, coin laundry, cable TV, putting green, fishing lake. **Westpark Hotel** (1600 Richmond Rd., 23185, tel. 804/229–1134, fax 804/229–3215). 163 rooms; restaurant, indoor pool, video games, bellhops, cable TV.

CAMPGROUNDS

Most area campgrounds (around Jamestown and along I–64, at least 5 miles from Williamsburg) are open March–mid-November. Advance reservations for June–August are needed at all of them. Contact the Visitors Bureau (tel. 800/368–6511) for information.

Williamsburg KOA Kampground. This camp near a lake provides free van service to Williamsburg and sells tickets to the attractions. *Exit 55 from Rte. 646 at Lightfoot, 23188, tel. 804/565–2907 or 800/635–2717. 17 cabins that sleep 4, 3 cabins that sleep 6, 65 RV sites, full and partial hookups, 75 tent sites, showers, bathrooms, laundry, solar heated pool, lake fishing. MC, V.*

DINING

Chesapeake Bay yields seafood in abundance for the restaurants of Williamsburg. The beloved blue crab appears au gratin, in crab cakes, crab imperial, and crab *ravigote*. Oysters are served in stew, scalloped, and fried, and the delicate shad roe, caught fresh in March and April, is served with new potatoes and fresh asparagus. Traditional tidewater cooking shows up in the Smithfield ham, kale, turnip greens, and hot breads served in a few restaurants.

At the Colonial Taverns, four authentic 18th-century eating places in the Historic Area, visitors dine in the atmosphere of Colonial times, with costumed waiters and oversize napkins and cutlery. The fare is hearty early American and differs in each tavern. All offer outdoor dining and accept AE, MC, and V. Price categories per person, excluding 8½% tax, service, and drinks, are Moderate, $15–$25, and Inexpensive, under $15.

MODERATE Colonial Taverns: **Christiana Campbell's** (Waller St., near Capitol, tel. 804/229–2141) features Virginia fish, crab, and oysters. **Chowning's** (Duke of Gloucester St. at Queen St., tel. 804/229–2141) specializes in Brunswick stew, duckling, and prime rib. **King's Arms** (Duke of Gloucester St., across from Raleigh Tavern, tel. 804/229–2141) offers game pie, peanut soup, and Virginia ham. **Shields** (Duke of Gloucester St., near Capitol, tel. 804/229–2141) serves spit-roasted chicken and broiled beef tenderloin.

Golden Horseshoe Clubhouse Grill. Good, simple lunches and dinners are served to golfers and others on the second floor of a luxurious white-brick Georgian clubhouse with a porch that overlooks a pond. *S. England St., tel. 804/220–7696. AE, MC, V, D.*

Nick's Seafood Pavilion. This famous Mediterranean-style eatery in Yorktown offers fresh seafood and Greek specialties. Try the bluefish, flounder, spot (a delicate ocean fish), or crabmeat. *Water St., Rte. 238 at south end of Yorktown Bridge, tel. 804/887–5269. AE, MC, V.*

The Trellis. This California-style restaurant serves an unusual array of entrées (specializing in Chesapeake seafood) in the spacious, plant-filled restaurant or outdoors in good weather. *Merchants Sq., tel. 804/229–8610. AE, MC, V.*

INEXPENSIVE **Back Fin Seafood Restaurant.** This unpretentious family-type restaurant with booths and tables serves good fresh fish, clams, and chicken to a nautical theme, with fishnets and oars on the walls. *1193 Jamestown Rd., tel. 804/220–2249. MC, V.*

Chickahominy House. Home-style southern breakfasts (Virginia ham, eggs, hominy grits) and Miss Melinda's Lunch (Brunswick stew, ham biscuits, and homemade pie) are served amid antique furnishings, which are for sale. *1211 Jamestown Rd., tel. 804/229–4689. MC, V.*

Morrison's Cafeteria. This southern chain serves such varied daily fare as Florida shrimp, roast beef, spoon bread, fried okra, and sweet-potato pie, in a large, airy room with greenery and colorful Colonial decor. *1851 Richmond Rd., tel. 804/253–0292. AE, MC, V.*

Polo Club Restaurant and Tavern. Polo equipment decorates this stylish bistro specializing in fresh fish, steaks, oversize burgers, and unusual sandwiches. *Colony Square Shopping Center on Jamestown Rd., tel. 804/220–1122. AE, MC, V.*

SHOPPING

Bargain hunters flock to the **Williamsburg Pottery** (tel. 804/564–3326), 5 miles west on Richmond Road. In 32 buildings are stacks of china, glassware, household goods, clothing, garden furniture, plants, and lots more—most of it at bargain prices. Near the Pottery are countless outlet malls and discount shops. More expensive reproduction 18th-century furnishings are sold at the **Craft House at the Williamsburg Inn** (tel. 804/220–7749) and at **Merchants Square** (tel. 804/220–7747).

OUTDOOR ACTIVITIES

BIKING The Historic Area limits auto traffic, thus affording space for pedestrians and bicyclists. Bicycles can be rented at the **Williamsburg Lodge** on South England Street (tel. 804/229–1000).

CARRIAGE RIDING For a leisurely view, ride through Williamsburg in an 18th-century horse-drawn carriage. Reserved tickets may be purchased on the day of the ride at the **Greenhow Lumber House** on Duke of Gloucester Street (tel. 804/229–1000).

GOLF There are good courses in town at the **Williamsburg Inn and Lodge** (tel. 804/220–7696), at **Fords Colony** (240 Fords Colony Dr., tel. 804/258–4130), and at nearby **Kingsmill Golf Club** (100 Golf Club Rd., Kingsmill, tel. 804/253–3906).

HIKING The 5-mile nature trail on Jamestown Island is an ideal place for exercise, with the added possibility of seeing wildlife. At both the Jamestown and Yorktown ends of the Colonial Parkway, turnoffs lead to waterfront recreation areas, where people walk, picnic, or play volleyball.

SWIMMING The nearest surf bathing is at Virginia Beach, 50 miles east on I–64; many area lodgings have pools.

ENTERTAINMENT

CONCERTS Folksingers, the Fife and Drum Corps, and costumed interpreters perform frequently in the buildings and on the greens of Williamsburg (general information: tel. 804/220–7645). Many wonderful evening concerts and Colonial-style programs take place throughout the Historic Area. Professional and student performers also grace the boards of Phi Beta Kappa Hall (tel. 804/221–2674) at the College of William and Mary. Check the "Visitors Companion" to see what's going on, or call 804/220–7645 for special events.

Wisconsin Dells

Wisconsin

Updated by Kristin Visser

Native American legend claims a giant serpent created Wisconsin Dells, one of the most scenic spots along the 400-mile-long Wisconsin River. Scientists say the 15-mile stretch of soaring rock formations was created over thousands of years by glacial waters cutting through soft Cambrian sandstone to a depth of 150 feet. Yet whatever their origin, the majestic dells of the Wisconsin River are one of the state's foremost natural attractions, and one of the Midwest's most popular tourist destinations.

In the 1850s, the community of Kilbourn City grew up at the Dells, and pioneer photographer H. H. Bennett settled here. Bennett's outstanding photographs of the Dells began to draw tourists as early as 1868, and to publicize the geologic novelty of the Dells, Kilbourn City was renamed Wisconsin Dells in 1931.

Once home to rivermen, trappers, lumberjacks, and Native Americans, the area today known as the Dells encompasses the small, adjacent communities of Lake Delton (on the west bank of the river) and Wisconsin Dells (on the east bank). Set some 3 miles apart, north to south, they are connected by Wisconsin Dells Parkway (U.S. 12/Route 23), a bustling, four-lane strip teeming with attractions. While the sandstone cliffs and majestic river remain the Dells' highlights, man-made enticements run a close second, and the region is filled with water parks, rides, stage shows, Indian ceremonials, specialty shops, and other amusements. And you'll have no trouble finding your way around—there are signs everywhere.

ESSENTIAL INFORMATION

WHEN TO GO While Wisconsin Dells holds the state's record-high temperature of 114°, the average temperature during peak tourist season (June–August) is just under 70°, and nights are pleasantly cool. The region is especially lovely from late September to mid-October, when the weather cools down, the foliage hits its peak of color, and the crowds of youngsters that throng the Dells' children-oriented attractions have returned to school. During the cold, snowy season (November–March), when nearly all attractions are closed, Wisconsin Dells becomes popular with skiers and snowmobilers.

TOURIST OFFICES Wisconsin Dells Visitor & Convention Bureau (701 Superior St., Wisconsin Dells 53965, tel. 608/254–4636 or 800/223–3557). **Wisconsin Division of Tourism** (Box 7606, Madison 53707, tel. 608/266–2161 or 800/432–8747).

EMERGENCIES Police, fire, and ambulance: Dial 911. **Doctors:** Dells Clinic (1310 Broadway, tel. 608/253–1171). **Hospitals:** St. Clair Hospital (707 14th St., Baraboo, tel. 608/356–5561).

ARRIVING AND DEPARTING

BY PLANE Madison's Dane County Regional Airport (tel. 608/246–3380), 45 miles southeast of the Dells (an hour's drive via I–90/94), has daily scheduled flights by major U.S. carriers.

BY CAR I–90/94, traversing the state from west to southeast and skirting the Dells, is

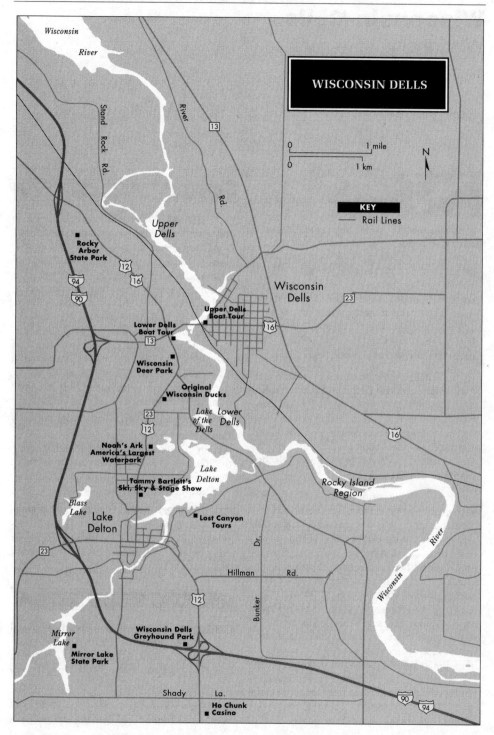

WISCONSIN DELLS

KEY
— Rail Lines

Wisconsin River

River

13

Stand Rock Rd.

Upper Dells

Rocky Arbor State Park

94
90

12
16

Wisconsin Dells

23

Upper Dells Boat Tour

16

Lower Dells Boat Tour

13

Wisconsin Deer Park

Original Wisconsin Ducks

Lake of the Dells

Lower Dells

23
12

Noah's Ark America's Largest Waterpark

Lake Delton

Tammy Bartlett's Ski, Sky & Stage Show

Rocky Island Region

Blass Lake

Lake Delton

Lost Canyon Tours

23

Dr.

Hillman Rd.

Bunker

Wisconsin River

12

Mirror Lake

Wisconsin Dells Greyhound Park

Mirror Lake State Park

Shady La.

Ho Chunk Casino

90
94

the fastest route across southern Wisconsin. U.S. 12, which passes through rolling hills and river valleys as it travels north, is a favorite route with travelers arriving from the south.

BY BUS Greyhound Lines (tel. 800/231–2222) stops regularly in the Dells.

BY TRAIN Amtrak (tel. 608/254–7706 or 800/872–7245) offers twice-daily rail service to the Dells.

GETTING AROUND

BY CAR AND RV You'll need a car for traveling along the strip (Wisconsin Dells Parkway). The major attractions offer ample parking for both cars and RVs. To avoid strip traffic between Lake Delton and Wisconsin Dells, take I–90/94, using Exit 92 (U.S. 12) to reach Lake Delton and Exit 87 (Route 13) to reach Wisconsin Dells.

REST STOPS Public rest rooms can be found adjacent to the Wisconsin Dells Convention and Visitors Bureau (701 Superior St.). Rest rooms and picnic facilities are available at Rocky Arbor State Park (just north of the Dells on U.S. 12) and Mirror Lake State Park (just south of the Dells on Ferndell Rd.).

EXPLORING

You can "do" the Dells in a day or a week, depending on your pace and interests. A power dam on the Wisconsin River near the Route 13/23 bridge divides the river into the Upper Dells and Lower Dells. A number of tours cover the Dells' natural attractions, and Rocky Arbor State Park (with hiking trails) provides a respite from the crowds. If you're traveling with children, you'll want to spend time at the water parks, miniature golf courses, and the like.

Dells Boat Tours offers a two-hour Upper Dells tour (departing from the docks just east of the bridge in Wisconsin Dells), which includes stops to view the fantastic rock formations from up close and to stroll through fern-filled canyons and along nature trails. The one-hour, nonstop Lower Dells tour (leaving from the docks at the west end of the bridge), cruises by the Rocky Islands, caverns, and rock formations. You'll save money if you purchase a combination Upper and Lower Dells boat-tour ticket, but if you take only one boat tour, make it the Upper Dells tour—it's more scenic. *11 Broadway, tel. 608/254–8555. Tours mid-Apr.–Oct., daily. Admission charged.*

Ho-Chunk Casino and Bingo, the area's largest Indian-operated casino, offers blackjack, video poker, slot machines, and high-stakes bingo. *S3214A Hwy. 12, 3 mi south of I-90/94, tel. 800/746-2486. Open daily. Admission free.*

Lost Canyon Tours organizes horse-drawn wagon tours of this narrow, mile-long, 80-foot-high sandstone canyon in Lake Delton. Picnic facilities are available. *720 Lost Canyon Rd., tel. 608/253–2781. Tours mid-May–mid-Sept., daily. Admission charged.*

Noah's Ark, along the strip, bills itself as America's largest water park and offers water slides, wave pools, and raft rides, along with go-cart tracks, miniature golf, and a host of other diversions. *1410 Wisconsin Dells Pkwy., 1½ mi south of bridge, tel. 608/254–6351. Open Memorial Day–Labor Day, daily. Admission charged.*

Rocky Arbor State Park offers a break from the crowds and hubbub of the Dells. Tucked away among stands of white and Norway pines, this 225-acre park has picnic areas; a children's playground; campsites; a 1-mile, easy walking nature trail; and soaring rock formations dating back thousands of years. *U.S. 12, 1½ mi north of the Dells, tel. 608/254–8001. Open Memorial Day–Labor Day, daily. Admission charged.*

Tommy Bartlett's Ski, Sky, and Stage Show puts on three shows daily, featuring waterski acts, acrobats, racing speedboats, precision hang gliding, and other family entertainment. A laser light show is enacted at night. *560 Wisconsin Dells Pkwy., tel. 608/254–2525. Open late May–Labor Day, daily. Admission charged.*

Wisconsin Deer Park, on the strip in Wisconsin Dells, is a 28-acre wildlife exhibit in a forest setting. You might spot several varieties of deer, including rare white deer—many of which you can pet and feed—along with elk, buffalo, and other wildlife. *583 Wisconsin Dells Pkwy., tel. 608/253–2041. Open May–mid-Oct., daily. Admission charged.*

Wisconsin Dells Greyhound Racing Park is Wisconsin's first pari-mutuel betting facility. Dog-racing programs are held most evenings, with occasional matinees, and doubleheaders on many weekends. There is both indoor and outdoor seating. A Beginner's Welcome Booth offers help to novice bettors. *Winner's Way, U.S. 12 and I–90/94, Lake Delton, tel. 608/253–3647. Open Feb.–late Nov., daily. Admission charged.*

Original Wisconsin Ducks are not waterfowl but World War II amphibious vehicles that take you on an action-packed, 7½-mile land-and-water drive through Fern Dell, Red Bird Gorge, and the Lower Dells. *1890 Wisconsin Dells Pkwy., 1 mi south of bridge, tel. 608/254–8751. Open May–Oct., daily. Admission charged.*

HOTELS AND INNS

Accommodations in the Dells range from bed-and-breakfasts in historic homes to modern resorts, housekeeping cottages, and motels, which frequently offer bargain rates. Off-season rates are generally in effect from mid-September to June 1 or later. Some two-thirds of the region's accommodations are closed November–April. Reservations for peak season (June–August) should be made at least two months in advance, and some facilities require a minimum stay during this time. Price categories for double occupancy in the summer season, excluding 10% tax, are Expensive, over $100; Moderate, $50–$100; and Inexpensive, under $50. Prices are as much as 50% lower at other times of the year.

EXPENSIVE **Monte Carlo Resort Motel.** In a quiet, secluded wood only two blocks from the strip, this resort motel on the shores of Lake Delton is popular with families and offers rooms with lake views (some with kitchenettes), apartments, and cottages (some with fireplaces). *350 E. Hiawatha Dr., Wisconsin Dells 53965, tel. 608/254–8761. 40 units. Heated outdoor pool, beach, fishing boats, tennis courts, volleyball court, game room, playground, picnic facilities, some rooms with whirlpool baths. MC, V.*

Copa Cabana. Located right in the heart of the lively strip, within walking distance of major attractions and restaurants, this tropical-theme motel is designed for families. *611 Wisconsin Dells Pkwy., Wisconsin Dells 53965, tel. 608/253–1511 or 800/364–2672, fax 608/253–7327. 160 units. Heated indoor pool and whirlpool, water activity park, kiddie pool, game room, sauna, fitness center. AE, D, MC, V.*

Polynesian. This motel started the trend toward ever-more amenities and mini-water parks at Dells motels. Located at the intersection of Highway 13 and I–90/94, ½ mile from the strip and from downtown Dells, the motel, one of the Dells newest, makes up for its somewhat remote location with lots of on-site activities for families. *857 N. Frontage Rd., Wisconsin Dells 53965, tel. 608/254–2883 or 800/272–5642. 170 units. 2 outdoor pools with water slides, 2 kiddie activity pools, heated indoor pool, indoor and outdoor whirlpools, coin laundry, microwave and refrigerator in rooms, whirlpool rooms available. AE, D, MC, V.*

MODERATE **Baker's Sunset Bay Resort.** Rooms in this tranquil, lakeside family resort feature kitchenettes and private decks. Large, modern, housekeeping cottages (some with fireplaces) have screened porches and views of Lake Delton. *921 Canyon Rd., Wisconsin Dells 53965, tel. 608/254–8406 or 888/435–6515. 67 units. Beach, 2 heated outdoor pools, heated indoor pool, free rowboats, pontoon boat rental, fishing, outdoor game area. MC, V.*

Bennett House B&B. Listed on the National Register of Historic Places, this restored 1863 Greek Revival structure was the home of early Dells photographer H. H. Bennett. Filled with antiques, the house has a gazebo and a Victorian garden. *825 Oak St., Wisconsin Dells 53965, tel. 608/254–2500. 3 rooms, 1 with private bath. Full breakfast included, fireplace in country kitchen and dining room, screened porch. No credit cards.*

Sherman House B&B. This two-story, 14-room home with a large lawn, an adjacent park, triple bay windows, and views of the river was built by one of Frank Lloyd Wright's associates in 1904 and adheres to the clean, classic style of Wright's Prairie School architecture. *930 River Rd., Wisconsin Dells 53965, tel. 608/253–2721. 4 rooms, 2 with private bath. Continental breakfast and afternoon refreshments included, large veranda. No credit cards.*

Aloha Beach Resort & Suites. Formerly the Tiki Hawaiian Motel, this resort property overlooking Lake Delton has large, modern rooms, including family and efficiency units, as well as luxury suites with whirlpool baths. It's also close to attractions along the strip. *1370 E. Hiawatha Dr., Wisconsin Dells 53965, tel. 608/253–7441. 63 rooms, most with private bath. Heated indoor and outdoor pool, sauna, private beach, rowboats, playground. AE, D, MC, V.*

INEXPENSIVE Gables Motel. Centrally located in downtown Wisconsin Dells (one block north of Broadway), this two-story motel is within easy walking distance of the boat docks and downtown attractions, restaurants, and shopping. *822 Oak St., Wisconsin Dells 53965, tel. 608/253–3831. 30 rooms. Heated outdoor pool, winter plug-ins. AE, D, MC, V.*

Indian Trail Motel. Away from the Dells' hustle and bustle, but within pleasant strolling distance of downtown attractions, this quiet, family motel offers large, comfortable rooms and suites, and the largest motel grounds in town. *1013 E. Broadway, Wisconsin Dells 53965, tel. 608/253–2641. 45 rooms. Heated indoor and outdoor pool, sauna, large playground, nature trail, some rooms with whirlpool bath and microwave ovens. AE, D, MC, V.*

CAMPGROUNDS

Three state parks near Wisconsin Dells offer camping and spectacular scenery: Devil's Lake State Park (near Baraboo), Mirror Lake State Park, and Rocky Arbor State Park. While each park offers a number of campsites on a first-come, first-served basis, you can't count on sites being available during peak travel times; reservations are necessary. Full payment for a campsite must be included with a reservation application, along with a registration fee.

In addition to camping fees, a vehicle sticker is required for admission to all Wisconsin state parks. Both daily and annual stickers are available.

Devil's Lake State Park. This 9,000-acre park is one of Wisconsin's oldest. These 500-foot bluffs, believed by scientists to be among the most ancient rock outcroppings in North America, ring a 360-acre lake offering two sand beaches with changing houses, fishing, and boating. Fifteen miles south of the Dells off U.S. 12, the park has 15 miles of hiking trails and several children's play areas and is home to nearly 900 plant communities and more than 100 species of birds. *S5975 Park Rd., Baraboo 53913, tel. 608/356–8301. 415 RV and tent sites, 121 with electrical hookups. Showers, flush toilets, picnic tables and grills, wheelchair-accessible rest rooms and picnic and camping facilities, nature center, interpretive programs. Reservations by mail only.*

Mirror Lake State Park. Just a 10-minute drive from Wisconsin Dells, Mirror Lake is surrounded by sandstone bluffs and is frequented in autumn by migrating waterfowl, including several species of ducks, grebes, and great blue herons. White-tailed deer, rare pileated woodpeckers, mink, and beavers are also seen here. Hikers will find 20 miles of trails, and there are nine miles of off-road bicycle trails. Evening nature programs, guided nature hikes, and lectures by visiting naturalists are offered in summer. The park is ½ mile south of I–90/94 on U.S. 12 and 1½ miles west on Fern Dell Road. The campgrounds are closed November through March. *E10320 Fern Dell Rd., Baraboo 53913, tel. 608/254–2333. 144 RV and tent sites, 27 with electrical hookup. Showers, sand beach, picnic tables, grills, wheelchair-accessible rest rooms and picnic and camping facilities, nature center, interpretive programs. Reservations by mail only.*

Rocky Arbor State Park. One-and-a-half miles north of the Dells on U.S. 12, Rocky Arbor State Park is tucked away among stands of towering white and Norway pines. The small (225 acres) park has soaring rock formations some 500 million years old and a 1-mile self-guided nature trail. Open Memorial Day–Labor Day, the park handles the overflow of campers from Devil's Lake and Mirror Lake. *Rocky Arbor State Park (c/o Mirror Lake State Park, E10320 Ferndell Rd., Baraboo 53913, tel. 608/254–2333). 89 wooded RV and tent sites, 18 with electrical hookups. Showers, picnic tables, grills, wheelchair-accessible rest rooms and picnic and camping facilities. Reservations accepted by phone June–Aug. (tel. 608/254–8001) or by mail. MC, V required for phone reservations.*

DINING

Wisconsin is the dairy state—milk, butter, and cheese are among its most prolific products. In line with this rich character, the cuisine of the Dells tends to be hearty, stick-to-the-ribs fare, but menus usually include such lighter dishes as seafood, chicken, and veal—and salad bars are available in all but the smallest restaurants. Price categories per person, excluding 5% tax, service, and drinks, are Moderate, $15–$25, and Inexpensive, under $15.

MODERATE **Fischer's Supper Club.** This longtime Dells favorite has been serving lean steaks, seafood, and chicken dishes to appreciative patrons for more than 45 years. This is one of the places where you'll find the locals. *441 Wisconsin Dells Pkwy., Lake Delton, tel. 608/253–7531. MC, V.*

House of Embers. Famous for its hickory-smoked ribs, prepared in the restaurant's own smokehouse, this supper club's menu also includes fresh fish, veal, and flame-broiled steaks. Candlelight dinners are held in the garden gazebo. *935 Wisconsin Dells Pkwy., tel. 608/253–6411. AE, MC, V.*

Jimmy's Del-Bar. This spacious supper club, designed in the style of Frank Lloyd Wright, has been packing in both locals and tourists since 1943. Though known for its steaks, Jimmy's also serves seafood, chicken, pasta, and veal. One dining room has a pianist and a singing hostess. *800 Wisconsin Dells Pkwy., tel. 608/253–1861. AE, D, MC, V.*

Ishnala Supper Club. Giant Norway pines grow right through the dining room and cocktail lounge of this rustic restaurant and nightclub set atop a bluff overlooking secluded Mirror Lake. Pre-dinner pontoon boat rides on the lake are available. Prime rib, grilled steak, lobster, and other seafood dishes are featured on the extensive menu. *Ishnala Rd., Lake Delton, tel. 608/253–1771. AE, MC, V.*

Thunder Valley Inn. This rural restaurant serves wonderful daily breakfasts that feature fresh-baked breads and cinnamon rolls and an old-fashioned Friday-night fish fry. Dining on Saturday is by reservation only. *W15344 Waubeek Rd., tel. 608/254–4145. MC, V.*

INEXPENSIVE **Dells Grill.** This local favorite, with its Formica-and-chrome decor, serves up sandwiches, light plate lunches, and homemade soups and desserts to hungry crowds of locals. *318 Broadway, tel. 608/254–2727. No credit cards.*

The Cheese Factory. This elegant eatery in a historic building serves a gourmet vegetarian menu, including soups and salads, sandwiches, and international specialties such as Greek spinach-feta pie, as well as pizza. It's also a great place for breakfast. Its coffee offerings are the best in the area. *521 Wisconsin Dells Pkwy. S, tel. 608/253–6065. AE, MC, V.*

SHOPPING

Broadway Street, Wisconsin Dells' main shopping street, is lined with T-shirt emporiums, fudge shops, souvenir shops, and shops selling such local specialties as Wisconsin cheese and Indian crafts.

ANTIQUES AND GIFTS Oak Street Antiques Mall (725 Oak St., tel. 608/254–4200) specializes in antique dolls, jewelry, toys, prints, and furniture. The **Loonery** (714 Oak St., tel. 608/253–7131) has 24 crafts stores featuring wildlife items; **Parsons Trading Post** (370 Wisconsin Dells Pkwy., tel. 608/254–8533) has a display of Indian artifacts and a range of modern Indian crafts for sale; and the **Winnebago Indian Museum Gift Shop** (Rte. 13 and River Rd., tel. 608/254–2268) sells a wide range of Indian crafts and deerskin footwear.

OUTDOOR ACTIVITIES

BOATING One way to explore the Wisconsin River is to rent a canoe, paddleboat, or sailboat. **Holiday Shores** (3900 River Rd., Wisconsin Dells, tel. 608/254–2878) and **Lake Delton Water Sports** (U.S. 12, Lake Delton, tel. 608/254–8702) provide safety equipment and instruction along with rentals.

GOLF Christmas Mountain (S944 Christmas Mountain Rd., tel. 608/254–3971) and **Dell View Golf Course** (511 E. Adams St., Wisconsin Dells, tel. 608/253–4653) are challenging 18-hole courses; **Coldwater Canyon** (4065 River Rd., tel. 608/254–8489) is a nine-hole course. Call ahead to arrange tee times.

HORSEBACK RIDING Christmas Mountain Ranch (5944 Christmas Mountain Rd., tel. 608/254–3935) offers English- and Western-style riding lessons and riding trails. Beginners are welcome. **OK Corral Riding Stable** (Hwy. 16, 1 mi south of Wisconsin Dells, tel. 608/254–2811) offers Western-style riding for adults and children on 100 acres of trails.

SKIING Mirror Lake State Park (tel. 608/254–2333), 1 mile south of I–90/94 on U.S. 12 and then east 1½ miles at E10320 Ferndell Road, has 18 miles of groomed cross-country trails; **Christmas Mountain** (5944 Christmas Mountain Rd., tel. 608/254–3971) has seven downhill runs ranging from beginner to intermediate and 12 miles of groomed, partially lighted cross-country trails ranging from beginner to expert.

ENTERTAINMENT

The weekly *Wisconsin Dells-Lake Delton Area Guide,* available free throughout the Dells area, lists regional events and activities.

CONCERTS The **Wisconsin Opry** (E10964 Moon Rd., tel. 608/254–7951) features nightly country cookouts and country-music shows Memorial Day–mid-September; nationally known country-and-western performers occasionally make appearances.

Yellowstone National Park
Wyoming

Updated by Candy Moulton

Where else but Yellowstone can you pull off an empty highway at dawn to see two bison bulls shaking the earth as they collide in battle before their herd, and, an hour later, be caught in an RV traffic jam? For 120 years, Yellowstone, the oldest national park in the United States, has been full of such contrasts that usually revolve around its twin role as America's preeminent wildlife preserve and its most accessible one.

Yellowstone is a high plateau, ringed by even higher mountains; the park lies mostly in northwestern Wyoming and extends into Montana and Idaho. Roadside elevations range from 5,314 feet at the North Entrance to 8,859 feet at Dunraven Pass. The Gallatin Range to the west and north, the Absaroka and Beartooth ranges to the north and east, and the Tetons to the south all have peaks higher than 10,000 feet. Scenery in the park ranges from near-high desert around the North Entrance to lodgepole pine forests around the South Entrance, and otherworldly landscapes of stunted pine and shrub around thermal areas.

From whichever direction you approach the Yellowstone plateau—larger than Delaware and Rhode Island combined—you'll see signs of the massive summer 1988 fires. Beyond the South Entrance along dizzying Lewis River Canyon, a landscape of charred trees to the west fit the media portrait of what happened: an unprecedented disaster to America's original natural preserve. Past the North Entrance along the Gallatin Range, the multicolored mosaic of burned and unburned pine and aspen offers the bigger Yellowstone picture. Right now, Yellowstone visitors have a rare chance to see nature's massive regeneration. Roadside exhibits near Lewis Lake, south of Tower Falls, and at five other locations explain that process.

ESSENTIAL INFORMATION

WHEN TO GO Yellowstone's midsummer average temperatures hover in the 70s at midday and around 40° at night. Snow is possible in high elevations year-round. June and September are often wet and cloudy in the park's lower elevations, but September, and to a lesser extent October, can also have delightfully sunny days—albeit 5° to 20° cooler than midsummer. Winter and spring are Yellowstone's best-kept secrets—the former for cross-country skiing, solitude, and wildlife encounters; the latter for viewing baby bison, moose, and other new arrivals. January afternoon highs average in the 20s, with nighttime average lows around zero.

The park's crowds can be daunting in July and August, when reservations are essential for most lodging. Only one stretch of road, from the North Entrance to Cooke City, Montana, on the northeast, is open year-round to wheeled vehicles; other roads open between early April and late May.

FESTIVALS AND SEASONAL EVENTS **Mid-Mar.:** The Rendezvous Ski Race in West Yellowstone is one of eight segments in the cross-country Great American Ski Chase. **Early Apr.:** Cowboy Range Ballads in Cody is a weekend of western entertainment. **Late**

June–early July: Plains Indian Pow-Wow and Cody Stampede in Cody celebrate the Indian and Cowboy heritages of the Northern Plains. **July 4:** Home of Champions Rodeo is a major rodeo circuit event in Red Lodge, 69 miles from Yellowstone's Northeast Entrance on the spectacular Beartooth Highway (other park gateway towns hold summer rodeos—check with tourist offices, listed below). **Mid-Sept.:** Western Design Conference in Cody featuring fashion, furniture, and western-style activities.

BARGAINS Free and varied ranger-led activities inside the park, usually held during summer months and listed daily at visitor centers, include photography workshops, map-and-compass workshops, and bird- and wildlife-watching. TW Recreational Services (*see* Tourist Offices, *below*), the park concessionaire for restaurants and lodging, offers some attractive deals if you're willing to rough it a bit: "Budget," "Rough Rider," and "Rustic Shelter" cabins cost $19–$25 per night at Mammoth, Roosevelt, and Old Faithful. TW Services also offers a two-night winter package (about $129 per couple) at Mammoth Hot Springs Hotel, including dinner and a half day of ice skating, plus discounts on guided ski and Snowcoach tours.

TOURIST OFFICES Yellowstone National Park Service information (tel. 307/344–7381). Information and reservations for lodging and activities: **TW Recreational Services** (Yellowstone National Park 82190-9989, tel. 307/344–7311). **Wyoming Division of Tourism** (tel. 307/777–7777 or 800/225–5996). **Travel Montana** (tel. 406/444–2654 or 800/541–1447). **Bozeman Chamber of Commerce** (Box B, Bozeman, MT 59715, tel. 406/586–5421). **Cody Country Chamber of Commerce** (Box 2777, Cody 82414, tel. 307/587–2297). **Jackson Hole Chamber of Commerce** (Box E, Jackson 83001, tel. 307/733–3316).

EMERGENCIES Police, fire, and **ambulance:** Dial 911. **Hospitals:** Yellowstone Lake (tel. 307/242–7241). **Doctors:** National Park Service emergency medical technicians and park medics are on duty at all times. Outpatient clinics operate Memorial Day through mid-September at Yellowstone Lake (tel. 307/242–7241) and Old Faithful (tel. 307/545–7325). Mammoth Hot Springs Clinic (tel. 307/344–7965) is open year-round.

ARRIVING AND DEPARTING

BY PLANE The two most convenient airports are **Jackson Hole Airport** (tel. 307/733–7682), outside Jackson, and **Yellowstone Regional Airport** (tel. 307/587–5096) in Cody, 50 and 52 miles from the South and East Entrances, respectively. Both have daily flights connecting to Denver or Salt Lake City on several national and commuter airlines. **Gallatin Field** (tel. 406/388–6632) in Bozeman, Montana, 90 miles from the West Entrance, also has daily flights connecting to Minneapolis or Denver. Some lodgings in the area offer free airport shuttles. From Yellowstone Regional Airport, Cody Connection Taxi (tel. 307/587–9292) takes passengers into town for about $5. One-way taxi fares from Bozeman's or Jackson Hole's airports are about $12; for a taxi in Jackson contact Buckboard Cab (tel. 307/733–1112) or Eagle (tel. 307/739–9999).

BY CAR All five park entrances join the Grand Loop Road. The most spectacular entry is from the northeast on U.S. 212, the Beartooth Highway. The 69 miles from Red Lodge, Montana, traverse the 11,000-foot-high Beartooth Pass, the nation's highest mountain highway pass with dizzying switchbacks. The northern approach on U.S. 89 is a straight shot through Paradise Valley, flanked by the Absaroka Range on the east and Gallatin Range on the west, to the original stone entry arch in the funky old tourist town of Gardiner, Montana. The South Entrance (U.S. 89), which is ideal for anyone also stopping at Grand Teton Park, the West Entrance on U.S. 20 through West Yellowstone, and the East Entrance on U.S. 14–16–20 from Cody are the most heavily trafficked.

BY BUS Greyhound Lines (tel. 800/231–2222) connects Bozeman, Montana, to points nationwide. **Cody Bus Lines** (tel. 800/733–2304) provides daily service from Billings.

89 TO LIVINGSTON

MONTANA

GALLATIN NA
FORES

YELLOWSTONE NATIONAL PARK

GALLATIN NATIONAL
FOREST

Gallatin Range

Yellowstone River

**North
Entrance**

**Mammoth Hot Springs
Park Headquarters**

Albright Visitor Center
*Undine
Falls*

Bunsen Peak
*Swan
Lake*

**Blacktail Deer
Plateau**

Roosevelt Lodge

Tower-R

Tower Cr

Antelope Creek

**Indian
Creek**

**Tower
Fall**

Indian Creek

Lava Creek

Tower Creek

**Mount
Washburn**

Dunraven Pass

191

287

*Hebgen
Lake*

191

287

Grand Canyon of the Yellowstone

**Norris
Geyser
Basin**

Norris

**Canyon
Village**

**Steamboat
Geyser**

Inspiration Point

Artist Point

*Lower Falls
Upper Falls*

Central Plateau

*Hayden
Valley*

TO ASHTON

20

Madison River

**West
Entrance**

Madison

Firehole Falls

Firehole River

Mud Volcano

Rec
Veh

**Fishing Bridge,
Lake Village,
and Bridge Bay**
Lake Yellowstone

Fis

IDAHO

**Lower Geyser
Basin**

Fountain Paint Pot

Imperial Geyser

Great Fountain Geyser

Fairy Falls

Fairy Creek

Midway Geyser Basin

Bridge Bay

Hotel

**Lake
Village**

M

**TARGHEE
NATIONAL
FOREST**

Biscuit Basin
Firehole River
Mystic Falls
Sapphire Pool
Black Sand Basin

Upper Geyser Basin

Old Faithful
Old Faithful Inn

*Yellowst
Lake*

**Lone Star
Geyser**

**West Thumb and
Grant Village**

Craig Pass

West Thumb

*Shoshone
Lake*

Grant Village

Continental

*Lewis
Lake*

Lewis Lake

*Heart
Lake*

Lewis Falls

KEY

Highways

Minor Roads

Unpaved Road

Trail

Ranger Station

Campground

Picnic Area

Restaurant

Lodge

Bechler River

0   10 miles

0   10 km

287
191
89

South Entrance

Flagg Ranch

TO JACKSON,
GRAND TETON
NATIONAL PARK

From downtown Cody, **Powder River Transportation** (tel. 307/527–6223) leaves daily for Old Faithful and other Loop lodgings.

Holiday Tour and Travel (tel. 307/733–4152) offers a daily winter shuttle from downtown Jackson to Flagg Ranch near the South Entrance. These shuttles connect to Snowcoach tours into the park (*see* Guided Tours, *below*).

GETTING AROUND

Despite a few good bus connections in the park, a car remains the most practical way to see Yellowstone. Some Yellowstone roads are steep with sharp drop-offs: Be especially careful south of Mammoth Hot Springs near Bunsen Peak, north of Canyon Village at Dunraven Pass, and just past the South Entrance along the Lewis River Canyon. Off-road parking is plentiful at all major sites.

REST STOPS The park has 50 picnic areas, most with nonflush toilets. Rest rooms with flush toilets are provided at Grant Village, Old Faithful, Madison, Norris, Mammoth Hot Springs, Tower-Roosevelt, Canyon, Fishing-Bridge, and Yellowstone Lake visitor centers.

GUIDED TOURS TW Recreational Services (*see* Tourist Offices, *above*) schedules bus tours from various park locations between mid-May and mid-September and from the Gardiner, Montana, bus depot. In winter, it offers orientation tours on tractored Snow-coaches; a half-day snowmobile tour; cross-country ski tours; and a winter wildlife bus tour. Free ranger-led activities, listed at visitor centers, include guided walks ranging from a stroll through Old Faithful's geyser system to a strenuous hike up Specimen Ridge at Mammoth Hot Springs.

EXPLORING

Admission to Yellowstone Park also allows entrance into Grand Teton Park for up to one week; entry fee at press time was $10 per vehicle or $4 per individual on foot or bicycle. National Park Service Golden Age and Golden Access Passports enable free entry to people over 62 and people with disabilities.

You can drive the 142-mile Grand Loop in a day—but it's easier to explore it over a few days. Major park attractions can only be seen by driving to parking areas and walking to the features. If your time is limited, consider concentrating on just one area—the Grand Loop's two halves are ideal for segmenting a visit like this.

Yellowstone Lake, 22 miles from the South Entrance, is North America's largest mountain lake, with 110 miles of shoreline. **Fishing Bridge** at the lake's northern end was named for the thousands of anglers who were allowed to fish from its rails until 1972. **Fishing Bridge Museum,** an example of early park architecture, contains bird displays; it's also an ideal place from which to start a lakeshore stroll. **Lake Butte,** a wooded promontory rising 615 feet above the lake, is reached by a 1-mile spur road 10 miles east of Fishing Bridge: try catching a sunset here. *Fishing Bridge Visitor Center, tel. 307/242–2450. Open late May–mid-Sept., daily. Scenicruiser tours leave Bridge Bay Marina daily early June–mid-Sept. Fee charged.*

Old Faithful, the punctual geyser, is Yellowstone's most famous attraction. A lobby sign in historic Old Faithful Inn tells when the next eruption is due (approximately every 65 minutes); the inn's deck and benches around the geyser itself are the best viewpoints. The geyser lies at the southern terminus of a 50-mile-long road that winds north toward Mammoth Hot Springs alongside one of the world's greatest concentrations of thermal features. Dozens of other thermal areas dot Old Faithful's immediate vicinity and are accessible by boardwalks and trails. Observation Point Trail (1.1 mile) crosses bubbling Firehole River, passes Solitary Geyser, and returns to the Upper Geyser Basin Trail, which offers other walking options. The Three Senses Trail off Firehole

Lake Drive is recommended. *Old Faithful Visitor Center, tel. 307/545–2750. Open June–Oct., daily; winter season dates vary.*

Mammoth Hot Springs is the park headquarters. The Terrace, an eerily colored travertine (calcium carbonate) plateau, towers over the hot springs. Take the Upper Terrace Loop; drive 2 miles south of Mammoth, where you'll pass 500-year-old gnarled limber pine trees growing atop extinct thermal features. You can walk down from here to the Main Terrace past formations such as the Liberty Cap, with the aid of a 25¢ map available in the parking area. Five miles south of Mammoth, a rough, one-way dirt road circles Bunsen Peak. *Albright Visitor Center, tel. 307/344–2263. Open daily, with movie and slides throughout day. Mammoth General Store open daily; service station open mid-May–mid-Oct., daily; hotel, fast food, horseback riding (fee charged), photo shop open May–Sept., daily.*

Tower-Roosevelt area, 18 miles east of Mammoth, centers around Roosevelt Lodge, another early park structure. Blacktail Plateau Drive, a one-way dirt road paralleling the main road eastward, traverses sagebrush hills and pine and aspen forests. A few miles south of the lodge is 132-foot-high Tower Falls, named for nearby volcanic pinnacles. *Roosevelt Store and Tower service station open early June–early Sept. Horseback rides, stagecoach rides, Old West cookout available early June–early Sept. (fee charged).*

Grand Canyon of the Yellowstone is reached driving south from Tower-Roosevelt. The road crosses Dunraven Pass (8,850 feet), covered in wildflowers and subalpine fir. At Canyon Village, a 2½-mile one-way loop road leads first to a spur road out to Inspiration Point, where the Yellowstone River plunges 1,000 feet below. The canyon's colors were created by hot water acting on volcanic rock. Next is Grandview Point, affording a distant view of the 308-foot drop of the Lower Falls, and Lookout Point, with a steep trail descending close to the Falls. Back on the main road, turn left after about ⅓ of a mile to view the edge of the 109-foot Upper Falls. Another .6 mile south, Artist Point Road's trails lead to views of both falls. Artist Point, at road's end, involves minimal walking and offers spectacular views of the canyon and Lower Falls. *Canyon Visitor Center, tel. 307/242–2550. Open mid-May–Sept., daily. Service station open late May–early Sept., daily; general store open late May–late Sept., daily; horseback rides (fee charged) available mid-June–early Sept.*

THE NATURAL WORLD Elk come right into Mammoth and the Old Faithful Geyser Basin, especially in early morning and evening—generally the best times to view Yellowstone's wildlife. Just below Tower Falls, as you drive up Mt. Washburn, look east, downslope, into prime grizzly bear country on Antelope Creek. This area is closed to human travel. The Hayden Valley between Fishing Bridge and Canyon is prime moose, bison, and waterfowl territory. Watch for elk, bison, antelope, and coyotes in the Lamar Valley. Bighorn sheep frequent Mt. Washburn in summer.

HOTELS AND INNS

While surrounding towns have plenty of accommodations (*see* Motels, *below*), staying in the park keeps you close to the action. It's wise to make reservations at least two months in advance for Old Faithful Inn, Lake Yellowstone Hotel, and Mammoth Hot Springs Hotel. Old Faithful Inn opens in early May, while most other park lodgings open in late May or early June; only the Inn and Old Faithful Snow Lodge stay open into October. Old Faithful Snow Lodge and Mammoth Hot Springs Hotel accommodate winter guests from mid-December to early March. Rates are slightly higher in summer. Price categories for double occupancy, excluding 2% tax, are Moderate, $40–$85, and Inexpensive, under $40.

Yellowstone visitor areas have a mix of Moderate and Inexpensive rooms. All reservations must be made through the Reservations Department of TW Recreational Services (*see*

Tourist Offices, *above*). Guests arriving within 14 days of the date of the reservation may use credit cards.

GRAND CANYON AREA **Canyon Lodge.** This busy property, the park's largest, consists of uninspired, single-story plain pine-frame cabins in clusters of four or more. Its size, however, means Canyon Lodge is one of the last to fill up. *North Rim Dr. 580 units. 3 restaurants, cafeteria, gift shop. Inexpensive–Moderate.*

LAKE AREA **Grant Village.** The newest park lodging, built in 1984 at the south end of the lake, proves they don't make 'em like they used to: It's gray on the outside and dull on the inside. Still, half the rooms overlook the lake and have private baths. *Grant Village Rd. 299 rooms. 2 restaurants, gift shop. Moderate.*

Lake Lodge. This peaceful property has cabins nestled in the trees with good views of the lake. *Lake Village Rd. 186 rooms. Cafeteria, gift shop. Inexpensive–Moderate.*

Lake Yellowstone Hotel and Cabins. This elegant colonial-style building with 50-foot Ionic columns overlooks the lake. The rooms—decorated with peach carpeting, pine furniture, and brass beds—are some of the nicest you'll find in the park. *On Yellowstone Lake. 287 rooms and cabins. Lakeview restaurant, lobby bar, gift shop, nearby marina. Moderate.*

MAMMOTH AREA **Mammoth Hot Springs Hotel and Cabins.** Built in 1937, with one wing dating back to 1911, this hotel, with a spacious lobby and smallish rooms, is generally less crowded than the other two historic park hotels. Although it shares grounds with the park headquarters, this spot is a little far from some of the main attractions. *5 mi from park's north entrance. 223 rooms and cabins. 2 restaurants, gift shop. Inexpensive–Moderate.*

OLD FAITHFUL AREA **Old Faithful Inn.** A National Historic Landmark, this inn has soaring log-beam construction, four hanging balconies, and a giant stone fireplace rooms in the 1904 section are furnished with brass beds; the newer upper-range rooms in the east and west wings have Victorian cherry-wood furniture; and the motel-style midrange rooms come decorated with ranch oak furniture. All have baths, and an elevator serves the upper floors. *First left off Old Faithful Bypass Rd. 359 rooms. 2 restaurants, Native American crafts gift shop. Inexpensive–Moderate.*

Old Faithful Lodge and Cabins. This budget choice is nicer than some of the park's midrange options; the lobby has a giant fireplace and a commanding view of Old Faithful. *At far end of Old Faithful Bypass Rd. 122 cabins. Cafeteria, 2 snack shops, gift shop. Inexpensive.*

Old Faithful Snow Lodge. This compact, drab-looking building, open in winter, is one of two Yellowstone properties that stay open in winter. The rooms are nondescript motel style, but the lobby's modern stone fireplace is a popular gathering spot on windy winter nights. *Old Faithful Bypass Rd. next to visitor center. 31 rooms, 34 cabins. Restaurant, gift shop. Inexpensive–Moderate.*

Roosevelt Lodge. Simple frame cabins surround a cozy two-fireplace log lodge with rocking chairs on the porch. In the dining room, big bowls of coleslaw, beans, and corn are passed around family style. *At Tower-Roosevelt Junction on Grand Loop Rd. 80 cabins. Restaurant, gift shop. Inexpensive–Moderate.*

MOTELS

MODERATE **Buffalo Bill Village** (1701 Sheridan Ave., Cody 82414, tel. 307/587–5544). 79 r̶ ̶ ̶ ̶staurant, pool. **Cedar Mountain** ̶heridan Ave., Cody 82414, tel. ̶. 45 rooms; pool. **Cody Motor** ̶ridan Ave., Cody 82414, tel. ̶0 rooms. **Days Inn** (1321 ̶an, MT 59715, tel. 406/ ̶325–2525). 80 rooms. ̶ (Box 972, Jackson ̶58). 41 rooms; pool.

Super 8 Motel (730 Yellowstone Rd., Cody 82414, tel. 307/527–6214). 64 rooms. **Super 8 Motel** (1520 S. Hwy. 89, Jackson 83001, tel. 307/733–6833). 97 rooms.

INEXPENSIVE **Big Bear Motel** (Hwy. 14–16–20, Box 2015, Cody 82414, tel. 307/587–3117 or 800/325–7063). 42 rooms; pool; pets allowed. **Motel 6** (1370 W. Broadway, Jackson 83001, tel. 307/733–1620). 155 rooms; pool.

CAMPGROUNDS

Yellowstone has 11 park-service campgrounds and one RV park operated by TW Recreational Services. All campsites are available on a first-come, first-served basis, except Bridge Bay, which is on the nationwide MISTIX (tel. 800/365–2267) reservation system from mid-June to Labor Day. Canyon Village is restricted to hard-sided units because bears frequent the area.

Bridge Bay. The largest park campground, set back from the lake in a wooded grove 3 miles southwest of Lake Village, features a marina, rental boats, fishing, campfire talks, and guided walks. Don't expect solitude. *434 RV and tent sites (under $15), no hookups; showers 4 mi away, bathrooms, picnic tables, barbecue areas.*

Canyon. One-quarter mile east of Canyon Village and near a laundry and visitor center, this area is popular with families and accessible to many short trails. *273 RV sites (under $15), no hookups; showers, bathrooms, picnic tables, barbecue areas. No reservations.*

Fishing Bridge RV Park. This is the only full RV facility in the park, at Fishing Bridge junction. Trailers must be under 40 feet with no canvas. Make reservations through TW Recreational Services (*see* Tourist Offices, above). *345 RV sites (under $25), hookups (no extra fee); showers, bathrooms, picnic tables, laundry nearby.*

Mammoth Hot Springs. The sites on a sagebrush hillside are also popular with elk and mule deer, just below the Mammoth complex and near its amphitheater, where rangers hold evening talks. *85 RV and tent sites (under $15), no hookups; bathrooms, picnic tables, barbecue areas. No reservations.*

Slough Creek. A small, creekside campground 10 miles northeast of Tower Junction off a spur road, this is about as far from Yellowstone's beaten path as you can get without actually camping in the backcountry. *29 RV and tent sites (under $10), no hookups; pit latrines, picnic tables, barbecue areas. No reservations.*

DINING

The Northern Rockies have come far from the days when roadside signs advised, "This is cow country—eat beef!" You'll still find some of the best steaks around, cut from grass-fed beef, however, healthier eating habits have taken hold here, too. Rocky Mountain trout is served at several park restaurants, and pastas outnumber fried potatoes nowadays. Expect less formality than you'd find elsewhere, even in the fanciest restaurants. Along with the informality come better prices. Price categories per person, excluding 6% tax, service, and drinks, are Moderate, $10–$20, and Inexpensive, under $10. All park restaurants are operated by TW Recreational Services (tel. 307/344–7311). (For Jackson restaurants, *see* Grand Teton National Park chapter.)

INSIDE YELLOWSTONE **Canyon Lodge Cafeteria.** You'll find long lines, but it's worth the wait for cheap and hearty soups, chili, and lasagna. *Canyon Lodge, tel. 307/344–7311. No credit cards. Inexpensive.*

Old Faithful Inn Dining Room. Lines form early at the park's premier restaurant—a big, friendly place that serves an impeccable trout almondine as well as a generous Sunday-brunch buffet. *Old Faithful Inn, tel. 307/344–7901, ext. 4999. Reservations required. AE, D, DC, MC, V. Moderate.*

Old Faithful Lodge Cafeteria. Lasagna, pizzas, and other staples are served here, but it's the table-side views of Old Faithful that draw the crowds. *Old Faithful Lodge, tel. 307/344–7311. No credit cards. Inexpensive.*

Roosevelt Lodge Dining Room. Pine chairs and tables set the rustic tone at this popular restaurant with a "family menu." Each entrée comes with bowls of coleslaw, mashed potatoes, corn, baked beans, and corn muffins. *Roosevelt Lodge, tel. 307/344–7311. AE, D, DC, MC, V. Moderate.*

Terrace Dining Room. Overlooking what was once the Army's parade and drill field at Mammoth Hot Springs, this restaurant serves excellent pastas and chicken dishes. *Across from Mammoth Hot Springs Hotel, tel. 307/344–7311. AE, D, DC, MC, V. Moderate.*

OUTSIDE YELLOWSTONE **Casa Sanchez.** The best Mexican food in Yellowstone—everything from tamales and burritos to beans, eggs, and tortillas—is served in three downstairs rooms of a converted house. *719 S. 9th Ave., Bozeman, MT, tel. 406/586–4516. D, DC, MC, V. Inexpensive.*

Chico Hot Springs. This lodge-saloon-hot springs resort also houses one of Montana's best restaurants; dinners can get expensive, but the more moderate, all-you-can-eat Sunday brunch features custom-made omelets, cereals, freshly baked rolls and breads, and fruits. *East River Rd. (follow signs on U.S. 89 35 mi north of North Entrance), Pray, MT, tel. 406/333–4933. D, MC, V. Moderate.*

Irma Hotel. Hearty breakfasts, various lunchtime sandwiches, and hearty dinners (with a salad-bar option) are offered in this historic hotel named for Buffalo Bill's daughter. *1192 Sheridan Ave., Cody, tel. 307/587–4221. AE, D, DC, MC, V. Moderate.*

La Comida. This small restaurant in downtown Cody has both shaded sidewalk tables and indoor seating where you can enjoy large servings of home-style Mexican dishes. *1385 Sheridan Ave., Cody, tel. 307/587–9556. AE, D, DC, MC, V. Moderate.*

Patsy Ann's Pastry and Ladle. Come here for whole-grain baked goods, soups, and sa wiches. *1243 Beck Ave., Cody, tel. 307/527–6297. No credit cards. Inexpensive.*

Trapper's Inn. Amid pine furniture and mountain-man memorabilia, diners linger over thick soups, sourdough pancakes, biscuits and rolls, and hearty entrées such as grilled steak or chicken with potatoes and beans. *315 Madison Ave., West Yellowstone, MT, tel. 406/646–9375. AE, MC, V. Moderate.*

SHOPPING

Yellowstone and its surroundings have two tiers of shopping possibilities for travelers: souvenirs and the real thing. Among the latter are genuine Northern Plains Indian beadwork, fine leather cowboy boots and coats, distinctive woolens, and local crafts. Souvenirs include rubber tomahawks and tom-toms that have acquired their own kitsch tradition, fake six-guns and other cowboy "paraphernalia," more Yellowstone sweatshirts and T-shirts than you could possibly imagine, and decorated mugs. (Some of the region's best shopping is in Jackson; *see* the Grand Teton National Park chapter.)

GIFT SHOPS **Old Faithful Inn**'s gift shop offers Native American beadwork and western regional art, along with mugs, sweatshirts, and calendars. Also at Old Faithful, the **Hamilton General Store** sells outdoor gear and souvenirs (some of the bear-related sweatshirts are truly funny). **Mammoth Hot Springs Hotel** has an interesting Christmas gift shop.

Outside Yellowstone, the **Buffalo Bill Historical Center** (720 Sheridan Ave., Cody, tel. 307/5_ _ _ \771) has the region's preeminent _ _ _ Plains Indian crafts and jewelry. _ _ _ **Bookshelf** (28 W. Main, Boze-\06/587–0166) stocks a wide ntemporary and historical

\enetton Factory Outlet \on, WY, tel. 307/733–\ing. **London Fog Fac-**

tory Store (485 W. Broadway, Jackson, WY, tel. 307/739–1819) specializes in men's and women's sportswear. The **Montana Woolen Shop** (3100 W. Main St., Bozeman, MT, tel. 406/587–5261) sells sweaters and other woolens, plus some expensive leathers.

OUTDOOR ACTIVITIES

BIKING Some 300 miles of roadway are available to bicyclists; bikes are prohibited on trails and in the backcountry. If you bike on the Grand Loop Road, keep in mind its notable climbs at Craig Pass between Old Faithful and Grant Village; Sylvan Pass between East Entrance and Fishing Bridge; and Dunraven Pass between Tower and Canyon. The gravel Bunsen Peak Road near Mammoth and Blacktail Deer Plateau Road between Mammoth and Roosevelt Lodge allow two-way bike and one-way auto traffic. Some roads restricted to bicycle and foot travel are: the abandoned railroad bed paralleling the Yellowstone River near Mammoth (5 miles); the Riverside Trail starting at the West Entrance (1 mile); the paved trail from Old Faithful's Hamilton Store to Morning Glory Pool (2 miles); and Natural Bridge Road near Bridge Bay (1 mile). Bikes can be rented and repaired in the gateway towns of West Yellowstone, Livingston, and Bozeman, Gardiner, Montana, as well as Cody and Jackson, Wyoming.

FISHING Cutthroat, brook, lake, and rainbow trout, along with grayling and mountain whitefish, can all be caught in Yellowstone's waters. Catch and release is the general policy, though you can keep some of the cutthroat, rainbow, and brookies, and all of the whitefish—get a copy of the fishing regulations at any visitor center. No live bait is allowed and only lead-free tackle may be used. Prime fishing areas include the upper Yellowstone River (north of Canyon), and Yellowstone, Sylvan, and Shoshone lakes and their tributaries. Literally dozens of backcountry and roadside rivers and creeks throughout the park provide good fishing, too: Try the Lamar River (north), Madison

River (west), and Lewis River (south). **TW Recreational Services** (tel. 307/344–7311) rents boats at Bridge Bay Marina; fishing supplies are available at all Hamilton Stores (Old Faithful, Bridge Bay, Fishing Bridge, Canyon, Tower-Roosevelt Lodge, Mammoth).

HORSEBACK RIDING TW Recreational Services (tel. 307/344–7311) runs easy one- and two-hour group trail rides from corrals at Roosevelt Lodge, Canyon Lodge, and Mammoth. Check at visitor center and park hotel activities desks for times and prices. A number of outfitters offer three-, five-, and nine-day horseback trips into the backcountry; try **Schmalz Outfitting** (Box 604, Cody 82414, tel. 307/587–5929 or 800/587–5929).

SKIING Besides guided ski tours (see Guided Tours, above), individual cross-country skiing options are limited only by your ability. At Old Faithful, the easy Lone Star Geyser Trail (9 miles) passes thermal features and links to several other trails ranging from easy to difficult. The Riverside Trail starts at the West Entrance and follows the Madison River; it involves one traverse up a short, steep hill. The canyon area has several trails for beginner to intermediate skiers, with some awesome rim-side views as well as dangerous switchbacks for advanced skiers only. Detailed brochures and maps are available from visitor-center ranger desks. You can rent touring and telemark skis, or snowshoes, at Mammoth Hot Springs Hotel and

Old Faithful Snow Lodge (see Hotels and Inns, above). Skier shuttles are available at both locations.

WALKING AND HIKING Possibilities abound in Yellowstone: Your only problem will be choosing walks to suit your ability. Always check at a visitor-center ranger desk before hiking to gauge a trail's difficulty (hikers should have Yellowstone topographical maps, available at visitor centers), and never wander out of sight of your trail. Beginners should concentrate on the many marked walkways at major attractions: The Upper Geyser Basin at Old Faithful can keep you busy for hours with fairly gentle boardwalk trails, as can the boardwalks at Norris Geyser Basin and Mammoth Hot Springs Terrace. Two easy backcountry hikes are the trail along the Lamar River Valley in the park's northeast and the 4-mile trail out to Shoshone Lake about 8 miles east of Old Faithful. A topographical map will forewarn you of difficulties on trails that might look easy on the maps handed out at the entrances: Both the Lost Lake Trail (which leaves from behind Roosevelt Lodge) and the Slough Creek Trail (departs from the Slough Creek campground) involve steep ½-mile opening climbs, followed by gentle terrain. If you're planning to camp as well as hike in the backcountry, you must obtain an overnight-use permit from a ranger station or visitor center.

Yosemite National Park
California

Updated by Sharron Wood

n one compact California valley—only 7 miles long and 1 mile wide—are two of the world's 10 highest waterfalls, the largest single granite rock on Earth (El Capitan), and one of America's most recognized peaks (Half Dome). And this spectacular valley is just a small part of 750,000-acre Yosemite National Park, which also contains in its southern tip the Mariposa Grove of Big Trees, a stand of giant sequoias towering 20 stories above the forest floor.

Toward the east is Yosemite's high country, an untamed expanse of rolling meadows, pristine forest, hidden lakes, and rocky domes.

In 1890, President Theodore Roosevelt, at the urging of conservationist John Muir and many like him, designated Yosemite one of our first national parks. Visitors from around the world, including royalty from Italy, Sweden, and Denmark, came here. They entered near Mariposa, gleefully riding a stagecoach through a tunnel bored into the trunk of a single sequoia. At the top of the rise south of Yosemite Valley, they saw America's Shangri-la—a deep, green canyon with walls of stone rising ⟨...⟩ feet into the clouds and graceful ⟨...⟩lummeting down from these ⟨...⟩s. It's the same vista that you ⟨...⟩hough these days your view is ⟨...⟩ured by a fleet of RVs and

⟨...⟩sit Yosemite every year. ⟨...⟩with the claim that, ⟨...⟩r, it's very crowded. ⟨...⟩has been written of

this valley (by John Muir and others) and so many beautiful photographs taken (by Ansel Adams and others), that you may wonder if the reality can possibly measure up. For almost everyone, it does; Yosemite reminds them of what *breathtaking* and *marvelous* truly mean.

ESSENTIAL INFORMATION

WHEN TO GO Although the high country is snowed in from late fall to late spring or early summer, Yosemite Valley is open year-round. In winter, the valley is often dusted with snow, but temperatures remain in the 40s during the day, dipping down to the 20s at night. Autumn and early spring weather in the valley is surprisingly mild, with warm days (60s and 70s) and crisp nights (30s and 40s). Summer in the valley brings hot, dry days with temperatures in the 80s and pleasant evenings with temperatures in the 50s. The high country is cooler, with daytime temperatures in the 60s and nighttime temperatures that dip into the 30s.

Summer is Yosemite's most crowded season, especially in the valley. More than 4 million people visited the park last year, the bulk of them between June and August. Many activities are offered, but you will have to contend with traffic jams, noxious tour buses, and lodging that is almost impossible to obtain. We recommend visiting during the off-season, when the autumn leaves turn, snow highlights the mountaintops, and deer and coyote make their winter homes in the valley. Even spring, when the mighty waterfalls reach their peak and flowering trees bloom in the valley, is less crowded than summer. However, summer is the only time of year when the Tioga Road into the high country is sure to be open.

FESTIVALS AND SEASONAL EVENTS Jan.: Chefs' Holidays (Holidays Hotline, tel. 209/454–2020) are free cooking demonstrations by well-known chefs for everything from exotic mushrooms to chocolate. A banquet dinner concludes the celebration. **Early May–late Oct.:** One of Yosemite's best-loved evening activities is Lee Stetson's portrayal of naturalist John Muir in his celebrated one-man shows. Performances of "Conversation with a Tramp," "John Muir's Stickeen and Other Fellow Mortals," and "The Spirit of John Muir" are held several days a week, early May through summer, at the Yosemite Theater for a nominal fee. **Mid-Nov.–mid-Dec.:** Vintners' Holidays (Holidays Hotline, tel. 209/454–2020), similar to Chefs' Holidays, are held midweek in the grand parlor of the Ahwahnee Hotel and feature free seminars by California's prestigious vintners, culminating in an elegant, albeit pricey, banquet dinner. **Dec. 23:** Yosemite Pioneer Christmas (tel. 209/372–0564) is a free, old-fashioned program of caroling, candlelight tours, and stagecoach rides at the Wawona area of the park.

BARGAINS Yosemite National Park offers a myriad of free and low-cost activities throughout the year. The admission fee to this national treasure is a bargain in itself— about $5 per car for a week's stay or about $3 per person if you don't arrive in a car.

Photo enthusiasts will delight in the free camera walks given each morning year-round by professional photographers. From early April through October, professional artists offer free workshops in watercolor, etching, drawing, and other mediums. Bring your own materials or purchase them for about $10. Rangers lead free discovery walks throughout the year and free snowshoe walks in winter. Children can participate in the free Junior Ranger naturalist activities. Free evening activities include films and slide shows on Yosemite. In winter, you can find 25% discounts off lodging and bargain ski packages, especially in midweek.

TOURIST OFFICES National Park Service, Information Office (Box 577, Yosemite National Park 95389, tel. 209/372–0200 or 209/372–0264). **Yosemite Area Road and Weather Conditions** (tel. 209/372–0200). **CalTrans Highway Information Network** (tel. 800/427–7623). **Yosemite Valley Visitor Center** (Box 577, Yosemite National Park 95389, tel. 209/372–0299).

EMERGENCIES **Doctors:** Yosemite Medical Clinic (Yosemite Village, tel. 209/372–4637) offers emergency care 24 hours daily. **Dentists:** The Dental Service (Yosemite Village, tel. 209/372–4200), next to the medical clinic, has been providing visitors with care since 1927.

ARRIVING AND DEPARTING

BY PLANE If you're coming from out of state, you will most likely fly into San Francisco or Los Angeles and then drive. An alternative is to fly into Fresno, which is the closest airport (97 miles away) but is not as well serviced by major airlines.

Between the Airport and the Park by Car or RV. Yosemite is a four- to five-hour drive from San Francisco and a six-hour drive from Los Angeles. From the west, three highways come to Yosemite; all intersect with Highway 99, which runs north–south through the Central Valley. Highway 120 is the northernmost and most direct route from San Francisco, but it rises higher into the mountains, which can be snowy in winter. Highway 140 from Merced is the recommended route in winter. It is the least mountainous route, and chains are not usually required. Highway 41 from Fresno is the shortest route from Los Angeles and offers the most dramatic first look at Yosemite Valley.

Coming from the east, Highway 120, the Tioga Road (known as Tioga Pass Road), climbs over the Sierra crest, past Tuolumne Meadows, and down into the valley. It's scenic, but the mountain driving may be

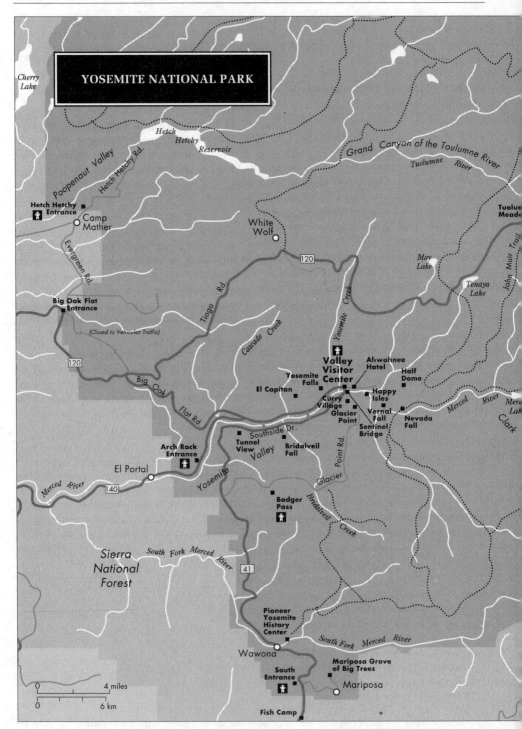

YOSEMITE NATIONAL PARK

Cherry Lake

Hetch Hetchy Reservoir

Poopenaut Valley

Hetch Hetchy Rd.

Grand Canyon of the Toulumne River

Tuolumne River

Hetch Hetchy Entrance
Camp Mather

White Wolf

120

Tuolu Meade

Evergreen Rd.

May Lake

John Muir Trail

Tenaya Lake

Big Oak Flat Entrance

Tioga Rd.

Cascade Creek

Yosemite Creek

120

(Closed to Vehicular Traffic)

Valley Visitor Center

Ahwahnee Hotel

Yosemite Falls

Half Dome

El Capitan

Happy Isles

Big Oak

Curry Village
Glacier Point

Vernal Fall

Merced River

Mer Lak

Flat Rd.

Sentinel Bridge

Nevada Fall

Clark

Arch Rock Entrance

Tunnel View

Southside Dr.

Valley

Bridalveil Fall

El Portal

140

Merced River

Glacier Point Rd.

Yosemite

Badger Pass

Bridalveil Creek

Glacier

Sierra National Forest

South Fork Merced River

41

Pioneer Yosemite History Center

South Fork Merced River

Wawona

Mariposa Grove of Big Trees

South Entrance

Mariposa

Fish Camp

0   4 miles

0   6 km

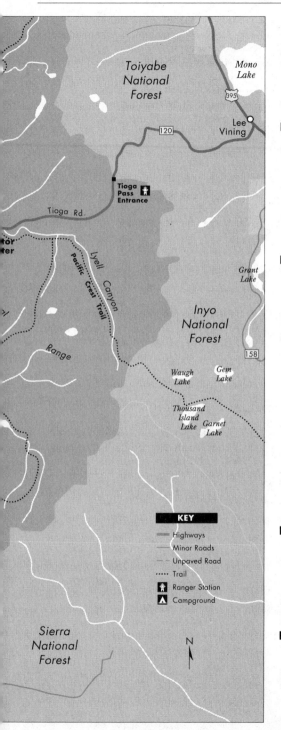

Toiyabe
National
Forest

Mono
Lake

395

120

Lee
Vining

Tioga
Pass
Entrance

Tioga Rd.

Grant
Lake

Pacific Crest Trail

Lyell Canyon

Inyo
National
Forest

158

Range

Waugh
Lake

Gem
Lake

Thousand
Island
Lake

Garnet
Lake

KEY

Highways

Minor Roads

Unpaved Road

Trail

Ranger Station

Campground

Sierra
National
Forest

N

stressful and it's only open in the summer due to heavy snow in the upper elevations. Carry chains no matter what your approach to Yosemite. They are often mandatory on Sierra roads during snowstorms. If you get caught in the valley and need to buy chains there, you'll pay twice the normal price.

BY BUS **Yosemite VIA** (tel. 209/384–2576) runs buses to Yosemite from Merced (about $30 plus $3 entrance fee round-trip, 2½ hours one-way) and Fresno (about $40 plus $3 entrance fee round-trip, three hours one-way). The Greyhound and Amtrak stations and the Fresno and Merced airports are regular stops, but call ahead to let the bus company know when you plan to arrive.

BY TRAIN **Amtrak** (tel. 800/872–7245) has train service to Merced, where you can connect with bus transportation.

GETTING AROUND

Although the most convenient way to travel to Yosemite is by car, you won't need an automobile once you arrive. A free shuttle bus circles continually (7:30 AM–10 PM in summer, 9 AM–10 PM the rest of the year) to all valley destinations. In winter, a free bus carries skiers from the valley to Badger Pass. In summer, there is one bus a day (for a fee) to the high country. If you do drive in the valley, parking lots are available at all major destinations. Finding parking, however, especially in summer, can easily take half an hour.

REST STOPS Rest rooms are few and far between on the forested mountain roads leading to Yosemite, but once in the park, you will find indoor bathrooms at the hotels and visitor centers. Portable toilets are available at the parking lots of many popular picnic spots, vista points, and trailheads.

GUIDED TOURS Yosemite offers tours that are run by Yosemite Park and Curry Company to fit every schedule and a variety of interests. Tickets may be purchased at the hotels' tour desks. Prices quoted are for adults; children 12 and under are half the quoted rates; and children under five ride free. Advance reservations (tel. 209/372–1240) are required for all tours except the Big Trees Tram Tour (*see below*). Tours are offered spring through fall, conditions permitting, unless otherwise stated. **Valley Floor Tour:** a 26-mile, two-hour tour of the valley's highlights with narration of the history, geology, and plant and animal life. It operates all year with open-air trams or enclosed motor coaches, depending on conditions. **Moonlight Tour:** a late-evening version of the Valley Floor Tour offered on full-moon nights and the three nights prior. **Glacier Point Tour:** a half-day trip to the vista at Glacier Point, 3,200 feet above the valley; operates approximately June through Thanksgiving. **Big Trees Tram Tour:** a one-hour, open-air tram tour of the Mariposa Grove of Big Trees. **Grand Tour:** a full-day combination of the Big Trees and Glacier Point tours, with lunch at the historic Wawona Hotel (meal not included in tour price). It is available from approximately June through Thanksgiving. **Tuolumne Meadows Tour:** a full day's outing across Tioga Pass Road to Mono Lake, with photo stops at highlights; operates July through Labor Day.

In addition to the commercial tours, rangers lead a variety of free tours ranging from snowshoeing at Badger Pass in winter to interpretive valley walks. For times, consult the visitor center (tel. 209/372–0299) or the *Yosemite Guide* newspaper, which is available for free at the park entrances and public buildings.

EXPLORING

The magnificent sites of Yosemite Valley are easily accessible by auto or free shuttle bus, with short trails to the bases of the powerful waterfalls. To experience the incomparable beauty of this national treasure, however, allow time for hikes off the well-beaten tourist paths (*see* Hiking, *below*).

Entering Yosemite Valley from the west: If you want to orient yourself, stop at the Valley Visitor Center, where a 20-minute audiovisual show offers an entertaining overview of the park's history and beauty; rangers on duty can recommend short hikes and direct you to other useful offices in the park. You'll pass some of the vista points on the way to the visitor center, and if you're really pressed for time, stop at them before going on because the circle road around the valley is one way and it would mean doubling back.

Bridalveil Fall should be your first stop. The parking lot is about 20 yards up Highway 41 from the valley road (Southside Drive). A paved ¼-mile trail with a slight, 100-foot rise will take you to the base of this graceful 620-foot cascade. The Ahwahneechee Indians called it *Pohono,* or spirit of the puffing wind, as breezes blow this lacy waterfall sideways along the cliff face.

El Capitan, the largest single granite rock on Earth, rising 3,593 feet, will loom to your left as you head farther into the valley. Turnouts along the road provide unbeatable vistas of the rock—rising more than 350 stories above you. Shadows of cloud set off patterns of light on its vertical striations, creating an ever-changing show. A pair of binoculars and keen eyes will allow you to spot rock climbers as they slowly ascend the sheer, vertical face of "El Cap."

Take a left over **Sentinel Bridge** and park. Walk to the center of the bridge for the best view of **Half Dome,** the most distinctive rock in the region, rising nearly 5,000 feet above the valley floor, and its reflection in the Merced River.

Drive back over the bridge and continue on Southside Drive. Hardy hikers may want to go straight to the Curry Village day-use lot, walk to the end of the shuttle bus road and climb the moderately steep (400-foot elevation gain) trail to the footbridge overlooking the 317-foot **Vernal Fall** (2½ miles round-trip, allow 1½ hours). Beyond Vernal Fall, the trail climbs up to the 594-foot Nevada Fall, then all the way to the top of Half Dome.

If you're not hiking, follow the road as it turns left across the Merced River. Take the short side road that dead-ends at the **Ahwahnee Hotel.** This stately 1927 lodge of granite-

and-concrete beams, stained to look like red-wood, is a perfect man-made complement to Yosemite's natural majesty. Visit the immense parlors with their walk-in hearths and priceless antique Native American rugs and baskets. The dining room is extraordinary, with high ceilings interlaced with massive sugar-pine beams.

Looping back toward the west, follow the signs for Yosemite Village. A large parking lot lends access to the gift stores, fast-food restaurants, and most important, the **Valley Visitor Center** (tel. 209/372–0299) with its exhibits on park geology and excellent selection of books on Yosemite. Behind the center is a small, re-created Ahwahneechee village as it might have appeared in 1872, 20 years after the first contact with non-Native Americans. Markers explain the lifestyle of Yosemite's first residents through the eyes of a young child. For more Indian lore, take a quick peak at the Indian Cultural Museum next door and its impressive collection of baskets.

Yosemite Falls is a short walk or drive from here. This is the highest waterfall in North America and the fifth-highest in the world. Though it looks like one cascade, Yosemite Falls is actually three waterfalls, a powerful chain of water twice the height of the Empire State Building. From the granite ridge high above you, Upper Fall drops 1,430 feet straight down. The Cascades, or Middle Fall, tumbles over another 675 feet, pouring into the steep 320-foot drop of the Lower Fall.

You can see the dizzying height of Yosemite Falls from the parking lot, but can only experience its power by following the ¼-mile paved trail to its base. The path leads to a footbridge, often showered with the mist of the mighty falls, that crosses the rushing waters with Lower Yosemite Falls towering above you. Many return to the parking lot at this point, but if you cross the bridge you'll come to a level, wooded 1-mile path that winds through the cool forest, meandering several times over creeks via footbridges. In a secluded spot, you'll discover the site of John Muir's cabin, with Yosemite Falls as a backdrop. The trail circles back to the falls parking lot.

Tunnel View, up Highway 41 on the way out of the valley, is a must for those with more time. The parking lots for this vista point are on either side of the road just before the tunnel. Below, tucked into 7 miles of pure inspiration is Yosemite Valley, with Bridalveil Fall on the right, El Capitan on the left, and Half Dome forming the backdrop to this deep, green canyon.

Farther up Highway 41 is the turnoff for the road to **Glacier Point** (open only in summer), another spectacular panorama of Yosemite, taking in the valley over 3,000 feet below and high country peaks on the horizon.

Highway 41 curves through the mountains south to the **Pioneer Yosemite History Center** at Wawona (30 miles, allow 45 minutes). Cross the New England–style covered bridge to this collection of late-19th- and early 20th-century log buildings that have been relocated here from their original sites around Yosemite. It is a vivid reminder of the park's first settlers and visitors, particularly in summer when costumed docents play the roles of the pioneers. The nearby Wawona Hotel, a whitewashed Victorian lodge built in 1879, is a pleasant stop for lunch.

Mariposa Grove of Big Trees is 6 miles south of Wawona. More than 20 giant sequoias are visible from the parking lot, but to get a true feel for the size of these trees, take the ¾-mile walk along the self-guiding nature trail to the Grizzly Giant. This gargantuan tree is 32 feet in diameter, 209 feet tall, and believed to be 2,700 years old.

Tuolumne Meadows is accessible in summer by driving east out of Yosemite Valley along Highway 120 (55 miles from the valley). This is the most extensive meadow system in the Sierra Nevada. Picnickers and day hikers enjoy the crystalline lakes, rolling fields, and rounded granite domes. Many hikers begin their journeys from here, but you'll need to get acclimated to the 8,575-foot altitude.

HOTELS AND INNS

Lodging in Yosemite ranges from the elegant Ahwahnee Hotel to spartan tent cabins. In the valley, Yosemite Lodge, made up of a variety of lodging alternatives, is the most populated area. It also has the most food, shopping, and restaurant services and is within easy walking distance of Yosemite Falls and the Valley Visitor Center. The secluded Ahwahnee Hotel is the only accommodation in Yosemite that offers color television and room service. Curry Village, a community of wooden and tent cabins, is within walking distance of the trails emanating from Happy Isles. In the summer, you can find rustic lodges at Tuolumne Meadows and White Wolf.

Reserve your room or cabin in Yosemite Valley as soon as possible. You can reserve exactly 366 days in advance of your arrival date. Hotel rooms and cabins with private bath are particularly popular. The Ahwahnee, Yosemite Lodge, and Wawona Hotel are regularly sold out on weekends, holiday periods, and all days between May and September within minutes after the reservation office opens. If you visit from November through March, especially midweek, you'll have a much easier time getting a reservation and will find rooms discounted up to 25%. All reservations for lodging in Yosemite are made through **Yosemite Concession Services Corporation** (Central Reservations, 5410 E. Home Ave., Fresno, CA 93727, tel. 209/252–4848).

Additional lodging is available in Yosemite's gateway cities, but the nearest town, El Portal, is still 14 slow mountain miles from the Valley Visitor Center on Highway 140. Farther away on Highway 140 are Midpines, 36 miles from Yosemite Valley, and Mariposa, 43 miles away. Farther north, on Highway 120, Groveland also has a number of lodging options. South of the park on Highway 41, the tiny town of Fishcamp is about 8 miles from Wawona. Another 14 miles south on Highway 41, the much larger town of Oakhurst has a larger selection of hotels. The

Mariposa County Chamber of Commerce (Box 425, Mariposa, CA 95338, tel. 209/966–2456) covering Mariposa, Midpines, and El Portal offers a free brochure listing all county hotels, motels, bed-and-breakfasts, restaurants, and sights. For hotels in Groveland, ask for the lodging guide from **Tuolumne County Visitors Bureau** (Box 4020, Sonora, CA 95370, tel. 209/533–4420 or 800/446–1333). For a free comprehensive guide to lodging and sightseeing options to the south of Yosemite, including Fishcamp and Oakhurst, contact the **Southern Yosemite Visitors Bureau** (Box 1404, Oakhurst, CA 93644, tel. 209/683–4636).

Price categories for double occupancy, excluding 9% tax, are Expensive, over $85; Moderate, $50–$85; and Inexpensive, under $50.

YOSEMITE NATIONAL PARK **Awahnee Hotel.** This grand 1920s-style mountain lodge—the most sought-after lodging in Yosemite—is constructed of rocks and sugar pine logs, with exposed timbers and spectacular views. The Grand Lounge and Solarium are decorated in a style that is a tribute to the local Miwok and Paiute Indians. The decor in the rooms continues that motif. *123 rooms. Restaurant, lounge, pool, tennis. DC, MC, V. Expensive.*

Wawona Hotel. This circa-1879 National Historic Landmark, located at the southern end of Yosemite National Park near the Mariposa Grove of Big Trees, has rooms that reflect their era—most are small and do not have private bath. The Victorian parlor in the main hotel boasts a fireplace, board games, and a pianist who plays ragtime tunes on weekend evenings. *104 rooms. Restaurant, lounge, pool, tennis, stables, golf course adjacent. Open daily Easter wk–Thanksgiving, during Christmas wk and weekends year-round. DC, MC, V. Moderate–Expensive.*

Curry Village. This is a large community of cabins, tent cabins, and basic hotel rooms in a woodland setting on the eastern end of Yosemite Valley in the shadow of Glacier

Point. The one-room cabins, spartan but adequately furnished, are a lower-cost alternative to Yosemite's hotels. Tent cabins have wood frames and canvas walls and roof. Those without bath share campground-style community bathrooms with showers available for a nominal fee. *183 cabins, 427 tent cabins, 18 hotel rooms. Fast-food restaurant, pool, skating rink. DC, MC, V. Inexpensive–Moderate.*

Yosemite Lodge. This property encompasses a variety of lodging alternatives, from rustic, one-room cabins (with electric heater) that share a camp-style bathroom with flush toilets to deluxe hotel rooms with cathedral ceilings and balconies overlooking Yosemite Falls. *495 rooms. 2 restaurants, cafeteria, lounge, pool, 2 gift shops. DC, MC, V. Moderate.*

MOTELS

OUTSIDE YOSEMITE NATIONAL PARK The following motels are 60–90 minutes by car from Yosemite Valley, unless otherwise noted.

Expensive: Berkshire Inn (19950 Hwy. 120, Groveland 95321, tel. 209/962–6744). 6 rooms; Continental breakfast included, Jacuzzi, common room with television. **Best Western Yosemite Gateway Inn** (40530 Hwy. 41, Oakhurst 93644, tel. 209/683–2378 or 800/528–1234, fax 209/683–3813). 118 rooms; heated indoor-outdoor pool, sauna, whirlpool, exercise room.

Moderate–Expensive: Cedar Lodge (9966 Hwy. 140, El Portal 95318, tel. 209/379–2612, fax 209/379–2712). 206 rooms; restaurant, indoor and outdoor pools, gift shop. 25 minutes from Yosemite Valley. **Shilo Inn** (40644 Hwy. 41, Oakhurst 93644, tel. 209/683–3555 or 800/222–2244, fax 209/683–3386). 80 rooms; pool, sauna, whirlpool, steam room, exercise room.

Moderate: Comfort Inn (4994 Bullion St., Box 1989, Mariposa 95338, tel. 209/966–4344 or 800/321–5261). 61 rooms; Continental breakfast included, pool, Jacuzzi, gift shop. **Miners Inn** (Rte. 140 at Rte. 49N, Box 246, Mariposa 95338, tel. 209/742–7777). 65 rooms; pool, Jacuzzi, movies, coffee in room.

CAMPGROUNDS

Yosemite Valley campgrounds are well maintained but crowded, especially in summer. Lack of undergrowth between tent sites means there's not much privacy. The campgrounds in Yosemite Valley are all in the eastern end with similar environments by the Merced River and have communal bathrooms with flush toilets. Showers are available for a nominal fee at Curry Village and at valley swimming pools in season.

The Recreational Vehicle limit is 35 feet in Yosemite. Rangers accommodate large RVs by matching them with the larger tent sites in each campground. There are no hookups in the National Park, but LP gas is available at the service stations. You'll find sanitary dump stations in Yosemite Valley and, in summer only, in Wawona and Tuolomne Meadows. Generators are permitted sparingly and only from 7 AM to 7 PM. Gravel and dirt RV sites are available in all park campgrounds except Upper River in the valley and the walk-in campgrounds.

All valley campgrounds, with the exception of Sunnyside Walk-in and Backpackers' Walk-in must be reserved through MISTIX (tel. 800/365–2267). You can reserve campsites no sooner than eight weeks in advance. Yosemite campgrounds consistently sell out within minutes of the time they become available during the high season. Call Mistix as soon as the office opens exactly eight weeks in advance to ensure a campsite for your visit. Campground choice is reserved, but individual sites are available only on a first-come, first-served basis, so arrive early for the best selection. Weather regulates the opening day of the seasonal campgrounds. Fees range from about $3 per person to about $14 per site.

Backpackers who want to avoid the Yosemite Valley crowds can hike to numerous backcountry areas. Wilderness permits, which cost about $5 per person, are required for overnight stays in the backcountry; you can get these at visitor centers and ranger stations or by writing the Wilderness Office (National

Park Service, Wilderness Office, Box 577, Yosemite National Park 95389) in advance of your trip.

Lower Pines and Upper Pines. Two similar campgrounds with some nice sites by the river; however, the road between the two has heavy traffic, which may be a consideration for families with young children. Upper Pines is the only Yosemite Valley campground that allows pets. *410 sites (about $15). Lower Pines open year-round. Upper Pines open Apr.–Nov.*

North Pines. Relatively scenic location between the Merced River and Tenaya Creek, with easy access to the Mirror Lake trail. *85 sites (about $15). Open Apr.–Oct.*

Sunnyside Walk-in. The only Valley campground available first-come, first-served and the only one west of Yosemite Lodge. It fills quickly and is typically sold out every day by 9 AM from spring through fall. *35 sites (about $5).*

Upper River. Ideal for tent campers who don't want to be next to RVs, this is the only drive-in valley campground for tents only. *124 sites (about $15). Open late Apr.–Oct.*

Wawona. A first-come, first-served campground with sites by the river, it's across the street from the Wawona hotel in the south end of Yosemite National Park. *100 sites (about $10).*

DINING

Food served in Yosemite, mostly standard American fare, tends to be overpriced. It's a good idea to stock up on groceries before you arrive at the park, though basic groceries and picnic fare are available at a number of stores throughout the park; see the *Yosemite Guide* for a list and the stores' open hours. Those on a budget should head for the cafeteria at Yosemite Lodge (open year-round) and the hamburger stand at Curry Village (open spring to fall). There are also several year-round fast-food options near the Valley Visitor Center. Summer-only restaurants are located in the Tuolumne Meadows Lodge and White Wolf Lodge.

All restaurants are run by Yosemite Concession Services Corporation (Central Reservations, 5410 E. Home Ave., Fresno 93727, tel. 209/252–4848). Operating hours vary by season and are listed in the *Yosemite Guide* newspaper.

Price categories per person, excluding 7¼% tax, service, and drinks, are Expensive, over $25; Moderate, $15–$25; and Inexpensive, under $15. All accept DC, MC, and V.

Ahwahnee Dining Room. This is the most dramatic setting in Yosemite, with its massive room, floor-to-ceiling windows, and soaring, 34-foot-high ceiling supported by immense sugar-pine beams. The restaurant glows with candlelight and serves such specialties as poached salmon with peppercorns and roast duckling with carmelized apples. *Tel. 209/372–1489. Reservations required for dinner. Jacket recommended. Expensive.*

Four Seasons Restaurant. Next to the Mountain Room Broiler, this large, casual restaurant is ideal for families looking for something more relaxed than the cafeteria, with entrées including grilled trout almondine (fresh when available) and steak. Vegetarian meals and a children's menu are available. Show up early for dinner or be prepared for a long wait. The restaurant is less crowded at breakfast, when omelets and pancakes dominate the menu. *Tel. 209/372–1269. Moderate.*

Mountain Room Broiler. Conveniently located at Yosemite Lodge, this restaurant offers casual fine dining away from the noise and crowds of other Yosemite Valley dining areas but is not as formal or expensive as the Ahwahnee and serves simply prepared fish such as salmon and trout. *Tel. 209/372–1281. Moderate.*

Wawona Hotel Dining Room. This is a romantic, nostalgic setting dating from the late 1800s, with pastel tablecloths, tabletop candles in hurricane lamps, and friendly service. Along with the rib-eye steak, trout, and daily chicken specials, selections include baked sea scallops and grilled polenta. A children's menu and Sunday brunch are also offered. *Tel. 209/375–6556. Moderate.*

Degnan's Pasta Place. On the second floor of the large A-frame building that also houses Degnan's Deli and Degnan's Fast Food, this is the only sit-down restaurant in Yosemite Village. At lunchtime you can glimpse Glacier Point and Yosemite Falls from large windows as you enjoy soups, salads, and simple pasta dishes. *Tel. 209/372–8381. Inexpensive.*

Village Grill. Open spring to fall, this casual, popular place serves hamburgers and sandwiches. *Tel. 209/372–1207. Inexpensive.*

SHOPPING

The **Ansel Adams Gallery** (tel. 209/372–4413), next to the Valley Visitor Center, is the most elegant store in the park, with Ansel Adams prints, fine artwork, and top-quality Indian crafts. The nearby **Village Store** (tel. 209/372–1253) offers the largest selection of goods, including groceries, magazines, film, clothing, camping supplies, postcards, gifts, and souvenirs. **Degnan's Nature Crafts** (tel. 209/372–1453), in the Degnan's complex in Yosemite Village, sells gifts.

At the Ahwahnee Hotel, the lobby **Sweet Shop** (tel. 209/372–1271) sells Ahwahnee logo merchandise. The **Gift Shop** (tel. 209/372–1205) in the Ahwahnee Hotel specializes in Indian jewelry and handicrafts. At the Yosemite Lodge, the **Gift/Apparel Store** (tel. 209/372–1297) offers Yosemite souvenirs, picnic supplies, and film. The **Indian Shop** (tel. 209/372–1438) at Yosemite Lodge features Indian artwork, handmade items, and moccasins. Curry Village has a year-round **Mountain Shop** (tel. 209/372–8396), with rock-climbing and backpacking supplies. Badger Pass Ski Area offers a winter-only **Sport Shop** (tel. 209/372–8430) with ski clothing, sunglasses, and sunscreen.

OUTDOOR ACTIVITIES

BIKING Yosemite Valley is ideal for biking, with more than 8 miles of scenic, mostly level bikeways. Bike rentals, with helmets, are available at **Yosemite Lodge** (tel. 209/372–1208), which is open year-round, conditions permitting, and **Curry Village** (tel. 209/372–8319), open from spring to fall, weather permitting.

FISHING In the Merced River in the valley and the Toulumne River in the high country, trout, mostly brown and rainbow, are available but not plentiful. Yosemite's stream and river fishing season begins on the last Saturday in April and ends on November 15, but be sure to inquire at a visitor center about exceptions; some waterways are off-limits to anglers at certain times of the year. Residents and nonresidents may purchase a one-day license at **Yosemite Village Sport Shop** (tel. 209/372–1286) next to the Village Store. For information, contact the **Department of Fish and Game** (3211 S St., Sacramento 95816, tel. 916/227–2244).

HIKING This is the reason to come to Yosemite. Though crowds may congest Yosemite Valley and RVs may fill every parking space in Yosemite Village, you can be sure that somewhere in the 750,000-acre park there is a trail populated with more blue jays that people. If ease of access is more important than solitude, however, you can always choose one of the many trails starting in Yosemite Valley, some of which take you to the base of those thunderous waterfalls you keep pulling over to look at. For an excellent map and description of the valley trails, invest in the colorful "Map & Guide to Yosemite Valley," available at the Visitor Center.

If you plan on hiking outside Yosemite Valley, you should definitely invest in an appropriate map. Maps of various areas are sold in almost every park store, though the best selection is at the Visitor Center in Yosemite Village. Books describing the flora and fauna of each of the park's varied regions will help you appreciate the uniqueness of the trails you choose to hike. Before you set out, be sure to ask a ranger about weather conditions, trail conditions, and any special precautions you should take in the area.

In the summer, Tuolumne Meadows, where sheer granite walls ascend from the subalpine meadows, is the hikers' favorite haunt. Backpackers can get lost in the high country for days, while day hikers can take advantage of shorter trails that are less congested that those in Yosemite Valley. Hikers should plan some extra time to adjust to the altitude here; the elevation ranges from 7,000 to 13,000 feet.

The sequoia graves at the southern edge of the park near Wawona are another good place to avoid the crushing crowds of Yosemite Valley, though the most popular trails through the Mariposa Grove can be extraordinarily congested. A number of less traveled trails, however, wind through the 2,000-year-old sequoias, the largest of all living things.

HORSEBACK RIDING All horses and pack animals must be accompanied by a guide. Scenic trail rides range from two-hour, half-day, and one- to six-day High Sierra saddle trips. Stables are open during the summer only in **Wawona** (tel. 209/375–6502) and **Tuolumne Meadows** (tel. 209/372–1327). Reservations must be made in person at the stables or at the hotel tour desks.

ICE-SKATING Skating is available from mid-November through mid-March depending upon seasonal conditions at an outdoor rink in Curry Village (tel. 209/372–8341).

SKIING Yosemite offers both cross-country and alpine skiing at Badger Pass in the winter months. Its gentle terrain is ideal for novices. Senior citizens over 65 and everyone exactly 40 years old ski free every day. Those staying in one of Yosemite's hotels also ski free Sunday through Thursday from January through March. Alpine and cross-country ski schools and rentals are available. Call 209/372–1244 for cross-country school information, 209/372–1000 for information on downhill ski school.

SNOWSHOEING Park rangers offer free snowshoe tours at Badger Pass during the winter months when the ski area is operating. These two-hour walks include rest stops, during which the ranger explains animal behavior in winter.

SWIMMING Several swimming holes with small, sandy beaches can be found along the Merced River at the eastern end of Yosemite Valley. Find gentle waters to swim; currents are deceptively strong and temperatures chilling. Do not attempt to swim above or near waterfalls or rapids—fatalities have occurred. Outdoor pools (summer only) are located at **Curry Village** (tel. 209/372–8324) and **Yosemite Lodge** (tel. 209/372–1250).

ENTERTAINMENT

In the evenings, ranger talks, slide shows, and documentary films present unique perspectives on Yosemite. Programs vary according to season, but there is usually at least one activity per night in the valley.

Zion and Bryce Canyon National Parks

Utah

Updated by Tom Wharton

nly 84 miles separate two of the most dramatically scenic national parks in the United States, Zion and Bryce Canyon, both found in southern Utah. Zion is Utah's most developed and busiest national park, with more than 2 million annual visitors. Close to major interstates, the park has a large lodge, spacious campgrounds, and extensive programs and services, all contributing to its popularity. It also has paved roads and easy hiking trails that allow for quick visits. Still, anyone who ventures from the main park roads will discover rugged trails in a true canyon with towering sandstone walls reaching 2,000 feet as well as a complex desert ecology.

The Virgin River, a muddy little stream that can turn into a violent red torrent during the spring runoff or after a summer thunderstorm, shaped the mighty canyon and its tributaries. Under a bright sky, a hiker can enter a side canyon barely 20 feet across and be sandwiched between high walls washed in shades of crimson, vermilion, tan, and orange and often streaked with dark "desert varnish" (oxidized minerals).

Bryce Canyon, on the other hand, is not really a canyon at all but a number of pink and white amphitheaters carved by rain, snow, and ice from the encircling cliffs. At 9,100 feet in elevation at its highest point, the park experiences four distinct seasons. Its brilliant red, buff, and tan limestone cliffs in strange and wonderful shapes change color with the season, the time of day, and the weather. Except during the height of the summer season, Bryce is a relatively quiet place in which to enjoy nature.

ESSENTIAL INFORMATION

WHEN TO GO Though both parks experience distinct seasons, the changes are more pronounced at Bryce Canyon, where its high elevation means more extreme temperatures. At Bryce, for example, the average high in January is 39° and the average low is 9°. In the summer, highs generally average in the low 80s, evenings in the mid-40s. January highs at Zion, on the other hand, range from 39° to 60°, with lows usually in the mid-20s. In April, the highs range between 62° and 80°, and lows from 37° to 59°. Summer heat can present problems to hikers, with temperatures between 93° and 103° in the middle of the day not uncommon.

About 75% of the visitors at both parks arrive during the summer, when trails can be crowded and lodging scarce. Spring and fall are the best times to visit Zion, when temperatures are moderate and crowds are smaller. Fall is probably the best season to visit Bryce; weather is clearer than at other times and the aspens begin to turn gold. For lower hotel rates, visit either park during the winter.

BARGAINS In both parks, ranger-naturalists sometimes offer free talks and guided nature walks; check park visitor centers for these activities. The Utah Shakespearean Festival (tel. 801/586–7880) is held July–early September at Southern Utah State College in Cedar City near Zion National Park. Many of

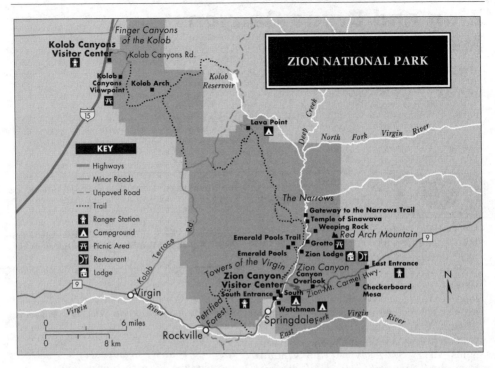

the activities surrounding the theater festival are free, including Greenshow, featuring puppets, storytellers, and musicians. You can also shop for unusual and rare rocks at fairly inexpensive prices at several shops in Springdale, near the entrance to Zion National Park or in small towns between the two parks on U.S. 89.

TOURIST OFFICES Superintendent, Zion National Park (Springdale 84767, tel. 801/772–3256). The Zion Canyon Visitor Center is near the park's south entrance, and the Kolob Canyons Visitor Center is in the northwest corner of the park just off I–15. **Bryce Canyon National Park** (Bryce Canyon 84717, tel. 801/834–5322). The visitor center is located near the park's main entrance.

EMERGENCIES Zion: For medical **emergencies,** dial 911, contact a park ranger, or call 801/772–3256 from 8 to 5; 801/772–3322 or 800/624–9447 after hours. Outside the park, from June through September, contact Zion Medical Clinic (Springdale, tel. 801/772–3226) or Dixie Regional Medical Center (St.

George, tel. 801/634–4200). **Bryce Canyon:** For medical **emergencies,** contact a park ranger or call 801/834–5322; first aid is available at the visitor center. Outside the park, contact Garfield County Sheriff (Panguitch, tel. 801/676–2678).

ARRIVING AND DEPARTING

BY PLANE SkyWest Airlines, the Delta Connection (tel. 800/453–9417), has regular flights from Salt Lake City and Las Vegas to St. George Municipal Airport, located 43 miles from Zion and 126 miles from Bryce, and to Cedar City Municipal Airport, located 59 miles from Zion and 78 miles from Bryce. Air Nevada (tel. 800/634–6377) flies April–mid-November, daily, from Las Vegas to Bryce, offering a package that includes airfare, a guide, and rim stops at Bryce.

From the Airport to the Parks: The easiest way to get to the parks from the airport is by car. In Cedar City, you can rent a car from **Avis** (Municipal Airport, tel. 801/586–7095),

Hertz (tel. 801/586–6096), **National** (tel. 801/586–7056), and **Speedy** (tel. 801/586–7368). In St. George, you can rent from **A-1** (tel. 801/673–8811), **Avis** (Municipal Airport, tel. 801/673–3451), **Budget** (tel. 801/673–6825), **Dollar** (tel. 801/628–6549), and **National** (Municipal Airport, tel. 801/673–5098).

BY CAR Salt Lake City and Las Vegas are the closest major cities to Zion and Bryce. I–15 runs from Salt Lake City, northeast of Zion, and from Las Vegas, to the southwest, and connects to Zion's Kolob Canyons Road entrance. The park's south and east entrances are located on Route 9, which branches off I–15 near St. George. A more scenic but slower route from Salt Lake City to the east entrances is U.S. 89, which also links Zion to Bryce Canyon and Grand Canyon parks. To reach the main entrance of Bryce, take U.S. 89 from the south via Kanab and Hatch or from the north via Panguitch. You'll have to turn east on UT 12 and south on Highway 63, which leads to the entrance (from U.S. 89 to the entrance is about 21 miles).

The drive from Las Vegas to Zion is 158 miles; to Bryce, 237 miles. The drive from Salt Lake City to Zion is 309 miles; to Bryce, 256 miles.

BY TRAIN **Amtrak** (tel. 800/872–7245) stops at both Salt Lake City and Las Vegas, where car rentals and bus tours are available.

BY BUS **Greyhound Lines** (tel. 800/231–2222) services St. George and Cedar City.

GETTING AROUND

Both parks are easily explored by car and allow opportunities for walking and hiking.

REST STOPS Public rest rooms at Zion and Bryce are found at the visitor centers. At Bryce, the only visitor center is right near the park entrance. At Zion, visitor centers are located near the south entrance and the Kolob Canyons entrance. The Grotto picnic area in Zion canyon near the lodge also has

rest rooms. Another small rest stop is located at the end of the Kolob Canyons Road.

GUIDED TOURS The **Utah Travel Council** (Council Hall/Capitol Hill, Salt Lake City 84114, tel. 801/538–1030) compiles an annual list of motor-coach tours into Utah from across the United States. **Scenic West Tours** (tel. 800/723–6429) offers regular and specialized package tours to the parks from Salt Lake City. Other companies offering more flexible schedules and personalized tours include **R&R Tours** (St. George, tel. 801/628–3643) and **Travel Regions West/ Toraco Enterprises** (St. George, tel. 801/628–8687 or 801/944–5736).

EXPLORING

Entrance fees for both parks for a seven-day pass are about $5 per vehicle and about $3 per person arriving on a bus, on foot, or on a bicycle. Entry is free to holders of Golden Eagle, Golden Age, and Golden Access Passports.

Zion and Bryce Canyon can both easily be seen by simply driving to major overlooks located off the highways that wind through both parks. Try to allow time for at least one or two short hikes on the park trails.

ZION **Zion Canyon Visitor Center.** The short multimedia program at this center has slides covering every season accompanied by narration by people who have lived and worked in the park. Rangers are available with helpful information on hiking, rock climbing, and other outdoor activities in the area.

Zion Canyon Scenic Drive. This 13-mile round-trip drive takes you along the floor of Zion Canyon, with brilliantly colored cliffs towering above you. The drive begins at the south entrance and proceeds north to the Temple of Sinawa parking area. Stop at the historic Zion Lodge about halfway on the drive for a snack or lunch. North of the lodge, past Red Arch Mountain, is the Grotto picnic area. Along this drive, you'll have access to several walking and hiking

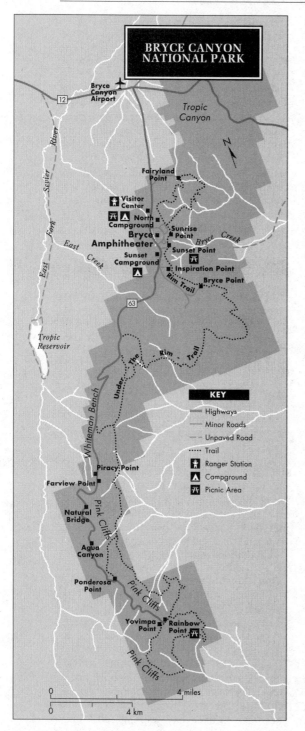

BRYCE CANYON NATIONAL PARK

Bryce Canyon Airport

Tropic Canyon

Sevier River

East Fork

Fairyland Point

Visitor Center

North Campground

Bryce Amphitheater

Sunrise Point

Bryce Creek

Sunset Point

Sunset Campground

Inspiration Point

Bryce Point

East Creek

Rim Trail

Tropic Reservoir

Under The Rim Trail

Whiteman Bench

Piracy Point

Farview Point

Pink Cliffs

Natural Bridge

Agua Canyon

Ponderosa Point

Pink Cliffs

Yovimpa Point

Rainbow Point

Pink Cliffs

KEY

Highways
Minor Roads
Unpaved Road
Trail
Ranger Station
Campground
Picnic Area

0   4 miles
0   4 km

trails, including the following (from south to north on the drive).

Emerald Pools Trail. This relatively easy one-hour, 1.2-mile round-trip hike begins opposite the Zion Lodge and ends at the Lower Emerald Pool, where three waterfalls cascade off the red cliffs. Another mile and a bit more energy will take you to the larger Upper Emerald Pool, at the base of some high cliffs.

Weeping Rock Trail. Beginning at the Weeping Rock parking lot, this easy half-hour, ½-mile round-trip trail leads to a spring that issues from a rock, with hanging gardens in spring and summer.

Gateway to the Narrows Trail. An especially beautiful route in spring and summer, when colorful wildflowers hang from canyon walls, the easy 90-minute, 2-mile round-trip trail follows the Virgin River to Zion Canyon Narrows. The way is shaded and the river keeps things cool; interpretive signs relate the natural history of the canyon.

Zion–Mt. Carmel Highway. This segment of Route 9 climbs 13 miles one-way from the bottom of the canyon at the south entrance up winding switchbacks and through tunnels carved out of the rock. It passes the petrified sand dunes of the Checkerboard Mesa before reaching the east entrance. This is the road that connects Zion to Bryce Canyon and the Grand Canyon. The easy, one-hour, 1.2-mile round-trip Canyon Overlook Trail, just east of the long tunnel, is one of the most attractive hikes off this road, ending at an awesome view of lower Zion Canyon.

Two other drives in the remote areas of Zion include the 15-mile round-trip journey along Kolob Canyons Road, from the Kolob Canyons Visitor Center to the Kolob Canyons Viewpoint, entering the red-rock walled Finger Canyons and the 50-mile round-trip drive from the town of Virgin north along the Kolob Terrace Road to Lava Point and Kolob Reservoir. The latter route runs along the western edge of the park, offering great views from the top of the canyon and passing farmhouses and bright green fields.

BRYCE CANYON The best time to explore the park is in the very early morning and the late afternoon, when the sun sets the rocks ablaze with color.

Visitor Center. Located near the park entrance, the center has a 10-minute slide show introducing the park. Rangers offer interpretative programs, and exhibits describe park flora and fauna.

Overlooks. You can drive on two main roads in the park—a section of Highway 12 in the northern end of the park and Highway 63, which leads south from the main entrance into the heart of Bryce and dead-ends after 18 miles at Rainbow Point, with a superb 270° view of surrounding canyon country. The park has 13 overlook points; Fairyland, Sunrise, Sunset, Inspiration, and Bryce points offer some of the best views of the unusual pinnacles, spires, and other rock formations.

Queen's Garden Trail. This short, one-hour, 1½-mile round-trip hike, beginning at Sunset Point, involves a moderately strenuous descent—and subsequent ascent—of 320 feet. Still, it allows you a closer view of the unique landscape.

Rim Trail. Although this easy to moderate trail stretches 11 miles along the rim of the amphitheater, hikers or cross-country skiers in the winter can access it at many different points. You can take a quiet stroll anywhere along the trail, which is paved between Sunrise and Sunset points.

HOTELS AND INNS

Lodging inside and near both parks is somewhat limited, making reservations almost a must during the busy tourist season of June–August and on any three-day holiday weekend.

The most convenient places to stay outside Zion are in Springdale, just outside the south entrance, or in neighboring Rockville. Bed-and-breakfasts in Springdale are surprisingly reasonable and allow visitors a taste of the local culture. The nearest town to Bryce of any consequence is Panguitch, 24 miles from the park entrance. Besides the historic lodges inside the two parks, the other accommodations near the parks, though clean, are simple motel rooms with two double beds and ordinary amenities. Price categories for double occupancy, excluding 6% tax, are Expensive, over $85; Moderate, $50–$85; and Inexpensive, under $50.

ZION **Cliffrose Lodge and Gardens.** A quarter of a mile from the park's south entrance and surrounded by botanical gardens and acres of lawns and trees, this serene hotel has spacious rooms and balconies with views of Zion Canyon and Watchman Mountain. *281 Zion Park Blvd., Springdale 84767, tel. 801/ 772–3234 or 800/243–8824. 36 rooms. Pool. AE, D, MC, V. Moderate.*

Handcart House Bed and Breakfast. This Mormon pioneer–style stucco home is filled with antiques; breakfast is generous. *244 W. Main St., Box 146, Rockville 84763, tel. 801/ 772–3867. 4 rooms. AE, MC, V. Moderate.*

Harvest House Bed and Breakfast. The first-rate Harvest House ranked as Utah's top B&B in recent surveys. A hot tub makes it an inviting place to return to after a long hike. Reservations are strongly suggested. *29 Canyon View Dr., Box 125, Springdale 84767, tel. 801/ 772–3880. 4 rooms. MC, V. Moderate.*

Zion Lodge. All rooms at the motel-like lodge have balconies that open onto splendid canyon views, but gas-burning fireplaces make the cabins more popular. *Zion National Park, Box 400, Cedar City 84720, tel. 801/586–7686 for reservations, 801/772–3213 to reach lodge; fax 801/586–3157. 121 rooms and cabins (no phones or TVs). Restaurant, snack bar, gift shop. AE, DC, MC, V. Moderate.*

Best Western Driftwood Lodge. This standard motel has well-manicured grounds and perhaps the best swimming pool in Springdale. *1515 Zion Park Blvd., Box 98, Springdale 84767, tel. 801/772–3262. 47 rooms. Restaurant, pool. AE, D, DC, MC, V. Moderate.*

Blue House Bed and Breakfast. This blue frame house with white trim is pleasantly decorated with plush carpets, floral bedspreads in the rooms, and wicker and oak furnishings. *125 E. Main St., Box 176, Rockville 84763, tel. 801/772–3912. 4 rooms, 2 with private bath. MC, V. Inexpensive–Moderate.*

Canyon Ranch Motel. The individual cabin units are unremarkable, but those with kitchenettes book up quickly. *668 Zion Park Blvd., Box 175, Springdale 84767, tel. 801/ 772–3357. 21 rooms, 5 have kitchenettes. Pool. D, MC, V. Inexpensive–Moderate.*

Flanigans. Kelly-green carpets and pastel southwestern furnishings contribute to the appeal of this modern wood-and-glass property. The most modern units resemble a big log cabin. *428 Zion Park Blvd., Box 100, Springdale 84767, tel. 801/772–3244 or 800/ 765–7787. 38 rooms. Restaurant, pool. AE, D, DC, MC, V. Inexpensive–Moderate.*

Under the Eaves Guest House. New owners of this small guest house, built of sandstone blocks cut from the canyon walls in 1935, have refinished the hardwood floors and painted the interior. The house offers rooms with antique furniture and a full breakfast. *980 Zion Park Blvd., Box 29, Springdale 84767, tel. 801/772–3457. 5 rooms, 3 with private bath. MC, V. Inexpensive–Moderate.*

BRYCE CANYON **Bryce Canyon Lodge.** This historic hostelry features lodgepole pine cabins with cathedral ceilings and stone fireplaces, and more contemporary rooms in the lodge. Reservations must be made at least three months in advance. *Bryce Canyon, Box 400, Cedar City 84721, tel. 801/ 586–7686, fax 801/586–3157. 114 rooms. Facilities: restaurant, shop. AE, DC, MC, V. Moderate.*

Ruby's Inn. A member of the Best Western chain, Ruby's is the largest lodging in the area, with a post office, service station, shopping complex, convention center, nightly rodeo in summer, horseback riding, and skiing in the winter. It's 1 mile north of the park entrance. *Hwy. 63, Box 1, Bryce 84717, tel. 801/834–5341 or 800/528–1234, fax 801/ 834–5265. 216 rooms. 2 restaurants, 2 pools,*

bakery, gift shops, RV park. AE, D, DC, MC, V. Moderate.

Bryce Canyon Pines Motel. This quiet, modern motel complex is situated 6 miles from the park entrance. *Hwy. 12, Box 43, Bryce 84764, tel. 801/834–5441. 52 rooms. Restaurant, pool, RV park. D, DC, MC, V. Moderate.*

Bryce Valley Inn. This motel features large rooms decorated with southwestern touches. It also provides shuttles to the park for guests. *200 N. Main St., Box 8, Tropic 84776, tel. 801/679–8811. 63 rooms. Restaurant, laundry, AE, MC, V. Moderate–Expensive.*

CAMPGROUNDS

For a complete listing of both public and private campgrounds in the area, send for a "Utah Travel Guide" from the **Utah Travel Council** (Council Hall–Capitol Hill, Salt Lake City 84114, tel. 801/538–1030). To make reservations in any Utah State Park, call 800/322–3770.

ZION During the summer months, Zion's main campgrounds, South and Watchman, fill almost every night. The best sites are closest to the Virgin River and farthest from the road. Neither campground takes reservations. For information, call 801/772–3256.

South Campground. Open spring through fall, this area near the south entrance is situated along the Virgin River and surrounded by large cottonwood trees. *140 RV and tent sites; no hookups (about $10). Running water, bathrooms, picnic tables, barbecue areas.*

Watchman Campground. This large area flanked by towering red cliffs is located near the south entrance. *270 RV and tent sites; no hookups (about $8). Running water, bathrooms, picnic tables, barbecue areas.*

Outside the park, some of the best campgrounds near Zion, especially for tenters, are found in nearby state parks. In contrast to the Zion Park campgrounds, those at **Coral Pink Sand Dunes State Park** (tel. 801/874–2408) and **Snow Canyon State Park** (tel. 801/628–

2255) are rarely crowded. A bit out of the way, these parks with showers and bathrooms are best for stopovers on the way into or out of Zion. Coral Pink Sand Dunes, near the town of Kanab on Highway 89, is a natural place to break during a journey between Zion and the Grand Canyon's North Rim. Snow Canyon is located to the east of Zion, not far from I–15 and St. George. The camping sites are set in pretty sandstone coves, surrounded by juniper trees. For RV hookups as well as tent sites, the closest private facility is the **Zion Canyon Campground** (tel. 801/772–3237), about ½ mile south of the south entrance, with showers, bathrooms, coin laundry, game room, and swimming.

BRYCE CANYON Bryce Canyon's two campgrounds, North and Sunset, generally fill every night from mid-May–mid-September; neither accept reservations, so you'll need to arrive by 2 PM the day you wish to stay. Both campgrounds are fine for tenters and maximum RV length is 30 feet. A store, laundry, and showers are located near Sunrise Point. For information, call 801/834–5322.

North Campground. Located east of the visitor center, this area, nestled under pine trees at an elevation of 8,000 feet, is open year-round, with one loop winterized for the cold temperatures. *55 RV and tent sites; no hookups ($5–$10). Running water, bathrooms.*

Sunset Campground. Open from May 15 to October 1, this area, situated 2 miles south of the visitor center, has a setting similar to North Campground. *50 RV and tent sites; no hookups ($5–$10). Running water, bathrooms.*

Outside the park are two relatively primitive but spectacular U.S. Forest Service camping areas: **Red Canyon** (tel. 801/676–2676 or 800/283–2267) on Highway 12, about 8 miles from Bryce, and **White Bridge** (tel. 801/865–3200) on Highway 143, 2½ miles from Panguitch and about 30 miles from Bryce.

Tenters will enjoy the alpine setting of **King's Creek Campground** (tel. 801/676–2676) in Dixie National Forest, about 11

miles west of Bryce. To get here, turn off Highway 12 west of the junction with Highway 63 and drive south for 7 miles down a dirt road.

Kodachrome Basin State Park (tel. 801/679–8562), 9 miles southeast of the town of Cannonville and about 23 miles east of Bryce, is an excellent campground with showers.

Private campgrounds close to the park include **Ruby's Inn** (tel. 801/834–5341), 1 mile from Bryce on Highway 63, with RV hookups, showers, coin laundry, and a pool; and **Bryce Canyon Pines** (tel. 801/834–5441), 6 miles from Bryce on Highway 12, with shady sites, a laundry, and horseback riding.

Bryce/Zion KOA (tel. 801/648–2490), 5 miles north of Glendale on Highway 89, is a good place to stop between Bryce and Zion, with tent sites and RV hookups, showers, bathrooms, coin laundry, and a pool.

DINING

Eating out in this corner of Utah is a down-home American affair; restaurants are neither fancy nor high-priced, but the food served is wholesome, filling, and western style. Menus tend to favor barbecue entrées and red meat, yet health-conscious diners should be able to find chicken and salad entrées that are prepared to their liking. The restaurants listed below are in the price category Inexpensive, under $15 per person, excluding tax, service, and drinks.

ZION **Bit and Spur.** The popular Bit and Spur, one of the best Mexican restaurants in Utah, serves innovative and healthy southwestern-style dishes such as fajitas and seafood enchiladas. *1212 Zion Park Blvd., Springdale, tel. 801/772–3498. MC, V.*

Driftwood Lodge. This establishment, with rustic ranch decor and picture windows framing a pasture and red cliffs, serves roasted chicken, trout, and homemade bread. *1515 Zion Park Blvd., Springdale, tel. 801/772–3262. AE, D, DC, MC, V.*

Electric Jims. This fast-food dining spot has the look of a '50s diner with a southwestern touch. Enjoy broiled chicken breast served with sprouts and Swiss cheese and a vegetarian sandwich with bean sprouts, pickles, tomatoes, cucumbers, and ortega chili. Jims is sometimes closed during winter; call for current hours. *Near park's south entrance on Zion Park Blvd., Springdale, tel. 801/ 772-3838. No credit cards.*

Flanigans. This pleasant place with southwestern pastel decor serves American and Continental cuisines, including pastas, trout, and grilled chicken. *428 Zion Park Blvd., Springdale, tel. 801/772-3244. AE, D, DC, MC, V.*

Pioneer Lodge and Restaurant. American food and a full salad bar are offered at this local favorite with an old fireplace. *838 Zion Park Blvd., Springdale, tel. 801/772-3233. AE, D, MC, V.*

Zion Lodge. In the park, fine American cuisine is served in a western-style dining room, with a wood-beamed ceiling, historic photos, and a wall of windows overlooking the canyon. *Zion Park, tel. 801/772-3213. AE, DC, MC, V.*

BRYCE CANYON **Bryce Canyon Lodge.** For the best food in the area, come to this rustic old stone-and-wood lodge, which serves such specialties as rabbit pollo with goat cheese and savory barbecued ribs. *Bryce Canyon Park, tel. 801/834-5361. AE, DC, MC, V.*

Bryce Canyon Pines Restaurant. Popular with families, this small establishment serves uncomplicated dishes such as fish-and-chips, homemade soup, and chili. *Hwy. 12 (6 mi from park), tel. 801/834-5441. D, DC, MC, V.*

Doug's Place. Doug's is located in the tiny hamlet of Tropic, east of Bryce. Typical diner fare is punctuated with taco salads and sticky sweet rolls. *141 N. Main St., Tropic, tel. 801/679-8633. AE, D, DC, MC, V.*

Hungry Coyote. Stop in for hearty southwestern dishes—grilled chicken and fajitas,

among them—served in an atmosphere thick with antiques and faded old pictures. The Hungry Coyote is located inside the Bryce Valley Inn in Tropic, east of the park. *200 N. Main St., Tropic, tel. 801/679-8811. AE, MC, V.*

Fosters Family Steakhouse. This clean, relatively quiet and modern steak house—with a stone fireplace and bright picture windows—features a standard menu of chicken and seafood. *Hwy. 12 (4 mi from park), tel. 801/834-5227. AE, D, MC, V.*

Ruby's Inn. This historic motel, store, and dining complex has a good soup and salad bar and an all-you-can-eat buffet. *Hwy. 63 (1 mi from park), tel. 801/834-5341. AE, D, DC, MC, V.*

OUTDOOR ACTIVITIES

BIKING A new paved bicycle trail, Pa'rus, leads along the Virgin River for about 2 miles. The trailhead is to the left on the entrance road to Watchman Campground. Other roads in Zion are quite narrow and are often quite crowded. Bryce Canyon's roads are wide enough, however, to accommodate cyclists safely. **Ruby's Inn** (tel. 801/834-5341), a mile from the park's entrance, rents bicycles. **Backcountry BicycleTours** (Box 4029, Bozeman, MT 59722, tel. 406/586-3556) and **Backroads Bicycle Touring** (1516 5th St., Dept. Q612, Berkeley, CA 94710, tel. 800/245-3874) organize bicycle trips to both parks.

BIRD-WATCHING May through July is the best time to observe birds in the parks. More than 270 species of birds have been identified at Zion; 170 species at Bryce. The park visitor centers carry a checklist for bird-watchers.

HORSEBACK RIDING **Canyon Trail Rides** (Box 128, Tropic 84736, tel. 801/834-5291 or 801/ 679-8665 after June 1) offers guided horseback trips from mid-March through October in Zion and April through September at Bryce.

SKIING AND SNOWSHOEING Some cross-country skiing and snowshoeing is available on Zion's higher plateau; Wildcat Canyon and the upper West Rim Trail have the best conditions.

Bryce is an excellent winter-sports area, with cross-country skiing available both inside and directly outside the park. You can rent skis from **Ruby's Inn** (tel. 801/834–5341). Free snowshoes can be obtained at the Bryce visitor center; Queen's Garden and Navajo Loop trails are recommended for snowshoers.

Fodor's Travel Publications

Available at bookstores everywhere, or call 1–800–533–6478, 24 hours a day.

Gold Guides

U.S.

Alaska

Arizona

Boston

California

Cape Cod, Martha's Vineyard, Nantucket

The Carolinas & the Georgia Coast

Chicago

Colorado

Florida

Hawaii

Las Vegas, Reno, Tahoe

Los Angeles

Maine, Vermont, New Hampshire

Maui

Miami & the Keys

New England

New Orleans

New York City

Pacific North Coast

Philadelphia & the Pennsylvania Dutch Country

The Rockies

San Diego

San Francisco

Santa Fe, Taos, Albuquerque

Seattle & Vancouver

The South

U.S. & British Virgin Islands

USA

Virginia & Maryland

Waikiki

Washington, D.C.

Foreign

Australia & New Zealand

Austria

The Bahamas

Barbados

Bermuda

Brazil

Budapest

Canada

Cancún, Cozumel, Yucatán Peninsula

Caribbean

China

Costa Rica, Belize, Guatemala

Cuba

The Czech Republic & Slovakia

Eastern Europe

Egypt

Europe

Florence, Tuscany & Umbria

France

Germany

Great Britain

Greece

Hong Kong

India

Ireland

Israel

Italy

Japan

Kenya & Tanzania

Korea

London

Madrid & Barcelona

Mexico

Montréal & Québec City

Morocco

Moscow, St. Petersburg, Kiev

The Netherlands, Belgium & Luxembourg

New Zealand

Norway

Nova Scotia, New Brunswick, Prince Edward Island

Paris

Portugal

Provence & the Riviera

Scandinavia

Scotland

Singapore

South Africa

South America

South Pacific

Southeast Asia

Spain

Sweden

Switzerland

Thailand

Tokyo

Toronto

Turkey

Vienna & the Danube

Fodor's Special-Interest Guides

Branson

Caribbean Ports of Call

The Complete Guide to America's National Parks

Condé Nast Traveler Caribbean Resort and Cruise Ship Finder

Cruises and Ports of Call

Fodor's London Companion

Gay USA

France by Train

Halliday's New England Food Explorer

Healthy Escapes

Italy by Train

Kodak Guide to Shooting Great Travel Pictures

Shadow Traffic's New York Shortcuts and Traffic Tips

Sunday in New York

Sunday in San Francisco

Walt Disney World, Universal Studios and Orlando

Walt Disney World for Adults

Where Should We Take the Kids? California

Where Should We Take the Kids? Family Adventures

Where Should We Take the Kids? Northeast